The Collected Writings of Walt Whitman

G.W. Waters
1877

WALT WHITMAN

The Correspondence

VOLUME III: 1876–1885

Edited by Edwin Haviland Miller

 NEW YORK UNIVERSITY PRESS 1964

The frontispiece is a drawing of Whitman by George A. Waters in March, 1877, made during the poet's visit at the home of John H. Johnston, a New York jeweler.

The Collected Writings of Walt Whitman

GRATEFUL ACKNOWLEDGMENT IS MADE TO

Mr. Charles E. Feinberg,

WHOSE ASSISTANCE MADE POSSIBLE THE ILLUSTRATIONS
IN THIS VOLUME AND WHO ALSO MADE
AVAILABLE TO THE PUBLISHER THE RESOURCES
OF THE FEINBERG COLLECTION.

Preface

Although it is often stated, and is all too true, that the humanities receive less financial support than do other kinds of research, the cooperation of curators, librarians, fellow scholars, and interested individuals is a rich dividend. My debts are great and the payment I render here is inadequate. For many people have given, collectively, many hours of their time to answer my queries and to find information for me in remote libraries.

My debt is greatest to Charles E. Feinberg, the unacknowledged "dean" of Whitman research, whose home and heart I have selfishly imposed upon.

I am also indebted to the following Whitman specialists: Gay Wilson Allen, Edward F. Grier, Emory Holloway, F. DeWolfe Miller, and Rollo G. Silver. I herewith acknowledge my obligations to the following: the American Antiquarian Society of Worcester, Massachusetts; Rodney Armstrong, librarian at Phillips Exeter Academy; Lillian R. Benson, of the Lawson Memorial Library at the University of Western Ontario; Martina A. Brown, of the Minneapolis Public Library; Mrs. Leslie V. Case, curator of the Historical Society of the Tarrytowns, Inc.; Anne Freudenberg, of the University of Virginia; Ethel B. Goldy; Dr. John D. Gordan and his staff, in the Berg Collection at the New York Public Library; Freda Gray, of the Carnegie Library of Pittsburgh; Mrs. F. D. Griffith, of the Public Library in Galesburg, Illinois; Elinor J. Harrington, of the Otis Library in Norwich, Connecticut; Donald R. Haynes, of the University of Virginia; Ethel L. Hutchins, of the Public Library of Cincinnati and Hamilton County; Ridgway McNallie, of the Buffalo and Erie County Public Library; John D. F. Morgan, Executive Director of the Camden County Historical Society; Mrs. Doris Neale; Harold Olmstead; Robert L. Patten; Margaret Rose, of the City Library Association in Springfield, Massachusetts; Mrs. William F. Schneider, of the Brandon (Vermont) Free Public Library; G. W. Spragge, Archivist of Ontario, Canada; Mrs. Elaine W. Walker, Director of the Huntington (New York) Historical Society; Conrad F. Weitzel, of the Ohio Historical Society; Dr. D. M.

Wickware, Superintendent of the Ontario Hospital at London, Ontario; and James S. Wroth.

For annotations in this volume I have been most fortunate in having access to a genealogy of the Stafford family which has enabled me to clarify Whitman's relations with the family. I have also utilized copiously material from Whitman's unpublished *Commonplace-Book* in the Feinberg Collection. This diary, which the poet began in 1876 and used until his death in 1892, has been invaluable in establishing dates, identifying correspondents, and clarifying many details in his life.

I am indebted to the following institutions for permission to print Whitman letters in their collections: Abernethy Library of American Literature, Middlebury College; the American Academy of Arts and Letters Collection; the Barrett Literary Manuscripts Collection, the University of Virginia; Henry W. and Albert A. Berg Collection, the New York Public Library; the British Museum; the University of Buffalo; the University of California at Berkeley; the Camden County (New Jersey) Historical Society; the John Carter Brown Library, Brown University; the University of Chicago; the William Andrews Clark Memorial Library of the University of California, Los Angeles; Columbia University; the Royal Library of Copenhagen; the Estelle Doheny Collection of the Edward Laurence Doheny Memorial Library, St. John's Seminary; the Furness Collection, the University of Pennsylvania; the Walter Hampden Memorial Library, The Players, New York; the T. E. Hanley Collection, the University of Texas; Harvard University; the Henry E. Huntington Library; the Library of Congress; Lincoln Memorial University; the Oscar Lion Collection, the New York Public Library; the Amy Lowell Collection, Harvard University; the Maine Historical Society; the Massachusetts Historical Society; the Missouri Historical Society; the Pierpont Morgan Library; the New York Public Library; Northwestern University; Ohio Wesleyan; the University of Pennsylvania; the Historical Society of Pennsylvania; Rutgers University; the Slack Collection, Marietta College; Smith College; Stillman Letters, Union College; Syracuse University; the University of Texas; the Trent Collection, Duke University; Washington University, St. Louis; Wellesley College; Wesleyan University; the Walt Whitman Birthplace; the Whitman House, Camden; Williams College; the State Historical Society of Wisconsin; and Yale University.

The following individuals have graciously permitted me to include letters in their collections: the William E. Barton Estate, Ben Bloomfield, Dr. R. J. H. DeLoach, Charles E. Feinberg, Horst Frenz, Rosamond Gilder, Mr. and Mrs. Stephen Greene, Dr. Cornelius Greenway, Mrs. Barbara Halpern, Florence A. Hoadley, Dr. Alma Howard, Professor

Thomas Ollive Mabbott, A. J. Marino, John S. Mayfield, Percy Muir, Professor G. Ross Roy, Louis H. Silver, Professor Rollo G. Silver, Gregg M. Sinclair, Robert H. Taylor, and the late Dr. Max Thorek.

The New York University Arts and Science Research Fund has been generous in its support of my research. My typist, Dorothy E. Buck, has from the beginning taken a more than professional interest in these volumes.

Lastly, I fondly trust that this volume is worthy of my most loyal supporters—Rosalind and Pamela.

E. H. M.

CONTENTS

Introduction

These were years of recovery and consolidation. Slowly Walt Whitman regained his health after the crippling physical paralysis which struck in January, 1873, and the emotional collapse following the death of his mother four months later. Although he never recovered complete use of his limbs, the poet was sufficiently strong in the late 1870's to travel to the West and to make occasional public appearances. The furore surrounding *Leaves of Grass*, of course, was not over, as the suppression of the Osgood edition in 1882 indicated, but Whitman was about to pass into literary history. Visitors, both American and foreign, came in increasing numbers to Camden to do homage to the first great native "original." Magazines and newspapers requested poems and prose as they never had before, and he was continually in the news, both because he was an avid self-publicist and because he was by all odds the most exciting literary personality in the United States. Idolators found him more godlike in these twilight years, though his walk could not conceal his paralysis. His presence provoked an awe and worship that, even if we perhaps in our shrunken age prefer to be skeptical of the magnetism of personality, we must take cognizance of. For Whitman's person had a radiant dimension not unlike that of his best poetry. The letters, particularly from young English admirers, attest to the fact that readers found Whitman's almost the only poetry of the period related to their individual crises and aspirations. God may have been dead, as Nietzsche was to aver about this time, but the godlike in Whitman was vibrantly alive in the hearts of his lovers.

In 1876 Mrs. Anne Gilchrist came to Philadelphia with three of her children. Although Whitman had forbidden the trip, her genuine passion was not to be checked by a male's fear: she trusted that her physical presence would achieve the consummation her body and soul longed for. Her erotic fantasy of the poet, based upon the erotic fantasy of his poems, shortly gave way to the painful recognition that the man could fulfill neither her fantasy nor his own. Her disappointment she never revealed, even to her children, and after she returned to England in 1879 she continued to write and occasionally to confess her feelings for the bachelor bard of love. In the months before her death in 1885 she composed a second defense of the American poet, and as she was dying she instructed her son to notify Walt. She was faithful to the last. He was faithful after his kind to her memory.

The ten-year estrangement of Whitman and O'Connor ended in 1882, when the poet's most vitriolic defender unleashed his verbal gunnery in assailing the Boston authorities. During the years of silence Whitman frequently sent books and magazine articles, perhaps in an attempt to heal the wounds. But O'Connor's anger, like Anne Gilchrist's disillusionment never put in writing, was not to be assuaged until his sense of justice was outraged by the attempts to censor. Then with the excessive fervor of a man whose hate knows few bounds, O'Connor charged into battle: "I will exterminate them"; "I burn to resume the thunder and let the levin flay"; "I gave him cantharides, or, as the Long Island boys say, 'hell under the shirt.'" In 1888 Whitman said of O'Connor: "What a fighter! I won't say that: I will say: What a lover!" But Whitman was rarely acute in his evaluations: Burroughs and the Gilchrists recognized and deplored the intemperateness of O'Connor's outbursts and the projection of his own emotional instability, and perhaps self-hatred, upon the "enemy."

The most meaningful event in these years was not the arrival and departure of the disappointed Mrs. Gilchrist or the renewed relationship with O'Connor, which was primarily confined to correspondence. That Camden attracted celebrities and hangers-on of genius was certainly gratifying, and the response to his lectures was pleasing to his ego, but no man, and certainly not Walt Whitman, can find emotional fulfillment in the personal or published adulation of people who are attracted to the public image. Life with George and Louisa Whitman, with whom he lived until 1884, was lonely, for the poet's brother was about to become the most prosperous of the Whitmans and less and less understanding of Walt's poetic greatness and human wants. Thus a familiar story was about to be repeated: At fifteen Whitman had left home to make his way in the world; obviously the home had frustrated cravings and aspirations which he did not understand at the time and perhaps never fully comprehended. In 1876 he again in effect left his family when he met Harry Stafford, and he was shortly spending a great deal of his time with the Staffords on their farm in Kirkwood, New Jersey. The farm provided him with a creek and with a lovely natural setting, which he duly commended in *Specimen Days*. But the physical environment was least important. He could have found this if he had accepted John Burroughs' invitation to move to Esopus, along the Hudson River, and in addition could have enjoyed intellectual companionship. But Whitman never ran away from home to seek out intellectual or artistic society. He left home to find another home among people who resembled his parents and his brothers and sisters.

Among the Staffords he found almost an exact duplication of his early life. The father, George, was hard-working but not very prosperous. Family life centered around the mother. Of Mrs. Stafford, Susan, Whitman wrote to her son: "There is not a nobler woman in Jersey." There were seven living children, five boys and two girls, a situation that paralleled closely the six boys and two girls in the Whitman family. Like his brothers and sisters, the Stafford children did not have time to be educated, and they had to pitch in and help with the chores in order to keep the family going.

In this familiar setting Whitman commanded respect. That probably no one read or at any rate understood his poems, as was the case in his own family, mattered not at all. He felt secure in the simple society and activities of the Staffords, just as he felt secure with conductors, pilots, and tradespeople who accepted him as a man, not as a poet. Since he knew that a poet was an anomaly, perhaps a freak, in the eyes of ordinary people, he frequently concealed his vocation. What the Staffords provided —and therefore what he needed—was the environment of his childhood without the frustrations of oedipal longings and sibling rivalry. Here he fulfilled the desires reflected in his early poems of being at once father, mother, and brother. He quickly became a father to the restless Stafford boys, who confided in him and sought his advice, and he participated as an older "brother" in the social life and recreations of the family. It is not surprising, then, since his ailments were in part emotionally based, that his health began to improve noticeably.

"*You, my darling boy*," Whitman wrote to Harry Stafford years later, "*are the central figure of them all*." Apparently he met Harry early in 1876, while he was employed in the printing office of the Camden *New Republic*. Harry was eighteen, uncertain of his goals, emotionally troubled as he was crossing the bridge from childhood to manhood, subject to the "blues." Again we perceive a pattern. For Harry was the counterpart of the soldiers whom Whitman met in the Washington hospitals during the Civil War, of Peter Doyle, and probably of many others in the early years who have escaped literary detection. (During the time he was preoccupied with Harry, he also established intense, but brief, friendships with John R. Johnston, Jr., the son of a Philadelphia artist; Edward Cattell, a friend of Harry Stafford; and Albert Johnston, the son of a New York jeweler.) These young men were invariably semiliterate, emotionally insecure, and desirous of establishing a dependent relationship with an older man. Whitman instinctively understood them, since he discovered in them a great deal of his own troubled youth, as revealed particularly in the poems of 1855. Since he offered these boys advice on education and employment, and since he sometimes even chose and purchased clothes for them, he was both father and mother. This bisexual role, safely removed from the threats of literal paternity and of mature sexuality, he fulfilled in "Calamus" friendships, the only relationships that were emotionally satisfying to him or for that matter possible.

Many of Harry Stafford's letters are in the Feinberg Collection, and, interestingly, were not destroyed as Peter Doyle's must have been; and many of the poet's replies, but unfortunately not the early ones, are in various collections, particularly in the Berg Collection. These letters are being published for the first time. Because Harry was too artless to conceal or to be "indirect," as Whitman invariably was, both in his poetry and in life, we are able to observe the development of a "Calamus" relationship as we cannot do in the case of Peter Doyle, and are thus able to understand better one of the deepest needs of the poet.

Harry came eagerly for guidance to a fatherly figure, and Whitman attempted to teach him penmanship and to obtain jobs for him. But the poet was not able to play the paternal role consistently; like a brother or a buddy he indulged in roughhousing with the lad. Burroughs in 1877 complained in his diary after Harry and Whitman had visited him: "They cut up like two boys and annoyed me sometimes." On November 24, 1878, after a visit to Camden, Harry wrote about his team of horses: "they wanted to troot all the way home, they felt good I guess, . . . so they wanted to show off, you know how it is you'r self when you feel like *licking* me; but I held them down as I do you, when you feel that way."

Whitman, who was seldom naïve, although his admirers frequently were, generally referred to their relationship guardedly. That he was aware of the construction that could be placed upon it was apparent when, in accepting an invitation to visit John H. Johnston in New York, he informed his host that he was to be accompanied by "my (adopted) son" in one letter and in another: "My nephew & I when traveling always share the same room together & the same bed." Just before Christmas in 1876 Whitman sent Johnston a check for $35 for a *"gold watch"*—"a Christmas present for a young man." In a letter on February 22, 1878, he mentioned Harry cryptically through concealed initials, much as years earlier he had alluded to Peter Doyle in a diary jotting through the use of numbers. The indirection that Whitman spoke of as characteristic of the new American poetry is paralleled by the secretiveness with which he, of painful necessity apparently, camouflaged his troubled emotions. Fearfully he trod untrod-den paths.

Although the bard and the boy could caper like children, relations were not always smooth. On May 1, 1877, Harry wrote:

> Dear Friend—
>
> You know how I left you at the station to-day. I have thought of it and cannot get it off my mind, so I have come up to ask your forgivness. I know how I have served you on many occassions before. I know that it is my falt and not yours. Can you forgive me and take me back and love me the same. I will try by the grace of God to do better. I cannot give you up, and it makes me feel so bad to think how we have spent the last day or two; and all for my temper. I will have to *controol* it or it will send me to the states prison or some other bad place. Can't you take me back and me the same.
>
> Your lovin but bad tempered
>
> Harry.

In April and May Harry was looking for employment. On May 21 he sent a letter from the Camden depot, where he had waited for the poet to return from Kirkwood.

> Dear friend—
>
> You cannot imagin how bad I was disappointed in not seeing you to night. I went down to the depot to meet you, and not finding you, I thought perhaps you came on the 1 O'clock train, so I went down to the house but did not find you. . . . You may say that I dont care for you, but I do, I think of you all the time, I want you to come up to-morrow night if you can. I have been to bed to night, but could not sleep fore thinking of you so I got up and *scribbbled* a few lines to you, to go in the *morning* mail. I hope you will not disappoint me. I want you to look over the past and I will do my best to-ward you in the future. You are all the true friend I have, and when I can-not have you I will go away some ware, I dont know where. . . . Good bye. *Believe* me to be your true and loving friend,
>
> Harry Stafford.

While he was staying in Mrs. Gilchrist's Philadelphia home, on June 18–19, Whitman wrote in his first extant letter: "Dear Harry, not a day or night passes but I think of you . . . Dear son, how I wish you could come in now, even if but for an hour & take off your coat, & sit down on my lap . . . I want to see the creek again—& I want to see you, my darling son, & I can't wait any longer—Your old Walt."

Whitman stayed with the Staffords from July 13 to 20, and in his *Commonplace-Book* he made this entry: "July 20th '77 in the room at White Horse 'good bye.' " Evidently he wanted to terminate or at least de-emotionalize the relationship much as in 1870 he wanted to free himself from Peter Doyle. On the following day Harry wrote:

> I thought I would write a few lines to you and let you know how I am. I cannot get you off my mind somehow. I heard something that made me feel bad, and I saw that you did not want to bid me good bye when you went away yesterday. I will tell you what it was. I heard that you was going to Washington and stay and be gon fore some time, is it so? I thought it was strange in you, in not saying anything to me about it, I think of it all the time, I cannot get my mind on my work the best I can do. I should like to come up to Camden next week, and stay all night with you if I could, but I suppose I can not do it. I wish you would write to me soon and let me know how you are.

But the poet could not disengage himself. In August, Harry was working in Woodbury, New Jersey, and Whitman was with the Stafford family. On August 14 Harry hoped that Whitman would soon return to Camden: "for I then will have some place to go. I want to get up to see you once a week at least and have a good time, for I cant let my self out here, they are too nice for that." On October 4 Harry wrote: "I want to come [to Camden] bad, dont know how I will stay away. I want you to have some place to go when I come down, some place where there is plenty of girls, I want to have some fun when I come down this time." On October 17 he boasted of defeating a friend in a wrestling match. "There is one more fellow who I want to take the conceat out of, and that is B. K. Sharp [his employer], he thinks he could do what he pleased with me but I want to show him he cannot do it." Harry continued: "I don't get much time to think about anyone, for when I am not thinking of my business I am thinking of what I am shielding, I want to try and make a man of myself, and do what is right, if I can do it."

The poet as the young man's confidant had to shoulder his problems, including his uncertain relations with the young ladies. But Whitman's own emotional involvement propelled the relationship in dubious ways. When George Stafford was ill in November, the poet went to Kirkwood. Harry wrote on the day Whitman left because "the folks and I have commenced to miss you already." Then he added: "I wish you would put the ring on my finger again, it seems to me ther is something that is wanting to compleete our friendship when I am with you. I have tride to studdy it out but cannot find out what it is. You know when you put it on there was but one thing to part it from me and that was death."

Harry's letters clearly reveal how meaningful the relationship had become to him; Whitman's, as one would expect, were affectionate but more cautious. About January 18, 1878, Harry was annoyed because his friend had failed to answer a letter. "Do you know," he wrote, "that I cannot enjoy myselfe any more at home, if I go up in my room I always come down feeling worse than I do when I go up, for the first thing I see is your picture, and when I come down in the sitting room there hangs the same, and whenever I do anything, or say anything the picture seems to me is always looking at me; so I find that I am better sattesfied when I am here [at the Stafford store] than when I am home." In this letter Harry mentioned Lizzie, possibly a cousin, in a portion which is badly water-soaked: "we have had many good times togeather, but none that hangs with me like those you and I have had."

He visited Whitman on January 22 and 23. On the following day, in a passage which is only partly legible because of water stains, he asked: "You did not give me what you said you was going [to?. is?] it because [I had accepted ?] this one, if so I will give it back to Lizzie." Possibly Harry referred to the ring. Three days after Whitman's visit on March 23, the young man wrote: "I have been thinking of the suit of cloths which I am to have like yours; I have had myselfe all pictured out with a suit of gray, and a white slouch hat on about fifty times, since you spoke of it; the fellows will call me Walt then. I will have to do something great and good in honor of his name, What will it be?"

If Harry was bewildered at times, it is no wonder. In addition to his own restlessness, mood swings, fear for his masculinity, and his relationship to young ladies, he had to cope with the perplexing behavior of an older man—sometimes a father who wrestled with him like a chum, occasionally a mother, but also a kind of husband.

Yet it seems clear that in 1878 the intensity of the relationship had slowly begun to alter. Harry, for example, wrote on July 27, 1878: "Times have become settled, and our love sure (although we have had very many rough times to-gather) but we have stuck too each other so far and we will until we die, I know." In the following year when Whitman visited Burroughs he took with him Albert Johnston. From the Johnston home, on May 28, he summed up his New York visit in a letter to Harry:

> All good for a change, & a little excitement—*but I wish I was with you this minute, down by the creek or off in the woods somewhere*—I have

> been here now away since April 9 & every thing & every body has
> been so loving & kind—I have been happy in it all—& yet, Harry,
> my heart & wishes turn to my old friends, (& to old Jersey)—

Some of the old ardor was present, to be sure, but the tone was less personal, less compelling.

During succeeding years the poet wrote frequently to the young man, but for the most part confined himself to chitchat and topical matters. To a letter from Harry, "a little wild & nervous & uncertain some parts," Whitman replied on February 28, 1881:

> Harry, you certainly know well enough you have my best honorable
> loving friendship settled—Of the past I think only of the comforting
> soothing things of it all—I go back to the times at Timber Creek be-
> ginning most five years ago, & the banks & spring, & my hobbling
> down the old lane—& how I took a good turn there & commenced to
> get slowly but surely better, healthier, stronger—Dear Hank, I realize
> plainly that *if I had not known you*—if it hadn't been for you & our
> friendship & my going down there summers to the creek with you—
> and living there with your folks, & the kindness of your mother, &
> cheering me up—I believe *I should not be a living man to-day*—I
> think & remember deeply these things & they comfort me—*& you, my
> darling boy, are the central figure of them all*—
>
>   Of the occasional ridiculous little storms & squalls of the past I
> have quite discarded them from my memory—& I hope you will too—
> the other recollections overtop them altogether, & occupy the only per-
> manent place in my heart—as a manly loving friendship for you does
> also, & will while life lasts—

A year later, in reply to a *"blue letter,"* the poet wrote:

>   I wish it was so you could all your life come in & see me often
> for an hour or two—You see I think I understand you better than any
> one—(& like you more too)—(You may not fancy so, but it *is* so)—
> & I believe, Hank, there are many things, confidences, questions,
> candid *says* you would like to have with me, you have never yet
> broached—me the same— . . . God bless you, my darling boy—
> Keep a brave heart—

At last Whitman assumed a paternal role: he was kind and affectionate and generously gave the young man the emotional support he obviously needed. It was healthier that way both for the older man's sensitive, easily overwrought nature and for Harry's self-doubts.

The change was also apparent in Harry's letters. When he wrote while Whitman was in Boston in 1881 to give his Lincoln lecture, he joshed and without emotion mouthed the friendship theme; he was plainly moving out of Whitman's orbit and was about ready to cross the bridge into marriage.

> Dear Walt:
>
> I have watched and waited for some friendly line from you, for about one month yet not a line have you pened. I suppose you have forgotten your rural friend, in the bustle and fashion [?] of Boston life. I don't blame you very much; yet it seems to me that you would occasionally think of the loving times we have had in days gone by. I notice that is the way you always use me, but I will get square with you when I go off on my lecturing trip, not a line will I write you, and dont you forget it. Here I have been waiting in this dry and dusty office for some account of you and your happy trip, and this is the way you serve me is it. Well I have a new *gal* and a mighty nice little thing she is too; Just such a one as you would like, and I know if you were to see those pretty rosy lips you would be charmed beyond measure with them, yet you shan't see her now that you used me so. She is a wild rose, plucked from the busom of the forest, pure as a lily and gentle as the summer breeze's.

Harry did not suddenly marry and live happily ever after. He continued to drift from job to job. He went to Canada for a few months and worked in the asylum of Whitman's friend, Dr. Richard Maurice Bucke. Then he set out bravely for Detroit, but suddenly altered his plans and returned to the Stafford farm. In 1884 he married and Whitman accompanied him to the civil ceremony. In succeeding years the poet visited the couple at intervals and always interested himself in their affairs.

This *was* the emotional experience of the period between 1876 and 1885—the last of the intense "Calamus" friendships.

This alphabetical list includes all the recipients of extant letters written between 1876 and 1885. The name is followed by the letter number.

Abdy-Williams, Ellen M., 1307
Almy, Frederic, 978
Baldwin, O. S., 1251, 1252
Bartlett, Dr. J. W., 1279
Bartlett, Truman Howe, 1241
Baxter, Sylvester, 1048, 1069, 1128, 1163, 1320, 1324
Beers, Henry A., 1029
Bellows, Edward D., 840
Bloor, Alfred Janson, 921
Bogue, David, 1081
Bolger, Peter, 1277
Booth, Edwin, 1288, 1289
Brockie, W., 763.1
Bryant, William C., 1298
Buchanan, Robert, 730, 747, 762, 775
Bucke, Richard Maurice, 1095
Burroughs, John, 735, 752, 786.1, 792, 796, 798, 799, 801, 803, 811, 819, 820, 848, 850, 852, 854, 856, 870, 872, 888, 898, 902, 905, 910, 911, 926, 929, 932, 933, 941, 943, 946, 954, 986, 988, 1002, 1018, 1038, 1044, 1059, 1061, 1108, 1150, 1152, 1191, 1197, 1202, 1209, 1229, 1243, 1268, 1317, 1327, 1361
Burroughs, Ursula, 872
Callicot, T. C., 1123

Camden *Daily Press*, 951.1
Carpenter, Edward, 738, 741, 834, 835, 837, 841, 886, 970, 1033, 1072, 1146, 1333, 1335
Cattell, Edward, 797
Chainey, George, 1137
Child, Josiah, 881, 897, 925, 1077, 1182
Childs, George W., 900, 906, 1090
Cincinnati *Commercial*, 717
Clark, Henry H., 1060
Conway, Eustace, 1010
Conway, Moncure D., 724, 763
Critic, The, 995, 1106
Cunningham, John S., 1093
Dana, Charles A., 1104
Denver *Tribune*, 959
Doggett, Edward G., 984
Donaldson, Blaine and Mary, 1304
Donaldson, Thomas, 1246, 1347, 1349
Dowden, Edward, 713, 720, 767, 1172
Dowe, Mrs. F. E., 823
Doyle, Peter, 708, 710, 781, 785, 787, 817, 821, 829, 849, 858, 887, 927, 939, 964, 1362–1364
Eldridge, Charles W., 1272, 1343
Ellis, F. S., 764
Elwell, Miss, 1285
Ford, Elizabeth, 1274, 1334, 1339

*

Additional Letter Not by Whitman

ABBREVIATIONS

AL	*American Literature*
Allen	Gay Wilson Allen, *The Solitary Singer* (1955)
Allen, *Handbook*	Gay Wilson Allen, *Walt Whitman Handbook* (1946)
Asselineau	Roger Asselineau, *L'Évolution de Walt Whitman* (1955)
Barrett	Clifton Waller Barrett Collection, University of Virginia
Barrus	Clara Barrus, *Whitman and Burroughs—Comrades* (1931)
Berg	Henry W. and Albert A. Berg Collection, New York Public Library
Binns	Henry Bryan Binns, *A Life of Walt Whitman* (1905)
Blodgett	Harold Blodgett, *Walt Whitman in England* (1934)
Bucke	Richard Maurice Bucke, *Walt Whitman* (1883)
Calamus	*Calamus: A Series of Letters Written during the Years 1868–1880 by Walt Whitman to a Young Friend (Peter Doyle),* ed. Richard Maurice Bucke (1897)
CB	*The Commonplace-Book*
CHAL	*The Cambridge History of American Literature*
CT	Complete Text
CW	*The Complete Writings of Walt Whitman* (1902), 10 vols.
DAB	*Dictionary of American Biography*
DNB	*Dictionary of National Biography*
Doheny	Estelle Doheny Collection of the Edward Laurence Doheny Memorial Library, St. John's Seminary
Donaldson	Thomas Donaldson, *Walt Whitman the Man* (1896)
ESQ	*Emerson Society Quarterly*
Feinberg	Charles E. Feinberg Collection
Frenz	Horst Frenz, ed., *Whitman and Rolleston—A Correspondence* (1951)
Furness	Clifton Joseph Furness, *Walt Whitman's Workshop* (1928)
Gilchrist	Herbert Harlakenden Gilchrist, *Anne Gilchrist: Her Life and Writings* (1887)

Gohdes and Silver	Clarence Gohdes and Rollo G. Silver, eds., *Faint Clews & Indirections* (1949)
Hanley	T. E. Hanley Collection, University of Texas
Harned	Thomas B. Harned, ed., *The Letters of Anne Gilchrist and Walt Whitman* (1918)
Holloway	Emory Holloway, *Whitman—An Interpretation in Narrative* (1926)
Huntington	Henry E. Huntington Library
Kennedy	William Sloane Kennedy, *Reminiscences of Walt Whitman* (1896)
Knortz	Karl Knortz, *Walt Whitman der Dichter der Demokratie* (1899)
LC	The Library of Congress
LC #	*Walt Whitman—A Catalog Based Upon the Collections of The Library of Congress* (1955)
Lion	Oscar Lion Collection, New York Public Library
Manchester	The John Rylands Library, Manchester, England
Morgan	Pierpont Morgan Library
NAR	*The North American Review*
NB	*November Boughs* (1888)
NEQ	*New England Quarterly*
Nonesuch	Emory Holloway, ed., *Walt Whitman—Complete Poetry & Selected Prose and Letters* (1938)
NYPL	New York Public Library
Pennsylvania	University of Pennsylvania
Perry	Bliss Perry, *Walt Whitman* (1906)
PT	Partial Text
SB	*Studies in Bibliography*
SD	*Specimen Days*, ed. Floyd Stovall (1963)
SDC	*Specimen Days & Collect* (1882)
Syracuse	Syracuse University
Traubel	Horace Traubel, ed., *With Walt Whitman in Camden* (1906–1953), 4 vols.
Trent	Trent Collection, Duke University
UPP	*The Uncollected Poetry and Prose of Walt Whitman*, ed. Emory Holloway (1921), 2 vols.
WW	Walt Whitman
WWR	*Walt Whitman Review*

The Correspondence of Walt Whitman

VOLUME III: 1876-1885

1876

708. *To Peter Doyle*   *1.15. [1876]*[1]

ADDRESS: Pete Doyle, | M street South bet 4½ & 6th |
Washington, D.C. POSTMARKS: Camden | Jan | 15 |
N.J.; Carrier | 16 | Jan | 8 AM.

431 Stevens st. | cor West. | Camden, |
N. Jersey | Jan 15.

Nothing very new or different. Was much relieved when I heard
you was *out* of that smash up on the road. John Burroughs is here on a
visit—we have just had dinner—Cold & wintry here, but bright & clear—
I go out some—your letter & paper came—am feeling quite comfortable—

WW

709. *To Ellen M. O'Connor*   *1.15. [1876]*

ADDRESS: Mrs. E. M. O'Connor | 1015 O st. near 11th
N.W. | Washington, D.C. POSTMARKS: Philadelphia |
Jan | 15 | 10 PM; (?) | 16 | Jan | 8 AM.

431 Stevens st. | cor West. | Camden, |
N. Jersey. | Jan 15.

Glad to get your letter, this morning. Am about as at last writing—
every thing more favorable than unfavorable. John Burroughs is here on a
visit. Cold & clear here, snow & sleighing—I am going out a little—

WW

1. The year is established by Burroughs' visit; see 711. Writing to Dowden on
April 9, Burroughs spoke of this visit and of his impression that WW "had mended
decidedly since I had seen him in the spring before" (Barrus, 120, and note 121).

710. *To Peter Doyle*   *1.22.* [*1876?*][2]

ADDRESS: Pete Doyle, | M street South—bet 4½ & 6th |
Washington, D.C. POSTMARKS: Camden | Jan | 22 |
N.J.; Carrier | 23 | Jan | 8 P.M.

431 Stevens st. | cor West. | Camden, |
N. Jersey. | Jan. 22.

All is going on with me full as comfortably as I can expect. A
dark, drizzly, very slippery day here—Keeps me in. Your papers & letter rec'd.

WW

711. *To William Michael Rossetti*

431 Stevens st. | cor West. | Camden, | N. Jersey, |
U.S. America | Jan. 26, | 76

My dear friend,

I send you the enclosed piece (printed in a paper here, with my
consent)[3]—quite willing you should have it put, if convenient, in the
Academy, or any other literary gazette, your way, if thought proper. My
theory is that *the plain truth* of the situation here is best stated. It is even
worse *than* described in the article.

With me, things are going on as for a year or two past—am no worse
—work a little—still remain in Camden. I rec'd your letter—have seen of
late months Joaquin Miller,[4] M. D. Conway, Lord Houghton,[5] &c. I have
lately heard from, but not seen, Marvin,[6] my Boston friend. John Burroughs was here with me last week. He is well. I have about got ready my

2. This post card appears to have been written one week after 708, as evidenced
by the descriptions of WW's health and of the weather.
3. "Walt Whitman's Actual American Position," which appeared in the *West
Jersey Press* on January 26, was WW's anonymous reply to the article in the Springfield
Republican of January 18, which attacked the "loose talk" of Joaquin Miller and others
that WW was "a neglected martyr," and averred that WW was "not yet in want, though
three years of illness and enforced idleness have used up his savings." In the *West Jersey
Press*, WW protested his neglect by American readers, publishers, and poets. He had
recently printed, he declared, a two-volume edition of his complete writings " 'to keep the
wolf from the door' in old age." See Furness, 245–246, and note letter 698. Rossetti
printed excerpts from the article in *The Athenaeum* on March 11, and also quoted the
last two sentences of the first paragraph of this letter. According to Rossetti's letter on
February 28 (Feinberg), the editor of *The Academy* had showed no interest in publishing the account.
4. Miller had visited WW in June, 1875; see 678.
5. For accounts of the visits of Conway and Houghton, see 696.
6. Marvin had recently returned from England; see 691 and 696.
7. In his letter of December 23, 1875, Rossetti had described a dinner given in
honor of Marvin (Feinberg); see 691.
8. Peter Bayne (1830–1896), a Scots journalist, in *The Contemporary Review*,

two Volumes—"Leaves of Grass" remains about the same, (a few new bits)—"Two Rivulets," the other Vol., has some new stuff—will write further to you soon anent of the books.

Was interested & pleased with your letter about the dinner[7]—sent it to Marvin to read. I have seen Peter Bayne's piece[8]—have also seen the friendly & glowing article of Arthur Clive in the *Gentleman's Magazine.*[9] Who is A. C.? When you write tell me something about him.

Walt Whitman

712. *To Rudolf Schmidt*

431 Stevens st. | cor West. | Camden, | N. Jersey. |
U.S. America | Jan 27 | 76

My dear Rudolf Schmidt

It is now some time since I have written to you, or heard any thing from you.[10] I still remain here laid up unwell from my paralysis—but keep much the same—no worse. I enclose you some slips—those relating to my-self, (which tell their own story) because I know you will be interested in any thing about me[11]—and the humorous pieces because I remember you are curious about American dialect & fun literature.[12]

As I write, it is a dark, rainy, muddy day. I am to recite a piece to-night for the benefit of the poor fund[13]—it will be printed in the paper, & I will send it to you. I tell you this partly to show you I still take some part in affairs, though I am badly shattered & old.

Remember your letters are always welcome to me.

Walt Whitman

xxviii (December, 1875), 49–69, attacked WW's English admirers, Rossetti, Dowden, and Buchanan, as well as *Leaves of Grass:* "While reading Whitman, . . . I realized with bitter painfulness how deadly is the peril that our literature may pass into conditions of horrible disease, the raging flame of fever taking the place of natural heat, the ravings of delirium superseding the enthusiasm of poetical imagination, the historians of tetanic spasm caricaturing the movements, dance-like and music-measured, of harmonious strength." Bayne's diatribe was reprinted in *The Living Age,* cxxviii (January 8, 1876), 91–102. See also *The Nation,* xxii (January 13, 1876), 28–29. In the *West Jersey Press* WW referred to "the scolding and cheap abuse of Peter Bayne" (Furness, 246). See also Barrus, 121 and 126.

  9. "Walt Whitman: the Poet of Joy," by the Irish poet, Standish James O'Grady, appeared in *The Gentleman's Magazine,* xv, n.s. (1875), 704–716. See 422 and 720; also Traubel, I, 399–400.

  10. WW had written on July 31, 1875; see 683.

  11. Undoubtedly the articles in the Springfield *Republican* and the *West Jersey Press;* see the preceding letter.

  12. See 589.

  13. On this occasion WW read Schiller's "The Diver" (Furness, 205). The program for the "Musical & Literary Entertainment, under the auspices of the Walt Whitman Debating Club of Camden, N. J.," is in the Lion Collection.

713. *To Edward Dowden*   [*1.(?). 1876*][14]

TRANSCRIPT.

431 Stevens St | &c

My dear friend,
        Enclosed I send you a piece printed here to give a *true* statement
of the situation—& which I should be well satisfied to have printed in
Britain. I ought to have written you before. I have read your "Shakspere"[15]
& ought to have thanked you for it. I find it full of vitality & suggestive-
ness, on themes that might be supposed exhausted years ago—but are not
at all exhausted.
        As I write I am feeling pretty comfortable—much the same as for last
two years—no worse. John Burroughs was here with me last week. He is
well. . . .[16]
        M D Conway has called upon us. He is a good & intellectual man, but
I don't think I either got hold of him, nor he of me, *at all.* My friend, I
must still put off for another letter some things I have had in my mind
for months to say to you. Your letters past—what John Burroughs told
me—(and your Shakspere book)—have *grafted* you more on my good will
& memory than you perhaps know. I write in haste.
                                                         Walt Whitman

714. *To Benjamin Perley Poore*[17]

ADDRESS: Ben: Perley Poore, | Clerk Printing
records, | Congress, | Washington, D.C. POSTMARK:
Camden | Feb | 7 | N.J.

431 Stevens st. | cor. West. | Camden, | N. Jersey. |
Feb. 7, | 76
        Thanks for the copy Directory, (which I was wanting)—& best
remembrances to you.
                                                         Walt Whitman

        14. This letter must have been written about the same time as the one to Rossetti
(see 711), for the following reasons: WW referred to the article in the *West Jersey
Press*, to Burroughs' visit in the middle of January, and to Conway's recent interview.
Dowden apparently replied to this letter on February 16 (Feinberg; Traubel, I, 301–303).
However, Dowden's letter on February 6 (Feinberg; Traubel, I, 299) also noted receipt of
a communication referring to his book on Shakespeare.
        15. See 673.
        16. Probably at this point WW mentioned the publication of *Leaves of Grass* and
Two Rivulets.

715. *To Whitelaw Reid*   [*2.8. 1876*]

ENDORSED (by Reid?): "8 Feb. 1876."

private

Calculated to make from 2¼d to 2⅔d columns, in the ordinary nonpareil, (or minion, is it?) you use for reading matter.

If convenient, when in type, send me a (revised) proof, which I will return by next mail.[18]

                                            Walt Whitman

431 Stevens st. | Camden, | N. Jersey.

716. *To William Michael Rossetti*

431 Stevens st. | cor West. | Camden, | N. Jersey, |
U.S. America. | Feb. 11 | 76

W. M. Rossetti: | My dear friend,

I would ask of you the favor to see, if convenient, whether the enclosed article (The American War) would be available for the *Academy*[19]—(or any where else if you think preferable.) I would like pay for it—would be satisfied with 25, or $30.

I am getting along much the same. My new book wont be out yet, publicly, for a month.

                                            Walt Whitman

I also send a little hitherto unpublished poem, *The Man-of-War Bird*[20]—which I can't sell here—I wonder if you could sell it for me, in London? It is not in my new book, & is entirely fresh.

---

17. Poore (1820–1887), a well-known columnist and author, was at this time editor of the Congressional Directory and clerk of the Senate committee in charge of printing public records.

18. WW sent Reid, the editor of the New York *Tribune* (see 644), a lengthy review of his new edition, which appeared in the New York *Tribune* on February 19; see *SB*, VIII (1956), 243–244.

19. "The American War" appeared in *The Examiner;* see 753.

20. The poem (later retitled "To the Man-of-War-Bird") appeared in *The Athenaeum*, I (April 1, 1876), 463, which paid WW £3.3 (*CB*). It was later published in *Progress* as "Thou who hast slept all night upon the storm"; see *CHAL*, II, 557.

717. *To the Editor, Cincinnati Commercial*

Private

431 Stevens st. | cor West. | Camden N Jersey | Feb 12 | 76
Editor Commercial. | Dear Sir:

Wouldn't these articles be available for the paper. The price is $60. for the two. Of course they are hitherto unpublished—(my book in which they go, will not be out for at least three or four weeks.)[21]

Walt Whitman

718. *To Ellen M. O'Connor*   *2.24. [1876]*

ENDORSED: "Ans'd." ADDRESS: Mrs. E. M. O'Connor, |
1015 O street, W, | Washington, | D.C. POSTMARKS:
Camden | Feb | 24 | N.J.; Carrier | 25 | Feb | 8 AM.

431 Stevens st. | cor. West. | Camden, |
N. Jersey, | Feb. 24.

Dear Nelly,

I am sitting here alone in the front room—a cold, gusty, wintry day outside, but bright & sunshiny—have just read your good letter of the 22d—Nothing special or different about my sickness or condition—I keep on much in the same way—gastric & liver trouble pretty grave, & (as a resultant) head distress more than half the time—go about though—The baby[22] is getting along well—though there are better, & fatter, & handsomer babies, this one is fine enough for all practicable purposes, is well formed, & has (I think) an especially fine pair of eyes—Knows me, & seems to like to be tended to occasionally held by me—begins to laugh, & [   ][23] [not at] all nervous or scareable—[   ] though (cant [   ] altogether satis[factory] [   ] [de?]formed one, has been [   ] foot, but is now nearly [   ] been steady—I have tended it—

My sister and brother Geo: are well—My other sisters, nieces, &

21. On March 16 WW noted receipt of $50 from Marst Halstead of the Cincinnati *Commercial* (*CB*). The newspaper had printed "extracts" from *Memoranda During the War* on February 16. For this information I am indebted to Ethel L. Hutchins, of The Public Library of Cincinnati and Hamilton County.
22. His nephew, Walter Orr Whitman; see 696.
23. The letter is mutilated for the next several lines because someone cut off WW's signature.
24. See 708.
25. WW had known Miss Hillard's writings since 1871 (see 512). He sent her a copy of *Leaves of Grass* on July 27 (*CB*).
26. Professor J. Peter Lesley was appointed state geologist of Pennsylvania in

brother Jeff, were well at last accounts. I am glad you wrote me about
your mother. John Burroughs[24] visited me some weeks since, on his way
home from Wash'n. Miss Kate Hillard[25] wrote me she is to be in Phila.
on her way to Wash'n 26th to 29th Feb. in Clinton st. near 10th, & I am
going over, 27th, to spend a couple of hours, as I know the folks. (Mrs.
and Prof. and Miss Lesley.)[26] As Hector Tyndale[27] lives only two or
three doors from there, I shall look in on him, or at least make some in-
quiry—& will send you word. The N. Y. Tribune of last Saturday (19th
Feb.) had the 2½ column synopsis of my new book, pretty full & fair[28]—
I suppose the *Star* extracts you mention must have come from it—

M. D. Conway[29] has not yet gone back to London—goes on two or
three weeks—How about Chas: Eldridge? Remembrance to Mrs. Brow-
nell,[30] Mrs. Huntington,[31] Mrs. Johnson[32] & Miss Donaldson, & best love
to you, Nelly dear—

719. *To Ellen M. O'Connor*   2.29. [*1876*]

ENDORSED: "Ans'd." ADDRESS: Mrs. E. M. O'Connor, |
1015 O street n. w. | Washington, | D.C. POSTMARKS:
Camden | Feb | 29 | N.J.; Carrier | 1 | Mar | 8 AM.

431 Stevens st. | cor West. | Camden, |
N. Jersey | Feb: 29.

Dear Nelly:

About me, my ailments, no great difference. (A queer old doctor
here—did I tell you?—sticks to it that, although the trouble has taken the
form of paralysis, & instigated far back, the basic & origin are of *stomachic*
nature—at any rate the derangement & suffering *now* are mostly gastric &
liver business—telling in distress of head)—

I went over to Phil: yesterday, & had a nice, good, I may almost say
happy afternoon, with dear Mrs. Lesley, Kate Hillard, & the two Miss
Lesleys, daughters[33]—us four, only, no men-critters but me—I was there
some four hours, filled with animated talk—we had dinner, very nice, a

1874. He was also secretary of the American Philosophical Society. Mrs. Gilchrist spoke
glowingly of the "delightful family circle" of the Lesleys (Gilchrist, 228–229). Miss
Maggie Lesley, an artist, visited Mrs. Gilchrist in 1881 (LC; Harned, 198).
27. An old friend; see 12 and 719.
28. See 715.
29. Conway had arrived in America for a lecture tour in September, 1875; see 689.
30. An unidentified Washington friend of Mrs. O'Connor; see 580.
31. Probably Mrs. William S. Huntington; see 580.
32. Mrs. Nancy M. Johnson, listed in the 1875 Directory as a widow. See also 725.
33. WW also recorded this visit in one of his notebooks (LC #108). See also the
preceding letter.

nice glass of wine—Mrs. L. a fine gentle, sweet-voiced, handsome black-eyed New England woman, (of the Lyman family, daughter of Judge Lyman.)[34] With Miss H[illard], though the first meeting, I got along capitally—found her a jolly, hearty girl—evidently seen life & folks, & read lots—she talked much about the London literati, & the (I suppose I may say) *personal* friends of mine there, both men & women, nearly all of whom she knew well, giving me, among the rest, descriptions of *Personnel* that were new & very interesting to me. She goes to Wash[ington] to-morrow, to stay there (1734 I st.) a month—reads a series of twelve papers on English poets.

I made a short call on Hector Tyndale, 1021 Clinton st—he came down to see me, in the parlor—(I did not see Mrs. T.)—Hector did not seem much different, physically—had the tone, I thought, of one who is *dreary* of life, to whom it is all an *ennui*, a settled morbidity—of course that was the worst. I rec'd a letter from Marvin to-day—from Peter Doyle yesterday—snowing here as I write—the baby fine, fat, bright to-day, but raising his voice lustily just this moment—You got my letter three days since?[35]

Walt—

720. *To Edward Dowden*

431 Stevens st. | cor West. | Camden, | N. Jersey. |
U. S. America. | March 4, | 76

Dear friend,

Yours of Feb. 6 with draft reach'd me which I responded to sending new edition "Leaves of Grass" and "Two Rivulets," two or three days since, by mail, same address as this, which you ought to have rec'd now lately—sent postal card briefly notifying you, & asking you to send me word (by postal card will do) immediately on their reception.[36]

To-day comes your affectionate, hearty, valued letter of Feb. 16, all right, with enclosure, draft 12£. 10s.[37]—all deeply appreciated—the *letter* good, cannot be better, but, as always, the *spirit* the main thing—

34. Professor Lesley married Susan I. Lyman, the daughter of Judge Samuel Fowler Lyman of Northampton, Mass.

35. The letter written on February 24.

36. Dowden enclosed a draft for $10 on February 6 (Feinberg; Traubel, I, 299). WW sent the two books on March 2 (*CB*). The post card is lost, but Dowden received it on March 14; see *Fragments of Old Letters, E. D. to E. D. W., 1869–1892* (1914), 149.

37. On February 16 Dowden ordered six copies of the new edition for friends, including Professor Atkinson of Trinity College, Dublin, and Stoker (Feinberg; Traubel, I, 301–303). WW mailed the volumes on March 14 (*CB*).

(altogether like some fresh, magnetic, friendly breath of breeze, 'way off there from the Irish Coast)—I wonder if you can know how much good such things do me. I shall send the six sets (six "Leaves" and six "Rivulets") by express, very soon, (probably by next Philadelphia steamer.) The extra copies of "Memoranda of the War" not being ready bound, at present, I will send by mail—six copies, before very long. (I hope the set above mention'd I mailed you by last steamer, will have reach'd you before you get this.) I saw O'Grady's article in the December "Gentleman's"[38] & from my point of view, he dwells on *what I like to have dwelt on.* I was deeply pleased with the article, & if I had O'Grady's address I would like to send him my photograph. I also read the Peter Bayne article. (It was copied in full here at once, & circulated quite largely.)[39] As I write this, I have not read Abraham Stoker's letter,[40] but shall do so, & carefully. (The names shall be written in the Vols. as you mention.) I read with great zest the account of the discussion at the "Fortnightly"[41] —I have learn'd to feel *very thankful* to those who attack & abuse & pervert me—that's perhaps (besides being good fun) the only way to bring out the splendid ardor & friendship of those, my unknown friends, my best reward, art & part with me, in my pages, (for I have come to solace & perhaps flatter myself that it is *they* indeed in them, as much as *I*, every bit.)

My condition physically is pretty much the same[42]—no worse, at least not decidedly. I get out nearly every day, but not far, & cannot walk from lameness—make much of the river here, the broad Delaware, crossing a great deal on the ferry, full of life & fun to me—get down there by our horse cars, which run along near my door—get infinite kindness, care, & assistance, from the employés on these boats & cars—My friend, next time you write say more about yourself, family & Mrs. Dowden, to whom with yourself best love & regards—

Walt Whitman

38. See 711. WW sent the photograph to O'Grady about October 19 (*CB*).
39. See 711.
40. See the following letter.
41. On February 16 Dowden mentioned a discussion of "The Genius of Walt Whitman" at the Fortnightly Club two days earlier (Feinberg; Traubel, I, 302–303).
42. This part of the letter was erroneously placed in 672, because Dowden's transcription in the Berg Collection included, without any indication, parts of 672 and the present letter. The correct and complete text of 672 will appear in the Addenda to the final volume of the *Correspondence*.

721. *To Abraham Stoker*

ADDRESS: Abraham Stoker | 119 Lower Baggot
street | Dublin, | Ireland. POSTMARK: Camden | Mar |
6 | N.J.

431 Stevens st. | cor West. | Camden, |
N. Jersey, U. S. America. | March 6 | 76
'Bram Stoker,[43] | My dear young man,

Your letters have been most welcome to me—welcome to me as
Person, & then as Author—I don't know which most—You did well to
write to me so unconventionally, so fresh, so manly, & so affectionately
too. I too hope (though it is not probable) that we shall one day personally
meet each other. Meantime I send you my friendship & thanks.

Edward Dowden's letter containing among others your subscription
for a copy of my new edition, has just been rec'd. I shall send the books
very soon by express in a package to his address. I have just written to
E. D.[44]

My physique is entirely shatter'd—doubtless permanently—from paralysis & other ailments. But I am up & dress'd, & get out every day a
little—live here quite lonesome, but hearty, & good spirits.

Write to me again.

Walt Whitman

722. *To William Michael Rossetti*

431 Stevens st. | cor West. | Camden, | N. Jersey, |
U. S. America—March 17, | '76
W. M. Rossetti—Dear friend,

Yours of the 28th Feb.[45] rec'd, & indeed welcomed & appreciated.
I am jogging along still about the same in physical condition—still certainly no worse, & I sometimes lately suspect rather better, or at any rate
more adjusted to the situation—Even begin to think of making some move,

---

43. Stoker (1847–1912) was the author of *Dracula*, secretary to Sir Henry Irving,
and editor of *Personal Reminiscences of Henry Irving* (1906). As a young man, on
February 18, 1872, Stoker wrote a personal, eccentric letter to WW which he did not
send until February 14, 1876 (Feinberg; Traubel, IV, 180–185). In the earlier letter he
had written: "How sweet a thing it is for a strong healthy man with a woman's eyes and a
child's wishes to feel that he can speak so to a man [WW] who can be if he wishes,
father, and brother and wife to his soul" (Feinberg; Traubel, IV, 185). Stoker visited
WW in 1884 (Allen, 516).
44. See the preceding letter.
45. Although previously confused by conflicting press reports as to WW's financial

some change of base, &c. (The doctors have been advising it for over two years, but I hav'n't felt to do it, yet.) My paralysis does not lift—I cannot walk any distance—I still have this baffling, obstinate, apparently chronic affection of the stomachic apparatus & liver—Yet (as told in former letters) I get out doors a little every day—write & read, in moderation—appetite sufficiently good, (eat only very plain food, but always did that)—digestion tolerable—& spirits unflagging. (As said above, I have told you most of this before, but suppose you might like to know it all again, up to date.) Of course, & pretty darkly coloring the whole, are bad spells, prostrations, *some pretty grave ones*, intervals—& I have resigned myself to the certainty of permanent incapacitation from solid work—but things may continue at least in this half-and-half way, for months—even years.

My books are out, the new edition, a set of which, immediately on receiving your letter of 28th, I have sent you (by mail March 15)[46] & I suppose you have before this rec'd them.

My dear friend, your offers of help, & those of my other British friends, I think I fully appreciate, in the right spirit, welcome & acceptive —leaving the matter altogether in your & their hands—& to your & their convenience, discretion, leisure & nicety—Though poor now even to penury *I have not so far been deprived of any physical thing I need or wish whatever—& I feel confident I shall not, in the future.* During my employment of seven years or more in Washington after the war (1865–'72) I regularly saved a great part of my wages—& though the sum has now become about exhausted, by my expenses of the last three years— there are already beginning at present welcome dribbles hitherward from the sales of my new edition which I just job & sell, myself, (as the book agents here for 3 years in New York have successively, deliberately, badly cheated me)[47] & shall continue to dispose of the books myself. And *that* is the way I should prefer to glean my support—In that way I cheerfully accept all the aid my friends find it convenient to proffer—(Prof. Dowden has sent me the money for seven sets—which I have forwarded to him at Dublin.[48] I wish you to loan this letter to him to read.) I wish you to

straits, Rossetti in this letter accepted WW's statements in the *West Jersey Press* and in 711; "There are some of us who wd really be glad to exert ourselves to the extent of our moderate means, to prove that we are not insensible of our obligations we owe you" (Feinberg). Yet in this letter WW was silently modifying his own earlier accounts; in fact, his position as now stated did not materially differ from that in the Springfield *Republican* which had led to the reply in the *West Jersey Press*. Rossetti distributed facsimiles of this letter to English admirers.

   46. On February 28 Rossetti informed WW that Mrs. Gilchrist and he would shortly send £10 (approximately $50) for sets of WW's new edition (Feinberg).

   47. For WW's account of this alleged embezzlement, see 698.

   48. See 720.

notify me—by postal card will do—soon as you receive your books sent on the 15th—I wish you also to loan this letter to Mrs. Gilchrist, first of all. I shall write to her to-day or to-morrow—but briefly.

To repeat a little, & without undertaking details, understand, dear friend, for yourself & all, that I heartily & most affectionately thank my British friends, & that I accept their sympathetic generosity in the same spirit in which I believe (nay, *know*) it is offered—that though poor *I am not in want*—that I maintain good heart & cheer—& that by far the most satisfaction to me, (& I think it can be done, & believe it will be,) will be to live, as long as possible, on *the sales, by myself, of my own works—* & perhaps, if practicable, by further writings for the press.

Walt Whitman

There is a small fury & much eructive spitting & sputtering already among the "literary coteries" here from Robt. Buchanan's lance-slash at them anent of me, in his letter in the London D[aily] News, of March 13,[49] (synopsis cabled here to Associated press, & printed everywhere)—the "coteries" resenting it madly by editorials here & there already in the papers—they fall to berating R. B. first, & then *me*—say, if *I* WERE *sick, or* WERE *poor, why then,*—&c. &c. &c.

(If convenient, I should like to have this letter loaned to Mr. Buchanan also. I am prohibited from writing too much, & I must make this candid statement of the situation serve for all my dear friends over there.)[50]

723. *To Anne Gilchrist*

431 Stevens st. | cor West. | Camden, | N. Jersey, |
U. S. America—March 17 | '76

Dearest friend,

To your good & comforting letter of Feb. 25th[51] I at once answer, at least with a few lines. I have already to-day written (answering one

49. Buchanan had written in praise of WW as early as 1867 (see 262 and 421). His account in the London newspaper was based on excerpts from the *West Jersey Press* which Rossetti had inserted in *The Athenaeum* on March 11. Rossetti's letter in support of Buchanan appeared in the London *Daily News* on March 14.

50. Except for this final paragraph, which was probably added later, the letter differs from the draft version only in insignificant verbal changes.

51. Poor Mrs. Gilchrist continued to ignore the obvious: WW wanted her (and her passion) three thousand miles away. On January 18 she informed him that she was sailing for America on August 30 (LC; Harned, 139). On February 25 she was ecstatic: "Soon, very soon I come, my darling. . . . this is the last spring we shall be assunder—O I passionately believe there are years in store for us— . . . Hold out but a little longer for me, my Walt" (LC; Harned, 141). Mrs. Gilchrist wrote again, on

just rec'd from him) a pretty long letter to Mr Rossetti, & requested him to loan it to you for perusal. In that I have described my situation fully & candidly.

My new edition is printed & ready. On receipt of your letter I have mailed you a set, two vols., which you ought to have rec'd by this time. I wish you to send me word soon as they arrive.

My health I am encouraged to think is perhaps a shade better—certainly as well as any time of late. I even already vaguely contemplate plans, (they may never be fulfilled, but yet again they may,) of changes, journeys—even of coming to London, of seeing you, of visiting my friends, &c.

My dearest friend, I do not approve your American trans-settlement[52] —I see so many things here, you have yet no idea of—the American social & almost every other kind of crudeness, meagreness, (at least in appearance)—Don't do any thing toward such a move, nor resolve on it, nor indeed make any move at all in it, without further advice from me. If I should get well enough to voyage, we will talk about it yet in London— You must not be uneasy about me—dear friend, I get along much better than you suppose. As to my literary situation here, my rejection by the coteries—& my poverty, (which is the least of my troubles)—I am not sure but I enjoy them all. Besides, as to the latter, I am not in want. Best love to you, & to your children.

Walt Whitman

724. *To Moncure D. Conway*   3.19. [1876][53]

431 Stevens st | cor West | Camden | N Jersey |
U S America—March 19

My dear friend,

I did not know at all till supper with my sister-in-law *last evening* that you had had a conversation with her about, & special interest in, my

March 11 after she had seen some of WW's poems in the London *Daily News* (LC; Harned, 143–144).

52. In her reply on March 30, Mrs. Gilchrist refused WW's advice: "I can't exactly obey that, for it has been my settled steady purpose (resting on a deep strong faith) ever since 1869" (LC; Harned, 147). After reading *Two Rivulets*, she could not curb her ardor, on April 21: "sweetest deepest greatest experience of my life—what I was made for, surely I was made as the soil in which the precious seed of your thoughts & emotions should be planted—they to fulfil themselves in me, that I might by & bye blossom into beauty & bring forth rich fruits—immortal fruits" (LC; Harned, 149). Mrs. Gilchrist sent birthday greetings on May 18 (LC; Harned, 152–153).

53. The year is established by the references to the 1876 edition. Perhaps Conway visited WW on March 18. According to 718, he was to return to England about the middle of March. For the subsequent controversy, see 732.

pecuniary condition, &c. If I had known it at the time I should have spoken about it, & freely, to you, by word of mouth—as that would have been, & is, best in such things.

When I came to Camden in '73, paralyzed, I felt, (& the feeling has since been confirmed,) that I had retired for good from the active world, but that I might linger along for years yet. I bought a pleasant little cheap lot here, paid for it, & my plan was to put up a small three or four room house on it, in which I might live plainly & comfortably the rest of my days—& that is still my plan & desire.[54] I had saved up quite a fund from my earnings '65 to '72 as clerk in Washington—but they have now become about exhausted by expenses of three years, (for I just take board & lodging here & pay for them scrupulously same as in some temporary inn.) My great wish still is to put up for myself this little three or four room home for the rest of my days, independently, in a sort. I suppose it would cost 700 or 800 dollars.

I have managed to get out complete my new edition both Vols. which I now begin to sell & job myself—intend to continue doing so—(have somehow an idea that I should then, in my own shanty, & for time to come, be able to live on the moderate steady income of the sales of my own works—*which is most satisfactory to me*)—

I was in hopes to have seen you again before you sail'd—I was at Mrs Lesley's again about three weeks since (to meet Miss Kate Hillard)[55]—had a very pleasant afternoon with Mrs. L & the rest—

Things go on much the same with me in physical condition—I send you a paper & some slips, same mail with this—I have written very lately to W M Rossetti about my affairs, books, &c.

Walt Whitman

725. *To Ellen M. O'Connor*   3.23. [1876][56]

ADDRESS: Mrs E M O'Connor | 1015 O street | Washington | D. C. POSTMARKS: Camden | Mar | 23 | N.J.; Carrier | 24 | Mar | 8 AM.

Camden—March 23—noon—

Yours rec'd—I am around, much the same—nothing very new, or different—the b[aby] doing well, grows well, hearty & bright—the rest well

54. See 630. WW did not move into his own "shanty" until 1884.
55. See 718–719.
56. The year is established by Mrs. Nancy M. Johnson's letter to WW on March 15 (Feinberg), in which she ordered the 1876 set, as well as by the reference to his

as usual— E[dward][57] recovered, & all right—my (new Edition) books out at last—(sent a set to N. M. J[ohnson] 506 12th st.)—comfortable to-day— write this in haste—

W.W.

726. *To William Michael Rossetti*   3.23. *[1876]*

ADDRESS: W M Rossetti | 56 Euston Sq | London | n w | England. POSTMARKS: Camden | Mar | 23 | N.J.; London N.W. | C 10 | Paid | (?) | 76.

Camden, N. Jersey—U. S. America—March 23

Yours of March 5[58] recd. with enc.—Books will be sent hence by Baldwin's Express (office in London, H. Starr & Co. 22 Moorgate st)—will probably arrive there somewhere ab't 10th or 12th April.

I sent a set (L of G and Two Riv. *Two Vols.* in one package) to you by mail March 15—& another set *two Vols.* same date, to Mrs. G[ilchrist][59] —but have since learn'd that such packages are *overweight*, & fear they may not have been forwarded from N. Y.

I wrote you letter March 17—I sent a single Vol. (Two Riv) by mail, March 20—I continue about the same.

W.W.

727. *To William Michael Rossetti*

431 Stevens st. | cor West | Camden | N Jersey | U. S.
America | March 29 '76

Dear friend,

As I should like to have you prepared for any thing that *might* happen, now or in future—As it may be that out of this hubbub, some one in London may take a notion to rush & crudely reprint my books—I send you (same mail with this) full & corrected copies of my two volumes, prepared for the printers, for a London edition, with an especial Preface note—& altogether as I should like to have the books brought out, for permanent reading & investigation in Europe.

My dear friend, I authorize you to make any arrangement about pub-

---

nephew. WW sent the volumes to Mrs. Johnson on March 17, and *Memoranda During the War* on April 20 (*CB*); see also 718 and 138.

    57. WW's brother.   58. Rossetti's letter is apparently lost.

    59. These transactions are confirmed in *CB*.

lishing, terms, &c. you think best—only the books must be printed verbatim & entire, if at all, & in Two Volumes—(You will see what I have authorized to be put at bottom of title pages.) [60]

Dowden wrote to me lately a word on this matter, relating however only to *Two Rivulets* (proposed Chatto & Windus, at a venture) [61]—I shall tell D. that I have placed these copies in your hands—& shall (if you have no objection) consider him to be join'd with you in the matter of deciding, negotiating, terms, &c. of the publishing, (should such come to pass)—& whatever you twain think well to do, under those conditions, in said matter, I hereby warrant & endorse.

Walt Whitman

728. *To William Michael Rossetti*

431 Stevens st | cor West | Camden N Jersey | U S
America March 30 | '76

Dear friend—

I have already acknowledged yours of 16th [62]—Mine of 17th will have advised you of the situation here, & the general character of my wishes, the way things have shaped themselves in London—Whatever I should do, if I had the planning of it *de novo*, the question is now (like a general making the best of the turn the battle has taken in its own hands, & compell'd to decide quickly & definitely,) what to direct & authorize under the circumstances—While I unhesitatingly accept such kind offerings as Chas W Reynell's [63] (No 1. in your transcript) and J Leicester Warren [64] (No 2)—& authorize you or any of my friends to continue to accept the like, in my name, where offer'd readily & properly, I'd rather you would, after receiving this, either, (to use nautical lingo,) *take in sail*, or at least don't crowd on any more sail at all. The whole business requires to be done with perfect candor to my generous friends—to you & the other mediums of that generosity—& to myself—& must & shall be so done. Of the cheque (No 1) or any other, or any thing of the kind sent by you or through you or any of my friends, the most convenient to me would be to have them remitted to me, to

60. Nothing came of this proposed English edition until 1881, when it was published by David Bogue.
61. Dowden made this proposal on February 16 (Feinberg; Traubel, 1, 303). He wrote again on March 16, after receiving WW's new edition (Feinberg; Traubel, 1, 122–123).
62. Probably a reference to the preceding letter. Rossetti's letter is not known (see 732).
63. WW sent the Centennial Edition to Reynell on May 18, and *Memoranda*

my address here, drawn on some well-known New York or Philadelphia banker, *payable to my order*—(if in Philadelphia, on Drexel & Co. bankers, 34 south 3d street.)[65] Then the p. o. international money order is also a good & safe way to remit—I should like in all cases to have the full & explicit address of the friend & giver, to send him or her at least one special autograph copy, or set, of my books—

As told you in former letter,[66] although I am indeed poor, with means exhausted, I am by no means in a condition of pinching want, nor likely to be. I am boarding here, under the usual, unavoidable expenses. I accept the kind gifts, first for my own help, then perhaps somewhat for the still graver needs of others, forever falling in my way. For the future I really think the income from my books, if it can be utilized, promises amply enough for my support—& *that* decidedly would be most satisfactory to me—

Probably from the tinge of Quaker breed in me the inner convictions & silent dictates of *the spirit* settle these cases, & what I must do in them, more than reason, convention or even delicacy—& those inner dictates I have now obeyed in the decisions of this letter, as *a higher reason & delicacy*, & the final arbiter of the question.

Walt Whitman

If perfectly convenient I should like Buchanan to see this letter—also Dowden—Indeed you can make what use of it, in your discretion, you think best—

A line further about the publication copy, Two Volumes, I sent a couple of days since.[67] I couldn't rest until I had sent that copy to provide for any thing that might happen (my affairs are in such a chaotic state here in America—my health, mentality, from week to week, even *existence*, uncertain)—Now you have it, I feel relieved, & shall consider that the thing is secured, & cannot be lost—*But there is no haste about it*—If you should hear of any proposed London reprint, then try & get my copy published at once, making any decent terms you can—But if there don't appear to be any danger, take your leisure, & hold on. See if you can get any one to pay me something down ahead—I revoke what I said about the *shilling edition*[68]— let the books, when printed, be at a price suitable to the trade & market—

W.W.

During the War on June 14 or 15 (CB).

64.   John Byrne Leicester Warren (1835–1895), third Baron de Tabley, was a poet. WW sent the 1876 edition on May 18, and *Memoranda During the War* on June 14 or 15 (CB).

65.   Rossetti noted in the margin: "superseded by letter of 31 March."

66.   See 722.

67.   See the preceding letter.

68.   WW evidently alluded to this edition in a lost letter.

There is a precious row here over *your* row in London—all the curs & kennels of literary New York and Boston are in full chorus after you fellows —after Buchanan especially—then you, Dowden, & the rest—(of course *I* catch it roundly)[69]—

729. *To William Michael Rossetti*

DRAFT LETTER.

> 431 Stevens st. | cor West. | Camden, | N. Jersey, |
> U S America | March 31, '76

My dear friend,
        (Later than my letter dispatched last evening I wish merely to say) make cheques, orders or drafts payable by Brown brothers, bankers, Philadelphia, U. S. A., corner Chestnut and Strawberry streets, *on my endorsement.*[70]

> Walt Whitman

I am feeling quite comfortable to-day—I wish this information—the address above—conveyed to Robert Buchanan—

730. *To Robert Buchanan*

ENDORSED: "to Buchanan | April 4 '76 | Sent[71] B
the N Y | letter of July 4 '78 | (to Olean
Scotland)." DRAFT LETTER.

> 431 Stevens st | cor West | Camden | N Jersey |
> U S America | April 4 '76

Robert Buchanan— | My dear friend—
        I merely want to say that I have read your letter in the London *Daily News*[72]—all your three letters—& that I deeply appreciate them, & do

69. See 735.
70. Rossetti duly cited Brown Brothers in a circular he issued on June 1 (Donaldson, 27–28).
71. This part of the endorsement was added two years later. WW referred to "A Poet's Recreation," published in the New York *Tribune* on July 4, 1878; see 875.
72. Buchanan's article of March 13; see 722
73. A copy of *Memoranda During the War* in the Feinberg Collection is inscribed: "To Dan: Whittaker from his friend the Author." Whittaker, a printer, was employed in the office of the Camden *New Republic*, where Harry Stafford was an errand boy.

not hesitate to accept & respond to them in the same spirit in which they were surely impelled & written.

May God bless you & yours,

Walt Whitman.

731. *To Daniel Whittaker(?)*[73]   *4.4. [1876?]*

431 Stevens st Camden | April 4

Dear Dan:

I take an interest in the boy in the office, Harry Stafford—I know his father & mother—There is a large family, very respectable American people—farmers, but only a hired farm—Mr. Stafford in weak health—

I am anxious Harry should *learn the printer's trade thoroughly—I want him to learn to set type as fast as possible*—want you to give him a chance (less of the mere errands &c)—There is a good deal really in the boy, if he has a chance.

Don't say any thing about this note to him—or in fact to any one—just tear it up, & *keep the matter to yourself private.*

Walt Whitman

732. *To William Michael Rossetti*

431 Stevens st. Camden, N. Jersey | U S America—
April 7 '76

Dear friend,

This is to acknowledge yours of the 25th March—those of the 16th and of the 20th,[74] duly rec'd, were previously acknowledged. My letters (that of March 17, in which I outline the situation & my wishes—that of 23d, postal c'd.—that of 29th, on sending the Two Volumes, publication copy L. of G. and Two R[ivulets]—that of April 1 conveying fuller & more detailed statement of views & wishes—& a short letter afterward, same date) have conveyed I think substantially all I desire to say on the whole affair.[75]

If the cable telegram in the evening papers of Tuesday last here cor-

(Since WW became acquainted with the Staffords in 1876, the year appears to be correct.)

When Mrs. Stafford wrote to WW on May 1, 1876, she was worried because Harry "left the New Republic office in such A hurry at least untill he had another place as he does not like to work on A farm. he spoke of getting A situation In the park" (Feinberg).

74. Rossetti's three letters are apparently not extant.

75. The letters referred to were written on March 30 and 31. The draft of the former, which WW retained in his possession, is dated March 31, with the additional notation: "went in steamer Baltic April 1."

rectly synopsizes M D Conway's letter about my case in some London paper or papers of that date, *I do not approve his letter.*[76] It seems singularly *malapropos*—& in the face of my friends—their efforts there.

I believe I ought to look over your two last letters again, & say something further about the transcripts of my kind & generous friends—but cannot to-day—will soon.

Send me, at your convenience, the papers that print my things—also any *notable* criticism or letter, (of course don't mind the small fry.)

I know I am troubling your time & activity a good deal, but I won't make any apology about it further than to say that I am sure I deeply appreciate it. Good bye for this time & God bless you, my dearest friend.

Walt Whitman

Your parcel of books by express has been delayed—not yet gone—will go in two or three days—You must have rec'd the 3 copies by mail?

I am still, still up & around, not much different in condition—[77]

733. *To Various Friends*   *4.12.* [1876][78]

ENDORSED: "letters to | Wm Swinton[79] | Ward[80] | Stedman[81] | J Miller | Dr Seeger[82] | Mr Jardine[83] | John Swinton[84] | Sent | April | 12." DRAFT LETTER.

Dear Sir,

In a letter from my friend John Swinton as he speaks of your kind desire to subscribe for some copies of my new edition books, I send you the

76. Conway was reported in the London *Daily News* as saying: "On the strength of a letter just received from Mr. Whitman, that the idea that he is in distress or dependent upon his relatives is unfounded" (Traubel, I, 345, and see I, 346). On April 24 Conway informed WW that he was attempting to protect the poet and his relatives from the "insults" of his British admirers (Feinberg; Traubel, I, 347). On April 17 the New York *Tribune* paraphrased Conway's remarks in the *Daily News*, and quoted him on April 26: "Having recently visited the poet in his comfortable quarters in Camden, I am compelled to deny Buchanan's gross exaggerations."

In the margin WW wrote: "sent this to C[onway]—2 of 4 [newspaper accounts]."

77. The postscript does not appear in the draft of this letter.

78. This is WW's copy of a form letter he sent to various friends at the suggestion of Swinton in order to sell copies of his new edition.

79. A war correspondent and later a professor of English; see 37.

80. See the following letter.

81. See 89. Stedman visited WW on March 18 (LC #108). Buchanan wrote to WW on April 18: [Stedman] "is most hostile to your *poetic* claims. . . . Stedman is a clever versewriter, without backbone or virility" (Feinberg). O'Connor, in 1876, however, termed Stedman "very friendly" (Doheny; Barrus, 132). See also 981.

82. Dr. Ferdinand Seeger, of New York City, sent checks for $5 on April 15 and 18 (Feinberg), and WW forwarded two volumes on April 21 (CB).

83. Jardine wrote to WW on April 26 (Feinberg).

84. See 37. On April 1 Swinton published in the New York *Herald* a previously unnoted article written after a recent visit to WW: "Walt Whitman's long and grievous

enclosed slips. Of course I should be happy to furnish you with any copies.

I am still jogging along here in the two-thirds ill, one-third well condition, of these late years.

734. *To John Quincy Adams Ward*[85]   *4.12.* [*1876*]

TRANSCRIPT.

April 12

. . . your kind desire to subscribe for some copies of my new edition. . . .
Of course I should be happy to furnish you with any copies.

Walt Whitman

735. *To John Burroughs*   *4.13.* [*1876*]

TRANSCRIPT.

April 13.

Your letter in 'Tribune' today headed 'W. W.'s Poetry'[86] is like an
artillery and bayonet charge combined—is splendid, earnest, and terribly
live—(Wonder the T—— ever printed it)—Bad spell this forenoon—F. B.

illness has placed him in such a position as to justify the appeal of Mr. Buchanan."
Swinton referred to the help given to WW by Colonel Johnston (see 554), James M.
Scovel (see 774.1), and Samuel Bowles (1826–1878), the editor of the Springfield
Republican. He concluded: "Now, sir, it seems to me that Walt Whitman's countrymen
should not allow him to suffer from penury in his old age. . . . his closing days should
be cheered by those kindly memories, which, I hope, are not to reach him wholly from
Great Britain." An envelope addressed to Swinton, postmarked April 12, is in the
Feinberg Collection.
    85. Ward (1830–1910) was, according to DAB, "the first native sculptor to create,
without benefit of foreign training, an impressive body of good work." Ward informed
WW on April 23 that on May 1 he would order five sets of the new edition (Feinberg;
Traubel, II, 278). The order was sent on June 1 (Feinberg); WW noted receipt of
$50 from Ward on June 6 (CB).
    86. Although the New York *Tribune* had printed WW's review of his own books
earlier in the year (see 715) as well as sympathetic reports on January 29 and February 25 and excerpts from *Two Rivulets* on March 1, the newspaper, probably through
the influence of Bayard Taylor (see 199), began to publish hostile notices. On March 28
the London correspondent assailed Buchanan's article in the London *Daily News*. An editorial on March 30 also attacked the recklessness of Buchanan's charges, and maintained
that if WW failed to save money from his Washington days, "the cause thereof was
certainly not 'persecution.'" Another hostile editorial appeared on April 12. Burroughs'
defense was published on April 13. On April 22 O'Connor, WW's estranged friend,
wrote an extravagant, and garrulous, encomium. Later the *Tribune* resumed its friendly
attitude toward WW.

Sanborn[87] visited me today—Am going out and will see if I can get the T—— to send you—am not sure—

W.W.

736. *To John H. Johnston* 4.19. [1876]

431 Stevens St. | Camden, N. Jersey | April 19

Dear friend,[88]

I have rec'd your letter, money, & order for Joaquin Miller's books, & had just prepared them to send, when I have rec'd a letter from J. M. saying he will soon be in Philadelphia[89]—& that I must lay the books aside *for him to take*, when he calls personally on me, which will be soon.

I am much annoyed about the postage mishap. I have written to the P. M. at New York, & hope he will make restitution—as the package was *not sealed* at ends, (only wrapt over & tied, to protect the gilt edges)—at least twenty packages have been sent *in precisely the same way* (one or two to N. Y.) and this is the only one that has been served so. If the P. M. don't *restitute* I must be allowed to pay it—not because it is important, but because it is my affair—& *business*—

I send you an extra copy of my little War book, same mail with this— Shall write you soon definitely about coming on—

Love to you, my friend, & to Mrs. J.

Walt Whitman

87. Franklin B. Sanborn (1831–1917) was an abolitionist and a friend of John Brown. In 1860, when he was tried in Boston because of his refusal to testify before a committee of the U. S. Senate, WW was in the courtroom (Allen, 242). He reviewed *Drum-Taps* in the Boston *Commonwealth* on February 24, 1866 (Miller, *Drum-Taps*, lviii). He was editor of the Springfield *Republican* from 1868 to 1872, and was the author of books dealing with his friends, Emerson, Thoreau, and Alcott. "A Visit to the Good Gray Poet" appeared without Sanborn's name in the Springfield *Republican* on April 19.
88. This is the first letter in a fairly extensive correspondence with this New York jeweler (1837–1919), who was also a friend of Joaquin Miller (Traubel, II, 139). WW visited the Johnstons for the first time early in 1877. In 1888 he observed to Traubel: "I count [Johnston] as in our inner circle, among the chosen few" (Traubel, II, 423). See also Johnston's letter, printed by Charles N. Elliot, *Walt Whitman as Man, Poet and Friend* (1915), 149–174.
89. Miller had written to WW on April 16 (Feinberg; Traubel, II, 139–140). He was in Camden on May 11 (*CB*).

737. To Edwin Stafford[90]   *4.19. [1876]*

DRAFT LETTER.

431 Stevens st | Camden | April 19

Dear Ed:

I send the little book I promised you.[91] The little box of *papetrie* is for Debbie. My love to mother, father, & all the children.

Walt Whitman

I want Harry to come up Friday, & stay over till Sunday with me[92]—I will not be down Saturday with you this week.

738. To Edward Carpenter

ADDRESS: Edward Carpenter | 3 Wesley Terrace |
Shaw Lane | Headingly | Leeds, England.
POSTMARKS: Camden | Apr | 23 | N.J.; Leeds | 162 |
10 My | 76.

431 Stevens St | Camden N Jersey | U S America |
April 23 '76

Dear Sir[93]

I have rec'd the P.O. money order, & the money (£4—$21.97) has been paid me—for which accept warmest thanks.—No letter has yet reached me, specifying an order for my books, new edition—but if one does not come in a few days, I believe I will send the Two Vols. to same address as this note—As, I take it, that will be agreeable to you.

I am middling comfortable these times—Again thanks—

Walt Whitman

90. The year is established by the fact that this draft was written on the verso of 740. Harry's brother, Edwin, was born on May 6, 1856, and died in 1906.
    91. Undoubtedly *Memoranda During the War*.
    92. In her letter of May 1 Mrs. Stafford was concerned about Harry's instability and, specifically, his lack of employment. She thought that it was "better still for him to be with you but I fear he is to much trouble to you all ready. I do not think it right to impose on the good nature of our friends. I hope Harry will ever be Greatfull to you fore your kindness to him" (Feinberg).
    93. Like many other young disillusioned Englishmen, Carpenter (1844–1929) deemed WW a prophetic spokesman of an ideal state cemented in the bonds of brotherhood. On July 12, 1874, he wrote for the first time to WW: "Because you have, as it were, given me a ground for the love of men I thank you continually in my heart. . . . For you have made men to be not ashamed of the noblest instinct of their nature" (Feinberg; Traubel, I, 160). On January 3, 1876, Carpenter sent another impassioned letter (Feinberg; Traubel, III, 414–418). On April 8 he sent £4 for the 1876 volumes (Feinberg). See also 810.

739. *To William Michael Rossetti*   *4.23. [1876]*

ADDRESS: Wm M Rossetti | 56 Euston Sq | London |
n w | England. POSTMARKS: Camden | Apr | 23 |
N.J.; Philadelphia | Apr | 24 | (?); London N W |
C 7 | Paid | My 8 | 76.

431 Stevens st | Camden N Jersey   U S America |
April 23

I have to-day sent by mail my new Vol. *Two Rivulets* to T. C. S. and
E. J. S. M.[94] (the Scotch l's) 1 Alva st, Edinburgh—

W.W.

have not yet sent any express parcel to London—

740. *To C. P. Somerby*[95]   *[4.23. 1876]*

ENDORSED: "Sent to C P Somerby | April 23 '76."
DRAFT LETTER.

Your letter of [   ] rec'd. I shall bear with you, trusting to
the future.

Please make a bundle of *all my books*, Burroughs's *Notes*, *As a Strong
Bird*, 67 Ed'n L of G, &c, & send here to me prepaid by Express.

Make out a full plain statement of our acc't exactly how much you owe
me, how it all stands &c. & send me.

Can you supply me with a copy of Websters Quarto Dictionary, latest
fullest edition, & Author's Classical Dictionary ditto?

94. On March 30 Theresa C. Simpson and Elizabeth J. Scott-Moncrieff sent orders
for books through Rossetti (Feinberg). WW sent *Two Rivulets* on April 23 and *Leaves
of Grass* on June 12 (CB).
95. Somerby was one of the book dealers whom WW termed "embezzlers." In
1875 Somerby assumed the liabilities of Butts & Co. (see 577). This proved to be a
matter of embarrassment to Somerby, who, in reply to a lost letter on March 16, 1875,
was unable "to remit the amount you name at present." On May 5 he wrote: "It is very
mortifying to me not to be in a position to send you even a small portion of the balance
your due." On October 4 Somerby sent $10—his only cash payment: "Have made every
exertion to raise the $200 you require, and find it utterly impossible to get it. . . . We
had hoped that you would accept our offer to get out your new book, and thus more than
discharge our indebtedness to you." On April 19, 1876, Somerby reported that "I have
been losing, instead of gaining." On May 6 he sent WW a statement pertaining to the
volumes mentioned in this letter. On May 12 he included a complete financial statement:
in eighteen months he had made only one cash payment, and owed WW $215.17. The
firm was still unable to make a payment on September 28. In August, 1877, WW
received a notice of bankruptcy dated August 8 from, in his own words, "assignee

741. *To Edward Carpenter*   4.25. *[1876]*

TRANSCRIPT.

431 Stevens Street, | Camden, | New Jersey, |
U. S. A. | April 25th.

I have to-day forwarded by mail in two parcels (same address as this card) my two volumes new edition, complete works.[96] Please send me word (by postal card will do) when they reach you safely. I shall send the others soon.

W.W.

742. *To S. W. Green*   *[5.4(?). 1876]*

ENDORSED: "Sample sent by S W Green |
May 3 '76." DRAFT LETTER.

S. W. Green | Dear Sir:

Yours of 3d rec'd,[97] with estimate, $157, for corrections (as per order & sample) and printing 600 copies, 384 pages, on paper as per sample—said copies to be ready for binder on 24th May—

This is to accept your estimate & to request & order the 600 copies—which I now do, & shall expect the sheets ready on the 24th—

Please make the corrections forthwith[98] & send me proofs thereof here, which will be promptly returned.

743. *To William Michael Rossetti*

431 Stevens st—cor West | Camden N Jersey
U S America | May 5 '76

My dear friend,
Yours of April 19[99] both rec'd—with draft on Drexel & Co. for £28.4

[Josiah Fletcher, an attorney] of the rascal Chas P. Somerby." These manuscripts are in the Feinberg Collection.
    96. See 738. In a letter to WW on March 1, 1877, Carpenter wrote: "Your two volumes with my name written in them are my faithful companions" (Syracuse). This presentation copy is now in the Feinberg Collection.
    97. On May 2, in a lost letter, WW asked Green, a New York printer, to give him an estimate, which Green supplied on May 3 (Feinberg). Probably WW accepted the offer on the following day. Green evidently delivered 600 copies to the binders on May 24, for in the Feinberg Collection there is a check for $157 made out to Green on May 31. Green had printed some of WW's earlier works; see 462.
    98. In the second printing of the 1876 *Leaves of Grass* intercalations included: "As in a Swoon," "The Beauty of the Ship," "When the Full-Grown Poet Came," and "After an Interval."
    99. Rossetti's letter is not known, but the receipt of money is noted in *CB*. On April 4 Rossetti had written to WW to inquire whether *Leaves of Grass* was available at less than £1 (Feinberg). Either WW's reply is not extant, or the second paragraph of this letter was intended as an answer.

—most acceptable. The books, according to list sent, will now be prepared, packed, & sent (together with your & Mrs. Gilchrist's copies, which have been waiting) probably to London express, of which I will advise you more explicitly by letter to follow this probably within two or three days.

I repeat what I have already written you—*accept all subscriptions*—all will be supplied, upon remittance—(I am already putting another small edition to press)[1]—the price will invariably be $10 the set—$5 each Vol.— can be had separately, or together, as wanted—Each will contain portraits & my autograph. The Two, *Leaves* and *Rivulets*, comprise my complete works (the latter Vol., as you see, includes *Memoranda of the War* as a constituent part.)

I do not approve of Mr Conway's letter of April 4[2]—it was unneeded, hurtful to my case,[3] & join'd with his allusions to the matter in his public American correspondence, an insult to Mr Buchanan, through me[4]—as such I decidedly resent & disavow it—Every point in B[uchanan']s March 11 letter to the *News*, is well taken, & *true without exception*—particularly all about the American critics, publishers, editors, "poets" &c—even what he says about my "impoverishment" is much, *much nearer the truth* than Mr Conway's and Lord Houghton's rose-colored illusion varnish—if Mr C. instead of intellectual possessed sympathetic delicacy & insight (I don't think he possesses either) he could have divined better about me & my affairs, not only now here in Camden, but times past in the beginning.

I send my love & thanks to W B Scott[5]—I shall try to write a line to him, to C W Reynell, to J L Warren, to A G Dew-Smith,[6] & one or two others, soon as I can. I heartily thank my good friends of the *Secularist*. I am glad you printed off, & furnish'd friends with copies of my letter of March 17— upon reading it in print, I find it exactly describes the situation, & my wishes—& I reëndorse it—(if you have any copies spare, send me two or three more in next paper you send.)

The drafting on Drexel & Co., the Philadelphia bankers, is perfectly convenient to me.

I am feeling pretty comfortable as I write—have been out a little nearly every day for a week—some days across the river here, the broad Delaware —This is one of my good mornings (it is now between 8 and 9), have

---

1. See the preceding letter.   2. See 732.

3. WW did not recopy the following passage in his draft: "(in diplomacy as some one has said, *the utterance markedly malapropos or ill-tempered* is worse than the worst untruth)."

4. WW did not include the following from the draft letter: "Buchanan stands to me as a fervid, affectionate & reverential friend and advocate."

5. William Bell Scott (1811–1890), an English poet and painter, became acquainted with *Leaves of Grass* through Dixon; see 365. WW sent the two 1876 volumes on May 18 and *Memoranda During the War* on June 14 or 15 (*CB*).

6. For Reynell and Warren, see 728. WW sent two volumes to Dew-Smith on

finished my breakfast, coffee, Graham bread & mutton chop—good night's sleep last night—occupy myself two or three hours every day, when not too ill, with my *book business*, letters, &c—also with *the baby boy*, my brother's 6 months infant, very fine & bright, (of course)—takes much of my time, & is a delightful diversion to me—the young one knows me *so well*, & is always happy when tended by me—& so, my dear friend, good bye for this time—& God bless you & yours.

Walt Whitman

744. *To John Swinton*[7]   5.5. [1876]

431 Stevens st | Camden N Jersey May 5 p m

Dear friend,

Nothing very notable to write about, but I thought I would send you a line—This is one of my comfortable days—good night's sleep last night—breakfast & dinner to-day with appetite—still get out a little most every day as formerly—my *book business*, & a little writing & reading give me three hours or so occupation (lazily) every day when I am not *too ill*—and then *the baby*, my brother's 6 mo's infant boy, very fine & bright (of course) is an unfailing delight & diversion to me—the young one knows me *so well*, & is never so happy as when I am tending him.

I adopted your suggestion of 3 or 4 weeks since—wrote with result as follows to

Wm Swinton—no answer

to E C Stedman, sent an order at once enc'g: $30

to J Q A Ward,[8] kind answer, will order presently

to Dr Seeger, answer, order 1 set, & money enc.

to Joaquin Miller,[9] ordered a set & sent the money.

to Mr. Jardine, answered a few days ago

I *did not write* either to G. A. Townsend,[10] or to W C Church[11]—have not sent the [*incomplete*][12]

May 19 (*CB*).

7. The following letter confirms that the recipient was John Swinton, who ordered books on April 24 (Feinberg).

8. See 734.   9. See 736.

10. George A. Townsend (1841–1914), a journalist who contributed to the New York *Herald* and to the Chicago *Tribune*. See also 236. Probably because of Townsend's affiliation, WW sent "Song of the Exposition" to the Chicago *Tribune* on this date (*CB*). On May 10 the newspaper returned the manuscript because it arrived too late for publication (Feinberg).

11. The editor of *The Galaxy*; see 242.

12. Only the first page of the letter is reproduced by Williamson. WW, after noting

745. *To John Swinton*   *5.6. [1876]*

ADDRESS: John Swinton | 134[13] East 38th Street |
New York City. POSTMARK: Camden | May | 6 |
N.J.

431 Stevens st. | Camden N Jersey | May 6—noon
I think I may be—nay *must be—wrong* in saying (Friday's letter)[14]
I wrote to Wm S[winton] with "no answer" result—I think I left writing
him to the last, & then omitted it by mistake. I will write to him in a day or
two—

W.W.

746. *To the Editor, New York* Herald   *5.7. [1876]*

DRAFT LETTER.

431 Stevens st. | Camden N Jersey | May 7
Editor Herald: | Dear Sir:
I merely write a line to call attention (lest it may be overslaughed
in the rush of a great office) to the poem I sent you some days since, *Song of
the Exposition*—(will make a column & a half close minion)—proposed
to be printed, if at all, *in the paper for May 10*, if acceptable at the price
named.
I believe I mentioned in my note at the time that it had also been sent to
the *London Times* and *Chicago Tribune*—& may, (or may not,) appear
May 10, in them.[15]

Walt Whitman

receipt of $50 from Swinton for five sets of books on May 4, sent two additional volumes
on May 6 (CB).
    13. Swinton's address was 124 East 38th Street; see 749.
    14. May 5 fell on Friday in 1876.
    15. In order to capitalize upon the formal opening of the Philadelphia Exposition
on May 10, 1876, WW sent the poem to various newspapers, among them the *Herald*
and the *Tribune*. According to a notation on May 5, the price was $50 (CB). "Song of
the Exposition" (formerly called "After All, Not to Create Only") was published in
1871; see 402 and 407.
    16. On April 18, in a letter marked "Private," Buchanan discussed the English
campaign on WW's behalf and, probably because he was perplexed by WW's contradic-
tory statements, pressed for a specific statement: "Moncure Conway has denied authorita-

747.   *To Robert Buchanan*

ENDORSED: "Robt Buchanan | (must have gone 17th
by Scotia | from N.Y.)"; "Buchanan | May 16 '76."
DRAFT LETTER.

May 16   '76

Your two letters including the cheque for £25 reached me, for
which accept deepest thanks.[16] I have already written you my approval of
your three communications in the L[ondon] D[aily] News[17] & will [say] that
in my opinion (& now with fullest deliberation reäffirming it) *all the points
assumed as facts on which your letter of March 13 is grounded, are substantially true, & most of them are true to the minutest particular*—as far as
could be stated in a one column letter.

Then let me quite definitely explain myself, about one or two things. I
should not have instigated this English move, & if I had been consulted,[18]
should have peremptorily stopt it—but now that it has started, & grown,
and under the circumstances, & by the person, & in the spirit, (& especially
as I can & will give, to each generous donor, my book, portrait, autograph,
myself as it were)—I am determined to respond to it in the same spirit
in which it has risen—to accept most thankfully, cordially & unhesitatingly
all that my friends feel to convey to me, which determination I here deliberately express once for all. This you are at liberty to make known to all who
feel any interest in the matter.

The situation at present may be briefly & candidly told. I am, & have
for three years during my paralysis, been boarding here, with a relative,
comfortable & nice enough, but steadily paying just the same as at an inn—
and the whole affair in precisely the same business spirit. My means would
by this time have entirely given out, but that have been temporarily re-
plenished from sales of my new edition and as now by this most welcome
present & purchase—the £25 herein acknowledged.

Though without employment, means or income, you augur truly that I
am not in what may be called pinching want—nor do I anticipate it.

tively that you wanted money, & I have been waiting & wondering what to do. . . . I
wish I were a rich man . . . and you should certainly never want anything your heart
craved . . . Be happy, Whitman, in the serene certainty that you have fulfilled your
life, & spoken—in tunes no thunders can silence—the beautiful message you were
fashioned to bring!" (Feinberg).

On April 28 Buchanan sent WW a check for £25, including a contribution of £5
from Tennyson, with a list of those who had subscribed £22.15 (Feinberg). WW sent
books on September 5 (see 762).

17. See 730.

18. WW deleted the following passage: "There is doubtless a point of view from
which Mr. Conway's statement of April 4th might hold, technically—but, essentially, &
under the circumstances, . . . " Despite the poet's denials, Conway's statement (see
732) was justified.

My object I may say farther has lately been & still is to build a cheap little[19] three or four room house on a little lot I own in a rural skirt of this town—for a nook, where I can haul in & eke out in a sort of independent economy & comfort & as satisfactorily as may be the rest of my years—for I may live several of them yet. To attain this, would be quite a triumph, & I feel assured I could then live very nicely indeed on the income from my books.

I shall (as I see now) continue to be my own publisher & bookseller. Accept all subscriptions to the New Edition. All will be supplied upon remittance. There are Two Volumes. Leaves of Grass, 384 pages, poems, $5, has two portraits. Then *Two Rivulets*, poems & prose, (including "*Memoranda of the War*") with photos, altogether 359 pages—also $5. Each book has my autograph. The Two Volumes are my complete works, $10 the set.

I wish the particular address of each generous friend given, so as he or she can be reach'd by mail or express—either with the autographic volume *Two Rivulets*, or a complete set of my works in Two Volumes, with autograph & portraits, or some other of my books. It may be some while before the books arrive, but they *will* arrive in time.[20]

748. *To Edmund W. Gosse*[21]   *5.19. [1876]*

ADDRESS: E W Gosse | Townsend House North Gate | Regent's Park | London England. POSTMARKS: Camden | May | 19 | N.J.; London. N W | F 6 | Paid | My 29 | 76.

431 Stevens st | Camden New Jersey | U S America | May 19

I have this day forwarded to you by mail—same address as this card —*my new edition, Two Volumes* (separate parcels)—Please notify me (by postal card will do) when they arrive safely—

W.W.

19. Originally WW wrote: "a little 100, 6 or $700 house."
20. WW struck out the following: "I should like Wm M Rossetti, and Prof. Dowden of Dublin to see this letter."
21. Gosse (1849–1928) had written to WW on December 12, 1873: "I can but thank you for all that I have learned from you, all the beauty you have taught me to see in the common life of healthy men and women, and all the pleasure there is in the mere humanity of other people" (Feinberg; Traubel, I, 245–246). He reviewed *Two Rivulets* in *The Academy*, IX (June 24, 1876), 602–603, and visited WW in 1885 (see 1306). In

749. *To John Swinton*   *5.31.* [*1876?*][22]

ADDRESS: John Swinton | 124 East 38th st |
New York City. POSTMARK: Camden | May | 31 |
N.J.

431 Stevens st | Camden N J | May 31

Letter & enc: recd—Thanks—will write more fully soon—middling
comfortable to-day—

W.W.

750. *To Alexander Ireland*[23]

ADDRESS: A Ireland | Inglewood | Bowdon |
Cheshire | England. POSTMARKS: Camden | Jun |
13 | N.J.; Manchester | U 33 | Ju 24 | 76.

Camden, New Jersey | *U S America June 13* 1876.

Your subscription for my Book is received—for which hearty
thanks. Excuse delay, should there be any—the small first edition being
exhausted, and another now in press. Your Volumes will be sent *by mail,
soon as ready,* (*which will not be very long*)—

W.W.

751. *To G. F. E. Pearsall*

ADDRESS: G F E Pearsall | artist & Photographer |
298 Fulton street | Brooklyn | N York. POSTMARK:
Camden | Jun | 15 | N.J.

June 15 '76

Dear Sir[24]

Thanks for your kind consent, & offer of the negative. The printing

---

a letter to Bucke on October 31, 1889, WW characterized Gosse as "one of the amiable
conventional wall-flowers of literature" (Feinberg).

22. Though the text of this post card is not helpful, it seems to refer to Swinton's
support of WW's 1876 edition; see 744–745. (This post card also resembles the earlier
one in appearance and in handwriting.)

23. Ireland (1810–1894), an English author and one of Emerson's early biographers, was also one of the organizers of the Manchester Free Library. His most popular
book was *The Book-Lover's Enchiridion* (1882).

24. WW sent *Two Rivulets* to Pearsall on September 10 (*CB*).

from it shall be done with very great care & the plate duly returned to you. Please send it to me by express, at once, well enveloped, directed

Walt Whitman

431 Stevens street | cor. West | Camden | New Jersey

752. *To John Burroughs*   6.17. [1876]
ADDRESS:John Burroughs | Esopus-on-Hudson | Ulster Co | New York. POSTMARK: Camden | Jun | 17 | N.J.

Saturday afternoon | June 17

John, I have just been reading your *Galaxy* article,[25] seated by the open window front room in my shirt sleeves, & must write a word about it —Your late pieces show *marked vitality—vivacity* (struggling, almost chafing, underneath a continent, respectable form or exterior) & *this is the best of them*—has those peculiarities, not without one or two foibles, but the *whole* of the piece is glorious—leaves the impression now upon me (after two readings) of the noblest piece of criticism on these things yet in America—as much nobler than the superb Emersonian pages on those subjects as lines & opinions with *the blood of life* & throb of hot conviction in them, are nobler than the superbest *Marble-statue lines*—

It would be possible that I might be swayed into a warm feeling about the piece by the magnificent & very 'cute page about me,[26] but as it happens by accident I had look'd over & read the piece in parts, *accidentally omitting at first the entire lines in the second column* of the page about me (which finally please me best)—& had made up my mind very decidedly as aforesaid—then when I *did* read them, you can imagine *they* didn't hurt me much—nor my estimation of the piece—[27]

I have much to write—or tell you—about my own concerns—things in England—here too—&c &c—have been waiting for the chance to write you fully ever since I got your kind generous note & present[28]—but it dont seem to occur—Physically I am not much different—get along about as well as usual these times—am now just going down to an old farm house & big family, down in Jersey at *White Horse*,[29] to spend a couple of days—and it is now (4½ p m) while I am waiting for the hack to come & take me to the depot that I write this—

25. Burroughs published "A Word or Two on Emerson" and "A Final Word on Emerson" in *The Galaxy* in February and April. See also 665.
26. See *The Galaxy*, XXI (February, 1876), 258–259.
27. Of WW's "overpraise," Burroughs remarked in 1907: "I think he must have had a glass of whisky, or some champagne, when he wrote that" (Barrus, 135).
28. On May 10 WW noted receipt of $50 from Burroughs in CB.
29. WW did not record in CB any visits with the Staffords at this time.
30. Mannahatta and Jessie, Jeff's daughters, came from St. Louis to Camden in

George and Lou are well—baby only pretty well—hot weather, & teething—(but behaves like a little hero)—expect my two neices[30] here next week from St Louis—Love to 'Sula[31]—Write soon—

Walt

753. *To William Michael Rossetti*

431 Stevens st. | Camden N Jersey |
U S America June 26 '76

Dear friend,

Yours of June 14 just rec'd—also the corrected circulars. (Yours of the 16th, of the 25th, of the 26th, & of the 29th May, previously acknowledged)[32]—All gives me entire satisfaction & comfort—arousing my deepest gratitude. All here goes as well as could be expected—even better—except that the *new edition* is rather slow in getting ready to be sent to subscribers, but will very soon be ready, & all the good friends & subscribers will have their copies carefully sent to their addresses by mail prepaid, (as I find this is the best way)—There were really only 100 of the first edition printed, and they have become exhausted—that is the reason of some present delay—but, as said in former letter, *every order & purchase will be faithfully supplied* (*only let the address of the friend be full & plain, in every instance*, the same as they have been hitherto)—& all lagging copies—yours & Mrs. G[ilchrist]'s among the rest—will also be carefully sent in due time—

The Two Vols. of the new edition will be identically the same in every literary respect, text, pictures, autograph & photo. but a *different binding* —(substantial, but less showy—good strong, half-calf, marble paper, leather tips, no gilt)—I am printing of this new ed. 600 L. of G. and 650[33] *Two R[ivulets]*—They will soon be ready—I have notified you that Vols. have been forwarded to & rec'd, acknowledged by J. L. Warren, Reynell,[34] (thank him for his kind generous note), W. B. Scott[35] (him also), and to A. G. Dew-Smith—also to Therese Simpson,[36] of Edinburgh—also Geo. Wallis,[37] Kensington Art Museum—(& I believe one or two others)—

I sent 2 copies *Memoranda of War* (one bound, one in sheets) to N.

July and remained until October 25 (*CB*).
    31. Burroughs' wife, Ursula.
    32. Rossetti's letters and WW's reply, probably sent early in June, are apparently lost.
    33. WW probably intended to write 600; see 761.
    34. See 728.   35. See 743.   36. See 739.
    37. Wallis (1811–1891) was an artist and Keeper of the Art Collection at the South Kensington Museum from 1860 until his death. WW sent the two volumes to him on June 7 (*CB*).

MacColl,[38] *Athenaeum*, June 12. (Your special copy *Mem.* of course was for *you* to keep, as your name was written in it by me.)

I have not yet rec'd my pay for the little *Man-of-War-Bird* in *Athenaeum*[39] nor the prose piece on the *the War* in the *Examiner*.[40] If convenient the editors can send to me by p. o. money order, as I find that very straight & sure.

Joaquin Miller comes occasionally to see me[41]—his visits are pleasant to me—Did you get the *Pre-Raphaelite* article in the *Galaxy* I sent?[42] Also J[oseph] M[arvin]'s letter to me about it?[43] Longfellow has also been to see me—(a sort of one-horse visit)[44]—

Tennyson sent £5 at once to Buchanan (on the latter's letter) who sent it to me—I havn't written lately to T.,[45] as I supposed him abroad on the continent—but I intend to write soon—& send him a set of my books—I am not at all sure that A. T. *sees my poems*—but I DO HIS, & strongly, (& there perhaps I have the advantage of him)—but I think *he sees me*—& nothing could have evidenced more courtesy, & manliness, & hospitality, than his letters to me have shown, for five years.

Buchanan has sent me six or seven names, (& a cheque)—will all soon be supplied, with the rest—Let me know if you find Ch. Kent[46]—Has the *Secularist*[47] my address?—Middling well—very hot weather here—

Walt Whitman

754. *To William Michael Rossetti*   [7.3. 1876]

DRAFT LETTER.

[Sent letter] also July 3,
acknowledging £45.9.6 sent me in letter of June 20 '76 with list.[48]

38. Norman MacColl (1843–1904), the editor of the London *Athenaeum* from 1871 to 1900. WW noted sending the two books on June 12 (*CB*).

39. An undated entry in *CB* recorded the receipt of £3.3 from *The Athenaeum*; see also 716.

40. The *Examiner* was slow in paying for "The American War" (see 716). WW informed Rossetti on September 1 that he had not been paid by the *Examiner* (see 761). On June 15, 1877, Rossetti mentioned that William Minto, the editor of the journal, had promised to send the money "round to me at once" (Feinberg; Traubel, III, 170). WW noted in *CB* on October 11, 1877: "Wrote to Rossetti, spoke of the *Examiner* claim, told him to take no further trouble." On December 17, 1877, Rossetti promised to call the matter once more to Minto's attention (Feinberg).

41. Miller visited WW on May 11 (*CB*).

42. Justin McCarthy's "The Pre-Raphaelites in England," *The Galaxy*, XXI (June, 1876), 725–732.

43. Marvin met Rossetti in 1875; see 691.

44. If WW's recollection was correct, Longfellow came to Camden with George W. Childs, the owner of the Philadelphia *Public Ledger*, and, not finding him at home, finally encountered him at the wharf. WW was unimpressed with Longfellow (Traubel, I, 129–130). The New York *Tribune* noted the visit on June 3: "The two poets are said to bear a striking resemblance to each other."

45. WW's last letter to Tennyson was written on July 24, 1875 (see 681). WW

755. *To Whitelaw Reid*

Camden, New Jersey | July 7th, 1876

My dear Reid:

I send a piece for the paper, on Custer's death.[49] If you can give me $10. for it, well and good—if not, not. If it comes in time, get it in tonight, as earliness is everything.

Walt Whitman

756. *To Philip Hale*   *7.11. [1876]*

431 Stevens st | Camden N Jersey | July 11

My dear Philip Hale[50]

I have rec'd your p o order for $10 for my books—for which hearty thanks. I send by same mail with this, One Vol. *Leaves of Grass*—the other Vol. *Two Rivulets* I will send soon as some copies of a new batch are ready, (the old ones being all exhausted.) Please inform me (by postal card will do) if this Vol comes safe.

Walt Whitman

replied to a letter from Tennyson on September 14, 1876; both letters, unfortunately, are lost.

46. Kent was the editor of the London *Sun;* see also 289.

47. See also 743.

48. This is WW's summary of a letter, or post card, which apparently is not extant. Rossetti's letter, which included a list of English subscribers to the 1876 edition, is also unknown.

WW received the following sums from Rossetti: £28.4 on April 20, £45.9.6 on June 20, £21.18 ($116.01) on October 9, and $23.30 on September 10, 1877. See *CB* and 768.

49. "A Death-Sonnet for Custer" (later entitled "From Far Dakota's Cañons") appeared in the New York *Tribune* on July 10. Reid acknowledged WW's note on July 10 (Feinberg; Traubel, II, 212). John Hay (1838–1905), who was Lincoln's private secretary and an historian as well as Secretary of State under Theodore Roosevelt, praised this poem on July 25 (Feinberg; Traubel, I, 60). WW sent the 1876 edition to Hay on August 1 (*CB*).

50. Philip Hale (1854–1934), a music critic and program annotator for the Boston Symphony Orchestra, wrote to WW for the first time on September 14, 1871 (Feinberg; Traubel, III, 533). Hale wrote again on October 7, 1875 (LC), to praise the "Calamus" poems and to enclose a copy of "Walt Whitman," which he published in *The Yale Literary Magazine* in November, 1874, 96–104. WW sent *Two Rivulets* on September 3 (*CB*).

757. *To Ellen M. O'Connor*   *7.13.* [1876]

431 Stevens | Camden July 13

Nelly, this is a sad house to-day—little Walt[51] died last evening about ½ past 8. Partially sick but sudden at last—suddenly turned to water on the brain—is to be buried to-morrow afternoon at 4—

George and Lou are standing it pretty well—I am miserable—he knew me so well—we had already such good times—& I was counting so much— My St. Louis nieces are here—they are well—Nelly dear, send me back their photos & Jeff's—the heat here has been & is dreadful—Love to you— write—

W W

758. *To Whitelaw Reid*

431 Stevens st. | Camden N Jersey | July 18 '76

My dear Reid,

The cheque has reached me $10. as pay for the little poem[52]—Thanks —I enclose a ¶ for the "Personals"—if thought proper.[53]

Walt Whitman

759. *To Rudolf Schmidt*   *8.11.* [1876]

ADDRESS: Rudolf Schmidt | 16 Klareboderne | Copenhagen | Denmark. POSTMARKS: (?) | Aug | 11 | N.J.; New York | Aug | 12.

431 Stevens st | Camden, N. Jersey—U. S. America | Aug 11

Yours of July 24 rec'd, also your previous one six weeks before—I wrote to you two months ago[54]—also sent papers—I send paper, also my *War Memoranda* &c by same mail as this—same address (is it right?)—I

---

51. His nephew, Walter Orr Whitman; see the following letter.
52. "A Death-Sonnet for Custer" (see 755).
53. The "Personal," which appeared on July 19, was a sentimental account of the death of WW's nephew; see SB, VIII (1956), 244–245. According to Bucke (55n.), the notice appeared in the Philadelphia *Public Ledger* on July 20.
54. On July 24 Schmidt (see 412) reported his recent marriage to "my dear faithfull little wife, to whom I have been betrothed since some years" (Feinberg). The letter written "six weeks before" may be Schmidt's letter of April 18, in which he admitted his failure to sell WW's books in Denmark (Feinberg). WW's reply, probably written late in May or early in June, is not known.

remain much the same—bad spells enough—*I congratulate you both—
love to both—*

W.W.

760. *To William Michael Rossetti*   8.22. *[1876]*

ADDRESS: Wm Michel Rossetti | 56 Euston Square |
London N W | England. POSTMARKS: Camden |
Aug | 22 | N.J.; London (?) | C 1(?) | Paid |
Sp 7 | 76.

431 Stevens st—Camden—N Jersey | U S America—
Aug 22

I send *you* to-day the Vol. specified for *"Mrs. Mathews, Birming-
ham"*[55]—As this is too indefinite, I have directed it to your care, to forward
to Mrs. M. The other Vols. will be sent by mail to the addresses given—All
about as usual—

W W

761. *To William Michael Rossetti*

431 Stevens St—Camden, N Jersey | U S America—
Sept 1, '76

My dear friend,

At last I am beginning to receive from the bindery the second
batch of my late Two Volume edition (I print 600 copies each Vol.) &
send you a set in the new binding, by this mail. I am now at last also
supplying my English subscribers & friends their Vols.—have sent their
books, postpaid, by same mail with this to several of them (see list
appended)[56]—& the rest will follow, until every one will be sent—probably
within the next ten days. I sent *you* the Vol. for Mrs. Matthews,[57] as the
address was too indefinite—How about G. W. Foote[58] and J. T. Nettleship
mention'd by you & giving extracts, under date of May 23d?[59] Their

55. WW sent a copy of *Leaves of Grass* (CB).
56. The list is not with this draft letter, but see 768.
57. See the preceding letter.
58. George William Foote (1850–1915), a freethinker, was the author of many
pamphlets attacking Christianity. Foote did not forward £3 to WW. Rossetti mentioned
on August 17, 1877, that he had called the failure to pay to Foote's attention (Feinberg).
On February 12, 1878 (CB) WW cited a letter from Foote, who promised to send the
sum, which he alleged had been stolen by an employee (Feinberg). After the entry the
poet later wrote *"fraud."*
59. See 422. Rossetti's letter of May 23 is not known.

names do not appear in the lists you have given me to send books to. The *Athenaeum* folks have sent me good pay for the little poem,[60] but I have had nothing, & heard nothing from the *Examiner*.

I expected to have heard of Mrs. Gilchrist's arrival in The U. S.[61] & to have had perhaps ere this the great happiness of meeting her—but have heard nothing up to date.

My letter of June 26, speaking of the situation, the delay in printing this second batch, &c.—And my letter of July 3d acknowledging yours of June 20, enclosing one £45–9–6, & list—you have.

I enclose herewith a later circular—will send you a dozen or so soon.

My dear little baby-nephew, & namesake, is dead, & buried by the side of my mother, a bitter cup to me—Otherwise things are about the same with me as before—& I am jogging along about the same.

Walt Whitman

762. *To Robert Buchanan*

ENDORSED: "R Buchanan." DRAFT LETTER.

Sept. 4 '76

I forward you by Express to-day, same address as this letter the package of Books (see list on other side)[62]—I wish Tennyson to have a set & have enclosed one, & would ask you to do me the favor of seeing that it is safely transmitted to him.[63] Notwithstanding the disclaimer in yours of April 28 I also send a set for Richard Bentley[64] in response to his kindness & generosity: (if any thing I know not of prevents its reaching him, I wish *you* to keep it for yourself.)

Please see that the photograph is given to the School of Art, with my affectionate respects.

Trusting to your kindness to see that they are carefully sent to the subscribers.

60. £3.3 (see 753).
61. Mrs. Gilchrist and her children arrived in Philadelphia on September 10 (*CB*). Though Mrs. Gilchrist had come to America to accomplish in person what she had not been able to accomplish in her letters—to become Mrs. Whitman—she was practical enough to arm herself with letters of introduction to various Americans. Rossetti, her shrewd and somewhat snobbish advisor, wrote on August 23 and 24 to various painters and to Charles Eliot Norton (Feinberg).
62. The list, which is not with the draft letter, appears in *CB* under September 5: two volumes were sent to Tennyson, Richard Bentley, Roden Noel, and Drummond; *Two Rivulets* was sent to Robinson, Salaman, Marks, Townsend Mayer, Thomas Ashe, Mrs. Dickens, and Henry Lobb; *Memoranda During the War* was sent to Newton, Cole-

763. *To Moncure D. Conway*   9.5. *[1876]*

TRANSCRIPT.

Camden, New Jersey—U. S. America | Sept. 5th
I send today, same address as this card my two volumes. Please notify me by postal card soon as they reach you safely. Mrs. Taylor's and Mr. Ireland's sets have also been sent.[65]

W. W.

Condition with me much the same.

763.1 *To W. Brockie*   9.7. *[1876]*

ADDRESS: W Brockie | Olive Street | Sunderland | England. POSTMARK: Camden | (?)p | 7 | N.J.

Camden, New Jersey—U S America | Sept 7
I send you to-day by mail, to same address as this card, my Volume, *Two Rivulets.*

Please let me know, (by postal card will do) soon as it reaches you safely.

W Whitman

764. *To F. S. Ellis*[66]   9.7. *[1876]*

ADDRESS: F S Ellis | 29 New Bond Street | London W | England. POSTMARKS: Philad'a | Sep | 8 | Paid; (?) | Paid | Sp 19 | 76.

Camden, N Jersey—U S America | Sept 7
I send you to-day by mail, to same address as this card, my Volume,

man, and Hirsh; and a photograph was sent to the School of Art in London. Buchanan's letter of April 28, in addition to these names, cited a contribution of £2 from Browning and his desire for a complete set of the 1876 edition (Feinberg). Buchanan acknowledged receipt of the volumes on January 8, 1877 (Feinberg; Traubel, I, 2–3).

63. See 753.
64. Richard Bentley & Son were London publishers. According to Buchanan's letter of April 28 Bentley was among those who "do not want copies, some having them already" (Feinberg).
65. On September 5 (CB), WW sent the 1876 edition to Mrs. Mentia Taylor, of Brighton, England, and to Alexander Ireland (see 750).
66. See 403. The date is confirmed by an entry in CB.

Two Rivulets. Please send me word, (by postal card will do,) soon as it reaches you safely—

W Whitman

765. *To Philip Bourke Marston*[67]   *9.7.* [1876]

ADDRESS: P B Marston | 20 Ladbroke Grove Road | London W England. POSTMARKS: Camden | Sep | 7 | N.J.; Philad'a | Sep | 8 | Paid.

Camden, N. Jersey—U S America | Sept 7

I send you to-day by mail to same address as this card, my Volume, *Two Rivulets.* Please let me know (by postal card will do) soon as it reaches you safely.

W. Whitman

766. *To Charles G. Oates*   *9.7.* [1876][68]

TRANSCRIPT.

Camden, | New Jersey, | U. S. A. | Sept 7th.

I send you to-day by mail, to same address as this card, my volume, "Two Rivulets".

Please send me word, (by postal card, will do), soon as it reaches you safely.

W. Whitman.

767. *To Edward Dowden*

TRANSCRIPT.

431 Stevens St | Camden | Sept 8 '76

I send you by mail to-day, same address as this note, 1 copy "Leaves of Grass" and two copies "Two Rivulets"—Also the set, Two Vols. for

67. Marston (1850–1887) was an English poet of the Rossetti school. The transaction was recorded in CB.

68. On June 3 Carpenter ordered books for Charles G. Oates (Feinberg). Evidently Oates himself wrote for a copy of *Two Rivulets,* which WW sent on September 7 (CB). The transcription of this note in the Stanford Library is dated "Sept 7th, 1881," which, in view of the entry in CB, is an error. When the post card was sold at the Rains Galleries on April 14, 1937, the year was cited as 1876.

69. Grosart (1827–1899) was a clergyman and also the indefatigable editor of Elizabethan texts.

70. On October 4 Dowden acknowledged receipt of the volumes, and discussed

. . . per A. B. Grosart[69]—"My Second Batch" of the new edition (600 copies each Vol.) is at last now ready, & I *promptly* supply orders henceforward. I have many things to say to you, my dear friend. I am sitting here by the open window, writing this, 'most sundown—feeling pretty well for me, as things go—Often think of you & yours & the friends in Ireland—Must close as I want to catch to-morrow's New York mail.[70]

Walt Whitman

768. *To William Michael Rossetti*

Camden, New Jersey—U S America | Sept 10, '76

Dear friend,

I wrote to you three [or] four days ago,[71] by which you must have recd partial list. The list on the other sheet will more fully show you what books I have sent, *comprising I believe all the names & remitting subscribers you have sent me*—Your two (principal) remittances £28.4 (April 19) and £45.9.6. (June 20) were accompanied with lists of subscribers' am'ts & addresses—the names on which lists & addresses I have carefully followed & sent to. I hope & think I have not missed any. *If you discover or know of any so missed, pray notify me at once.*

Looking over the pretty voluminous correspondence & extracts you have sent me so kindly, the last six months, there appear to be *a number of other names*, both men's & women's, mentioned, or writing themselves, as ordering the books in letters to you. But of course *I have exclusively confined myself to the names & addresses specified in the lists accompanying your remittance-letters*, above alluded to. I have been somewhat exercised about those *other names*.

Prof Atkinson[72]
    " Armstrong[73]
A G B[74]
G L Cathcart[75]
Mrs. Deschamps[76]

the impending publication of a volume of his poems (Feinberg; Traubel, II, 90–91).
    71. WW probably meant the letter of September 1.
    72. Probably Robert Atkinson (1839–1908), professor of romance languages at Trinity College, Dublin.
    73. Probably Edward Armstrong (1846–1928), English historian and lecturer at Oxford.
    74. Perhaps A. C. de Burgh, to whom WW sent two volumes on September 7, in care of T. W. H. Rolleston in Dublin; the entry, however, was later deleted (CB).
    75. Probably the son of Sir George Cathcart (1749–1854).
    76. Perhaps Chrissie Deschamps, mentioned in 553.

J D[77]
Lady Hardy[78]
Harold Littledale
C W S[79]
Dr Todhunter,[80]
☞ Nothing has been sent to any of these
(D G Rossetti
C A Howell
J T Nettleship[81] for self & others
H G Dakyns[82]
Herbert Herkomer[83]
Roden Noel[84]
A C Swinburne
G W Foote[85]
Cicely Marston[86]
    & several others)

—but know no other course than to *confine myself to sending to the addresses on your remittance lists only*—which I have done. Any errors or oversights will be gladly & promptly corrected on information. *I have now plenty of Books, & orders will be complied with promptly.* The delay of the last two months in getting ready my second instalment of the 1876 Edition, has annoyed me much—but it is past—& I have as I believe forwarded now every British paid subscriber his or her books, (duplicate sets are yet to go to three or four)—A parcel of 17 Vols. has gone by Express to Robt Buchanan[87] to subscribers, sent through him to me—Prof. Dowden's 4 sets specified in your list have been sent to his subscribers to their addresses, & Mr. Conway's 3 sets (ordered in his letter to me) to theirs[88]—It is now some weeks since I have heard from you. *I want to hear about Mrs. Gilchrist.*[89]

                                                    Walt Whitman

77. Probably Edward Dowden's brother, John (see 422).
78. WW sent the 1876 set to Lady Hardy in London on October 24 (*CB*). She was probably the wife of Herbert Hardy, first Baron Cozens-Hardy (1838–1920), an English judge.
79. WW sent two volumes to C. W. Sheppard at Horsham, England, on September 6 (*CB*).
80. A friend of Edward Dowden (see 422).
81. See also 761. WW sent two books to Nettleship on October 24 (*CB*).
82. WW mailed two volumes to Dakyns at Clifton College, Bristol, on October 24 (*CB*).
83. Sir Hubert von Herkomer (1849–1914), a Bavarian painter who resided in England and was professor of Fine Arts at Oxford from 1885 to 1894. He was correctly cited as "Hubert" in the draft of this letter as well as in *CB*, in which WW noted forwarding two volumes on October 24.
84. A poet and the author of a critical notice of WW in *Dark Blue* in 1871 (see 426). Noel was hurt because Bucke did not include the essay in his biography; see

769. *To an Unidentified Printer*   *9.23.* [*1876*][90]

Camden   Sept 23

I send over two copies of Two Rivulets—Can't you have the pictures properly pasted on the frontispieces prepared for them (see front of the vols)—& send them over again by this boy, & I will put my autograph on them—

Walt Whitman

770. *To Damon Y. Kilgore*   *9.24.* [*1876*]

431 Stevens street | Camden New Jersey Sept 24
D Y Kilgore[91] | Dear Sir

Send me word immediately *when* (day & hour) & *where* the Paine bust affair is to come off. I see an announcement in the paper that I am to read a poem on the occasion. I do *not* propose to read a poem—but I will promise to be there, & speak just a little (say 10 minutes)—if I can be put on the early part of the program (as waiting fags me out entirely)—& perhaps it would be necessary that I should be sent for in a carriage. I would advise that you have some good music, & no long-winded address at all. (Couldn't you get some good baritone singer to sing Paine's fine lively old song of "the Liberty Tree"?)

Walt Whitman

best respects to Mrs Kilgore—love to Charley—

Noel's letters to WW on March 30 and May 16, 1886 (Feinberg; Traubel, I, 432–433, 394).
    85. See 761.
    86. The sister of Philip Bourke Marston (see 765).
    87. See 762.
    88. Conway's letter to WW is not extant; see also 763. He had received £6 from Conway on June 12 (CB).
    89. Mrs. Gilchrist arrived in Philadelphia on September 10 (CB).
    90. There is no reason to question the date that Furness assigned to this note (249–250).
    91. Damon Y. Kilgore (1827–1888) was a well-known Philadelphia lawyer and a member of the Liberal League of Philadelphia. In 1875 he prepared a petition to exclude the Bible from the public schools. In the following year he married Carrie S. Burnham, who was the first woman admitted to the bar in Pennsylvania. For this information I am indebted to Kilgore's granddaughter, Florence A. Hoadley. While WW was at Kirkwood, from September 19 to 23, he "composed the Tom Paine bit" (CB). See also 794–795.

771. *To Helen and Abby H. Price*

ADDRESS: Miss Helen Price | (or Mrs Abby Price) | Red Bank | New Jersey. POSTMARK: Camden | Oct | 6 | N.J.

Camden | Oct 6 1876.

Dear Helen, Dear Abby, & all[92]—

I am still jogging along here—still just holding on—sometimes (perhaps a quarter of the time) tolerably fair—the rest, by the skin of my teeth—but upon the whole with a spirit of cheerfulness & content with what comes that quite surprises myself.

My new edition 2 Vols is out & bound, & *pictured* & *autographed*. I sell a few, mostly to England[93]—gives me a little occupation—got your letter—write again—believe me, Helen and Abby dear, I appreciate the letters, & most of all your persistent & faithful friendship.

Walt Whitman

772. *To Anne Gilchrist*   *10.11. [1876]*

Oct 11   p m

Dearest friend

I am spending a few days down at the old farm, "White Horse"[94]—wandering most all day (well clad & shod, for it is cool weather here) about the banks, trees, grass &c. by the very secluded beautiful druidic creek—have just picked up a few leaves that seem'd to offer themselves to send specially to you, which I enclose.

I am feeling middling well, for me. Shall send you word—or rather shall send *myself*—soon as I come back to town—Meanwhile love to you all—

Walt Whitman

92. This is the last letter WW wrote to Mrs. Abby H. Price, who was dead when he wrote to Helen on April 21, 1881. WW, who had lived with the Prices at various times in the 1860's, evidently did not visit them after his mother's death in 1873 until he journeyed to his birthplace in 1881.

93. This is one of WW's characteristically misleading statements. He had exhausted the first printing of 100 to 150 copies of the 1876 edition, but he sent, as CB and his letters reveal, many copies of the second printing to English and American admirers.

94. WW was at the Stafford farm in Kirkwood from October 10 to 19 (CB). WW called on the Gilchrists frequently in Philadelphia after their arrival on September 10, and was accompanied by John Burroughs on September 14 and 15 (CB). Perhaps WW had to retreat to Kirkwood occasionally in order to escape the importunities of his passionate admirer.

95. Theobold was a London art collector or dealer, probably a friend of Rossetti's brother.

96. Stillman (1828–1901), an American painter and art critic, visited WW in

773. *To H. S. Theobold*[95]   *10.23.* [1876]

ADDRESS: H S Theobold | 20 Talbot Road |
Bayswater | London W | England. POSTMARK:
Camden | Oct | 23 | N.J.

Camden New Jersey | U S America | Oct 23
I send to-day to same address as this card my Vol. *Two Rivulets*—
Please notify me, (by postal card will do) soon as it reaches you safely—
W W

774. *To William J. Stillman*[96]   *10.24.* [1876]

ADDRESS: W J Stillman | St Helen's Cottage |
Ventnor | England. POSTMARKS: Camden | (?) |
2(?) | N.J.; Ventnor | (?) | No 6 | (?)6.

Camden New Jersey | U S America | Oct 24
I send you to-day to same address as this card my Vol. *Two Rivulets*
—Please notify me, by postal card will do, soon as it reaches you safely—
W W

774.1 *To James Matlack Scovel*[96.1]   [*11(?).1(?). 1876(?)*]

TRANSCRIPT.

Dear S.:—
    It seems the bottle I left for you was broken by accident. Here is
another. Don't mind the tart puckery taste. It is the taste of the grape-skin

Washington in December, 1869, and wrote to his friend Rossetti of WW's "remarkable
personal qualities"; see *Rossetti Papers*, 492, and Traubel, I, 380–381. An intimate of
Ruskin and Turner, he was in the diplomatic service from 1862 to 1868 and a correspondent for the London *Times* from 1875 to 1898. An entry in CB corroborates the
date.
    96.1. James Matlack Scovel began to practice law in Camden in 1856. During
the Civil War he was in the New Jersey legislature, and became a colonel in 1863. He
campaigned actively for Horace Greeley in 1872, and was a special agent for the U. S.
Treasury during Arthur's administration. In the 1870's WW frequently went to Scovel's
home for Sunday breakfast, as he did on December 2 and 9, 1877 (CB). For a description of these breakfasts, see *Walt Whitman's Diary in Canada*, 59–60. For Scovel, see
George R. Prowell's *The History of Camden County, New Jersey* (1886).
    Apparently WW sent this note to Scovel, who was hospitalized shortly before the
presidential election in 1876. The Camden lawyer included it in an article entitled
"Walt Whitman. | A Symposium in a Sick Room," which appeared in the Camden
Daily Post on November 18, 1876. Scovel was one of WW's publicity agents at this time
(see 683). Professor F. DeWolfe Miller called my attention to this newspaper article.

in the Virginia wine. Hope you are getting all right. Love to you and the household.

W. W.

775. *To Robert Buchanan*

ENDORSED: "to Robt Buchanan | Nov 21 | '76."
DRAFT LETTER.

431 Stevens street | Nov. 21 '76

My dear R B

I sent you over two months ago (Sept 5),[97] by express prepaid direct to same address as this letter, a package of some 17 or 18 vols of my books, in wrappers, with names on them. As up to this date I have heard nothing of them from you, and Messrs. Strahan have not acknowledged them either, I am a little uneasy about them. Have they arrived? Have they been distributed?[98]

I am jogging along much the same. My limbs still lamed from paralysis —but I get around yet—strength a little more reliable—spirits cheerful.

Your letters of April 18 and 28th were very comforting to me. I have read them several times—& they are before me now.

I wrote to you Sept. 4, announcing the Vols. That was my last. Did it reach you? Your letter of April 28th is the last I have rec'd from you.

776. *To Herbert Gilchrist*   *11.21. [1876]*

431 Stevens street | Camden Nov 21

My dear Herbert

I had a safe little jaunt home yesterday afternoon[99]—What a long-drawn-out storm—cloudy yet this morning.

---

97. See 762.
98. On January 8, 1877, Buchanan informed WW that he had neglected to acknowledge the books because "the tone adopted by certain of your friends here became so unpleasant that I requested all subscriptions etc. to be paid over to Rossetti, and received no more myself" (Feinberg; Traubel, I, 2).
99. A reference to his return from a visit to the Gilchrists in Philadelphia from November 18 to 20 (*CB*).
1. WW sent *Two Rivulets* on September 7 (*CB*) to Justin H. McCarthy, Jr. (1860–1936). On September 23 (Feinberg), McCarthy thanked him for the volume, and recalled that his father, the novelist, had met the poet in 1870; see also Allen, 418–419, and Justin McCarthy, *Reminiscences* (1899), I, 258–261. McCarthy's unsigned review of *Two Rivulets*, "Songs Overseas," appeared in *The Examiner* on October 21.

Upon talking more fully with my sister about the colored woman Rosy, I am convinced she *would not do*—so I think we will give up any further thought of her as a help to you—

J T Nettleship's address is 233 Stanhope street, Regents' Park N W— The criticism in the *Examiner* was written by J H McCarthy.[1] I am feeling pretty well (for me) this morning—Affectionate regards to all—

                                                    Walt Whitman

777. *To Ellen M. O'Connor*   11.23 [1876?][2]

ADDRESS: Mrs Ellen M O'Connor | 1015 O street n w | Washington | D C. POSTMARK: Camden | Nov | 23 | N.J.

                                    Camden New Jersey | Nov 23
I continue pretty well for me this fall—All about as usual with all of us—

                                                    W.W.

778. *To Ellen Louise Chandler Moulton*[3]   [12.11. 1876]

ADDRESS: Mrs Louise Chandler Moulton | care Philip Bourke Marston | 20 Ladbroke Grove Road | Notting Hill W | London | England. POSTMARKS: Camden | Dec | 11 | N.J.; London | F Z | Paid | De 23 | 76.

                                Camden New Jersey | U S America
I send to-day, to same address as this card, my Vol. L of G— Please notify me, (by postal card will do) soon as it reaches you safely.

                                                    W W

After praising WW's description of Lincoln's death, McCarthy observed: "Could he apply this power to the whole as to this chapter, Walt Whitman might abandon all other titles for that of America's first historian."

2. Although the text furnishes no clues as to the date, 1876 appears plausible. WW apparently did not correspond with Mrs. O'Connor between 1876 and 1887; there are no extant letters from her to WW between 1865 and 1888. Because of the continued estrangement between WW and O'Connor, probably neither his wife nor the poet was completely at ease in writing to the other.

3. Mrs. Moulton (1835–1908), an American poet, was staying with Philip Bourke Marston (see 765), whose works she edited after his premature death in 1887. See Lilian Whiting, *Louise Chandler Moulton, Poet and Friend* (1910). An entry in CB confirms the date.

779. *To Anne Gilchrist*   *12.12.* [*1876*][4]

431 Stevens st | Camden N J

Thanks, my dear friend, for your hospitable & affectionate letter, & invitations. I too want to come & see you all, & be with you from time to time—hoping it may be good & a comfort to all of us—to *me* surely—

As (though better this winter) decidedly sensitive to the cold—how would it do for me to have a little sheet-iron wood stove, & some wood sawed & cut, & carried up in the south room, immediately adjoining the one I before occupied? Could it be done? Is there a hole in the chimney in that room—or place for stove pipe?

I am getting along quite well—& shall be over very soon—possibly Thursday—

Walt Whitman

(A pretty good fire—& a wood fire—is to me I find the greatest physical comfort I can have this weather—I should want to select & purchase, & have put up myself, the stove, wood, &c.)

Dec 12

780. *To Josiah Gilbert Holland*   *12.12.* [*1876?*]

431 Stevens st. | cor West. | Camden, |
N. Jersey, | Dec. 12.

Dr. Holland,[5] | Dear Sir,

Would these pieces—or either of them—be available for the Magazine? The price is $50—(40 for the first—10 for the other.) I have had them put in type for correctness & my private use.

Walt Whitman

4. Because this letter is among the other Gilchrist correspondence, formerly in the possession of Mrs. Frank J. Sprague, there can be no doubt that it was addressed to Mrs. Gilchrist. Since the Gilchrists were in Philadelphia in December, 1876, and since WW accompanied Eldridge to the Gilchrists' on December 12, 1877 (see 843–844), this letter was written in 1876.

5. See 250. At this time Holland was editor of *The Century Magazine*. On two occasions WW recalled that he had sent poems to Holland at the suggestion of John Swinton (Traubel, I, 184; IV, 326–327). Since one of the poems was "Eidolons," which was composed in 1876, the date of this letter is almost certain. However, it is strange that WW submitted poems after Holland's hostile criticism in the May issue of *Scribner's*

781. *To Peter Doyle*   *12.13.* [1876][6]

Camden N J | Dec 13—

Dearest Pete,

I ought to have written to you before—but I believe lazy & listless
fits grow stronger & frequenter on me as I get older—& then I dont do
anything at all, especially just the things I ought to do—But I often, often
think of you, boy, & let that make it up. I certainly am feeling better this
winter—more strength to hold out, walking or like, than for nearly now
four years—bad enough yet, but still *decidedly better*—(My loving boy,
I underscore the words, for I know they will make you feel good, to
hear) —

I heard about the accident on the road at the time two weeks ago—&
was uneasy enough until I heard definite particulars—such things seem
the fortune of RR travel, which I sometimes think more risky than the
"fortune of war," which the knowing ones know well is more chance &
accident (I mean the victory in battles) than it is generalship—

Pete, I am sitting up here alone in my room, 8 o'clock p m, writing this
—I am feeling quite comfortable—I stood the cold snap of the last three
days very well—to-day has been moderate & nice here—Nothing new or
special in my affairs—I am selling a few of my books (the new 2 Vol. 10
dollar edition) from time to time—mostly to English & Irish purchasers
—it is quite funny how many of my books are sent for from Ireland[7]—
Love to you, dearest son—

Walt

782. *To John H. Johnston*   *12.13.* [1876][8]

Camden N J | Dec 13—

Thanks, my dear friend, for your cheery letter, & for your warm
& hospitable invitations—I am, though crippled as ever, perhaps *decidedly*

Monthly, XII (1876), 123–125. Holland's lengthy (lost) reply "was offensive, low,
bitter, inexcusable" (Traubel, IV, 327). In an interview in 1879, WW complained that
many American magazines were "in the hands of old fogies like Holland or fops like
Howells" (*AL*, XIV [1942–43], 145–146).

    6. That this letter was written in 1876 is evidenced by WW's references to his
paralysis in the first paragraph and to the 1876 edition in the last paragraph and by an
entry in *CB*.

    7. A reference to Edward Dowden, who was primarily responsible for WW's
popularity among students in Dublin.

    8. The year is established by an entry in *CB* as well as by the fact that WW
visited Johnston for the first time early in 1877.

better this winter—certainly in the way of strength & general vim—& it would be very pleasant to me to come on & stay at your house for about a week, if perfectly convenient, & if you have plenty of room—My (adopted) son,[9] a young man of 18, is with me now, sees to me, & occasionally transacts my business affairs, & I feel somewhat at sea without him—Could I bring him with me, to share my room, & your hospitality & be with me?

Glad to hear in your note from Joaquin Miller—first news of him now for three months[10]—Will sit to Mr Waters with great pleasure[11]—& he & you shall have every thing your own way—

I am selling a few copies of my Vols, new Edition, from time to time —most of them go to the British Islands—I see Mr Loag[12] occasionally— Loving regards to you, my friend, & to Mrs Johnston no less—

Walt Whitman

783. *To John H. Johnston*   *12.19. [1876]*

Camden | Dec 19

My dear Johnston,

Yours of yesterday rec'd. Every thing will suit me, just that way— would like to come during or before the close of January—would like to have a room where I could have a fire, table, &c. My nephew[13] & I when traveling always share the same room together & the same bed, & would like best to do so there. I want to bring on a lot of my books, new edition, & sell them, so I can raise a little money—(& that is what my young man is for.)

Fix the time to suit Waters & yourself, that way.

Thanks & affection—

Walt Whitman

9. Undoubtedly Harry Stafford, with whom WW was establishing a "Calamus" relationship; see Introduction.

10. Miller had visited WW on September 24 (*CB*).

11. George W. Waters (1832–1912), a portrait and landscape painter.

12. Samuel Loag, a Philadelphia printer and friend of the Johnstons. See *The Bookman*, XLVI (1917), 412.

13. Harry Stafford. WW was hardly accurate since there is no evidence that Harry and he had taken a trip together.

14. After visiting their uncle for four months, the nieces had returned to St. Louis

784. *To Mannahatta and Jessie Louisa Whitman*

431 Stevens street | Camden New Jersey | Dec 20 '76
Dearest Hattie | (& Dearest Jessie too,)

Your letter came this morning, & not until we got it could we believe in the change—so different from what we supposed the programme was arranged to be, in St Louis, housekeeping &c. Dear Hattie, it is real lonesome here since you went away[14]—it is more a "receiving vault" to me than ever. Thank God though I am certainly better this winter, & more like a prospect for me physically, than for now nearly four years. (It will be now four years the 23d of January, since I was paralyzed.) This makes me more cheerful & buoyant under the chilling atmosphere, (both moral & meteorological) of this house. Dear girls, I sometimes lately feel as if I was going out in the world, to take some hand again in some work that suits me, even if ever so little. Wouldn't it be a blessed thing? You see, dear girls, I just talk freely & confidentially to you both—I want some one to talk to—& it does me good—

Hattie, I have just got your pictures (after some delay) from the photographic printers.[15] I will send you one *very soon*—& will send your father one, & your Aunt Hannah at Burlington wants one. Your Aunt Lou *has* one in the parlor already, & it looks very nice—it is a plain head only, looks like an engraving, no fixings or bows or jewelry, but a simple fine classical head, just as I wanted it—But you will see when I send it you.

Your Uncle George, Aunt Lou & Cousin Eddy are all well as usual. Tip[16] is also well as usual—It has been & is very cold here—the ground is all covered with snow—but it is bright to-day. I have just been out about three blocks off in an alley, to see a poor young man, James Davis,[17] who is dying of consumption—You know I like to visit the sick—I have to stay in most of the time just now though, as it is very slippery—Little Helen Ewing is staying here now—

If I keep as well as now I think of going on to New York on a visit next month. Lou will write to you soon. Love to you, dear, dear Hattie, & Love to you, dear dear Jessie, from

Uncle Walt

on October 25 (*CB*). On September 16, WW had attended with Hattie a performance of *La Favorita* at the Philadelphia Academy, in which Brignoli (see 231) had sung (*CB*). On October 24, he had gone to the Exposition in Philadelphia with Mrs. Fannie L. Taylor, of St. Louis, who probably had come to Camden to escort the young ladies home (*CB*).

15. Mannahatta's picture had been taken on October 25, and on November 12 WW had paid a Mr. Spieler $5 (*CB*).

16. WW's dog.

17. See 787.

785. *To Peter Doyle*   *12.20. [1876?]*[18]

ADDRESS: Pete Doyle | M Street South | bet 4½ &
6th— | Washington | D.C. POSTMARK: Camden |
Dec | 20 | N.J.

Camden N J | Dec 20

Letter rec'd—(& very glad every way—& thanks)—I think I am
really better this winter—The cold & snow & ice keep me in the house—
else I should have been over to the W Phil[adelphia] depot—it would
have done me good, even to have a minute, & a good hold of you once
more—Nothing new in my affairs—I am doing well enough—Tell Mr &
Mrs N[ash][19] I want to come to Wash[ington] once more, & I have
not forgot the pictures—

W W

786. *To John H. Johnston*

Dec 20   '76

My dear Johnston
    Enclosed find check for $35 for which send me on *immediately*
as good a *gold watch*, hunting case, middling showy in appearance &
best inside you can give me for that sum. (Let me have it at wholesale
price, only paying yourself what you pay for it). I want it for a Christmas
present for a young man[20]—*Can't you send it by express to-night or to-
morrow morning early?*

Walt Whitman
431 Stevens st cor West
Camden New Jersey

    I might as well leave you some margin. If you think of something a
little more [in] price or different any how, better, send it along, as it can
be changed, paid for, or made right when I come on in January—
    I find I have no revenue stamp to put on check & cannot go out to
get one—

18. Although the executors dated this post card 1878, 1876 seems more plausible;
note the similar phraseology in 781 and the reference to the weather in the preceding
letter. In 1877 the weather late in December, according to CB, was perfect, and WW
visited the Gilchrists almost daily. In 1878 there is no indication in CB that WW wrote
to Doyle, or that the weather kept WW indoors (note 902). Probably Doyle had answered

786.1 *To John Burroughs*   *12.20.* [*1876*]

ADDRESS: John Burroughs | Esopus | Ulster Co |
New York. POSTMARK: Camden | Dec | 20 | N.J.

                    431 Stevens st Camden N J | Dec 20
    Glad to hear from you—as by your card of 17th just rec'd. Very
glad to hear of S[ula] having got home "well & hearty"—Sheets you
speak of, not yet come to hand.
    I am better this winter, *seems almost decidedly*—banged bad enough
yet, but the bad deathly spells are very rare, (almost unknown) the last
three months—I want to go to N Y city in January—to J H Johnstons
(in 10th street)—his jewelry store is at 150 Bowery, cor Broome—call &
see him—quite a lull in my book selling, & in my affairs, & literary doings, generally—
                                                        W W

787. *To Peter Doyle*

                    431 Stevens street | Camden Dec 27 '76
Dear son
        The money came all right, & I will keep it for the present, & use
it for myself—*but only to return it at some future time, when I am flush.*
Nothing very new with me. I still feel pretty well, for me, (& considering
the past four years.) Who knows? May be after this winter, I shall feel
well enough to come on to Washington & make out several weeks—&
we'll have a good time together, my loving son—(no more long *walks*, to
be sure—but we can be happy other ways)—
    Beautiful, mild, sunny, thawing afternoon to-day [&] I have been out
a little—down to see a poor young man, an oysterman, Jim Davis, very
low with consumption, took him some stew'd chicken for his dinner—
then went to a nice reading room & library we have here, very handy—
then home to my own dinner, stew'd chicken & nice roast potatoes—&
now (2½) up stairs in my room writing this, & feeling very fair—
    O Pete, you get that arm chair (with the broken arm) I left at Mrs
Nash's—perhaps the broken arm is still there, if so get it put on—then

WW's letter of December 13.
    19. Old Washington friends of WW and Doyle. The poet stayed at their home
in 1875 (see 694).
    20. Johnston was a jeweler. The watch was intended either for Harry Stafford or
Edward Cattell (see 797). Note also 788.

take the chair home for you as a new year's present, & for your mother to sit in, & you afterwards—you know I used the chair for a year, & if I recollect right, it is a good strong one, though plain—I am glad to hear what you wrote about your mother—Every thing about fellows' old mothers is interesting to me—

Give my love to Mr & Mrs Nash—your loving old

Walt

788. *To John H. Johnston*   *12.31.* [*1876*]

431 Stevens st Camden | New Jersey |
Sunday afternoon Dec 31

My dear Johnston

Supposing you may receive this Monday morning, I feel to say to you & Mrs. J. & all the childer too, *Happy new year, for the first thing* —& you take this home to Mrs. J to read the printed letter on the other side—(it is one I sent to Rossetti in London, & he had some copies printed as a sort of circular)[21]—

The watch[22] came last evening, & I received and examined it this forenoon—I think it is going to do just right—thanks—very cold here, the gale whistling & blowing about the house, as I write—but the sun shining bright enough. Note in the box rec'd & welcomed—I am feeling quite well for me—If you see J Miller tell him *I like much* his piece to me in the January Galaxy[23]—it is full of the fieriest horses, held well in hand— tell him to write to me—I shall send you a newspaper to-morrow with some little poems to me extracted, Miller's among them—When you read it & are through, give it to J M—

Walt Whitman

789. *To an Unidentified Correspondent*[24]   [(?).(?)]. *1876*

DRAFT LETTER.

Camden, New Jersey | 1876

Your subscription for my Book is received—for which hearty thanks. Excuse temporary delay—the small first edition being exhausted, & [another being in the] press. Your Volume [*incomplete*]

21. The letter of March 17 (see 722).
22. See 786.
23. "To Walt Whitman" appeared in *The Galaxy*, XXIII (January, 1877), 29.
24. After the first printing of the 1876 edition was exhausted, there was a delay

790. *To an Unidentified Correspondent*[25] *[(?).(?). 1876?]*

431 Stevens Street Camden New Jersey | U S America

Yours rec'd—Many thanks—shall be happy to supply you with the Books—the best way is by mail—the price is £2 sent me here by p. o. order—it is entirely safe and easy—

Walt Whitman

Thanks for your offer of "the Poetry of the Period"—I have not seen it—

until WW had 600 additional copies printed (see 761). This note undoubtedly was the draft of a letter which WW sent to those people who had to wait for the second printing.

25. This note was sent to an Englishman to inform him of the price of the 1876 edition.

1877

791. *To Herbert Gilchrist*   *[Early 1877]*[1]

431 Stevens Street Camden | Sunday afternoon

My dear Herbert

Though I am pretty well physically it is very lonesome & dreary to me here, & I have been thinking all day how much I would like to come over & see you all, & stay awhile with you. Herbert, see about the stove & have put up soon as convenient—& have some *dry oak wood* sawed the right length, split, & carried up there, & piled in the room. Send me word before the end of the week. I wish much to come—Love to all—

Walt Whitman

(rec'd yesterday a letter from Wm Rossetti, which I will just enclose —& take again when I come over)[2]

792. *To John Burroughs*

January 16, 1877

I have been over here with the Gilchrists for a week[3]—go back to Camden this afternoon or tomorrow—I have a nice room here with a stove and oak wood—everything very comfortable and sunny—most of all *the spirit* (which is so *entirely lacking* over there in Camden, and has been for more than three years)—

We often speak of you—I received your letter of the 7th. . . .[4]

Love to you and 'Sula.

Walt Whitman.

1877
    1. The text does not aid dating. However, the letter was written during the winter months, and it seems reasonable to assume that it was sent shortly after the arrival of the Gilchrists in Philadelphia. Note also the similarities to 779 and 792. According to *CB*, WW stayed with the Gilchrists from January 10 to 16 and from January 25 to February 2.
    2. Probably a fragment of this letter is in the Feinberg Collection (December 15?, 1876).
    3. WW's increasing dissatisfaction with life in George's home (see 784) is ap-

793. *To Anne Gilchrist* *1.19.* [*1877*][5]

White horse N J | Jan 19

My dear friend

I jaunted down here last evening, to spend a couple of days. I think of being over with you (in all probability) Sunday next, say to dinner about 2.

I am feeling about as usual.

Love to all—

Walt Whitman

794. *To Damon Y. Kilgore*

431 Stevens street | Camden N J | Jan 23 '77

My dear Kilgore

Do your folks intend having a Paine meeting on the 29th instant? Would you like to have me present & make some off-hand remarks, (agreeable to you, & doubtless to all) for ten minutes? Answer forthwith[6]—

Walt Whitman

795. *To Mr. and Mrs. Damon Y. Kilgore*

Jan 24 '77

My dear Damon Kilgore | & Mrs Kilgore

I will be at the Commemorative meeting. I would like to speak from ten to twenty minutes *before* Mr Phillips's address. What I have to offer might be called *A true Reminiscence of Thomas Paine.* I shall be to-morrow evening & night, and all Friday, & the following night & forenoon, *at 1929 north 22d street, Phila.* (north of Berks)[7]—& if it would be convenient for you to send a carriage *there* for me at about 1½ p m Sun-

parent in the frequency of his absences. He was with the Staffords from January 6 to 10 and January 18 to 23 (*CB*); and observe his stays with the Gilchrists cited in note 1.

 4. This letter is not known.

 5. The year is established by the reference to his visit to the Staffords on January 18. WW did not return on January 21, Sunday, but he was with the Gilchrists on the following Sunday (*CB*).

 6. See 770 and the following letter. See also *SD*, 140–142.

 7. WW was with the Gilchrists from January 25 to February 2 (*CB*).

day it would suit me—Call on or address me there Friday forenoon or evening, or Saturday forenoon before 12—

Walt Whitman

Thanks for the hospitality—hearty thanks—I will accept if I can Sunday—but it is not certain—

796. *To John Burroughs*

ADDRESS: John Burroughs | Esopus-on-Hudson | New York. POSTMARKS: Camden | Jan | 24 | N.J.; New York | Jan | 25 | 8 AM.

431 Stevens street | Camden New Jersey Jan 24 '77
I think *Birds and Poets* not only much the best name for the book, but a first-rate good name, appropriate, original & fresh, without being at all affected or strained. The piece you put 4th should then be *first*—should lead the book, giving it its title, & having the name of the piece changed to "Birds and Poets"—which I think would be an improvement. The whole collection would be sufficiently homogeneous, (and it were a fault to be too much so)—You just want *a hint* for the name of a book—Only it must be in the spirit of the book—& not too much so either. *"Nature and Genius" is too Emersony altogether.*[8]

I will think over the name of the piece devoted to me, & will in a couple of days write you the result. May-be I can think of a better name. I have not rec'd the MS from Church.[9] You send on any thing—any MS—which I will cheerfully read & will return with any suggestions that may occur to me—I keep pretty well for me—

W W

8. Burroughs accepted WW's suggestion; and "Birds and Poets," which had appeared in *Scribner's Monthly* in 1873 (see 523), became the first chapter in the book. For over a month Burroughs sent to WW the manuscript of this book for comment and correction; see 798, 799, and 801. WW's emendations, particularly in the chapter devoted to himself, "The Flight of the Eagle," are discussed at length by Barrus (160–163).

9. Possibly a reference to "Our Rural Divinity," which appeared in *The Galaxy* in January (XXIII, 43–51).

10. Cattell was a young, semiliterate farm hand and a friend of the Staffords. WW met him evidently in May, 1876: "about 25 or 6—folks mother, father &c. live at Gloucester—his grand, or great grandfather, Jonas Cattell, a great runner, & Revolutionary soldier, spy." (WW referred to Jonas in the Philadelphia *Times* on January 26, 1879.) Later in the same diary the poet wrote: "the hour (night, June 19, '76, Ed & I.) at the front gate by the road." Two days later he noted "the swim of the boys, Ed.

797. *To Edward Cattell*

ENDORSED: "letter to | Ed Cattell"; "letter sent to |
Ed Cattell." DRAFT LETTER.

Jan 24th | '77

Dear Ed[10]

I want to write you a few lines particular. Do not call to see me
any more at the Stafford family, & do not call there at all any more—
Dont ask me why—I will explain to you when we meet. When you meet
any of the family I wish you to use them just the same as ever, but do not
go over there at all. I want you to keep this to yourself, & not mention it
nor this letter to any one & you must not speak about it at all to any one.

There is nothing in it that I think I do wrong, nor am ashamed of,
but I wish it kept entirely between you and me—&—I shall feel very much
hurt & displeased if you don't keep the whole thing & the present letter
entirely to yourself. Mr and Mrs Stafford are very near & kind to me, &
have been & are like brother & sister to me—& as to Harry you know how
I love him. Ed, you too have my unalterable love, & always shall have. I
want you to come up here & see me.[11] Write when will you come.

798. *To John Burroughs*   2.3. *[1877]*

ADDRESS: John Burroughs | Esopus-on-Hudson |
New York. POSTMARK: Philadelphia | Feb | 3 |
10 PM | Pa.

1929 north 22d St Phila: | Feb 3

I send the second MS back to-day.[12] The first I sent some four or
five days ago. I am pretty well for me.

WW

[Stafford?], Ed. C. & Harry" (*Diary Notes* in Feinberg). In 1877 WW cited "Sept
meetings Ed C by the pond at Kirkwood moonlight nights" (*CB*), and in *Diary Notes*
on October 29, "Ed. Cattell with me." On November 26, 1877, Cattell, who generally
called WW "old man," wrote: "Would love to See you once moor for it seems an age
Since i last met With you down at the pond and a lovely time We had of it to old man
. . . i love you Walt and Know that my love is returned to" (Feinberg). In another
letter dated simply Sunday 21, perhaps written in November, Cattell said: "Went with
Some Boys up the Pond to day and i Seen your old Chir floting down the Strem. . . . i
would like to See you and have a talk. i love you Walt and all ways Will. So May God
Bless You is my prayer" (Feinberg).

    11. WW deleted the following: "Or come over to 1929 north 22d street Phila-
delphia [Mrs. Gilchrist's house] & see me."

    12. *Birds and Poets* (see 796).

799. *To John Burroughs*   2.13. [1877]

431 Stevens st Camden Feb 13—p m

Dear John Burroughs
    Yours of 6th only rec'd this afternoon by me—as I have just return'd to-day from a week down at a farm in Jersey—
    I hope you will adopt *Birds & Poets*—& then the *Flight of the Eagle*[13] —As the more I think of them, the better I like both—(I mean directly & indirectly, & for wear)—Come on to Mrs. Gilchrist's 16th or 17th[14]—I will prepare them—I will be there—it is 1929 north 22d street—I still keep pretty well for me—

WW

800. *To Anne Gilchrist*   2.14. [1877]

431 Stevens Street Camden | Feb 14—p m

Dearest friend
    I returned last evening from a week's stay at White Horse[15]—am feeling pretty well for me—heard of your call during my absence—Think of coming over *to-morrow, Thursday, afternoon* (say about 4)—As you will see by the enclosed card Mr Burroughs is to be in Phila: on a flying visit, & expects to be at your house to-morrow afternoon at 5. So long till to-morrow—& love to all—

Walt Whitman

801. *To John Burroughs*   2.27. [1877]

Camden | Tuesday night | Feb 27

    I have gone over the chapters—got quite in the spirit of them— added & suggested a few lines or words here & there—and *pruned* a few

---

13. "The Flight of the Eagle" is the chapter devoted to WW in *Birds and Poets* (see 796).
14. Burroughs arrived in Philadelphia on February 15; see the next letter. In his journal on February 17, Burroughs recorded his visit with WW: "It is a feast to look at Walt's face; it is incomparably the grandest face I ever saw—such sweetness and harmony, and such strength . . . If that is not the face of a poet, then it is the face of a god. None of his pictures do it half justice" (Barrus, 160).
15. WW was with the Staffords from February 7 to 13, and stayed in Philadelphia from February 15 to 21 (CB).

passages, even pages, remorselessly.[16] I like them all—they are very *living* —the "Beauty" chapter I think especially fine.[17]

Do you say the final chapter is already in print? the one about me? If so, *send me the proof*, which I will return by next mail. I am feeling quite well for me.

WW

802. *To Anne Gilchrist*   *3.4.* [*1877*]

113 east 10th Street | New York | March 4—evening

Dear friend

We arrived here safely, (Harry Stafford is with me) Friday evening and are very comfortably situated with hospitable friends[18]—I am feeling well as usual—go out sufficiently, & meet with many old acquaintances—Only write this time to report myself in safety, & to send love to all—

Walt Whitman

803. *To John Burroughs*   *3.13.* [*1877*]

ADDRESS: John Burroughs | Esopus-on-Hudson | New York. POSTMARK: New York | Mar 13 | 9 PM.

113 east 10th Street | N Y City—March 13

Dear friend

Yours of yesterday rec'd—Shall be very glad to go up with you Friday for a couple of days or so[19]—Should like to fetch my boy Harry Stafford with me, as he is my convoy like—We occupy the same room & bed—

We had another reception here last night—very successful—lots of artists, many fine ladies & not a few ministers & journalists—I am feeling pretty well, but can't stand these things long—Dull half rainy day here—

---

16. For WW's emendations in Burroughs' manuscript, see 796.

17. "Before Beauty" is the fifth chapter of *Birds and Poets*.

18. WW, accompanied by Harry Stafford, stayed with the New York jeweler, John H. Johnston (see 786). He was in New York from March 2 to 27 (*CB*).

19. WW was at Burroughs' home in Esopus from March 16 (Friday) to March 20. Burroughs noted the "great event" in his journal on March 21: "[WW and Harry Stafford] cut up like two boys and annoyed me sometimes. Great tribulation in the kitchen in the morning. Can't get them up to breakfast in time. Walt takes Harry with him as a kind of foil or refuge from the intellectual bores" (Barrus, 164).

have been in all day—sitting muchly for my picture[20]—which gets on well—

    'Sula, love to you—

                                                          W W

    I wrote you a Postal Card yesterday but believe (although I am not *sure*) that it got lost before it was mailed[21]—

804. *To John H. and Amelia Johnston*   *3.17.* [*1877*]

                                    Esopus-on-Hudson | March 17
Dear friends
    We arrived here all safe at last—(after adventures)—had to cross the river late of a dark night in broken ice, in a little row boat, mid a furious snow storm (this house is on the west bank Hudson)—the natives advised us not to try it, but Harry & I said *cross*, & Mr. Burroughs consented—it was quite interesting—It looks like winter here, snow 8 inches deep in every direction—but I like it much—a far view from my window of miles of river, mountains, rocks & woods—quite a change of scene from N Y—We are very comfortable here, folks are (as every where) very kind to us—Harry has gone across the river in a row boat with Mr B. all the forenoon—& I have spent mine alone in the library writing, & frequently looking out at the grand show of scenery, in winter garb—
    Love to *you all*, to Al and May, and the childer—to Mr Waters— (& even the picture)—May return either Tuesday or Wednesday for a couple of days or so[22]—

                                                    Walt Whitman

805. *To Anne Gilchrist*   *3.17.* [*1877*]

                            Esopus-on-Hudson | New York | March 17
Dearest friend
    After a couple of weeks in New York, Mr Burroughs has brought me up here, where I am to stay for a few days—Every thing goes well—

---

20. WW had agreed in 782 to sit for a portrait by Waters. Burroughs, understandably, was not fond of the painting: "It gives Walt's benevolent look, but not his power—his elemental look. It makes him look rather soft, like a sort of Benjamin Franklin" (Barrus, 164). The portrait appears as the frontispiece to the fifth volume of the Camden Edition. Waters' sketch also idealizes the poet (*CW*, I, 202).
    21. This post card is not known.

I am very comfortably situated, & it is not only a great change from N Y —but a great relief—I mean the excitement of so much company—every thing is quiet & secluded here—all winter too, the snow white & deep in every direction—as I look from my window, river & mountains & trees & rocks—far & vast—

I only write a hurried line to let you know my whereabouts—Shall (probably) be returning to Camden latter part of next week—Love to all—

Walt Whitman

806. *To Anne Gilchrist*   *3.23.* [*1877*]

ADDRESS: Mrs Gilchrist | 1929 north 22d Street | Philadelphia. POSTMARK: New York | Mar | 23 | 7 PM | N. Y.

New York | March 23
Still here & feeling pretty well for me—Shall return to Camden to-morrow or Monday[23]—

W. W.

807. *To Scribner and Company*   [*3.30. 1877*][24]

ENDORSED: "R | 4 | 2 | 77."

431 Stevens street | Camden New Jersey
Messrs Scribner & Co
    I send you to-day by mail one copy *Burroughs's Notes on Walt Whitman*, as ordered by yours of yesterday.
    The price is $1, which please send me by mail here—

Walt Whitman

22. WW returned to New York on Tuesday, March 20, and stayed with the Johnstons until March 27. See also Furness, 207.
23. WW returned to Camden on March 27, Tuesday. Mrs. Amelia Johnston died on Monday evening, March 26, in giving birth to Harold; see Elliot, *Walt Whitman As Man, Poet and Friend* (1915), 153. An account of WW's New York trip appeared in the Camden *Daily Post* on March 29.
24. WW sent Burroughs' book on March 30 (*CB*).

808. *To Anne Gilchrist*   *4.2.* [*1877*]²⁵

Camden | Monday evn'g April 2
Think of coming over to-morrow Tuesday (say by 1½ o'clock) —
to stay perhaps till Thursday afternoon—

WW

809. *To Anne Gilchrist*   *4.10.* [*1877*]²⁶

ADDRESS: Mrs. Gilchrist | 1929 north 22d Street |
Philadelphia. POSTMARKS: Kirkwood | (?) | (?) |
N.J.; Philad'a, Pa. | Apr | 12 | 2 (?)M | (?).

White Horse N J | April 10

Dearest friend,
    I am having comfortable times down here for me—spend many
hours in the open air, though it has been furiously blustering the last two
days here—& pretty cold—Still it is *spring* here—evidences every way,
every day—Much singing of birds, on some of my visits at the pond. *The
Pond* I have more joy & comfort from than ever—I shall not be up with
you for a week, as I am to go down to the sea-shore Saturday with Mr
Stafford—(not to stay however)—Hope to be with you next week—Will
(probably) send you a postal card—
    This review of Hugo I cut from a late Weekly ed. *London Times*—
You may have it already, but as also you may not, I send it—Seems to me
good—
        Love to all—

Walt Whitman

810. *To Anne Gilchrist*   *5.1.* [*1877*]²⁷

Camden May 1

My dear friend
        I have come up from White Horse, & think of visiting you to-

---

25. April 2 was on Monday in 1877. WW did not record this visit in *CB*.
    26. Since WW was in Camden on April 10, 1878 (*CB*), this letter was un-
doubtedly written in 1877. He made no entries in *CB* between April 1 and 24, 1877.
    27. WW had been with the Staffords from April 24 to 30, and Edward Carpenter
was in Camden on May 1 (*CB*). This was WW's first meeting with his fervid English
admirer (see 738). On March 1 Carpenter wrote to WW about his intended visit: "I
think there are reasons *why we should meet*. . . . What must be done—and what you
have largely (for a foundation *entirely*) done—is to form a new organic centre for the
thought growth of this age. All seemed clear to me at times, so simple, so luminously
clear—I have no more doubt or trouble for myself—but then to *express* it: that is an

morrow Wednesday—towards the latter part of the afternoon. Will be then to supper. Have met Edward Carpenter of Brighton, England, & have taken the liberty of inviting up to your house to spend a couple of hours—to be there at 6—I am keeping up well in health for me.

                                                            Walt Whitman

811. *To John Burroughs*   *5.17. [1877]*[28]

ENDORSED (in unknown hand): "5 | 18 | '77."
ADDRESS: John Burroughs | Esopus-on-Hudso[n] | Ulster County New York. POSTMARK: Philadelphia | May 18 | 1 PM | Pa.

                                                Kirkwood N J | May 17
Dear John Burroughs
        I am passing a good part of my time down here at the farm I believe I mentioned to you. Still keep well for me & jolly—am all tann'd & sunburnt—Eat my rations every time—
        I was up yesterday to Camden to get my mail—& found *the book*[29] —read it all over with appreciative & I think critical eyes—my impression of liking it, as a curiously *homogeneous* work—(just enough radiations to make it *piquant*)—& in connection *liking the name* &c—all deepened & clinched. I especially much like—& more like—the chapter about me. There has certainly been nothing yet said that so makes the points—(& eloquently makes them—) I most want brought out & put on record—Are you coming to the Gilchrists? & when?[30]

                                                            WW

812. *To George W. Waters*   *5.17. [1877]*[31]

ADDRESS: George W Waters | artist | Elmira | New York. POSTMARK: Philadelphia | May 18 | 1 PM | Pa.

                                                Kirkwood N J | May 17
        The picture arrived in perfect order, & is much admired—I think it *grand*—Was only opened night before last, as I am down in the coun-

endless business—a thing never finished" (Syracuse). In *Days with Walt Whitman* (3–4), Carpenter erred in dating his visit May 2. A few days later he followed WW to Kirkwood, where he was charmed by the poet's naturalness among the earthy Staffords.
        28. WW had been with the Staffords before he returned to Camden on May 15; he went back to Kirkwood on the following day and remained there until May 22 (*CB*).
        29. Burroughs' *Birds and Poets*. According to *CB*, however, WW received the book on May 23.
        30. Burroughs was expected to visit the Gilchrists in June (see 814), but he apparently was unable to come to Philadelphia.
        31. Waters evidently sent the completed oil portrait (see 803), which John H. Johnston later purchased from WW for $200 in 1884 (see 1269).

try now most of the time. (My address though is still at Camden)—I am still keeping well, for me—

W. W.

Get the little new book "Birds & Poets" by John Burroughs—

813. *To Anne Gilchrist*   *6.11.* [1877][32]

at Geo: Stafford's | Kirkwood | Monday
forenoon June 11

Dearest friend

I send you a hurried line as Herbert is going up for a few days—I want to come up & be with you all awhile—I am getting much nearer to Herby, & he is already a great comfort to me—I keep well as lately, & enjoy the creek &c as much as ever—but perhaps a little variation would be acceptable & salutary to me—I shall come up soon—let us all be together awhile if agreeable, (I am not willing to have Herby absent when I am there)—

Have you been over to Camden since? I was so much obliged to you for your good letter about my sister & all, & your kind invitation to my neices which I have sent on to them. This morning is cloudy & a little chilly—Love to you, dearest friend, & to Bee & Giddy[33]—We will all see each other soon—

W. W.

814. *To Anne and Herbert Gilchrist*   *6.12.* [1877]

at Geo: Stafford's Kirkwood | N J | Tuesday p m
June 12

Dearest friend

After dinner, now, seated out in an arm chair under the tree, the grass below, & the good breeze laving me, I have just read (& reread)

32. June 11 was on Monday in 1877. According to an entry dated May 15, Herbert Gilchrist visited WW at Kirkwood (*CB*).
33. Mrs. Gilchrist's daughters, Beatrice and Grace. WW was fond of both girls, especially of Beatrice, whom he termed "the noble one" (see 816).
34. These letters are not known.
35. Evidently Burroughs changed his plans (see note 59).
36. Mrs. Gilchrist had written to Burroughs early in May inviting him to meet

the three letters, yours & Herby's & Mr Carpenter's—sweet, & welcome & bracing all of them somehow[34]—

Yes, dear friend, I will be up by Thursday evening, in time for tea, if nothing happens—Count much on seeing you all, & the cluster of friends —May-be while there are so many with you I had better sleep over in Camden, & Herby & Mr Burroughs[35] take my room & bed—but we will see when I come—the days I shall surely be there—

Love to you, Herby & the girls—& to John Burroughs & Mr Carpenter[36] if they get there before me—

W W

Herby, to-day is cloudy & threatening here though no rain yet—(I shouldn't wonder if Mr Stafford's prophecy ab't the week proved true)— You ought to have been here yesterday & be here to-day for one thing— we have oceans of *delicious strawberries* most every meal—

(The camp-out *project* in Aug: with J[ohn] B[urroughs] is magnificent[37]—O that I were well & hardy enough, to go with you—but it is out of the question)—

815. *To Ida Johnston*   *6.14.* [*1877?*][38]

ADDRESS: Miss Ida Johnston | 434 Penn street | near 5th | Camden. TRANSCRIPT.

431 Stevens st. | June 14—11 a m

Dear friend

I am afraid to venture out much in the heat of the day (as part of my trouble of the head is *sun affection, & susceptibility*)—so I give up the *Congress* visit *to-day*.

We will see about it, either *next Wednesday*, or indeed most any other (cloudy) day—as I want to go aboard—& you shall go, if you wish to. Love to mother, father & Jack.[39]

Walt Whitman

Carpenter. According to his next letter of May 16, Carpenter was to visit Burroughs at the latter's home. On June 5 Burroughs mentioned a three-day visit: "I like him much—a modest, sensible man and a great admirer of W. W." (Barrus, 140–141).

37. Herbert went to Esopus with Burroughs in September (see 830).

38. Ida was the daughter of Colonel John R. Johnston, the artist, whose home WW visited almost every Sunday evening (see 654). The year is, of course, conjectural, although entries in CB warrant the elimination of the next five years.

39. Her brother, John, Jr. (see 818).

816. *To Harry Stafford*   6.18–19 [1877]

1929 north 22 st Phila: | Monday June 18

Dear Harry,

I am still stopping here,[40] & we are having quite nice times, all of us, (Mrs Gilchrist, Mr. Carpenter, Herbert and the two girls and I)—but I miss the creek, a good deal—yesterday, (Sunday) I thought if I could only go down to the creek, & ramble about in the open air by myself & have a leisurely wash & some exercise, it would do me more good than any thing—but I staid in all day. Still it is all very pleasant here, every thing is so gentle & smooth, & yet they are all so jolly & much laughing & talking & fun—we have first rate times, over our meals, we take our time over them, & always something new to talk about. Mr Carpenter has travelled much in England, & met many people & he is one of a large family of brothers & sisters, all in active life in various parts of the world, & he shows us their pictures & tells us about them—

Dear Harry, not a day or night passes but I think of you—I dont suppose it would be so much fun for you here—but it suits an old man like me, (& then it pleases one's vanity to be made so much of)—Harry, I suppose you get the papers I send you—I don't know whether you care about them, but I thought they might amuse you a moment there for a change—I want you always to take them home for your father—At present it is about 11½ o'clock—Herbert is down stairs painting—The girls are sewing—Mrs G is out shopping & at the groceries—Mr Carpenter has gone upstairs to write some letters—& I am sitting here in my front room in the great bay window at a big table writing this—a nice cool breeze blowing in—Why there it goes, the bell for 12 o'clock—right opposite us, the masons &c building a big house, all knock off work, & there are groups sitting down in shady places & opening their dinner kettles—I too will knock off for this time—Dear son, how I wish you could come in now, even if but for an hour & take off your coat, & sit down on my lap—

Tuesday afternoon | June 19

Every thing about the same with us—was over to Camden yesterday afternoon—Mrs Gilchrist went over too, & my brother took her out on a

---

40. WW remained at the Gilchrists' until about June 25, when once again he visited the Staffords (*CB*).

41. Louisa, George's wife, was in poor health (see the next letter). On July 4 WW noted that Louisa was "very sick" (*CB*). She had a miscarriage about July 7 (see 823).

42. Grace and Beatrice Gilchrist, respectively.

43. Apparently Harry was drifting from job to job. According to some notes he

good drive about the country—My sister was up & in good spirits[41]—Herbert & Mr Carpenter went out to the park & didn't get back till 9—I came [home?] to Phil. by myself—The girls & I had our supper together, & had a jolly time—the younger daughter came out finely, & she showed that she could make herself very agreeable & interesting when she has a mind to—but the elder one is the noble one[42]—the more I see of her the better I like her—

Harry, how are you getting along there? I suppose you are learning —& I hope you are having good times[43]—Something Mr Carpenter has told me about the effect working at telegraphing has on a person disturbs me a little—but I will talk with you more particularly about it when we are together again—I send you the enclosed from Mr C[44]—I shall be down *Friday*[45] in the 6 o'clock train—I want to see the creek again—& I want to see you, my darling son, & I can't wait any longer—

Your old Walt

817. *To Peter Doyle*   6.20. [1877]

1929 north 22d street Philadelphia | Wednesday
June 20—

Dear, dear boy Pete

I am stopping here now for a week or two in the house I believe I have mentioned to you before, & where I wanted you to come & see me— (& *still want you, if you have a chance.*) But I spend most of my time down at an old farm down in Jersey where I have a fine secluded wood & creek & springs, where I pass my time alone, & yet not lonesome at all (often think of you, Pete, & put my arm around you & hug you up close, & give you a good buss—often)—

I am still keeping pretty well for me, have improved much indeed, quite fat, and all sun burnt brick red in the face, & hands as brown as nuts—am pretty lame & paralyzed yet, but walk or rather hobble sometimes half a mile, & have no more (or hardly ever) of those bad prostrated, gone-in, faint spells I used to have most every day—so you see I am doing pretty well, my dear—I still make my brother's house at Camden my

wrote on April 21–22, he was working for the *West Jersey Press*. On May 21 Harry was looking for a job in Philadelphia or Camden. When he wrote to WW on July 9, he said: "I wish that I coul[d] get a situation in a good printing office. Try the Democrat of Camden for me, will you?" (Feinberg).

44. Carpenter had called on WW at Kirkwood about May 15 and had met Harry Stafford at that time (CB).

45. Apparently WW did not go to Kirkwood until June 25, Monday (CB).

headquarters, & keep my room there—address my letters to Camden always—But my sister is not well, has not been for some weeks, (is soon to lie confined)—Upon the whole, am getting along pretty well, & good spirits—

The new edition of my books I sell enough of to pay my way very nicely—so I get along all right in that respect—(I don't need much)—how are they getting along at the Navy Yard? I send them my love—(I havn't forgotten the pictures, but they are a long while a-coming)—When you see Mr Noyes[46] tell him I should like to come on & pay him a visit this fall—& now good bye for this time, my own loving boy—

Your Old Walt

818. To John R. Johnston, Jr.   6.20. [1877]

1929 north 22d Street | Phila: June 20

Dear boy Jack,[47]

I thought of coming round to see you all last Sunday, but it was so hot & I didn't get over to Camden—didn't feel like walking up from the ferry—Jack, I am stopping up here in 22d street for a week or two—they are very kind to me, & very jovial & we have real good times—the young man, about 21,[48] he & I are very thick—then there are two grown daughters—the eldest one is a *first class trump*, she is my favorite every way—she is studying at the woman's Medical University here—the mother, Mrs Gilchrist, is a very fine lady—We have good meals, & take our time over them—I have the best room in the house, breezy & cool (& the water in it)—& a young English college Professor, Mr Carpenter, is staying here for a few days—though a stranger he is a great friend of mine & indeed has come over from England to see me—(But I have written enough of all that—)

Dear Jack, I wonder if I shall ever be with you, or rather have you with me, so that we can have some good times together on land or water —I used to think of having a shanty of my own there in Camden, & I thought I shouldn't be satisfied without having you & Ida up there to take

46. Crosby Stuart Noyes, the editor of the Washington *Star* (see 314).
47. According to WW's notation on Jack Johnston's calling card, the young man was employed about this time by A. R. McCown & Co., a hosiery store in Philadelphia (see 846). Later he was employed by Ziegler & Swearingen, sellers of notions in Philadelphia (*CB*). In Jack's autograph book WW wrote in 1875: "In memory of the good times, Sunday evenings, in Penn street, 1875, '4, & 3." On January 18, 1880, he wrote again: "Good times, Sunday Evenings, continued, '76, '77, '78, '79, &c. W W" (Feinberg).
48. Herbert Gilchrist.

supper with me *two evenings* in the week at least—I wonder if it is ever coming to pass—

Mean time I shall come around *next Sunday*, if you are all at home— Tell Ida to put her hair in curl papers Saturday night—& though I do not wish the fatted calf slaughtered on Sunday morning—*I hope there will be some spearmint ready to pull in the garden*—Johnny, how does it go with you? Love to mother & father & tell 'em I'm coming round next Sunday—Here is a kiss for you, Jack, & take care of yourself, & don't forget your loving friend

Old W W

819. *To John Burroughs*   6.22. [*1877*]

ADDRESS: John Burroughs | Esopus-on-Hudson | Ulster County New York. POSTMARK: Philadelphia | June | 22 | 3 PM. TRANSCRIPT.

1929 north 22d st Phila | June 22

Am here having a good time—Carpenter[49] returns to Europe in Saturday's steamer—the G[ilchrist]s all well—my folks in Camden all doing well[50]—Marvin comes here (to the G's) on 6th of July[51]—Shall come and visit you & S[ula][52] this summer—

W.W.

820. *To John Burroughs*

TRANSCRIPT.

Kirkwood, N. J., July 2, 1877.

Am down here for a couple of weeks on a farm with friends, enjoying things.[53] Still keep pretty well this summer. Marvin is coming to Mrs. G[ilchrist]'s on the 6th & 7th. I shall be there. That "Eagle" grows, grows.[54]

W. W.

49. It was "with real reluctance" that Carpenter returned to England after coming under "the added force of bodily presence" (*Days with Walt Whitman*, 32).

50. Apparently WW, with his customary optimism, considered that Louisa's health had improved (see 823).

51. Joseph B. Marvin, one of WW's Washington friends (see 645), visited Mrs. Gilchrist shortly after her arrival in Philadelphia in September, 1876 (Gilchrist, 228).

52. Ursula, Burroughs' wife.

53. WW was with the Staffords from June 25 to July 6 or 7 (*CB*).

54. "The Flight of the Eagle" in *Birds and Poets* (see 796).

821. *To Peter Doyle*   *7.2.* [*1877*]

Kirkwood New Jersey | July 2—

Dear boy Pete

I still keep pretty well, & am again down here at the farm in the country, for a couple of weeks, & to stay over 4th of July. Nothing particularly new in my affairs. As I write this (Monday 10 a m) it is a beautiful bright breezy forenoon—& I am going now down to the creek & spring to take a bath—it is about 90 rods distant, & I walk there & back —Love, love, love,

Your old Walt

I still make my headquarters in Camden—

822. *To Anne Gilchrist*   *7.2.* [*1877*]

ADDRESS: Mrs Gilchrist | 1929 north 22d Street | Philadelphia. POSTMARK: Kirkw[ood] | Jul | 3(?) | (?).

Kirkwood noon July 2

A beautiful day, & we are enjoying it—H[erbert] is painting[55] —I am well, for me—We expect to come up Friday—(possibly *I* not till Saturday)—

WW

823. *To Mrs. Emma Dowe*[56]   [*7.12(?). 1877*]

TRANSCRIPT.

Dear Emmy:

Lou wishes me to write you a line. She is very weak yet, but . . . in good spirits and comparatively free from pain, for now five days and nights. The babe ceased to live before it was delivered. That Lou's life was saved and that she will recover (as now seems every way probable)

55. Herbert spent part of July painting at Kirkwood (*CB*, and see 824). In a news article in the Camden *Daily Post* on August 2, which quoted from the Washington *Star*, WW, who was obviously the anonymous author, referred to Herbert's portrait of himself: "The painting, which is now well advanced, and promises to be an excellent likeness, represents Mr. Whitman sitting in an easy chair under a favorite tree." WW expected to return to Camden on Friday, July 6, as noted in 819.

56. Mrs. Dowe was Louisa's sister. Her husband Francis E. Dowe operated dry goods stores in Norwich, Conn., from 1872 to 1918. For this information I am indebted to Miss Elinor J. Harrington, librarian of the Otis Library in Norwich. This letter was preserved by Mrs. Dowe's daughter Amy, who wrote "A Child's Memories of the Whit-

is something to be devoutly thankful for. The case is curiously solemn and sad—to me—Everyone says it was the most beautiful, perfect, and well-developed babe, boy; unusually large, had black hair, nose and features like its father. Today is the anniversary of little Walter's death here. Emmy, isn't it a sad world, after all.

824. *To Herbert Gilchrist*   7.22. [1877][57]

ADDRESS: Herbert Gilchrist | Kirkwood | Camden County | New Jersey. POSTMARK: Camden | Jul | 22 | N.J.

431 Stevens Street | Camden Sunday noon July 22

Dear Herbert

Here I am at my room & haunts in Camden, so different from the creek, & bathing & exercising in the open air—yet I keep myself busy at one thing & another—& am feeling pretty well so far. (Yet I attribute my feeling pretty well now to my visits for the last year & a half to the creek & farm, & being with my dear friends the Staffords.)

We had a nice healthy ride up from Kirkwood, Mrs S[tafford] and I, Friday morning, & I enjoyed it much—(am glad I came up that way, instead of the RR). I went over to your mother's yesterday afternoon about 5½ & staid till after 8—nothing specially new with them—your mother & Bee & Giddy are all well & in good spirits—We had a good tea —I punished a fearful quantity of good oatmeal mush & stewed black-berries—then we sat & talked for an hour & a half, in the cool of the evening on the front stoop—then a delightful jaunt home to Camden, a most lovely evening (the moon & Jupiter in conjunction, & I *speering* them all the way home & especially on the river)—

I am partially busy at some writing—feel *most first rate* for me, to-day—Herb, you will see by the enclosed piece that J. Bur[roughs] is in Canada (or *en route* thither)[58]—Write to me—

Your old Walt.

I have written to-day to Mrs Stafford—

mans" (unpublished). The first child of George and Louisa Whitman died on July 12, 1876 (see 757).

57. WW was with the Staffords from July 13 to 20; he "came up in the light wagon with Mrs. S July 20." (CB). For an account of a scene with Harry Stafford, see Introduction. Evidently WW was considering a trip to Washington, for on November 9, 1877, Elmer Stafford, Harry's sixteen-year-old cousin, wrote to WW: "I would like to be with you all the time if i could. i would like very much to go with you on your trip to Washington" (Feinberg).

58. Burroughs wrote to WW on August 10 after a three-week trip to Canada and a brief visit to Boston and Concord (Feinberg; Traubel, II, 318–319). He was in Camden about the middle of September (see 830).

825. *To F. Leypoldt*[59]

431 Stevens Street Camden N J | July 23 '77

F Leypoldt   Dear Sir

In answer to your circular I send you the following—

My works as they now stand (in the latest edition published by me at Camden N J about a year ago, June 1876) consist of Two Volumes

LEAVES OF GRASS, copyrighted 1876, 384 pages 12 mo, (with portraits)

—The first edition 72 pages, small quarto, was pub in Brooklyn N Y in 1855

—Second New York City 1857—third 1860 (by Thayer & Eldridge Boston)

—fourth New York City 1865—fifth Washington D C 1871—Sixth & last as above.

(—all the editions except the third by me)

TWO RIVULETS, copyrighted 1876, 350 pages 12 mo. with photo. —including *Democratic Vistas*, *Memoranda of the War*, and *Passage to India*

I publish & sell these Vols. at $5 a piece. Each Vol contains autograph & portrait—I enclose proofs of the title pages of the above two Vols. Also a circular or adv. If needed will cheerfully furnish you any further information on the matter—Address me here—

Walt Whitman

825.1 *To Herbert Gilchrist*   [7.28. 1877][60]

1929 north 22d Street | Saturday—6 p m

Dear Herb

I will just write a line to put in your mother's letter—I am well as usual—We have had three awful hot days & nights, (but I have stood 'em capitally) up to last evening, when it rained hard, & though warm enough yet again, it is now quite tolerable—

I have been here 24 hours—(go back to Camden this evening)—Your

59. F. Leypoldt & Co. were bookdealers with a store at 37 Park Row in New York City. There are no references to book orders from this firm in *CB*.

60. On Saturday, July 28, WW stayed at the Gilchrists', and Herbert was at Kirkwood with the Staffords. WW also noted in *CB* that from July 22 to 30 it was *"very hot* —therm 90–96—in Camden." See also note 55.

61. August 7 was on Tuesday in 1877. Until August 12 WW remained in Camden, where Harry had visited him on August 4 and 5 (*CB*).

62. Probably with Jack Johnston and his friends (see 818).

63. After staying with WW in Camden on August 4 and 5 (*CB*, and see 824), Harry wrote from Kirkwood on August 6: "Herbret cut me pretty hard last night at the

mother, & Bee & Giddy are very well—I am writing this up in the bow
window room—it is jolly up here—I slept like a top last night—We all
sat in the big room in the dark, till 10—(had to put down the windows
it was so coolish & windy)—

Herb, your creek picture looks steadily good—don't give out the
more you are acquainted with it, & examine it—seems to me indeed a
true bit of nature—I miss the creek & spring—Miss my dear friends at
the house—shall write to Mrs Stafford probably same mail with this—
rec'd your letter—& thank you for it—As I close it is 6 o'clock, & a fine
evening—

Love to you from your old Walt

826. *To Harry Stafford*   *8.7.* [*1877*][61]

431 Stevens Street | Camden Tuesday Aug 7

Dear Comrade & Dear Son

Your letter came this morning, & as I think my loving boy is so
touchy ab't it, (he says he has writ *three* letters, but I can't make out but
two) I will sit right down & send him a letter. I am feeling well—only
as I was out with some friends Sunday night,[62] I was foolish enough to
take a good strong drink, & eat a couple of slices of rich cake late at
night—& *I shan't do any thing of the kind again*. But I am pretty well,
dear son, & feel more able & sassy every day—& we will have some good
times yet. Harry, I don't know the particulars about the Herbert scrape,
but you must let up on him—I suspect you said something pretty tantaliz-
ing before he call'd you that—Let it go—Of course I shan't say any thing
about it to any one[63]—

There is quite a stir here in Camden to-day as the 6th New Jersey
Reg't. is coming home this afternoon or evening, & they are going to
give the boys a reception & sort of supper. A good many of the young
fellows are friends of mine—I am invited, but it will be too boisterous for
me, & I shan't go—If you was here you should go, as it would suit you.

I wish I was down by the pond to-day for a couple of hours, to strip
& have a good bath—It is very close & hot here—

supper table, you must not let on if I tell you; he called me a 'dam fool,' I wasn't talking
to him any way! we was all talking of telegraphing, and father said he was reading of
a man who was trying to overdo it and I said that I did not think he could do it and
the[n] Herbret stuck in that, it did not sit very well, and if I had been near enough to
smacked him in the 'Jaw' I would of done it. you must not say anything about it to him or
any one, he thinks he can do as he wants to with me but he will find out sometime [t]hat
he is fooling with the wrong one. . . . I will be up to see you on Thursday to stay all
night with you. dont want to go any wair[?] then, want to stay in and talk with you.
did not get time to say anything to you when I sawe you, did not have time to say
scarcely anything" (Feinberg). See also 839 and Introduction.

There is a great rush now to the country—every train most is full—it is quite a sight to go to the ferry, Philadelphia side, & see the stream of people, men, women & children, old & young, some really funny characters—I go once in a while & take a look at the sight—

We are all well—as soon as I finish this I shall go out for a couple of hours before dinner—(it is now between 11 and 12)—

Here is an item about your old friend Mr Moore, of Bingham's school & printing office:[64]

> Henry W. Moore, Esq., formerly of the Philotechnic Institution of this city, and at present a resident of St. Louis, has been spending a few days with his friends in this vicinity, leaving Wednesday night for home. He intends departing, in company with Mrs. M., *nee* Vandergrift, one of our former school teachers, for Venezuela shortly, in the interest of St. Louis merchants.

And here is one about the little girl that was run over, & your father picked up & carried home:

> Monday morning about 11 o'clock Lizzie Linkenheil, 6 years of age, living at 126 Market street, was run over in front of her home by a farmer's Sheldon wagon, loaded with truck, and instantly killed. George Sheer, the driver, was taken into custody and released afterwards by the Coroner. The child's father is a member of the 6th N. J. Regiment, and was absent with the command at the time.

And here is one about your old Woodbury friend, I suppose

> The residence of Mr. Barber, editor of the Woodbury *Constitution,* at Woodbury, was discovered to be on fire about 9½ o'clock Sunday morning, and damaged to the extent of $1,000. The good folks of that delightful little place were about proceeding to church when the alarm was given, but they turned in nobly to save the furniture, which was removed little damaged.

Good bye for a couple of days, my own loving boy. I shall look for you Thursday[65]—

Your old Walt

64. WW pasted three newspaper clippings in his letter from the Camden *New Republic* of August 4.
65. There is no notation in *CB* of Harry's visit on Thursday, August 9. WW returned to Kirkwood on August 12 and, except for a flying visit to Camden on August 15, remained there until September 10 (*CB*).

Harry, I want you to tell (above every one) your mother and father I have written to you & that I send them my love particular, & I will be down again one of these days—

827.   *To Anne Gilchrist*   *8.20. [1877]*[66]

                                        Kirkwood N J | Monday afternoon Aug 20
My dear friend,
        I forward you the accompanying rec'd to-day by me. *The other two* will you please take, or mail to my sister in Camden, soon as you have read?[67]
        I am here yet, living a free outdoor life, alone with the pond & trees, lots of wild flowers, lots of butterflies (those in season now)—Shall report myself to you soon as I come up—

                                                                        WW

828.   *To Anne Gilchrist*   *[9(?).4(?). 1877]*[68]

                                        By the Pond | Tuesday 4½ p m
        I have just been reading your Monday note for the second time— & will write a line in rejoinder, with my French water pen, moistened out of the gurgling brook, just as I sit here, half shade, half in the warm sun, as I sit here after my lavations—
        I am still pretty well—Still enjoy my natural days here, by the creek (but they are now drawing to a close)—Nothing new.
        The papers have all arrived I think—the News, with the Plevna battle letter, &c. I have here to-day, & am reading with interest. Herby is well & brown—Shall be up in good time to be with my dear neices & all of you— I wonder if you have the same splendor of days & nights as we here the week past.
        I suppose you will have Edward Carpenter's letter to Herby by this time & will find it indeed cheery & interesting.[69]
        Love to all—

                                                                        W. W.

66.   August 20 was on Monday in 1877, and see the preceding note.
67.   The enclosures, probably letters, are not with the manuscript.
68.   This letter was written shortly before WW's return to Camden on September 10, probably on Tuesday, September 4. On September 3 the New York *Tribune* noted the fighting between the Turks and Russians near Plevna.
69.   Carpenter returned to England late in June (see 819).

829. *To Peter Doyle*   *9.16.* [*1877*][70]

ADDRESS: Pete Doyle | M Street South | bet 4½ &
6th | Washington | D C. POSTMARK: Camden |
Sep | 16 | N.J.

431 Stevens St Camden | Sunday Sept 16 4:30 p m

Dear Son

I will write you a line or two any how—(it is so long since I have written any thing in an envelope)[71]—Pete, if you was to see me to-day you would almost think you saw your old Walt of six years ago—I am all fat & red & tanned—have been down in the country most of the summer, return'd the past week—feel real comfortable for me—only I am still paralyzed left side, & have pretty bad stomach troubles still at times—but thankful to God to be as well & jolly as I am[72]—

I am all alone in the house to-day, & have had a good time—fine bright warm day—been out twice for short walks, (my little dog accompanying me)—rest of the time up here alone in my 3d story south room—done up & sent off my two books to a subscriber in England[73]—Eat my dinner alone, *wished you could be with me then, & for a couple of hours, if no more*—Pete, your papers all come regularly, & I am pleased to get them—About coming on I cannot say now, but *I shall come*, & before long[74]—Love to Mr and Mrs Nash—Love to you, my darling son, & here is a kiss for you—

WW

830. *To Anne Gilchrist*   *9.19.* [*1877*]

431 Stevens Street Camden | Wednesday Sept 19

Nothing special to write about—& yet I thought I would send you a line—A good, long, kind, hearty, satisfying visit from John Burroughs & Herby last evening—I suppose they are now on the RR to New York[75]—

70. September 16 occurred on Sunday in 1877. WW had returned from Kirkwood on September 10 (*CB*).

71. Most of WW's communications with Doyle were written on post cards.

72. Much more romantically, and inaccurately, WW had written on August 27 in a little piece entitled "Convalescent hours": "Come, ye disconsolate, in whom any latent eligibility is left—come get the sure virtues of creek, shore, and wood and field. Two months (July and August) have I absorbed them, and they already make a new man of me. Every day, seclusion—every day at least two or three hours of freedom, bathing, no talk, no bonds, no dress, no books, no *manners*" (Yale; *CW*, IV, 182).

73. WW sent the 1876 two-volume edition to James Anderson Rose in London (*CB*).

74. WW made only one visit, in 1875, to Washington after going to Camden in

And you? I hope you are feeling in good heart & physique—Your note to my sister rec'd & read with sympathy & love by all—

We are all well—My brother is off to his labors, (which are still quite pressing)—My sister has gone out to market—Hattie & Jessie are down stairs sewing—I am sitting up here in my 3d story south room by the open window writing this—feeling quite well for me—

Love to you & the girls, & God bless you all—

Walt Whitman

Bee, dont neglect to write us word—tell us when we can come over for at least a momentary call—& could I or any of us be of any service to you?[76]

831. *To Beatrice Gilchrist*   9.21. [1877]

ADDRESS: Miss Beatrice Gilchrist | 1929 North 22d Street | Philadelphia. POSTMARKS: Camden | Sep | 21 | N.J.; Philad'a, Pa. | Sep | 21 | 9 PM | Rec'd.

Camden Friday | afternoon Sept 21

Dear Bee

Your letter came an hour ago, & we have all read it with deepest interest—Praying that all will go well with your dearest Mother—& having no doubt it will—Hattie has been quite unwell for two nights, & yesterday—a sort of *Cholera morbus* & fever—but is pretty well to-day—is dress'd & down stairs again—the rest all well—

I rec'd a letter from Herby—he said he had written to you all, at the same time with mine—He had arrived at Esopus, & was having good times—

As I was down by the market here three hours ago I met Mr Stafford, & have had a talk & a short ride with him—he came up with a load of cabbages, which he sold, & has just started for home—All are well, (al-

1873, but he apparently was considering another trip in 1877 (see notes to 824).

75. Herbert stayed with Burroughs at Esopus-on-Hudson until about October 4 (see 835).

76. Mrs. Gilchrist had, as she wrote to one of her English friends on December 23, "a somewhat severe operation (under ether) to cure an injury received at the birth of one of my children which has always troubled me—The success depended largely on skilful nursing afterward and this Bee accomplished" (Feinberg). In the same letter Mrs. Gilchrist made an interesting comment upon her stay in America: "I rejoice that we came—to see it all with our own eyes, but I also rejoice very much that I do not feel as if I ought to stay—as I should have done if it had offered manifestly better advantages and opportunities for Herby and Bee than England." Not a word about her disillusionment with the person who, not mentioned by name, was simply "an American poet."

though Mrs S is hardly so, either, I think overworked & too much tasked & nervous)[77]—

I have rec'd I think from Edw'd Carpenter the *Daily News* (London) with a long very fine resumé article on *Thiers*—which I will bring or send you, for yourself & (by & by) your mother's reading—

I am feeling comfortable—go out some hours every day, enjoying the fine Sept: weather—

Affectionately

W.W.

832. *To Anne Gilchrist*   9.25. [1877]

431 Stevens Street | Camden Sept 25

Dearest friend

Bee's card rec'd this morning—glad & thankful to hear all is going well with you—have abstained from coming over, for fear of being in the way—but hope I may come soon—Mannahatta and Jessie went off in the 11:45 train from Phil: to-day[78]—in good spirits, & excellent well, and have had a jolly good visit both to you & yours & over here—My sister is well—She went over with the girls to the depot—saw them off safely, & returned to dinner—No further news rec'd by me from Herby—I am well as usual—doing nothing particular—

W.W.

832.1 *To John H. Johnston*   9.25. [1877?][79]

431 Stevens Street | Camden New Jersey | Sept 25

Dear Johnston

How are you—& all?—I want to hear about Al and May—& I want to hear about the baby—Please do a little thing for me—there was a white tea-cup & saucer, a "moustache-cup," given me by a soldier, & I left it at your house—if it is unbroken & still there, please have some of your fellows box it neatly & express it here to me—How are all your fellows in the store? Tell them I remember them all so well & so pleasantly—

77. On the same day WW recorded in *CB*: "Saw Geo Staf[ford] at the market, (sent the little dinner basket to Ruth—Geo: wanted me to go down with him)."
78. According to *CB*, the girls left on September 24 for Ellicott City, Md., where they attended Patapsco Seminary (see 833).
79. Since this letter apparently refers to WW's extended visits to Kirkwood in 1877 and to his stay with the Johnstons in March, the year is almost positive. The

I have been down in the country at a secluded primitive farm all summer, living much of the time outdoors by a solitary woody pond, (half the time naked or half-naked)—am now quite fat & all tanned & red—Love to you, my friend—

Walt W

Where & how is Waters? Where is the picture?

833. *To Mannahatta and Jessie Louisa Whitman 10.2.* [*1877*]

ADDRESS: Miss Mannahatta Whitman | Care of
Mrs Archer | Patapsco Seminary | Ellicott City |
Maryland. POSTMARK: Camden | Oct | 3 | N.J.

431 Stevens Street | Camden Oct 2

My dear girls (for this letter is for you both)

I will just write you a few lines without formality—

It is evening—has just struck 8—I am sitting up in my room alone—I still feel pretty well for me—went over to Phila: & took a long pleasant ride out to the Park in the open car, this afternoon—return'd about an hour ago, & had my supper—

Lou is well—she went over to Phila: this forenoon, & this afternoon & evening she has had company, (Aunt Libby, & her daughter & daughter's husband—they are down stairs now)—George is well—he has been to New York to-day, & has just return'd, & is down stairs eating his supper—Eddy is well & hearty—Tip ditto—We all get along pretty much in the old way—To-day I rec'd an order for five full sets of my books from England, *accompanied by the money*[80]—(which of course doesn't hurt my feelings a bit)—

I havn't been over to the Gilchrists' for about two weeks, as they are all deeply absorbed in Mrs. G's illness (from the operation)—but Lou was there a few minutes to-day—didn't see Mrs G, she is doing well, & will probably be up in a couple of weeks, or so—Lou saw Beatrice—Herbert is in New York, (up the Hudson) visiting at Mr Burroughs's—

I have rec'd a good letter from your father, dated Sept 24[81]—he was well, & busy in his new office—So, my darlings, you see I have just

---

reference in the last line to Waters, who had recently painted the poet's portrait, also points to this year.

80. The book order from Carpenter referred to in the following letter.

81. This letter is apparently lost. However, on July 22 Jeff had written to inform WW that he was about to lose his position at the St. Louis Water Works because of political pressures, but that he was actively engaged in consultation work for Henry Flad & Co., civil engineers (Feinberg).

rattled off all the domestic gossip & have now only room to send love from

Uncle Walt[82]

834. *To Edward Carpenter* *10.2.* [*1877*][83]

TRANSCRIPT.

Camden, | New Jersey, | U. S. A. | Oct 2nd.
I merely write to say at once that your letter and the postal order have both been safely received. The books (to the addresses given) will be sent immediately. I am well for me. H[erbert] G[ilchrist] is at John B[urroughs]'s on the Hudson. Mrs G[ilchrist] is ill in bed. Harry[84] is well.

Thanks and love.

W.W.

835. *To Edward Carpenter* *10.5.* [*1877*]

ADDRESS: Edward Carpenter | 45 Brunswick Square | Brighton | England. POSTMARKS: Camden | (?) | N.J.; Paid | Liverpool | U S Packet | 18 Oc (?)7 | 5 A.

Camden New Jersey | U S America | Oct 5
I have to-day sent by mail post paid, the Volumes to Messrs *Thompson, Templeton, Teall* and *Haweis*,[85] (seven Vols in all)[86]—*Many thanks to you*—I am well, for me—I am just going over to the G[ilchrist]s to spend the evening[87]—H[erbert] has return'd—

W W

82. Shortly after WW wrote, he received a letter from Charles Heyde, dated October 10, in which he complained that "the trouble I have with her [Hannah] is past endurance." Haunted by sexual fantasies, Hannah "smells my coat, when I come home, my gloves, my handkerchief and declares that I have been abed somewhere. . . . A evening she goes out, in the rain and darkness and returns at bed time, with scandal stories, of sexual demonstration—whoring truly, and she does not take the smallest interest or thought how I am to maintain myself, keep this shelter over her and the sheriff from fore-closing" (Trent).

83. WW noted receipt of $50.12 from Carpenter on this date (CB). Carpenter sent a letter on September 17 and a post card on September 20 about the book orders from his friends (Traubel, IV, 204–205, and see 835). At WW's request Carpenter had examined a volume of Augusta Webster (1837–1894), an English poet, and had found her verse commonplace.

84. For an account of Harry's letters to WW, see Introduction.

85. Seymer (Seymour?) Thompson was at Christ's College, Cambridge; Clement Templeton was a concert manager in London; J. J. Harris Teall taught science at

836. *To J. J. Harris Teall*   *10.5.* [*1877*][88]

ADDRESS: J J Harris Teall | University Extension
Lecturer | Nottingham | England. POSTMARKS:
(?) | Oct | 5 | N.J.; Philadelphia | Oct | 5 | Paid.

Camden New Jersey | U S America | Oct 5
I have to-day sent by mail same address as this card my Volume
Two Rivulets—Please notify me (by postal card will do) soon as it reaches
you safely—

Walt Whitman

837. *To Edward Carpenter*

TRANSCRIPT.

Camden, | New Jersey, | U. S. A. | October 25th, 1877.
I send to-day to same address as this card, one L of G, one T[wo]
R[ivulets], and four copies Dem[ocratic] Vistas.[89]

I am pretty well and getting along as usual. I saw the G[ilchrist]s
last evening.[90] They are well.

If you want another copy or two, send me word, and write when you
can.

W. W.

838. *To Anne Gilchrist*   [*10.30. 1877*][91]

ADDRESS: Mrs Gilchrist | 1929 North 22d Street |
Philadelphia. POSTMARK: Philadelphia | Oct | 30 |
1 PM | Pa.

431 Stevens Street | Camden Tuesday forenoon
As I write (9–10 o'clock) it looks so stormy it is probable I shall

Nottingham; and the Rev. H. R. Haweis was "a popular London preacher"; see *CB* and
Carpenter's letter to WW on December 19 (Feinberg; Traubel, I, 189–190). Haweis and
his wife called on WW in Camden on December 3, 1885 (*CB*); "A Visit to Walt
Whitman" appeared in *The Pall Mall Budget* on January 14, 1886, and in *The Critic*
on February 27 (VIII, 109).
    86. Except for Teall, the men had ordered the two-volume edition; see the following
post card.
    87. In *CB* WW noted: "Oct 5 after three weeks absence visited Mrs G's—Mrs G
temporarily sitting up—Herbert returned."
    88. See notes 85 and 86.
    89. This transaction is confirmed in *CB*.
    90. WW had supper with Mrs. Gilchrist every evening from October 22 to
26 (*CB*).
    91. The date of this post card is established by the postmark. October 30 occurred
on Tuesday in 1877. On November 1 WW wrote in *CB:* "walked a-foot in Phil: and
C[amden]—more than for four years, at any one time."

not be over this evening—I had a good night, & have just had a good breakfast, & am feeling comfortable—

W.W.

839. *To Anne Gilchrist*   *11.11.* [1877]

ADDRESS: Mrs Gilchrist | 1929 North 22d Street |
Philadelphia. POSTMARK: Camden | Nov | 11 | N.J.

Camden Sunday noon—Nov 11

Harry came up yesterday—staid the afternoon—went back home
in the 6 train—his father is sick in bed—they are quite anxious about
him[92]—(H[arry] wished me to explain to you & Herby[93]—then it was
very stormy here Sat: p m)—I am well—have been out this forenoon for a
hundred-rod-walk—the painting upside-down still continues here—I will
be over Monday, by 5½ or 6—

W.W.

839.1 *To John Lucas*   *11.13.* [1877?][94]

TRANSCRIPT.

November 13.

[WW introduced a young friend in the hope that he might find a
place of employment with Lucas.]

840. *To Edward D. Bellows*

ADDRESS: Edward D. Bellows | 356 Fifth Street |
bet Monmouth & Brunswick sts | Jersey City | N J.
POSTMARK: Camden | Nov | 20 | N.J.

431 Stevens Street | Camden New Jersey Nov 20 | 77

Dear Sir[95]

I rec'd the letter with the money—& yesterday I sent you by

92. After Harry Stafford visited WW on November 10, and informed the poet that
his father was "quite unwell," WW sent "an affectionate letter" and a small bottle of
whisky to Mr. Stafford (CB). On November 13 Harry urgently suggested that WW
come immediately to Kirkwood (Feinberg). During his stay there from November 14 to
17, WW learned that George Stafford suffered from stomach hemorrhages—hematomesis
(see 841). For Harry's letter to WW, see Introduction.
93. Since Herbert Gilchrist walked to Kirkwood on November 4 and returned on
the following day (CB), Harry wanted him to be informed of his father's condition.
Herbert and Harry, however, were not on amicable terms (see 826). On October 24
Harry complained to WW: "H. G. is down yet, he will be down for several days by the
way he talks. him and our folks get along well, Mother thinks him tip top, and it
makes her mad if I say any thing against him. she told me the other day if I did not want
to sleep with him I could go somewhere else for she was not going to keep a bed for me
by myselfe" (Feinberg). Evidently the two young men were later on better terms, for,
according to Harry's letter to WW on November 7, Herbert invited him to spend the

Adams' express, paid, to same address as this letter, a set of my books *Leaves of Grass* and *Two Rivulets* with John Burroughs's *Notes*—Should like to have you notify me if they reach you safely—I can lend you a copy of Mr O'Connor's pamphlet *Good Gray Poet*, which you can have for a month, if you wish & then return by mail to me—or if you want rather to purchase a copy I will get you one at the store of rare books in Philadelphia where they sell it at $1 a copy—

Walt Whitman

841. *To Edward Carpenter*   *11.27. [1877]*

ADDRESS: Edward Carpenter | Cobden Road |
Chesterfield | Derbyshire | England. POSTMARKS:
Camden | Nov | 27 | N.J.;(?) | De 10 | 77.

Camden New Jersey | U S America | Nov 27
Your card of Nov 13 rec'd—have to-day mailed Mr Vines'[96] books—Your card of a week or ten days previous rec'd—Many & sincere thanks—

I still keep pretty well, & every thing goes on with me much as usual —Geo: Stafford has been very ill with hemorrhages from the stomach (hematemesis) but is over it, & out, though feeble[97]—the rest well—the Gilchrists are all well—Mrs G is here with us in Camden today to dinner[98] —We often speak of you—

W W

842. *To A. Williams and Company*

431 Stevens Street | Camden New Jersey | Nov 30 '77
A. Williams & Co[99] | Dear Sirs
     In compliance with your request of Nov 28 I send by Adams's

weekend with the Gilchrists (Feinberg).

     94. Lucas was a manufacturer of paint with a store at 1028 Race Street in Philadelphia. The family had a zinc and color works near Kirkwood; see *Proceedings of the New Jersey Historical Society*, LXVI (October, 1948), 148. Harry Stafford probably was not the young man referred to, since he wrote to WW on June 5, 1878, about an offer made to him by Lucas (Feinberg).

     95. WW sent advertising circulars to Bellows on November 13, after which Bellows sent an order for books (undated fragment in LC), and on November 18 WW forwarded the two-volume edition and Burroughs' book (CB).

     96. On this date WW sent the 1876 edition to Sidney H. Vines, a lecturer at Christ's College, Cambridge (CB).

     97. See 839.

     98. WW also mentioned this visit in CB.

     99. Owners of the "Old Corner Bookstore" in Boston from 1864 to 1883 (Gohdes and Silver, 88*n*.).

Express three copies of the only edition of *Leaves of Grass*,[1] of the few copies at my command to fulfil your order—(the retail price is $3)—below see bill, the am't which please remit me here.

Walt Whitman

Bill

Camden N J Nov | 30 '77

A Williams & Co
To W Whitman
   To three copies Leaves of Grass @ $1.75—$5.25
   —Rec'd payment—

---

843. *To Herbert Gilchrist*   *12.12. [1877]*[2]

ADDRESS: Herbert H Gilchrist | 1929 north 22d Street | Philadelphia. POSTMARK: Philadelphia | Dec | 12 | 1 PM | Pa.

Camden   Dec 12 a m

I have invited Mr Eldridge, a Washington friend, to come up to your house & spend a couple of hours this evening—Please have a fire made ready in the stove up in the room—Shall be over rather earlier—

W W

844. *To Beatrice Gilchrist*

Camden Dec 13 '77

Dear Bee

My sister told me at breakfast to say to you she would be happy to have you come over Saturday p m & spend the night, & take a ride Sunday, if agreeable to you—

---

1. The 1872 edition of *Leaves of Grass* (CB).
2. The year is confirmed by the following (dated) letter. Eldridge was an old friend of WW and copublisher of the 1860 edition of *Leaves of Grass*. He had last visited WW on October 19, 1876 (CB).
3. Beatrice was a medical student. WW was almost clairvoyant: Beatrice committed suicide in 1881 (see 1054).
4. Here WW gave the more plausible explanation of his paralysis and physical collapse; for public consumption, however, he invariably attributed his ailments to infections received during his visits to the wartime hospitals.

Bee, I have been thinking much the few hours past of what Mr Eldridge told me of a young Mrs Needham (an intimate friend of my Washington friends, & two years ago a fine healthy woman of 26) who too overwhelmingly swamped herself as a student at your Phila: medical school, a year & a half since, (crowding too much & too intense study into too short a time) resulting in terrible brain troubles & a general caving in, & now (as Mr E told me last night on our journey down) of *death lately in a lunatic asylum*—just from sheer overwork, & too intense concentration, ardor, & continued strain[3]—

My own trouble is an illustration of the same danger, & I feel peculiarly sensible of it in others near to me[4]—

Always yours

Walt Whitman

I shall be over at ½ past 5[5]—

844.1 *To an Unidentified Correspondent* [(*?*).(*?*). *1877*(*?*)][6]

James M Scovel
113 Arch Street
Camden

9½ a m

Come over by Market st ferry—about 80 rods from the Camden landing ferry—

5. According to *CB*, WW spent most evenings with the Gilchrists from December 10 to 30, and had Christmas dinner with them. In December WW introduced the Gilchrists to Joaquin Miller and took them on December 27 to see Miller's play, *The Danites*, at the Walnut Street Theatre (*CB*). WW himself had attended the opening of the play on December 24; see Miller's letter to WW (Feinberg; Traubel, III, 225). Herbert Gilchrist reported that at a tea given by his mother Miller exclaimed upon WW's arrival: "He looks like a god, to-night" (Gilchrist, 231).

6. This note, probably directing an acquaintance to a Sunday morning breakfast at Scovel's home, was written on the verso of an invitation to a farewell reception for the sculptor, W. W. Story, on December 24, 1877.

1878

845. *To Anne Gilchrist*   2.18. [*1878*]

ADDRESS: Mrs A Gilchrist | 1929 North 22d
Street | Philadelphia. POSTMARKS: Kirkwood |
Feb | 1(?) | (?); Philad'a, Pa. | Feb | 19 | 7
PM | (?).

Kirkwood N J | Monday evening Feb 18

Dear friend, & Bee, Herby & Giddy—

I am down here at Kirkwood—Came down here some four days ago[1]
—am having a real hearty old-fashioned time, for me—Harry came up for
me in the light wagon, the day but one after I was last at your house—a
delightful ride down here—& yesterday afternoon one of those nice long
rambling drives with George Stafford, in the roomy old light wagon, (a
good part of the road through the piney woods, which I always enjoy so
much)—

The weather has been & is pleasant—a little cool to-day, but the sun
shining out as I write—I was down by the creek most of the forenoon—&
shall go down for an hour again this evening—bright moonlight nights—
I am quite happy here, for me—We live well, keep good wood fires—&
have plenty of chicken, eggs & fresh pork (they kill a hog about every
two or three weeks)—Mr Stafford is pretty well—he has been out all day
with the team hauling marl—Mrs Stafford is well—Harry & the rest ditto
—Mrs Stafford thanks you kindly for the medicine—I don't know what
day I shall come up—Love to you all—

W.W.

846. *To John R. Johnston, Jr.*   2.18. [*1878*]

ADDRESS: John R Johnston Jr | care of McCown &
Co: | 623 Market Street | Philadelphia. POSTMARKS:
(?) | Feb | (?); Philad'a, Pa. | Feb | 19 | 7 PM.

Kirkwood N J | Monday evn'g Feb 18

Dear Jack[2]

I am down here for a few days—Came down last Saturday fore-

1878
    1. According to the following letter, WW arrived in Kirkwood on Saturday,
February 16, and in *CB* he mentioned his stay with the Staffords from "16th to 23d
inclusive." WW was with Mrs. Gilchrist on February 13, and George and Louisa dined
with her on the following day (*CB*). Mrs. Stafford had written on January 26 urging
that WW come to Kirkwood (Feinberg).
    2. See 818.

noon—am with folks I love, & that love me—have had a real good old-fashion'd time, first-rate for me—It is a farm, every thing plain & plenty, & blazing wood fires—in the eating line, lots of chickens, eggs, fresh pork &c: (they kill a hog every two weeks)—

You ought to be here with me a day or so—(likely one day would be enough *for you*, as there is no city excitement or fashions—no *sogering* & no balls or theatres—but quite lots of *gals*, & some real nice ones)—I take an old man's liberty of *kissing them all*, (especially the handsome ones) when I go around where they are—as I have been coming down here off & on for nearly two years & have got acquainted—

I go out walking a good deal down a lane & by a beautiful pond & creek I am very fond of—spend two or three hours there first-rate, even this weather, all by myself—I am quite happy here for me—the weather was very fine for two days, but is a little cooler to-day—I can't walk far you know, but I go stumping about & enjoy it—yesterday they took me out on a long ride—went through the piney woods, which I always like—Jack, I thought you might like to get a line from me, from here—Every thing is so different from Market st or Chestnut or Penn st—but there is no difference in your loving old friend & comrade

Walt Whitman

847.   *To Anne Gilchrist*   2.22. *[1878]*

Kirkwood | Friday night Feb 22

Dear friend

I am still here—Your kind letter & the papers arrived at noon to-day—Thanks—They are the first visitations of the sort from *the outside world* for a week—

Sunday Mr S[tafford] and I took a long ride (did I tell you before) —Tuesday another, this time to a *farm-auction*, where all the neighbors were gathered, 100 or more—quite a scene, and a real study of character, looks & manners here—I scanned it all well, (& was doubtless scanned in return)³—Mr S was to go up last night with a load of straw for market, but it rained furiously, & he did not go—Rain all day till middle of this afternoon, since which we have had a glorious four hours, grand rainbow

3.   During the auction, WW, "pinched by the cold," took "refuge in the house, by a window, whence I get a full view of the crowd." He observed the people, "old & young, a hundred or more, mostly men & young fellows, but a few housewives & young women . . . Very well they look too, in my opinion—not only handsome & open-eyed, and fresh & independent, with wit enough, movements a little sluggish, but none the less artistic for that—always evidencing power—but with a certain heroic, rugged element through all" (Barrett).

& gorgeous sunset—but now, as I write, (8½) it looks like rain again—I still keep well—appetite any how quite magnificent—At least two hours forenoon, & two afternoon, down by the *creek*—Passed between *sauntering* —the *hickory saplings*—& "*Honor* is the *subject* of my story"—(for explanation of the last three lines, ask Herby—)[4]

I am glad Bee gets on so well (but I expected it) & my prayers *might* go up, (if it were not for Tyndal)[5] not only toward the success of the *second* negative,[6] but for you & Giddy in *that* ("up to your ears" of) *needle-work*—I shall be up before many days[7]—May be soon—at any rate I think I shall take supper with you by next Tuesday—

W W

848. *To John Burroughs*

431 Stevens Street | Camden N J Feb 24 '78

Dear J B[8]

I am agreeable to the Lecture project—*if it could be well put through*—About the middle of April (the anniversary of the eve or night of Lincoln's murder) might be a good night—Every thing would depend on how it was fixed up & prepared for & put through—Let me hear more particulars—I could be ready to splurge April 14th or 15th—

I am well, considering—in good flesh, appetite & trim generally— Only return'd last night from a long jaunt & absence down at my secluded creek—

Write me immediately, & I will you—
I am thoroughly willing & agreeable—
Yours as always

Walt Whitman

4. A cryptic reference to Harry Stafford ("*hickory saplings . . . Honor . . . subject*"). Perhaps the c in "*creek*" referred to Edward Cattell, another one of his young Kirkwood friends (see 797), to whom the poet had written on February 10 (*CB*). Herbert Gilchrist noted that WW was fond of quoting Cassius' speech to Brutus, "Well, honour is the subject of my story" (*Julius Caesar*, I, ii; Gilchrist, 241). WW placed a large bracket about this passage in the margin.

5. A reference to the investigations of John Tyndall (1820–1893), the British physicist.

6. Probably an allusion to an experiment conducted by Beatrice at the medical school.

7. WW returned on the following day (*CB*).

8. On February 3 Burroughs informed WW that Richard Watson Gilder (see 852) wanted to organize a "benefit" in New York at which the poet was to lecture on Lincoln. Burroughs suggested that Stedman and Swinton should be invited to support

849. *To Pete Doyle*   2.26. [*1878*]⁹

ADDRESS: Pete Doyle | M Street South—bet 4½ & 6th |
Washington | D C. POSTMARK: Camden | Feb | 26 |
N.J.

431 Stevens Street | Camden N J Feb 26
    Paper rec'd (as always—thanks)—Well as usual—nothing new—
have been down in the country the last week—It is now noon & I am just
going out & over the river—

W. W

850. *To John Burroughs*

431 Stevens Street | Camden N J March 5 '78
Dear John Burroughs¹⁰
    John Swinton lives at 134 east 34th Street. (He is married lately
to Mrs Dr Smith)—Yes [J. H.] Johnston's taking part in the lecture enterprise would be perfectly agreeable to me¹¹—the name of the lecture,
would be *The death of Abraham Lincoln.*
    (In my last letter among the names proposed was S S Cox,¹² M C—
I wish that name cancelled)—I should well like to have, if the letter to me
is carried out, a real mixture of names, representing the young blood, &
all the parties, various professions, (especially as I said, *journalists, artists,
actors,* &c &c—perhaps *some women*)—
    I shall be home here all the following two weeks except next Saturday
& Sunday¹³—

Walt Whitman

the project (Lion; Barrus, 171). The envelope of Burroughs' letter was marked by WW:
"(first suggestion of lecture)."
    9. The year is confirmed by the allusion to the stay with the Staffords and by a
reference to this communication in *CB.*
    10. WW also wrote to Burroughs on February 27 about the New York lecture
(*CB*), and evidently listed the names of possible sponsors. WW had been with the
Staffords from March 2 to 4 (*CB*).
    11. Burroughs on February 28 asked for Swinton's address and inquired about
Johnston (Feinberg).
    12. Samuel S. Cox (1828–1889) served in the House of Representatives from
New York from 1869 until his death. Burroughs, when asked why WW wanted Cox's
name deleted, could not recall any reason (Barrus, 172).
    13. WW was with the Staffords again on Saturday and Sunday, March 9 and
10 (*CB*).

851. *To Herbert Gilchrist*   *3.8. [1878]*[14]

ADDRESS: Herbert Gilchrist | 1929 north 22d Street |
Philadelphia. POSTMARK: Philadelphia | Mar | 8 |
3(?) PM | Pa.

Camden March 8   a m

Will be over to tea at ½ past 6, & will give you a good long sitting
for the pict[ure] if you wish—("Improve the time" saith the little busy
bee)—

W W

852. *To John Burroughs*   *3.11. [1878]*

TRANSCRIPT.

March 11

Yours of 7th from N.Y. rec'd last night. I will scratch off some
suggestions:

In composing the letter, let it be brief, and don't mention the subject
—or, if you do, *just say indefinitely that it is about Abraham Lincoln*
(which you may do, if you think proper)—

I would like Gilder's[15] name on the letter—

The suggestion (Gilder's) *about 8 or 10 names only—good ones only*
—should be carried out. About the Hall I leave to your selection (not the
very biggest ones, however, would seem to me best)—

I would like Whitelaw Reid's[16] name to cap the list—Couldn't the
World man, Schuyler[17] (if he is there yet?) come next?

Elliott F. Shepard the lawyer,[18] might be a good name.

Take [J. H.] Johnston into your councils, in any business and pe-

14. Since WW was in New York on this date in 1877, and since the Gilchrists
were not in Philadelphia in March, 1879, the note was sent in 1878.
15. Richard Watson Gilder (1844–1909) was the assistant editor of *Scribner's
Monthly* from 1870 to 1881 and editor of its successor, *The Century*, from 1881 until
his death. WW had met Gilder for the first time in 1877 at Johnston's (Allen, 482).
He attended a reception and tea given by Gilder after Bryant's funeral on June 14; see
"A Poet's Recreation," in the New York *Tribune*, July 4, 1878. WW considered Gilder
one of two sane men, the other being Stedman, "in that New York art delirium"
(Traubel, II, 93).
16. The editor of the New York *Tribune*.
17. Montgomery Schuyler (1843–1914) was associated with the New York *World*
from 1865 to 1883 and with the New York *Times* from 1883 until his retirement in
1907. He was also managing editor of *Harper's Weekly* from 1885 to 1887.
18. Shepard, a colonel in George's regiment during the Civil War, was now a
New York attorney (see 163 and *Wilson's Business Directory of New York City* for

cuniary arrangements—he is very 'cute and I consider him a true friend of mine.

I am particular about the names. Let [Joel] Benton[19] have my letters, take as much as possible my point of view, and he might write to me here.

Walt Whitman

Private

I care little—or rather nothing at all—about Bayard Taylor's[20] or G. W. Curtis's[21] names on the letter. Don't want them. If they get on, let them be, of course—but don't you make any point about getting them. I suppose you understand me.

Of course the letters I write you are for perusal by all my friends— Gilder, Swinton, Benton, &c.—but if I write *private*, it is for you alone.

853. *To Herbert Gilchrist*   3.18. *[1878]*

ADDRESS: Herbert Gilchrist | 1929 North 22d Street | Philadelphia. POSTMARKS: Camden | Mar | 18 | N.J.; Philad'a, Pa. | Mar | 18 | 10 PM | R(?).

Camden March 18   5 p m

Dear Herby

I have just come up this afternoon from White Horse[22]—Friday & Saturday good outdoor days there—Have had a pretty severe attack of what appears to be (mostly) rheumatism in my right shoulder—more pain to me last night than I have before felt any time, I think, in my whole life —besides unnerved & generally *clumsied* more than usual[23]—Expect to come over to-morrow, Tuesday, to a 6½ supper, as usual—

No news particular with the Staffords—Mrs S, Ed, Harry & Debby,[24] &c. well—Mr S. pretty well—

1878–1879).
    19. Joel Benton (1832–1911) was a poet and a friend of Burroughs (see Barrus, 18, 174).
    20. See 735 and 199.
    21. George William Curtis (1824–1892), the editor of *Harper's Monthly*, was disliked by WW's friends. Burroughs termed Curtis "an orator that fairly leaned and languished on the bosom of the graces" (Barrus, 173). Speaking of Curtis's criticisms of WW in *Harper's* "Easy Chair" in June, 1876 (141–142), O'Connor observed in a letter to Burroughs, "The artificial mountain in Brooklyn park has labored and produced a toy mouse!" (Barrus, 131).
    22. WW was at Kirkwood from March 15 to 17 (CB).
    23. From March 17 to 25 WW noted "much suffering from rheumatism & prostration" (CB and see the following letters). Later he consulted Dr. S. Weir Mitchell (see 857).
    24. Mrs. Stafford's children, Edwin, Harry, and Deborah.

Saturday & Sunday lots of Company[25]—Am writing this in my 3d story room—where I shall remain in the evening & recuperate—

> Walt Whitman

I enclose a slip from the *Tribune*[26]—may interest you—
Love to all—

854. *To John Burroughs*   3.21. *[1878]*

TRANSCRIPT.

> March 21.

For the last four days I have been and am now quite severely down again with muscular and nervous prostration, somewhat like formerly—aggravated this time by a painful and obstinate rheumatism . . . count on it soon passing over and leaving me about the same possession of my powers as of late—but it occurs to me to say to you that while I wish the prospecting for the N.Y. lecture to go on—I think it would be best so—don't make any pledge about hall, or any other thing involving obligation, until further notice and advice from me.

I have just got a letter from Johnston, the jeweller, asking me to come on to his house & make it my home in N.Y. for the lecture trip. Very kind and acceptable.

> Walt Whitman

855. *To Herbert Gilchrist*   3.23. *[1878]*

ADDRESS: Herbert Gilchrist | 1929 North 22d Street | Philadelphia. POSTMARKS: Camden | Mar | 23 | N.J.; Philad'a, Pa. | Mar | 23 | 8 PM | Rec'd.

> Camden March 23 a m

Dear Herby

Last night the best night for a week & I count on getting better now—only weakness very pronounced & general, & a little sickish—rheu-

---

25. Evidently the "Company" included Ben Pease, Will Fox, Will and Rachel Morgan, and Lizzie Hider (*CB*).

26. Perhaps the account of "The American Water Color Society" in the New York *Tribune* of March 18, since Herbert undoubtedly was acquainted with some of the artists mentioned.

27. Herbert's drawing of WW (see 851). Herbert visited WW on the following evening, and Mrs. Gilchrist called on March 27 (*CB*).

matic pains in shoulder & wrist still present, but much modified—tell Bee I am wearing the flannel sleeve constantly—it was just about what I was wanting—

Herb, I hope you will lay on while your hand is in & finish the black & white drawing all up[27]—hope you will put in to-morrow some good licks, Lord willing—I am making great *calculations* about it—hope I shant be disappointed—

Love to all—

Hope to be over Monday evening next—

WW

856. *To John Burroughs* 3.29. [*1878*]

ADDRESS: John Burroughs | Esopus-on-Hudson | New York. POSTMARK: Camden | Mar | 29 | N.J.

Camden | Friday even'g March 29

Dear friend

Your card just rec'd—I am still badly under the weather—spells of prostration like those of two years ago—& now for more than a week the restless wretched *nights* of the rheumatic—Still a good heart & not only a hope *but confidence*—having pass'd through worse spells several times—that I shall get round soon & be the same as before ill—I am up, & feeling quite jolly this evening—

Instead of 15th of April I think it would be safer to fix the lecture night, any where between the 10th & 20th May—If you & the rest feel to, go on that understanding, *as a settled thing*—

What is Benton's address in N Y? If convenient, I should like to see the list of names, & the draft of the letter, before formally put out—if you think well of this, either send me the list, or *tell Benton to send it me forthwith*—

Beatrice Gilchrist is over here with us this evening—the G's break camp here in three or four weeks—spend the ensuing year excursively in America[28]—

Write me the moves—I shall be home here all the time—Every thing

---

28. On May 1 Mrs. Gilchrist informed Burroughs that they were in Northampton, Mass., and mentioned her sorrow in leaving Philadelphia: "We had planted our tent so firmly and spread our possessions around us so, at 1929. However it stands empty and forlorn now" (Barrus, 145). This description of her former home undoubtedly characterized her own emotional state after an association with WW for eighteen months during which she had learned, how painfully she never divulged in her correspondence, the **impossibility of establishing a physical relationship with the poet.**

(p o, or telegram) comes here, (431 Stevens Street Camden N. J.) as un-
erringly as fate, & very promptly[29]—

                                                            W W

857. *To Louisa Orr Whitman*   [*4.13–14. 1878*][30]

ADDRESS: Mrs Louisa O Whitman | Care of F E
Dowe | Norwich | Conn:. POSTMARK: Camden |
AP(?) | 14 | N.J.

                                           Camden Saturday 6 p m
Dear sister
        We have had a wonderful fine day—I feel much better—had the
best night's sleep last night for four weeks—Miss Hillard[31] came at 10
this forenoon, & took me over in the coupé to Philadelphia—went & saw
the great Dr Mitchell,[32] I was very well pleas'd with him—I am to go
again—He did not express any opinion particular—said he would tell me
next time—examined my heart by auscultation—said there was nothing at
all the matter with *that*—Then I went to Mrs Perot's[33] & we had dinner—
Mrs P brought me home in the coupé—had a very good 4 or 5 hours—
        Harry is up spending the afternoon with me—brought a chicken—your
card to Bell[34] & letter to George came this forenoon—George has not yet
got home—
        Lou, my old grand-aunt 97 years old in New York, Mrs Sarah Mead[35],
died last Tuesday—I got a letter from her son-in-law Thursday—will finish
this, & send it off to-morrow—Sunday—

                                    Sunday afternoon—3–4 oclock—
        George got home about dark last evening, & is away up to the farm
to-day—he seems all right as usual—
        Bell has been to church this morning—She continues to get along

        29. Burroughs came to Camden to see WW on April 1 (*CB*).
        30. The date is confirmed in the notes below. Louisa left for Norwich, Conn., to
see her sister (see 823) on April 10 and returned on April 20 (*CB*).
        31. See 718.
        32. Dr. S. Weir Mitchell (1829–1914) was a specialist in nervous disorders as
well as a poet and a novelist. On April 18 WW had his second interview with Dr.
Mitchell, who attributed his earlier paralysis to a small rupture of a blood vessel in the
brain but termed WW's heart "normal and healthy." WW also noted that "the *bad
spells* [Mitchell] tho't recurrences by *habit* (? sort of automatic)" (*CB*). Mitchell was
the first physician to indicate the psychosomatic nature of many of WW's ailments.
Probably the impending lecture on the death of Lincoln unconsciously brought back the
emotional involvements of his hospital experiences with comrades whom he had come to
love only to be separated from them.
        33. Mrs. Elliston L. Perot, evidently a friend of Miss Hillard, called on the poet
on April 3, according to WW's notation on her calling card mounted in *CB*.
        34. Louisa's servant.

excellently well—We have quite a good many callers[36]—I am not so well to-day—my rheumatism makes itself felt nearly all the time, yet not so severe —Fine sunny weather yet—

Brother Walt

5:30—Have been out for over half an hour's walk (I & Tip[37]) up to Broadway—pleasant warm evening—met Mr Elverson[38] & Alise, (I think she looks & behaves finer than ever)—George not home yet from the farm —I smell Bell's *strong tea* cooking on the stove, for supper—I will now go out to post office & mail this—

858. *To Peter Doyle*   *4.22. [1878][39]*

ADDRESS: Pete Doyle | M Street South—bet 4½ & 6th | Washington | D C. POSTMARK: Camden | Apr | 22 | N.J.

Camden April 22   3 p m

Am getting better—have had a bad time—shoulder grumbles a little now & then (rheumatism) but I feel much better—strength improving —& expect to soon be about as before—thankful for that—Nothing very new in affairs—*I get along*—Still think of coming to W[ashington] for a month or so—

W W

859. *To George W. Waters*   *4.23. [1878?][40]*

ADDRESS: George W Waters | artist | Elmira | New York. POSTMARK: Philadelphia | Apr 23 | 6 PM | Pa.

431 Stevens street | Camden N J April 23

Nothing very new with me. Paper rec'd. Thanks. I still keep pretty

35. WW noted on February 25 in *CB* that he had been reading a letter about his aunt in the New York *Evening Post* of February 22, in which the author mentioned that Mrs. Sarah Mead had seen George Washington (Trent). From a member of Mrs. Mead's family or from a friend WW received a letter on April 11 announcing her death (fragment of letter in Feinberg).

36. In addition to Harry Stafford, Debbie Stafford and her future husband, Joseph Browning, called on April 10 (*CB*).

37. WW's dog.

38. Probably Joseph Elverson, Jr., assistant editor of the *Saturday Night* (Philadelphia).

39. WW listed this post card in *CB*, and the text refers to WW's recent rheumatic attack. He did not visit Washington after 1875; the *West Jersey Press* on January 16, 1878, noted that the poet contemplated "trips to Washington, D. C."

40. The major objection to assigning this post card to 1878 is the absence of a reference to his recent indisposition. After his visits to Mitchell, WW began to improve, and he resumed his frequent visits to the Stafford family (see note 42 below).

well for me—perhaps even improve. Change my base a good deal—but *this* is my centre & p o address.

W.W.

860. *To Henry Festing Jones*

Camden New Jersey | U S America | April 29 '78

Dear Sir[41]

In answer to yours of 14th—I send by mail postpaid my complete works verse & prose, Two Vols: for $10 (Two pounds sterling I believe) —Address me here—I enclose circular—

Walt Whitman

861. *To William J. Linton*

431 Stevens Street | Camden New Jersey | May 8 '78

My dear Linton

I returned last evening from a jaunt to the country[42]—feel middling well again (about half-&-half)—after a bad spell during March & most of April—thought I was going to have a relapse to my old state, but the doctors say it was either only or mostly a bad case of *rheumatism*[43]— (the best point about which seems to be that if it be ever so bad a devil itself, it generally keeps the coast clear of all other devils)—However, I am better at this writing, & look forward to a tolerably fair summer—

The "Poetry of America" arrived, & I am well content & pleased with the part I am made to bear in it—Surely you have made a capital compilation & condensation—the best thing of its sort & size I have seen[44]—

Our friends the Gilchrists have broken camp in Philadelphia, & gone (more or less temporarily) to Northampton, Mass:[45]—You will probably soon hear from (perhaps see) Herbert, the artist, the son—

I enclose a little printed slip—(or did I send it you before?)[46]—Since

---

41. Jones (1851–1928) was the author of *Samuel Butler* (1919) and the editor of many of Butler's manuscripts. WW evidently forgot that he had promised to mail the two books (see 865 and 874). In *CB* he noted that he had sent an advertising circular. The inscription in *Leaves of Grass* was dated by Jones "July 1878"; both volumes are now in the Feinberg Collection.

42. In April WW resumed his visits to the Staffords. He was at Kirkwood on April 20 and 21, April 25 to 27, May 1 and 2, and May 6 and 7 (*CB*).

43. Interestingly, WW did not repeat Dr. Mitchell's diagnosis (see 857).

44. Linton, a wood engraver, published *Poetry of America, 1776–1876* in London. The volume contained eight of WW's poems and Linton's engraving of the poet. See also

my late sick spell, it is not so likely the programme will be carried out[47]
—but I want to go about somewhat this summer—

With Love—

Walt Whitman

862. *To Anne Gilchrist*

> ADDRESS: Mrs Anne Gilchrist | Round Hill Hotel |
> Northampton | Mass:. POSTMARK: Camden | May |
> 10 | N.J.

431 Stevens Street | Camden N J   May 10 '78

Dear friend

Yours rec'd, & much pleas'd to hear you are in such satisfactory quarters—there is nothing very new or different with me—Though the rheumatism is not severe—any thing like its first attack—it still keeps its hold—my knees, & indeed whole joint & muscular power are affected— Was down at White Horse Monday & Tuesday, (two perfect days)[48]—& I expect to be down there next Sunday—

The Staffords are all about as usual—My sister & brother are well— I have rec'd Mr Linton's book "Poetry of America"—(it is a Vol: of Bohn's Standard Library)—It is a good collection—he gives my picture for frontispiece—

Miss Hillard has returned from Annapolis, after a fine visit, improved still in health[49]—is at Germantown, at "the Cocoonery"—Nothing in the way of letter lately from England—

I have written to Herby to-day, to Brooklyn[50]—As I write I am sitting up in my third story room—just after 4 p m—my sister down stairs sewing—it is very quiet in the house, almost lonesome—my brother away far in Pennsylvania at his work—& no, or very few visitors lately—The weather is fine day & night, for a rule—I am now going out for an hour [or] two—

Love to all—

Walt Whitman

I return the letter—I found it interesting—

438.
    45. The Gilchrists had left Philadelphia evidently late in April, since apparently WW saw them for the last time in Philadelphia on the evening of April 22 and 23 (CB). Herbert went to Brooklyn (see 863).
    46. Unquestionably "Walt Whitman for 1878," which appeared in the *West Jersey Press* of January 16, 1878, as noted in CB.
    47. The New York lecture on Lincoln's death.
    48. May 6 and 7, characterized in CB as "two fine days." WW was at Kirkwood on Sunday, May 12.
    49. See 857.   50. See the following letter.

863. *To Herbert Gilchrist*

ADDRESS: Herbert H Gilchrist | Care of Mrs
Voorhees | 147 Remsen Street | Brooklyn | New
York. POSTMARKS: Camden | May | 10 | N.J.;
Brooklyn, N.Y. | May | 11 | 8 AM | Rec'd.

431 Stevens Street | Camden N J May 10 '78

Dear Herbert

Your good letter reach'd me yesterday—& I dont wonder you like,
& are exhilarated by, New York & Brooklyn—They are the places *to live*.

I was down at White Horse Monday & Tuesday last—expect to go
down again Sunday—Just as I left, your letter to Mrs S[tafford] arrived
—All were about as usual—Nothing very new with me—I am only middling well, but go about—rheumatism, not yet subdued—threatens to partially disable my right arm—(this writing probably shows it)[51]—I am interested in what you say of Eaton[52] and the sculptor O'Donavan[53] (is it?)
—should like to hear more about them—About the mulleins[54] & bumble-
bees I should like to have them *as soon as convenient*—

Pleas'd to hear that you go around with the New York artists, design-
ers, young fellows, & folk in the picture trade, publishing, &c—I think with
the superb *foundation* you have it will be just the thing for you, fetch you
up & make you aware what's going at latest advices, &c. which is very
desirable—

There is a book *"Stories from Homer,"*[55] just published by Harpers—
It is much praised in high quarters—I have wondered whether it doesn't
contain the hint-suggestion of what your mother should do with the
V[ictor] Hugo translations—You might look at the book in the book
stores—

I have written a few lines to your mother to-day—Write soon, Herby,
& tell me all about your moves, & about the artists you meet &c—

W W

51. The rheumatism had little discernible effect upon WW's handwriting.
52. Wyatt Eaton (1849–1896), an American portrait and figure painter, organized
the Society of American Artists in 1877. WW met Eaton at a reception given by
Richard W. Gilder on June 14; see "A Poet's Recreation," New York *Tribune*, July 4,
and *Walt Whitman's Diary in Canada*, 54.
53. William Rudolf O'Donovan (1844–1920) was an American sculptor.
54. See the discussion of mulleins in SD (148–149).
55. By Alfred J. Church (1829–1912), a prolific translator. I have not found the

864. *To Anne Gilchrist* 5.19. [*1878*]

ADDRESS: Mrs Anne Gilchrist | Round Hill Hotel |
Northampton | Mass:. POSTMARK: Camden | May |
19 | N.J.

Camden | Sunday afternoon | May 19

My dear friend

I came up last night from a three days visit to White Horse[56]—went down thinking only to spend the day, but the spring beauty of the creek, skies, weather, trees, birds &c. fascinated me—

I am feeling excellent well to-day, for me—have been out to a gay breakfast party (lawyers & ladies & lots of talk, & champagne)[57]—& enjoyed it very well—but *once* of such a thing will last me a long while—got home about one o'clock, (it has now just struck four)—consequence of my gay breakfast is, I have not eat any dinner—but shall go to Col. Johnston's to supper[58]—

Thanks to Herbert for his good letters of the 7th from Brooklyn—& the 16th from Northampton[59]—please give him the enclosed postal, I found at White Horse—May-be you will like to read Miss Hillard's letter—so I enclose it—The Staffords are mostly as usual—George S. not very well, but around at work—Debbie not married yet[60]—

You must have fine surroundings indeed at Round Hill—As I close we have the prospect of a fine evening—A cannon has just boomed out on the river, probably an ocean-steamer just come in, firing her signal gun—& I am just off to Col. J's, & to leave this at the P O—

Best love to all—

Walt Whitman

865. *To Henry Festing Jones* [*6.2. 1878*][61]

ADDRESS: Henry Festing Jones | 1 Craven Hill
Gardens | London W | England. POSTMARKS:
Camden | Jun | 3 | N.J.; London W(?) | F(?) |
Paid | 15 Ju (?) 8.

Camden New Jersey, | U S America

Yours of 21st May rec'd—You appear to have made a mistake—

edition referred to.

56. WW had been with the Staffords from May 16 to 18 (*CB*).
57. He had breakfast at the home of James Matlack Scovel (*CB*).
58. WW almost invariably went to Johnston's on Sunday evenings when he was in Camden.
59. These letters are not known.
60. Debbie was married on June 13 (*CB*).
61. See 860.

As near as I remember I sent you on the 29th of April last some circulars, slips, price-advertisements &c. of my books—but have not sent the books themselves—waiting until ordered, June 2—

Walt Whitman

866. *To Richard Watson Gilder*

TELEGRAM.

Penna Depot W Phila | June 13 1878

To Watson Gilder | at Scribner | 743 Bway

Am coming on to B[ryant]'s funeral[62] Come to Johnstons Jewelery Store one fifty Bowery at nine oclock a m for me if convenient

Walt Whitman

867. *To George and Louisa Whitman*   *6.15–17. [1878]*[63]

1309 Fifth Avenue[64] | New York June 15

Dear brother & Sister

I will just write you a line to let you know I am all right—I sent you a N Y paper the *Sun* of to-day with an acc't of the funeral[65]—

I am feeling pretty well for me—am stopping with Mr Johnston and his wife & family—there is a big family & they have moved up here in 5th Avenue—very grand—a big four or five story house, near 86th St overlooking the Park, cool & fresh as can be—all are very kind, especially Mrs J. (the new one)—the children all call me Uncle Walt—the baby is bright & interesting, but not rugged—(I hardly think its tenure of life secure)[66]—I have many invitations, but don't accept them—

I have seen John Burroughs & he wants me to go up there to Esopus,

---

62. The decision to go to New York was impromptu (*SD*, 165–167). Bryant was buried on June 14. After the funeral WW attended a reception and tea given by Gilder (*SD*, 329).

63. WW was in New York from June 13 to July 10 (*CB*).

64. Johnston had moved to this address after his marriage to Alma Calder on April 21; see Elliot, *Walt Whitman As Man, Poet and Friend* (1915), 152.

65. A lengthy account of the funeral of Bryant appeared in the New York *Sun* on June 15, one paragraph of which began: "The man most looked at was the white-haired poet, Walt Whitman, who presented a Homeric picture, in which were combined

but I don't think I shall go[67]—I find my gray clothes very seasonable here, as it is cool enough all the time except at mid-day—

I suppose Hattie and Jessie are there, all right[68]—Dear girls, I send you my best love, & I will soon be home & see you—I will finish to-night—

Sunday 3½ p m
West Point | 50 miles above N Y on the Hudson

I finish my letter here—having had a very pleasant 3 hours trip up here on the "Plymouth Rock," to Mr & Mrs John Bigelow's (he was U S minister to France)[69]—I met her at Mr. Bryant's funeral & she invited me up here—I came up for the sail, as well as to see the good folks & this beautiful spot—I think it the finest I have ever seen—Had dinner about an hour ago, and in about an hour more, shall return on the boat—Shall get to N Y before sundown.

The weather is perfect—I am feeling all right—shall probably mail this to you when I get in to-night—Hope you are all well &c—

Walt

Monday 17th | 11 a m

I was so tired out & got in so late from the West Point trip that I did not go to mail this last night—At present I am sitting alone in the front parlor with the Park opposite like a dense woods—is pleasant, but cloudy & *almost cold* to-day—(if I had not my old grays wearing I should be un-comfortable)—Lou, you would like the folks & everything here—especially Mrs Johnston—at meals there is a great big table & the little children sit up the same as any—toward the last the baby & the little 4 year old girl are generally down crawling around on the floor—the whole squad are model children lively & free & *children*, but no bother & no whimpering or quarrelling at all under any circumstances—they form a great part of my comfort here—Yesterday was such a strain that to-day I [am] going to keep still—Best love to you all—I enclose a card—write me about the girls & all—

W W

the easy good nature of Grandfather Whitehead and the heroic build of an antique statue."

66. Harold Johnston, the child whose birth caused his mother's death (see 806).
67. But see the following letter.
68. WW's nieces arrived in Camden on June 13 (*CB*).
69. John Bigelow (1817–1911) had been minister to France in 1865 and 1866 and had been coeditor, with William Cullen Bryant, of the New York *Evening Post* from 1848 to 1861. The account of WW's visit appeared in the New York *Tribune* on July 4, but was not included in *SD* (329).

868. *To Mannahatta Whitman*   6.22–26. [1878][70]

Esopus on the Hudson, 80 miles north | of New York
—Saturday June 22

Dear Hattie (& all the rest)

I came up here last Thursday afternoon in the steamboat from N Y —a fine day, & had a delightful journey—every thing to interest me—the constantly changing but ever beautiful panorama on both sides of the river all the way for nearly 100 miles here—the magnificent north river bay part of the shores of N Y—the high straight walls of the rocky Palisades—the never-ending hills—beautiful Yonkers—the rapid succession of handsome villages & cities—the prevailing green—the great mountain sides of brown & blue rocks—the river itself—the innumerable elegant mansions in spots peeping all along through the woods & shrubbery—with the sloops & yachts, with their white sails, singly or in fleets, some near us always, some far off—&c &c &c—

& here I am, this is now the third day having a good time—Mr Burroughs & his wife are both kind as they can be—we have plenty of strawberries, cream &c & something I specially like, namely plenty of sugared raspberries & currants—(I go out & pick the currants myself, great red things, bushels of them going to waste) —

Albert Johnston, (the Jeweler's son, I am staying with in N Y) is here too on a visit to the Burroughs's—& makes it still more agreeable—

Yesterday we all (Mr B, Al & I) went out on a long drive—I tell you it is very different country here from out west, or down in Jersey—the old stone fences, two feet thick—the scenery—the many splendid locust trees, often long rows of great big ones—the streams down the mountains, with waterfalls—"Black Creek"—the Cattskills, in the distance—all did me good. It is lucky the roads are first rate (as they are here) for it is up or down hill or around something continually—

We pass'd many *tramps* on the roads—one squad interested me—it was a family of five (or six) in a small flat ricketty one-horse open wagon, with some poor household traps huddled together, some new baskets for sale (they were basket makers I suppose) & some three young children— the man driving, the woman by his side, thin & sickly, & a little babe wrapt in a bundle on her lap, its little feet & legs sticking out towards us as we went by—

---

70. Much of the material in this and the following letter appeared in similar form in "A Poet's Recreation" in the *Tribune* on July 4, and later in SD (165–172). The phrasal similarities between the letters and the printed versions are indicated in the notes to the

On our return at sundown a couple of hours afterwards, we met them again—they had hauled aside in a lonesome spot near the woods, evidently to camp for the night—the horse was took out & was grazing peacefully near by—the man was busy at the wagon, with his baskets & traps, & the boy of 11 or so had gather'd a lot of dry wood & was building a fire on the open ground—As we went on a little on the road we encounter'd the woman with the little baby still in her arms, & her pretty-eyed 6 year old barefoot girl trotting behind, clutching her gown—the woman had two or three baskets she had probably been on to neighboring houses to sell—we spoke to her & bought a basket—she didn't look up out of her old sunbonnet—her voice, & every thing seem'd queer, *terrified*—then as we went on, Al stopp'd the wagon & went back to the group to buy another basket—he caught a look of the woman's eyes & talked with her a little—says she was young, but look'd & talk'd like *a corpse*—the man was middle aged—

I am having a good quiet time here—eat lots of strawberries, raspberries & currants—(O I wish Lou could have a lot of the latter to do up)—I am well—To-day for a change it is raining—but altogether I have enjoyed fine June weather for my trip—Will finish my letter in New York—

1309 Fifth av. near 86th St | New York June 26—p m

Came away from Esopus Monday afternoon 4th, by RR, & got here at dark—Still keep pretty well & shall stay here a few days longer—I find it hard to get away—(then I take things quiet, & a change is good for me) —Jeff's telegram came & Mr Johnston tells me he telegraphed back Monday late in the afternoon—I should much have liked to see Jeff—I suppose he has gone back[71]—I suppose you women folks are having great times all to yourselves—

Yesterday I went out on a steamboat sail down the bay to Sandy Hook with a party of Sorosis ladies—very pleasant—a real sea-sail, sea-breeze &c—(I went up with the pilots in the pilot house)—we had dinner aboard—got back before dark—the weather keeps fine—plenty cool enough for me—Love to you, dear Hat, & dear Jess & dear Aunt Lou, & every body—

Uncle Walt.

next letter.
71. On October 27 Jeff wrote to WW about an epidemic of yellow fever during the warm months in St. Louis and about Hattie's illness (Feinberg).

869. *To Anne Gilchrist*   6.23–26. [*1878*]

Esopus on the Hudson 80 miles | north of New York—
Sunday June 23

Dear Mrs Gilchrist (& all the rest)

I sent you a postal card from N Y & a paper with an acc't of the
Bryant funeral, which I suppose you rec'd[72]—I came up here last Thursday afternoon, in a fine steamboat[73]—had a delightful journey—a fine
day & everything to interest me—the constantly changing but ever-beauti-
ful panorama on both sides of the river all the way, (nearly 100 miles up
here)—the magnificent north river bay part of the city—the high straight
walls of the rocky Palisades—the never ending hills—beautiful Yonkers—
the endless succession of handsome villages & cities—the prevailing green
—the great rocky mountains, gray & brown—the river itself, now expanding, now narrowing—the glistening river with continual sloops, yachts, &c.
their white sails singly or in fleets, some near, some in the distance—the
numberless elegant mansions in spots peeping through the woods, or
perch'd somewhere back on the hills—&c &c &c—& here I am—this is now
the fourth day, having a good time—Mr Burroughs & his wife are as kind
as they can be—We have plenty of strawberries, cream, &c. and something
I specially like, namely plenty of sugared raspberries & currants mixed
together (I go out & pick the currants myself, great red things, bushels of
them going to waste)—

Albert Johnston, (the gentleman's son, at whose house I am staying in
N Y) is here too on a visit to the Burroughs's—makes it more agreeable[74]
—Yesterday we all (Mr B, Al, & I) went out on a long drive—I took in
every thing—the old stone fences two feet thick—the peculiar scenery,
hilly & broken & rocky—the long rows of splendid locust trees—the "balm
of Gilead" perfuming the road—the streams down the mountains, with
waterfalls—"Black Creek" brawling along—the Cattskills in the distance,
with mist around their peaks—All did me good—It is lucky the roads are
first [rate] here, (as they are) for it is either up or down hill constantly, &
often steep enough—We pass'd many *tramps* on the road—this seems
a great region for them—One squad specially interested me—it was a
family of five (or six) in a smallish, flat, ricketty one-horse wagon, with a

72. This card is evidently not extant. The newspaper must have been the New
York *Sun* of June 15 (see 867).

73. The parallels with the published account of this trip in the *Tribune* on
July 4 indicate that WW retained a draft of this or of the preceding letter. The account
in SD is condensed (167).

74. The printed version in the *Tribune* adds the detail that upon rising "I have a

few poor household traps, & some baskets (the folks were basket makers), in the midst of all of which were huddled two or three young children— On a low board in front of the wagon, the man (gaunt dirty middle aged) was driving—the woman by his side, thin & sickly, & a little babe wrapt in a bundle on her lap, its little red feet & legs sticking out toward us as we passed—

On our return at sundown we met them again—they had hauled aside at a lonesome spot near the woods evidently to camp for the night—the horse was unhitched & taken out, & was grazing peacefully near by—the man was busy at the wagon with something—the little boy had gather'd a lot of dry wood & was building a fire on the open ground—& as we went on a little on the road we encounter'd the woman still carrying her baby, & a pretty-eyed 6 year old girl trotting barefoot behind, clutching her by the gown—the woman was carrying two or three baskets (she had doubt-less been on to the neighboring houses to sell, & was now returning)—We stopt & spoke to her & bought a basket—She didn't look up at all out of the recesses of her old sunbonnet—her voice, manner, seem'd so queer, terrified—then as we went on Al stopt the wagon, & ran back to the group to buy another basket—he caught a look of the woman's face, & talk'd with her a little—says she was young, but seem'd more like an animated corpse than any thing else—poor woman—what was her story?[75]

Shall go back to New York to-morrow afternoon—will finish my letter there—To-day, Sunday (now 11½ a m) Mrs B[urroughs] has driven to church—Mr B is off somewhere—Al ditto—I seem to be alone in the house, every thing quiet, only natural sounds, birds, &c. for nearly an hour —a beautiful expanded view from the large open windows as I write— Before Mr B went out I told him I was going to write to you—He told me to send you & all his love, & say he got Herbert's letter yesterday—

1309 5th avenue near 86th St. |
New York—June 26 p m

Dear friend—

Here I am back again in N Y—Came down the river Monday night, & shall stay here a few (but not many) days longer—I find it hard to get away—Yesterday went on a sail down N Y bay to Sandy Hook with a party of Sorosis ladies—they spoke of Miss Hillard—had a fine sail, good sea

capital rubbing and rasping with the flesh-brush—with an extra scour on the back by Al: J., who is here with us—all inspiriting my invalid frame with new life, for the day." (See also SD, 168.) For Albert Johnston's recollection of this trip, see Barrus, 176–177.

75. The *Tribune* account of the gypsy concluded: "Poor woman—what story was it, out of her fortunes, to account for that inexpressibly scared way, those glassy eyes, and that hollow voice?" (See also SD, 169.)

air—dinner on board—got back at dark[76]—rec'd your letter yesterday morning—thanks—

Debby[77] was married June 13th—my dear nieces are at Stevens st. Camden—all well, including my sister & brother—

Best love to you, & to Bee, Herbert, & Giddy—

Walt Whitman

870. *To John Burroughs* 7.5. [1878]

ADDRESS: John Burroughs | Esopus-on-Hudson | New York. POSTMARK: New-York | Jul 5 | 6 PM.

1309 Fifth av. 2d house | south of 86th St. | New York July 5

Still here—still quite well—sent you a paper yesterday with my "June" letter in[78]—Shall go back to Camden ab't the 10th (or 9th)[79]— Fiery weather here, but I stand it well so far—

W W

871. *To Harry Stafford* 7.6–7. [1878]

1309 Fifth [av]: near 86th St | New York Saturday July 6 | p m

Dear son[80]

I suppose you rec'd a paper from me lately with an acc't of some of my movements &c. here, as I sent you one—I had no idea of staying so long when I left 13th June—thought only of staying a couple of days— [but then?] it will be most a month soon—But I shall return to Camden next Tuesday—or Wednesday at furthest—

I keep well & hearty considering—it has been very hot weather here for a week, but I havn't minded it any to hurt—to-day it has been a little more moderate—I have been down this forenoon to Sarony's,[81] the great photographic establishment, where I was invited to come & sit for my picture—had a real pleasant time—I will bring you on one of the pictures—

76. The version of this trip which appeared in the *Tribune* mentioned the owner of the boat, David G. Croly, the editor of the New York *Daily Graphic* (see 486).

77. Deborah Stafford had married Joseph Browning.

78. "A Poet's Recreation" appeared in the New York *Tribune* on July 4. On the preceding day WW read proof in the *Tribune* office (Feinberg; *Walt Whitman's Diary in Canada*, 55).

79. He returned to Camden on July 10.

80. The letters from Harry Stafford to WW in 1878 reveal the troubled relations

My darling boy, I want to see you very much, & I know you do me too —Harry, I meet many, many friends here, some very fine folks—some tip-top young men too—& there is no end to hospitality, & places to visit &c.—everybody seems to know me—it is quite funny sometimes—but I believe I am as contented down by the old pond as any where—(I wish I was there this afternoon—at least for a couple of hours)—

Well, I see Hunter[81.1] was convicted—we will see now whether he is hung—I see an item in the paper that [Emma?] Bethel had confessed to poisoning the Bishops—I will finish my letter & send it off to-morrow—

Sunday July 7—The little 15 months old baby, little Harry (that was born that night there in 10th street,) is a fine, good bright child, not very rugged, but gets along very well—I take him in my arms always after breakfast & go out in front for a short walk—he is very contented & good with me—little Kitty[82] goes too—I had a good night's rest last night, & am feeling comfortable to-day—Good bye for the present, my loving son—It will not be long now before we are together again—

Your old W W

872. *To John and Ursula Burroughs*   *7.11.* [*1878*]

431 Stevens st Camden N J | July 11 p m

Dear John & 'Sula Burroughs,

I kept staying & staying in N Y—but left yesterday in the 4 p m train, had a fine run to Phila: & here I am to-day in my regular den—all the better for my month's trip—

Nothing very new—brother & sister well as usual—my two nieces, Jeff's daughters, are here & are a great comfort to me. Hot weather, awful —yet I am standing it well so far. I suppose you got the *Tribune* of July 4 with my letter in.[83] And the box of Graham biscuits by Express—(Of course you know they must be soak'd half an hour or more in milk or water —I sweeten mine with sugar, but some dont like it)—

How are you getting along this hot weather? & how is that baby?[84]

Walt Whitman

between the two men; see Introduction.
    81. On September 18 WW received 250 prints of this photograph (*CB*).
    81.1. Benjamin Hunter was convicted of the murder of John Armstrong on July 3.
    82. Harry (Harold) and Kitty were two of John H. Johnston's children.
    83. "A Poet's Recreation."
    84. Writing on the same day, Burroughs informed WW that "we got our baby just as the heat began, July 1st, & we have had our hands full. . . . He is a bright little fellow & expect we shall 'set a store' by him as the old women say" (Feinberg). This adopted child was Julian.

I eat my biscuits *for supper* only—have two or three of them in a bowl soak'd for an hour, & the water pour'd off, & then a little milk, & plenty of sugar—they must be fixed *just right*, or they ain't good—

873. *To Anne Gilchrist*   7.11. [*1878*]

431 Stevens street Camden N J | July 11 p m

My dear friend

I kept staying & staying in N Y (four weeks altogether)—but took the 4 p m train yesterday & had a fine run to Philadelphia—So here I am to-day in my regular den—find a great accumulation of letters—all those of the past month—so you will understand several things (my not sending regards & love to Miss Hillard for instance)—

Nothing new to write about—brother & sister well as usual—fearfully hot weather still, but I stand it fairly yet—I have rec'd a letter from Rossetti, a scrap from which I enclose[85]—I think of going down to White Horse Saturday[86]—No letter from Bee yet—I suppose you rec'd the Tribune of July 4 with my printed letter in.[87]

Best love to you & all—

Walt Whitman

874. *To Henry Festing Jones*   7.12. [*1878*][88]

ADDRESS: Henry Festing Jones | 1 Craven Hill
Gardens W | London W | England. POSTMARKS:
Camden | Jul | 12 | N.J.; London N. W. | (?) 7 |
Paid | (?) 78.

Camden New Jersey | U S America | July 12

Your letter of June 20 reach'd me, with enclosure—thanks. I have to-day forwarded by mail, to same address as this card, my Two Vols. Please notify me (by postal card will do) soon as they reach you safely.

Walt Whitman

85.   There are no extant letters from Rossetti to WW between 1877 and 1885. See 876.
86.   WW was with the Staffords from July 14, Sunday, to 17 (*CB*).
87.   "A Poet's Recreation."
88.   See 860. WW noted receipt of $9.70 from Jones on the preceding day (*CB*).
89.   WW mentioned in *CB* this letter and *Passage to India* (1871), in which

875. *To Whitelaw Reid*   *7.12.* [*1878*][89]

431 Stevens Street | Camden New Jersey | July 12
My dear Reid

I forward you same mail with this the little "Passage to India" we spoke of, with the "Captain" bit in.

If convenient have the pay for my letter of July 4 in *Tribune* ($20) sent me here.[90]

I am well, for me—All the better for my pleasant NY jaunt.

                                        Walt Whitman

876. *To William Michael Rossetti*   *7.12.* [*1878*]

ADDRESS: Wm M Rossetti | 56 Euston Square |
London W | England. POSTMARKS: Camden |
Jul | 12 | N.J.; London N.W. | C 7 | Paid | 23
Jy 78.

                Camden New Jersey | U S America | July 12
Yours of June 3d, with enclosure,[91] rec'd. Thanks. The books will be sent next mail. I still keep pretty well, for me—just returned here from a month's jaunt, New York-ward—(I sent you a paper with a descriptive letter)—The G[ilchrist]s[92] are at Northampton, Mass:—all well—(B[eatrice] is at the Woman's Hospital Boston)—This place is still my headquarters—but I get off a good deal.

                                        W W

877. *To Oscar Tottie*   *7.26.* [*1878*][93]

                Camden New Jersey | U S America | July 26
I have to-day sent, same address as this card, my Two Volumes—Please notify me (by postal card will do) soon as they [reach] you safely.

                                        Walt Whitman

"O Captain! My Captain!" appears. On July 17 Reid thanked WW for the book (letter in possession of Mrs. Doris Neale).
    90. WW received the payment on July 19 (CB).
    91. A money order for $24 (CB). See 878.   92. "A Poet's Recreation."
    93. WW mentioned sending these books on this date to Tottie at 64 Seymour Street, London (CB), who acknowledged receipt of the volumes on August 11 (LC).

878. *To William Michael Rossetti*

ADDRESS: Wm M Rossetti | 56 Euston Square |
London N W | England. POSTMARK: Camden |
Jul | 28 | N.J.

Camden New Jersey | U S America | July 28 '78
I have to-day forwarded by mail Two Sets of my works—four Vols.
Please notify me soon as they reach you safely.

W W

879. *To Anne Gilchrist*   *8.1.* [*1878?*][94]

Camden Aug. 1
I will send only a line this time—as I have written to Herb at some
length, & ab't in response to yours the same—Best love to you as always.
I will keep you posted, dear friend, of any literary utterance or personal
news—

Walt Whitman

880. *To Herbert Gilchrist*   *8.3–5.* [*1878*]

Down at White Horse | At the Staffords'—Aug 3
My dear Herb
I came down here yesterday afternoon in the 4½ train.[95] Mrs Stafford has been for over a week, & yet is, quite ill—in bed most of the time
—She lies in Deb's room—the one you used to occupy—She is pretty comfortable—is thinner, & more brunette than ever—Keeps pretty cheery—
Will get around I think this coming week—had a good night last night &
a fair forenoon to-day, (sitting up in the easy chair by the window) but is
not quite so well this afternoon (it is now 3)—They have had no doctor
so far—I think the *immediate* trouble is of stomach & bowel nature, deeply
seated—& the general *basic* & more or less remote trouble is being fearfully
& for a long time overwork'd in body & worried in mind—Still, as I said,
I think she will be about again in a few days[96]—As at present, though a
quite sick woman, nothing serious indicated—Debby[97] has been home the

94. Although there seems to be little doubt that WW wrote "Aug. 1," it is possible
that he intended to write "Aug. 7." If that were the case, the allusion to the lengthy
letter to Herbert would clearly be to 880. WW was in Camden on August 1 and 7 (*CB*).
  95. WW was with the Staffords from August 3 to 6, 10 to 13, and 17 to 20 (*CB*).
  96. Mrs. Stafford was still ill on August 10 (*CB*). She was "only middling" on
August 30 (see 885).

past week, but is to go away to-night—Mr Stafford is well as usual—was up to the city with a load of straw yesterday.

Sunday forenoon Aug 4

I am writing this down by the pond, in the cool of the willows close by the gurgling brook—a hot walk down the lane & across the big field, but the strong sun welcome to me, for all that—Here I sit (have hung my shirt on a bush to dry) —

All here just as you used to see it—only more so—more luxuriant, untrimm'd, bushy, weedy than ever—the locust (cicada) sounds firmly to-day here—

Mrs S[tafford] down in the kitchen this morning—I rose early & made the fire, & assisted Ruthey[98] in getting the breakfast—We had a fine meal —I made the coffee & (*of course*) it was good—No mail to-day & I must wait to send this to-morrow—

August 5th

I am writing this up in Harry's & my room at K[irkwood]—Mrs S is much better to-day—She is about seeing to things somewhat as usual—(A great part of her illness is some peculiar trouble, or breakage or rupture to which *women* only are liable—in her case aggravated by overwork)—

It is a wet foggy forenoon—Debby went away with Jo Saturday night —George has gone up to the City with a load of sugar-corn—Harry has gone over to his work at the station—Ed to the store—Lizzie Hider[99] was over here Saturday afternoon & evening—Bill Peak (epileptic), the miller's son at Tomlinson's, has been arrested for purloining a lot of Camden & Atlantic RR tickets—Old Mr Morgan[1] has been dead six weeks—you knew that Mrs Lizzie Stafford (Ben's wife)[2] was dead & buried—

Shall send this over by Harry to mail after dinner—Much obliged for the designs on the block—very nice—also the letter—both arriving safe— Give my best love to your mother—tell her I am well, & shall branch off somewhere (I hardly know where) for the rest of the summer, & will not forget to send some written or printed sign of my whereabout, if any chances—Her letter of a week since was rec'd just as I was starting out— I shall go up either this afternoon or to-morrow.

Walt Whitman

let me hear whether this comes safe to you—

97. Deborah had married Browning on June 13.
98. Mrs. Stafford's daughter (1866–1939), later Mrs. William Goldy.
99. See 1005.
1. He died on June 13 (*CB*).
2. Benjamin Franklin Stafford, a cousin of George, was married to Elizabeth Allen.

881. *To Josiah Child*

ADDRESS: Josiah Child | care of | Trübner & Co: |
publishers &c | 57 & 59 Ludgate Hill | London |
England. POSTMARKS: Camden | Aug | 9 | N.J.;
London E.C. | Paid | (?) | 20 Au 78.

Aug 9 '78 | 431 Stevens Street | Camden
New Jersey | U S America

My dear Mr Child

I rec'd your kind letter of June 25th—you say:

"I hope you rec'd the a/c of your doings & saying at Alfred Tenny-son's son's wedding, which I sent you some time ago."

No, I did not receive any such acc't, & I cannot tell what you mean, or what occurr'd—If convenient tell me—

Ab't the *London Times'* comments on Mr Bryant's death (American poetry, with something about me, as I understand) I wish you had sent it me—as I have not seen or heard of it[3]—

I live very quietly here—am at present pretty well, considering, go about daily. Keep cheery, but remain a partial paralytic—

I have now an edition of my works in Two Volumes (see Circular herewith) which I have got out here & job & sell *myself*—(as the publishers positively wont publish me & my agents here in New York during 1873, '4 & '5 regularly embezzled the proceeds)[4]—I only print small editions, & the price is very high, $5 a Vol:—but they sell moderately well—it all gives me something to do—& then the income supports me.

If Trübner & Co: should wish any, the price would be $3.50 a Vol:[5]—I send you a copy of *Two Rivulets*, as a little present, with my best regards—

Any thing you meet alluding to me, or criticizing, or that you think will interest me, send me, my friend, when convenient (any *real* thing—of course don't bother about the flippant & pointless)—Address as at the top of this letter—I find the P O here entirely reliable—

Walt Whitman

3. WW quoted from this editorial in the London *Times* in "Poetry To-day In America" (*CW*, v, 214–215), which appeared as "The Poetry of the Future" in *The North American Review*, CXXXII (February, 1881), 195–210.

4. For WW's account of his relations with bookdealers, see 698.

5. For WW's transactions with Trübner, see 891.

6. This letter is apparently lost. It is strange that WW did not keep a draft.

7. See 747.

8. Lionel (see 884).

9. On August 14 (*CB*) WW applied for a situation for Harry Stafford to Bartram

882. *To Alfred, Lord Tennyson*

ENDORSED: "Sent to Tennyson | Aug 9 '78 |
Aldworth | Blackdown | Haslemere | (or
elsewhere) | England." DRAFT LETTER.

August 9 '78

My dear Tennyson
        The last letter I sent you was Sept 14 '76,[6] (nearly two years ago)
to which I have received no response. I also sent my Two Vols: new edition—having rec'd your subscription of 5£ (with an intimation from
Robert Buchanan that no books were expected in return—but I preferr'd
to send them)[7]—
        I am still in the land of the living—much better & robuster the last two
years, & especially the last six months, (though a partial paralytic yet)—
I find the experiences of invalidism & the loosing of corporeal ties not
without their advantages, at last, if one reserve enough physique to, as it
were, confront the invalidism—But all this summer I have been & am well
enough to be out on the water or down in the fields & woods of the
country more than half the time and am quite hefty (as we say here) and
sunburnt.
        Best regards & love to you, dear friend. Write me first leisure & op-
portunity. Havn't you a son, lately married[8] I have heard about? Pray tell
me something about him—& the respected lady, your wife, whom you
mention'd in your last as prostrated with illness—& yourself most of all—

883. *To Harry Stafford*   8.15. [1878][9]

ADDRESS: Harry L Stafford | Kirkwood | Camden
County | New Jersey. POSTMARK: Camden | Aug |
15 | N.J.

Camden Aug 15—3 p m

Dear Harry
        I wrote Bart Bonsall a note yesterday about getting you a situation,
& stopt there ab't noon to see him to-day—but they told me he was away &

Bonsall, coeditor of the Camden *Daily Post* with his father, Henry Lummis Bonsall (not
Harry as stated in 641). Henry established the Camden *New Republic* after the Civil
War and later founded the *Post*, which he sold to his son in 1883; see George R. Prowell,
The History of Camden County (1886), 325–326. Harry began to work at Haddonfield,
N. J., about August 20, either for a newspaper or in a printing plant (see 886). Probably
WW was seeking a position for Harry when he wrote on October 9 to William Taylor,
the editor of the Woodstown (N. J.) *Constitution* (CB). On November 13 WW noted
that Harry was at "Atco," but after his visit on December 31, the poet wrote in *CB*: "has
left Atco."

would not be back to-day—There is no news to write—all goes on pretty much the same with me—Harry, I send you a couple of to-day's papers—Things rather dull with me—I am only middling well—(have probably banged around too much the last three months & too much excitement)—

WW

I will be down Saturday in the 4½ p m train[10]—

884. *Alfred, Lord Tennyson to WW*

August 24th 1878

My dear Walt Whitman

I am not overfond of letter-writing—rather hate it indeed—I am so overburdened with correspondence that I neglect half of it—nevertheless let me hope that I answered your last of September 14 '76—& that it miscarried.[11] I am very glad to hear that you are so improved in health, that you move about the fields & woods freely & have enjoyment of your life.

As to myself I am pretty well for my time of life—sixty nine on the sixth of this month—but somewhat troubled about my eyes—for I am not only the shortest-sighted man in England—but have a great black island floating in each eye, & these blacknesses increase with increasing years. However my oculist informs me that I shall not go blind, & bids me as much as possible spare my eyes, neither reading nor writing too much.

My wife is still an invalid & forced to lie on the sofa all day but still I trust somewhat stronger than when I last wrote to you.

My younger son Lionel (whom you inquire about) was married to the daughter of F. Locker[12] (the author of London Lyrics) in Feby—the wedding was celebrated in our old grand historical Abbey of Westminster—there was a great attendance of literati &c of all which I read an account in one of your New-York papers—every third word a lie! Trübner wrote to me this morning, stating that you wished to see a parody of yourself, which appeared among other parodies of modern authors in a

10. WW was at Kirkwood from August 17, Saturday, to 20 (*CB*).
11. WW's letter and Tennyson's reply are unknown.
12. Frederick Locker-Lampson (1821–1895), an English poet, corresponded with WW in 1880 (see 947).
13. WW noted receipt of letters from Carpenter and Herbert Gilchrist on August 30 (*CB*).
14. WW's most recent visit to the Staffords had been from August 17 to 20 (*CB*).
15. Beatrice had sent to WW a lengthy account of her activities at the New

paper called 'The London'—I have it not or I would sent it you. Goodbye, good friend. I think I have answered all your questions.

Yours ever

A Tennyson

885. *To Beatrice Gilchrist*   *8.30.* [*1878*]

ADDRESS: Beatrice C | Gilchrist M D | New
England Hospital for Women | Codman Avenue |
Boston Mass:. POSTMARKS: Cam(?) | A(?) | 3(?) |
N.(?); Boston Mass. | Aug | 31 | (?) | Carrier.

431 Stevens St Camden New Jersey | Aug 30 p m

Dear Bee

I send you Edward Carpenter's letter to Herby, as requested—
Also H's to me (as he may not have written to you)[13]—Your E[dward]
C[arpenter]'s letter rec'd this morning—thanks—Nothing very new with
me—I continue well—have had the best summer for several years—My
brother & sister are well—he, *plus*—she only measurably. I think Mrs Stafford is only middling—(I havn't been at White Horse now for a fortnight)[14]—My nieces are still with us (though just now at Atlantic City for
a few days)—they return to their school latter part of Sept—Your letter
of Aug 12 was rec'd & has been read by all of us[15]—have you rec'd papers?

W W

886. *To Edward Carpenter*   *9.1.* [*1878*]

TRANSCRIPT.

Camden, | New Jersey, | U S A | Sept 1st, 5 p.m.

Just a word any how to let you know I am real well and hearty
considering, and haven't forgotten you a bit. Received your kind letter
(to which I know this is a poor return).[16] Have a photo: though which I
like, taken in N.Y.[17] Will send you one soon as I get them. The G[il-
christ]s [are] well. Herbert is here in New Jersey.[18] B[eatrice] at the

England Hospital for Women, and had also mentioned visits with Joseph B. Marvin and
Sidney Morse, who was "working away desperately at the bust of you" (LC; Harned,
156–158). WW received the head from Morse on February 16, 1879: "head rec'd—
bad—wretchedly bad" (CB).
16. Carpenter's letter is not extant. But earlier in the year, on May 13, he had
written to WW about his lectures in England (Barrett; Traubel, IV, 391–392).
17. The one taken by Sarony (see 871).
18. Herbert was in Kirkwood on August 22 and in Camden on August 24, after
which he returned to the Staffords'. He was in Atlantic City on August 29 (CB).

hospital.[19] Harry S[tafford] is back at printing. Mrs. S[tafford] not well.

W. W.

Thanks for your suggestion in Bee's letter, which she sent me.

887. *To Peter Doyle*   9.1. [*1878*][20]

ADDRESS: Pete Doyle | M Street South bet 4½ |
& 6th | Washington D C. POSTMARK: Carrier | Sep | 3 |
(?) AM.

Camden Sunday Sept 1 5 p m

Still keep real well & hearty considering—Anticipate visiting Wash[ington] sometime this winter—Saw your friend Ch: Johnson[21] a few evenings since on the ferry—had quite a talk about you, &c—

Nothing very new in my affairs—(nothing to complain of)—Very hot here to-day—bad for yellow fever if prevalent, & continuous—

W W

888. *To John Burroughs*   9.20. [*1878*][22]

ADDRESS: John Burroughs | Esopus-on-Hudson |
New York. POSTMARK: Camden | Sep | 20 | N.J.

Camden New Jersey | Sept 20

Am well as usual, & getting along all right—Came up yesterday from ten days down at the Jersey farm & creek—I send you some English papers which I wish return'd to me (especially the *Times*)[23]— Your card rec'd.

W W

19. Beatrice was at the New England Hospital for Women in Boston (see the preceding letter).

20. WW mentioned this post card in *CB* on this date.

21. According to a notation in *CB*, Charles Johnson was a railroad man who had been on a train with Doyle for six months. WW met him on the Federal Street ferry boat on August 28.

22. WW noted sending this post card and "papers" in *CB*. He had been at White Horse, N. J., from September 11 to 18 (*CB*).

23. In commenting upon Bryant's death, the London *Times* had referred to WW (see 881). On September 9 WW noted receipt of the article from Josiah Child (*CB*).

24. WW sent "Gathering the Corn," which appeared in the New York *Tribune* on October 24. It was later reprinted in *Good-bye My Fancy* (*CW*, VII, 14–17). See also 890 and 895.

25. See the preceding letter. WW returned the article to the *Tribune* on October 3 (*CB*).

889. *To Whitelaw Reid*   *9.21. [1878]*

431 Stevens Street | Camden New Jersey | Sept 21
My dear Reid,
    Won't the herewith do for an editorial these days?[24]
The price is $10—

                                              Walt Whitman

I am keeping quite well & hearty yet for me—

890. *To Whitelaw Reid*   *9.30. [1878][25]*

431 Stevens Street | Camden New Jersey | Sept 30
My dear Reid
    Yes—put my name to the piece, if you like it better that way—But
I think you had first better send the M S back to me, & let me fix it up for
an October article—
    Yours

                                              Walt Whitman

891. *To Trübner & Company*

                        431 Stevens Street | Camden New Jersey
                              U S America | Oct 1 '78—
Dear Sirs
    Yours of Sept 14 with $14 for Two Sets (4 Vols) of my books has
come safely to hand[26]—Thank you sincerely—

26. WW's dealings with Trübner & Co. were handled through Josiah Child (see
881). On May 31, 1877, Trübner sent WW $7.57, in payment for copies of *Democratic
Vistas*, and noted that 61 copies of that work were still on hand (LC). On November 8
WW recorded that Trübner owed him $70 for ten sets and "also something due me for
Dem: Vistas." On December 6 he received $47.55 from Trübner in payment for six sets
and for fifteen (twelve according to 899) copies of *Democratic Vistas;* the balance due
was $28 for four sets and $17.02 for forty-six copies of *Democratic Vistas*.
    WW received a payment from Trübner on June 9, 1879, through Josiah Child
and an order for books (see 925). Probably the payment amounted to $24.50, since in
making a tally of the books in Trübner's possession as of June 27, he noted thirty-seven
volumes (including thirty-six sent on June 25 or 27) and forty-six copies of *Democratic
Vistas*. On March 4, 1880, he received in payment $37.22; on July 22, 1880, $80.50,
at which time he sent thirty-four volumes; on March 4, 1881, $105.37, at which time he
sent an additional twenty volumes; and on December 8, 1881, he received $80.50. At that
time the balance due was $14.43 for thirty-nine copies of *Democratic Vistas*. At a later
date WW added to this entry, "all paid in full" (CB).

I to-day forward to Wiley & Sons, New York, Twelve Sets (24 Vols) of my books, to be sent you—which please acknowledge as soon as received—Two of the Twelve Sets being paid for, there are Ten Sets, for which you are to acc't to me at $7 the set—& you are not to furnish them to purchasers at less than $10 the set, or $5 the Vol.

Walt Whitman

892. *To John H. Johnston*   *10.23. [1878]*

ADDRESS: J H Johnston | Jeweler | 150 Bowery cor
Broome St | New York City. POSTMARKS:
Philadelphia | Oct | 23 | 5 PM | Pa.; New York | (?)
24 | 12(?)M | 78 | Recd.

Camden New Jersey | Oct 23
I am well, for me—Have been down at the old Jersey farm by the pond nearly all summer—start again to-morrow[27]—Am writing some— Shall come to N Y to lecture—Al: I got your letter down in the country four **days** after due—I return the Goethe Club ticket—

W W

H—l of a gale here this morning—great destruction—

893. *To Anne Gilchrist*   *11.10. [1878]*

Camden New Jersey Nov 10
Dear friend
I am still well, for me, & having good (or at any rate not *ill*) times —Return'd from Kirkwood yesterday[28]—Am there half the time—(have a room all to myself, good bed, good stove, &c)—Must tell you about Herb's picture, he calls *September Days*—(name not very good, but will do)—Picture itself, in my opinion, *very good*, the best he has painted, such opulence, mellowness of color that would be your first feeling, & would fill you as it did me—it is a very simple scene (story) only well

27. In October WW was with the Staffords from October 5 to 7, 10 to 12, 16 to 21, and 24 to 28 (*CB*). He mentioned "the furious gale & storm" in *CB*. Herbert Gilchrist was also with the Staffords; see Mrs. Gilchrist's letter to him on October 10 (Feinberg) and the following letter.
28. According to *CB*, WW returned from Kirkwood on November 8.
29. On October 25 Mrs. Gilchrist had written from Concord, Mass., about her visit with Emerson, and had inquired about Herbert's portrait of WW and his landscape

shaded opening in the creek, with water 'way to the foreground, & five or six ducks & drakes—foliage meeting at top, no sky, every thing very broad, foliage in masses, all the handling easy & large, yet sufficiently defined—really a *fine*, *original*, rich picture, & in treatment no following of any thing Herb has done before[29]—

Our folks are well as usual—(it is toward noon)—My sister is off to church somewhere—brother down stairs balancing his acct's—I up here in my 3d story front room writing this—the Nov. wind whistling sharp, but sun shining—

The Staffords about as usual—crops & every thing pretty fair this fall, with them—Mrs S keeps about, works hard, devotes all to her family & friends, (woman like)—Debby & her husband all right—Harry well & at work at printing—I saw Arthur Peterson,[30] they are all well—Return me Tennyson's and John Burroughs' letters—(no hurry though, only be careful of T's)—Best love—

W W

Tennyson's letter was delayed, sent back as you will see—I only rec'd it a week ago[31]—

894. *To George W. Waters*

Camden New Jersey | Nov 10 '78

Dear George Waters

Yours of 4th rec'd (I only came up yesterday from the country, where I go more than half the time)—I am pretty well for me, & have had a good summer—

Will the enclosed little bit do for your publication? Success to it[32]—

Walt Whitman

George, if you print it be very careful of the proof—they have lately made some bad work in that respect for me—

(LC; Harned, 161–162). On November 13 she expressed her delight with the description of Herbert's painting but wondered whether WW was satisfied with the portrait (LC; Harned, 164).

29. Probably the poet (1851–1932), whose *Songs of New-Sweden* appeared in 1887. See also 942.

31. WW received Tennyson's letter of August 24 (see 884) on October 21 (CB).

32. WW sent "Roaming in Thoughts" (CB), a two-line poem which appeared in the 1881 edition of *Leaves of Grass*.

895. *To Whitelaw Reid*   *11.27. [1878]*

                          431 Stevens Street | Camden New Jersey Nov 27
My dear Reid
    If convenient please send me the pay for the *Gathering the Corn*
article ($10) published Oct: 24³³—
    All goes about as usual with me—
                                               Walt Whitman

896. *To Anne Gilchrist*   *[12].6. [1878]*³⁴

    ADDRESS: Mrs Anne Gilchrist | 177 Remsen Street |
    Brooklyn N Y. POSTMARKS: Camden | Dec | 6 |
    N.J.; Brooklyn N.Y. | Dec | 7 | 9 AM | Received.

                              Camden New Jersey | Nov 6 evening
    Have just returned this afternoon from White Horse—(a week's
visit—)—nothing very new—Mrs S[tafford] only middling—Folks here
well—found your Boston letter of Nov 29, (enclosing T[ennyson]'s)—
Tell Herb I rec'd his two letters from N Y—(welcome letters)—I am
well—no rheumatism *yet*—Shall write more fully soon—
                                                    W W

897. *To Josiah Child*

                       431 Stevens Street | Camden New Jersey |
                                    U S America | Dec 10 '78
My dear Josiah Child
    Yours of Nov: 23d duly came to hand with Trübner & Co's remit-
tance of $47.55, & statement of acc't³⁵—Thanks—I send by same

    33. See 889. WW received payment on December 6 (*CB*).
    34. WW erred in writing "Nov 6." Upon his return from Kirkwood on December 6
he sent a post card to Mrs. Gilchrist in Brooklyn (*CB*). There are no extant letters
from Mrs. Gilchrist or from Herbert.
    35. For WW's transactions with Trübner, see 891.
    36. WW sent photographs, undoubtedly Sarony's, to Cecil C. Brooks and W. J.
Ham Smith (*CB*).
    37. WW mailed the journal to Burroughs on December 12 (see the next letter).
    38. See 893.
    39. See the preceding letter.
    40. Smith Caswell was one of Burroughs' hired hands (Barros, 178). In the New
York *Tribune* on May 17, 1879, WW described Caswell ploughing in a raspberry field
(*SD*, 340).

mail with this the Photos: to Messrs: Ham Smith and Brooks, as re-quested[36]—

Won't you also accept (for your Christmas trifle) a large & small Photo: which also goes—(Should the mat on the larger Photo: not please your eye, It does mine though—just as it is—you can remove it for a different sized one—or remove it altogether)—

The *New Quarterly Magazine* also came safely[37]—Grateful thanks— I still keep around well as usual—

Walt Whitman

898. *To John Burroughs*   *12.12.* [*1878*]

Camden Dec 12 Evening

Dear friend
        Nothing new or particular to write about—I thought I would send you Tennyson's last letter—(written some time since but by misdirection had to be ret'd & only reached me lately)[38]—Send it back to me when through—I send you a muddled sort of criticism in a late English maga-zine, of no particular interest[39]—Send it back also—

How are you getting along? How is 'Sula? how the baby? Tell me, when you write, about Smith[40]—give him my love—I still keep well & bustling for me—have been down in the country much of the fall, but am now here probably for the winter—Wish I was with you & 'Sula for a few weeks—often think about you all—

Got a letter from London from Trübner day before yesterday for six sets of my books, remitting the (wholesale) price—I sell a set now & then—

The Gilchrists (Mrs G. and Herbert & Grace) are at 177 Remsen street Brooklyn—Jeannette Gilder[41] has written to me that she is going to write my life & asking for items &c—

I rec'd the Scribner for Nov:[42] I suppose from you—Three days

After Burroughs informed WW of the death of Caswell's brother, Charles, the poet copied verbatim Burroughs' sketch of the young man in "Three Young Men's Deaths," printed in *Cope's Tobacco Plant* and later in SD (157–158). WW sent the article to John Fraser, the editor of *Cope's Tobacco Plant*, on November 27, through Josiah Child (*CB*). See also 926.

41. Jeannette Leonard Gilder (1849–1916) was Richard Watson Gilder's sister. WW met her, probably for the first time, at a reception given by her brother on June 14, although he wrote to her in 1875 (see 698). At this time Miss Gilder was writing a literary column for the New York *Herald*. With her brother Joseph, she founded *The Critic* in 1881 and was its editor until 1906. WW wrote to Miss Gilder, evidently about the biographical sketch, on December 20, 22, and 30 (*CB*). See also 902.

42. Burroughs' "Picturesque Aspects of Farm Life in New York" appeared in the November issue of *Scribner's Monthly*, XVII (1878), 41–54.

storm & gale here, but beautiful & clear to-night—I am going out for an hour—

Walt

899. *To Anne Gilchrist*   12.12. [1878]

431 Stevens Street | Camden Dec 12 4½ p m

Dear friend

All about as usual—Rec'd a London letter day before yesterday, purchasing six sets of my books & a dozen *Democratic Vistas* (separate) —& remitting the pay[43]—(come in good for Christmas pocket money)—

Spent last evening till midnight with my friend Dr Bucke, of Canada, Supt of the great Gov't Insane Asylum, & Mrs B, who are over here just for a day or so at Continental Hotel, Phila:[44]—They return to N Y this afternoon, & will call upon you—I have known Doctor B for a couple of years, & what I know, I *like well*—Mrs B, mother of a large family of children, seems to me a woman one would *love & respect more & more* as one knew her—But you will see them—they return to London, Canada, in a few days—Your & Herby's letters rec'd—My sister & brother well— heavy storms & gales here, but brighter to-day—

Walt Whitman

900. *To George W. Childs*   12.12. [1878][45]

DRAFT LETTER.

431 Stevens Street | Camden New Jersey Dec 12

My dear friend

As the holidays come on I would like to make to from 40 to 50 [*incomplete*]

43. The transaction with Trübner & Co. (see 897).
44. On this occasion Dr. Bucke presented to WW a copy of *Man's Moral Nature* (1879): "I dedicate this book to the man who inspired it—to the man who of all men past and present that I have known has the most exalted moral nature—to WALT WHIT- MAN." During the year Bucke sent to WW his pamphlet entitled *The Moral Nature and the Great Sympathetic* (1878) "with the author's affectionate regards" (presentation copy in the Feinberg Collection).
45. According to *CB*, WW sent a note on December 12 to George W. Childs (1824–1894), co-owner of the Philadelphia *Public Ledger;* and on December 17 he

901. *To R. J. Morrell(?)*   *12.18. [1878?]*[46]

431 Stevens Street Camden N J | Dec 18 a m
My dear Sir
    I want a nice *standing ratan work-basket* for my sister here—If
you are coming up any time this week or early next, you might bring one
—Or you might stop & take her order—a nice one with two handy
baskets—such as will probably cost 3½ or $4—*Please call soon—*
                                        Walt Whitman

    I am well as usual—I send my love to the little fellow & wish him
(& all of you)
    Merry Christmas—

902. *To John Burroughs*   *12.23–25. [1878]*

                                        Camden Dec 23
Dear John Burroughs
    Yours rec'd last week—Nothing new with me—I still keep well—
The lecture[47] is a *fixed fact* (to come)—but I shall wait till I get good &
ready—I suppose as I am writing this you & 'Sula are now home—I 'most
envy you—Very cold here to-day, but bright—& I am just going out for a
couple of hours—
    25th Christmas afternoon—Went out—also yesterday—but not long
or far, as we are having a sharp spell of cold & gusty winds here these
days—Rec'd a letter from Herbert Gilchrist this morning—they are at
315 West 19 Street, N. Y., now, in their own apartments, & I believe
expect to be for the winter—Call on them, & 'Sula call too, when down—
    Write me more fully about your proposed book of next spring—(it is
in the gestation of a book—the melting of the fluid metal, before the
casting—that it receives that something to make its idiosyncrasy, identity
—its "excuse for being" if it is to have any—)[48]

received "50 from G W C for the drivers' gloves." At Christmas WW sent gloves to
friends, relatives, and various drivers. He apparently had enough gloves to give them as
presents again in 1881. This draft letter appears on the verso of notes for "A County
Auction."
    46. This letter was probably sent to R. J. Morrell, a manufacturer of rattan
furniture at Newfield, N. J., or to Mr. Judson, one of his employees. Morrell's advertisement is mounted in *CB* opposite the entries for late November, 1878.
    47. The lecture on Lincoln which had been postponed earlier in the year because of
WW's health.
    48. Burroughs published *Locusts and Wild Honey* in 1879.

I have written to Jenny Gilder & sent her a small budget of printed slips &c. (I would like best to be *told about* in strings of continuous anecdotes, incidents, *mots*, thumbnail personal sketches, characteristic & true—such for instance as are in the 2d edition of your old Wash'n *Notes*)[49]—

Yours of 17th Dec. rec'd—Tennyson's & the criticism safely rec'd back—I suppose you rec'd the hat photo. you spoke of—(I sent it to you Oct 1st)—I mail'd you also a pair of buck gloves—& Smith a pair too—four days since[50]—I shall send this to Delaware County, as you say you are going home for a few days—Write me if you get it all right—

W W

Happy New Year to you & all

903. *To Herbert Gilchrist*   12.25. *[1878]*

ADDRESS: Herbert Gilchrist | 315 West 19th Street | New York City. POSTMARK: Philadelphia | (?) | 25 | (?) | Pa.

Camden New Jersey | Dec 25—p m

Yours of day before yesterday rec'd—I am well as usual, & bustling about—Sister and brother well—Bitter cold & gusty gales here for two days[51]—I don't go out so much—Went over Sunday morning to foot of Arch St. Phila. to breakfast on a steamer—bountiful breakfast—jolly democratic three hours[52]—I have written to Miss Jenny G[ilder]—I sent John Burroughs your Brooklyn address—he & wife are away spending Christmas holidays—I shall send him your present address—havn't seen E's[53] portrait yet—I am writing this up in my room—Sun shines out as I finish—

W W

Merry Christmas to you all

49. See 898.   50. See 900.
51. In CB WW mentioned that the "cold spell" lasted from December 24 to 29.
52. WW had Sunday breakfast (December 22) with John L. Wilson, the purser of the "Whildin" steamboat. Upon his return WW sent Wilson a photograph and a copy of *Memoranda During the War* (CB).
53. Probably Wyatt Eaton (see 863), who did a crayon drawing of Bryant for *Scribner's Monthly* (CB).
54. This post card was undoubtedly written in 1878 after the Gilchrists' depar-

904. *To an Unidentified Correspondent*   *12.30.* [*1878?*][54]

TRANSCRIPT.

December 30

[WW noted that the Gilchrists had moved to another address.]

904.1 *To Susan Stafford*   [*12(?).(?). 1878(?)*][55]

DRAW LETTER.

Dear friend

I enclose $5 for the past (over) a weeks board. (God bless you for your many sisterly kindnesses to me, which no money can ever repay. My love to Ed and Debby and the whole family.)

As I am going up & may not be down again soon, I wish Debby to take charge of my big pillow, as it was made by & given me by my mother, & she slept on it & I shall want it again. I may want the stove, to use, this winter, but don't know. The bedstead I give to Debbie if she will accept it—it an't worth much any how.

ture from Philadelphia in April. After their arrival in New York, at first they took rooms in Brooklyn (see 898), but, on December 29 (Feinberg), when Mrs. Gilchrist wrote to Beatrice, who was in Boston, she had just moved to 112 Madison Avenue, New York City (but note 903). Perhaps the note was addressed to Jeannette Gilder, as WW wrote a post card to her on this date (CB).

55. This letter was probably sent shortly after WW's visit from November 29 to December 6, 1878. He was not with the Staffords again until July 2, 1879 (CB). When he stayed with Mrs. Stafford, he ordinarily paid her $5 a week for his board. This draft letter was called to my attention by Professor Edward Grier.

1879

905. *To John Burroughs*   1.25. [1879]

ADDRESS: John Burroughs | Esopus-on-Hudson | New
York. POSTMARK: Camden | Jan | 26 | N.J.

Camden Jan 25

Dear John Burroughs

I havn't been able to think of any thing worth while in the way of a name—to my notion *Locusts and Wild Honey* is the best proposed[1]—(the *Speckled Trout* piece suggested to me whether the *fish* couldn't afford a name for one of your books, for a change)—

Nothing new with me—I am well, for me—I send you a Phila: paper with a letter[2]—Cold winter here—

Walt

906. *To George W. Childs*   1.31. [1879]

431 Stevens Street | Camden Friday noon Jan 31

Dear Mr Childs[3]

If nothing imperative prevents, I shall do myself the pleasure of accepting your invitation for to-morrow night—'Twould be a kindness to me if you would have one of your young men (Mr Johan[4] perhaps) come down & meet me at the foot of Market Street (Camden Federal Street Ferry reception room—Philadelphia side) at ¼ to 8, and convoy me up to your house—

Walt Whitman

1879
    1. On January 13 Burroughs wrote to WW about the title of his new book, which his publisher did not like (Feinberg). See Barrus, 181.
    2. "Winter Sunshine. A Trip from Camden to the Coast" appeared in the Philadelphia *Times* on January 26; reprinted by Herbert Bergman in *Proceedings of the New Jersey Historical Society*, LXVI (October, 1948), 139–154. See SD, 330–338.
    3. See 900. WW attended a reception at Childs' on the following day (CB). On April 9, 1878, D. W. Belisle, with the encouragement of Childs, had approached WW about an edition of *Leaves of Grass*, "*leaving out the objectionable passages . . .* (decided at once to decline on any such condition)" (CB).
    4. John A. Johann, of the Philadelphia *Public Ledger*, whose calling card appears in CB.
    5. In his letter to "Dear Darling Walt," Herbert mentioned the development of a "tenfold facility with my brush since the autumn" and receptions given by various New Yorkers which were attended by such people as Katharine Hillard and Joaquin Miller

907. *To Herbert Gilchrist*   2.6. *[1879]*

ADDRESS: Herbert H Gilchrist | 112 Madison Avenue |
New York City. POSTMARKS: Camden | Feb | 6 | N.J.;
New York | Feb 6 | 8 PM | 79 | (?).

431 Stevens Street | Camden Feb: 6 noon

Dear Herb

Yours of 2nd rec'd, & good to hear from you, & all—That you
improve in handling & dexterity is nothing more than I expected—You
have it in you I am sure[5]—

I am quite dismay'd to hear about John Burroughs's trouble—it is
far more painful & serious than I thought—his last letter (Jan 13) just
devotes a line to it—& I was in hopes all had passed over[6]—

Have you seen my friend Johnston the Jeweler? His store is at 150
Bowery, cor: Broome street—his house 1309 Fifth avenue, near 86th
street—he is a splendid *champagny* fellow, of the American type—

I met Mr Borody[7] the Russian in Chestnut st. Mrs Barry has had a
baby—Mr B. was to go to N Y, & I gave your address, to be call'd on—

Harry Stafford was up to see me ten days ago[8]—They are all going to
move from the Creek (as Montgomery S[tafford][9] wants the farm)—
They are going over to Glendale, to take the store there on the corner,
opposite the church—are to move early in March—They are all well—I
saw Capt. Townsend since[10]—all well yet—

Nothing new or different with me—I keep pretty well—My wrist,
right arm & shoulder &c are *symptomising* a little, possibly for another
March attack of that nerve-inflammation & rheumatism—(but I must not
cry till I am hurt)—My brother & sister are well—Love to you, Herb, boy
—& to your dear mother[11] & Giddy[12]—

Walt Whitman

(LC; Harned, 173–174).
    6. Burroughs was suffering from "painfully excruciating" attacks of neuralgia
(LC; Harned, 173).
    7. WW noted meeting Alexander Boroday, a "Russian gent, on Chestnut st.
Feb. '79" (CB).
    8. Harry had visited WW on January 22 (CB); see also his letter to WW on
January 13 (Feinberg).
    9. George Stafford's older brother, Montgomery (1820–1907).
    10. Captain Vandoren Townsend was married to Patience, George Stafford's
sister.
    11. After moving from Massachusetts to New York, Mrs. Gilchrist wrote frequently
and impatiently to WW. She wanted him to come to see her. "Are you never coming?"
she asked on January 27. "I do long & long to see you" (LC; Harned, 171). WW did
not hurry—he never did when he was importuned—and he arrived in New York on
April 9. In fact, he apparently did not write to Mrs. Gilchrist until March 27 (see 912).
    12. Grace, Herbert's sister.

Herb, why don't you all get a big cheap house in Brooklyn by the month or quarter, with the privilege of keeping it for two or three years? —room enough for all hands—Percy[13] & his if he chooses to come on—a room for me—I would come on & stay & pay a moderate board—Can't we make it pay?

908. *To Beatrice Gilchrist*   *2.21. [1879]*

ADDRESS: Dr Beatrice C Gilchrist | 33 Warrenton Street | Boston | Mass:. POSTMARKS: Philadelphia | Feb | 21 | 6 PM | Pa.; Boston Mass. | Feb | 22 | 11 AM | Carrier.

431 Stevens Street | Camden New Jersey Feb 21
Dear Bee
Your letter rec'd, & we all read it with interest[14]—my sister sends love—We are all about the same—I am continuing well for me—To-day is very clear, but cold & windy—I have been out some two hours enjoying it—cross'd the river—The Staffords, (with the exception of Mr H[15] who has a spell) are well as usual—Harry comes up to see me occasionally[16]—

A note from your mother yesterday forwarding the enclosed letter of Rossetti's which she wished me to post to you—So far my rheumatic (neuralgic) attack keeps off—But I am not out of the woods till April sets in—

WW

909. *To William Harrison Riley*   *[3.18. 1879][17]*

431 Stevens Street | Camden New Jersey U S America
My dear Wm Harrison Riley

13. Herbert's married brother, a metallurgist (1851–1935). On January 5 Mrs. Gilchrist informed WW that Percy was about to lose his position, and that she wondered about his making a career in America (LC; Harned, 167), but, on January 14, she had come to the conclusion that Percy should remain in England (LC; Harned, 169–170). Percy's problems created a great deal of uncertainty for Mrs. Gilchrist since she had to assist her son, as she wrote to Beatrice on January 28, "with a little of the money that was to have taken us back—so that even if he gets an opening in England & decides not to come, we may have to wait another year, & contrive to get a little forward in money matters somehow or other before we can go" (Feinberg). At this time Percy was engaged in experiments which led to the establishment of the Basic Bessemer Process; see *Obituary Notices of Fellows of the Royal Society*, II (1936–1938), 19–24.
14. In her letter on February 16 Beatrice described her work at the hospital and her decidedly favorable impression of Boston (LC; Harned, 175–176).
15. Perhaps a mistake for Mr. George Stafford, the father.
16. Harry Stafford had last visited WW on February 10 (CB).
17. The date is established by an entry in CB. This ardent young Englishman addressed WW as "My dear Friend and Master" on March 5. Twelve years earlier he had

Your letter has reach'd me here & I thank you for your affectionate warmth & appreciation.

I have long wanted to do myself the pleasure of sending a book of
mine to Mr Ruskin, & I have sent one—also a couple of photographs—
directed to him, to your care, by the same mail with this—same address—
Please send me word soon as they reach you & are delivered to Mr R—

Walt Whitman

910. *To John Burroughs*

ADDRESS: John Burroughs | Esopus-on-Hudson | New
York. POSTMARK: Philadelphia | Mar | 20 | 1 PM |
Pa.

Camden New Jersey | noon March 20 '79

Dear   John   Burroughs

How are you getting along? Havn't heard from you in a long time
—My splurge on the *Death of Lincoln* is all ready to be splurged—I
should like to deliver it on Monday evening April 14 in N Y—(or Tuesday
evening—if for any reason preferable)—How about making the arrangements—some respectable second or third class hall?

Is Gilder[18] off for Europe? Would not Chas: DeKay[19] be a good man
to help? I should have written you before—but I have been waiting a little
to see if this March–April attack I had last spring wan't going to give me
another hitch[20]—but I believe not—If the arrangements could be conveniently made, I shall *positively be on hand* for April 14 (or 15)—
Write forthwith—Love to 'Sula—How is the young one? How Smith[21] &
his?

Nothing very new with me—I keep well for me—have had a good
winter—Got a letter from one Riley, from Sheffield, Eng: day before

found a copy of *Leaves of Grass* "and saw a Revelation. . . . In all my troubles and
successes I have been strengthened by your divine teachings." Riley wanted a copy of
Leaves of Grass for Ruskin, who, upon reading a few extracts from WW's poems,
pronounced them "glorious": "He is a stern critic, and as honest as God or a tree." On
April 2 Riley noted receipt of the book and photographs, and on April 4 he quoted from a
note sent to him by Ruskin: "I am glad to know that I can give some pleasure to such a
man." (Riley's letters are in the Feinberg Collection.) Although Ruskin did not write to
the poet, WW informed the New York *Sun* on April 15 that "he did not feel at liberty to
divulge the exact contents of the letter." See also the Camden *Daily Post* of May 12.
These two newspaper items were brought to my attention by Professor F. DeWolfe
Miller. See also 946.

18.   Richard Watson Gilder (see 852).

19.   Charles de Kay (1848–1935) was the literary and art editor of the New York
Times from 1876 to 1894, and was the brother-in-law of Gilder (Barrus, 182). WW
met de Kay at a reception given by Gilder on June 14, 1878 (*SD*, 329).

20.   See 907–908.

21.   Smith Caswell.

yesterday—he is a friend & young chum of *Ruskin*—the latter accepts me, & goes it strong—he adjectives the word "glorious" for L of G[22]—

W W

911. *To John Burroughs*   3.27. [*1879*][23]

ADDRESS: *John Burroughs* | care J B Marvin[24] | Internal Revenue Bureau | Washington | D C. POSTMARK: Philadelphia | Mar | 27 | (?).

Camden New Jersey | March 27 p m

My dear friend

I could not conveniently come to the West Phil: Depot—I have just written to Johnston leaving the hall, &c to his selection (the night too, if necessary)—I am averse to a first class hall—(I shall certainly be on hand, if alive & able, but the thing is yet a *prospecting*, & we are not at all sure what we shall find.)

I am as usual—was over to Phila: last evening to a nice dinner party, all men, artists, &c, Horace Furness, (a good fellow)—his brother Frank, architect[25]—my friend Forney[26]—Kirke,[27] (of Lippincott's Mag:) & eight or ten others—a jolly time—No imminent intention of going south or to California—Love to all inquiring Wash'n friends—

W W

912. *To Anne Gilchrist*   3.27. [*1879*][28]

Camden New Jersey | March 27 p m

My dear friend

Yours of yesterday rec'd—Also the previous ones[29]—I keep well—

---

22. See the preceding post card.
23. That this letter was written in 1879 is confirmed by an entry in CB and by the reference to the New York lecture.
24. Marvin had visited WW on February 24 (CB).
25. Furness (1833–1912) was the distinguished editor of the Variorum Shakespeare, and was one of the honorary pallbearers at WW's funeral. See also Traubel, III, 520. Frank Furness designed the Pennsylvania Academy of Fine Arts and was the teacher of Louis Sullivan, who described his mentor in *The Autobiography of an Idea* (1926), 190–196.
26. John W. Forney (1817–1881) established the Philadelphia *Press* in 1857, the Washington *Sunday Morning Chronicle* in 1861, and the *Daily Morning Chronicle* in 1862. In 1878 he founded the Philadelphia *Progress*, a weekly magazine to which WW contributed; "The First Spring Day on Chestnut Street" appeared in the *Progress* on March 8 (SD, 188–190). During the Washington years WW's self-puffs had frequently appeared in Forney's newspapers. Later in 1879 the publisher accompanied WW to

no attack of the neuralgia-rheumatism so far this spring—So I fancy it has skipp'd me—havn't been down to Kirkwood since early in Dec: last —the Staffords have no doubt moved—Harry comes up about once a month to see me—I expect to come on to N Y to lecture (Death of Abraham Lincoln) the middle of April—Do you know of my friend Mr Johnston, jeweler, 150 Bowery? he is sort of engineering it—in conjunction [with] John Burroughs, (now in Washington)—

My brother & sister well—her sister[30] & two children staying with us this spring—the charmingest, fattest, lovingest, cunningest little five year old girl, with the sweet name of Amy[31]—

I dont know where I shall go this summer, but must strike off somewhere—Well pleased with the prospect of seeing you & all, in Phila:—Love to Herb and to Giddy—I shall now go over the ferry, & post this in the Phil: Office—return leisurely to C[amden] before dark—

So long, dear friend—

W W

913.   *To Herbert Gilchrist*   *4.8.* [*1879*][32]

ADDRESS: Herbert Gilchrist | 112 Madison Av: | New York City. POSTMARKS: Philadelphia | Apr | 8 | (?); F | 4–8 | 6 P(?) | (?).

Camden April 8

I leave here to-morrow Wednesday in the 2 p m train for N Y—to report at Mr J[ohnston]'s, 150 Bowery—All well—

W W

Kansas (see 934).

27.   John Foster Kirk (not Kirke) (1824–1904) was editor of *Lippincott's Magazine* from 1870 to 1886.

28.   The year is established by the reference to the Lincoln lecture on April 14.

29.   Mrs. Gilchrist wrote five letters to WW in 1879 before he replied: on January 5, 14, and 27, and on March 18 and 26 (see note 11 above).

30.   Mrs. Emma Dowe (see 823). Her arrival in Camden was noted in *CB* on March 6.

31.   WW sent Amy H. Dowe a valentine on February 14 (*CB*). According to information supplied by Miss Elinor J. Harrington, the librarian at Norwich, Conn., Amy taught school there from 1912 until 1918, when she moved to Philadelphia with her father.

32.   WW left for New York on April 9 and remained there until June 14 (*CB*). See also *SD*, 190–202. While WW was at Johnston's home in New York, G. M. Ottinger painted his portrait; see Elliot, *Walt Whitman As Man, Poet and Friend* (1915), 150–151.

914. *To a Newspaper Editor*

April 13 '79

My dear Sir

To break the tedium of my half-invalidism—& as an experiment—I have come on to N Y to try a lecture—Can't you give me a little lift in to-morrow's paper—Something like the below?[33]

Walt Whitman

915. *To Whitelaw Reid*   4.14. [1879]

TRANSCRIPT.[34]

Monday afternoon | April 14 | 1309 Fifth av:
near 86th st

My dear Reid—

As you might possibly have room in the paper—& a full report *might* hit—I send you a complete copy of my lecture, to take the chances *for to-morrows paper*—(As I calculate, it would make about three quarters of a column of small type)[35]—

My plan is to break the tedium of my half invalidism from time to time (& also collect a few shekals) by getting engagements as a lecturer & reader—& this is an attempt to break the ice.

Walt Whitman

916. *To Herbert Gilchrist*   4.29. [1879]

ADDRESS: Herbert Gilchrist | 112 Madison avenue | New York City. POSTMARK: Esopus | (?).

Esopus April 29

All goes well—enjoyed my journey up the river that afternoon &

33. Probably WW sent an account of his lecture to this unidentified editor similar to the one mentioned in the following letter.

34. This transcription was sent to Professor Rollo G. Silver years ago by the secretary of Ogden Reid.

35. The two-column report of WW's address—"A Poet on the Platform"—in the New York *Tribune* on April 15, began: "The poet Walt Whitman made his beginning as a lecturer last night at Steck Hall, in Fourteenth-st. His subject was the death of President Lincoln. He reads from notes, sitting in a chair, as he is still much disabled from paralysis. He desires engagements as a reader of his own poems and as a lecturer."

36. WW stayed with Burroughs from April 23 to May 3 (CB). A report of his journey appeared in the New York *Tribune* on May 17 under the heading "Real Summer Openings"; most of the material was included in SD (190–196, 339–341). Burroughs was particularly delighted with what was to be WW's last visit to Esopus-on-Hudson: "The weather has been nearly perfect, and his visit has been a great treat to me—April days with Homer and Socrates for company" (Barrus, 184).

evening—10½ when I got in—Every thing soothes, comforts, invigorates me here—the hills, rocks, sky, river, nearer & more to me than ever[36]—

All well here—the baby superb[37]—yesterday we spent at Po[ugh]-keepsie & in Vassar College[38]—I return to N Y Friday or Saturday—

W W

917. *To Whitelaw Reid*   *5.8. [1879]*

1309 Fifth av. near 86th st | Thursday afternoon
May 8

My Dear Reid

Can you use this *for Saturday's paper?*[39] (Will make a column & a third or half about)—If put in type please have me the proof (which I will return forthwith) sent *to-morrow afternoon* any time before 7 o'clock to above address—

Walt Whitman

918. *To Whitelaw Reid*   *5.12. [1879]*

1309 Fifth av: near 86th street | Monday noon May 12

My dear Reid

If you put this in type perhaps you could send me a proof *to-morrow Tuesday afternoon say by 2, (if convenient order it so, specifically)*—It will make, I think, from 1½ to 1¾ columns—Can you use it in Wednesday's paper?[40]

---

37. The report in the New York *Tribune* included two paragraphs describing Burroughs' son, Julian, passages omitted in SD (339–340).

38. On April 28 WW visited Professor Frédéric Louis Ritter (1834–1891), professor of music and art at Vassar College. Mrs. Ritter, a musician and a friend of William D. O'Connor, invited WW to visit her in a letter to O'Connor on April 26, 1876 (Traubel, III, 483–484). Her letter "was on rose tinted paper in a pale green envelope, and perfumed like Arabia Felix," so O'Connor described it to Burroughs on May 4, 1876 (Doheny). Professor Ritter composed a musical setting for "Dirge for Two Veterans" (see 946 and Barrus, 355).

39. "Broadway Revisited" appeared in the New York *Tribune* on May 10, and, rearranged, in SD, 16–21, 338–339. This was the first of three chatty (and embarrassingly trite) letters WW submitted to the *Tribune* in May. See also the following letter. On May 29 WW received from D. Nicholson $45 for the three articles (LC).

40. "Real Summer Openings," which appeared in the *Tribune* on Saturday, May 17, described WW's trip to Burroughs' home (see 916).

I have another screed—*Central Park jottings*, &c[41]—which I think of offering you for Saturday's paper—I return to Camden in a few days—
Walt Whitman

919. *To Harry Stafford*   5.13. [1879]

1309 Fifth av: near 86th street | New York May 13
Well, Hank, here I am yet—I went up to Esopus & had a real good time nearly two weeks—rode out somewhere every day—Came back here a week ago Saturday—I am writing a little for one of the papers here[42]—that's one thing keeps me—another is I may as well stay here, if they wish me to, & I like them & they me, which is the case—

Summer is upon us—I have been out in Central Park all the forenoon —It is beautiful as money can make it (but I would rather be down by the old creek)[43]—I suppose Herb is stopping with you at present—I send him a paper—tell him I saw his mother and Giddy at the theatre last night—

Dear son, how are you getting along—& how are your dear father and mother?—how does the store go? Rec'd your letter & was glad to get it— Shall stay here perhaps a week longer yet—On the other side is an acc't of a great wrestling match here last night[44] I thought might interest you— best love to you & all—
Your old friend

W W

920. *To General James Grant Wilson*

TRANSCRIPT.

New York | May 21, 1879
[WW thanked Wilson for two books, one a gift, the other to be returned; the latter request WW would comply with after his return to Camden.][45]

41. The piece was entitled "These May Afternoons" when it appeared in the *Tribune* on May 24. It discussed a visit to Central Park and to the "U. S. Minnesota." Much of the material later appeared in *SD*, 196–202, 341–342.
    42. The New York *Tribune* (see the preceding two letters).
    43. WW's remark here contrasts sharply with his idyllic account of Central Park published in the *Tribune* on May 24 (see *SD*, 197–198). Note also the differences between his public and private accounts of St. Louis in 936.
    44. WW attached two accounts of a wrestling match between Professor William Miller and John McMahon, both of whom "belonged to the sect of muscular Christianity," as it was termed in the days before television. McMahon was the victor.
    45. Wilson (1832–1914) served in the Civil War, was an editor of *Appleton's Cyclopaedia of American Biography*, and author of biographies of Grant and Fitz-Greene Halleck. Probably Wilson sent to WW *The Poets and Poetry of Scotland* (1876). WW

921. *To Alfred Janson Bloor*

TRANSCRIPT.

New York | May 24, 1879

In a letter in the "Tribune" of to-day[46] I have printed (as I some time since notified you)[47] what you said (well said) about actors . . . Shall count on getting extracts from your Journal about Mr. Lincoln's murder and funeral soon as you can conveniently send them.[48]

922. *To Harry Stafford*   5.28. [1879]

1309 Fifth av: near 86th Street | New York May 28
Dear Son

Your letter dated 27th has reached me here, & glad to get it—glad to hear you are having such good health this summer—as to that spell you speak of, no doubt it was the devilish lemonade & cake—I always told you you was too heedless in the eating & drinking, (sometimes going without too long, &c)—(I tell you what, Harry, it is the *stomach*, *belly* & liver that make the principal foundation of all *feeling well*—with one other thing)—

The little piece "Will it Happen"? is real good—stick away at it, dear son—write little pieces of your thoughts, or what you see, off-hand, *at the time*—(that *always* puts *life* into 'em)—Keep pegging away[49]—

Day before yesterday I spent aboard the great ship *Minnesota*, (big enough for a thousand people)—it was all very enjoyable—the officers all my friends right off—I took dinner with them at a big table in what they call the Ward Room—Some splendid young fellows—some jolly old roosters—lots of fun, yarns &c—every thing good to eat, & plenty of it— What I liked best though was rowing in the boat to & from the ship, man-of-war fashion—(In my last letter in *Tribune* you will see a ¶ about the *Minnesota*, my first visit)[50]—

wrote to Wilson again on December 8, 1886.
    46. Bloor (1828–1917) was, he informed WW on June 9, a member of the architectural staff that designed Central Park (LC). He was a poet as well as the author of a number of architectural treatises. WW quoted from Bloor's letter at the conclusion of his article in the *Tribune* on May 24 (see SD, 342). Bloor had taken exception to WW's contemptuous references to actors in his lecture on Lincoln's murder.
    47. A lost letter written on April 29.
    48. On June 9 Bloor sent to WW "a copy of the selections you made from my journal, and also an account of the information Miss Harris [daughter of Senator Ira Harris] gave me as to what she knew of Mr. Lincoln's assassination" (LC).
    49. Harry occasionally wrote short compositions as exercises in penmanship and writing which he submitted to WW for criticism.
    50. See SD, 201–202.

I got a letter from my sister yesterday from Camden—all as usual there—Mrs Gilchrist was there last Saturday, she said—I suppose Herbert is still with you—I rec'd his letter—he seemed to be having royal times there—Beatrice G[ilchrist] is here—she called on me here—Hank, you speak about my not writing oftener—this is the *third* letter[51] I have written to you from here, & papers three or four times—Yours of yesterday is the *second* rec'd here from you—*let them read this letter if they care to*—I shall probably be back last of next week—come up, my darling boy—

Your old W W

Wednesday evening

John Burroughs was here last evening—went home this morning —I go about middling—take things very easy—am as well as usual—(have some sort o' bad spells, still)—am all tann'd & red—wear my gray clothes, (my new suit, pretty good yet)—Al and May[52] are well, have grown well & finely, (we three pass a good deal of the time together, as we all like each other first rate)—

Mr and Mrs Johnston are now away for some days on account of the death of the latters father, Monday last—wish'd me particular to stay till they returned—I have lots of visitors—some every day—quite a good many ladies—invitations, dinner parties &c (seldom go to them though)— All good for a change, & a little excitement—*but I wish I was with you this minute, down by the creek or off in the woods somewhere*—I have been here now away since April 9 & every thing & every body has been so loving & kind—I have been happy in it all—& yet, Harry, my heart & wishes turn to my old friends, (& to old Jersey)—weather fine nearly all the time—I go out in Central Park frequently—Harry, give Herbert this enclosed slip[53]—

923. *To Herbert Gilchrist*   [5.28. 1879][54]

Herb, yours rec'd & welcomed—Nothing very new with me here— have enjoyed the past seven weeks hugely—but am quite ready to go back —You must be having first-rate times there—Bee was here to see me

---

51. Only two letters are extant (see 919). Harry's letters are apparently lost.
52. Two of the children of John H. Johnston.
53. The following note to Herbert Gilchrist.
54. The "Tom Moore Centenary" took place on May 28, 1879. This note to Herbert was included in the preceding letter to Harry Stafford.
55. The artist (see 863). According to Mrs. Gilchrist's letter of March 18, Eaton had urged Herbert to continue his art studies in Paris (LC; Harned, 177–178).
56. The Moran brothers, Edward (1829–1901), Thomas (1837–1926), and

Monday—looks well—Eaton[55] is still in Canada, I hear—Some artists here, last evening—(one of the Morans,[56] & wife)—Herb, I suppose you get the papers I send you[57]—I am well—great *Tom Moore Centenary* here in N Y to-night—I have been formally invited—but shall not attend—

W W

924. *To Samuel Van Wyck*[58]

ADDRESS: Sam'l Van Wyck | 65 New York Avenue | Brooklyn | N Y. POSTMARK: New York | May 28 | 5 PM | 79.

1309 Fifth av: near 86th Street | May 28 '79

My dear Sir

Yours of May 23d has reach'd me here—I am unable to give you any information on the genealogic points you speak of—wish I could —I have an idea there are town records or documents at Huntington, that are accessible, & that might throw light on the Van Wyck and Whitman families—I have seen such records alluded to, & printed extracts from them—where they are, or what office, in Huntington I think, or who keeps them, I can not say—Yes I was born at West Hills—my father Walter Whitman—I trace the Whitmans there four generations—my grandmother (father's mother) was Hannah *Brush*[59]—

I am here on a visit—go back, last of next week, to Camden New Jersey, my regular p o address.

Walt Whitman

925. *To Josiah Child*

TRANSCRIPT.

New York June 9, 1879

[WW acknowledged receipt of a payment and an order for copies of his books.[60] He mentioned his article in *Cope's Tobacco Plant*

Peter (1841–1914), were British-born painters who had emigrated to the U. S. in 1844.

57. WW's recent articles in the New York *Tribune*.

58. Van Wyck (1824–1900) was born in West Hills, Long Island. He later became the president of the Lafayette Fire Insurance Company of Brooklyn, and was a member of the Long Island Historical Society.

59. See Allen, 595.

60. WW received $24.50 from Trübner & Co. (see 891). On June 25 he shipped thirty-six volumes at $3.50 each, as he informed the firm two days later (CB).

("Three Young Men's Deaths"), and promised to prepare "other two pieces."][61]

926. *To John Burroughs*   *6.11. [1879]*

1309 Fifth avenue | New York | June 11
Dear John Burroughs
    As you see I am still here—but I leave for Camden next Saturday —I still keep ab't the same as when I last saw you—The Johnstons all well—The Gilchrists sailed last Saturday in the Circassia[62]—
    I send you the *"Tobacco Plant"* with a piece of mine will interest you —(you'll see I have used one of your letters of last winter)[63]—How nicely those English get up their print things—
    This has been a good visit for me—it sort o' *rehabilitates* me for speaking & literary handling, writing, off-hand, more than I anticipated— half-paralytic as I am—henceforth I feel more at ease, more self con- fidence—which is always half the battle—
    I hope 'Sula is comfortable this hot weather (very hot here to-day)—& the babe—When you write direct to Camden—I send Smith[64] a paper, with my love—
                                         Walt

927. *To Peter Doyle*   *6.16. [1879]*[65]

ADDRESS: Pete Doyle | M Street South—bet 4½ & 6th | Washington | D C. POSTMARK: Camden | (?) | 17 | N.J.

431 Stevens Street | Camden New Jersey June 16
Have just got back here—All right—have been in (& around) New

61. The article appeared in the April issue (II, 318–319); see also 898. WW sent the article on November 27, 1878, to John Fraser, the editor of the magazine (CB), and see 928. "The Dalliance of the Eagles" appeared in this magazine in November, 1880 (II, 552).
62. The Gilchrists sailed for Glasgow on June 9 (CB). See also 931. Before em- barking, Mrs. Gilchrist and WW had a private farewell at Johnston's home—a farewell which neither was willing to discuss (Barrus, 146–147). Though she undoubtedly kept her emotions under control, the meeting was Anne Gilchrist's final defeat, as she "learned of finalities | Besides the grave."
63. "Three Young Men's Deaths" (see 898).   64. Smith Caswell.
65. The year is confirmed by the reference to the post card in CB and by his

York ever since I saw you that night—have had a good time—I send you a paper[66]—yours regularly rec'd—So long—

W W

928. *To John Fraser*

ADDRESS: John Fraser | 10 Lord Nelson Street |
Liverpool | England. POSTMARKS: Camden | Ju(?) |
17 | N.J.; Paid | Liverpool | US Packet | 28 Ju 79 |
5 B.

431 Stevens Street | Camden New Jersey
U S America | June 16 1879
Your postal order duly received to-day ($15.30)—payment in full
—thanks[67]—

Walt Whitman

929. *To John Burroughs*   *6.20. [1879]*

Camden New Jersey | June 20

Dear John Burroughs
I have got back here after ten weeks' absence, & find myself all the better for my trip (& for what it has developed, & sort o' *crystallized*) —but discover that I need a spell of quiet and slip shod—Thought I should like the Delaware river trip, & have been deferring to write decidedly, in hopes to go—but have concluded it is best for me *not to try it*—Write to me soon as you get this—Al Johnston would be a good one to take[68]—there is *manliness* in the boy—& he needs such a trip—

Nothing very new with me. I am well. I get a stray order now & then from England[69]—a long letter yesterday from Edward Carpenter (I shouldn't wonder if he panned out finely)[70]—I have sent you papers from here which of course you have rec'd—I enclose the baby's photo. returned[71]

recent New York trip.
66. WW sent a copy of "Three Young Men's Deaths" (CB).
67. Payment for "Three Young Men's Deaths" from the editor of *Cope's Tobacco Plant.*
68. Albert, John H. Johnston's son, accompanied WW to Burroughs' home in 1878 (see 869).
69. WW sent the 1876 two-volume edition to E. D. Mansfield and James W. Thomson on June 16 and to W. G. Brooke on June 20 (CB).
70. Upon his return to England, Herbert Gilchrist spent a week with Edward Carpenter and his family (LC; Harned, 183).
71. Burroughs' son, Julian.

—my sister thinks of her own lost darling whenever she looks at it—If you get others any time, send me one to keep—I am taking it easy—sleep & eat well—Splendid days & nights here lately—

How is 'Sula? How the *plantation?* Remembrances to Smith—

Walt

930. *To Ruth Stafford*   6.24. *[1879]*

Camden June 24

Dear Ruthey

I received your letter and was glad to hear from you by your own writing. You must be having good times over there at Glendale. Do you all like it there as well as the old farm? Well, Ruth, it is now over six months since I have seen any of you except Harry.[72] The last three I have been away in New York—return'd only a few days ago—I am well and fat, & have been so, & my visit & lecture & jaunts on the water & seashore &c. all did me good.

Tell your mother that the baby born over two years ago when Mrs Johnston died there in N Y is still living & though not rugged is a nice sweet little child—He is named Harry[73]—

To-day a friend from Philadelphia has made me a half-hour call, with his four nice girls, one of them about your age, two a little older, & one younger. He has four boys and four girls. First he takes the four boys out, & then the four girls—I enjoyed their call—They were going off on a little excursion—

My brother & sister are well as usual—My nieces are now here[74]— have left school—they are grown, tall hearty girls—

Tell Mont[75] I want to see him—I often wished he was with me to see the sights, when I was in New York—It is very hot here to-day—I want to come down soon, probably next week, & see you all & see the new place— I will send word a day or two before, so Mont or you can come to the station for me. Love to you & all, Ruthy dear. I shall come soon.[76]

Walt Whitman

72. WW was last with the Staffords from November 29 to December 6, 1878 (*CB*). Ruth was Harry's sister.
73. See 806.
74. Jeff's daughters, Mannahatta and Jessie Louisa, came to Camden almost annually.
75. Ruth's brother, Montgomery.   76. WW went to Glendale on July 2 (*CB*).
77. Mrs. Gilchrist wrote after landing in Glasgow on June 20 and on August 2 from Durham, where her son Percy was living. Both were chatty letters about her travels

931. *To Anne Gilchrist* 8.18. [*1879*]

ADDRESS: Mrs Anne Gilchrist | Lower Shincliffe |
Durham | England. POSTMARKS: Philad'a Pa. | Aug |
18 |Paid All; Durham | H | Au 29 | 79; Haslemere |
A | Sp 1 | 79.

431 Stevens Street | Camden August 18

Dear friend

Yours of 2d just rec'd (the one from Scotland came also)[77]—I am pretty well—full as well as when I last saw you in New York—(if any thing perhaps a little plus)—

I went down last month to spend a while with the Staffords at their new farm, but I miss'd my main attraction & comfort, *the Creek*, & did not make a long visit[78]—Mrs S and the rest are as usual, except Debbie, who was not at all hearty—

Brother & sister here well—sister seems to be engaged this morning with her new girl, (who seems to be doing marvellous!) in early fall house cleaning—at any rate I noticed every thing tumbled & heaped just now, as I have been down stairs to see what the post man left me—

I am sitting up in my room Stevens Street writing this—copious rains all the morning, and last night—(& indeed this is the third day of them)—Hattie and Jessie left for St Louis last Thursday night—Lou and I went over to the West Phil: depot and saw them off—(dear girls, how we miss them)—

I am busy a little leisurely writing—think of printing soon a smallish 100 page book of my accumulated memoranda down at the Creek, & across the Ferry, days & nights, under the title of

Idle Days & Nights of a half-Paralytic

prose, free gossip mostly, (you saw some specimens in that Jersey letter, last winter in the Phila: *Times*)[79]—

Isn't that sad about the sudden death of our young Mr Sartoris in your country? Something strange too (I hope nothing uncanny will turn out)—

Thank you, dear friend, for your letter—(came in just right)—how I

and various points of interest (LC; Harned, 181–185).

　　78. WW visited the Staffords from July 2 to 9. It was an uneventful summer except for an "Evening at Exposition Building, at National Teachers' Reception—saw the *phonograph* and *telephone*" (CB, and see *SD*, 203).

　　79. "Winter Sunshine. A Trip from Camden to the Coast" (see 905). In her letter of October 6–12, Mrs. Gilchrist hoped "you would reconsider the title—so far, that is, as to leave out the clause 'by a half paralytic' . . . for health and vigour, dear Friend, are and ever must remain synonymous with our Walts name" (Barrett; Barrus, 147).

should indeed like to see that *Cathedral*—I dont know which I should go for first, the Cathedral, or *that baby*[80]—

Best love to you—to Bee, Herb, Giddy and all—I write in haste but I am determined you shall have a word at least promptly in response—

932. *To John Burroughs*   8.20. [*1879*]

431 Stevens Street | Camden N J Aug 20

Dear John Burroughs,

Postal of 18th just rec'd, & glad enough to hear from you all—the interval has been a long one—I supposed you were off some where—

Nothing special with me—After I returned from N Y middle of June, went down to my Jersey farm friends a couple of weeks—but they have moved into a new place, superior for their purposes, but to me the attraction had ceased, & I left—Otherwise have been here in Camden all summer (I feel now as though I ought to have gone up & room'd in your house & boarded with Smith[81] the last two months)—I still keep well—about the same as when you last saw me—may be a trifle ruggeder yet—

All here well—I enclose you two letters from Mrs Gilchrist[82] in England, & one from my friend Mrs Botta,[83] may interest you—I shall send you papers to-morrow—Weather fine yesterday & to-day here—& I am out enjoying it—(after fair[84] days of pouring rain)

I often see your name, & extracts, (sometimes quite long ones) in the papers hereabouts—

Love to Sula—

Walt Whitman

That Del: river boat trip? Did it come off? You know I have heard nothing about it since[85]—

80. On August 2 Mrs. Gilchrist described her grandson and the Durham Cathedral (LC; Harned, 183).

81. Burroughs' hired hand, Smith Caswell.

82. Mrs. Gilchrist's letters of June 20 and August 2 (see note 77 above).

83. The poet and sculptor (see 387 and 388.1; letter 388 was erroneously assigned to Mrs. Botta). Burroughs informed Mrs. Barrus that WW attended some of Mrs. Botta's receptions (Barrus, 186). WW sent her a photograph and a copy of *Democratic Vistas* on July 20 (*CB*).

84. WW undoubtedly intended to write "four" or "five." He noted "rainy days & nights" in *CB* from August 16 to 18.

85. See 929. On August 24 Burroughs described his trip on the Delaware River late in June (Feinberg; Traubel, III, 260).

933. *To John Burroughs*   *8.29.* [*1879*]

Camden Aug 29

Dear Jack

As I sit here—the weather is now perfect, day & night—I have jotted off the enclosed & send you—(of course use it or *not.*)[86] Your letter arrived with the enclosures. I keep well—go out most every day. I suppose you rec'd the *Tribune* (27th I think) with your letter in, which I sent you[87] —& the other papers I occasionally send. No news particular—I sell a book now & then—

No, I have not been to any watering place—they are no company for me—the *cities* magnificent for their complex play & oceans of eager human faces—But the country or sea for me in some sparse place, old barn & farm house—or bleak sea shore—nobody round—Meanwhile I get along very well here—

Walt

934. *To Louisa Whitman*   *9.12–13.* [*1879*]

St. Louis | Friday noon Sept 12[88]

Dear Lou

Came through here all right—seems to be much as I was mentioning to you the other day—at any rate I feel better here now at the end than I did the two days before I started, & on Wednesday night & morning—Found it comfortable & easy on the sleeping car—suited me perfectly—I see now that *you ought to have come*—you would have enjoyed every thing—it is really nothing difficult to come—To make it more interesting we had a smash about 5½ Thursday p m on our train, just escaped being something very bad indeed—the two locomotives all shivered to splinters—nobody hurt however, (only one man who jumped,

86. WW enclosed a note for inclusion in Burroughs' article, "Nature and the Poets," in which he discussed his own poetry and quoted Symonds' opinion that WW "is more thoroughly Greek than any man of modern times!" (Doheny; Barrus, 111, who also quotes Burroughs' adaptation of the passage). WW reread Symonds' *Greek Poets* while he was at Esopus in April (SD, 340). Burroughs' article appeared in *Scribner's Monthly*, XIX (December, 1879), 285–295, and later in *Pepacton* (1881).
87. Burroughs' "Harvest Time." On August 24 Burroughs mentioned sending a "Pastoral Letter" to the New York *Tribune* (Feinberg; Traubel, III, 260).
88. WW, accompanied by Colonel Forney (see 911), left for St. Louis on September 10 after accepting an invitation to address the Old Settlers of Kansas Committee at Lawrence. He arrived in St. Louis on September 12, and proceeded on the following day to Lawrence, where he stayed with Judge John P. Usher (1816–1889), Secretary of Interior in Lincoln's administration and at this time mayor of Lawrence (see 945).

the mail agent)—detained us there 2½ hours[89]—I didn't mind it at all—the last 400 miles since we did fly! I never rode so fast before in my life—strangely enough too I slept quite well—only woke up every hour or two—When we got here in St L an hour & a half ago, on alighting from the cars, found Jeff waiting for me—he looks fat & dark, & like work —(which I guess he has plenty of)—We all rode immediately to the Planter's Hotel, where we were expected, & have just had a royal breakfast, perfect beefsteak, broiled chicken, oysters, good coffee &c—enjoyed it, for I hadn't eat any thing since yesterday at 3½—This great hotel is crowded with guests—the proprietor puts his private parlor & room at my disposal, & it is in it I am writing this—Jeff is coming in about an hour to take us on a long ride around—I shall stay with him & the girls to-night—To-morrow morning at 8.50 we start for central Kansas, 350 miles further (we are here 1000 miles from Phila:)—

Lou, I will write again, what moves I make—dont exactly know—most likely I shall come back with Col. F[orney] soon, as I find it mighty convenient & nice—every thing seen to—

Saturday—8 a m—I have been stopping at Jeffs—they are very nicely fixed—slept like a top—have just had a first rate breakfast—the girls are well, & send love—they much wish you had come—

I now start in an hour for Kansas, (Lawrence)—shall get there about 10 to-night—

Brother Walt

935. *To Louisa Orr Whitman*   *9.19.* [1879]

Sept 19

On the cars on the great Plains on the eastern frontiers
of Colorado

Well, Lou Dear, I suppose you got my letter from St Louis, here I am on the great Plains of Colorado (and Kansas)—We ride and ride all day & all night, & it is nothing but plains—but I enjoy it all very much indeed—as I sit in the cars writing this, (have a leaf-table before me to write on) 1 p m flying along, I can [look? u]p[90] with my eye, including both sides, a radius [of t]wo hundred miles—emigrant wagons—quite frequently herds [of] cattle, some large ones—settlements 15 or 20 miles

89. WW described this accident at Urbana, Ohio, in an interview in the St. Louis *Republican* on September 13 (reprinted in *AL*, XIV [1942–1943], 143).

90. A small piece at the side of this letter is missing.   91. See also *SD*, 207–208.

92. In an "interview" which WW himself prepared for a Denver newspaper, he

apart—no improved farms, no fences—(I mean along here)—but 600 miles of rolling prairie land—the pure cool mountain air delicious to breathe, (it is 3000 feet higher level here than Phila:)—I am in a sleeping car—(we left St Louis Saturday morning, came through Missouri—staid 4 days in Kansas)—left Topeka yesterday at 5 p m, & will be in Denver this evening—I have got along very well—(two days in Lawrence, Kansas, & two in Topeka)[91]—we are now about 1800 miles or over west of Phila:—I have good meals—

There is a very sick lady aboard the cars—her husband is taking her to Colorado, hoping it will help her—two beautiful little children—she is groaning as I write—

Denver Colorado[92] | Evening

I finish my letter at the hotel, the American House, where I am comfortably housed—This is evidently a fine large busy city, beautifully situated—Every thing goes all right so far with me—Shall stay here about four days—Col Forney hasn't come on here, but turned [back] at Topeka & has gone home—I am feeling well—better than before I started—hope you & George & Ed are all right—

Brother Walt

I have seen the mountains just before sunset—It was only ten minutes but I shall never forget it—

936. *To Louisa Orr Whitman* *10.11.* [*1879*]

2316 Pine street | St Louis Oct 11—noon

Dear Sister

I have been quite unwell, a bad spell with my head, worse than usual, nine or ten days—I kept up, but had no comfort—the last two days it is easier, & it is passing over apparently, for the present[93]—

Lou, I think I would like to have you or George put up my letters (not the books or papers) in a package & send them to me here, 2316 Pine street, if it dont make too big a package, *send by mail*, (postage will be 6 cts an ounce by mail)—(or if George thinks best, send by express—that is if the parcel is too big)—please do it soon as convenient—there is brown wrapping-paper & string in my room—I shall stay here perhaps two weeks

spoke ecstatically of the beauties of Denver (Doheny; *AL*, x [1937–1938], 84–87). See also *SD*, 209, 214–216.

93. WW had a serious relapse while he was in the West, and was not able to return to Camden until early in January, 1880.

longer—It is very hot here for this season, indeed as hot as we had it in July there in Camden—I go out most every day, Jeff has taken me out riding very often, & I have been everywhere within several miles, & in all the outer parts of the City which are the roomiest & the pleasantest by far of any city I have ever seen—Jeff is very kind indeed, & I am agreeably fixed here—& since I am here so far, & shall probably never come again, I have concluded to stay awhile—The girls are well & hearty & send their love—Hatty is down stairs piano-practising as I write—I have not written any thing for publication yet here, as I have not felt well, but I want to, before I leave, as this trip is a great revelation, especially the Colorado journey, & the mountains—

Lou, your letter was rec'd, & very glad to get it—Write again soon after receiving this—I have written to Hannah[94] and Mary[95] from here—I have just written to the Camden post office to send my letters on here for the present—Lou, this is a wonderful, wonderful country, & the richest city upon the whole (thousands and thousands of fine comfortable 5 or $6000 well built brick or stone houses, with gardens around them) & streets ahead of Chestnut st[96] & more crowded, &c &c—but there are just two things here you & I w'd never get used to, & would spoil all, that is the air you breathe is always tainted with coal smoke & pungent gas—& a perpetual dust & smut & little black motes, that forever smut your clothes & hands & face, all the time, night & day—So you see there are always some bad points, even to the greatest & best—But the folks here don't seem to mind it, or think it is any thing[97]—

So good bye for the present, Lou dear, & love to all—

Walt

937. *To William Torrey Harris*

2316 Pine Street | St Louis Oct 27 | '79

My dear Mr Harris[98]

Thank you for the Magazine & for the newspaper extracts, & especially for the Memoranda of the Concord school. I have looked over

94. Possibly on January 2 of this year Hannah had written one of her querulous, neurotic letters to WW. She was "anxious" because her husband, who, so she said, had written recently to WW, "cannot or does not say *one word of truth*" (LC).

95. Though WW wrote several times a year to Mary and never failed to send her a Christmas gift, usually $5, few of his letters to her are extant, and only two of her letters are known. See Gohdes and Silver, 207–208; Appendix C, December 23, 1883 (Yale).

96. Chestnut Street in Philadelphia.

97. In SD WW made no references to these liabilities (228).

98. Harris (1835–1909), the editor of *The Journal of Speculative Philosophy* from

all, & thoroughly read a great part—(the "School of Athens" in the magazine,[99] & the thoughts, & statistics about the Mississippi River, & about Chicago.)

I am better this fine morning—Should like to spend an hour in one of your public schools.

Walt Whitman

938. *To Robert Underwood Johnson*

2316 Pine street | St Louis Oct 29 '79

Dear Sir[1]

Your note has just reached me here, where I am temporarily stopping—I could not well tell you the names of "the young men referred to," because I spoke mainly of a class, or rather of a leaven & spirit—

My talk to the newspaper here the other day has been extracted from in so dislocated & awry a manner—was printed here indeed so badly—that I enclose you herewith a hastily corrected slip—If you know some N Y paper or literary publication in whose line it might come, & that would like to print it, use it for that purpose, at your discretion—& send me a couple of copies, (to Camden)—If not available that way, let it go—

I am laid up here disabled. My permanent address is 431 Stevens street Camden, New Jersey—shall return there about Nov 15—

Walt Whitman

939. *To Peter Doyle*   *11.5. [1879]*

2316 | Pine Street | St. Louis Missouri | Nov 5

Dear Pete

You will be surprised to get a letter from me away off here—I have been taking quite a journey the last two months—have been out to the Rocky Mountains and Colorado (2000 miles)—(Seems to me I sent

1867 to 1893, was the leading interpreter of Hegel and German philosophy in America and superintendent of schools in St. Louis. See also 941 and Traubel, I, 191.

99. Gertrude Garrigues' "Raphael's School of Athens," *The Journal of Speculative Philosophy*, XIII (October, 1879), 406–420.

1. Johnson (1853–1937) was on the staff of *The Century Magazine* from 1873 to 1913, and was U. S. ambassador to Italy in 1920 and 1921. WW included in this letter a news release based on an interview printed in the St. Louis *Post-Dispatch* on October 17, in which he criticized Bryant, Whittier, and Longfellow (reprinted in *AL*, XIV [1942–1943], 144–147). See also Johnson, *Remembered Yesterdays* (1923), 336, and *SD*, 224–225.

you a paper six weeks ago from Denver)—I got along very well till about three weeks ago when I was taken sick & disabled, & hauled in here in St Louis for repairs, have been here ever since—am fixed comfortable—Still somewhat under the weather, (but have no doubt I shall be well as usual for me before long)—Shall stay here probably two or three weeks longer, & then back east to Camden—

Pete, this is a wonderful country out here, & no one knows how big it is till he launches out in the midst of it—But there are plenty of hard-up fellows in this city, & out in the mines, & all over here—you have no idea how many run ashore, get sick from exposure, poor grub &c—many young men, some old chaps, some boys of 15 or 16—I met them every where, especially at the RR stoppings, out of money & trying to get home —But the general run of all these Western places, city & country, is very prosperous, on the rush, plenty of people, plenty to eat, & apparently plenty of money—Colorado you know is getting to be the great silver land of the world—In Denver I visited a big smelting establishment, purifying the ore, goes through many processes[2]—takes a week—well they showed me silver there by the cart load—Then in middle Colorado, in one place, as we stopt in a mining camp I saw rough bullion bars piled up in stacks outdoors five or six feet high like hay cocks—

So it is—a few make great strikes—like the prices in the lottery—but most are *blanks*—I was at Pike's Peak—I liked Denver City very much— But the most interesting part of my travel has been *the Plains*, (the great American *Desert* the old geographies call it, but it is no desert) largely through Colorado & Western Kansas, all flat, hundreds & even thousands of miles—some real good, nearly all pretty fair soil, all for stock raising, thousands of herds of cattle, some very large—the herdsmen, (the principal common employment) a wild hardy race, always on horseback, they call 'em *cow-boys* altogether—I used to like to get among them & talk with them—I stopt some days at a town right in the middle of those Plains, in Kansas, on the Santa Fe road—found a soldier[3] there who had known me in the war 15 years ago—was married & running the hotel there—I had hard work to get away from him—he wanted me to stay all winter—

The picture at the beginning of this letter is the St Louis bridge over

2. See also *SD*, 215.
3. E. L. (Ed. Lindsey), who lived in Sterling, Kansas, with whom WW stayed on September 24 and 25 (*SD*, 219; *WWR*, VII [1961], 10).
4 WW referred to the picture of the bridge on the stationery he used.
5. Mrs. Gilchrist's post card contained her address (University of California at Berkeley; *WWR*, VII [1961], 12). In her letter of October 6–12 she noted a recent

the Mississippi river[4]—I often go down to the river, or across this bridge —it is one of my favorite sights—but the air of this city don't agree with me—I have not had a well day, (even for me,) since I have been here—

Well, Pete, dear boy, I guess I have written enough—How are you getting along? I often think of you & no doubt you often do of me—God bless you, my darling friend, & however it goes, you must try to keep up a good heart—for I do—

So long—from your old

Walt

940. *To Anne Gilchrist*

> ADDRESS: Mrs Anne Gilchrist | 1 Elm Villas | Elm Row
> Heath street | Hampstead | London | England.
> POSTMARKS: Saint Louis | Nov | 10 | 2 PM | Mo.;
> London, N(?) | (?) | Paid | 24 No 79.

St Louis Missouri | (1000 miles west of Philadelphia) |
Nov 10 '79

My dear friend

Just rec'd your postal card—(your letter of a month ago from Haslemere rec'd—both forwarded here)[5]—Two months ago I started off (make or break) on a long jaunt west—have been to the Rocky Mountains (2000 miles) and Denver city, & Colorado generally—with Kansas and Missouri—wonders, revelations I wouldn't have miss'd for my life, the great central area 2000 miles square, the Prairie States, *the real America* I find, (& I find that I wasn't realizing it before)—but three weeks ago I was taken down sick & have come back & stopt here in St Louis ever since—am quite comfortable in quarters & shall soon be well enough to return home to Camden—

I enclose a rude map which will show you the line of my jaunt—the red lines are of my present trip, while the blue lines are of former journeys of mine, may interest you, & give you some idea[6]—

I shall probably be able to send you papers of my jottings before long

luncheon with Tennyson and the preparation of a new edition of her husband's *Life of William Blake* (Barrett; Barrus, 147–148).

6. The map is reproduced by Gilchrist, 253. Of this map Mrs. Gilchrist wrote to WW on December 5: "You could not easily realize the strong emotion, with which I read your last note and traced on the little map—a most precious possession to me which I would not part with for the whole world—all your journeyings—both in youth & now" (LC; Harned, 187).

—(my sickness has prevented hitherto what I designed to write)⁷—My sister, brother & neices are well—

Best Love

Walt Whitman

Lived a couple of weeks on the Great Plains (800 miles wide, flat, the greatest curiosity of all)—50 years from now this region will have a hundred millions of people, the most comfortable, advanced, & democratic on the globe—indeed it is all this & here, that America is for—

941. *To John Burroughs* *11.23.* [1879]

ADDRESS: John Burroughs | Esopus-on-Hudson | Ulster County | New York. POSTMARK: Saint Louis | Nov | (?) | Mo.

2316 Pine Street | St Louis Missouri |
Sunday afternoon Nov 23

Dear friend

I am still here—not yet (as an old Long Island aunt used to say) "not yet out of my misery" but I go out on the streets, or to the Public Library, most every day, & have no doubt I shall be as well as usual before long—I believe I told you I was in nice quarters & very comfortable here⁸—I send you Mrs Gilchrist's letter, which you needn't return⁹—Gilder's, which I also enclose, I wish you to send back, some time¹⁰—Upon receiving this, post me a card—tell me how the mother is & 'Sula, also the baby, also Smith¹¹—Just got a postal from Mrs Gilchrist giving her address.

1 Elm Villas   Elm Row
Heath street   Hampstead
London   Eng:

7. As his health improved, WW wrote articles for various newspapers. On November 12 he sent a letter to Marvin with a "piece" for Noyes, the editor of the Washington *Star*. "A Poet's Western Trip" appeared in the *Star* on November 15; for this information I am indebted to Professor F. DeWolfe Miller. On November 20 he forwarded a "piece" to Bonsall, the editor of the Camden *Daily Post*, perhaps the item on November 29 referring to a volume of prose based on his Western journey. In a letter to Erastus Brainerd on December 9 he enclosed a poem, "What Best I See in Thee," and a "¶ for Personal—in answer to request"; they appeared in the Philadelphia *Press* on December 17. See *WWR*, VII (1961), 10, 12.

8. Apparently WW wrote to Burroughs two days earlier about O'Connor; see the cryptic entry in his diary, *WWR*, VII (1961), 11.

9. Her letter of October 6–12 (see the preceding letter), which Burroughs gave to Mrs. Barrus.

10. R. W. Gilder, writing to WW from England on October 1, mentioned

The rough map enclosed gives you some idea of my present jaunt, on the red line (the blue lines are old travels of mine)[12]—I have seen the December *Scribner's*—What you say of me in *Nature & the Poets* thoroughly delights, satisfies & *prides* me[13]—I saw in the Library a late London *Fortnightly* in which J A Symonds, touching briefly but very commendingly & mentioning my name, makes quite an extract from *Dem[ocratic] Vistas* (summing up the general spirit of British literature as being markedly sombre & bilious)[14]—A B Alcott is expected here, to talk—I may see him—This is quite a place for the most toploftical Hegelian transcendentalists, a small knot but smart—the principal of them, W T Harris,[15] editor of *Speculative Philosophy*, has been often to see me, has been very kind, & I like him much—Probably ten days more will end my stay here, (but I am not fixed)[16]—A fine day as I write, & I am feeling comfortable. Best love to 'Sula—

Walt Whitman

942. *To Herbert Gilchrist* *12.15.* [*1879*]

ADDRESS: Herbert Gilchrist | 1 Elm Villas Elm Row |
Heath Street Hampstead | London | England.
POSTMARKS: Saint Louis | Dec | 15 | 6 PM | Mo;
London N. W. | C 7 | Paid | (?) 79.

St Louis Missouri U S A | Dec 15

Yours of 1st inst: rec'd, forwarded from Camden here—Have been & am quite ill here, getting better, & then bad relapses[17]— yesterday & to-day decidedly improving—Soon after you receive this shall probably be back in Camden—Will try to send you a photo such as you desire—I hear from John Burroughs—he is well—Arthur Peterson has gone to the Pacific, bound round the world, 3 years trip—Merry Christmas to you & all—

Walt Whitman

Charles Bonaparte Wyse, a young Irish poet, who wanted to visit, in his own words, "this most sympathetic of poets, for whose large & lofty nature my admiration is merged with love" (Historical Society of Pennsylvania).

11. Smith Caswell, to whom WW wrote (lost) on November 4.

12. Reproduced by Barrus, 188.

13. WW, in short, approved of his own contribution to Burroughs' article in *Scribner's Monthly* (see 933).

14. In his review of Arnold's *Selections from Wordsworth*, in *The Fortnightly Review*, n.s., XXVII (1879), 686–701, Symonds quoted WW's indictment of English literature as "no model for us," but added that if WW had read Wordsworth, "he would have made at least a qualified exception in his favor."

15. See 937.

16. WW did not leave St. Louis until January 4, 1880.

17. According to his diary, WW had "*very bad spells*" from December 7 to 10, "(sometimes tho't it all nearing the end)" (*WWR*, VII [1961], 12).

1880

943. *To John Burroughs*   *1.2–[3]. 1880*

St. Louis Jan 2 '80—4½ P M
Dear friend
        Yours of 29th Dec. with *the present* came safe to-day—Believe me
I feel the gift, & it comes just right too—John, please forward the enclosed slip to unknown friend[1]—
        The above is a fair picture of the great Mississippi Bridge, East St
Louis, where I have loafed many hours—only it sets up *much higher* than
the print gives—I dont believe there can be a grander thing of the kind
on earth[2]—

Jan 4[3]
        I leave here Sunday morning at 8, on my return east, & shall be due
in Philadelphia Monday evening, before 8—The last two or three weeks
I have been well, for me, & am so now—
        Your letter was deeply interesting to me, made me see Emerson no
doubt just as he is, the good pure soul—
        John, I sympathize with you in the arm, & the treatment too—
        A great thaw & dense fog here as I write—
                                                                    Walt Whitman

944. *To Anne Gilchrist*   *1.3. [1880]*

        ADDRESS: Mrs Gilchrist | 1 Elm Villas Elm Row |
        Heath Street Hampstead | London | England.
        POSTMARK: Saint Louis | Jan | (?).

St Louis, Missouri U S America | Jan 3d—evening
        I leave early to-morrow (Sunday) morning to go straight through

1880
        1. James T. Fields wrote to Burroughs on December 22, 1879, about sending
WW "a small Christmas remembrance in money [$100] . . . There is no occasion for
his being told who sends it" (Barrus, 189). On December 29 Burroughs sent the gift
without mentioning the donor's name (Manchester). On November 9 Bucke had offered
the poet $100 as a gift or a loan. WW wrote on the letter: "Kind letter from Dr
Bucke offering money (declined with thanks)" (Feinberg).
        2. The Eads Bridge.
        3. WW undoubtedly meant to write "Jan 3," since Sunday was the fourth.

east—due in Camden Monday evening, 7:30—Have been quite well the last three weeks, & am so now—All the folks well[4]—

W W

945. *To John P. Usher, Jr.*[5]

TRANSCRIPT.

431 Stevens Street | Camden, New Jersey Jan 14 '80

After I left you I went to Colorado, & there & in Missouri have spent the time since—came back here about a week ago—I sent you a little Volume—also two little pictures—You take the one you prefer & give the other to Linton—Send me word if they come safe. I am all right in health.

Walt Whitman

946. *To John Burroughs*   *2.21. [1880]*

ADDRESS: John Burroughs | Esopus-on-Hudson | Ulster Co: | New York. POSTMARK: Camden | Feb | 21 | N.J.

431 Stevens Street | Camden New Jersey Feb: 21

Dear friend

Yours of 20th, with enclosure, came safely[6]—Best thanks—Yours of four days previous also, telling me of Smith[7] and family's removal—which quite put me out too—Nothing very new with me, since my return—I have not written out for print any notes of my jaunt yet—I am well, considering—

Addington Symonds has sent me a copy of the American edition of

4. Mrs. Gilchrist replied to this post card on January 25: "Welcome was your post card announcing recovered health & return to Camden! . . . I wish one of those old red Market Ferry Cars were going to land you at our door once more! What you would have to tell us of Western scenes & life!" (LC; Harned, 190).

5. The son of Judge Usher, with whom WW had stayed at Lawrence, Kansas (see 934). On the same day he sent to the son a copy of *Memoranda During the War* and two photographs, one of which was intended for Linton J. Usher, probably the brother of Judge Usher (CB).

6. WW received a check for $25 from Burroughs on February 20 (CB).

7. Smith Caswell (see 898).

his "Greek Poets"[8]—Ruskin has sent to me [for] five sets of my books[9]—
Does Mrs Gilchrist write to you?[10] They are well—are all in London,
except Beatrice, who is in Switzerland—As I write (near noon Saturday)
it is snowing heavily here—Dr Bucke, of London, Canada is writing *my
life*—I suppose he has sent you his printed circular, asking information
&c. What do you think of the project?[11]

Walt Whitman

rec'd a letter from Mrs Ritter—She speaks of a musical composition
of her husband, to go with my "Two Veterans"—& asks if I am willing it
should be published—I answered expressing my consent[12]—

947. *To Frederick Locker-Lampson*

ADDRESS: Frederick Locker | 25 Chesham Street |
London S W | England. POSTMARKS: Camden |
Mar | 23 | N.J.; Philad'a, Pa. | Mar | 23 | Paid All.

431 Stevens Street | Camden New Jersey

U S America | March 21 '80

I send today same address as this card, my Vol: *Two Rivulets*
(as requested by Mr Rossetti)—Please let me know soon as it reaches
you safely[13]—

Walt Whitman

8. *Studies of the Greek Poets* was published in a two-volume edition in 1879–
1880 in Boston.
9. On February 16 WW received from Ruskin £10 for five sets of books through
Herbert J. Bathgate, to whom the books were sent on February 19 (*CB*). In a letter on
January 31, Bathgate quoted a recent communication from Ruskin: "The reason neither
he (yourself) nor Emerson are read in England is first—that they are deadly true—in
the sense of rifles—against all our deadliest sins. The second that this truth is asserted
with an especial colour of American egotism which good English scholars cannot, and
bad ones will not endure. This is the particular poison and tare by which the Devil has
rendered their fruit ungatherable but by gleaning and loving hands, or the blessed ones
of the poor" (O'Connor's transcription of the letter in Berg). The first sentence of this
letter was quoted in *The Athenaeum* on March 20, 1880. See also 909.
10. In her letter on January 25 Mrs. Gilchrist added this postscript: "Please give
my love to John Burroughs when you write or see him" (LC; Harned, 192). Beatrice
Gilchrist was studying medicine in Switzerland.
11. On January 19 Dr. Bucke asked for "a sketch of your interior life—especially
in relation to the conception and elaboration of 'Leaves of Grass.'" On February 3 he
acknowledged receipt of articles about the poet by O'Connor, Burroughs, and Mrs.
Gilchrist, and again requested more "inward and outward" facts about the poet's life.
On February 6 Bucke noted his recent lectures on WW's poetry and his arrangements
for the sale of his works, a subject to which he again referred in letters on March 18
and 23 (Manchester). In his "circular" soliciting information about the poet, Bucke
wrote: "I am myself fully satisfied that WALT WHITMAN is one of the greatest men, if
not the very greatest man, that the world has so far produced" (Berg).
12. Ritter (see 916) composed a setting for "Dirge for Two Veterans." The

I have also mailed to you a little photograph—

948.   *To Robert G. Ingersoll*[14]   4.2. [*1880*]

ADDRESS: Robert G Ingersoll | 1421 New York
Avenue | Washington D C. POSTMARK: Camden |
Apr | 3 | N.J.

431 Stevens Street | Camden New Jersey April 2
Thanks, dear Colonel, for your kind letter & for your books, which
have reached me safely—many thanks—I am well as usual of late years—
Walt Whitman

949.   *To Horace Howard Furness*   4.8. [*1880*][15]

ADDRESS: Horace Howard Furness | 222 West
Washington Square | Philadelphia. POSTMARK:
Camden | Apr | 9 | (?).

431 Stevens Street | Camden N J April 8 evn'g
Yours rec'd with the 5 from Roberts—All right, & thanks—I have
just returned from a short trip down in the Jersey Woods—all well—
W. W.

compilation of Henry S. Saunders, "Whitman Music" (typescript, 1938), lists Ritter's
composition: "Piano accompaniment for recitation, Op. 13. Schuberth, N.Y., 75¢."
    13.   Locker-Lampson acknowledged receipt of the book on April 7 (Donaldson,
236–237).
    14.   Ingersoll (1833–1899), the noted lawyer and agnostic, sent on March 25 (Man-
chester) what WW termed a "cordial, flattering, affectionate letter" (*CB*):
    "My dear Sir: | For years I have been your debtor. From you I have received
thousands of noble and splendid thoughts. You have been true. You have expressed your
honest thought. You have nobly defended the human body and the sacred passions of
man from the infamous placebos of the theologian. For this I thank you.
    I have taken the liberty to send you three small volumes of my own. You may not
agree with me. That will make no difference. I am battling for the right of people to dis-
agree.
    Thanking you again & again for all your noble words and wishing you many years |
I remain | Your friend | R. G. Ingersoll"
    WW heard Ingersoll lecture, evidently for the first time, on May 25: "talked
afterward with him a few minutes" (*CB*). On May 26 the Philadelphia *Press* noted that
"Walt Whitman . . . drank deep draughts of the orator's eloquence," and interpolated
into its reprint of the text at several points, "['Amen' from Walt Whitman.]" On the
following day Bucke, who had accompanied the poet, denied that WW had showed
either approval or disapproval. See also WW's comments on Ingersoll's religious views in
1000.
    15.   WW returned from a visit with the Staffords on April 8 (*CB*). On April 15
he sent the volumes to Howard Roberts (1843–1900), a sculptor whom he met on
March 12, 1879, at a dinner attended by Furness (*CB*).

949.1 *To Horace Howard Furness* [*4.13. 1880(?)*]¹⁶

ADDRESS: Horace Howard Furness | 222 West
Washington Square | Philadelphia. POSTMARK:
Camden | Apr | 13.

Camden Tuesday | noon
Yours rec'd—thanks, dear H—most likely I will come to the Club
Wednesday evn'g—but it is not certain—

W. W.

950. *To Harry Stafford* *4.13. [1880]*

ADDRESS: Harry L Stafford | (Glendale) | Kirkwood |
New Jersey. POSTMARK: Camden | Apr | 14 | N.J.

Tuesday evening April 13
Harry, if come up Thursday (say by the 5.13 p m train) go up to
the hall by 7 oclock, and make yourself useful, if you feel like it—Give this
note to the one it is address'd to¹⁷—ask for him there—(I will mention it
to him—he is bossing the thing for me)—act as usher, or door keeper, or
help in the box office—it will be fun for you—

Walt

951. *To William Reisdell* [*4.13. 1880*]

ADDRESS: William Reisdell | at the door Association |
Hall, cor 15th & | Chestnut | Phila:.

The bearer is a young friend of mine, Harry Stafford, who will
do any thing appropriate to assist at the Lecture, Thursday evening¹⁸—

Walt Whitman

16. April 13 fell on Tuesday in 1880. Perhaps WW was acknowledging receipt of
money for a set of his books which he sent to Furness on March 30 (*CB*).
17. See the following letter.
18. WW delivered "Death of Abraham Lincoln" at Association Hall, Philadelphia,
on April 15. He sent the lecture to the Chicago *Tribune* and to the Cincinnati *Commercial* on April 13 (not published), and forwarded to many of his friends the account of
the speech which appeared in the Camden *Daily Post* on April 16, the introductory
paragraphs of which are quoted in Basler's edition of *Memoranda During the War*
(1962), 30–33. See also 954.
19. This note is written at the top of a proof sheet entitled "Walt Whitman Last
Night," which WW had obviously placed in type before he gave his lecture. Although the

951.1 *To the Editor, the Camden* Press(?)   *[4.13(?). 1880]*[19]

I send you an authentic copy, so that if you care to you can print in *Friday morning's paper* (as I deliver it on the evening previous)—
W. W.

952. *To Harry Stafford*   *[4.19. 1880]*

> ADDRESS: Harry L Stafford | (Glendale) | Kirkwood | Camden County | New Jersey. POSTMARK: Camden | Apr | 19 | N.J.

Harry, I shall come down on Wednesday in the 4 p m train (as I said)—Nothing new—I am well—I had a good day yesterday (Sunday) perfect day—went over to late breakfast to the Steamer *Whillden*, Arch Street wharf[20]—every thing jolly and plentiful & sailor-like—there four hours—then in the evening to Col: Johnston's family[21]—I have got your blue flannel shirts for you—
W W

—love to your father & mother—

953. *To Herbert Gilchrist*   *4.24. [1880]*

> ADDRESS: Herbert Gilchrist | 5 Mount Vernon | Hampstead | London England. POSTMARKS: Haddonfield | Apr | 29 | N.J.; Philad'a Pa. | Apr | 25(?) | Paid All.

Kirkwood (Glendale) New Jersey | U S America |
April 24

Down here on one of my visits[22]—Mr and Mrs S[tafford] and all the young folks well as usual—E[dwin] is still over at Laurel

---

letters are not extant, probably the poet sent similar notes to the editors of the Chicago *Tribune*, the Cincinnati *Commercial*, and to the Philadelphia *Press*. There is, of course, the possibility that WW prepared this copy but did not send it. At the bottom of the sheet WW appended a note: "*to printer* dont mind the different type."

20.   On this visit WW was the guest of John L. Wilson, the ship's purser. See also 903.

21.   The artist whom WW visited frequently. (See *SD*, 235.) Apparently the Johnstons became annoyed at something WW said in his (lost) letter to their son on June 9, for on June 21 Scovel informed the poet that "Johns[t]on called here Sunday with your letter to his Boy." Scovel urged WW to apologize to the mother and thus "stop Johns[t]on's blathering" (Manchester).

22.   WW was at Glendale from April 23 to May 4 (*CB*).

Mills, & is well & hearty—H[arry] runs the store here—(the store is doing middling well)—M[ontgomery] and V[an Doran] and R[uth] and G[eorge][23] all right & growing fast—

Begins to look like spring—apple trees all in bloom, & the sprouting wheat a rich emerald, beautiful—(but just to-day is raw and half-raining & darkish)—the l[ecture] went off fairly, it was good fun for me, grave as the subject was—I sent you a short report—I am surprised about B[eatrice][24]—my health & strength fair—

W W

954. *To John Burroughs*

ADDRESS: John Burroughs | Esopus-on-Hudson | New York. POSTMARKS: Camden | May | 9 | N.J.; New York | May 10 | 5 AM | 80(?) | Recd. TRANSCRIPT.

May 9, 1880

I have just returned from a two weeks' visit down in the Jersey pine woods and had a good time in the simple, savage way I like. Am well for me, sunburnt and fat. (Some twitchings, but I don't dwell on them.) Nothing very new in my affairs, sell a couple of books occasionally.

I suppose you saw my Riddle Song in the first number of Sunnyside Press[25]—if not, I can send you the "Progress" with it in.

I delivered my Lincoln lecture last April 15 in Philadelphia—the same as the N.Y. version. I took it very coolly and enjoyed it—(No great audience—$90, after paying expenses).

Mr. Abbott of Boston wrote to me for a poem for his May 22d "Emerson Number" of the "Literary World." I could not write him a poem, but I sent him a little prose criticism which I believe he is to print in said number.[26]

Dr. Bucke is coming here to Philadelphia about May 22.[27] Eldridge

23. Harry's brothers, Montgomery (1862–1926?), Van Doran (1864–1914), and George (1869–1924). For Ruth, see 880.
24. WW sent to Mrs. Gilchrist the account in the Camden *Daily Post* on April 16 (CB). On March 28 Mrs. Gilchrist wrote at length about Beatrice's decision to give up her medical studies. Evidently during her stay in Switzerland Beatrice had decided that because she was intellectually incapable of becoming an ideal physician, she preferred to abandon the profession. Her sympathetic (but possessive) mother observed that "the profession was like a great man that swallowed her up from me" (Manchester). A year later she was a suicide (see 1054).
25. "A Riddle Song" appeared in the Tarrytown *Sunnyside Press* on April 3. For this information I am grateful to Mrs. Leslie V. Case, Curator of the Historical Society of the Tarrytowns, Inc.
26. "Emerson's Books (the Shadows of Them)" appeared in *The Literary* World on May 22 (XI, 177–178); it was reprinted in the New York *Tribune* on May 15, 1882, and later appeared in SDC (CW, v, 265–270). Edward Abbott was evidently associated

passed through here day before yesterday, returning to Washington . . . .

I had the May "Scribner" and read it leisurely down in the woods—
Stedman's Poe, and your "Notes."[28] (Scratched off my Emerson screed
down there, as it was there I rec'd Abbott's letter.)

I hear from the Gilchrists; they are in London; the daughter Beatrice
has suddenly abandoned her medical pursuits and intentions. Herbert
thrives.[29]. . .

I hear at second remove, and vaguely, that Symonds is writing a book,
or something, about me.

. . . When you write, send me Smith Caswell's exact post office
address, so I can send him papers.[30] Don't forget.

Is it *you* who says so emphatically the blackbirds don't sing? What
they call here the Virginia blackbird, with red dabbed shoulders—Harry
Stafford says they do, at times, and very finely (and I say so, too)—How
are you? How the arm? how the babe? Love to 'Sula—

955. *To Frederick Locker-Lampson*

ADDRESS: Frederick Locker | 25 Chesham Street |
Belgrave Square | London S W | England.
POSTMARKS: Camden | May | 28; Philad'a Pa. |
May | 28 | Paid All.

Camden New Jersey—U S America | May 26 1880
Frederic Locker | Dear friend

I rec'd yours of April 7th & believe me I fully respond to your
cheery greetings & kind wishes—I am pretty well for me (call myself now
a *half-paralytic*)—am much of the time in the country & on the water[31]—
yet take deep interest in the world & all its bustle, (though perhaps keeping it at arm's length)—I send you a Boston paper same mail with this, an
"Emerson number" that may interest you—a piece by me in it[32]—After

with *The Literary World*.
    27. Bucke arrived in Camden on May 25 (*CB*).
    28. Stedman's "Edgar Allan Poe" and Burroughs' "Notes of a Walker" appeared in
Scribner's Monthly, xx (1880), 47–64, 97–102.
    29. According to *CB*, WW sent to Burroughs Herbert Gilchrist's letter of May 9,
in which he described a visit to the studio of Dante Gabriel Rossetti (Barrus, 148–149).
    30. WW sent Caswell a copy of the Lincoln lecture on May 13 and other
clippings on May 23 (*CB*).
    31. WW was with the Staffords from May 19 to 23 (*CB*). His trips "on the
water" were confined to his rides on the ferry from Camden to Philadelphia.
    32. See the preceding letter. On June 15 Locker-Lampson acknowledged WW's
letter as well as the receipt of the Emerson article and "The Riddle Song" (Manchester).
On July 3 he requested that WW write a few lines in a Sir Walter Scott manuscript
(Manchester). In both letters he wrote about Tennyson's travels. The poet's son, Lionel,
was married to Locker-Lampson's daughter (see 884).

you are through with it, send it to Mr Tennyson, if you think proper—& should you do me kindness to write me again (I hope you will) send me Mr T's post office address (a good permanent one that whatever sent to will finally reach him)—

We are having a dash of the hottest weather here ever known, & I am standing it finely. I believe I sent you a month ago a little paper with my late piece "Riddle Song." The early summer is very fine here, & I am enjoying it, even heat and all—I live on the banks of the Delaware river like —I wish you could know my dear friend Mrs Gilchrist & her family, now 5 Mount Vernon, Hampstead—they were three years here in America— Best respects & love to you—

Walt Whitman

956. *To Anne Gilchrist*

ADDRESS: Mrs Gilchrist | 5 Mount Vernon
Hampstead | London England. POSTMARKS:
Camden | Jun | 3 | N.J.; Philad'a Pa. | Jun | 4 | Paid
All; London(?) | D6 | Paid | Ju 14 80.

Camden June 3 '80

I start at 8 this evening for Niagara Falls[33]—& so on farther west, North, &c. My address for six or eight weeks to come will be *care of Dr Bucke, London, Ontario, Canada.* I am well as usual—

W W

957. *To the New York* Tribune

Camden N J June 3 '80

N Y Tribune:

Find two dollars enclosed. Send me the *Daily Tribune* to that amount. Direct *Walt Whitman London, Ontario, Canada.*

W W

33. WW was accompanied by Dr. Bucke, who had come to Camden on May 25. See also SD, 236–237. On June 1 WW made a new will in which he appointed George and his wife as executor and executrix. At the time he had approximately $1000 in the Brooklyn Savings Bank and about $800 in the National State Bank in Camden. He bequeathed four-sevenths of his estate to Edward and one-seventh each to Mary Van Nostrand, Hannah Heyde, and his nieces, Mannahatta and Jessie (Whitman House, Camden).

Lengthy interviews with WW upon his arrival in Canada appeared in the London *Advertiser* and London *Free Press* on June 5. For transcriptions of these articles I am indebted to Miss Lillian R. Benson, of the Lawson Memorial Library, the University of Western Ontario in London.

34. C. H. Sholes, a shorthand reporter in Des Moines, Iowa, requested the 1876 edition on March 12, 1880. WW noted receiving an "ardent letter from him" in the

957.1 *To C. H. Sholes*[34]   *6.9.* [*1880*]

ADDRESS: C H Sholes | Short-Hand Reporter | Des
Moines | Iowa | U S A. POSTMARK: London | (?) |
Ju 10 | 8(?) | Ontario.

London Ontario Canada
    I have journey'd out here from my home in Camden, & this will
be my head-quarters & P O address for the next two months—(making
short leisurely visits to different parts of Canada, but coming back here)—
I have rec'd the two Iowa papers, with my soldiers' poem commemorative
of Decoration day—believe me I appreciate your kind mention—
    I am well as usual—Best remembrances—June 9—
                                                    Walt Whitman

958. *To Whitelaw Reid*

London Ontario Canada | June 17 '80
My dear Reid
    Herewith find a letter for the paper. The price is $12—If used *it
must be printed in the paper of Tuesday, June 22*[35] (or afterward)—The
letter is sent in the same manner as this *to several other papers* in Canada
& The States—(no *two* papers in same city)—one each in Boston, Phila:,
Cincinnati, Denver, &c—on the same condition—*this condition being a
point of honor*—It is sent to *no other but you* in New York—
                                                    Walt Whitman

    I am well for me—& having a good time—fine country, many fine
people here—I go all about leisurely but *this* will be my headquarters &
p.o. address all summer—

same month. Sholes on June 30 "saw Dr B[ucke] and myself in Dr B's library—London" (*CB*).
    35. "Summer Days in Canada" appeared in the London (Ontario) *Advertiser* on
the date stipulated. The article did not appear in the New York *Tribune*. It later was included in *SD*, 236–241, 345–346. According to *CB*, the article was sent to the following
papers, in addition to the two mentioned: Boston *Herald*, Philadelphia *Press*, Cincinnati
Commercial, Chicago *Tribune*, Detroit *Free Press*, Louisville *Courier-Journal*, Washington *Post*, and to Canadian newspapers in New Brunswick, Halifax, Toronto, and
Montreal. The price, except for the *Tribune*, was $10. WW offered the piece to the
Woodstown (N.J.) *Register* for $7, however, and to the Camden *Daily Post* without
charge. So far as I have been able to determine, after checking depositories in this
country and in Canada, only the Camden *Daily Post* and the Philadelphia *Press* printed
the piece.

959. *To the Editor, Denver* Tribune

London Ontario Canada | June 17 '80

Editor *Denver Tribune:*

Herewith find a letter from me for the paper. The price is $10—If used *it must be printed in the paper of Tuesday, June 22* (or afterwards) —The letter is sent in the same manner as this to several other papers (*one* each in New York, Boston, Philadelphia, Cincinnati, Chicago) on the same imperative condition—*this condition being a point of honor—* If used, please send me the pay by mail here, as this place will be my head-quarters for the ensuing two months.

Walt Whitman

960. *To the Editor, Toronto* Globe

June 17, 1880

[WW offered "Summer Days in Canada" to the Editor of the *Globe* at $10, and mentioned several other newspapers to which he was sending the article.]

961. *To Tilghman Hiskey*[36]   *6.20. [1880]*

ADDRESS: Tilghman Hiskey | Care of Ed: Lindell | ferry foot of Federal St: | Camden New Jersey | U S A. POSTMARK: Sarnia | (?).

Lake Huron June 20

Here I am way off in Canada West at a place called Sarnia[37] (800 miles northwest of Phila:)—I am writing this on Lake Huron. Weather fine, country ditto—these noble waters, the lake, & the St Clair river, dotted with steamers & sail craft, suit me first rate. Everybody is

36. Hiskey and Captain Respegius Edward Lindell worked for the Camden ferries (*SD*, 183). Lindell, who was also a viola player (*CB*), wrote to WW on July 4: "The boys read your little postal cards with much pleasure" (Manchester).

37. WW was in Sarnia, Canada, from June 19 to 24 (*CB*). See also *Walt Whitman's Diary in Canada*, 3–10.

38. WW's printed accounts of his activities in Canada were more colorful than his personal letters, usually cards, as also was his Canadian diary, printed by Kennedy in 1904. As was to be expected, WW was especially attracted to a number of young Canadians; see his letters to Thomas Nicholson. A young man named Norman McKenzie, a high school student in Sarnia, wrote to WW on June 29: "Do you remember the nice sail we had that night on the lake and river, I will never forget it, you, and I had such a pleasant time up in the bow of the boat when I sat on your lap and asked you questions

kind & hospitable. To-morrow I visit a Chippewa Indian village—next day an excursion up the lake—Thursday back to London.[38]

W W

962. *To John H. Johnston*   6.20. [*1880*]

ADDRESS: J. H. Johnston jeweler | 150 Bowery cor: Broome St | New York City U S A. POSTMARK: Sarnia | Ju(?) | (?).

Lake Huron June 20

Have come on here 100 miles further west (from London) & am very pleasantly quarter'd at Sarnia, Canada West, at the fine mansion of Mr Pardee,[39] (one of the Dominion officers.) Weather fine, country ditto —am especially pleas'd with these noble waters dotted with steamers & sail craft. I am writing this on Lake Huron—I am well so far—every body kind & hospitable—Al,[40] I wish you were here with me. To-morrow I go visiting a Chippewa Indian town. Return to London Thursday—

Love to Alma[41]—

W W

963. *To George and Susan Stafford*   7.13. [*1880*]

London Ontario Canada | July 13 p m

My dear friends all

I am still laid up here quite sick[42]—last week has been about the same as the previous one with me—I am up & drest, but dont go out—the weather is in my favor here—if it was as hot here as it seems to be most of the time in Philadelphia, it would go hard with me—They are as kind & good as can be, both Dr and Mrs Bucke—then I have a horse & little basket-wagon appropriated to me, to go out by myself, or be driven out

about the which you wrote about in your book named Two Rivulets" (Manchester). McKenzie wanted to visit WW in London, Canada, during the school vacation period. The poet undoubtedly met the boy when he visited a public school in Sarnia (*Walt Whitman's Diary in Canada*, 8–9); probably McKenzie accompanied the poet on "A Moonlight Excursion up Lake Huron" (7–8). WW replied (lost) to the boy's letter on July 4 (*CB*).

39. Timothy Blair Pardee was Commissioner of Crown Lands (*CB*).
40. Johnston's son, Albert.
41. Johnston replied to this card on June 26 (Manchester).
42. There is no reference to WW's illness in *CB*, but in a letter to O'Connor on July 1, Dr. Bucke noted that WW "has not been very well for a few days" (Trent). Though WW and O'Connor remained estranged until 1882, Bucke as well as Burroughs apparently kept O'Connor informed about the poet's activities.

just whenever I like—but to be deprest & sick prevents any thing being enjoyed—But enough of this—I have no doubt it will pass over, as it has times before—

The country here is beautiful with hay & wheat—they are just now in the height of harvest for both, & I watch them from my windows—We have rain every third or fourth day (just now a little too much)—Dr Bucke has a big house & a great many visitors—from two or three to five or six here nearly all the time—two fine young ladies staying all the time, with Mrs B & a governess for his younger children—I tell you if I felt well I should have great times—even as it is we have some jovial hours— last evening nothing would do but I had to come in the parlor & sing a couple of verses of "Black Eye'd Susan"—

If I get all right, the plan is three of us, Doctor & another man & myself, to go down the Lakes, and all down the St Lawrence, (the "Thousand Islands" &c) and so on far north to a great river, the Saguenay, I have always wanted to see—& so to Quebec—will take three weeks— but I will have to feel very different from what I do now—

Well I must close—How are you all? Is George well this summer? Is Harry well & in the store? This is about the *eighth* or *ninth* document I have sent to you from Canada—counting papers, letters, postal cards, &c. (one to Harry from Lake Huron) & *I havn't had a single breath of reply from any of you*—Susan, I enclose you an envelope—Love to all—
Walt Whitman

I shall get well, no doubt, & be coming back like a bad penny toward the end of the summer.

964. *To Peter Doyle*   7.24. [1880]

ADDRESS: Peter Doyle | M Street South bet: 4½ & 6th | Washington | D C | U S A.

London Ontario Canada | July 24 p m
Am all right again for me—was sick ab't three weeks—at times pretty bad—was well taken care of here—*the best of friends* both Dr and Mrs B[ucke] (as *human* as I ever met, both)—Monday morning next I start on a long Lake & St Lawrence river trip, 900 miles (mostly

43. WW left London on July 26 for his trip on the St. Lawrence River and returned to London on August 14. WW's account of this journey was published in the London (Canada) *Advertiser*, the Philadelphia *Press*, and the Camden *Daily Post* on August 26. He sent the article on August 23 to the Washington *Sunday Herald* (CB). Most of the material was later incorporated into SD, 241–245, 346–347. See also the

by steamer, comfortable, I reckon)—gone nearly three weeks, then back here[43]—May write you from Quebec. Your papers come—

W W

965. *To Franklin B. Sanborn*[44]   *7.25. [1880]*

TRANSCRIPT.

July 25.

Should be delighted to accept it [an invitation] and be with you all—but I start to-morrow morning on a three weeks' trip over the Lakes, the St. Lawrence & up the Saguenay—I have been pretty ill but am now better & the doctor thinks the trip will do me good.

966. *To Tilghman Hiskey*   *7.27. [1880]*

ADDRESS: Tilghman Hiskey | care of Ed: Lindell | ferry foot of Federal street | Camden New Jersey | U S A. POSTMARK: (?) | Jy 28 | 80 | Canada.

Toronto Canada | *July 27 a.m.—*

I have come on here, for a few days on my jaunt to the Thousand Islands at the mouth of St Lawrence—shall spend a week there, then to Montreal—then on to Quebec—then to the Saguenay river—am pretty well, considering—go all the way, 800 miles, by good steamboat—(the doctor thinks it will do me good)—This is a splendid city, right on Lake Ontario—I shall be back in September—I enjoy my journey & meet with plenty of friends—Show this to all the boys[45]—

Walt Whitman

967. *To Thomas Jefferson Whitman*   *8.1. [1880]*

ADDRESS: Thos: J Whitman | office Water Commissioner | City Hall | St Louis | Missouri | U S A. POSTMARK: (?) | (?) 2 | 80 | Canada.

Lakes of the Thousand Islands | St Lawrence River

Aug 1

I am here in a handsome little steam yacht (owned by the friend[46] I am staying with at Kingston.)—have been here some days cruising

account of this trip in *Walt Whitman's Diary in Canada*, 16–40.

44. WW noted sending this post card in *CB*.

45. Hiskey's fellow employees on the Camden ferries, many of whom were cited in *SD* (183). See also 961 and *Walt Whitman's Diary in Canada*, 19–20.

46. Dr. W. G. Metcalf; see the account in *Walt Whitman's Diary in Canada*, 17, 22–26. Metcalf was in Philadelphia with Bucke on May 25 (*CB*).

around—seems to me the most beautiful extensive lake & island region (over 1000 sq miles) on earth—I am pretty well—go to Montreal Tuesday —then to Quebec—then to the Saguenay river—back in London Aug 14—

W W

968. *To Albert Johnston*[47]   *8.16. [1880]*

ADDRESS: Al: Johnston | 1309 Fifth avenue | New York City | U S A. POSTMARKS: London | A.M. | Au 17 | 80 | Ont; K | 8–18 | 3–1.

London Ontario Canada | Aug 16—
Am back again here all right after my Quebec and Ha-ha bay trip—Have been away just three weeks & traveled over 1500 miles—the most comfortable & healthy trip I ever put in—Shall probably stay here a month yet—Write—Your old uncle & comrade

W W

969. *To Richard Worthington*

London Ontario Canada | August 21 '80
My dear Sir[48]
Some six months ago, you wrote me (I was then laid up ill in St Louis) that you had purchased the electrotype plates of the 1861 Boston ed'n of my *Leaves of Grass*—& making me some proposals about them— To which I made answer at the time, as you probably bear in mind.
Are you still the owner of those plates? Do you still hold to the offer then made by you? Please write me here.

Walt Whitman

970. *To Edward Carpenter*

ADDRESS: Edward Carpenter | 45 Brunswick Square | Brighton | England. POSTMARKS: (?) | Sp 28 | 1880 | U.S.A.; Brighton | 1 | Oc | 80 | E.

Niagara Falls America | September 28 1880
Dear Edward Carpenter[49]
I will just write you a line or two—it will be very short—but show

47. On June 26 Johnston informed WW of his son's recent activities (Manchester). The address on WW's card was crossed out, probably by Albert's father, and the card was redirected to "Equinunk, Wayne Co | Pa."

48. For a discussion of the Worthington affair, see 985, where Worthington's letter, which WW misinterpreted, is quoted. The poet's letter, probably written in October, 1879, is not known.

you that I am still in the land of the living, & have not forgotten you—
My four months jaunt in this noble ample healthy Canada country is done
(it has been a great success to me)—I have traveled several thousand
miles—mostly on the Lakes & St Lawrence, very comfortably & I am now
on my way back home to Camden, stopping here only a short time. I am
feeling heartier physically than for years—Camden will be my permanent
P O address—Love to you—

Walt Whitman

971. *To Anne Gilchrist*

Niagara Falls, America | September 28 '80

My dear friend

I must write you a line or two but it will be a short letter—I am on
my way back to Camden, stopping here only temporarily. Have had a
very successful summer trip—have jaunted over 3000 miles, no mishaps,
and generally everything working in well—have met with many friends,
& kindness & good will everywhere—I am as well as usual again the last
two months, indeed I think I am better than usual—the climate, country
&c agree with me & I almost hate to leave them. Dr and Mrs Bucke have
been like brother & sister, unvaryingly kind & helpful & affectionate—Dr
has several times spoken of you—

I rec'd your letter of a month since[50]—My brother & sister are well, &
matters as usual with them—Dr B wishes to be remembered—he has
come on to the Falls with me. Peter Doyle has also come on from Washington, to spend a short time here & then return with me to Philadelphia.
Love to you, dear friend, & to Beatrice, Herbert & Grace—

Walt Whitman

972. *To William Torrey Harris*

ADDRESS: W. T. Harris | p o box 2398 | St Louis |
Missouri U S A. POSTMARK: St. Louis (?) | Sep |
(?) | 10 AM | Received.

Niagara Falls Sept 28 '80

Have finished my summer tour of St Lawrence & the Thousand
Islands &c.—have jaunted over 3000 miles mostly river & Lakes—(I

---

49. Carpenter had written to WW twice in 1880, on March 28 and on July 1
(Manchester). In the former he asked whether WW approved the publication of an
inexpensive English edition of *Leaves of Grass*.

50. On August 22 Mrs. Gilchrist wrote to WW about her family, and concluded:
"Send me a line soon, dear Friend—I think of you continually & know that somewhere &
somehow we are to meet again & that there is a tie of love between us that time & change
& death itself cannot touch" (LC; Harned, 194).

believe I sent you a couple of my current letters here in Canada)⁵¹ & am now on my way home to Camden N J (stopping here a short time)—I am unusually well & robust for a half-paralytic—Camden will still remain my address. Thanks for the *Journals*⁵² which have reach'd me—

Walt Whitman

973. *To Frederick Locker-Lampson*   9.28. [*1880*]

ADDRESS: Frederick Locker | 25 Chesham Street | London S W | England. POSTMARK: Hamilton | Sp 28 | 80 | Canada.

Niagara Falls America | *Sept: 28—*

I have been spendin[g] the whole summer in Canada, mostly on the Lakes & St Lawrence river—have had a good time—& it has done me good—have leisurely traveled over 3000 miles land & water—now on my way home to Camden New Jersey, my permanent address—Am now pretty well for a half-paralytic, better than for some years⁵³—

Walt Whitman

974. *To Rudolf Schmidt*

ADDRESS: Rudolf Schmidt | Baggesen's Gate No 3 | Copenhagen | Denmark. POSTMARKS: Hamilton | Sp 28 | 80 | Canada; K | Omb. 1 | 14–10–80.

Niagara Falls—America | *Sept 28 '80*

I have been spending the summer in Canada, especially on the Lakes, & the Thousand Islands, & the river St Lawrence—have jaunted leisurely over 3000 miles—It is a singularly healthy, beautiful interesting country, this Canada, (it is as large as the U S—population, 4½ millions, very advanced, very sound, a good race, ⅔ds English ⅓ French)—I am now on my way home to Camden—address me there as formerly—I am unusually well for a half-paralytic—

Walt Whitman

51. The newspaper accounts of his journey (see 958 and 964).
52. *The Journal of Speculative Philosophy*, of which Harris was the editor (see 937).
53. Locker-Lampson noted receipt of WW's post card on October 13 (Donaldson, 237). In January, 1881, WW sent copies of his article in *The North American Review* (see 994), one of which was to be forwarded to Tennyson. The Englishman acknowledged the gift on January 31 (Historical Society of Pennsylvania).
54. WW was with the Staffords from October 9 to 13 (*CB*). "Home Again" appeared in the Camden *Daily Post* on September 30 and was reprinted with the title "Walt Whitman Safe Home" in the London (Ontario) *Advertiser* on October 4. For

975. *To Herbert Gilchrist*   10.10. [*1880*]

ADDRESS: Herbert Harlakenden Gilchrist | Keats'
Corner Wells Road | Hampstead | London | England.
POSTMARKS: Haddonfield | Oct | 12 | N.J.;
Philadelphia | Oct | 12.

Kirkwood (Glendale) New Jersey | U S America
Oct 10

Have come back all right from my Canadian trip, & now spending
a few days down here[54]—A fine autumn sunny hazy peaceful Sunday—
woods, field, sky, delightful—The S[tafford]s much as usual—Mrs S
quite well—if you were here you would not see any difference from over
at the Creek—Mr S has had a very fair summer, but is not very rugged—
Ed has just been home, with his nag, looks fine—M[ontgomery] well,
up in Camden—D[ebbie] and J[oseph Browning] well, having good
times riding about the same as of old—rec'd your paper—

Walt Whitman

976. *To Thomas Nicholson*   10.14. [*1880*][55]

ADDRESS: Thomas Nichelson | Asylum for the Insane |
London | Ontario Canada. POSTMARKS: (?) | Oct |
15 | N. J.; London | Oc 16 | 80 | Ont.

431 Stevens Street | Camden New Jersey U S A |
Oct: 14

Dear Tom

I got home all safe—We stopped a day & a night at Niagara &
had a first rate time—Started the next morning early in an easy comfortable palace car & went on like a streak through New York and
Pennsylvania—got into Philadelphia after 11 at night—(we were an
hour late,) but the city looked bright & all alive, & I felt as fresh as a
lark—

I am well, my summer in Canada has done me great good—it is not

this information I am indebted to G. W. Spragge, archivist of Ontario.

55. In *CB* WW noted sending this letter. Nicholson, who was twenty-one, was an
attendant in Bucke's asylum from April 12, 1880, to September 14, 1882. In his only
extant letter to the poet, on December 6, 1881, Nicholson urged WW to come to London,
Ontario: "Every body *loves you*, and you waunt be no Stranger this Time" (Feinberg).
Perhaps Nicholson, or one of his friends, is referred to in the following description in
Gosse's *Critical Kit-Kats* (1896), 104–105: "The other . . . was a photograph of a very
handsome young man in a boat, sculling. . . . He explained . . . that this was one of
his greatest friends, a professional oarsman from Canada, a well-known sporting
character."

only the fine country & climate there, but I found such good friends, good quarters, good grub, & every thing that could make a man happy—

The last five days I have been down on a jaunt to the sea-shore[56]— got back last night—It is a great change from the beautiful grass and spacious lawns there around the Asylum—for miles as far as the eye can reach nothing but flat gray sand & the sea rolling in—& then looking off at sea, always ships or steamers in sight out in the offing—I sat hours enjoying it, for it suits me—I was born & brought up near the Sea, & I could listen forever to the hoarse music of the surf—Tom, I got your paper & handbill—*Good for you, boy*—believe me I was pleased to know you won—best respects to Tom Bradley, Batters—and Dick Flynn & O'Connor[57]—Show them this letter—also Canuth[58]—Write to me—I hope you practice & write as I told you—

                                            Walt Whitman

977. *To Isaac Hull Platt* (?)   **10.22. [1880?]**[59]

                    431 Stevens Street | Camden New Jersey | Oct 22 p m
Dear Sir

Thanks for your kind letter, just rec'd & read with greatest interest & pleasure—I sell my books, Centennial or author's edition, myself— Circular enclosed—will I think give you the information you ask—
                                            Walt Whitman

978. *To Frederic Almy*[60]

ADDRESS: Frederic Almy | 151 Pawtucket Street | Lowell | Mass:. POSTMARKS: Camden | Oct | 30 | N.J.; Lowell Mass. | Nov | 1 | 9(?) AM | Carrier.

                            Camden New Jersey Oct: 30 '80
I to-day forward by mail (same address as this card) my two Vols:

56. According to *CB*, WW was with the Staffords from October 9 to 13, not at the seashore, unless he was with Harry in Atlantic City.

57. These young men, like Nicholson, were employees in Bucke's hospital. Thomas Bradley, age 23, served at the asylum from September 6, 1876, to April 30, 1877, when he was discharged. He rejoined the staff on June 1, 1877, and was employed until April 30, 1882, holding such positions as mail driver, assistant baker, and messenger. He again returned to the asylum on July 1, 1882, only to resign three months later.

Edward Batters, who was 42, worked at the hospital in 1873 and 1874, until he was discharged. He was rehired in 1875 and remained until March 31, 1881, at which time he was a supervisor.

Richard Flynn, age 24, was employed from 1875 to 1885, working as a messenger, a gardener, a night watchman, and a stoker.

Henry O'Connor, age 22, was an attendant from August 15, 1879, until he was discharged on November 12, 1880.

according to your letter (enc[losure] rec'd: thanks)—Will you please
send me a postal notifying me on their safe arrival.

Walt Whitman

979. *To Harry Stafford*   *10.31.* [*1880*]

431 Stevens street | Camden Sunday noon Oct | 31

Dear Hank

I have just written a postal to your folks to say I wouldn't be down
till Saturday afternoon (Ashland Station) & I thought I would write you
a line—Every thing goes well with me these times considering—health &
feelings better since I come back from Canada than for nine years past—
(one of the ferry men told me he heard a lady say to another on the boat
yesterday as I went off, "He looks older & savager than ever, dont he?
but there is a something—I dont wonder that Aleck is all taken up with
him" &c &c—*Aleck*, the ferry man thought, was her husband)—

I am selling quite a good many of my books now[61]—gives me something to do every day—so you see I have enough to put me in quite a good
humor. Then upon going to look where I had my bound books boxed &
stored away, up in the garret at Mr. Scovel's, (I hadn't been to look after
them in three years)—I found them not only in good condition but found
I had twice as many as I calculated—yesterday I had the express man to
bring two boxes of 'em home, & left three boxes there still. I got a letter
from the PM General, Canada[62]—the missing letter not there—I am convinced it came to Haddonfield—

2.40 afternoon

I have just had my dinner & am up here in my third story room
finishing this—it is a bright sunny day here, after the three days' storm—
I have been alone all day, but busy & contented—my room is just right

For this information I am grateful to Dr. D. M. Wickware, the superintendent of
the Ontario Hospital at London, Ontario.

58. Probably WW referred to Gomley Canniff, an eighteen-year-old attendant,
who worked at the asylum from January 1 to November 30, 1880.

59. In *CB* WW noted sending a circular to Platt on October 22, but on the following page, on Platt's calling card, he wrote: "Oct 23—Letter from, *very warm ab't poems,*
& asking ab't books—I sent circular . . . (I sent the letter to Dr Bucke)." Platt
(1853–1917) was a New York attorney, a Baconian, and an early biographer of WW
(1904). The poet sent the 1876 edition on October 27 (*CB*).

60. Almy was a graduate of Harvard College, a friend of Jane Addams, and the
founder in 1885 of the Saturn Club in Buffalo. For this information I am indebted to
Harold Olmstead. Almy sent $10 to WW on October 27 (Feinberg).

61. The records of book sales in *CB* are numerous at this time.

62. WW had written to the Postmaster General at Ottawa, Canada, about October 13 (*CB*).

for all the year except the very hottest months—the sun pours in here so nice, especially afternoons—I wish you was here to-day, Hank (I havn't got any *wine* though)—I see Hoag[63] yesterday, & Seigfried too—every body is flying around—Election excitement now, very hot. Sports, newspaper men, & politicians busy as the devil in a gale of wind—Love to you, dear son—I shall be down Saturday[64]—

Your old Walt

980. *To A. Williams & Company*

ADDRESS: A Williams & Co: | Booksellers | 283 Washington Street | Boston Mass:. POSTMARK: Camden | Nov | 1 | N.J.

431 Stevens Street | Camden New Jersey Nov 1 '80

According to your letter just rec'd I forward the two Vols. L of G and T[wo] R[ivulets] by same mail with this. Please send me the pay $7 here by mail[65]—

Walt Whitman

981. *To Anne Gilchrist*   11.10–16. [1880]

ADDRESS: Mrs Gilchrist | Keats' Corner | Wells Road | Hampstead | London | England. POSTMARKS: Camden | Nov | 17 | N.J.; London, N.W. | Z A | No 29 | 80.

Nov: 10th—Down at the Staffords |
Kirkwood (Glendale)

I still keep quite well considering—have been down here the past week[66]—every thing much the same as of old with our friends the S[tafford]s—Mr and Mrs S, and all their sons and daughters—Harry is down at Atlantic City, telegraph operator at a RR station but is going to Camden, same position—

---

63. F. A. Hoag was a young reporter who died on June 17, 1890, at age thirty-five.
64. WW was at Glendale from November 6, Saturday, to November 16 (*CB*).
65. This transaction with the Boston book dealer was noted in *CB*. The card was marked by the bookseller—"Paid Nov. 3/80 $7.00."
66. WW was in Kirkwood from November 6 to 16 (*CB*).
67. Stedman's "Walt Whitman" appeared in the November issue of *Scribner's Monthly* (47–64); it was reprinted in *Poets of America* (1885), 349–395. For the reactions of WW's friends to Stedman's article, see Barrus, 192–195, and letter 986.
68. On July 17, 1880, Mrs. Gilchrist informed Louisa Whitman that some Americans had purchased Percy's "Dephosphorization process"; see Amy Haslam Dowe, "A Child's Memories of the Whitmans" (unpublished). See also 907.
69. Analysis of WW's records in *CB* of book sales in 1880 shows that purchasers

A fine week down here for me—the finest sort of mellow sunny autumn weather—the old woods fine & I in it for hours every day (sometimes I think it as good in its way as the Creek)—I go about nearly the same, my lameness no better (occasionally pretty bad, worse) but my feelings of comfort & strength in general better than former years—often decidedly better—

13th Saturday—Still here—We drove over yesterday (Mrs S and I) to the old place at Timber Creek & down by the pond—I thought it beautiful as ever along the creek and banks—

This month *Scribner* has a long criticism by E C Stedman on L of G & author, quite funny—"I would & I would not" style, with a bad portrait[67] —Dr. B[ucke] is furious—Burroughs thinks it well enough & will do good—probably the truth between the two—

I see in the papers allusions to "the Gilchrist Thomas process" & its adoption in some of the great works & foundries—So I think it must be a permanent triumph—I congratulate you all & of course Percy especially (for all I dont know him)[68]—

Sunday 14th

Rather cold, the feeling of snow, but dry & pleasant in a way— I sell some of my books occasionally—have quite a supply left—of late have had more *American* purchasers than foreigners—(different from previous experience)[69]—

Rec'd your letter of two months since in Canada—it was very welcome—I wrote a postal card from here to Herbert, over a month ago[70]— Did he get it? Is the address on *this* right? Do you see any thing of my friend Josiah Child?[71] A gentleman named Ingram[72] (in the Engineer's office, London General Post Office) has written to me twice in the interest of publishing a Vol: of my prose writings in London[73]—He seems to be a nice sort of man (is the author of an edition of Poe in London)—I think I shall give him your address & ask to call on you.

Love to you all—where is Beatrice, & how?

Walt Whitman

were chiefly Americans.

70. See 975.

71. On July 10 Child informed WW that Trübner & Co. had exhausted its supply of *Leaves of Grass*. He sent a draft for $80.50, and ordered ten copies of *Leaves of Grass* and five of *Two Rivulets* (Manchester).

72. WW wrote on September 19 (*CB*) to John H. Ingram (1848–1916), who, in addition to the edition of Poe's writings, wrote *Chatterton and His Circle* and *Christopher Marlowe and His Associates*.

73. After reading this letter to his mother, Herbert Gilchrist wrote on November 30 about the publication of WW's prose writings in England. He wanted to illustrate the volume which he thought was to be entitled "Pond Musings by Walt Whitman" (LC; Harned, 195–196).

Nov 16—I return home to Camden to-day—Every thing as usual—I am well—fine November weather, crisp & sunny—

WW

982. *To Harry Stafford* *11.12.* *[1880]*

At the Store Glendale Friday afternoon Nov: 12

Dear Hank

I am staying here yet—Yesterday Deb[74] came over here about 2 o'clock & we took Modoc & went over (your Mother & I) to the old place[75]—went down to the pond & all around—I thought the pond, & creek, the big part there to the west, looked beautiful as ever—the big spring, the other way (east) is all stopped up, disappeared altogether—the big south field Wes has got in wheat—otherways things look not much different—pretty lonesome though, as we didn't see chuck nor child nor any living thing on the premises—(but I suppose it will be different when Lizzie[76] gets there)—but the jaunt about there & the ride, made us a very pleasant three hours—Nothing new here—Your folks have been up to town twice this week—Van once & your father once—they were all gathering apples for cider yesterday, & to-day are burying the cabbages—Hieniken[77] comes over as usual (likes his cider)—this morning I went over to the school library & got six or seven books—he took me—

I go around here the same as ever—jaunt in the woods & loafe about a good deal, (but always sure to be back at meal time)—heavy storms this week two nights, but the days bright & clear every time—

& you, dear son, how do you make out down there? We think & speak about you often—as I write, the wind is blowing a south west gale around here—I suppose it is pretty cold at Atlantic[78]—It is now ¼ after 1—the school children are playing & making a great racket, & I see Hiniekin just come down from his dinner—the shoemaker has been over for his pitcher of cider—and there I hear Ruth calling me to come to my dinner—so I must bid good bye to you for the present, & God bless you, my darling son—

W W

I think of going up to Camden to-morrow or Sunday—most likely Sunday—Mont expects to go over with Ben Sharp soon—

74. Harry's married sister, Deborah Browning.
75. The former home of the Staffords, where WW had recuperated in the late 1870's.
76. Lizzie H. Hider was shortly to marry Wesley Stafford, Harry's cousin (see 1005). They occupied the former home of Susan and George Stafford (*CB*).
77. Theodore Hieniken, apparently a friend of the Staffords, was occasionally men-

983. *To Richard Watson Gilder*   *11.17.* [*1880*]

ADDRESS: R W Gilder | office Scribner's Magazine |
743 Broadway | New York City. POSTMARKS:
Camden | Nov | 17 | N.J.; New-York | Nov 17 |
8 PM | Rec'd.

431 Stevens street | Camden New Jersey Nov: 17
My dear friend
    I do myself the real pleasure of presenting you with a set of my
books—which are sent by same mail with this—I have inscribed Mrs G's
name with yours on the fly leaf, & please show her this as a testimony of
my remembrance & affection to you both⁷⁹—
                                                        Walt Whitman

    I am well for me—have been down two weeks in the Jersey woods
—return'd last evening—

984. *To Edward G. Doggett*⁸⁰

                          431 Stevens Street | Camden New Jersey
                                       U S America | Nov: 23 '80
    Yours rec'd with Enc: thanks—I forward to day by mail (to same
address as this card) my Two Vols: as requested—Will you please send
me a postal soon as they reach you safely notifying me?
                                                        Walt Whitman

985. *To Richard Watson Gilder*

                          431 Stevens street | Camden New Jersey |
                                              Nov: 26 '80 p m
My dear Gilder
    I wonder if you can help me in the matter of wh' the enclosed two
pp. are a statement—Havn't you connected with your establishment some

tioned in *CB*, but spelled Heineken, Hieneken, and Hinieken.
    78. Harry was working at the time in Atlantic City, N. J.
    79. Mrs. Gilder thanked WW for the books on November 20 (Feinberg; Traubel,
II, 118–119). Inscribed copies of the two books—"from the author | with love"—are
in the possession of Gilder's daughter, Rosamond Gilder.
    80. Doggett lived in Bristol, England (*CB*).

one learn'd in copyright law & its infractions, that could take the thing in hand? *injunct* Worthington or something?[81]

I have sent a duplicate of the two pages to John Burroughs—& asked him to call & see you—I am ab't the same as of late years but unable to travel & mainly helpless.

Walt Whitman

Nothing must be done involving heavy fees, as I couldn't pay them—

NOV: 26 1880

R Worthington 770 Broadway New York about a year ago bo't at auction the electrotype plates (456 pages) of the 1860–'61 edition of my book *Leaves of Grass*—Plates originally made by a young firm *Thayer & Eldridge* under my supervision there and then in Boston, (in the spring of 1860, on an agreement running five years.) A small edition was printed and issued at the time, but in six months or thereabout Thayer & Eldridge failed, and these plates were stored away and nothing further done—till about a year ago (latter part of 1879) they were put up in N Y city by Leavitt, auctioneer, & bought in by said Worthington. (Leavitt, before putting them up, wrote to me offering the plates for

---

81. WW's account of his dealings with Richard Worthington ("Holy Dick" was the poet's epithet later), a New York publisher, is somewhat garbled. (WW's version in 1888 was filled with inaccuracies; see Traubel, I, 195–196, 250–251). Worthington bought the plates of the 1860 edition after they had been sold at auction by George A. Leavitt & Co. for $200 "to a Mr Williams" (see 988). After the plates came into Worthington's hands, he wrote to the poet on September 29, 1879: "As the edition is not complete although subject as I understand to a copyright of ten per cent it seems to me that it would be better for all parties to have it completed. If this idea meets your views on the subject I would be willing to make you an immediate payment of $250.00 on account and will do everything in my power to make the book sell" (Yale). Despite WW's rejection of Worthington's offer, the publisher began to run off copies from the plates.

On August 20, 1880, Dr. Bucke informed Eldridge that he had lately discovered many copies of the 1860 edition (Barrus, 197–198). Probably at Bucke's suggestion WW wrote on the following day to inquire whether Worthington still owned the plates (see 969). He probably wrote to the same effect on September 19 (*CB*). After WW was offered a copy of the pirated book in Philadelphia on November 20, 1880, he decided to take action against Worthington.

Early in December Scovel went to New York and compelled Worthington to pay a royalty of $50. On December 6 WW sent a receipt to the publisher: "Rec'd from R Worthington (thro Jas M Scovel) Fifty-Dollars on account of royalty in selling(?) my book *Leaves of Grass* W. Whitman" (*CB*). It would appear, despite the poet's later observations, that the settlement permitted Worthington to continue his sales (perhaps only of bound copies) so long as he paid a royalty. On December 6 Scovel asked to be reimbursed: "I expended $9.50 in pursuit of the *recalcitrant, pirate* Worthington, in New York City" (Feinberg). WW paid Scovel $10 (*CB*).

On May 20, 1881, WW informed Osgood & Co. that Worthington had "sold languid surreptitious copies—can be stopt instantly by me & will be" (see 1030). On August 11, 1881, WW "call'd on R Worthington . . . & had an interview of over half an hour—I told him emphatically he must not print and publish another copy of L. of G. from the '60–'61 plates—if so it would be at his peril—he offered $50 down if I would warrant his printing a new edition of 500 from said plates, which I peremptorily

sale. I wrote back that said plates were worthless, being superseded by a larger & different edition—that I could not use them (the 1860 ones) myself, nor would I allow them to be used by any one else—I being the sole owner of the copyright.)

However it seems Leavitt did auction them & Worthington bo't them (I suppose for a mere song)—W. then wrote to me offering $250 if I would add something to the text & authenticate the plates, to be published in a book by him. I wrote back (I was in St Louis at the time, helpless, sick) thanking him for the offer, regretting he had purchased the plates, refusing the proposal, & forbidding any use of the plates. Then & since I thought the matter had dropt. But I have to add that about September 1880 (I was in London Canada at the time) I wrote to Worthington referring to his previous offer, then declined by me, and asking whether he still had the plates & was disposed to make the same offer: to which I rec'd no answer. I wrote a second time; and again no answer.[82]

I had supposed the whole thing dropt, & nothing done, but within a week past, I learn that Worthington has been slyly printing and selling the Volume of *Leaves of Grass* from these plates (must have commenced early in 1880) and is now printing and selling it. On Nov. 22, 1880, I

declined—Mr Williams & one or two clerks in the store heard the conversation—R. W. paid me $25 due me on back sales—I shall not trouble him for any thing past—but shall hold him to strict account for what is done after this date" (*CB*).

Apparently WW again must have consented to Worthington's selling bound copies, for on July 25, 1882, the publisher wrote to the poet: "I Enclose you check for 44.50 being Copyright on Leaves of Grass sold since you last received check" (Yale). In 1888 WW recalled only the first payment and "another twenty-five dollars paid at another time—I don't know when. I acknowledged both, on account, as royalty" (Traubel, I, 250).

During the 1880's Worthington ran off additional copies. In 1885 WW, again disturbed about the publisher's activities, wrote about the piracy in a lost letter to Eldridge, who advised him on August 17 to write to a firm in New York which made "a specialty of copyright cases" (Feinberg). Evidently WW did not write to the firm, but again availed himself of the services of Scovel. About November 5 he noted "from R Worthington $24: through J M S" (*CB*).

David McKay, the Philadelphia publisher of WW's writings, became concerned about the plates. On February 12, 1886, WW noted "a visit from D McKay, ab't the Worthington plates—subscription to purchase" (*CB*).

In a letter to the editor of *The Critic* on June 2, 1888 (XII, 272), Kennedy, without mentioning Worthington's name, asserted: "Mr. Whitman has not received a cent of copyright on them. . . . I hope that this note may be the means of inducing some rich friend of Whitman's to put a lawyer on the case, and bring the New Yorkers who are issuing the spurious books to justice." Interestingly, WW neglected to inform Kennedy of the royalties ($143.50) he had accepted (Traubel, I, 250). It is also noteworthy that, despite Kennedy's remarks, WW refused to stop the publisher: "I am averse to going to law about it: going to law is like going to hell: it's too much trouble even if we win" (Traubel, I, 195, and see I, 251). But he was willing to go to law at someone else's expense.

Worthington continued to use the plates until they were purchased by the literary executors after WW's death (*CW*, VIII, 280).

82. The lost letter of September 19 (*CB*).

found the book, (printed from those plates,) at Porter & Coates' store, cor: 9th & Chestnut Sts. Philadelphia. P & C told me they procured it from Worthington, & had been so procuring it off & on, for nearly a year.

First I want Worthington effectually stopt from issuing the books. Second I want my royalty for all he has sold, (though I have no idea of ever getting a cent.) Third I want W. taken hold of, if possible, on criminal proceeding.

I am the sole owner of the copyright—& I think my copyright papers are all complete—I publish & sell the book myself—it is my sole means of living—What Worthington has done has already been a serious detriment to me. Mr Eldridge, (of the Boston firm alluded to) is accessible in Washington D C—will corroborate first parts of the foregoing—(is my friend)—

Walt Whitman
431 Stevens Street
Camden New Jersey

986. *To John Burroughs*

431 Stevens Street | Camden New Jersey |
Nov 26 '80 |p m

Dear John

What could you do, towards helping me in the matter by these two pages?—badly copied, but I can't write them out—I have sent duplicates of the two pp to Watson Gilder & said I requested you to see him soon as convenient.

I am ab't as usual, except the locomotion business is worse, making a bad drawback, rendering me indeed at times practically helpless. I rec'd your letter—I thought Stedman's article full as good as could be expected[83]—Marvin call'd here yesterday, but I was absent & didn't see him—

Walt

83. Burroughs on November 2 informed WW of Stedman's difficulties in getting his article printed in *Scribner's Monthly* over the objections of Holland, the editor, and observed: "The article is candid & respectful & that is all we can ask. . . . it seems to me that the adverse criticisms in the paper are all weak & ineffectual, & that he is truly at home only when he is appreciative. How gingerly he does walk at times to be sure, as if he feared the ground underfoot was mined" (Hanley). Interestingly, WW did not

987. *To Harry Stafford*   *12.1.* [*1880*]

Camden | Wednesday Evn'g Dec: 1—

Dear Hank

Nothing very new with me the last two weeks—how has it been with you? Are you on the C & A[84] again—& how about that Medford Station? Write soon—(it will do you good to write & fully & carefully—I wish you would oftener)—

I have had something of a set-back—A rascally publisher in New York named Worthington has been printing and selling a cheaper edition of my book for his own profit, no benefit to me at all—& it has been going on privately for a year—I only found it out for certain about ten days ago —of course it is quite a hurt to me—will lead to a law suit, as I shall have to sue him, & I hate getting into law—it is almost as bad to me to sue, as to be sued—then it cost[s] money—

I am jogging along here about the same—keep pretty well, & eat my allowance every time—went over to 41st st: Phila: to eat my Thanks-giving dinner, with an old friend of mine, (his wife & two young ones)— had a good time—Came back home in a rousing snow storm, but got along all right—Sunday morning went to breakfast at Mr and Mrs Scovel's[85]—

I am sitting up here 3d story—warm & nice, every thing as still as can be—it has struck 8 and the wind outside moans & whistles by starts— have been reading the evening paper, & today's N Y *Tribune*—& I thought I would write to you, but I am afraid I havn't made out a very interesting letter—It was well I was down there the good weather middle of November—it has been bad enough since, some bitter cold— I have got my new overcoat, it is thick & warm & I like it—have you got the *new cider?* Love to your father & mother, not forgetting your share, dear son—

Walt

988. *To John Burroughs*

Dec: 7 '80

In the letter I sent you yesterday ab't the Worthington matter, I spoke of W probably buying with the plates a lot of the old Boston edition

comment on the following passage in Burroughs' letter: "Dr Bucke is a good fellow, but between me & you, I am a little shy of him: I fear he lacks balance & proportion & that his book will not be pitched in the right key. But I hope I do him injustice."

84. Camden & Atlantic Railroad.

85. According to entries in *CB*, WW often had Sunday breakfast with the Scovels. Though there is no entry in the notebook for November 28, he was at the Scovels' on December 5. The poet spent Thanksgiving with the Kilgores (*CB*).

in sheets—Dr Bucke[86] yesterday stopt at Leavitt's (the auctioneer's) in N Y. & to-day I receive from B the following postal:

"Leavitt sold the plates to a Mr Williams (for Wentworth of Boston) in Sept: 79 for $200—Leavitt never saw or heard of any *sheets*—Worthington must have bo't the plates from Williams—He must have printed from them

R M B"

I thought I might as well let you know every new discovery &c—and shall continue to do so—

Bitter cold here, but clear—

W W

989. *To Richard Watson Gilder*   *12.9.* [*1880*]

ADDRESS: R W Gilder | *Scribner's Magazine* office |
743 Broadway | New York City. POSTMARKS:
Camden | Dec | 10 | N.J.; D | 12–10 | 3 P.

Camden N J Dec: 9

Dear G:

Don't bother ab't that matter[87]—it is in hands that have already put it in fair train—You have my best sympathies—Am coming to N Y before long, & shall notify you or call—

W. W.

990. *To Thomas Nicholson*   *12.17.* [*1880*][88]

431 Stevens Street | Camden New Jersey
U S A—Dec: 17

Dear Tom

I was glad to have word from you, once more, & glad to get the particulars of that race—this is the first full account I have heard, & I am real pleased, Tommy, first at the satisfaction of your winning, and next at your raking in the good stakes—altogether it must have been quite a time—

Yes Dr Bucke was here, and we had a very pleasant afternoon and evening together—had a first rate dinner—and then in the hotel sitting

---

86. Dr. Bucke was in Philadelphia on December 5, evidently on his way to New York, where he apparently investigated the Worthington matter (CB).

87. The Worthington matter (see 985).

88. WW noted this letter to Nicholson in CB. The poet sent the young man a newspaper account of a "N Y walking match" on January 30, 1881 (CB).

room some of the tallest kind of talking & arguing you may be sure.[89]

I live very quietly & plainly here, board with my brother & sister-in-law —have a nice little room up in the third story fronting south (I am sitting here now in a great rocking chair, & the sun is pouring in bright and warm as you please—I wish you was here, Tommy, to spend the afternoon with me)—

I have some work to-day, most every day a little, but I take it easy, content if I can make enough to pay my expenses—I never cared to be rich, (no possibility of that any how) but I dont care to be too poor either.

I get out on the river, (the Delaware) or over in Philadelphia most every day—lately I go down to the Ferry at nights & cross over & back two or three times. The river is full of ice & the boats have a pretty tough time—but the nights are light, the full moon shining like silver, and I enjoy it all—(Know the pilots and boat hands intimately.) Last night was perfect, & only middling cool—I staid crossing till 12 o'clock—felt good —& then got hungry & went and got a dozen nice oysters & a drink (Dont that make your mouth water, Tommy boy?) I often think of you and the boys & girls—give my best respects to all of them, Dick Flynn, Tom Bradley[90] & all the cricket boys—that was the best summer there in Canada, & among you all & the Asylum grounds, & the daily rides into London & all, that I ever put in & I am feeling the benefit of it yet. My love to you, Tom, & am glad you dont forget me, as I won't you—try to write to me regular—

Walt Whitman

Did George England's picture come all safe?

991. *To an Unidentified Correspondent*[91]

DRAFT LETTER.

431 Stevens Street | Camden New Jersey | Dec: 28 '80

Dear Sir

I shall be glad to supply you with a set (Two Volumes) of my books—There is only one kind of binding—

Walt Whitman

89. WW had spent the afternoon of December 5 with Dr. Bucke at the Girard House in Philadelphia (*CB*).

90. These two friends of Nicholson are mentioned in 976.

91. The only clue to the identification of this correspondent is the reference in *CB* to the fact that WW sent his two-volume edition to John P. Woodbury of Boston on this date. This draft was written on the verso of "Embers of day-fires smouldering."

992. *To Jeannette L. Gilder*

TRANSCRIPT.

Camden, Dec 31, '80.

Yes, my friend, I will supply you with some little out-door sketches —three, possibly four—for your paper at the price you propose. . . . You can rely on it within a week.[92]

Walt Whitman

92. WW agreed to write a series of sketches for *The Critic*, a new magazine of which she was editor. On January 5, 1882, he sent her the first instalment (see CB and 996). The series, entitled "How I Get Around at 60, and Take Notes," was printed during the following eighteen months: January 29, 1881 (2–3), April 9, 1881 (88–89), May 7, 1881 (116–117), July 16, 1881 (184–185), December 3, 1881 (330–331), and July 15, 1882 (185–186).

1. An oil portrait of Whitman by Percy Ives. This illustration and all others in this volume are from the Feinberg Collection.

2. A photograph of Whitman with two of John H. Johnston's children. The boy's mother, Amelia, died giving birth to the child on March 26, 1877.

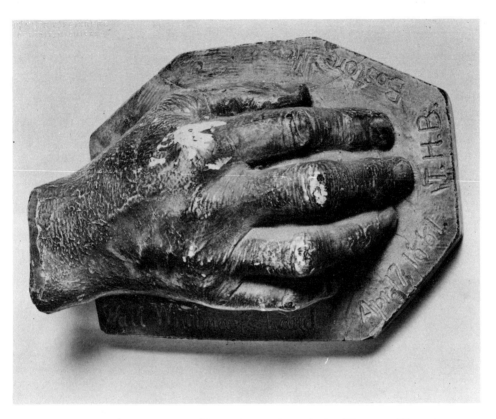

3. A plaster cast of Whitman's hand made by Truman Howe Bartlett two days after the poet's lecture on Abraham Lincoln in Boston on April 15, 1881.

4. A photograph of Harry Stafford, probably made shortly after the beginning of their friendship in 1876.

5. A letter to Whitman from Harry Stafford's mother, Susan M. Stafford, of whom the poet wrote: "There is not a nobler woman in Jersey."

4

1

6. A letter from Harry Stafford to Whitman, May 21, 1877.

Kirkwood N.J.
October 17-77

Dear Friend Walt:

I don't know as I have any thing to say that will interest you, but I feel as if I would like to write something, and so I will begin by telling you about the fun I had last night, it was with a fellow that has been thinking for a long time he could throw me, so last night him and I came together for the first; he said he could throw me and I said if he thought so he was welcome to try his hand, so we buckled in, he his first holt and mine second, his holt we pulled around for a short time and then I let loose on him and down he went, then came my holt he did not want me to have it but I got him in to it and I asked him if he was ready and he said he was so I stood him on his head, he got up and said he would go home, but he did not have much to say all the way home, I guess that I hurt his back by the way he went, but he did not say anything. There is one more fellow who I want to take the conceit out of and that is B.K., hurt, he thinks he could do what he pleased with me but I want to show him he cannot do it. I was out Sunday night had a good time, went to church and there came home, Cousin Lizzie was over to our house this week and went to Sunday school, I been carrying, eat our supper and then went out for a ride. I will be down to see you Saturday if nothing happens more than I know of, you will be down on the (5½) train, perhaps on the (12) I don't know yet for certain.

The folks are all well, and myself the same, I think of you when ever I have a moment to think, I don't get much time to think about any one, for when I am not thinking of my business I am thinking of what I am should-ing, I want to try and make a man of my-self, and do what is right if I can do it, I have not said from C. Allenges. I will have to stop writing now for my sheet is giving out and I must go to work.

4   1   2   3

7. A letter from Harry Stafford to Whitman, October 17, 1877.

June – first part at White Horse
" Last part at north 22d st (E Carpenter there

June 25 – went down to White Horse
July 4 – Lou very sick – (I return'd 6th or 7th)
July 13 to 20th '77 – down at White Horse
(came up in the light wagon with Mrs S July 2d)
July 20th '77, in the room at White Horse "gold eagle"
Herbert's paintings at the creek – July '77

last of June or early in
ab't July 12 – Two Riv: to Gen Carse for
Mr Kearsbey – (paid)

July 27 – E J Loomis   sent Two Riv +
Nautical Almanac Office   paid $5?
Washington DC

July 21st)
July 29 (wrote Mrs S – (28th over at 22d st)

July 22d to 30th '77 – very hot – therm 90 – 96 –
in Camden – feeling pretty well, for me –

Aug 4 '77 – For the last 3 or 4 days Herbert
home (at 1929 no 22d st) from White Horse
– I am over there for a couple of hours eve, evening – Aug 3 – letter from Mrs S rec'd – &   4.
sent Mrs S the big photo. by Herbert –   .5
– still feeling well for me

8. A page from Whitman's *Commonplace-Book* in 1877, when
the poet was spending a great deal of time with the Staffords at
White Horse, New Jersey, and with the Gilchrists, who were
living at 1929 North 22nd Street in Philadelphia. Both Herbert
Gilchrist and Edward Carpenter, who was making his first trip
to America, accompanied the poet to the Stafford farm.

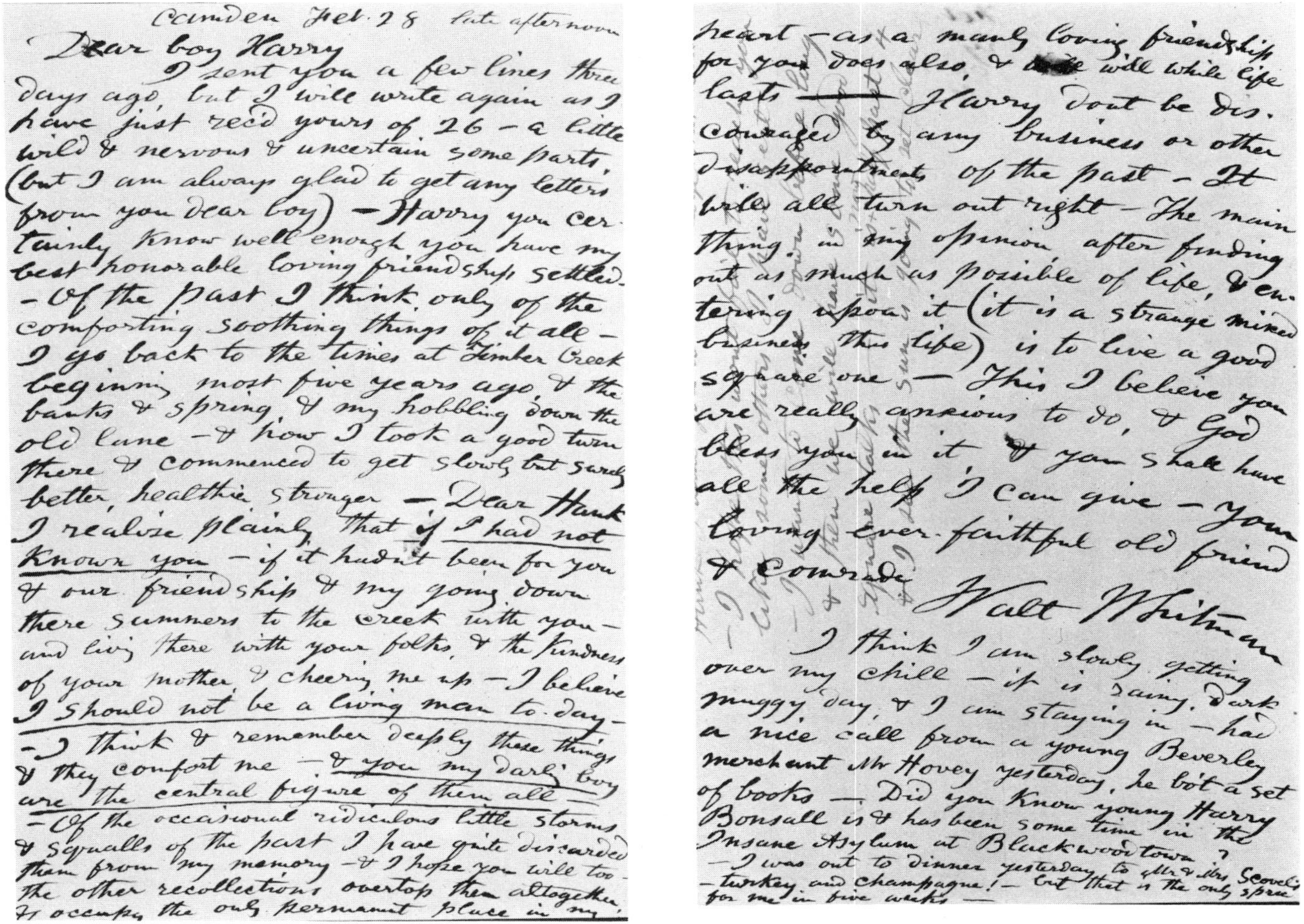

9. A letter from Whitman to Harry Stafford, February 28, 1881.

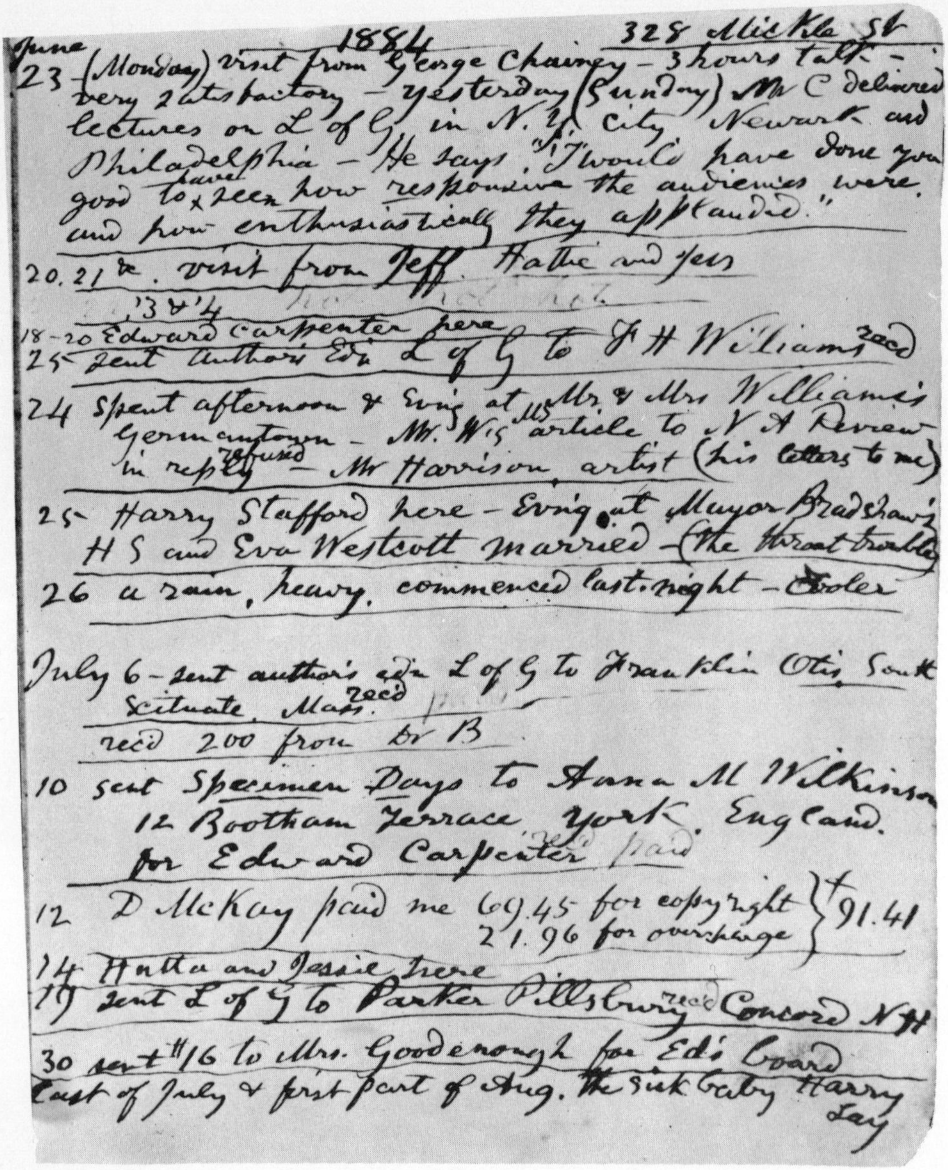

[Handwritten diary page, 1884]

328 Mickle St

June 1884

23 (Monday) visit from George Chainey — 3 hours talk — very satisfactory — yesterday (Sunday) Mr C delivered lectures on L of G in N. Y. City, Newark and Philadelphia — He says "Twould have done you good to x seen how responsive the audiences were, and how enthusiastically they applauded."

20. 21 &c. visit from Jeff, Hattie and Jess

'3 & '4

18-20 Edward Carpenter here

25 sent author's Ed'n L of G to J H Williams (rec'd)

24 Spent afternoon & Ev'ng at Mr. & Mrs Williams's Germantown — Mr. W's article to N A Review in reply — Mr Harrison, artist (his letters to me)

25 Harry Stafford here — Ev'ng at Mayor Bradshaw's H S and Eva Westcott married — (the throat trouble)

26 a rain, heavy, commenced last night — cooler

July 6 — sent author's ed'n L of G to Franklin Otis, South Scituate, Mass. rec'd

rec'd 200 from Dr B

10 sent Specimen Days to Anna M Wilkinson 12 Bootham Terrace York, England. for Edward Carpenter paid

12 D McKay paid me 69.45 for copyright } 91.41
21.96 for overcharge }

14 Hattie and Jessie here

19 sent L of G to Parker Pillsbury rec'd Concord N H

30 sent #16 to Mrs. Goodenough for Ed's board last of July & first part of Aug. the sick baby Harry Lay

10. Another page from the _Commonplace-Book,_ recording on June 25, 1884, Harry Stafford's marriage to Eva Westcott. In his diary Whitman carefully recorded the sales of his books, the receipt of royalties from David McKay (July 12), his payments for his brother Edward's board (July 30), and the visits of friends and relatives.

328 Mickle street (Camden
Ev'g Nov. 18 '84

My dear friends

Your kind letter (Eva's) came
this afternoon & it gave me real
comfort both to hear from you &
have such loving remembrance &
friendly invitation — Harry dear boy,
I hardly think I shall be able to
come down & be with you this
Thanksgiving — but I will come
one of these times — Since I have
got into this shanty, although I go
out every day, I don't go any distance
— I haven't been away this past summer,
only one short trip to Cape May —
— My lameness increases on me — it
probably won't be long before I shall
be unable to get around at all —
— General health otherwise about the
same as usual — Eva, my dear friend
it would be a true comfort for me
if it was so I could come in every
few days, and you and Harry and I

could be together — I am sure it
would be good for me —
— Nothing very new in my affairs —
not much sale for my books at
present, or for the last fifteen months
— Harry your mother call'd here last
Monday, but I was not in, was over
to Germantown — I was sorry to be
away — I am writing this up in
my room — am alone most of the
time — write a little most every
day — sell a piece once in a while —
— maintain good spirits and a first-
rate appetite — My dear friends
indeed I appreciate your loving wishes
& feelings, & send you mine the same,
for both of you —

Walt Whitman

Eva would you like to have
me send you some papers now
& then? Write me whenever you can.
Harry I am sorry about the neck — I
think it will get right & heal in time

11. A letter from Whitman on November 18, 1884, to the newly married couple,
Mr. and Mrs. Harry Stafford.

Harry L and Eva Stafford
RR Station
Marlton
New Jersey

12. A drawing of the poet by a young American artist, Percy
Ives, whom Whitman met in 1880.

1881

993. *To Anne Gilchrist*

ADDRESS: Mrs Gilchrist | Keats corner 12 Well Road | Hampstead | London | England. POSTMARKS: Camden | Jan | 2 | N.J.; (?)N.W. | E | Paid 20 Ja 81.

> 431 Stevens Street | Camden New Jersey
> U S A—Jan: 1 '81

Was sorry—extremely sorry—to hear of your illness—trust you are well again by this time, (as fore-indicated by H[erbert]'s last)[1]—all H's books for Mrs S[tafford] came safely[2]—also letters & p.o. order—rec'd the good, long, fine letter from B[eatrice][3]—The S's are all well as usual—I am getting along capitally for me this winter so far—have been & am writing quite a deal *to order* (astonishing, isn't it?)[4]—will surely send you when in print—I wish you would send the *Cedar-Plums like*[5] to Rossetti—(I suppose you rec'd it)—what silly fictitious items appear about me in some of the English papers—(about as bad as *here*)—trust you all had merry Christmas & New Year's—Cold & deep snow here—

> WW

994. *To Harry Stafford*

> Camden Jan: 2 '81

Dear Hank

I hear from you indirectly once in a while by Hoag,[6] (& saw Debbie & Jo[7] some days since)—I suppose you got the postal I sent you about 12

1881

    1.   Herbert informed WW about his mother's health on December 13, 1880 (Feinberg). On February 16 Mrs. Gilchrist wrote about her "bronchitis & cardiac asthma" (Pennsylvania).

    2. See 1001.   3. Apparently this letter is lost.

    4. A reference to the articles for *The Critic* (see the preceding letter).

    5. "Cedar-Plums Like" probably appeared late in 1880 in the Philadelphia *Press*. It was included in SD (245–248). On February 16 Mrs. Gilchrist referred to the notes in *The Critic* and "Cedar-Plums Like": they "are especially precious to me & I doubt not will be so to all friends & lovers of yours" (Pennsylvania).

    6. See 979.   7. Harry's sister and brother-in-law, the Brownings.

days ago[8]—the weather has been so bad, or I should have come down—
I have had quite a good deal to do writing—have finished quite a piece for
a big magazine in N. Y.—the *North American Review*—it was ordered—
I get $100 for it—I read the proof last night & sent it off[9]—then I have
a little poem *the Patrol at Barnegat* probably in next Harper's[10]—(but I
think I told you about it)—then to-day I am busy on another order[11]—So
you see I have something to do—I will send you the *Review* piece when
printed—I am feeling better and *sassier* this winter so far than for some
years, am very comfortable here, plain & quiet though—eat my allowance
every time—& have a little jug of *good Jamaica rum* from which I take a
sip now & then—(but not very often)—came in chill'd & dumpy late
yesterday afternoon—made myself a good mug of hot rum, & felt better—

Hank, I hope you are having fair times on the road—I am glad you
stick to it—perseverance will conquer. Horner[12] was here again a few
evenings ago, an hour—How do you get on with Col: Ingersoll's book?[13]
(You mustn't take too much stock in him)—If there is any book particular
you want, you tell me, & I will try to get it—Lots of sleighs out, good
sleighing—my brother was out day before yesterday, & got overturned—
I wanted to go yesterday, but he was afraid for me to venture it—his
nag is pretty lively, (but I should have liked that all the better)—

1½—just had dinner, hot soup, cold roast beef, apple pie—all good—
the sun is out real warm, & I shall go at my piece for the N Y order—it is
for a lady, a friend of mine—she has been for years principal literary
editor of the *Herald*, & now she is going to start a paper of her own—
pays me[14]—

Is Ed[15] home? I should just like to have a ten mile ride behind his
nag with the sleigh bells—Dear boy, I send you my best love & dont you
forget it—

Your old Walt

8. This card is evidently not extant.
9. "The Poetry of the Future" appeared in *The North American Review* in
February (195–210). It was later called "Poetry To-day In America" (*CW*, v, 205–229).
On January 15 WW received $100 in payment for the article (*CB*).
10. "Patroling Barnegat" was sent to *Harper's Monthly* on October 9, 1880
(*CB*), and appeared in the April issue (LXII, 701). The poem had appeared in *The
American* in June, 1880 (*CHAL*). On May 20, 1881, WW sent to *Harper's Monthly* "A
Summer's Invocation," which was returned (*CB*); it appeared, however, in *The Ameri-
can* (see 1026).
11. The articles for *The Critic*.
12. As evidenced by an address mounted in *CB*, Horner was the nickname of
Jacob H. Stafford (1850–1890), Harry's cousin, whose mother was Mary Horner.

995. *To the Editor*, The Critic   *[1.5(?). 1881]*[16]

follow copy in Capitalization, punctuation & ¶'s—& please send proof to

Walt Whitman 431 Stevens St Camden New Jersey
which will be returned immediately—

996. *To Jeannette L. Gilder*   *1.8. [1881]*

431 Stevens Street | Camden New Jersey Jan: 8
My dear Miss G

Yours of yesterday rec'd—glad you like the papers—the $20 rec'd —thanks—Send the *proof* (which is important) & it will be sent back the same night, so that you will get it next forenoon—

Yes, you shall have two more[17]—

Walt Whitman

997. *To Jeannette L. Gilder*

431 Stevens Street | Camden New Jersey | Jan: 15 '81
My dear friend

As I have not rec'd the proof,[18] I take it things are lagging or postponed a little with *the Critic* (is that the name?)

In the Feb: *N A Review* there is a piece of mine about Poetry (a good many of my private sentiments publicly expressed)[19]—Of course I should like to have it exploited—& by you if handy—Should you think proper, would it be worth while to get it in advance, for the *Herald?*[20] (Should the *Review* not be out when you get this) you can send to Mr Rice,[21] the editor, or Mr Metcalf,[22] the business manager, & I think get the sheets— you can use my name—

Walt Whitman

13. Apparently WW gave Harry one of the books which Ingersoll sent on March 25, 1880 (see 948).

14. The articles for Jeannette L. Gilder of *The Critic* (see 992).

15. Harry's brother, Edwin.

16. WW sent the manuscript of "How I Get Around at 60, and Take Notes" to *The Critic* on January 5 (*CB*).

17. WW sent the next two articles in the series on April 9 (*CB*).

18. WW returned the proof of his article on January 20 (*CB*).

19. "The Poetry of the Future" (see 994).

20. Miss Gilder had been associated with the New York *Herald* (see 898).

21. Charles Allen Thorndike Rice (1851–1889) purchased *The North American Review* in 1876. See also 1002.

22. Perhaps Lorettus S. Metcalf, listed in the directories as a journalist.

Should you notice, send to me—

In my last I addressed you at 757 Broadway—is either that, or the address to this letter, all right? Send me word more definitely about the *Critic* & mind *the proof*—send it in a letter, letter postage—& it will be returned *same night*—

I am feeling really well for me this winter—

WW

998.   *To George and Susan Stafford*   *1.16.* [*1881*]

431 Stevens Street | Camden Sunday afternoon
Jan: 16

My dear friends

You havn't sent for the two big books Herbert sent you, So as I have been snowed in a good deal lately, I have opened them & read quite a good deal in them—they are queer books, the very finest of printing & paper & some odd pictures[23]—I got a postal from Mrs Gilchrist yesterday —she **is** improving—the rest all well—

We have had a rough hard winter, all around—Keeps me in mostly, but I make a dash out now & then—I still keep pretty well this winter—if it hadn't been so cold I should have been down to see you—Ed, how do you like being home again? But I think you are contented most any where—how is the nag? I was out once or twice sleighing—my brother took me—his mare Nelly is in fine condition—pretty lively—makes things fly sometimes—

I have been in all day reading & writing—I have put up two sets of my books, to send off this evening's mail, to purchasers[24]—a very quiet day, but I have enjoyed it—outside it is cold and half-cloudy, not an inviting day out—

Well, Mont, have you found any chance yet at telegraphing? I think the best thing a fellow can do this weather, is to stay home & keep warm— but when the spring opens then make a dash somewhere—Van I suppose will make a farmer—well if he is satisfied, it is about as good as anything, I don't know but better—

There comes my call to dinner, & I shall go for it, without delay & finish my helter-skelter letter afterwards—

---

23. See 1001. Mrs. Gilchrist's "postal" has not been located.
24. In *CB* WW noted sending two volumes to John A. Scott in London; on the following day he forwarded a set to Miss Harriet W. Robinson in Brooklyn.

Dinner all right, baked beef pie—

I am now going out to see one of the ferry men, a friend, very sick— I have provided a bottle of brandy to take him, as I understand the doctor orders milk punch—there is a good deal of sickness around here, much diphtheria—Well I must stop—Good bye & God bless you, friends, Susan, George, & Harry dear—

W W

999. *To D. M. Zimmerman*

431 Stevens Street | Camden Jan: 26 '81
Thanks for the '81 ticket which has come safe to hand.[25] I am not certain whether I sent the enclosed slip at the time—so send it now—

Walt Whitman

1000. *To Harry Stafford*   *1.27.* [1881]

ENDORSED (in unknown hand): "1881." ADDRESS:
Harry Lamb Stafford | Kirkwood | Glendale | New
Jersey. POSTMARK: Camden | Jan | 27 | N.J.

431 Stevens Street Camden | Thursday noon Jan: 27[26]
Dear Hank—

Dear boy—your letter rec'd & read—Take it easy about the minister & the Ingersoll business[27]—the best answer you can make is to be quiet & good natured & even attentive & *not get mad worth a cent—* True religion (*the most beautiful thing in the whole world*, & the best part of any man's or woman's, or boy's character) consists in *what one does* square and kind & generous & honorable all days, *all the time—*& especially with his own folks & associates & with the poor & illiterate & in devout meditation, & silent thoughts of God, & death—& not at all in what he *says*, nor in Sunday or prayer meeting *gas*—My own opinion is that Ingersoll *talks* too much on his side—a *good life, steady trying to do fair*, & a sweet, tolerant liberal disposition, shines like the sun, tastes like the fresh air of a May morning, blooms like a perfect little flower by the road-side—& all the blowing, talking & powowing *both sides* amounts to little or nothing—Glad, dear boy, you had a good little visit, you &

25. D. M. Zimmerman, the secretary and treasurer of the Camden & Atlantic Railroad, sent the poet a railroad pass (*CB*).
26. WW referred to this letter in *CB*. January 27 was on Thursday in 1881.
27. See 994.

Mont,[28] with me—I enjoyed it too—I am writing this up in the room—the sun shines, but sharp cold & the wind whistling—

Your Walt

1001. *To Susan Stafford*   *1.30.* [*1881*]

Camden Sunday afternoon Jan: 30—[29]

My dear friend,

I rec'd your good letter some days since, & would like indeed to be down with you & George & all—but the bitter cold continues so I think I'd better stay close here for the present—but it won't be long before I shall be with you all—I suppose you & the rest are reading Herbert's books from time to time—though they are very queer in the story of Blake's life and works, there is a deal that is interesting & good to chew on—then they are such beautiful specimens of paper & printing, it is a pleasure to read them[30]—

I had a nice visit from Harry and Mont—there is nothing new or interesting to write you—it is now ½ past 2, after dinner, & I have been writing & fixing up a composition alone in my room, since breakfast—it is a cloudy, cold raw day here, rather lonesome, but still I make out—(but I could make out better if I have the rest of the day on a visit to Glendale, & a good strong cup of tea with you & Ruth, to cheer me up)—I am still feeling pretty well so far this winter, bless the Lord—I send Debbie a book "*the Old Curiosity Shop*"—love to her and Joe—have you had any more *hog-killings*—which is the most fun? them or the Glendale church?

W W

1002. *To John Burroughs*

TRANSCRIPT.

February 1, 1881

Yours rec'd and very opportunely[31]—all today has been the dis-

---

28. WW did not note in *CB* this visit with Harry and his brother.
29. On January 30 WW sent this letter to Mrs. Stafford as well as a " 'wrestling' slip to Harry" and *Old Curiosity Shop* to Deborah Browning (*CB*).
30. Presumably the new and enlarged two-volume edition, *Life of William Blake, with Selections* (1880), containing the memoir of Herbert's father, Alexander Gilchrist.
31. Burroughs' letter is apparently lost.
32. A criticism of "The Poetry of the Future" appeared in *The American* (*CB*).
33. On January 21 Rice wrote to WW: "Permit me to thank you on behalf of the readers of the Review for the singularly interesting and valuable article you contribute

malest of this grim winter here, furious snow and wind howling, and I have not stirred out—the roads and rivers here all block'd with snow and ice—the last week my physical system block'd, too, with a chill and depression—right in the middle of the smoothest sailing I have had for years—but I feel that it will be a passing cloud (such indeed as comes to me every two or three months)—

Yes I am quite tickled and favorable to coming there and am about sure I shall come, accepting your good invitation right out—Will write again this week—I have one or two newspaper bits about the *Review* article which I will send you;[32] it has been extracted from considerable—the best thing is a letter from the *Review* editor, Allen Thorndike Rice, to me about a week after the piece appeared, one of the most eulogistic, solid acceptances of my theories possible[33]—he paid me $100 for the piece and supplied me with a hundred pamphlet copies of it. I have rec'd five or six letters from one and another, none of any acc't. I saw Marvin some weeks ago.[34] Eldridge is in Boston, in U.S. office. Dr. Bucke is writing his book.[35]

W. W.

1003. *To Louise Chandler Moulton*[36]

431 Stevens Street | Camden New Jersey Feb: 2 '81

Thanks for your kind note just rec'd—I think I had better send you the Two Volumes without further ceremony, which I do, same mail with this, same address. All the little pieces Stedman speaks of as *pasted* (in a very small prior edition) *are in this* being afterwards put in the plates[37]—Warmest thanks for your friendly words & invitation—I am a little more unwell even than usual these days & dont get out of the house—but with Spring & good weather shall no doubt be all right again —I truly hope, my friend, we shall meet—I shall be on the look out for you—

Walt Whitman

to the February number. With the cooperation of yourself and other American thinkers of the first note, the Review must become indeed a necessity for every thinking man in America. I hope to be able to afford the readers of the Review frequent opportunity of being instructed by you" (Yale).

34. Marvin had also called on WW in November (see 986).

35. Bucke's biography of WW (see 946).

36. See 778.

37. In the first printing of the 1876 edition of *Leaves of Grass* some poems were pasted in. As WW noted, they were included in the text in the second printing.

1004. *To Jeannette L. Gilder*

431 Stevens Street | Camden New Jersey Feb: 6 '81

My dear J L G

I send you the Carlyle piece as requested[38]—Mail me a proof, if possible—if Tuesday forenoon I can return it Tuesday night—If not possible pray read proof with extra care by copy—It ought to make just a page—I want without fail fifty impressions of just that page. It can easily be done in the printing office—Another thing I forget to mention before (& perhaps is not strictly needed any how) I reserve the right to print any of my pieces in future book—& to make it clearer, would you & J B[39] kindly, after signing, return to me the accompanying page?[40]

Walt Whitman

1005. *To Susan Stafford*   2.6. *[1881]*

ADDRESS: Mrs Susan M Stafford | Kirkwood | Glendale | New Jersey. POSTMARK: Ca(?) | Feb | 7 | N.J.

Camden Feb: 6   8 p m

Dear friend

I have had a sick week—two days pretty bad—last Sunday night had a strange chill, rattled me for two hours lively—one or two since but milder—the doctor thinks my system was got all chilled through—havnt been out for a week till this evening, went to the post office—am feeling better to-day, but weak—

How are you all? Was glad to have a call from Debbie & your neice Lizzie—So Lizzie Hider and Wes are to be married soon[41]—well if it is to come off at all the sooner the better & I hope it will turn out a happy marriage—should say there was the best reason to expect it to, for both have estimable qualities & I dont see how a woman can help loving the

38. "Death of Carlyle" appeared in *The Critic* on February 12, and was reprinted in *Essays from "The Critic"* (1882), 31–37. See also SD, 248–253. WW received $10 for the article on February 25 (CB). On February 7 (CB) he sent the piece to *The Literary World* (see 1007).
39. Miss Gilder's brother, Joseph.
40. Evidently a financial agreement.
41. Lizzie Hider and Wesley Stafford, Mrs. Stafford's nephew, were married on February 9 by the Reverend J. B. Wescott, according to the Camden *Democrat* of

good man she lives with as a wife—Best love to Harry, I got his good
letter & will answer it soon—love to George & all—

W W

Send me a chicken when you have a chance—

1006. *To Harry Stafford*   *2.11.* [*1881*]

> ADDRESS: Harry Lamb Stafford | Kirkwood |
> Glendale | New Jersey. POSTMARK: Camden |
> Feb | 11 | N.J.

Camden Friday Evening Feb: 11—

Dear Hank—
Yours of 9th rec'd—am a little surprised you take to L of G so
quickly[42]—I guess it is because the last five years had been *preparing
& fixing the ground*, more & more & more—& now that the seed is dropt
in it sprouts quickly—my own feeling ab't my book is that it makes (tries
to make) every fellow *see himself*, & see that *he has got to work out his
salvation himself*—has got to pull the oars & hold the plow, or swing the
axe *himself*—& that the real[43] blessings of life are not the fictions generally
supposed, but are real, & are mostly within reach of all—you chew on
this—
Hank, I am still feeling under the weather—My appetite is fair, (when
I can get what I like)—& sleep middling, but I am as weak as a cat, & dull
half-dizzy spells every day—I sent off two sets of books to-day, got the
money for them—one set to a big lady in England[44]—I enclose you a slip
of a piece out to-morrow in the N Y *Critic*, about the old man Carlyle,
85 years old, the grandest writer in England, just dead[45]—they sent for
me to write it ($10 worth)—You read it carefully—read it twice—then
show it to your mother, I want her to read it, without fail—(Hank, *you
do not appreciate your mother*—there is not a nobler woman in Jersey)—
Your Walt

February 19.
    42. Evidently when Harry visited WW on February 7 (*CB*), the poet gave him a
copy of *Leaves of Grass*, five years after they had become acquainted. WW noted
sending this letter in *CB*.
    43. WW may have stricken this word.
    44. According to *CB*, WW sent the books to Mrs. Edward Smithson in York,
England.
    45. See 1004.

1007. *To the Editor*, The Literary World

431 Stevens Street | Camden New Jersey Feb: 16 '81

Dear Sirs

Yours of 14th with the $5 enclosed, has arrived safely[46]—The slips came all right—Thanks—

Walt Whitman

If you have some spare numbers of your *World* running back six or seven weeks send them to me—

1008. *To Harry Stafford*   2.17. [*1881*]

ENDORSED (by R. M. Bucke): "1881."

Feb: 17th Evening[47]

Dear Hank

If you carefully write out the extracts I send you, & punctuate them correctly, & *read them slowly & carefully*, it will be a success I am sure—

George D Prentice[48] was a great Kentucky editor & writer—Coleridge was an Englishman—both dead—I hope you will read the piece yourself— that is part of the trade *that has got to be begun & gone through with*— read very slow, & mind the pauses—I want the extracts return'd to me as they were wrote out for me by a lady friend I think a great deal of— Pluck up courage & go ahead—

your W W

1009. *To Henry Wadsworth Longfellow*

431 Stevens Street | Camden New Jersey Feb: 20 '81

My dear Mr Longfellow

A friend in Canada—to whom I am indebted for great personal

46. *The Literary World* printed "The Dead Carlyle" on February 12 (see 1004).
47. WW wrote to Harry on this date (*CB*). Harry called on WW on February 15 and returned on the following day (*CB*).
48. Prentice (1802–1870) was editor of the Louisville (Ky.) *Daily Journal* from 1830 to 1868. His poetry was issued posthumously in 1876. During the Civil War he was a supporter of Abraham Lincoln, and, according to *DAB*, was largely responsible for keeping Kentucky in the Union.
49. On February 13 WW sent a "postal to Dr Bucke ab't Longfellow's autograph,"

kindnesses & affections—particularly desires your autograph[49]—Could you
furnish it to me, to send? & much oblige—

Walt Whitman

1010. *To Eustace Conway*

431 Stevens Street | Camden New Jersey Feb: 22 '81
My dear Eustace Conway[50]

I am sorry I was out when you called—have been hoping you
would come again—Are you going to stay in America? If so I shall be on
the look out for you & trust you will the same for me—

Walt Whitman

1011. *To Susan Stafford*   2.22. *[1881]*

Camden Feb: 22 Evening[51]

My dear friend

I still keep around & have been over to Philadelphia this afternoon
for three hours, the day has been so fine & bright, (but I am weak & half-
sick yet)—over in Phila: I ride in the new Market st. coaches, the
Herdies[?] (they start from the ferry door, & I buy 25 tickets for a
dollar)—I was on Arch and Chestnut streets—such crowds—oceans of
women, drest to kill—I like to walk along & look in the windows, every
kind of article you can think of, & many you never thought of—always
something new & interesting—then I have a friend cor: 7th & Chestnut,
Col: Forney's office, a nice big old fashioned room—he keeps a great ratan
easy chair for me, by a bay-window, & I always stop there to rest, & read
the news—

How are you all getting along? We are at the beginning of another
spring, & I want to come down soon—The chicken was first rate—it made
me several good meals—(I expected to pay for it, & expect to yet)—the
strawberries good—they tasted like Glendale—as I close it is 9 oclock &
a lot of darkies are going along singing an old southern slave hymn—

W W

which apparently was intended for one of Bucke's friends (*CB*). On February 22 Long-
fellow wrote to WW: "It gives me great pleasure to comply with your request"
(Berg); and on February 24 WW sent the autograph to Bucke (*CB*). On January 16
WW wrote to *The Literary World* "declining to write an article on Longfellow" (*CB*).

50.   The uncle of Moncure D. Conway; see *Autobiography . . . of Moncure
Daniel Conway* (1904), I, 38. According to a jotting in *CB*, Conway was associated
with Bangs & Stetson in New York.

51.   WW wrote to Mrs. Stafford on February 22 (*CB*). Harry brought the poet a
chicken and strawberries on February 15 (*CB*).

1012. *To Harry Stafford*   *2.24. [1881]*

ENDORSED (by R. M. Bucke): "1881."

Camden Feb: 24 Afternoon[52]

Dear Hank—

I feel to write you a card, but I guess it will be a dry one, for I have nothing to write about, & I havn't got very smart yet—I go out though —(Seems to me if I couldn't go out in the sun & open air I should give up entirely)—How did you make out with the piece for the Lyceum? I suppose you rec'd what I sent you—the extracts on poetry—did you make a piece *and read it* as I told you?[53] (I'll bet five dollars you didn't do any thing of the kind)—

I rec'd a pamphlet from Edward Carpenter to-day—his forthcoming lectures for 1881—perhaps he sent you one—I have been in all day, occupying myself reading & writing a little—Shall go out now for a couple of hours—There I told you this would be a dry letter—

Walt

1013. *To William Sloane Kennedy*[54]   *2.25. [1881]*

Camden N J Feb: 25 | Evening

Thanks—If convenient then send me the Carlyle Tribune[55]—& I will return.

Walt Whitman

1014. *To Harry Stafford*   *2.28. [1881]*

Camden Feb. 28 late afternoon[56]

Dear boy Harry

I sent you a few lines three days ago, but I will write again as I have just rec'd yours of 26—a little wild & nervous & uncertain some

---

52. The year is established by the reference in the second paragraph and by a notation in *CB*.

53. See 1008.

54. This card marks the beginning of WW's extensive correspondence with Kennedy (1850–1929), who at this time was on the staff of the Philadelphia *American* (*DAB*), and who later published biographies of Longfellow and Whittier. Apparently Kennedy had called on the poet for the first time on November 21, 1880 (Kennedy, 1). Though Kennedy was to become a fierce defender of WW, in his first published article he admitted reservations about the "coarse indecencies of language" and protested that WW's ideal of democracy was "too coarse and crude"; see *The Californian*, III (February, 1881), 149–158. Yet, according to Burroughs' letter to WW on November 2, 1880, Kennedy was angered by Stedman's article in *Scribner's Monthly* (see 986), and thought

parts, (but I am always glad to get any letters from you, dear boy)—Harry, you certainly know well enough you have my best honorable loving friendship settled—Of the past I think only of the comforting soothing things of it all—I go back to the times at Timber Creek beginning most five years ago, & the banks & spring, & my hobbling down the old lane—& how I took a good turn there & commenced to get slowly but surely better, healthier, stronger—Dear Hank, I realize plainly that *if I had not known you*—if it hadn't been for you & our friendship & my going down there summers to the creek with you—and living there with your folks, & the kindness of your mother, & cheering me up—I believe *I should not be a living man to-day*—I think & remember deeply these things & they comfort me—*& you, my darling boy, are the central figure of them all*—

Of the occasional ridiculous little storms & squalls of the past I have quite discarded them from my memory[57]—& I hope you will too—the other recollections overtop them altogether, & occupy the only permanent place in my heart—as a manly loving friendship for you does also, & will while life lasts—Harry, dont be discouraged by any business or other disappointments of the past—It will all turn out right—The main thing, in my opinion, after finding out as much as possible of life, & entering upon it (it is a strange mixed business this life) is to live a good square one—This I believe you are really anxious to do, & God bless you in it, & you shall have all the help I can give—Your loving ever-faithful old friend & comrade—

                                        Walt Whitman

I think I am slowly getting over my chill—it is rainy, dark, muggy day, & I am staying in—had a nice call from a young Beverley merchant Mr Hovey[58] yesterday, he bo't a set of books—Did you know young Harry Bonsall[59] is & has been some time in the Insane Asylum at Blackwoodtown? I was out to dinner yesterday to Mr & Mrs Scovel's—turkey and champagne!—but that is the only spree for me in five weeks—

that his own article did WW "fuller justice" (Hanley). He vigorously defended his views in a letter to Burroughs on February 26, 1881 (Barrus, 201–204).
    55. Excerpts from articles about Thomas Carlyle appeared in the New York *Tribune* on February 21. WW returned the clipping from the newspaper on February 28 (*CB*).
    56. This letter was mentioned in *CB*.
    57. Relations between the poet and the young man were frequently strained; note the earlier letters to Harry, and see Introduction.
    58. Franklin H. Hovey was a salesman in Philadelphia (*CB*).
    59. The son of Henry Lummis Bonsall, editor and politician. According to WW's letter to Mrs. Stafford on February 6, 1889, Bonsall died in the asylum in the preceding month (Feinberg); the poet's brother was in the same institution at the time.

Hank, I want you to acknowledge this letter—I hope this won't fail to reach you like some others I have sent—I want to come down before long & then we will have some good square talks—it is now half past 4 & I see the sun is going to set clear—

1015. *To Harry Stafford*   *[3].7. [1881]*

Camden Feb: 7[60]

Dear boy Harry,

Your letter rec'd to-day—I am sorry you didn't go in & read the piece your own self—it has got to be done, speaking in public, & the more you hang back & dread it, the worse it grows—after trying it on once or twice, you find it is nothing to be afraid of—

I have been busy all the forenoon fixing one of my little pieces *"How I get around at 60 and take notes"* for the N Y paper, the *Critic*—they give me $10 a piece for them, & want several more—I make use of my notes—at Timber Creek and Glendale and every where—I shall use them in a book at a future time—Hank, dear boy, I hope you are all right again by the time this reaches you—It is now noon & I must get out a bit—

I went out & took a short stroll, but my knees gave out & I had to turn back—beautiful day here—I saw, had 10 minutes talk with, the young lady lives next door but one above us in Stevens street, (I have spoken to you about) a great friend of mine, lived here ever since we have —I think she is the handsomest woman & pleasantest ways for young, I ever knew—full figure, blonde, good hair, teeth, complexion, ab't 19, a worker too, cooks & scrubs, but when she dresses up, she takes the shine off of all—(O that I was young again)—always feel better the whole day, when I can see & talk with her—

8½ Evening—after supper, I will finish—Have been over in Phila— went out a ways on Market st cars—nothing to write about particular— Shall be down Friday in the 4½ p. m. train, to Kirkwood—So long, dear son—

W W

---

60. WW erred in writing "Feb: 7." According to *CB*, he sent Harry a letter on March 7 and went to Glendale on Friday, March 11.

61. This "letter-card" was sent on Wednesday, March 9 (*CB*). The visitor from Boston was George Parsons Lathrop (see 1018). I have not been able to identify the

1016. *To Ruth Stafford*   *3.[9. 1881]*

Camden Wednesday afternoon | March 8[61]

Dear girl Ruth

Your nice letter came all right, & I was glad to hear from you, & the news around there—I put in quite a busy day yesterday—in the forenoon, 9 to 10, went to the funeral of a valued friend of mine—then had three visitors, made long calls during the day—I was glad to see them all—one from Boston, I had long wanted to see—then middle of the afternoon went to the polls to vote, (election day here yesterday)—and went over to Philadelphia on a jaunt & visit from 4 to 6½—But today it is raining & blowing at a great rate, & I am staying in writing—give my love to your father & mother—I am sorry to hear by your letter she is not very well—I hope you fly around & spare her as much as possible in the work—I shall be down Friday in the 4½ afternoon train to Kirkwood if it dont storm—

Your friend

Walt Whitman

1017. *To an Unidentified Correspondent*

431 Stevens Street | Camden New Jersey
March 15 | '81

Yours of 12th rec'd. No, I have had no call to deliver my Lincoln lecture in New York or Brooklyn this Spring—& no arrangements made.

Walt Whitman

1018. *To John Burroughs*   *[3.16. 1881]*[62]

Camden Wednesday Evn'g

Dear friend

Yours rec'd with the good 10—God bless you—I half-moped along all through February, but am coming round, same as before —I go down three or four days at a time to my friends the Staffords, & get out in the woods a great deal—It is only half an hour's journey—go

"valued friend."

62. WW referred to this letter in *CB*. On March 14 Burroughs sent "a little remembrance—enough to pay your expenses up here when you get ready to come" (Feinberg; Traubel, I, 43).

again Friday if it dont storm[63]—Should have come up there with you a month ago, but was hardly able—I got a bad chill six weeks ago, struck in —(was quite well up to that time)—

Your letter *don't contain* the slip about the Emerson business you allude to[64]—The just published Carlyle *Reminiscences* so well & strongly praised in the *Herald*, the *Critic* & every where, don't confirm or add to my estimation of C—*Much the contrary*[65]—

Kennedey comes here quite often & is disposed to be friendly—I guess he is a pretty good man, but has *the fever called literature* & I shouldn't wonder if he was in for it, for life[66]—Lathrop[67] has visited me—very pleasant—Shall be glad to supply you with a set of books of course—I have plenty yet[68]—

Walt Whitman

1019. *To Thomas Nicholson*

Camden New Jersey U S America | March 17 '81

Dear Tom

Your letter has just come all right & I am glad to hear from you again. Every thing seems to go lovely there with you & the boys & Dr B[ucke] (which is as it should be)—Tom, I often think of you all, & of the last night we all got together, & of the friendly parting drink we all had out there on the lawn—seems as if I only got to know you & all best & then time for me to clear out—

I have some good times here in moderation—I cant go around very lively, but I enjoy what's going on wherever I go—This 31st of May coming I shall be 62—but thank the Lord I still feel young at heart & cheery as ever—After I returned last fall from Canada I was first rate all along—put in four good months—had some rare old times—will tell you when we meet, Tom—but some six weeks ago was careless enough to get badly chill'd all through my whole body, & repeated the next day— So I have been since quite under the weather—But I am getting over it & feeling quite myself again—I find I can be well enough if I take very particular care of myself, how I go, &c—

63. WW again went to Glendale on March 18 and remained there four days (*CB*).
64. Burroughs enclosed, or thought he had, a copy of Emerson's "Impressions of Thomas Carlyle in 1848," which was to appear in the May issue of *Scribner's Monthly*, xxii, 89–92.
65. A review of James Anthony Froude's volume appeared in *The Critic* on March 12 (1, 59–60). Of Carlyle, "a towering and god-like man," Burroughs wrote eulogistically on March 14 (Feinberg; Traubel, 1, 43).
66. Burroughs observed on March 14: Kennedy "is a good fellow but he needs hatcheling to get the tow out of the flax" (Feinberg; Traubel, 1, 44).

An old doctor here said to me "Whitman you are like an old wagon, built of first rate stuff, & the best sort of frame & wheels & nuts—& as long as you are mighty careful, & go slow, & *Keep to good roads*, you will last as long as any of us—but if you get on bad roads, or cut up any capers, then *look out*"—I go down every week or two (I go tomorrow again) about 20 miles from here right into the country, with a family of farmers, dear friends of mine, named Stafford—Keep a country store also—a big family of boys & girls, & Mrs S one of the kindest & best women in the world—how much happier one can be when there is good women around —Does me good to be with them all. Every thing is very old fashioned, just suits me—good grub & plenty of it. My great loafing place out there is a big old woods, mostly pine & oak, but lots of laurel & holly, old paths & roads every where through the thick woods—I spend hours there every day—have it all to myself—go out there well-protected, even in a snow storm—rabbits & squirrels, & lots of birds beginning already—Tom, you would laugh to see me the way I amuse myself, often spouting terrible pieces Shakspere or Homer as loud as I can yell. (But that always was a favorite practice of mine—I used to do it in the din of Broadway New York from the top of an omnibus—at other times along the seashore at Coney Island)—

Tom, my paper is fill'd & I must close—I wanted to write something about the running & matches, but must postpone it—Give my love to all my friends there & you yourself, dear boy—

Walt Whitman

1020. *To Anne Gilchrist*

> ADDRESS: Mrs Gilchrist | Keats' corner Well Road |
> Hampstead | London | England. POSTMARKS:
> Philadelphia | Mar | 21 | (?); London (?) | D |
> Paid | 4(?) Ap 81.

Kirkwood New Jersey U S America | March 20 '81

I am down here spending a few days[69]—Every thing continues very much the same—Our friends the S[tafford]s still at Glendale,

---

67. George Parsons Lathrop (1851–1898) was a journalist and the biographer of his father-in-law, Nathaniel Hawthorne. WW received a letter from Lathrop on March 23 (lost) inviting him to come to Boston to give his lecture on Lincoln (*CB*). According to Kennedy (3), Lathrop was in Philadelphia on March 8 in order to arrange for WW's lecture. Lathrop wrote to the poet for the first time on April 20, 1878 (Feinberg; Traubel, II, 315–316). On March 31, 1885, he urged WW to give a reading from his own poetry in order to raise funds in aid of international copyright laws (Feinberg).

68. According to Barrus (200), WW enclosed a proof of "Patroling Barnegat."

69. WW was at Glendale from March 18 to 22, March 26 to 30, and April 2 to 7 (*CB*).

farming & store-keeping—Mr and Mrs S. & all the boys & girls as usual—

Nothing very new with me—I suppose you have rec'd my pieces, slips, papers &c. sent the past winter[70]—I rec'd your good letter ab't ten days ago[71]—trust you are yourself again in sound health by this time[72]—I believe I wrote last ab't my being somewhat unwell[73]—got badly chill'd —felt the effects two months—am now pretty well over it, & expect to be as usual till next time—My brother & sister well—J[ohn] B[urroughs] is reading the proofs of new book *Pepacton* (the Indian name of a beautiful little river)[74]—I am out in the woods a great deal—to-day mild but damp & cloudy—a little bird they call the rain-bird is singing softly & coyly on a bush over the road—

W W

1021. *To Susan Stafford*   *3.31. [1881?]*[75]

ADDRESS: Mrs Susan M Stafford | (Glendale) | Kirkwood | Camden County | New Jersey. POSTMARK: Camden | Mar(?) | 31 | N.J.

Camden March 31

Shall come down Saturday afternoon in the 4 o'clock train—to Kirkwood—

W.W.

1022. *To the Staffords*   *4.15 [–17. 1881]*

Well here I am in a grand old hotel, the finest in town—the proprietor Mr Ferrin[76] (a stranger too) sent and invited me to stop here as the guest of the house & no bill to pay—nice room large, fire in it, first rate grub (too good, I am tempted too much)—When I got up this

---

70. One of the pieces WW sent to Mrs. Gilchrist was "Death of Carlyle," to which she referred in her reply (LC; Harned, 198).

71. Mrs. Gilchrist's letter was sent on February 16 (Pennsylvania).

72. In her answer on April 18, Mrs. Gilchrist wrote: "I am well again so far as digestion &c goes; but bronchitis & asthma of a chronic kind still trouble me—My breath is so short, I cannot walk, which is a privation" (LC; Harned, 197).

73. WW wrote last to Mrs. Gilchrist on January 1 (see 993) before his illness. She noted his error in her reply.

74. Burroughs mentioned this fact in his letter of March 14 (Feinberg; Traubel, I, 43). *Pepacton* includes "Nature and the Poets" (see 941).

75. Since WW went to Glendale on Saturday, April 2 (CB), the year appears to be

morning, snow falling thick & every thing dark & cloudy & wintry—but looks a little brighter now—I am feeling pretty well—went out around yesterday & last night—great bright stirring city, this—great people, these Yankees—I like them—I am used tip top here—friends call all the time[77] —lecture comes off to-night.

Saturday Evening Lecture went off first rate last night—best I have had yet, better audience (better than New York or Philadelphia)—I am enjoying myself well—have been out riding today & shall go again to-morrow. I dont know that I can tell you anything particularly to interest you but I suppose you will like to have a word. I am to stop here till Tuesday or Wednesday next. Love to Harry & Ed—I send you a paper—

Walt Whitman

Boston Friday now April 15

1023. *To Helen E. Price*

ADDRESS: Miss Helen E. Price | Woodside | Long Island | New York.

431 Stevens Street | Camden New Jersey April 21 '81
Dear Helen Price
    Your good letter has come, & I am glad indeed to hear from you, & sister & father, & have you *located*—All sorrowful, solemn, yet soothing thoughts come up in my mind at reminiscences of my dear friend, your dear mother[78]—have often thought of you all, since '73 the last time I saw you so briefly—so sadly—
    About Dr Bucke—(he is a long-established *medical doctor* & head of the Asylum for the Insane, at London, Ontario, Canada)—you can write to him freely & send him what you feel to—he is a true & trusted friend of mine—I know him well[79]—
    I have just returned from Boston, where I have been the past week—

correct.
    76.   Charles B. Ferrin, the proprietor of the Revere House. WW was in Boston from April 13 to 19. The proceeds from the lecture amounted to $135 (*CB*).
    77.   For the Boston visit, see *The Critic* of May 7, 1881; SD, 264–269, 347–348; Allen, 491. An account of WW's lecture appeared in the Boston *Herald* on April 16, reprinted in part in *Memoranda During the War*, ed. Basler (1962), 34–35.
    78.   Abby H. Price, an old friend of the Whitman family, had died on May 4, 1878; see *Putnam's Monthly*, v (1908), 163–169.
    79.   Undoubtedly Helen Price wrote to WW after receiving a request from Dr. Bucke for material to be included in his study of the poet. Her reminiscences appear in Bucke (26–32). WW and Dr. Bucke visited Miss Price from July 23 to 28, 1881 (see 1044).

went on to read my annual *Death of Abraham Lincoln* on the anniversary of that tragedy—

I am pretty well for me—am still under the benumbing influences of paralysis, but thankful to be as well as I am—still board here (make my head quarters here) with my brother & his wife—Eddy, my brother, is living & well, he is now boarding ab't 40 miles from here[80]—Yes, Helen dear, when I come to New York, I will send you word sure—Best love to you, Emmy, father & all, especially little Walter[81]—

Walt Whitman

1024. *To Jeannette L. Gilder*   4.27. [1881]

Camden Wednesday noon | April 27

My dear Jeannie

Yours just rec'd here sent on from Boston—Yes, I will give you a page or more of Boston notes[82]—will send them on by mail to-morrow night—so you will get them Friday morning & be able to send me a proof Saturday afternoon & I will return Sunday night, so you will get it Monday morning—

Walt Whitman

1025. *To Ruth Stafford*   4.29. [1881]

Camden Friday noon April 29[83]

Dear Ruth

Yours rec'd & accordingly I will not come down now until I hear from you—Pretty warm dry weather here & I suppose you have the same —The woods must be coming out—have you gathered any arbutus?

Give my love to your father & mother, & to Harry, Ed & all. I am sorry the mother is sick—hope when this comes she will be all right again—I am about half-and-half, have had several little jobs of writing to do—the

80. Edward, WW's feeble-minded brother, went on March 23 to an institution at Glen Mills, Pa. WW sent $16 monthly to William V. Montgomery for Ed's care (*CB*).
81. Helen's sister, Emily, who had married in 1869 (see 341), probably named one of her sons after the poet.
82. The "Boston notes" became the third instalment of "How I Get Around at 60, and Take Notes," which appeared in *The Critic* on May 7 (see 992). WW was paid $15 for the article (*CB*).
83. WW referred to this letter in *CB*, "postponing visit until I hear from them."
84. For Horner, see 994, and for Hieniken (not Hinieken), see 982. I have not identified Burr.
85. This letter was noted in *CB*. For Harry's letter to WW on April 4 (or 14), see Introduction.

hot weather makes me hanker for the country—I see Horner & Burr occasionally—How is Hinieken?[84] Good by, Ruthy dear—

W.W.

I had written a postal before I rec'd yours postponing till Tuesday—but now I will postpone until I hear from you—

1026. *To Harry Stafford* 5.5. [*1881*]

Camden May 5th Evening[85]

Dear Hank

Yours of yesterday rec'd this afternoon, & glad to hear from you & the folks—I hear from you now & then by Hoag[86] or Burr, who tell me they meet you up here frequently—(I wish you had said how Hieneken is getting along—is he getting better?)

Well, Hank, my Boston tramp, lecture, &c. turned out far ahead of what I had any idea of—it was not a very large room, but it was packed full (at $1 a head) & they say there never was a more *high toned crowd* collected in the town—full half were ladies, & I never saw finer ones—I had good quarters at the principal hotel, the Revere House, (dead-headed, the proprietor, Mr Ferrin invited me to stay as long as I liked)—& callers all the time—So, boy, you see how your uncle was *set up*—& yet I am going to speak to all my old friends just the same! !

Have had several little jobs writing lately—Phila: and N. Y. papers[87]—(will send you the *Critic* of the latter city next Monday or Tuesday with my piece in)—Havn't felt very well lately—a real bad spell last night & this forenoon—don't feel right living in the city any how, after the summer comes on—very possibly shall go off to Canada again, as Dr and Mrs B[ucke] wish me to, & write strongly—

I sent you a little book of poetry by a boy 13 years old, in Pennsylvania, he sent it to me with a nice letter[88]—Well, Hank, my sheet is short & most

86. See 979.
87. WW sent on May 3 "Bumble-Bees and Bird Music" to W. R. Balch of *The American* (Philadelphia), for which he received $20 (*CB*). It appeared on May 14, and was later included in *SD* (263). The poet sent "My Picture-Gallery" to Balch on October 8, 1880, for which he received $5, and which appeared in *The American* on October 30. On May 27, 1881, he sent to the same newspaper "A Summer's Invocation" (later called "Thou Orb Aloft Full-Dazzling"), and received $12 from Balch. The poem was printed on June 14. For this information I am indebted to Miss Freda Gray of the Carnegie Library of Pittsburgh.
Unless WW meant *The Critic*, it is not clear which "N. Y. papers" he referred to. The third instalment of "How I Get Around at 60, and Take Notes" appeared on May 7.
88. On May 3 WW sent Harry "Newspaper ballads" (*CB*).

full, & I must come to a close—I gather by your letter that you are in good spirits—love to you & God bless you—I am sorry enough to hear your mother is unwell—Susan, my dear friend, I hope when this comes you will be all right—

Walt Whitman

I suppose your mother got a letter & some papers from Boston,[89] as I sent them, & of course supposed you would all read them—my best love to your mother & father & I want you to let them read this—

1027. *To James R. Osgood*

431 Stevens Street | Camden New Jersey May 8 '81
My dear Mr Osgood[90]

I write in answer to the note on the other side from my dear friend O'Reilly[91]—My plan is to have all my poems, down to date, comprised in one 12 mo: Volume, under the name "Leaves of Grass"—I think it will have to be in brevier (or bourgeois) solid—and I want as fine a (plain) specimen in type, paper, ink, binding, &c. as bookmaking can produce—not for luxury however, but solid wear, use, reading, (to carry in the pocket, valise &c)—a book of about 400 pages to sell at $3—The text will be about the same as hitherto, occasional slight revisions, simplifications in punctuation &c—the main thing a more satisfactory consecutive order—a better *ensemble*, to suit me—some new pieces, perhaps 30 pages—

Fair warning on one point—the old pieces, the *sexuality* ones, about which the original row was started & kept up so long, are all retained, & must go in the same as ever[92]—Should you, upon this outline, wish to see the copy, I will place it in your hands with pleasure—

Walt Whitman

89. See 1022.

90. James R. Osgood (1836–1892) was the publisher of Browning, Arnold, Holmes, Henry James, and Howells; see Carl J. Weber, *The Rise and Fall of James Ripley Osgood* (1959).

91. John Boyle O'Reilly (1844–1890) was a fervent Irish patriot who joined the British Army in order to sabotage it. He was arrested and sentenced to be hanged in 1866. Later the decree was altered, and O'Reilly was sent to Australia, where he escaped on an American whaler in 1869. In 1876 he became the coeditor of the Boston *Pilot*, a position which he held until his death in 1890. See William G. Schofield, *Seek for a Hero: The Story of John Boyle O'Reilly* (c. 1956).

On April 26 O'Reilly informed WW that "James R Osgood wants to see the material for your complete book" (Huntington). WW's letter to Osgood was written, as he indicated, on the verso of O'Reilly's.

92. Osgood did not pay sufficient attention to WW's "warning," since he was not prepared to resist the censors who succeeded in protecting Boston's dubious morality by making it a national joke.

1028. *To Ruth Stafford*   *5.10.* [*1881*]

ADDRESS: Miss Ruth Anna Stafford | Kirkwood
(Glendale) | New Jersey. POSTMARK: (?)am(?) |
[*indecipherable*].

Camden Tuesday night May 10[93]
Yours rec'd—All right—I will come down Friday afternoon in the
4½ train to Kirkwood—

W W

1029. *To Henry A. Beers*[94]

ADDRESS: Henry A Beers | New Haven | Conn:.
POSTMARK: Kirkwood | May | 21(?) | N.J.

May 20 '81
Your pleasant note of 16th rec'd—glad you wrote—just now I am
down in the country temporarily—in the Jersey woods[95]—am well for me—
Walt Whitman

1030. *To James R. Osgood*

Camden New Jersey | May 20 '81
My dear Mr Osgood
Yours rec'd,[96] & accordingly I am fixing up the copy, which I will
send on to you in a few days—perhaps it will be a week—
Walt Whitman[97]

93. May 10 fell on Tuesday in 1881, and WW went to Glendale on Friday,
May 13 (*CB*).
94. Beers (1847–1926) was a poet and professor of English literature at Yale.
On May 16 he wrote to thank WW for quoting his verses in *The American* on May 14:
"To a young writer, uncertain of himself, the slightest notice from an older & distinguished brother in the craft is very precious. . . . because it gives him heart in his
work" (LC). Beers in 1898 termed WW "a great sloven" (see Kennedy, *The Fight of a
Book for the World* [1926], 136). Similar reservations appear in his *Four Americans*
(1919), 85–90.
95. WW was at Glendale from May 13 to 26 except for a brief visit to Camden
on May 17 (*CB*); see also *Walt Whitman's Diary in Canada*, 58–59.
96. On May 12 Osgood asked for "the copy" in order to make "careful estimates
as to its size, style etc. and give you our views." He also inquired about the plates of the
Thayer & Eldridge edition (LC; *CW*, VIII, 277).
97. This part of the letter was not printed in *CW*. The final sentence of the second
paragraph was also omitted.

Yes—a new one Vol: edition would supersede all others not only legally (I am sole owner of the copyright, which I have kept thoroughly fortified from the beginning) but by superiority, additions, modernness, &c— The Thayer & Eldridge plates of 1860 *are* in existence in the hands of R Worthington[98] N Y (a bad egg) who has sold languid surreptitious copies—can be stopt instantly by me & will be—(The matter is not of any moment however)—The plates were offered to me two years ago & I refused them as worthless—

1031. *To James R. Osgood*   5.26. [1881]

431 Stevens street | Camden New Jersey May 26   8 p m

My dear Osgood

Just returned from a week down in the Jersey woods—& find yours—Will send on the copy so you can have it in Boston Monday forenoon next at furthest[99]—

Walt Whitman

1032. *To James R. Osgood*

431 Stevens Street | Camden New Jersey | May 29 '81

My dear Mr Osgood

I suppose you rec'd the copy yesterday (Saturday) as I sent it the previous day. You already have my plan—a volume of say 400 pages, (not over 450) handy size, first class (but I know you wouldn't issue any other) in paper, print, binding &c: but markedly plain & simple even to Quakerness—I have a desire that all through even in capitalization, punctuation &c it shall be so—no sensationalism or luxury—a well made book for honest wear & use & carrying with you—to retail at $3—

The book has not hitherto been really *published* at all—the issues have been *reconnoisances*—printings in proof for zealous friends &c.

The British market is an important consideration.

The copy I sent will have to be returned before very long to me, for complete minor & technical revision, as I did not wait to finish it after receiving your last letter.

98. See 985.

99. This note was written in reply to Osgood's letter of May 23, in which he asked for "the copy *this* week, as I sail for Europe in a fortnight" (LC; *CW*, VIII, 278).

1. Osgood informed WW on May 31 that the firm would be "glad to publish the book" and proposed a royalty of ten per cent. Again he inquired about Worthington's pirated books: "We should like to feel clear that you can control the old Thayer & Eldridge plates, so as to stop the issue of any books printed from them" (LC; *CW*, VIII, 278–279). Osgood returned WW's copy at the same time, and enclosed a copy of *Our*

But I reserve any thing further until I hear your definite decision on the main point—the publication[1]—

Walt Whitman

1033. *To Edward Carpenter*

ADDRESS: Edward Carpenter | Bradway | near
Sheffield | England. POSTMARK: Camden | May |
30 | 12 M | N.J.

431 Stevens Street | Camden New Jersey U S
America | May 30 '81

My dear Edward Carpenter,

Yours of May 14 rec'd, with the £3[2]—Many thanks—I send the three L of G by same mail with this, same address—please notify me soon as they reach you safely—

I am much as usual—Pretty well a good deal of the time—go down to the Staffords' farm often—was there two weeks of this month—they are well—have not forgotten you—Harry still works at telegraphing—

I was on in Boston five weeks since—but I believe I sent you a little printed item of my jaunt—

I sympathize with you in the loss of the dear mother—I have drunk of that cup—Commend me faithfully in good wishes to my unmet friends you come across—to Robert Sharkland, whose name I have written as you desired, in the Volume—

Write to me as often as you can, my dear friend—& I will try the same to you—

Walt Whitman

1034. *To James R. Osgood*

431 Stevens Street | Camden New Jersey | June 1 '81

My dear Mr Osgood

Yours of May 31 just rec'd—Thanking you warmly for willingness, promptness, &c. my terms are:

25 cts on every copy sold if the retail price is put at $2

30 cts on every copy sold if the retail price is put at $2.50[3]

Poetical Favorites as a sample of what the firm proposed to do with WW's book (LC, unpublished).

2. Carpenter's letter is not known. On July 1 Carpenter wrote from Sheffield what WW termed a "good letter": "These friends that I have here and my more natural open air life seem to have made a difference to me. I feel as if I had touched the bottom at last, and had something firm to go upon—after floundering about so long. Thanks for all that also to you" (Feinberg).

3. This was WW's counterproposal to Osgood's offer of ten per cent. The publisher accepted WW's terms on June 3 (LC; *CW*, VIII, 279–280).

If these suit you the bargain is settled—you shall be fully fortified as sole publisher with all legal authority—& you can act accordingly in England—If they do not suit no harm done—the thing is off—but with perfect good feeling left on both sides.

Walt Whitman

1035. *To James R. Osgood*

431 Stevens Street | Camden New Jersey | June 4 '81

My dear Mr Osgood

Yours of yesterday rec'd, which settles the engagement. I shall forward the copy soon. The name will be *Walt Whitman's Poems*—with the sub-title *Leaves of Grass* in its place or places inside. I suggest a 400 page book—in size, thickness, general appearance &c: closely like Houghton & Mifflin's 1880 edition of *Owen Meredith's Poems*, only better paper & print, & at least one size larger type—I think in solid bourgeois (or long primer)—ought to be new type—page the same size as the Owen Meredith (see outline in blue lines on the picture I send) with the same rather narrow margin, which I prefer to wide—in the make up every thing the reverse of free spacing out or free leading—of course not crowding too close either, but with an eye to compacting the matter (for there is quite a good deal to go in the 400 pages)—plain green muslin binding—binding costing say 15 or 16 cts.—no gilt edges—a handsome, stately, *plain book*—

I shall get a new copyright out—Shall probably write to you in London about the English sale[4]—Can I get a British copyright by going to Canada? If so I will go—How would the enclosed picture do for a frontispiece? I like it—It is made by Gutekunst 712 Arch St Philadelphia—I think he would furnish them at three to four dollars a thousand.[5]

Walt Whitman

Who of your house shall I specially see & deal with if I should take a notion to come on to Boston in person with the copy—or after the type setting commences?

4. Osgood advised WW on June 3 to write to him in care of Trübner & Co., London.

5. Benjamin H. Ticknor, who replied to this letter on June 8, liked the "photo-

1036. *To James R. Osgood & Company*

431 Stevens Street | Camden New Jersey June 7 '81

Dear Sirs

Would you have set up for me from the copy enclosed two sample pages size of the below diagram? I think—am pretty sure—the book (400

this is the size of the printed

    page, without the *folio & running* title

— — —

set up a sample one page from the copy

    in long primer solid

— — —

then another sample, one page, in

    bourgeois solid,

      & send me

type": "should be quite inclined to use it, and perhaps also the first, steel, portrait" (LC). After noting his letter to Osgood on June 4 in *CB*, WW added: "(mistake about price of lith[ograph] corrected next day)."

pages about) will go in long primer solid. But I would like to have a sample page in bourgeois too for my calculations—I hope it will be new type —the typographical show of my poems—how they shall show (negatively as well as absolutely) on the black & white page—is always in my idea in making them—I am printer enough for that[6]—

Walt Whitman

1037. To James R. Osgood & Company

431 Stevens Street | Camden New Jersey June 16 '81

Dear Sirs

I have been down in the Jersey woods the last ten days—just returned[7]—have finished my copy which is now ready to put in hand—*all plain sailing & all complete*—When do you want to begin? & will it go ahead pretty fast when actually begun?

I have spoken about the type—*ought to be new or substantially new long primer*—I sent on the proof page for a little change, last night on my return—I have pretty well decided to come on to Boston & see it through[8]—

Walt Whitman

1038. To John Burroughs

TRANSCRIPT.

June 17, 1881

. . . I have just concluded a contract with J. R. Osgood and Co of Boston for the publishing of my poems complete in one volume, under the title of "Walt Whitman's Poems" (the old name of "Leaves of Grass" running through the same as ever) —to be either a $2. book or a $2.50 one —if the former, I to have 25 cts royalty, if the latter, 30 cts) —The proposition for publication came from them. The bulk of the pieces will be the

---

6. The firm sent on June 10 "3 sample pages of the size you indicated" (LC).
7. WW was with the Staffords from June 11 to 15 (CB).
8. Osgood & Co. sent "three new proofs" to WW on June 21 (LC).
9. On May 23 Burroughs wrote to WW inviting him to Esopus, N. Y., and promising to visit Camden shortly (Hanley). With his letter WW sent a copy of "A

same as hitherto—only I shall secure now the consecutiveness and *ensemble* I am always thinking of—Book will probably be out before winter.

Nothing very new otherwise—you must have kept posted about my Boston jaunt, for I sent you papers—it was altogether a curious success —not so much in quantity as quality—

Last January, I think it was, I took a bad chill—bothered me for over two months, lingering along—but I believe the Boston jaunt drove the last of it away. . . .

My forthcoming summer movements are not exactly decided—probably go on to Boston for two or three weeks, as I like to keep a sharp eye on my proofs and typography—then I must go a month in Canada—I will keep you posted, and will try to pay you a visit, too[9]. . . .

1039. *To Thomas Nicholson*

Camden New Jersey U S A | June 19 '81

Dear Tom

I am still here & am well as usual—have just returned from some twelve days down in the Jersey woods[10] where I like to go this time of year (I believe I have told you about it)—Plenty of woods here in Jersey & plenty of sea-shore—& I like them both—& get a good deal of comfort out of them both—Things are going on pretty much the same with me as when I last wrote—that was an awful affair on the river, & I tell you I looked over the lists of names the next two or three days with fear & trembling—I dont seem to remember Wm Hardy you mention—but I dare say I knew him among the men, poor fellow—

It is now late Sunday afternoon, been a very hot day here, & there is just now a lively little thunderstorm coming on, (& over almost as soon as on)—I must finish my letter quickly, for I must go the P.O. here as it shuts at 6 Sundays—Tommy, dear boy, this is only an apology for a letter but it will show that I bear you in mind & all the rest too—I shall be on there at the Asylum this summer—not perhaps for a long visit, but for two or three weeks[11]—I am having some work to do this summer at writing

Summer's Invocation" (*CB*).

    10. WW was at the Staffords' only from June 11 to 15 (*CB*). He spent twelve days in Glendale in May.

    11. WW was too occupied with printing the Osgood edition to make the trip, but he met Nicholson and Dr. Bucke in Jersey City, N. J., on July 23 (*CB*).

—I rec'd the paper—good luck to you if you run on the 28th—Tom, I must end—love to you & the same to all the boys—& girls too—

Walt Whitman

1040. *To James R. Osgood & Company*   [6.23. 1881][12]

ENDORSED (by WW): "sent | June 23 '81." DRAFT LETTER.

Specimen page rec'd—seems to me just about right. My copy will come in about 400 pages of it—perhaps a trifle more. Copy is all ready—Shall come on personally with it soon as you are prepared to begin the type-setting—Please make the arrangements, & write me forthwith.[13]

1041. *To Louisa Orr Whitman*   7.6. [1881]

ADDRESS: Mrs Louisa Whitman | Care of F E Dowe | Norwich | Conn:. POSTMARKS: Camden | Jul | 6 | 5 (?)M | N.J.; Norwich | Jul | (?) | 12 M.

Camden July 6—Afternoon

Dear Sister Lou

There is nothing very new & I suppose George has written to you, as he returned about 6 p m yesterday all right—but I thought I would drop a line[14]—

Of course the shooting of President Garfield[15] is the general subject, & has depressed me much, but for the last twenty four hours, his case is so much more favorable—We had the most horrible *celebration* here I ever knew, commenced at dark Sunday night, continued all night & of course next day, ruffians yelling, crackers, and all the old guns & pistols of all Jersey, with all the bad elements of humanity completely let loose &

12. The date is also confirmed by an entry in *CB*.
13. The publishing house replied on June 25: "If you desire to personally oversee the beginning, (or all, if you prefer), shall be happy to see you at any time, & do our best to facilitate matters" (LC; *CW*, VIII, 282).
14. George's wife left for Connecticut on July 2 (*CB*).
15. WW knew Garfield when he was in Washington (see 103). Later in the year he wrote "The Sobbing of the Bells," which appeared in the Boston *Daily Globe* on September 27, and was included in *The Poets' Tribute to Garfield* (1881), 71. See also *Poet-Lore*, x (1898), 618.
16. Beginning July 2, WW took his meals with Mrs. Caroline Wroth, the wife of a

making the most infernal din possible to conceive for over thirty hours without a moments intermission—Over in Philadelphia perfectly quiet, (all the bad stuff probably came over here)—very hot indeed here the last four days, & continues still—I am standing it well—I take my meals at Mrs Wroth's[16] & find it a very good place—it was a good move, my going there—Mrs W is very kind—Tip has been all right & has had his meals regular—a little off his feed & off *his bark* this morning, I suppose from the great heat, & folks away—Arthur Stanley lives now over at the Chevaliers, with his new wife[17]—his little boy bro't me over a nice piece of wedding cake Sunday which I took down to Alice Wroth[18]—

The *house* is all right so far—I try to keep as cool as I can—what with bathing & ventilation, & of course you will find some litter when you come back—

I send some *Ledgers*—I am writing this in the dining room, by open window—George was writing early forenoon, but has gone out—Tip has commenced a good barking at last (11½ oclock) after being quiet all the forenoon—I was afraid something was the matter with him—

I am busy five or six hours yet every day with the copy of my book— hard work to get it in the shape I want it.

As I finish it is after noon & very hot & oppressive—Love to you & all— tell little Amy[19] I have not forgotten her, & that I am going to give Tip a nice sweet coffee-cake for his dinner—George has just returned—

W.W.

1042. *To Harry Stafford*

Camden July 14 '81

Dear boy Harry

Glad to hear from you by your letter, & hope the Ashland job may lead to something better in both pay & hours—I am not very well—the fearful heat has struck in to me, & I have had a miserable two weeks past[20]

Philadelphia importer who lived at 319 Stevens Street, Camden (*CB*). I am indebted for this information to Mrs. Wroth's grandson, James S. Wroth, to whom WW sent a post card on July 28, 1887.

17. Arthur Stanley was an oilcloth painter; according to "A Child's Memories of the Whitmans" by Amy Haslam Dowe, some old ladies, the Chevaliers, lived across the street from WW.

18. Mrs. Wroth's daughter.

19. Louisa's niece, Amy Dowe (see 912).

20. On July 15 WW wrote in *CB*: "quite unwell these days—prostrated with the heat & bad, bad air of the city."

—shall get away soon, but don't know exactly when & where—will write to you soon as I get anywhere & have any thing to say[21]—

I have been staying alone here in the house, as the folks have gone off on summer trip—My sister is at the White Mountains—I take my meals at Mrs Wroth's 319 Stevens—I like it—An old lady I knew quite well died there very suddenly—funeral to-day (this forenoon) there.

How are you all? I have not seen or heard any thing from you all since Ruth's letter telling me not to come down, & that your mother was going away—I see Ben Stafford[22] last evening over in Market street Phila: he told me he was standing in the market—had been at it for a week, & liked it—I see Hoag[23] once in a while—it was a good little squib he put in the *Press* and *Courier* about you at Ashland—

Well, Harry, dear son, I believe that is all, (& not much either)— Love to you & all—

Your old W.W.

Keep a good heart through botherations—I will write to you from somewhere again before long—

1043. *To James R. Osgood & Company*

431 Stevens Street | Camden New Jersey |
July 17 '81

Dear Sirs

I have been unwell & disabled the last fifteen days from the heat & several little things happening. Am pretty well shattered any how—Am busy with the copy of the book—thought I had finished—but I find it will bear about as much work as I can put on it—& I can't hurry—But it is about in printing office shape—

How will it do to have this definite arrangement—that I come on by (or just before) 1st of September to Boston—& we make a clear start with it at once then? Ought to be put through I suppose in two months—say by the end of October—

I was thinking something might be done with an extra bound edi-

21. WW left Camden on July 23 to meet Dr. Bucke (*CB*).
22. George Stafford's cousin (see 880).
23. See 979.
24. On July 18 the firm was ready to "start the book whenever you wish, and should consider six to eight weeks sufficient time for it" (LC; *CW*, VIII, 283).
25. WW met Dr. Bucke and Thomas Nicholson in Jersey City on July 23, and went to Woodside, Long Island, where he stayed with Helen and Arthur Price until July 28. He spent the following four days at West Hills near Huntington. On August 1 he went to New York City, where he stayed with Edgar M. Smith, listed in the Directory

tion for the holiday book trade for '81–2 for gift books—Couldn't we get it out early half of November if I am in Boston with the copy complete on or before 1st September sure?[24]

Walt Whitman

1044. *To John Burroughs*   8.3. [1881]

ADDRESS: John Burroughs | Roxbury | Delaware County | New York. POSTMARK: New York | Aug 3 | 9 30 PM | 81.

5 East 65th street | New York City Evn'g Aug 3d
Your postal of 29th rec'd—I am here for a few days, after spending a week down on Long Island, mostly at West Hills and Cold Spring, my parents' places of nativity—& my own place.[25] Dr Bucke has been with me—he has return'd to Canada—I am about as usual—I go on to B[oston] before long, about the book—

W W

1045. *To the Editor, the New York* Tribune

ENDORSED (by WW): "Personal."

5 East 65th Street New York | noon Aug. 3 '81
My dear Sir
I send you a letter for *Summer Leisure* column[26]—say for the paper of to-morrow—the price is $10 & 30 papers—I will call at the office about 9 this (Wednesday) evening to see the proof—

Walt Whitman

1046. *To Harry Stafford*   8.5. [1881]

TRANSCRIPT.

New York City. Aug. 5[27]
. . . have been (a little) at Long Branch and Rockaway, but most of the time down on Long Island exploring the place where I was

as a secretary, until August 6 (*CB*). See also *SD*, 273. In *The Long Islander*, on August 5, appeared a lengthy article on the poet by Mrs. Mary E. Wager-Fisher, who drew upon an earlier piece in *Wide Awake Pleasure Book*, VI (February, 1878), 109–115, in which she was greatly indebted to WW. In an adjacent column of the same issue of the newspaper was a report entitled "Walt Whitman in Huntington."

26. On August 4 "A Week at West Hills" appeared in the *Tribune;* it was later included in altered form in *SD* (5–8, 352–354).

27. WW noted sending a "postal" to Stafford. While he was at West Hills, he spent one day at Long Branch and another at Far Rockaway (*CB*).

born (& the Whitmans &c for 250 years)—had a good time—am now here in New York—am going on to Boston very soon to print book . . .

1047. To Jeannette L. Gilder 8.6. [*1881*]

Aug 6 p m[28]

After correcting please take *five slip impressions* (proofs) & send me—direct to me, *care of J H Johnston Jeweler, 150 Bowery*—that will be my address for 10 days to come—as I have left 65th street.[29] I am stopping for the present out at Mott haven—

No objection to mentioning the Osgood Volume, the new & complete *Leaves of Grass*—If mentioned say while including all the old pieces, it will comprise many fresh poems—will for the first time fulfil what has been W W's main object for twenty years, completeness and relative proportion—and will be essentially a *new Volume*[30]—

Walt Whitman

1048. To Sylvester Baxter

Mott avenue & 149th Street | Station L
New York City | Aug: 8 '81

My dear Baxter[31]

Yours rec'd, & glad to hear from you. Wonder if you—or you & Guernsey[32]—couldn't help me a little. I am coming on to Boston in ten or twelve days to remain about two months—& I want a plain boarding-house or good furnished room secured, so I can go right there—Let me give you fuller particulars. Osgood & Co: are going to publish a complete & new volume of my poems, & I am coming on to see to & oversee it, every page—will take six or eight weeks. *I want quarters near, or eligible to get at, their printing office,* so I can be there two or three hours every day, handy—What I want of you is to ascertain (if you dont know already

28. The year is confirmed by the notes below. WW was at the office of *The Critic* on August 3 (*CB*). He undoubtedly was returning the corrected proof of "Spirit That Form'd This Scene," which appeared in *The Critic* on September 10. After the poem was rejected by *The North American Review*, WW sent it on May 28 to Miss Gilder, who paid him $5 (*CB*).
29. WW left the home of Edgar Smith on August 6, and stayed with his old friend until August 19, when he went to Boston (*CB*). Johnston's summer home was at Mott Avenue and 149th Street. WW described Mott Haven in the New York *Tribune* on August 15 in "City Notes in August."
30. The announcement of WW's new edition appeared in *The Critic* on August 13: "Walt Whitman's poems will soon have the recognition of a well-known pub-

—is it Cambridge?) where their printing is done, & then secure me either board in full, not more than 6, 7 or $8 a week—or a nice furnished room handy as I said. I trust you or Guernsey to know what would suit me & do for me—Try to write me here, so I can get it by first of next week, say 15th or 16th—as I shall want to be coming on within two or three days after that—If you go to Osgood's show them this letter. I am well as usual of late—have been jaunting about the Long Island & Jersey shores &c. last two weeks.

                                                            Walt Whitman

1049. *To Harry Stafford*

                                                  Boston. Aug: 20 1881.

Dear Hank

I am here seeing to the setting up & stereotyping of my book in a big printing office, (Rand & Avery.)[33] Every thing goes satisfactory enough, so far. I suppose you rec'd the paper (or papers?) I sent—they will give you some acc't of two or three little happenings in my jaunt—I was down on Long Island at the spot where I was born where I had spent my summers in youth from time to time—went around to all the old places I hadn't seen before for 40 years—seems to me now the most beautiful region on earth—Dr Bucke was with me & he thought so too—Before I went there, I was at Rockaway (L[ong] I[sland])—& at Long Branch (N J)—The last two weeks I have been in N Y City—So you see I have been the rounds—I am pretty well—& have been so—

I shall probably stay here a month or more—Dear boy, I wish you would write to me a good long letter & tell me all the news, especially about yourself. Direct to me *care of Osgood & Co: 211 Tremont street, Boston, Mass:* and I shall get it.

I have not been much about Boston this time, but it is a lively place to be in—the streets all crumpled up, short, and more corners & angles than any thing else, but clean & handsome—this forenoon I have been some

lishing house. James R. Osgood & Co. will publish 'Leaves of Grass' without any expurgations, the author having made that a condition of his contract. The book will contain many new poems, and will for the first time fulfil what Mr. Whitman says has been for years his main object in relation to the publication of his works—namely, 'completeness and relative proportion.' "

    31. Baxter (1850–1927) was on the staff of the Boston *Herald.* Apparently he met WW for the first time when he delivered his Lincoln address in Boston in April, 1881; see *PMLA,* LXIII (1948), 268. Baxter wrote many newspaper columns in praise of WW's writings, and in 1886 attempted to obtain a pension for the poet.

    32. Like Baxter, Frederic R. Guernsey was associated with the Boston *Herald.*

    33. This firm had printed the third edition (see 18). WW arrived in Boston on August 19 (*CB*).

time on *the Common* (an old Park of 60 or 70 acres right in the midst of the city with lots of fine very old trees)—I am now writing this in Osgood's place in Boston (they are the publishers of my book)—

How are you & all getting along? I wish you to give my love to your father & mother—Debbie & Jo, Ed, Mont, & Van—Ruth & little George—& tell them I remember the good times I have had, past summers—& show this letter to them, if they wish—

It is now nearly 1, & I must go off to my dinner—God bless you, dear boy, & farewell for this time—I shall write again before long—

Your old Walt

1050. *To James R. Osgood & Company* [*About 8.22. 1881*]³⁴

ADDRESS: Osgood & Co: | 211 Tremont St.

Rand & Avery's | 117 Franklin st:
Please send my mail, by bearer, & please send the same down to me here in future every morning about 10 if convenient—

Walt Whitman

1051. *To Louisa Orr Whitman*   *8.27.* [*1881*]

Boston | Saturday Evn'g | Aug: 27
Dear Sister Lou

All goes satisfactory here—I keep as well as usual—have a very good room & board in a kind of half hotel half boarding house, the hotel Waterston—the landlady, Mrs Moffit,³⁵ has a hundred guests when full, mostly families, very nice—capital table, (most too good for me, tempts me too much)—

My book is getting on swimmingly—I have got it (after considerable worrying & doing & undoing) into a shape that suits me first-rate,

34. About August 22 WW began to spend part of the day at Rand & Avery's so that he could supervise closely the printing of his book (*CB*).

35. WW paid $8 a week for his board to Mrs. Eva E. Moffit. On September 30 WW paid Mrs. Moffit $41.44 "for six weeks, up to date" and $21 on October 19 (*CB*).

36. On August 22 WW spent the morning at the printing office: "the superintendent Mr [Henry H.] Clark very kind & thoughtful—appears as though I was going to have things all my own way—I have a table & nook, in part [of] a little room, all to myself, to read proof, write, &c." In an inclusive entry, "Aug 20 to 30," WW noted: "the book well under way—I am at the printing office some hours every day." On September 1 WW sent Dr. Bucke "proofs up to page 143" and on September 4 "proofs to p 176" (*CB*). See also Furness, 263–265.

37. A lengthy interview with WW, entitled "The Good Gray Poet," appeared in the Boston *Globe* on August 24, in which the poet discussed the architectural structure of

and this printing office is putting it into typographical shape too that satisfies me well—nearly 100 pages already set up & cast—So you see that's working all right—I am mostly here at the printing office, five or six hours every day, reading proof & seeing to things[36]—Mr Osgood the publisher & Rand & Avery the printers are very friendly indeed, I couldn't have better ones to deal with. I suppose you get the papers I send—the Boston *Globe* of four or five days ago[37]—& others—I get my letters very well here, sent on from Camden—Lou, I send a small package by mail, directed to you, please put it up on my table—Shall send occasionally same way, to be put up there & kept for me—I go out riding now & then, am to go for a couple of hours this evening—havn't got any thing from you since (I believe) Monday last.

Address me either *here* (see outside of this envelope)—or care Osgood & Co: 211 Tremont Street—Of course the greatest anxiety about the President[38]—thought here to-day there is no hope—it is terrible—

Brother Walt

1052. *To an Unidentified Correspondent*   [8(?).(?). 1881]

Of course this will be crude to you—yet it is in parts suggestive—I have marked in blue pencil what might be dwelt upon or touched[39]—

1053. *To Lewis T. and Percy Ives*   9.7. [1881][40]

TRANSCRIPT

8 Bullfinch Place | Wednesday Evening |
September 7th

My dear Mr. Ives, and dear boy Percy:

I am compelled to go out to Brookline and wonder whether you could not come around here and see me tomorrow (Thursday) forenoon,

Leaves of Grass; averred that "the large magazines are still shy of me," citing a recent rejection by *Harper's Monthly* ("A Summer's Invocation"; see 994); praised Emerson as the most important American poet and termed Tennyson "in every respect the poet of our times."

38. President Garfield lingered in a critical condition until September 19.

39. This note was written in the margin of the notice in the Boston *Globe* on August 24 (see note 37 above). Undoubtedly WW sent it to one of the many newspapermen he knew.

40. Father and son, both artists. In a notation late in 1880 WW referred to Percy, "age 16, a student, intends to be an artist . . . Academy of Fine Arts" (*CB*). On December 21, 1881, Percy made several pencil sketches of WW, and in his letter to his grandmother, Mrs. Elisa S. Leggett, on December 25, he drew a sketch for her of the picture which was "in a promising condition" (Detroit Public Library). His oil painting of WW is now in the Feinberg Collection. See also Mrs. Leggett's letter to WW on July 19, 1880 (Manchester).

say before ten—9½ would suit me—I hope you can—should like well to have you.

Walt Whitman

1054. *To Harry Stafford*

Boston Sept: 9 '81

Dear Harry

I keep about the same in health—am & have been very busy with the printing of my book, it goes on all right & suits me—246 pages are up (& mostly electrotyped)[41]—

That was a sudden and dreadful piece of news, the death of Beatrice Gilchrist[42]—your mother's letter informing me was sent on here from Camden P O—Harry, please tell her I rec'd it, & thank her for sending me word—

Harry, I do not know the Secretary of the Navy or Treasury either[43] —do you still think of getting in one of the coast life-saving stations? I will write to any one you wish me to, for that purpose—fix on some particular person, who has the appointment, if you decide to try for it—I will do any thing I can for you—(By the by, tell Van I went twice to see a man in Camden, a boss plumber, three months ago—he said he could not take on any boy just then, but he probably would want one, & would send me word)—I am having good times here—have a good room & boarding house, the landlady[44] is first rate & kind [to] me, (as often happens I find my best friends among the women)—then I have a friend here, a man of leisure, who has a good horse & phaeton, takes me out riding afternoons or fine evenings[45]—So you see I am putting in *good* papers—

Well, dear boy, how does it go with you? I hope all right—I rec'd your letter here—tell Mont if he feels disposed to write to me, (if he is in the store & has a spare hour) I will answer it—if he does, I want him to tell me all the news—(I get the *Phil: Ledger*, a friend in the office there sends it to me)[46]—Hot, hot as the devil here three days the past week—but

41. The entry in CB for this date read: "have just read proof to page 245 of the book."

42. In CB WW commented: "some gloomy news—sad, sad—the death of Beatrice Gilchrist—as accomplished and noble a young woman as I ever knew." Yet he did not write to the mother until November 28. On December 14 Mrs. Gilchrist wrote to WW: "Herby wrote to Mrs. Stafford first—thinking that so the shock would come less abruptly to you" (LC; Harned, 203).

43. See 1056.
44. Mrs. Moffitt.
45. Probably one of his new Boston friends mentioned in CB: Colonel Frank E. Howe, Captain Milton Haxtun, or Ed Dallin.
46. Probably a reference to Richard E. Labar, who, according to an entry in CB,

I don't seem to melt yet—pleasant & cool now—I shall stay here three weeks yet—if you write direct same address (care J R Osgood & Co: 211 Tremont Street Boston)—Love to you, Harry boy, & keep a good heart— you know the verse of the old song

> "A light heart & thin pair of breeches
> Goes through the world my brave boys"

Well the office has just sent me a fresh batch of proofs & I must go to work & tackle them—

W W

Later—half an hour—I was keeping this, all enveloped &c. to take to the box when yours dated Sept: 3d has just come—so I open it to add a line—yes, I got the letter of over two weeks since (as above)—dear boy, I feel sorry about the ailing—write me about it all, soon as you get this —I send the papers you request, same mail with this[47]—Harry boy, if you want a little money write me & I will supply you—(Son, why did you send your letter to Camden?)

Always your old Walt

hope you will get this before Sunday—

1055. *To James R. Osgood & Company*

Boston Sept: 12 '81

J R Osgood & Co: | Dear Sirs

The documents rec'd—but I cannot agree or convey copyright as therein specified. Of course you must be thoroughly fortified in your investment & publication of the book—& I will do any & every thing to secure you to your fullest satisfaction (if not already—which I thought the case—distinctly, amply, legally secured by my letters in the correspondence between us *ante*)—But the copyright of *Leaves of Grass* must remain absolutely & solely in my own hands as hitherto.[48]

was associated with the Philadelphia *Public Ledger*. WW wrote (lost) to Labar on August 21 (*CB*). Upon his return to Camden, on November 10, he made a "visit through the *Ledger* office with Dick Labar" (*CB*).

47. According to *CB*, WW sent copies of *The Long Islander* (see 1044), the Boston *Daily Globe* (see 1051), and his article "City Notes in August," which had appeared in the New York *Tribune* on August 15. For the last-named article, included in abridged form in *SD* (273–276, 354–355), he received $10 (*CB*).

48. The firm agreed on the following day to make the changes (*LC*; *CW*, VIII, 284). The contract was executed on October 1: the price of the edition was to be $2, the royalty was twenty-five cents on every copy sold, the copyright was to remain in the poet's hands, and Osgood & Co. was to be the sole publisher for ten years (*LC*; *CW*, VIII, 285–286).

The steel engraving—just as good as new I believe—I send herewith. It is required in the book (to face page 29)—in fact is involved as part of the poem. If desired I will sell it to you, as a necessary part of the stock for issuing the book—price $50 cash, & 20 copies of book (without royalty)—I shall want 200 prints from the plate also—(the printer can make that number extra & give me)[49]—

The book will make 390 (to '95) pages. Seems to me every way best for us both that it sh'd be put at *two dollars*—& that it can well be afforded at that price.

Before putting in any thing in adv't'mt or circular advertising L. of G. let me be consulted—Show me first.

Dont forget carefully attending to the English copyright through Trübner—as we concluded about it the other day.

I want to say over again that while I reserve to the fullest degree all my own rights & the means to maintain them, you are to be, & I hereby make & confirm you, the sole issuers and publishers of my completed *Leaves of Grass*—that I shall coöperate strenuously & loyally in the enterprise—& to add that I do not fix any term or limit of years, because it is my wish that the publication by you, on the conditions & payments of royalty already settled between us, may, while those conditions are fulfilled, continue on and on, quite indefinitely & without limit, as being (I hope) better for you, & better for me too.

Should you wish any thing more in detail let me know. Of course any further points, specifications &c. that may arise as time elapses, or as circumstances or our wishes require, are open to both of us, to be added, modified, revoked or what not, as we may join & agree.

Walt Whitman

1056. *To Harry Stafford*   9.14. [1881]

ADDRESS: Harry Lamb Stafford | Kirkwood | Glendale | New Jersey. POSTMARK: Boston | Sep | 14 | (?)PM | N. (?).

Boston Sept: 14

Dear Hank

Yours of 11th just rec'd—I enclose you a note to Secretary of War, at a venture—If you go on, you get to see the Secretary. It wouldn't be any

49. Osgood & Co. replied on the next day that the plate (the portrait in the first edition) was worn, and that it would cost "$15. or $20. to put it into a condition suitable to use" (LC). WW received $40 from the firm on September 30 (CB). See also 1057.

use to send it by mail—(as you requested)[50]—I shall be through here in nine or ten days—Keep well yet—Shall stop a week or so in New York— then home to Camden for two or three weeks—then to Canada for some time.

Your Walt

I suppose you got the papers—

1057. *To James R. Osgood & Company*

ENDORSED: "James R. Osgood & Co. | Boston . | Sep | 16 | 1881."

Boston Sept: 15 '81

J R Osgood & Co: | Dear Sirs
     Yours of 13th rec'd. About the plate my impression still is that in the hands of a good expert steel plate printer it will be found to be not only not worn, but just about as good as new. There have been less than 2000 impressions struck off from it altogether, & it has been carefully preserved. However let us say $40 (instead of 50) as the price (with the books & prints before specified).
     My notion is against getting up any further portrait (this steel plate will have to *permanently* continue in all issues) for this issue, or at present[51]—let that be kept for something to give added zest to a future issue—perhaps a year or two from now. Besides we would have to hurry too much—for I think the book better be thrown on the market forthwith— all the favorable stars are apparently just now in conjunction—
     The press-work (which I hope will be *very carefully done*, & with good ink)—& the binding, color, style, (strong, plain, unexpensive, is my notion, nothing fancy) are now about to be prepared for immediately, & the plate printing to be at once put in hand. The book will not make more than 390 pages (most likely 385 to 390.) I am in favor of its being so trimmed & bound that it will be as eligible as possible for the pocket, & to be carried about—& I am *not* in favor of wide margins.
     I have no objection for any specific time for the contract to continue if you wish. I think of calling Friday noon 16th at your place—

Walt Whitman

50. See 1054.
51. The firm suggested on September 13 the inclusion of "another plate—a portrait of yourself as now" (LC). Why WW decided against using the Gutekunst portrait which he originally suggested in 1035 is not clear.

1058. *To Louisa Orr Whitman*

Concord Mass: Sept: 18 | '81

Dear Sister Lou

I still remain well—Am out here in Concord on a visit[52]—spent last evening with Mr Emerson very pleasantly indeed—am to take dinner with him to-day—Every thing very agreeable here—I am at F B San-born's—(the little picture at the top is the house)[53]—as I write (Sunday forenoon 11 o'clock) I look out on the Concord river—something like the Schuylkill—

The book is almost finished—I am on the last pages of the proof— will be ready in the stores ab't last of October—will be issued first in England, to secure the copyright there—as that is required, & I consider it important—Shall leave here (Boston) in about ten days—(perhaps less)[54] —expect to stop in New York probably a week or so, & then on home—I sent your letter to Mrs. Gilchrist—I have not written yet—it is so sudden & dreadful[55]—I thought I would wait a while—rec'd your letter & as always was glad to get it—it is a sunny, Indian summery spell of weather here now, cool enough, but just suits me—I go back to Boston probably to-morrow—

Yes I rec'd the wedding invitation cards from Mr [&] Mrs Elverson for Alice[56] & the happy (proposed) bride groom—I think him a lucky man—

Well I must close at once, for here comes a fine lively team of white horses to take me out to ride, to be driven by the owner, Miss Mann,[57] herself—With love as always—

Brother Walt

1059. *To John Burroughs*

ADDRESS: John Burroughs | Esopus-on-Hudson | New York. POSTMARK: Concord | Sep | 19 | Mass.

Concord Mass: | Sept: 19 '81

Dear John

I keep on fairly in health & strength—have been out here a few days the guest of Mr & Mrs F B Sanborn—& everything most affection-

---

52. WW's account of this visit to Concord, during which he met A. Bronson Alcott and Louisa and the Emersons as well as visited the graves of Hawthorne and Thoreau, appeared in *The Critic* on December 3 (330–331) and later became part of SD (278–282). See also the following letter.

53. WW wrote on Sanborn's stationery, which had a sketch of his home at the

ate & hospitable from them both—& from others—Have had a curiously full and satisfactory time with Emerson—he came to see me Saturday evening early, Mrs E also, & staid two hours—Yesterday I went there (by pressing invitation) to dinner, & staid two hours—a wonderfully good two hours—the whole family were very cordial, including Mrs. E. & the son, Edward, a doctor, a fine, handsome, 'cute, glowing young man, with a beautiful wife and child—I took to them all—I cannot tell you how sweet and good (and all as it should be) Emerson look'd and behaved—he did not talk, in the way of joining in any animated conversation, but pleasantly and hesitatingly & sparsely—fully enough—to me it seemed just as it should be—

The book is about through—will appear last of October—every thing satisfactory—I go from here in about a week to Johnston's, cor: Mott avenue & 149th St. N. Y.—then to Camden—shall go to Canada this winter—

Walt Whitman

1060. *To Henry H. Clark*

8 Bulfinch Place   Boston | Sept: 19th p m | '81

Dear Mr Clark[58]

I will come down myself to the office at 10½ to-morrow fore-noon, (Tuesday) & bring all the proofs—also give you the copy of the *contents* pages—also title—I have been away since Saturday noon—out to Concord to see Emerson—had a royal good time—dined with him yester-day—& only got back about two hours ago.

Walt Whitman

1061. *To John Burroughs*

Rand, Avery & Co., Printers. | *Boston*, Sept: 24   1881

Dear friend

Yours rec'd—I am now back here finishing up—only staid a few days in Concord, but they were mark'd days. Sunday, Emerson & his wife, son Edward & wife &c. gave me a dinner—two hours—every thing just

top of the sheet.
54. WW left Boston on October 22 (*CB*).
55. The death of Beatrice Gilchrist (see 1054).   56. See 857.
57. Probably one of the daughters of Horace Mann's brother, Thomas.
58. See 1051.

right every way—a dozen people there, (the family & relatives)—for my part I thought the old man in his smiling and alert quietude & withdrawness—he has a good color in the face & ate just as much dinner as any body—more eloquent, grand, appropriate & impressive than ever—more indeed than could be described—Wasn't it comforting that I have had—in the sunset as it were—so many significant affectionate hours with him under such quiet, beautiful, appropriate circumstances?

The book is done & will be in the market in a month or so—all about it has proceeded satisfactorily—& I have had my own way in every thing—the old name "Leaves of Grass" is retained—it will be a $2 book—

I shall probably go on to New York in about a week—shall stay at Johnston's, (address me there Mott avenue & 149th street N Y city) about a week or ten days—

Besides this general death-gloom of the nations[59]—have you heard of the sudden & dreadful death of our young friend Beatrice Gilchrist in performing some chemical experiment with ether?

Joaquin Miller is here—is with me every day—Longfellow has been to see me[60]—I have met O W Holmes & old Mr James.[61]

With love—

Walt Whitman

1062. *To Alma Calder Johnston*

ADDRESS: Mrs. Alma Johnston | Mott avenue &
149th Street | Station L | New York City. POSTMARK:
Boston | Sep | 23 | 2 PM | 1881 | Mass.

Rand, Avery & Co., Printers. | *Boston*, Sept: 24   *1881*

Dear Alma

Every thing is going on & has gone on satisfactorily—My book is finished in the type setting & plate-casting, & if things turn out wrong any way I shall have only myself to blame, for I have had my own way in every thing—

Spent a few days at Concord—had the good luck to light on the most blessed time that Emerson has had of late years—the old man came to see me Saturday evening, & made a long stay—Sunday he & Mrs E gave me a dinner—every thing just as it should be, & just suited me—I think Emerson more significant & *glorified* in his present condition than any of his former days—

59. The death of President Garfield on September 19. See also 1041.
60. WW had called on Longfellow on April 16 (*SD*, 266).
61. The father of the novelist.   62. Mr. Johnston's son, Albert.
63. This letter was sent to the Librarian of Congress during WW's Boston stay.

Joaquin Miller is here—I am with him every day—Longfellow has been to see me—I have met O W Holmes, Henry James Sr &c—Should like to come on to N Y abt 1st of October, & stay at your house a week or ten days—Write me & say if all right—Love to John, Ally,[62] & the girls & babies, address me Hotel Waterston, 8 Bullfinch Place here—

Walt Whitman

1063. *To Ainsworth R. Spofford*   [*9(?).(?). 1881*][63]

DRAFT LETTER.

My dear Mr Spofford

If convenient won't you inform me soon as possible by letter here, of the dates of my copyrights on *Leaves of Grass*—I think they were in 1856, 1860, 1866 (or 7) and in 1876—but want to know *exactly*—

Walt Whitman

If you have a printed slip or abstract of the copyright laws, please enclose that also.

address me Boston | care Osgood & Co: | 211 Tremont Street

1064. *To Trübner & Company*

ENDORSED (by WW): "sent to Trübner & Co | of London | Oct 5 '81 from Boston | ab't English Copyright." DRAFT LETTER.

Rand, Avery & Co., Printers. | U S America | *Boston,* Oct 5   *1881*

Trübner & Co: | Dear Sirs

Osgood & Co: of this city, who have set up & electrotyped a new, complete & markedly fuller edition (with several new pieces) of my *Leaves of Grass* inform me that by first *issuing* & *bona fide selling* in Great Britain, I can take out a copyright there, for this edition (such as it is.) We therefore send you a few copies at once, with the request that you will immediately have the book entered for copyright & secured in my name—(immediately after which the work will be published here.)[64]

Until Spofford's reply or WW's letter is found, it will not be possible to determine the precise date.

64. WW completed reading the proofs on September 30 and sent a complete set to Dr. Bucke on October 4 (*CB*).

I am under many obligations in the past to my friend, your Josiah Child, & should like to have this matter put in his hands—should like to have him write to me about it, direct as of old, to Camden New Jersey⁶⁵—

WW

1065. *To Alma Calder Johnson*

Rand, Avery & Co., Printers. | *Boston,* |
Monday noon | Oct: 10 '81

My dear friend
Yours rec'd, & thanks—I still linger along here—the printing of my book is finished—but one or two little things I want to see too—& then I am in no hurry—Shall probably finish up altogether this week—& then shall come on to your house⁶⁶—shall send you word a day beforehand—I am well as usual—Have had a very pleasant time here, & the book printed &c. to my entire satisfaction—Best love to John, Ally, & the dear girls—

Walt Whitman

1066. *To Thomas Nicholson(?)*   [*10.12. 1881*(?)]⁶⁷

ENDORSED (by R. M. Bucke): "Probably written 1881."

Wednesday Noon
Tom, here is a New York paper with an acc't of the great Cricket Match between the Canadians and Americans—I thought you might like to read—
I find I have no photo: here like the one I gave Tom Bradley, but I have some home, & when I go back to Camden, I will send you one sure.

W W

65. On October 31 WW received from Josiah Child "form of entry for English copyright," which he returned to Trübner & Co. on November 1 (*CB*).
66. WW did not leave Boston until October 22 (*CB*).
67. According to the New York *Times*, the Canadians defeated an American cricket team on October 11. October 12 was on Wednesday in 1881.
68. This letter was written on the stationery of the Grand Union Hotel, which was opposite the Grand Central Depot, between Forty-first and Forty-second Streets at Fourth Avenue.
69. Matilda Gurd (*CB*).
70. Apparently WW changed his mind later in the day, since, according to *CB*, he

1067. *To Louisa Orr Whitman* *10.23.* *[1881]*

> *Grand Union Hotel.* | . . . | *New York,*
> Sunday forenoon   Oct 23.

Dear Sister Lou

I am back here in New York, stopping for a couple of days at this hotel[68]—as Dr Bucke & his sister[69] are here (she is in poor health, & they are here to consult a special physician)—we wanted to be together till Monday or Tuesday, when they start back for Canada—Then I shall go up & stay with Mr & Mrs Johnston[70]—so if you write (& I wish you would soon after getting this—have you seen Eddy?) direct to me *Mott avenue & 149th street—Station L, New York City* (same as before I went on to Boston)—I havn't heard from you all now in a fortnight—

I came on yesterday from Boston[71]—As I told you in my last every thing went on there satisfactory[72]—& my treatment from Osgood has been of the best—the prospect for the book (sales &c) seems to be fair—there are already quite a number of orders—it is all ready, & will be delivered & for sale 4th Nov.—There will come a box (or bundle) by express to me probably to-day or to-morrow from Osgood, contains some of the books —Lou dear, you open & take one out for yourself, as I suppose you would like to see how it looks—leave the bundle tied up in the dark stout paper, as it contains only some MSS and stuff—also there may come a roll of printed matter for me, to be put up in my room—it will be directed to you "for W W"—(as any thing directed to *me* is liable to be forwarded here from Camden p o)—

I am well as usual—I shall stay here in N Y ten or twelve days & then home for a while[73]—Lou, I expect to spend a good part of the winter up in London, as I quite like it, & they have great plenty of room, grub, servants & every thing—I am enjoying the day & time (Sunday forenoon) here at this big hotel—& it is a *rouser*, (as you will see by the picture)— Dr B. and the Sister have gone over to church to Brooklyn to hear Beecher[74]—& I have been & am having a good nice time sitting here by

was at the Johnstons' on October 24 and 25.

71. During WW's last weeks in Boston he had entertained himself to his own satisfaction. On October 11, accompanied by Baxter, he attended a performance of *Romeo and Juliet* starring Ernesto Rossi, the Italian actor who was on an American tour (*CB*). On October 15 he held open house at Mrs. Moffitt's boarding house for the pressmen and friends. According to the report, undoubtedly written by WW, in the Boston *Daily Advertiser* on October 17, there were three hundred visitors. See also 1068.

72. A reference to a missing letter written on October 4 (?) (*CB*).

73. He returned to Camden on November 3 (*CB*).

74. The celebrated Brooklyn clergyman, Henry Ward Beecher.

myself reading the Sunday *Tribune*, & writing this & one or two more letters—affectionately—

Brother Walt

The books are *for sale* to any that want them—price $2—I will drop you a line a day or two before I come back—

1068. *To Ruth Stafford*   10.25. *[1881]*

ADDRESS: Ruth A Stafford | Kirkwood | (Glendale) | New Jersey. POSTMARK: Morrisania | Oct 25 | 6 PM | N.Y. City.

New York | Oct: 25   p m

Dear Ruth Stafford

Your letter has reach'd me here, & I am very glad to hear from you all—sorry your father suffers so from rheumatism—(but I believe every one has something.) You do not say any thing about your mother—I hope she is well.

I have been away now over three months—was down on Long Island last July & August and then for the last two months have been in Boston, seeing to the printing of my complete poems "Leaves of Grass" in one volume—which is all done to my satisfaction, & the book will be published now in about a week. I came back from Boston last Saturday, & expect to stay in New York ten or twelve days, & then back to Camden for a while. I got a letter from Harry six or seven weeks ago, wh' I answered[75]—& have sent him several other letters, also papers, which I suppose he has rec'd. I sent him a postal card last Sunday from here in N Y—also a paper to Mont—

I have been & am well as usual—see a great many people, & some how have to go around quite a good deal, but I often feel that I sh'd rather be alone out in the woods or especially if I could be down there by the old pond, & have no racket or hubbub around me—yet I ought not to complain, for I find lots of friends & the very best of good treatment continually wherever I go in New England & here in New York—I have had a long rambling ride this forenoon & midday all about the upper part of N Y island—it is like a fairy land, such hills and lanes and ponds & old

75. See 1056.
76. Baxter printed a lengthy review of *Leaves of Grass* in the Boston *Herald* on October 30.
77. The concluding part of Baxter's review, obviously inspired by WW himself, perhaps written by the poet, referred to Stedman's impression that his article in

trees & queer rocks—I just let the horse go his own way, most of the time —got home in time for dinner, (3 oclock) & found your letter among two or three others waiting for me—& thought I would answer it without delay—I will send you one of the little circulars of my book, although I sent one a week ago to Harry—When I was in New England I travel'd quite a good deal—had some splendid rides—good horses & good roads— one young lady I fell in with near where I was living had a team of her own, two handsome white ponies, & a good light wagon, & she had the *good sense* to ask to take me out every other day—of course I was nothing loth—Miss Mann—a very good driver too, & we did have some jolly times I tell you—

The Saturday evening before I came away I gave a reception to my Boston friends, especially the printers &c. We had a jolly time too— there were three hundred came & went—at 10 o'clock we had a supper —but one such affair will answer for a life time—I enjoy'd it, but I dont want any more—Such things will do better for you young folks—

By your letter I suppose Ed and Mont and Van are well as usual & all right—I should be real glad to see them & Deb too—When Harry comes home Sunday tell him I sent my best love to him, as always—& tell him to write to me—I expect to go to Canada this winter—Have you heard any thing from Herbert since? Well it is growing twilight & I must stop—

Walt Whitman

my address here for ten days will be
Mott av: & 149th street—Station L | New York City

1069. *To Sylvester Baxter*   *10.31.* [*1881*]

431 Stevens Street   Camden   New Jersey |
Oct 31—p m

Dear Baxter

I have seen your fervid and stirring criticism[76]—respond with thanks & love—if convenient mail me three or four copies here (see above) —please mail one to *E C Stedman*[77] *71 West 54th Street New York City* —one to *Dr R. M. Bucke, London, Ontario, Canada*—and one to *John Burroughs,*[78] *Esopus-on-Hudson, New York—*

Scribner's Monthly (see 981) had been "churlishly received": "Mr. Whitman has the warmest personal regard for Mr. Stedman, of whom he speaks with a genuine liking, and he felt the real worth of Mr. Stedman's article, but he also felt that Mr. Stedman had failed to grasp the wholeness of the work."

78. Burroughs was with WW on October 28 and 29 (*CB*).

252

I write in N Y, but *the above* is my main address, & I return there forthwith—I keep well as usual—

Walt Whitman

1070. *To John H. Johnston*

ADDRESS: John H Johnston | Jeweler | 150 Bowery | New York City. POSTMARK: Camden | Nov | 6 | (?) PM | N.J.

431 Stevens Street | Camden   New Jersey | Nov: 6 '81—Evn'g

Dear friend

I made a good smooth fast trip back to Camden that afternoon—find every thing here moving on about the same—life here is pretty monotonous any time, & especially after banging about & seeing so many folks & being made so much of as I for the last three or four months—but I feel pretty well & find myself enjoying most things & times—this beautiful day among the rest—(now toward sundown, & I am writing this alone up in my room, 3d story—have had a nice quiet day)—The valise came all right—Thought it best to write to Leibkeucher,[79] Newark, to ask whether I should send him the two vol. $10 edition, or the one vol. $2 one—which I have accordingly done—How are you, Alma? How are you, Ally boy?

Walt Whitman

1071. *To Helen E. Price*

November 9, 1881

I send you my new book (it is due you, you know) same mail with this . . .[80]

---

79. Arthur E. Lebknecker (not Leibkeucher), to whom WW sent the new *Leaves of Grass* on December 27 (CB).
80. In CB WW noted sending *Leaves of Grass* and a "letter card" to Helen Price.
81. WW also noted the "magnificent" review in CB. On November 20 he wrote a

1072. *To Edward Carpenter*

ADDRESS: Edward Carpenter | Bradway | near
Sheffield | England. POSTMARKS: Camden | Nov |
10 | 7 AM | N.J.; Philadelphia | Nov | 10.

431 Stevens Street | Camden New Jersey
U S America | Nov. 10 '81

I send you same mail with this the circular of my new & fuller
L of G.—& enclose printed slips of some of the newer pieces—the Volume
is copyrighted in England, & Trübner is the publisher & seller there—I
have been away all summer—just ret'd to Camden—I am well as usual of
late for me—H[arry] S[tafford] is well, he is still telegraphing—Write
me soon as you get this—How about our dear friends the G[ilchrist]s?
rec'd yours some six weeks ago—

Walt Whitman

1073. *To the Editor, the Springfield* Republican

Camden   New Jersey—Nov: 13 '81

I gratefully thank your paper & the writer of the Boston Literary
Letter in Nov: 10th's issue—I have never had more comforting words—
so noble & glowing in themselves & in their bearing on other things than
me & mine—I wish this card conveyed to the writer of them[81]—

Walt Whitman

1074. *To Anne Gilchrist*

ADDRESS: Mrs Anne Gilchrist | Keats Corner 12 Well
Road | Hampstead | London | England. POSTMARKS:
Philadelphia | Nov | 28 | Pa.; London | C M |
De 10 | 81.

431 Stevens Street | Camden New Jersey
U S America | Nov: 28 '81

My dear friend,

Have time & its influences at least helped to calm the terrible loss
& shock & dislocation? Have you got so that letters and all outside news

card of "thanks" to the New York *Sun* after the appearance of E. P. M.'s lengthy review,
"Walt Whitman and the Poetry of the Future," on the preceding day (*CB*). On November 14 Ticknor, of Osgood & Co., wrote to WW: "The first edition is all gone & we are
binding up the second" (LC).

are *not* altogether painful intrusions? Hoping so I send just a line. (For a while I thought it must be some false report—I was in Boston at the time —& waited & waited until confirmed.)[82]

I am as well as any of late years—or perhaps better. My brother & sister are well. The Staffords the same. I am writing this in the sunshine up in my old 3d story room—Best best love to you & to Herby & Grace—

Walt Whitman

I send a *Ledger* with Arthur Peterson's[83] letter—

1075. *To T. W. H. Rolleston*[84]   *12.2.* [*1881*]

ADDRESS: T W H Rolleston | Lange Strasse 29 | Dresden | Saxony. POSTMARKS: Philadelphia | Dec | 3; Dresden (?) | I. | 18 12 | 81 | (?).

431 Stevens Street | Camden   New Jersey

U S America | Dec: 2—Ev'ng

Rec'd to-day a copy of your *Encheiridion*—seems a little beauty of book-making. I suppose you have rec'd the copies of new L of G: I sent you over three weeks since, addressed same as this card.[85]

Walt Whitman

1076. *To an Unidentified Editor*

Camden   Dec. 3, 1881

Dear Sir,

I send you a fair proof[86] of my Emerson article visit in hopes it will be convenient for you to print it in full.

Walt Whitman

82.   WW was referring to the suicide of Beatrice Gilchrist. On December 14 Mrs. Gilchrist replied to WW: "Your welcome letter to hand. I have longed for a word from you—could not write myself—was stricken dumb—nay, there is nothing but silence for me still" (LC; Harned, 203). The intensity of Mrs. Gilchrist's grief cried in the lines of an undated and unsigned letter: "My dear Children, you would not wish me to live if you knew how I suffered. Not grief alone—that I could learn to bear, to be resigned— but *remorse*—that I should have left her; that is like an envenomed wound poisoning all my life. 'Weighed & found wanting' am I. And there where I thought myself surest. O the love for her shut up in my heart" (Feinberg). Probably Mrs. Gilchrist had encouraged Beatrice to abandon medicine (see 953).

WW apparently did not reply to Mrs. Gilchrist's letter of June 17, in which she apologized for not remembering his birthday: "it was past & I had not written one word—not just put my hand in yours as I would fain always do on that day." In the same letter she invited the poet to visit her: "a snug bed-room ready & waiting for you— as long as ever you will stay with us" (Pennsylvania).

83.   A friend of the Gilchrists (see 893).

84.   Rolleston (1857–1920) was one of Professor Edward Dowden's students, a

1077. *To Josiah Child* *12.8. 188[1]*

TRANSCRIPT.

Camden | Dec. 8, 188[1].[87]

First, thanks, heartfelt thanks, my friend, for your good will & deed—finding a publisher, &c—I wish to know specifically whether Mr. Bogue will take the Leaves . . .

1078. *To James R. Osgood & Company*

431 Stevens Street | Camden New Jersey | Dec: 8 '81

Dear Sirs

I suppose you have got word that Trübner & Co: decline being the London publishers or agents of our *Leaves of Grass*, & that a friend there (in whom I have great confidence) has in the mean time (I suppose until you can be consulted) placed the agency in the hands of David Bogue, St. Martin's Place, Trafalgar Square. My friend seems to speak in a very recommendatory manner of D. B., & thinks the transfer will be no detriment to the sale of L of G in the long run—(& somehow I get the same impression)[88]—

Let me know soon as it is settled, as I have frequent occasion to give the London place of issue & deposit. I keep in good health for me—

Walt Whitman

poet, the biographer of Lessing, and an historian of Irish myth and legends (Frenz, 7). The correspondence between the two men began in 1879 (see Rolleston's letters in Manchester), but the poet's replies (at least six) are missing.

On October 16, 1880, Rolleston sent WW a copy of his translation of Epictetus which he had printed at his own expense (Feinberg; Frenz, 16). The pamphlet is now in the Feinberg Collection. In the following year *The Enchiridion of Epictetus* was published in London by Kegan Paul, Trench & Co. In his copy, also in the Feinberg Collection, WW wrote in 1886 or 1888: "Have had this little Vol. at hand or in my hand often all these years." The markings in three different colors testify to the fact that WW perused the book.

85. WW sent a letter to Rolleston on November 9 (*CB*).

86. The article appeared in *The Critic* on December 3, the fifth part of "How I Get Around at 60, and Take Notes."

87. Though the auction record dates this letter "1880," this is clearly an error, for WW wrote to Child on December 8, 1881, about an English edition of *Leaves of Grass* (*CB*). See the following letter and 1081.

88. Ticknor replied for the publishing house on the following day, and noted "a cable order for 250 copies more" from Bogue (*LC; CW, VIII*, 287).

1079. *To James R. Osgood & Company*

431 Stevens Street | Camden New Jersey | Dec: 10 '81

Dear Sirs

Please send me here by express fifteen free copies *Leaves of Grass* for my disposal to editors, for notice—will send you list as disposed—Send also in same parcel thirty sets of the sheets of the new poems printed on one side—(see that *both sheets* are sent)—

Then another thing: I have a few copies remaining (between one & two hundred sets) of my old $10 centennial authographic two-Volume personal edition of L of G., moderately sought after *by collectors and specialists mostly in England*—which I should like to sell whenever applied to—price $10—You have no objections to my selling them? I dont think it would affect the new edition the slightest unfavorably—probably indeed do more good than harm to it—but is not of much importance any how—only (to me) as putting a few dollars in my pocket now & then—which I need—Shall not sell them if you object[89]—

Walt Whitman

1080. *To Ruth Stafford*

ADDRESS: Miss Ruth Anna Stafford | Kirkwood | Glendale | New Jersey. POSTMARK: Camden | Dec | 11 | (?) M | N.J.

Camden   Dec: 11 '81

Dear Ruthey

Yours rec'd—It seems a friend of mine who is in the *Ledger* office Philadelphia,[90] tho't I was down at Kirkwood—he was very anxious I should know of the bad illness of a particular friend of mine, & so wrote to Kirkwood—My friend died Friday morning—I go to the funeral tomorrow[91]—

I get a little news from you all, once in a while—(by a visit from Ed some time ago—& early last week by a visit from Harry.)

Thank you for the honey—it was very acceptable—we ate every drop of it, & enjoyed it—it was like the *singed cat*—a great deal better than it look'd—

---

89. The firm granted both of WW's requests on December 13, and included a list of thirty-eight newspapers and magazines to which review copies had been sent (LC).
90. Probably Richard E. Labar.
91. Colonel John W. Forney was buried on December 12 (CB).
92. WW was at Glendale from December 29 to January 9 (CB).
93. See 1078.   94. The "list of names in Eng[land]" (CB) is not with the letter.

I am well as usual—have a little work to do, but not much—Want to come down & see you all before long—will write a day or two before[92]—
                                                                Walt Whitman

1081. *To David Bogue*[93]

                        431 Stevens Street | Camden   New Jersey
                                        U S America   Dec: 14 '81
Dear Sir
    I wish you would have a little circular printed—(or some special paragraph inserted in your regular list, & *marked*)—announcing the new Osgood 1882 edition of *Leaves of Grass* with your place as the London agency & depository—*and send to the names on the accompanying list*[94]— all special friends of the book—
                                                                Walt Whitman

1082. *To Rudolf Schmidt*

                        431 Stevens Street | Camden   New Jersey
                                    U S America | Dec: 18 '81
My dear Rudolf Schmidt
    Yours of Nov: 27 rec'd. Console yourself for suffering f'm rheumatism—for it might be paralysis—I still keep around—am much more comfortable than four years ago, but am very lame & clumsy, (yet red and stout) —
    Bjornson[95] did not come to see me—America you know is a big country, & he had many places to go to—I think Clemens Petersen[96] is still some where in this country—very likely doing well—the last time I saw him he came up to me (personally looked well) in New York, between two & three years ago, in a crowd, & only a few words—he is a quite well known literary person & if he had died or any thing happened, I should have heard of it—
    I too mourn the death of Elster[97]—though unknown I had formed a

95. Björnson, the Norwegian poet (see 412).
96. A Danish critic who had emigrated to the U. S. (see 440). On November 27 Schmidt mentioned to WW that Petersen's family feared he was dead (Feinberg). WW met Petersen in New York; see the New York *Tribune*, March 6, 1877.
97. A Norwegian critic (see 607), whose death Schmidt lamented on November 27: "He was a heart's ease growing in the shadow" (Feinberg).

liking for him—I shall forward one of my books to Thorsteinsson[98]—Dr Bucke's book[99] will not be published for some months—perhaps a year —I send you, same mail with this, a copy of my new edition[1]—

As I write it is Sunday, just before sunset—& we have had a fine day —indeed a fine mild winter so far—have been in my room all day, writing &c, very comfortable—shall now walk to the post office, & probably sail once or twice across the river, the Delaware here, a mile wide—

The London publisher & agent for my new edition is David Bogue, St Martin's Place, Trafalgar Square—

I have heard that my book is to be translated into German, by some friends in Dresden[2]—also into Russian by some Russian exiles & a Mr Lee a Russ-English scholar[3]—I have been written to about both propositions & of course have expressed warmest assent—So good bye, my dear friend—& affectionate wishes to you & yours—

Walt Whitman

1083. *To Benjamin Ticknor*

Camden N J | Dec. 18 '81

My dear Ben: Ticknor
        Thank you for your (& O'Reilley's)[4] suggestion about Swinburne —I cannot consent however to solicit him to write a notice—& must decline to do so—But I have dispatched to him by mail an autograph copy of the new edition, & a little bundle of slips of the new pieces & some notices—without however any letter from me[5]—I have sent to David Bogue a list of some forty or more *special friends* of L. of G. (& author) in Great Britain & on the continent, & have requested him to inform them —by little printed circular or otherwise—that he is the London pub. & agent of the book—

Walt Whitman

☞ The 15 copies for editors have not yet reach'd me—perhaps they will come to-morrow—have they been sent?

98. Steingrimar Thorsteinsson (1831–1913), an Icelandic classical scholar and poet as well as an intimate friend of Schmidt, received a copy of *Leaves of Grass* from WW on March 26, 1882; see *Orbis Litterarum*, VII (1949), 58–59.
        99. Bucke's *Walt Whitman* was published in 1883.
        1. WW also sent a copy of *The Literary World* containing a review of recent Scandinavian books (*CB*).
        2. See 1075.

1084. *To Dr. John Fitzgerald Lee*[6]

431 Stevens Street | Camden New Jersey |
U S America—Dec: 20   1881

Dear Sir

Your letter asking definite endorsement to a translation of my *Leaves of Grass* into Russian is just received, and I hasten to answer it. Most warmly and willingly I consent to the translation, and waft a prayerful *God speed* to the enterprise.

You Russians and we Americans;—our countries so distant, so unlike at first glance—such a difference in social and political conditions, and our respective methods of moral and practical development the last hundred years;—and yet in certain features, and vastest ones, so resembling each other. The variety of stock-elements and tongues to be resolutely fused in a common Identity and Union at all hazards—the idea, perennial through the ages, that they both have their historic and divine mission— the fervent element of manly friendship throughout the whole people, surpassed by no other races—the grand expanse of territorial limits and boundaries—the unformed and nebulous state of many things, not yet permanently settled, but agreed on all hands to be the preparations of an infinitely greater future—the fact that both peoples have their independent and leading positions to hold, keep, and if necessary fight for, against the rest of the world—the deathless aspirations at the inmost centre of each great community, so vehement, so mysterious, so abysmic—are certainly features you Russians and we Americans possess in common.

And as my dearest dream is for an internationality of poems and poets binding the lands of the earth closer than all treaties or diplomacy— As the purpose beneath the rest in my book is such hearty comradeship for individuals to begin with, and for all the Nations of the earth as a result—how happy indeed I shall be to get the hearing and emotional contact of the great Russian peoples!

To whom, now and here, (addressing you for Russia, and empowering you, should you see fit, to put the present letter in your book, as a preface to it,) I waft affectionate salutation from these shores, in America's name.

Walt Whitman

3. See 1084.
4. WW misspelled O'Reilly's name. The letter referred to is apparently lost.
5. WW sent the book and slips to Swinburne's publishers, Chatto & Windus (CB). Wilde wrote to Swinburne on WW's behalf in January, 1882 (see 1091).
6. Lee was a student at Trinity College, Dublin, and a friend of Rolleston. On November 28 Lee wrote to WW requesting permission to translate *Leaves of Grass* into Russian (LC; Frenz, 48–50). Nothing came of Lee's projected translation.

You see I have addressed you as Russian—let it stand so—go on with your translation—I send you a book by this mail—advise me from time to time—address me here—

W W[7]

1085. *To William Sloane Kennedy*

431 Stevens Street | Camden New Jersey
Dec 21 '81

My dear W S K

Yours rec'd & glad to hear from you—have not forgotten those pleasant calls & chats, & hope they will one day be renewed—I read your (added to & somewhat changed) California magazine criticism[8]—the copy you showed Osgood—& thought it noble—

Am thankful to you & of course much pleased with your study of, & exploiting L of G—have just sent you a package by express of the late & other editions & Vols. of poems &c. as my Christmas offering[9]—with affectionate remembrances—

Walt Whitman

1086. *To T. W. H. Rolleston*   [*12.22. 1881*]

ENDORSED (by WW): "letter sent T W H Rolleston | Dresden, Dec 22 '81." DRAFT LETTER.

Yours of Nov: 28 rec'd.[10] My satisfaction with your proposed German trans[lation] increases the more you unfold it, and I think of it.[11] What you say against the two texts is sound, & I am content (retracting former suggestion) that it should be in the usual form, in German only. Want it by all means to be *Complete*. In the whole matter I freely trust to your intuitions and 'cuteness as to meanings, my dear friend— you have so long been a reader and lover of the book—& I fully empower you to go on & go your own way. I like of course what you say of getting the carefullest, technical, grammatical (and ? idiomatic) German assistance and collaboration as you go along.

7. The postscript is not included in earlier transcriptions of this letter.
8. "A Study of Walt Whitman," *The Californian*, III (February, 1881), 149–158.
9. WW sent three copies of *Leaves of Grass* (CB). Kennedy wrote at the conclusion of the letter: "I afterward sent him $5. as part payment for these   K" (Gohdes and Silver, 94*n*.).
10. LC; Frenz, 43–47.
11. On September 17 Rolleston had proposed a German translation of *Leaves of Grass* "as soon as I could find a proper German collaborateur" (LC; Frenz, 41). In his lost

I have received a good letter from Mr Lee[12] about the Russian translation, & have written him in answer.

I keep well for me, & shall remain here for the winter.

I suppose you recd a note from me weeks since acknowledging the *Encheiredion.*[13] My letter to Mr Lee was also as a preface to the Russian translation. Should that be fulfilled I will prepare & send you something of the same sort for the German Volume—I think so much of the internationality element (sentiment) which I have intended as one of the leading fibres of my book—

W W

1087. *To Herbert Gilchrist*   *12.30–31. 1881*

ADDRESS: Herbert H Gilchrist | Keats' Corner 12 Well Road | Hampstead | London | N W | England.
POSTMARKS: Haddonfield | Jan | 2 | N.J.; London, N.W. | C M | Ja 14 | 82.

Kirkwood Glendale | New Jersey
U S America | Dec: 30 '81

Dear friend

Down here for a few days[14] I thought you would like to get news right from the midst of people & scenes you loved so well—I came down yesterday amid sousing rain & cloudy weather—but this forenoon it is sunshiny & delightful—I have just returned from a two hours ramble in the old woods—wintry & bare, & yet lots of holly & laurel—& I only wish I could send you some cedary branches thick with the china-blue little plums, so pretty amid the green tufts—

The Staffords are all well—Mrs S is much as usual, looks in good condition—I heard her singing this morning at her work in the kitchen before I was up—George has been well, & is so—Ed & Debby & Harry & Mont & Van & Ruth & little George all right—Jo Browning ditto—Jo & D had some company here to supper last evening—Harry is away at the RR office at Clementon (Narrow Gauge)—likes it—is home only at long intervals—Ed tends the store, & the nag Ned[15] looks as well as ever—

letter written on November 9, WW approved the translation and proposed a double text. On November 28 Rolleston confessed that the "collaborateur" was too "pedantic," and that he had reservations as to a double text (LC; Frenz, 44–46). On January 7, in reply to this letter, Rolleston stated his "principle of rigid literality" (LC; Frenz, 54). The Rolleston translation was completed years later with the assistance of Karl Knortz.

    12. See 1084.   13. See 1075.

    14. WW stayed with the Staffords until January 9 (CB). Herbert replied to this letter on January 15, 1882 (Feinberg).

    15. The name of Ed's "nag."

it is now nearly 12—& we are going to have chicken for dinner—My morning paper has just come from Phila: & I will knock off & read it—

Dec 31—Saturday noon—Well this is the last day of the year, & it has grown freezing cold—Mr S is out at the wood-pile chopping away—I hear the sound of his axe as I write—Mont went off early, he goes over to Clementon and works at telegraphy, learning & assisting Harry—comes home quite late—Ed is busy with customers in the store—Ruth is in the kitchen making mince pies for New Year's—Mrs S is just sitting down a spell in the old rocking chair, reading to-day's Phila: Ledger—the acc't of the Guiteau trial[16]—(I don't know whether you read it or not, but of all the strange things of this strange century, I am not sure but that trial is the strangest)—

We had a flurry of snow last evening, & it looks wintry enough to-day, but the sun is out, & I take my walks in the woods. Hienikin was here yesterday—Wesley Stafford & his wife (Lizzie Hyder you know) have just drove up—they are very comfortable at the old place by the pond, & Lizzie is reconciled & happy—

Herb, I thought you would just like to hear all the small news & gossip & so I have written it—O how shocking I felt at the sad sad sudden death of the dear one[17]—was a long time before I realized it as true—hope your dear mother—to whom I send best love—is beginning to feel something like herself again—tell her I rec'd hers of Dec 14, & will write before long[18]—All here speak of you with love, & send affectionate remembrances—My best love to Giddy[19]—

Walt Whitman

1088. *To an Unidentified Correspondent*   [*1881?*]

TRANSCRIPT.

[WW referred to "My Long Island Antecedents"[20] and to Baxter's favorable review of *Leaves of Grass* in the Boston *Herald*, which he included in the letter.]

16. The trial of Charles J. Guiteau, the assassinator of President Garfield.
17. Beatrice Gilchrist.
18. WW did not write to Mrs. Gilchrist until July 22, 1882. She, however, wrote on January 29, 1882: "Your letter to Herby was a real talk with you. I dont know why I punish myself by writing to you so seldom now, for indeed to be near you, even in that way would do me good—often & often do I wish we were back in America near you" (LC; Harned, 205).
19. Herbert's sister, Grace.
20. WW sent "My Long Island Antecedents" to *The North American Review* on October 29, but it was returned (CB). For Baxter's review see 1069.

1 8 8 2

1089. *To Joseph M. Stoddart*[1]

TRANSCRIPT.

Camden, N. J., Jan. 11, 1882

[WW informed Stoddart that he would be at home for visitors at certain hours on the following Saturday, January 14.]

1090. *To Mrs. George W. Childs*

431 Stevens Street | Camden   Jan: 18 '82

My dear Mrs Childs[2]

Yours & Mr Childs', inviting me to dine & meet Mr Wilde received & appreciated—But I am an invalid—just suffering an extra bad spell & forbidden to go out nights this weather—Please give my hearty salutation & American welcome to Mr Wilde—

I much desire, my friend, to briefly report & give my respects in person to you & shall try to do so soon—

Walt Whitman

1091. *To Oscar Wilde and Joseph M. Stoddart*   *1.18. [1882]*

ENDORSED (in unknown hand): "1882."

431 Stevens Street | Camden   Jan: 18

Walt Whitman will be in from 2 till 3½ this afternoon, & will be most happy to see Mr Wilde & Mr Stoddart.[3]

1882

1.   Stoddart (1845–1921) published *Stoddart's Encyclopaedia America;* established *Stoddart's Review* in 1880, which was merged with *The American* in 1882; and became the editor of *Lippincott's Monthly Magazine* in 1889.

On January 11 WW received an invitation from Stoddart through J. E. Wainer, one of his associates, to dine with Oscar Wilde on January 14 (LC; Barrus, 235*n.*).

2.   The wife of the co-owner of the Philadelphia *Public Ledger* (see 906).

3.   In CB WW noted, "Oscar Wilde here a good part of the afternoon." An account of this interview appeared on the following day in the Philadelphia *Press.* WW was evidently pleased with Wilde's letter of March 1, 1882, in which he quoted Swinburne's praise of WW: "I have by no manner of means relaxed my admiration of his noblest works" (Feinberg; Traubel, II, 288). The quotation was from a letter written by Swinburne to Wilde on February 2 (Feinberg). Note also 1083. The meeting of Wilde and WW was satirized by Helen Gray Cone in "Narcissus in Camden," *The Century Magazine*, XXV (November, 1882), 157–159.

1092. *To Harry Stafford*

Camden Jan: 25 '82

Dear Harry

Yours rec'd—I am just starting off a few miles out from Phila—probably a day or two only[4]—will look up the book you require (if I can find one) soon as I come back—& send you—I am ab't as usual—nothing very new—

Hank, if I'd known you was coming home last Sunday would have come down Saturday & staid till Monday any way—You say you wrote a *blue letter* but didn't send it to me—dear boy, the only way is to dash ahead and "whistle dull cares away"—after all its mostly in one's self one gets blue & not from outside—life is like the weather—you've got to take what comes, & you can make it all go pretty well if only think so (& provide in reason, for rain & snow)—

I wish it was so you could all your life come in & see me often for an hour or two—You see I think I understand you better than any one—(& like you more too)—(You may not fancy so, but it *is* so)—& I believe, Hank, there are many things, confidences, questions, candid *says* you would like to have with me, you have never yet broached—me the same—

Have you read about Oscar Wilde? He has been to see me & spent an afternoon—He is a fine large handsome youngster—had the *good sense* to take a great fancy to *me!*[5] I was invited to receptions in Phila. am'g the big bugs & a grand dinner to him by Mr & Mrs Childs—but did not go to any —Awful cold here, this is now the third day, but you know all about *that*— (you say you know you are *a great fool*—don't you know every 'cute fellow secretly knows that about himself—I do)—God bless you, my darling boy— Keep a brave heart—

W W

---

4. There is no reference in CB to a visit to one of his friends. Jeff was with his brother on January 24 and 25, and apparently the poet was in Camden on January 26 and 28.

5. See the preceding letter. Burroughs, who also met Wilde in 1882, was less impressed (see Barrus, 235).

6. In CB WW referred to a "card-note" to Cunningham, whose name card was mounted opposite the entries for this period. There is only one other reference to Cunningham in CB: on June 22, 1882, he was stationed at Wakefield, R. I. The article in the Washington *Evening Star* of January 21 quoted Wilde: "I think Mr. Whitman is

1093. *To John S. Cunningham*[6]

ADDRESS: Paymaster | John S Cunningham | U S N |
Office 425 Chestnut Street | Philadelphia.
POSTMARKS: Camden | Jan | 27(?) | 7 AM | N.J.;
Philadelphia, Pa. | Jan | 27 | 8 AM | Rec'd.

431 Stevens Street | Camden   Jan: 26 '82—Evn'g
Thank you, my dear friend, for sending Washington Star with that good-tasting little paragraph (like the bouquet of a tiny glass of rare wine at the right moment.)

Walt Whitman

1094. *To Harry Stafford*   *1.31.* [1882]

ENDORSED (by Bucke): "1882."

Tuesday Evn'g | Jan 31[7]
Rec'd yours to-day—Sorry you didnt get the letter sent that day I met you, as I wanted you to have it particular[8]—but perhaps it has come to hand—that it went to Berlin p. o. I have no doubt, as I mailed it myself, addressed it to you "care of Sheriff Gibbs"[9] same as this envelope—

I hear Ed has sold the nag, & gone off to seek his fortune, newspaper canvassing &c.[10]—Whether he will make much money or not, I dont know, but I feel sure he will learn a good deal & get experience of the world & people, *& of himself* too—all of which is the *wisdom* described in scripture as better than riches—rec'd a long letter from Herbert Gilchrist, to-day[11]— he seems to be well, & working away hard at his painting—he describes to me some of his new pictures—says his mother was temporarily quite unwell, when he wrote—Edward Carpenter was visiting them—has a big beard—

Nothing new with me—I keep well as usual—you say when I have a *blue spell* I must write to you—I don't have any such spells—& seems to me it is time you grew out of them—my theory is that it is *in onesself* and not from outside circumstances one suffers such unhappy hours—the more one

in every way one of the greatest and strongest men who have ever lived."
  7. January 31 occurred on Tuesday in 1882. The year is also confirmed by the reference to Oscar Wilde.
  8. Apparently WW referred to 1092.
  9. In 1881 WW noted Harry's address as "care of T B Gibbs—Berlin N J" (*CB*).
  10. Evidently Edwin Stafford was in Indiana, Pa., since that was his address when WW wrote (lost) to him on February 3. He was in Kirkwood, however, on March 31 (see 1103).
  11. Gilchrist's letter of January 15 (Feinberg).

yields to them the frequenter & stronger they get until at last they take complete possession of a fellow—Harry dear, you are a good wrestler—see if you cant *throw them* & keep 'em thrown—

But I ought to write you something cheerful—I have been in all day—quite a deep snow & the wind blowing—I here in my big rocking chair at a job writing—Oscar Wilde sent me his picture yesterday, a photo a foot & a half long, nearly full length, very good—

As this letter has little or nothing in it I suppose it will be sure to reach you & not miss—like the other I wanted you to get—

Your old WW

1095. *To Richard Maurice Bucke*

ENDORSED: "Letter sent Dr Bucke—with his return'd
MS | My letter to Dr Bucke | Feb 7 '82 | returning his
MS." DRAFT LETTER.

Feb. 7 '82[12]

I have just sent the MS back by Adams express, same address as this letter.

You will be surprised, probably enraged, at the manner in which I have gone through it—

Upon first looking over it I was divided between two courses—whether to send it back without revision at all—or to go over it *with decision* making all the corrections & changes I felt entirely clear of. After deliberating I decided on the latter—I have acted upon it.

Without explaining each particular point of elision or addition, I will only say that I am convinced if you accept & print this copy as now arranged, you will bless your stars afterward—(printed in the old shape it would have turned out ill, and in very many things would probably have been unendorsed by you, as it certainly would by me.)

The character you give me is not a true one in the main—I am by no means that benevolent, equable, happy creature you pourtray—but let that pass—I have left it as you wrote.

You will see what I have substituted for your argument on the sexual theme. Upon looking it over (pages 166 to 168) after an interval I am

12. Only the photostat of the draft version of this letter is extant. The librarians at the University of Pennsylvania do not know where the original of the draft is. According to Holloway, the draft in 1917 was in the possession of the Bucke family; see *Free and Lonesome Heart*, 208–209. On February 1 WW was "reading Dr B's MS book (& a tough job it is)" (CB).

13. See Bucke, 163–167.

14. Bucke dedicated this book to WW (see 899).

15. According to CB as well as to the next letter, this communication was sent on

satisfied with it, and am willing to let those sections of my poems stand or fall on its support.[13]

I am sure as I can be all of those elaborated and lengthy parts from *Man's Moral Nature* should be ruled out of this book & referred to their own volume, where they are magnificent, (but an intrusion and superfluity here).[14] The whole MS. was far, far far too redundant—some things were often repeated three or four times—several long passages (very likely those you had set your heart on) were very much better out than in. Others would have been nuts to the caricature baboons—There were many errors or half-errors of fact.

But there is enough to make a very creditable, serviceable book—a permanent storehouse of many biographic, personal & other things, and of your glowing & penetrating criticism—

Upon the whole it will justify itself, and (as I have corrected it if you accept) will endure the test of both [readers?] & the best critics of one, ten or fifty years hence—which is the main thing.

Although the MS as it comes back may seem *in a state* to your eyes, I assure you that the printers could take it just as it is, (all numbered with the folios in blue pencil) and get along with ease.

Finally as all the excised pages of the MS are returned (& though it will need considerable writing &c.) it can be restored entirely to the original form, if you should decide to do so.

1096. *To James R. Osgood & Company*

Camden   New Jersey | March 7 '82[15]

I am not afraid of the District Attorney's threat—it quite certainly could not amount to any thing—but I want you to be satisfied, to continue as publishers of the book (& I had already thought favorably of some such brief cancellation.)

Yes, under the circumstances I am willing to make a revision & cancellation in the pages alluded to—wouldn't be more than half a dozen anyhow —perhaps indeed about ten lines to be left out, & half a dozen words or phrases.[16]

March 8.
  16. On March 1, Oliver Stevens, District Attorney in Boston, wrote to Osgood & Co.: "We are of the opinion that this book is such a book as brings it within the provisions of the Public Statutes respecting obscene literature and suggest the propriety of withdrawing the same from circulation and suppressing the editions thereof" (LC; *CW*, VIII, 290). In transmitting Stevens' letter to WW on March 4, the firm asked WW's "consent to the withdrawal of the present edition and the substitution of an edition lacking the obnoxious features" (LC; *CW*, VIII, 289).

Have just returned from a fortnight down in the Jersey woods,[17] & find your letter—

                                                            Walt Whitman

1097. *To James R. Osgood & Company*

                                            Camden   N J   March 19 '82
Dear Sirs
        I have been expecting response to my letter sent you some twelve days since (March 8) but no word rec'd—Are there any newer developements? Are you still proceeding with the sale of the book? I re-affirm my suggestions and disposition of March 8[18]—

                                                            Walt Whitman

1098. *To Jeannette L. and Joseph B. Gilder*

ADDRESS: J L & J B Gilder | *Critic* office | 30 Lafayette Place | New York City. POSTMARK: Camden | Mar | 21 | 4 PM | N.J.

                                    431 Stevens street | Camden   New Jersey
                                                            March 21 | '82
My friends
        I believe you have in MS one or two clusters of my Notes[19]—*yours*— they are paid for—I think I would like to look over them & touch them up to date (*perhaps*, or *not*, I could tell on seeing them)—I wish you would send the MS therefore immediately here—& I will at once make the im- provement-changes, (if any)—& return to you—

                                                            Walt Whitman

1099. *To James R. Osgood & Company*

                                    Camden   New Jersey | March 21 '82
Dear Sirs
        Yours of 20th rec'd, ab't Dr Bucke's book. I know something about it, & do not object. Dr B. has spent considerable on the illustrations (I have

---

17. WW was with the Staffords from February 16 to March 6 (*CB*).
18. On March 20 the firm replied: "We are waiting for an official indication in the matter of revisions" (LC; *CW*, VIII, 292).
19. Perhaps the sixth and last instalment of "How I Get Around at 60, and Take Notes," which appeared in *The Critic* on July 15, 1882 (see 992). WW noted sending

seen them, they are quite creditable) has gathered a variety of biographical information—criticises my poems from an almost passionately friendly point of view (as scientist, student of poetry, medical doctor &c)—& has included what as time goes on may prove a curiously valuable collection of cumulative opinions on L of G. from 1856 to the present day—& I should say it would be a safe publication-enterprise—but you must of course judge & decide for yourselves[20]—

Another thing I must broach—hoping you are not alarmed at the District Attorney episode, (as I am not at all,) but see your way clear to continue on in earnest—

I have about got into shape a volume (*It* at least will not be liable to any District Att'y episodes—) comprising all my *prose writings* to be called (probably)

Specimen Days
& Thoughts
by Walt Whitman

to be about same size as L of G. This little Dist. Att'y flurry blowing over, & we getting things into good shape—(as of course I suppose *it* surely will, & *we* will)—would you bring it out say late this summer, same terms as L of G? In that case there would be three Volumes gyrating together, the L of G—the S D & T—and Dr Bucke's book—

Upon the whole, & as my friend seems determined to bring out his book, I hope you will take it. I know Dr Bucke well, & have for some years —He is a perfectly honorable, reliable solid man to deal with—a linguist, well conversant with the best German, French & British poetry—of English stock & birth, but grown up in Canada and the California regions of America, & combining in my opinion the best traits of both nationalities. He is now & has been for some years, (in fact he built up & organized it) at the head of the largest & most complete & modernized Asylum for the Insane in America—(one of the largest in the world—1000 persons under his charge)—near London, Ontario, Canada—Though enthusiastic he has a careful eye to practical & business responsibilities—has a fine very large family of children—his social, professional, citizen &c reputation, all first class in Canada.

Walt Whitman

My last three letters to you have been

the sixth (revised?) article on April 2; evidently he returned the galleys of the "Notes" on April 9 (*CB*).

20. On March 20 Osgood & Co. wrote about Bucke's biography: "We do not know whether the book would appeal to us commercially but we of course prefer not to look at it without first being sure that it meets your approval" (LC; *CW*, VIII, 292).

One of March 8 (or 7)
"   "   19
& the present one
find Dr Bucke's letter to you herewith returned encl'd—

1100. *To George and Susan Stafford*   3.22. [1882]

ADDRESS: George and Susan Stafford | Kirkwood |
(Glendale) | New Jersey. POSTMARK: Camden |
Mar | 22 | 12 M | N.J.

Camden   March 22[21]

Dear friends
    I shall come down *Friday afternoon* in the 4½ train to Kirkwood—
for three or four days visit—

W W

1101. *To James R. Osgood & Company*

Camden   New Jersey | March 23 '82

Dear Sirs
    Yours of 21st rec'd, with the curious list—I suppose of course from
the District Attorney's office—of "suggestions" lines and pages and pieces
&c. to be "expunged." The list whole & several is rejected by me, & will not
be thought of under any circumstances.[22]
    To give you a definitive idea of what I meant in my notes of March 8
and March 19—& of course stick to—I mail you with this a copy of L. of
G. with the not numerous but fully effective changes and cancellations I
thought of making: see in it pages   84
                                      88
                                      89
                                  &   90

21. WW went to Glendale on Friday, March 24, and remained there until
March 31 (*CB*).
22. The publisher submitted the following list of "Passages to be expurgated
from Walt Whitman's 'Leaves of Grass,'" a list not accurately recorded by Bucke
(149*n*.): "Song of Myself" (p. 31, ll. 15–16; p. 32, ll. 19–22; p. 37, ll. 14–15;
p. 48, ll. 20, 28, 29; p. 49, ll. 11, 20; p. 52, section 28, beginning with l. 12; p. 59,
ll. 11–12; p. 66, ll. 15–16); "From Pent-Up Aching Rivers" (p. 79, ll. 21–22; pp.
80–81, ll. 14 to end); "I Sing the Body Electric" (p. 84, ll. 1–17; p. 87, ll. 13, 28);
"A Woman Waits for Me" (pp. 88–89, "entire"); "Spontaneous Me" (pp. 90–91);
"Native Moments" (p. 94, ll. 1–7); "The Dalliance of the Eagles" (p. 216, in
entirety); "By Blue Ontario's Shore" (p. 266, ll. 21–22); "To a Common Prostitute"
(pp. 299–300, in entirety); "Unfolded Out of the Folds" (p. 303, ll. 2–3); "The
Sleepers" (p. 325, half of l. 22; p. 331, ll. 9–10); and "Faces" (p. 355, ll. 13–17).
23. This copy of *Leaves of Grass* with WW's changes has either been lost or was

All those lines & passages marked in pencil to come out, & their places to be exactly filled with other matter—so that they will superficially present the same appearance as now.[23] The whole thing would not involve an expense of more than from 5 to $10—

My proposition is that we at once make the revision here indicated, & go on with the regular issue of the book—If then any further move is made by the District Attorney & his backers—as of course there are others behind it all—they will only burn their own fingers, & very badly—

I want the paper copy I send of L of G. returned to me when through.[24]

Walt Whitman

Let this whole matter be kept quiet in the house—no talk or information that may lead to newspaper items—the change to be just silently made—the book, & at casual view all its pages, to look just the same—only those minutely looking detecting the difference—

Inform the official people at once that the cancellation is to be made for future editions.[25]

WW

Write me at once & definitively if all this suits—

1102. *To Albert Johnston*

March 27 '82

Dear Al[26]

First—Love to you and all, May, Bertha, Grace, Kittie & Harry—Second, sorry to hear your mother has been down sick & hope the Florida jaunt will help her, (as it probably will)—

Third, it was I no doubt that sold the Cumberland Street Brooklyn house to Wineburgh[27]—What is it your friend wants me to do? Send me

destroyed. It will be noted that WW agreed to alterations only in "I Sing the Body Electric," "A Woman Waits for Me," and "Spontaneous Me." On his copy of a draft of the letter to Osgood & Co. WW wrote: "By this letter of W W March 23 several minor changes & alterations, words & lines in two or three cases are consented to in '*Children of Adam*' but J R O. & the officials not considering them as at all meeting the point they are entirely waived on both sides" (LC; *CW*, VIII, 295).

24. Osgood & Co. replied to WW on March 29: "We do not think the official mind will be satisfied with the changes you propose. They seem to think it necessary that the two poems 'A Woman Waits for Me' and 'Ode to a Common Prostitute' should be omitted altogether. If you consent to this we think the matter can be arranged without any other serious changes" (LC; *CW*, VIII, 295).

25. This final paragraph was included by the executors in the letter of March 7 (*CW*, VIII, 291).

26. The son of the jeweler, John H. Johnston (see 868).   27. See 20.

word when the coast is all clear, & every thing lovely, & I will come on to Mott Haven for a week's visit—I am well as usual—

Walt Whitman

I write this down in the woods in Jersey but go up to Camden to-morrow[28]—

1103. *To Herbert Gilchrist*

> ADDRESS: Herbert H Gilchrist | 12 Well Road |
> Keats' Corner Hampstead | London England.
> POSTMARK: Philadelphia | Mar | 31(?) | (?).

Kirkwood (Glendale)   March 31 '82 | U S A

Down here again spending a few days—nothing very different—pretty much the same story of all my letters—but I knew you would like to hear—Mrs S[tafford] and all the family well as usual—they often speak of you & of the old times—I was over to the creek and by the old walnut-trees last week—all beautiful & refreshing as ever—

Harry is still at Clementon—Mont is with B. S. at Kirkwood station—Ed has gone up to Phila: to-day for store goods—Do you know of David Bogue,[29] bookseller, Trafalgar Sq: who publishes my book in London? Have you ever been in his place? I go up to Camden this evening—Yours of last Jan: & your mother's of Feb. 6 rec'd[30]—

W W

1104. *To Charles A. Dana*

Camden   New Jersey | April 2 '82

My dear Dana[31]

Yes I am willing you should make extracts—Enclosed (suggestions of the moment) two or three slips from new edition—

Walt Whitman

28. But see the next letter.

29. On May 8 Mrs. Gilchrist informed WW that Herbert had visited Bogue (see 1077), and discovered that "the sale of Leaves of Grass was progressing satisfactorily." Bogue's father had published her husband's "first literary venture" (LC; Harned, 207). On November 24 Mrs. Gilchrist wrote: "I fear you will be a loser by Bogue's bankruptcy" (LC; Harned, 210).

30. Herbert wrote on January 15 (Feinberg); Mrs. Gilchrist on January 29–February 6 (LC; Harned, 205–206).

31. Dana (1819–1897) was the editor of the New York *Sun* (see 674). In *The Household Book of Poetry* (1882) Dana included six poems from *Leaves of Grass:* "Vigil Strange I Kept on the Field One Night," "A Sight in Camp in the Daybreak Gray and Dim," "Great Are the Myths," "The Mystic Trumpeter," and excerpts from "When Lilacs Last in the Dooryard Bloom'd" and "Song of Myself" (section 35).

32. When WW did not reply to their letter of March 29 (see 1101), Osgood &

1105. *To James R. Osgood & Company*

TELEGRAM.

April 5 | 82

Dated   Camden N J
To   Jas R Osgood & Co
          211 Tremont St Boston
          No I cannot consent to leave out the two pieces   I am only willing
to carry out my letter of March twenty third.[32]

Walt Whitman

1106. *To the Editors*, The Critic

TRANSCRIPT.

Camden, April 9, 1882
          I rec'd the $7 for the Longfellow bit[33]—thanks.

1107. *To James R. Osgood & Company*

Camden   New Jersey | April 12 '82
Dear Sirs
          Yours of 10th just rec'd[34]—If you desire to cease to be the publishers
of *Leaves of Grass* unless I make the excisions required by the District
Attorney—if this is your settled decision—I see indeed no other way than
"some reasonable arrangement for turning the plates over" to me—What
is the am't of royalty due me, according to contract, from the sales altogether? & what is your valuation of the plates?

Walt Whitman

Co. sent a telegram to the poet on April 5 (LC; *CW*, VIII, 296).
          33. "Death of Longfellow" appeared in *The Critic* on April 8; it was reprinted in
Essays from "The Critic" (1882), 41–45, and in *SD*, 284–286, 355. WW sent the article to the magazine on April 2 (*CB*).
          34. Osgood & Co. wrote to WW on April 10: "We have laid before the District
Attorney the alterations proposed by you. They are not satisfactory. . . . As we said
at the outset we do not wish to go into court in connection with this case. Therefore as
your views seem to be irreconcileable with those of the official authorities there seems no
alternative for us but to decline to further circulate the book. We should be open to any
reasonable arrangement for turning the plates over to you" (LC; *CW*, VIII, 296).
          On April 13 the publisher informed WW that the royalty due him was $405.50
and that the cost of the plates was $475. In return for a receipt for the royalty, the firm
was willing to turn over to WW the plates, the steel portrait and 225 copies of the book
in sheets (LC; *CW*, VIII, 297). As WW did not reply, the firm wrote again on May 4
(LC; *CW*, VIII, 298). The poet arranged better terms in the final settlement (see 1118).

1108. *To John Burroughs*

431 Stevens Street | Camden N J   April 28 '82

Dear friend

Just returned from a fortnight down in the Jersey woods[35]—not feeling well this month, (a bad cold, neuralgia, other head trouble, bowel trouble &c—yet nothing serious—will blow over in a few days)—went down for a change—had bad weather & nothing propitious—but I have just come back & am already better—shall get along—

So Emerson is dead[36]—the leading man in all Israel—If I feel able I shall go to his funeral—improbable though—A new deal in the fortunes of *Leaves of Grass*—the District Attorney at Boston has threatened Osgood with indictment "under the statutes against obscene literature," specifies a long list of pieces, lines, &c.—Osgood is frightened, asks me to change & expurgate—I refuse peremptorily—*he throws up the book & will not publish it any more*—wants me to take the plates, wh: I shall try to do & publish it as before—(in some respects shall like it just as well)[37]—Can you help me? Can you loan me $100?[38]

The next *N A Review* (June number) will have a piece *A Memorandum at a Venture* signed by my name in which I ventilate my theory of sexual matters, treatment & allusion in *Children of Adam*—I shall have some slips & will send you some to England[39]—

Am writing this in great haste, angry with myself for not having responded before to your good letter of April 10—Love to 'Sula & the kid—

Walt Whitman

35. WW was inaccurate: he was at Glendale from April 22 to 27 (*CB*). This was his "excuse" for not replying to Burroughs' (lost) letter of April 10.

36. Emerson died on April 26, 1882. On April 29 WW sent to *The Critic* "By Emerson's Grave," which appeared in the issue of May 6, along with Burroughs' "Emerson's Burial Day." The poet received $3 for the piece (*CB*). It was included in *SD*, 290–291.

37. With his letter of May 1, Burroughs included a communication from O'Connor dated April 28, in which the latter related how he had convinced associates in his office that the Boston censorship was "the greatest outrage of the century" (Feinberg; Traubel, III, 351). O'Connor wrote to Bucke about the matter on April 29 (Barrus, 212). On May 1 Burroughs wrote to Gilder, probably Richard, "So far as this is the wish of the city of Boston, I pray for the wrath of Sodom and Gomorrah to descend upon her" (Barrus, 211).

38. In reprinting Burroughs' letter of May 1, Traubel interpolated an explanation of the loan: "This was money in my possession belonging to Walt. J. B. 1912." (Traubel, III, 350). Burroughs and Traubel, however, were in error, for on January 27, 1883, WW noted: "returned $100 to John Burroughs" (*CB*). And see Barrus, 210.

39. WW had sent the article to the magazine on April 8, and on April 27 received

1109. *To the Editor, the Philadelphia* Press   *4.28. [1882]*

April 28

Couldn't you use this in Sunday's Press? Could you send me $8.oo for it? Although printed four or five months ago in N. Y. Critic[40]—I was thinking it might have the point now of *special opportuneness*—which is I suppose the main thing in paperdom—more than a freshly written piece.

Walt Whitman

1110. *To William D. O'Connor*   [*5.3. 1882*][41]

ENDORSED: "Forward all this budget 'A to L inclusive' to Dr. Bucke." ADDRESS: Wm D O'Connor | Life Saving Service | Bureau | Washington D C. POSTMARKS: Camden | May | 3 | 12 M | N.J.; Washington, D. C. | May | 4 | 4 AM | 1882 | Recd.

forward all this budget—keep together in envelope (*A* to *L* inclusive) after reading digesting &c. (no hurry however) to Dr Bucke | Asylum | London Ontario Canada | —who will be expecting them—

1111. *To William D. O'Connor*   [*5.3. 1882*]

ADDRESS: Wm D O'Connor | Life Saving Service Bureau | Washington D C. POSTMARKS: Philadelphia | May | 3 | 7 PM | Pa.; Washington, D.C. | May | 4 | (?)AM | 1882 | Recd.

In the just mailed Osgood and L of G budget, the date on the last slip (marked L) sh'd of course have been *May* 3—

$25 "with 'sincere thanks' " (CB).

40. Apparently WW submitted the account of his last visit with Emerson which had appeared in *The Critic* on December 3, 1881 (see 1058). On the verso of this letter Thomas Donaldson wrote on April 30 that he was in the office of the Philadelphia *Press* when WW's contribution arrived and that it was declined; see American Art Association, February 16, 1927.

41. It is unfortunate that WW's correspondence with Bucke at this time is lost, for it would presumably reveal that after the poet informed Bucke of Osgood's decision on April 19, the latter suggested that O'Connor be enlisted to reply to the charges of obscenity. Since the poet and O'Connor had been estranged for ten years, Bucke undoubtedly wrote to O'Connor to obtain his consent. Probably WW discussed the matter frankly in a "long letter" to Bucke on April 27 (CB). At any rate their correspondence resumed without mention of their misunderstanding.

Jottings in CB suggest that WW had attempted to heal the wounds for many years. He sent to O'Connor the following books and articles: *Memoranda During the War* in April, 1876; the Centennial Edition in March, 1879; his Emerson article in *The Literary World* in May, 1880; "Poetry of the Future" in December, 1880; *The Progress* of April 30, 1881; *The Critic* of May 9, 1881; the New York *Tribune* of August 4, 1881; and the Osgood edition on December 25, 1881.

1112. *To William D. O'Connor*

ENDORSED: "Answd May 9/82." ADDRESS:
Wm D O'Connor | Life Saving Service Bureau |
Washington | D C. POSTMARKS: Camden | May |
7 | 6 PM | N.J.; Washington, D.C. | May | 8 |
4 AM | 1882 | Recd.

431 Stevens Street | Camden   N J   noon   May 7   '82

Dear William O'Connor

Yours of 5th rec'd & welcomed.[42] To keep you posted I make notes at random of this Osgood affair, & send herewith.[43] I have an article *A Memorandum at a Venture* 5 or 6 pages signed by my name in the forthcoming June number *North American Review*, which, although hastily written & eligible to great additions, I consider a sort of rallying point or key note to my position in the *Children of Adam* business—will be out probably 12th to 15th of May—I shall have some proof copies, & will send you two or three soon as I get them—(It is a paid for contribution, my own price given)[44]—the newspapers specially like to have something *up at the moment*—this *N A Rev.* piece might give a current reason-why for your article—commencing by alluding to it[45]—

The skeleton-facts of the Osgood publication are these. Osgood & Co. wrote to me last May ('81) asking about a new & complete edition & suggesting that they were open to proposals. I wrote back that a new & complete edition was contemplated but I wanted it distinctly understood that not a line was intended to be left out or expurgated—that the book must be printed in its entirety & that those were prerequisites opening to any negotiation.[46] They wrote back asking me to send the copy. I sent it. In a few days they wrote me that they would publish it. The bargain was closed. I was to have 12½ per cent on the sales, and the contract was to run ten years. I went on to Boston (Sept. '81)[47] and saw the book through the press— pub last of Nov. '81—(I think [some?] 3000 must have been published by them since then.)[48]

In their penultimate letter (a month or so ago) Osgood & Co: wrote me that the pieces the District Attorney specially & absolutely required to be

42. O'Connor's letter is apparently lost.
43. The "notes" begin in the second paragraph.
44. The price asked was $25 (*CB*).
45. On May 9 O'Connor informed WW that he needed no excuse for the article he was writing for the New York *Tribune* (Syracuse; Traubel, IV, 331).
46. See 1027.
47. WW was slightly inaccurate: he arrived in Boston on August 19, 1881 (*CB*).
48. Probably WW overstated the number of copies printed by Osgood. In a letter to the poet on January 25, John H. Johnston quoted from a note he had received from

entirely expurgated were *To a Common Prostitute* and *A Woman Waits for Me*—those left out the rest could be arranged without trouble, & he would allow the publication to continue—*but the leaving out of those two pieces was indispensable.*

I shall write you again, dear friend, as any thing occurs or suggests itself that I think you ought to know bearing on this matter—I am well as usual now—after a pretty bad month of illness—but mainly getting along pretty well & in good spirits considering—

Walt Whitman

1113. *To the Editor*, The North American Review

TRANSCRIPT.

431 Stevens Street | Camden   New Jersey | Evening
May 12 '82

Dear Sir

Yours of yesterday rec'd—I could send the MS of *Carlyle from an American point of View* by the 20th or 21st a week from now[49]—It would make about nine or ten pages—What I said about its being "a candidate for the place of leading paper" &c was meant to be left entirely to the editorial exigencies of judgment—no *condition* at all—

Walt Whitman

1114. *To Susan Stafford*

Camden   Sunday Evn'g   May 14 '82

Dear friend

Yours of 12th rec'd & much welcomed—As I write the day [is] just closing & dark & the rain has been falling heavy & steady for hours—makes an undertone & music for me on the tin roof overhead—I have been

---

the publisher, who had "printed three editions, 2000 copies in all" (LC; *CW*, VIII, 288). The Springfield *Republican* on May 23 (see note 72 below) reported that 1600 copies of *Leaves of Grass* had been sold "during the winter and spring." When Osgood discontinued publication in April, the royalty due to WW amounted to $405.50 (see note 34 above). Unless there were a previous payment to the poet, Osgood sold 1622 copies of the book ($405.50 @ .25 per copy).

49. WW sent the article on May 18, and it was returned to him (*CB*); printed in *SD*, 254–262. *The North American Review* also rejected "The Prairies in Poetry" which the poet submitted on May 4 and for which he asked $50 (*CB*). This article included a number of sections in *SD* (219–224; and see Stovall's note, 219*n*.).

moderately busy for some time past & to-day writing—pieces I get fair pay for from the magazines—the more necessary now as quite a set-back & very bad piece of luck has happened to me in my new Boston book—but it would be quite a complicated story, & I will tell you the particulars when I come down—

Susan, I am sorry to hear of Howard Browning's death[50]—so young, & with life & pleasure all before him, as it would seem—such things bring up thoughts in one's mind that no words or writing can describe—I wish Jo and Debby to see this letter—& I send them my love—

I suppose Harry is not home to-day it is so stormy—I have sent him bundles of papers[51]—They say the old C[amden] & A[tlantic] road have bought the Narrow Gauge—will that affect Harry's position any? I can fancy you all there in the house to-day, if it rains there any thing like it does here—George I dare say has gone up in his room & is taking a good blessed sleep—I don't know what Ed would be doing, but I can fancy Mont reading some of Mrs Holmes's[52] books & perhaps Ruthey setting the table or frying something for supper—at any rate I hope you are all having a good time —& if I had the magic carpet of the Arabian Nights, I should come down & join your circle for a couple of hours, & then whisk myself back here again by nine o'clock, in time to finish the piece I have under way—Tell Mrs Rogers I send my best respects—I remember with pleasure the nice visit & dinner in Linden street—I have not forgotten Jane either[53]—

Susan, you speak of my not being well—somehow I seemed to have a real bad time, a mixture of troubles, neuralgia among the rest, for a month past—but I think I have got over the worst for the present, & for the last three or four days I feel about as usual—I went over a few days ago to a (Quaker) school in Philadelphia, where they teach well-grown children, *not* lessons by rote, but all sorts of practical things, such as would be appropriate and interesting to the young, but leading the way to occupations, for both sexes, drawing, painting, the use of carpenters' tools, cooking, sewing, cutting out clothes, &c. It was conducted by a gentleman and his neice, free—I tell you it opened my eyes to many new things—makes our ordinary schools ridiculous—Well, Susan, dear friend, I have filled

50. Probably the brother of Mrs. Stafford's son-in-law, Joseph Browning.

51. WW sent "papers" to Harry on May 7 (*CB*).

52. Mary Jane Holmes (1825–1907) was a popular novelist.

53. Mrs. Elizabeth W. Rogers, a widow, was Mrs. Stafford's sister. WW dined on March 11, 1882, with Mrs. Stafford at Mrs. Rogers' home at 431 Linden Street, Camden (*CB*). Mrs. Rogers died on March 30, 1888.

54. Ticknor, of Osgood & Co., telegraphed on May 16 for an appointment on the following day (LC). The settlement provided that Osgood turn over "the plates, dies, steel portrait, and 225 copies (more or less) in sheets of *Leaves of Grass*, and pay W. W.

out the sheet with writing, such as it is—I believe the first letter I have sent you now for a long time—God bless you & all—

Walt Whitman

1115. *To William D. O'Connor*   *5.17. [1882]*

ENDORSED: "Answd May 20/82." ADDRESS:
Wm D O'Connor | Life Saving Service | Bureau |
Washington | D C. POSTMARKS: Camden | May |
17 | 2 PM | N.J.; Washington, D. C. | May | (?) |
1882 | Recd.

Camden   May 17   noon

Ben Ticknor has just been here, to make a settlement of the L of G publication business between me and Osgood & Co.—which settlement has been amicably effected—and O & Co. have withdrawn & given it up for good, & made the plates &c over to me[54]—

What I write for is this:—Ben. tells me that the whole business originated from the State Attorney General Mr Marston, who (at the instance of certain parties) peremptorily instructed the Boston Dist. Attorney Stevens to proceed against L of G. As I wrote you before, the *betes noir* were *To a common prostitute* and *A woman waits for me.* Unless those were left out he was instructed to indict and arrest to the law's extremity. (I believe I told you that Osgood & Co. formally notified me that they would continue the publication if those were expurgated.)

I do not myself feel any resentment toward O & Co. for any thing done me or the book—They have acted with reference to conventional business & other circumstances.[55] *Marston* is the target for you[56]—If I learn more I will notify you—

WW

Have you seen my N A Rev. article?[57] I expect some proof-impressions & will immediately send you two or three—

the sum of $100.00 in cash" (LC; *CW*, VIII, 298).

55. Though O'Connor on May 20 approved of WW's "magnanimous" attitude toward Osgood & Co., he believed that "my part, and the part of all your friends, is to whale them" (Feinberg; Traubel, II, 14).

56. In his reply on May 20, O'Connor said that he had "focussed all my fire right upon Oliver Stevens, who, you know, is the only one that appears officially in the transaction." But "when we get Marston to the front, there will be augmented fire for his hide, and I hope to make it so intolerable for him, that he will in self-defence peach on the holy citizens who have egged him on" (Feinberg; Traubel, II, 13).

57. "A Memorandum at a Venture" (see 1108).

1116. *To Rand & Avery*[58]

431 Stevens Street | Camden New Jersey | May 19 '82

Dear Sirs

I suppose Benj: Ticknor has informed you that the Osgood & Co: plates of *Leaves of Grass* now in your charge have been transferred to me, & are henceforth subject to my order.[59]

Will you please prepare for me for casting a new title page, the copy for which is herewith enclosed—As it is a small job, could you make up (I should say in the same long primer as book, but I leave it to Mr Clark's[60] taste), & send the proof of it to me by next Monday night's mail—as I am waiting for new titles for 225 copies I have in sheets, & have an order for[61]— Will return proof immediately with word how many I want printed.

Walt Whitman

If convenient please place this matter in the hands of H H Clark to whom I hereby send *best remembrances* & respects—

W W

1117. *To Benjamin Ticknor*   [5.23 (?). 1882]

ENDORSED (by WW): "Sent May 24 '82."
DRAFT LETTER.

O & Co | Benj Ticknor

Enclosed find receipt which I believe closes the matter[62]—

I wish you would mail me the (brown paper bound) copy of "Leaves of Grass" I sent on about a month ago[63]—I mentioned my desire at the time for its return—

WW

58. WW noted in *CB* this letter to Rand & Avery, the firm which had printed the 1860 and Osgood editions. On June 8 WW sent "corrections" to the firm and "ordered 1000 copies printed," but the order was later "countermanded" (*CB*). Evidently Rand & Avery refused to run off the edition because of fears of legal action (see 1169). On July 24 WW paid Rand & Avery $13.75, presumably for the corrections (*CB*).

59. Ticknor, for Osgood & Co., on May 19 instructed Rand & Avery to hold the plates for WW (WW's copy of the letter in LC).

60. The superintendent of the Rand & Avery plant.

61. On the same day WW "sent order to Sanborn, Boston, to send the 225 sets sheets to James Arnold" (*CB*). Arnold, who had his plant at 531 Chestnut Street in Philadelphia, had bound the 1876 edition.

62. See the following letter. Ticknor had sent a check for $100 on May 20 (LC); he acknowledged WW's letter on May 25 (LC; *CW*, VIII, 299).

63. See 1101.

64. At the top of the page WW wrote: "? Under *Bits of Criticism* | in Sunday *Tribune* | *A defence of Walt Whitman* | *From the Philadelphia Press.*" Immediately below appeared the editorial from the *Press* of May 22. According to *CB*, WW sent similar letters (lost) to the editors of the Boston *Herald* (see 1122), the Boston *Globe*, the Boston *Post*, and to Crosley Stuart Noyes, an old friend and the editor of the Washington

1118. *To J. R. Osgood & Company*   5.23.1882

ENDORSED (by WW): "Copy of rec't sent O & Co
May 23 '82." DRAFT RECEIPT.

Copy
        Received of James R Osgood & Co: one hundred ($100:) dollars
in cash—and the plates, sheets, dies, &c. of "*Leaves of Grass*," in full of all
claims for copyright or otherwise, as per our agreement of May 19 1882
                                                        W W
Camden N J May 23—1882

1119. *To Whitelaw Reid*   5.23. [*1882*]

ENDORSED (in unknown hand): "Not answered."

                                        Camden   May 23d
My dear Reid
        Couldn't you feel to print the above say for instance in the *Bits of
Criticism* in next Sunday's *Tribune?*⁶⁴
                                        Walt Whitman

1120. *To William Sloane Kennedy*

                        Camden   New Jersey | May 24 '82
        Thanks for the beautiful & opportune book⁶⁵—just come to hand—I
am about as usual in health—
                                        Walt Whitman

Evening Star. The Camden *Daily Post* copied the article in the *Press* on May 22.
Though the *Tribune* apparently did not reprint the editorial, it published on May 15
WW's "Emerson's Books, (the Shadows of them)," which appeared in 1880 in *The
Literary World* (see 954).
    WW was supported, not without reservations in some instances, by the following
newspapers: the Philadelphia *Times* on May 23, the Chicago *Inter Ocean* on May 22
and 23, the Chicago *Herald* on May 23, the New York *Home Journal* on May 24, the
Boston *Liberty* and the Cambridge (Mass.) *Chronicle* on May 27, the Boston *Globe* on
May 28, the Audubon County (Iowa) *Sentinel* on May 31(?), and the Woodstown
(N. J.) *Register* on June 6. He was attacked, often with hysteria, by the following: the
Philadelphia *Evening Bulletin* on May 23, the Boston *Daily Advertiser* on May 24, the
Cincinnati *Ohio* on May 24, *The Christian Intelligencer* (quoted in the New York
Tribune on June 4), and the Philadelphia *Times* on July 17. For the Springfield
Republican and the Boston *Herald*, see 1122; for *The Critic*, see 1129.
    65. Kennedy's biography of Longfellow was published in Cambridge, Mass., in
1882. In an undated letter, written in late May or early June, Kennedy referred to the
Boston censorship: "I know you are as serene as a mountain, though you are a grand
old god, with all your faults. . . . It has taken me three years to get y'r parallax &
calculate your dimensions" (Feinberg).

1121. *To L. F. De H. Noble*[66]

431 Stevens Street | Camden   New Jersey |
May 25 '82

There is a late full edition of *Leaves of Grass* poems in one Vol. I can furnish you with a copy. The price is $3—

I have a few copies of the Centennial Edition, two Vols., poems & prose (described in printed slip herewith) & could furnish you a set should you prefer—price $10—

Which ever you wish—if either—send p o order & I will mail to you—

Walt Whitman

1122. *To William D. O'Connor*   5.25. [*1882*]

ENDORSED: "Answ'd May 29/82." ADDRESS:
Wm D O'Connor | Life Saving Service Bureau |
Washington | D C. POSTMARK: Philadelphia |
Pa. | May 25 82 | 7 PM.

Camden   May 25

My dear friend

Yours of 20th recd—At this present writing I don't think the *Tribune* will print your letter at all[67]—if it dont appear next Sunday, I doubt if it appears at all—the course of the T[ribune] towards me I think has been left to Wm Winter, who I have no doubt writes the squib in T. of 24th May —& also wrote (may be in conjunction with R H Stoddard,)[68] the notice of L of G in T. four or five months ago—After Stedman's *Scribner* article a year or two ago the T. extracted half a column of his condemnatory views & opinions on my treatment of amativeness in L of G.[69]—a few days after-

---

66. Noble, who lived in Elizabethtown, N. Y., ordered the Centennial Edition (see 1126 and *CB*).

67. But see the latter part of the letter.

68. Winter, the drama critic of the New York *Tribune*, and Stoddard, a writer and reviewer, were old enemies of WW (see 247). The brief note in the newspaper on May 24 consisted chiefly of adverse comments from the Boston *Transcript*.

69. "Walt Whitman's Naturalism," consisting largely of quotations from Stedman's article (see 981), appeared on November 7, 1880.

70. It is difficult not to be irritated at times by WW's carping at people like Reid, who gave him considerable space in the New York *Tribune* during these years, and who printed O'Connor's attack on the poet's critics on May 25. On May 29 O'Connor quoted what Reid had written to him: " 'I took great pleasure in printing your letter, because it was so cleverly done, and because, besides, I could not help having sympathy with it' " (Feinberg; Traubel, III, 284).

71. Another favorite target of the Whitmanites.

72. The editorial in the Springfield *Republican*, entitled "The Prurient Prudes and 'Leaves of Grass,'" quoted WW: "There is no bad personal feeling at all—W. W. considers himself treated by Osgood & Co throughout with courtesy and even liberality." The

ward, an extract, offering third of a column from Mrs Gilchrists *Woman's Estimate* was sent Reid, but he refused to print it[70]—I think, at present at any rate, that indicates their stand—(expediency, popular current &c)—carrying out the old enmity of Bayard Taylor,[71] &c &c—

Have you seen Dr Bucke's letter in *Springfield Republican* of May 23—and the vigorous editorial same number?[72] The Boston *Herald* May 24 (Supplement) takes the same ground[73]—both editorials would satisfy you perfectly—Shouldnt at all wonder if your guess about Rev T W Higginson[74] hits the nail—one nail—exactly on the head.

Your line about the Emerson talk on the Common[75] &c is very opportune—it was as you say—the *essential* matter, at the spine or abysm of all, such as the Bible often presents & in all primal poetry & attempt at returning to Creation's birth-innocence—let alone my attempt at the same result, based on modern science, biology & physiology—was not touched upon at all by Emerson—but it was a splendid & most sincere unfolding of the technical esthetic & conventional & technical literary points applicable—But you know, dear friend, my plan (hobby) is never to shirk the enemys fullest tactics but to state them over again if possible better than ever—*I shall mind your admonition though*—

As things are, I don't feel any resentment at all toward Osgood & Co. A sharp friend here suggests that they themselves (O & Co) had some hand in the Marston-Stevens proceeding & rather egged it on—that they were losing, paying me 25 cts royalty, &c &c—*But I havn't the least idea of any such thing*—I only mention it because I shouldn't wonder if it came up that way & you will hear it broached—

Dr Bucke is absent in Ottawa, Canada—from there he goes to Cincinnati—John Burroughs I suppose is in England[76]—(he went off in a depress'd humor—blue as indigo)—

<hr/>

newspaper again defended the poet on May 28 and on June 11.

73. On May 26 Guernsey, of the Boston *Herald*, asked WW to write to the editor, E. B. Haskell, "in acknowledgment of his defence of you" (Feinberg). The *Herald* supported WW against the Boston censors on May 24 and 28, and on June 2 it quoted Oscar Wilde's defense.

74. Colonel Thomas Wentworth Higginson (1823–1911), reformer and author, was a consistently hostile critic of WW. His first denunciation of the poet, "Unmanly Manhood," in *The Woman's Journal* on February 4, 1882, charged that WW, "with all his fine physique and his freedom from home-ties, never personally followed the drum, but only heard it from the comparatively remote distance of the hospital." O'Connor suggested on May 20 that "Reverend" Higginson was an "instigator" of the whole Boston affair. He promised "in due time [to] plant a javelin where it will do him good" (Feinberg; Traubel, II, 14).

75. The famous 1860 stroll in the Boston Common (see 18). On May 20 O'Connor advised WW to "be careful in what you say of Emerson's position" (Feinberg; Traubel, II, 15).

76. Burroughs left for England reluctantly when he discovered that the book of his friend was under attack (see Barrus, 212).

As I write—Thursday forenoon—it is raining again, with east wind & the heavens all lead-colored—but I am feeling well as usual & in good spirits—Sometimes I feel to welcome any *whack* that breaks the stupid monotony even of life's prosperous evenness—& as to this last & in some sense most marked buffeting in the fortunes of *Leaves of Grass*—why—if it cant stand it & throw it off & go on better than ever, why let it go under—of which I havn't the slightest idea though—but I feel sure the book will gather added, perhaps a main part, interest, from what it has gone through, from association—& I shall too—I tickle myself with the thought how it may be said years hence that at any rate *no book on earth ever had such a history*—

I shall keep you advised if I hear any thing—

Walt Whitman

later | Thursday—afternoon | May 25

I have just had the Tribune of to-day, in which I find *the letter*—I don't know but Charles Eldridge was right[77]—Being so much interested perhaps I am not a fair judge—but if ever Jupiter went into the press hurling the lightnings (& yet a sort of Jovian continence) *this letter* has got him in—It is apparently printed with wonderful correctness—don't need a single alteration—it will live in literature at least as long as Junius—God bless you[78]—

1123. *To T. C. Callicot*[79]

431 Stevens Street | Camden   New Jersey | May 26 '82

Dear Sir

Yours rec'd—I accordingly mail you a copy of my book—the price is $3 which please send by p o order—

Walt Whitman

77. On May 20 O'Connor informed WW that Eldridge, who had read the manuscript of his letter to the New York *Tribune*, considered it "the best thing I have done" (Feinberg; Traubel, II, 13).
78. On May 29 O'Connor expressed his gratitude for WW's praise: "I shall get nothing worth so much as your heartful 'God bless you,' flashing from the finale of your postscript" (Feinberg; Traubel, III, 282).
79. Callicot was the editor of the Albany *Evening Times*.
80. John White Chadwick (1840–1904), who termed himself a radical Unitarian,

1124. *To William D. O'Connor*

ENDORSED: "Answ'd | June 3/82." ADDRESS:
William D O'Connor | Life Saving Service | Bureau |
Washington | D C. POSTMARKS: Camden | May |
28 | 7 PM | N.J.; Washington, D.C. | May | 29 |
5 AM | 1882 | Recd.

Camden | Sunday   May 28 '82

Dear William O'Connor
    I like the big letter of May 25 the more I have read it—I think it
will never die—I am glad the Rev Mr Chadwick[80] appears with his *Tribune*
letter to you to-day (as enclosed) for the fine chance it affords to ventilate
the real account & true inwardness of that Emerson talk on the Common in
1860—& I at once send you the best synopsis of it I can recall—quite certainly the same in amount as I told you while it was fresh in my memory—
the which with hasty scribblings on my relations with Emerson—I hope
(working in as from yourself) you will incorporate in your answer to
Tribune—

Walt Whitman

for head

? *What were Emersons relations to Walt Whitman?*
    (for quoting entire in your letter if you think proper)
    "What made, and ever makes the argument of Emerson, in that walk
on the Common, so dear and *holy to me, was the personal affectionateness*
of it, as of an elderly brother to a younger. It was a vehement, even passionate well-wishing, which I felt then and feel to this hour the gratitude
and reverence of my life could never repay. Although perfect from an
intellectual and conventional point of view, it did not advance any thing I
had not already considered. And my arriere and citadel positions—such as
I have indicated in my June *North American Review* memorandum[81]—
were not only not attacked, they were not even alluded to.
    While I am on the subject, let me tell you I am sure the same process
went on with Emerson, in this particular (it was not needed any where

was the pastor of the Second Unitarian Church in Brooklyn from 1865 until his death.
He was also a reviewer for *The Nation* and the author of *A Book of Poems* (1876). In his
reply to O'Connor in the *Tribune* of May 28, Chadwick averred that Emerson had qualified his earlier praise of the poet. On May 29 O'Connor wrote to WW: "Of course I shall
answer this clerical blackguard, who has the audacity to accuse me of wilfully and
consciously lying, and I shall do my best to answer him with blasting effect" (Feinberg;
Traubel, III, 283).
    81. "A Memorandum at a Venture."

else) that goes on with many other of my readers. Certain am I that he too finally came to clearly feel that the "Children of Adam" pieces were inevitable and consistent—and in that sense, at least, proper—parts of the book. He was not the man to retract any utterance: whatever it had been, it had expressed the truth of the period.

That he said some transient things, from 1863 to 1873, which are in the critical direction and are acrid, (very likely your discussion will bring them out) there is no doubt. But he permanently loved me, and believed in my poems, of which the "Children of Adam" section, though difficult to unfold, is vertebral."

William, I submit to you whether it wouldnt be well, in your reply to *quote all this*, as extracted from a late letter to you from me[82]—

1125. *To William D. O'Connor*   5.30. *[1882]*

ENDORSED: "Answ'd June 3/82." ADDRESS: Wm Douglas O'Connor | Life Saving Service | Bureau | Washington | D C. POSTMARKS: Camden | May | 30 | 6 PM | N.J.; Washington, D.C. | May | 31 | 4 AM | 1882 | Recd.

Camden   Tuesday Evening | May 30—
The whole hinge of the Chadwick letter[83]—involving you and yours, with me, & including the question of veracity—seems to me to be essentially *What are the relations of Emerson to W W?* As permanently left by *the sum* of the transactions and judgments of twenty-five years—(yours of 29th recd)—(just the same as the Bible means its whole & final spirit, not one or two picked out verses or texts)—confirmed by a most deliberate and emphatic act of the last year of his E's life—seems to me the mood of your reply to the Chadwick letter may well be *different* from the other (which the more I read it, the more it unfolds—it is such a piece of *literary work*)[84] —I see clearly that the question above is more involved than that of veracity you speak of—see the other page I send—
Personal information—perhaps nothing but what you knew already—
☞ I suppose you know that the *Life of Emerson*—(& a very good

82. As directed, O'Connor quoted WW's remarks in his reply to Chadwick in the New York *Tribune* on June 18. Also see the following letter.
83. Here WW continued to assemble facts to refute Chadwick's article. On June 3 O'Connor wrote: "I have freely used the memoranda you sent, and got in as much of it as I could see my way to employ, and as much as I dared" (Feinberg; Traubel, I, 52). But, fortunately, O'Connor verified some of WW's erroneous information (see note 86 below).
84. O'Connor's letter in the New York *Tribune* on May 25.

one I guess)—published nearly a year ago by Osgood—*all with the sanc-tion & revision of the family & of E. himself*[85]—gives *in full the letter of 1856 you quote*—thus confirming & sanctioning it—See said *Life.*[86]

Seems to me would be good to bring in quite verbatim—it is certainly *true*—

Emerson had much more of a personal friendship for W W than has been generally known; making a determined visit to Brooklyn soon after the appearance of Leaves of Grass, twenty five years ago, walking out to the little cottage in the suburbs, several miles from the ferry where Mr W then lived. From that time regularly for years afterwards whenever he came to New York he appointed a meeting, and they two generally dined together and spent some hours.[87] When Mr Whitman was in Boston in 1860 Emerson was his frequent & cordial visitor. As time elapsed, though officious persons intervened, and there was a lull of some years, I doubt if it could be said that Ralph Waldo Emerson's affections (and few know how deeply he could love!) ever went out more warmly to any one, and re-mained more fixed, under the circumstances, than toward Walt Whitman.

Mr Chadwick evidently thinks that if the author of Leaves of Grass had any case to state, that walk on the common in 1860 was his time. But it is well known to his intimate friends that Walt Whitman, who has the most simplicity and good nature of any man alive, is also the haughtiest, the most disdainful at those periods when expected to talk loudest and best, and when he probably could do so, is apt to remain perfectly silent. The main reason certainly was, curious as it may seem, that Emerson's objections, on that famous walk, did not at all touch Whitman's principle of treatment which was a moral one, or rather it involved the verteber of all morals. I have heard the author of Leaves of Grass say that what he sought to do in "Children of Adam" seemed all the more necessary after that [conversa-tion?]. Though Emerson's points were of the highest and keenest order, they sprang exclusively from conventional and what may be called the usual technical literary considerations. I know from what he has told me that Whitman himself had long dwelt on these very points in his own mind— that he was anxious to hear the utmost that could be brought forward in their behalf. And now when he heard what the best critic of the age so brought forward, and his inmost soul and brain remained altogether un-

85. WW deleted: "as far as he did any thing."
86. In his reply on June 3, O'Connor corrected WW's misstatements in this para-graph. George W. Cooke reprinted Emerson's famous letter to WW (see 10) in *Ralph Waldo Emerson: His Life, Writings, and Philosophy* (Boston, 1881), 233–234; but it was obvious that Cooke's remarks about the relations between the two men were specula-tive, not official.
87. It is not known exactly how many times Emerson visited WW in Brooklyn. Probably WW overstated.

touched, his final resolution was taken, and he has never changed from that hour.

Then to clench the whole matter of the relations between these two men, I doubt whether there is any thing more affecting or emphatic in Emersons whole career—a sort of last coruscation in the evening twilight of it—than his driving over to Frank Sanborn's in Concord, Sept 1881, to deliberately pay "respects" for which he had obligated himself twenty five years before.[88] Nor was the unusual compliment of the hospitable but formal dinner made the next day for Walt Whitman, by Mr and Mrs Emerson, without marked significance. It was a beautiful autumn Sunday. And if that afternoon, with its occurrences there in his own mansion, surrounded by all his family, wife, son, daughters, son-in-law, nearest relatives, and two or three very near friends—some fourteen or fifteen in all—if that does not mean how Emerson, by this simple yet almost solemn rite, wished, before he departed, to reiterate and finally seal his verdict of 1856, then there is no significance in human life or its emotions or[89]—

1126. *To L. F. De H. Noble*[90]

431 Stevens Street | Camden New Jersey May 31 '82
In accordance with yours of 29th (the $10 have come safe—best thanks) I forward the two Vols. Centennial Edition, by same mail with this—Please send me word soon as they reach you safely.

Walt Whitman

1127. *To Karl Knortz*(?)[91]

TRANSCRIPT.

May 31, '82.
From to-day I enter upon my 64th year. The paralysis that first affected me nearly ten years ago, has since remain'd, with varying course—seems to have settled quietly down, and will probably continue. I easily

88. See the two letters written at the time of WW's visit to Concord (1058 and 1059).
89. Herbert Gilchrist did not know that WW had contributed to O'Connor's article when he wrote on August 16: "I and mother do not think very highly of O'Connor's blustering defence: we think that he is on the wrong tack when he justifies you by the classics and by what Emerson says as if that made any difference one way or the other" (Feinberg; Traubel, I, 227). See also Anne Gilchrist's letter to Burroughs on July 28 (Barrus, 220–221).
90. See 1121. This correspondence card is mounted in a copy of *Two Rivulets* inscribed by WW to Noble (Feinberg).
91. No entry in CB provides a clue to the identification of this person whom WW called in SD "a German Friend." However, in 1176 WW called the letter to Knortz's

tire, am very clumsy, cannot walk far; but my spirits are first-rate. I go around in public almost every day—now and then take long trips, by railroad or boat, hundreds of miles—live largely in the open air—am sunburnt and stout, (weigh 190)—keep up my activity and interest in life, people, progress, and the questions of the day. About two-thirds of the time I am quite comfortable. What mentality I ever had remains entirely unaffected; though physically I am a half-paralytic; and likely to be so, long as I live. But the principal object of my life seems to have been accomplish'd—I have the most devoted and ardent of friends, and affectionate relatives—and of enemies I really make no account.[92]

1128. *To Sylvester Baxter*

Camden   N J | June 2 '82

Dear Baxter

My friend John Sands,[93] a veteran magazine & newspaper writer, has just sent a lengthy—but I think very *meaty*, & *most readable*—article, for the forthcoming Sunday paper, about me & mine—I am quite sure it will please your folks, if they give it immediate *attention*—I am well as usual—have received your *Heralds* with feeling & gratitude—

Best remembrances to Guernsey[94]—

Walt Whitman

If printed send me three or four copies—

1129. *To Jeannette L. and Joseph B. Gilder*

ADDRESS: J L & J B Gilder | *Critic* office | 30 Lafayette Place | New York City. POSTMARK: Philadelphia | Jun | 3 | 9 PM | Pa.

Camden   New Jersey | June 3d '82

Yours of 2d rec'd, with the $10, hereby receipted[95]—

attention.
     Knortz (1841–1918) was born in Prussia and came to the U. S. in 1863. He was the author of many books and articles on German-American affairs and was superintendent of German instruction in Evansville, Ind., from 1892 to 1905. See *The American-German Review*, XIII (December, 1946), 27–30. His first published criticism of WW appeared in the New York *Staats-Zeitung Sontagsblatt* on December 17, 1882.
     92. WW could never resist the pose of the benign poet indifferent to his enemies. His publicity campaign after the banning of the Osgood edition hardly confirms the pose.
     93. "John Sands" was the pen name of William Hutchinson, a journalist (*LC #* 108).
     94. The Boston *Herald* vigorously supported WW (see 1122).
     95. Payment for "Edgar Poe's Significance," which appeared in *The Critic* on this date; included in *SD*, 230–233.

I appreciate the "Dogberry" article not only for its bearing on me & my book—it is the keenest bit of quiet razor-edged literary paragraphing I have read lately[96]—

I have rec'd from Boston the handsomely published *"Essays"*—hearty thanks to the writer of the criticism last of book on mine & me[97]—I am at present again well as usual (was quite ill all April & first half of May)—Send me please three copies last *Critic*—

Walt Whitman

1130. *To Van Doran Stafford*   *6.14.* [*1882*]

Camden | Wednesday Evn'g   June 14

Dear boy Van[98]

So you are back again—I heard that your folks had sent for you—How did you like New York & your trip & every thing? I got your letter & was glad to get it—write to me again if you feel like it—I saw Bill Engle & he told me they had sent for you, & that Ed was up here in Camden in a store —(I have not seen Ed yet)—Van, I send you a paper—read that story "the boy from Xenia"—it is very good—in fact there is lots of good reading in the little paper—I know you do not care much for reading, but I wish you would read more—read this paper I send any how—

I have had a good deal of trouble in business lately, but I guess it is going to be all right—I am not altogether out of the woods, but near it surely—I keep about as usual in health—I got a paper from Herbert—one of his pictures has taken a big prize, a gold medal—(probably he has wrote your folks all about it though)—A big fire up here last night, the Narrow Gauge Engine House & Depot, five engines burnt, bad luck—

Van, show this letter to your father and mother—my love to you, boy, & to all the rest, every one—I want to come down before long—Ruth, have you got *a chicken* ready? I will send you word—I dream'd night before last I was down by the old pond a long while—the old tulip tree was coverd with blossoms & the bees humming—

Walt Whitman

96. "The Massachusetts Dogberry," an editorial in *The Critic* on June 3, was indeed a "razor-edged" attack on the Boston censors of *Leaves of Grass*.

97. *Essays from "The Critic"* contained WW's "Death of Carlyle" and "Death of Longfellow" as well as an anonymous chapter entitled "Whitman's 'Leaves of Grass,'" in which the author judiciously appraised WW's poetry as "truly caviare to the multitude," defended the sexual poems, deplored WW's "lack of taste" in the use of foreign phrases, and compared him to Richard Wagner.

98. Van Doran Stafford wrote to WW on May 28 from New York, where he was

1131. *To Rees Welsh & Company*

431 Stevens Street | Camden   N J | p m June 17 '82

Dear Sirs[99]

Yours of 16th rec'd—Although delayed from calling upon you by one or two little matters, I still entertain your proposals—I have had several —For one point I should like some publishing & radiating spot near my own locality—for another to retain control of my book & personally advise in selling & publishing it—Will call upon you Monday bet'n 11 and 12—

Walt Whitman

What would you say to entering decidedly into the publishing field? Haven't you thought of it? I want to publish my *Prose writings* in a companion volume to L of G—Then there is a Canada man who has a book— "*Walt Whitman—a Study*"[1]—(Osgood & Co: had the MS. & would doubtless have issued it but for the flurry.)—Making *three Volumes* that ought to go out together, from the same house & hands—

How would it suit you to get up *this three-fold team* & dash into the fall publishing trade?

1132. *To William D. O'Connor*   *6.18. [1882]*

ENDORSED: "Answ'd June 19/82." ADDRESS: Wm D O'Connor | Life Saving Service Bureau | Washington | D C. POSTMARKS: Camden | Jun | 18 | 6 PM | N.J.; Washington, D.C. | Jun | 19 | 4 AM | 1882 | Recd.

Camden | June 18   p m

Only a word to catch this evening's mail—the second letter in to-day's *Tribune* fully follows up the first—& I should say settles the Chadwick points—Dear friend, I only wanted to say again how *entirely satisfied* I am with your championship, matter & spirit—

Walt Whitman

employed on the steamer "Plymouth Rock." He was enjoying New York and was not anxious to return since "Ruth Says She will have a situation for me when i get home to Scrub and wash dishes" (Feinberg).

99. Rees Welsh & Co., booksellers and publishers, wrote to WW on June 5 offering to print his book. On June 16 the firm wanted to proceed "*at once*" (Pennsylvania). See also 1133.

1. WW wrote to Bucke on June 10 "ab't '*motif*' of his book & ab't printing in Phila" (CB).

The "savage" letter of "*Sigma*" following seems a very curious one.[2] I am more than half inclined to think it some crafty friend who takes the mask of foe—

1133. *To Rees Welsh & Company*   [6.20. 1882]

ENDORSED: "Rees Welsh & Co | Sent Rees Welsh & Co June 20 '82." DRAFT LETTER.

Let me make my propositions as plain as possible.

Rees Welsh & Co: to publish Leaves of Grass, (in a style as good as the Osgood issue) from W W's electrotype plates to retail at $2—to pay W W a royalty of 35 cts on every copy sold. This agreement to remain in force [*inserted in pencil:* "blank"] and as much longer as both parties mutually agree. R W & Co. to have the privilege of purchasing from W W the plates of L of G., with the steel engraving & the wood cut, for the sum of 400. cash. After so purchasing W W's royalty to be at 25 cts a copy—

Rees Welsh & Co: to electrotype, in the best manner at their sole expense, & publish W W's Prose Writings, Specimen Days (now mostly in MS) as a companion volume to Leaves of Grass, to be of about the same s[ize & ?] in equally good type, paper & style & to retail at $2—R W & Co: to pay W W a royalty of 22 cents on every copy sold—said R W & Co. to have the sole right to publish *Specimen Days* for five years, and as much longer as mutually agreed—

A special edition of Leaves of Grass for holiday presents in handsome binding, (say half calf, gilt) may be published, price $5. For these W W's royalty to be 87½ cts a copy.

W W is to be the sole owner of the copyright of Specimen Days.

W W to have 25 copies of the first 1000 of *Specimen Days*, without charge.

R W & Co: to publish *Walt Whitman a Study*, by Dr R M Bucke of Canada, in a 12mo volume of about three hundred pages, on condition that Dr. B. secures an American copyright & royalty of [   ] to be paid Dr B. WW a Study to retail at $2—will call soon[3]—

                                        W W

2. On June 15 O'Connor notified WW of the appearance of his article in the New York *Tribune* and of what Reid termed "a savage article on the other side" (Feinberg). On June 19 O'Connor tentatively proposed that Spofford, the Librarian of Congress, was the author of the letter signed "Sigma" (Feinberg; Traubel, I, 314), but on June 29 he decided upon Richard H. Stoddard (Feinberg; Traubel, III, 49).

3. Rees Welsh & Co. agreed to WW's terms on June 21 with two stipulations: they were unwilling to accept *Specimen Days* until they had seen the manuscript, and they wanted to know about the copyright of Bucke's volume (Pennsylvania). Apparently the agreement to publish *Leaves of Grass* and *Specimen Days* was signed on June 28

1134. *To William D. O'Connor*   6.22. [*1882*]

ENDORSED: "Answ'd June 29/82." ADDRESS: Wm
D O'Connor | Life Saving Service Bureau |
Washington | D C. POSTMARKS: Camden | Jun | 23 |
5 PM | N.J.; Washington, D.C. | Jun | 24 | 4 AM |
1882 | Recd.

                                          Camden   June 22
   I send you the Phil: *Press* with an item—after reading please mail
to Dr Bucke.[4]

                                                 W. W.

1135. *To Ruth Stafford*   6.22. [*1882*]

ADDRESS: Miss Ruth Anna Stafford | Kirkwood |
Glendale | New Jersey. POSTMARK: Camden | Jun |
23 | 7 AM | N.J.

                                   Camden   June 22   Ev'ng
Dear young friend
   Yours rec'd to-day, & glad to hear from you—I have wanted to
come down for quite a while, but business has delayed me. I am pretty well
—& all goes well enough to be thankful for in my affairs. Only a short word
this time but I will be down soon & tell you all the news[5]—After I write this
I am going out on the river for an hour or two—

                                                 W W

1136. *To William D. O'Connor*   [*6.25. 1882*]

ENDORSED: "Answ'd June 29/82." ADDRESS: Wm
D O'Connor | Life Saving Service Bureau |
Washington | D C. POSTMARKS: Camden | Jun(?) |
26 | 7 AM | N.J.; Washington | Jun | 26 | 5 M(?) | (?)

                                   Camden   Sunday Evn'g[6]
   Yours of yesterday rec'd—I had heard nothing of the Boston P. M.
action—(it is not some mistake?—As you describe it?)[7]—The price of

(CB and see 1138).
   4. Probably WW sent an article entitled "The Condemned Poems," signed by
W. H. (apparently a woman), which appeared in the Philadelphia *Press* on June 16.
See also Traubel, III, 349.
   5. WW was at Glendale from July 3 to 5 (CB).
   6. June 25 was on Sunday in 1882. The year is also confirmed by the notes
below.
   7. On June 24 O'Connor reported that the Boston postmaster had halted a lecture by George Chainey on *Leaves of Grass* (Feinberg; Traubel, III, 349). Obviously
he meant the sending of the printed lecture through the mail (see the next letter).

the book such a volume as I sent you is $3—I sent one to Prof. Loomis⁸—
The heat here to-day has been awful, but I seem to stand it well—

                                                                    W W

I decidedly approve your non-answer to *Sigma*⁹—

1137. *To George Chainey*¹⁰

                431 Stevens Street | Camden New Jersey   June 26 '82
My dear friend—
    I to-day mail you a copy of "Leaves of Grass" as a little gift &
testimonial of thanks. Please send me word if it is safely delivered. I sent
you a little package of printed sheets last week by mail.

                                                            Walt Whitman

1138. *To William D. O'Connor*   6.28. *[1882]*

ENDORSED: "Answ'd | June 29/82." ADDRESS:
Wm D O'Connor | Life Saving Service Bureau |
Washington | D C. POSTMARKS: Philadelphia |
Jun | 28 | 3 PM | Pa.; Washington, D.C. | Jun | 29 |
5 AM | 1882 | Rec'd.

                                            Wednesday noon   June 28
    Publishers secured—(not in the front rank at all, but young, ex-
perienced, & I guess square & the proposition to take the book comes vehemently from them)—Rees Welsh & Co: 23 south 9th st: Phila: (dealers
in 2d hand books & pub: of law books & some others)—*Satisfactory to me,
as I see at present, & in prospect.* They are to publish L of G. same style as
O[sgood]'s ed'n, same price, from my plates, & pay me 35 cts a copy
royalty—They are also to publish immediately my prose writings, *Specimen
Days, & Collect*—a companion vol. to L of G. same price & ab't same size,
for which they pay me 22 cts royalty. They consider favorably the idea of
publishing Dr. Bucke's book also—& I think will do so—though they have
not pledged themselves—

    8. After O'Connor's request on June 15 (Feinberg), WW sent the volume
on June 20 to Professor Elias Loomis (1811–1889), the astronomer and Yale professor, who at the time was in the Nautical Almanac Office of the Navy Department in
Washington (CB). According to O'Connor's letter of June 19, Loomis knew that Emerson had never qualified his praise of *Leaves of Grass* (Feinberg; Traubel, I, 313).
    9. O'Connor "judged it prudent to withhold my reply to 'Sigma' " (Feinberg;
Traubel, III, 349).
    10. Probably WW met George Chainey, the publisher of *This World* (Boston),
in Boston in 1881. On December 22, 1881, the poet sent one of Chainey's sermons
to Mrs. Stafford (CB). Chainey printed on June 17, 1882, "Keep Off the Grass," a
lecture which he had delivered on June 11, as well as "To a Common Prostitute." Chainey
printed WW's letter and one from O'Connor on July 1. Interestingly, O'Connor deplored
Chainey's stupidity in a letter to WW on July 13 (Feinberg), although he had been

By what I hear since I wrote last I think the enemy (in Boston) have formally appealed to the Post Master General to order L of G. excluded from the mails under the Comstock[11] statutes—I think the P M G has it before him—perhaps has already decided—I keep well—

W W

The Boston *Herald* has articles strongly in my favor—Cambridge *Chronicle* also—Boston *Globe* also[12]—Yours rec'd yesterday—

1139. To Benjamin Ticknor

Rees Welsh & Co., | . . . | *Philadelphia,*
June 28 1882

My dear Ben: Ticknor
     I wish you would do me the favor to have *the steel plate,* (we used in L of G) properly enveloped & sent by express, directed to Rees Welsh & Co: 23 south 9th street, (as above.) I have forgotten the address of your plate printer in B[oston] who has it.[13]
     Yours (notwithstanding)

Walt Whitman

1140. To William D. O'Connor

ENDORSED: "Walt Whitman | Answ'd July 7/82."
ADDRESS: Wm D O'Connor | Life Saving Service Bureau | Washington | D C. POSTMARKS: Philadelphia | Jul | 6 | 6 PM | Pa.; Washington, D.C. | Jul | 7 | 5 AM | 1882 | Recd.

Rees Welsh & Co., | . . . | *Philadelphia,* July 6 1882
My dear friend
     If entirely convenient I wish you would find out whether there has been any consideration of the question of sending *Leaves of Grass* through

furnishing Chainey with information; see Chainey's letter to O'Connor, dated July 11 (Trent). Chainey discussed the censorship on July 1, July 6, and November 4; see Asselineau, 250–251n. Chainey lectured on *Leaves of Grass* in 1884 (CB, June 23).
     11. Anthony Comstock (1844–1915), the secretary of the Society for the Suppression of Vice in New York from 1873 to 1915, was the author of *Frauds Exposed* (1880) and *Morals Versus Art* (1887). On June 29 O'Connor informed WW that Ingersoll and he were drawing up a memorandum for the Postmaster General (Feinberg; Traubel, III, 50). On July 13 O'Connor reported that in Ingersoll's opinion Comstock "is not an honest bigot, but an arrant black-hearted scoundrel" (Feinberg).
     12. The Cambridge *Chronicle,* edited by Linn B. Porter, printed a vigorous defense of WW on May 27. For the Boston *Herald,* see 1122.
     13. On May 19 Ticknor advised J. W. Daniels, of Boston, to hold the plate subject to WW's orders (LC).

the mails, and decision thereon, at the P O Department—& send me word at
once—I am well as usual—

Walt Whitman

direct to me at Camden N J—

1141. *To William D. O'Connor*   [7.9. 1882]

ENDORSED: "Answ'd July 10/82 | [Answ'd July] 12
[82]." ADDRESS: Wm D O'Connor | Life Saving
Service Bureau | Washington | D C. POSTMARKS:
Camden | Jul | 9 | 7 PM | N.J.; Washington, D.C. |
Jul | 10 | 5 AM | 1882 | Recd.

Camden   Sunday noon
Yours rec'd—yes indeed it is a cheering & very important victory[14]—
most important coming just at this nick of time—vivifies Rees Welsh much
(as I saw yesterday) & gives an absolute cement to what perhaps was not
so entirely *set* as I could have wished—though as I get along with them, &
versed, I am well satisfied with R W & Co. and my prospect with them—
Though Thursday & Friday last were pretty dark, big clouds, big enemies
on the horizon, some bad letters sent them threats from the "Society," they
did not flinch but went on getting out the new edition as fast as possible—
Now of course they feel entrenched & good heart[15]—The printing is done at
Sherman & Co's. cor 7th & Cherry, the best printing office in Philadelphia.
My L of G plates having been sent on there from Rand & Avery's, Boston—
& I shall begin on "Specimen Days" there in about a week—
    I havn't emerged from the house to-day, (it is July heat, oppressive) —
but I shouldn't wonder if *the L of G. officially ordered to pass unmolested
through the mails* was itemized generally over the land everywhere to-day,
as the Telegraphic Associated Press chargé here in Phila told me yesterday
afternoon he intended to send it generally—the Phila: *Press* here is very
friendly—it has three short pieces in to-day, a first-rate acc't of the P O

14. On July 7 O'Connor wrote jubilantly: "The Boston Postmaster's action on
Chainey's lecture is reversed and disapproved! Furthermore in the letter to Tobey, the
Postmaster General takes the ground *that your book must pass unmolested through the
mails*—that a book, generally accepted by the public, admitted into libraries, and accepted by the literary class, cannot be brought under the operation of the statutes respecting taboo matter.
    "This is cheering. We owe this victory to the tact, bonhomie, energy and gallantry
of Ingersoll, who put the case to the Department in the best manner possible" (Feinberg).
15. On July 5 Rees Welsh & Co. wrote to WW: "Much to our surprise we are
threatened with an action. Please call at your earliest convenience and we will talk over
it" (Pennsylvania).
16. Williams (1849–1928), a journalist, worked for the New York *Sun* and

Dept. decision & commending it editorially—Talcott Williams[16] on the P[ress] is an ardent friend—

William, I wish you would get an authentic copy of the P. O. letter order & send me *soon*, if you can—When you see Col. Ingersoll say he dont know how deeply he has served me, & at a time when it told best—

W W

1142. *To William D. O'Connor*   *7.11.* [*1882*]

ENDORSED: "Answ'd July 13/82." ADDRESS:
Wm D O'Connor | Life Saving Service Bureau |
Washington | D C. POSTMARKS: Camden | Jul | 11 |
4 PM | (?); Washington, D. C. | Jul | 12 | 5 AM |
1882 | Recd.

Camden—noon—July 11—

Yours just rec'd—the acc't & formal letter shift the relative positions—but taking in Judge R[ay]'s remarks which are a part of it, the result seems to me absolutely & unequivocally what I took it to be, & what I suppose the papers (with some marked errors of detail) are stating[17]— Though I havn't seen the said papers (except the Phila "Press")—the weather here is so hot I dont go out or over to Phila:—

W W

1143. *To William D. O'Connor*   *7.19.* [*1882*]

ENDORSED: "Answ'd July 20/82." ADDRESS:
Wm D O'Connor | Life Saving Service Bureau |
Washington | D C. POSTMARKS: Philadelphia |
Jul | 19 | 6 PM | Pa.; Washington, D.C. | Jul | 20 |
5 AM | 1882 | Recd.

Phila: July 19—

Rees Welsh & Co:'s new ed'n L of G. *looks well*—is a fac-simile of the Boston ed'n—announced ready by 17th (being pretty cautious printed

World, and became an editorial writer on the Springfield *Republican* in 1879. He joined the staff of the Philadelphia *Press* in 1881. In 1912 he became director of the School of Journalism at Columbia University. See also Elizabeth Dunbar's *Talcott Williams: Gentleman of the Fourth Estate* (1936); Traubel, I, 202.

The Philadelphia *Press* vigorously supported the poet against the Boston censorship both in its news columns and in its editorials. A front-page story on July 15 quoted at length the defense of *Leaves of Grass* offered by the Reverend James Morrow, "a prominent Methodist."

17. O'Connor carefully explained on July 10 that he had given a slightly misleading impression of the Post Office's decision since the ruling applied only to Chainey's pamphlet, not to *Leaves of Grass* as a book. However, the interpretation offered by Judge Charles A. Ray, the law officer of the Post Office Department, meant in effect that *Leaves of Grass* was "*mailable*" (Feinberg).

only 1000) began to come in from the bindery late that day—Early this forenoon *they were all clean'd out—hadn't a copy left*[18]—are hurrying up their second batch—I have commenced type-setting on *Specimen Days*[19] —Keep well—awful hot weather—

W W

1144. *To William D. O'Connor*   7.21. [1882]

ENDORSED: "Answ'd July 24/82." ADDRESS: Wm D O'Connor | Life Saving Service Bureau | Washington D C. POSTMARKS: Philadelphia | Pa. | Jul 21 82 | 11 PM; Washington, D.C. | Jul | 22 | 7 AM | 1882 | Recd.

July 21—Evn'g

Yours of 20th rec'd[20]—Nothing very new—the 2d & larger Phila. ed'n L of G. will be ready ab't 26th or 7th[21]—(I like it best of all my ed'ns) —I will send you one soon as I can get it—also Florio's Montaigne if it can be had[22]—

W W

1145. *To Anne Gilchrist*

ADDRESS: Mrs Anne Gilchrist | Keats' Corner—12 Well Road | Hampstead | London England. POSTMARK: Phila. Paid All | Jul | 22 | 1882 | Pa.

Camden N J | U S A | July 22—'82

We are all still here & about the same—I am well as usual—your letters rec'd & dearly welcomed[23]—I am busy printing "Specimen Days"— the Staffords well—best love—

W W

18. WW wrote in *CB*: "The first Phila ed'n. . . . ready 18th—morning of 20th all exhausted—not a copy left."
19. Sherman & Co. began to set type on July 19 (*CB*). On July 23 WW "read first page proof 'Specimen Days'" (*CB*).
20. In 1888, speaking to Traubel, WW observed that he had read O'Connor's letter "a dozen times" (Traubel, II, 60). O'Connor was so vituperative in dealing with Comstock that Traubel omitted the following passage: "It is a disgrace to the Government that they should employ this vile maggot bred from carrion—the rat of the cloaca— this lump of devil's-dung" (Feinberg).
21. This edition appeared on August 4 (see 1149).
22. On July 7 O'Connor asked WW to see whether Rees Welsh & Co. had a copy of the first edition of Florio's *Montaigne* (Feinberg). See also Traubel, II, 496.
23. Mrs. Gilchrist wrote on May 8 and again on June 18. In the earlier letter she objected to WW's rearrangement of his poems and to the new titles in the 1882 edition (LC; Harned, 207). In the latter she praised "A Memorandum at a Venture": "It is as

first Phil. ed'n out last Wednesday—all sold in twenty four hours—not one left—2d ed'n ready soon—

1146. *To Edward Carpenter*

TRANSCRIPT.

431 Stevens Street, | Camden, | New Jersey, |
U. S. A. | July 24th, 1882.

Yours received with enclosure.[24] Thanks, dear friend.

I am well. H[arry] S[tafford] is well.

I shall send you both books, soon as the S.D. is ready. The present edition L of G. satisfied me more than any hitherto. I am now printing Specimen Days.

W. W.

1147. *To Ainsworth R. Spofford*   [*8.1. 1882*]

ENDORSED: "Aug 1 '82 | sent to Librarian of
Congress | ans'd—see note | copyright entrance of |
1860–'61—acknowledged | & on file." DRAFT
LETTER.

In your letter to me of Sept. '81, (herewith enclosed) you tallied all my several copyrights for "*Leaves of Grass*"—*except the 1860-61 edition of Thayer & Eldridge, Boston*—saying that one was not "entered" in your office. I enclose it herewith to show that it was taken out regularly, & is in existence.

What I send now for is to ask you to enter that edn for the extension of fourteen years further from expiration & send me certificate of such entry— find $1 enc.[25]

clear as daylight to me that you speak truth—invigorating ennobling truth, full of hope & promise & impetus for the race. I have never for a moment wavered in my belief in this truth since it burst upon me a veritable sunrise in reading your poems in 1869" (Pennsylvania).

On July 28 Mrs. Gilchrist in a letter to Burroughs offered her defense of WW, which she was willing to have submitted to the New York *Tribune* (Barrus, 220–221). The newspaper, however, declined to publish it (Barrus, 242).

24. WW referred to Carpenter's letter of March 16, in which he enclosed a letter from a friend named Sharp(?), who termed *Leaves of Grass* "a barbaric work" and WW "the poet of anarchy, confusion, lawlessness, disorder, 'anomia,' chaos," who was not even "*cosmopolitan*" (Feinberg; Traubel, I, 252–253). WW was amused and impressed: "I kind o' take to the man: he tumbles me clear over as a matter of conscience—I respect him for it" (Traubel, I, 253).

25. On the following day Spofford, the Librarian of Congress, acknowledged that the 1860 edition had been entered, but the request for renewal of copyright could not be made until May 24, 1888 (LC).

1148. *To William D. O'Connor*   8.3. [*1882*]

ENDORSED: "No answer." ADDRESS: Wm D O'Connor |
Life Saving Service Bureau | Washington D C.
POSTMARKS: Philadelphia | Aug | 3 | 5(?) PM |
Pa.; Washington, D.C. | Aug | 4 | 4 AM | 1882 |
Recd.

Camden—Aug 3—noon

Thank you for sending me Herman Grimm on *Emerson*[26]—Seems to me, (colloquial & rather hurried as it is) it is the only fine & worthy utterance on the subject I have yet seen—I am well (upon the whole)— "Specimen Days" is getting along to the 100th page in the foundry—the second & a little larger ed'n L of G. launch'd to-day[27]—

W W

1149. *To William D. O'Connor*   8.6. [*1882*]

ENDORSED: "Answ'd Aug 19/82." ADDRESS:
Wm D O'Connor | Life Saving Service Bureau |
Washington D C. POSTMARKS: Camden | Aug | 6 |
6 PM | N.J.; Washington, D.C. | Aug | 7 | 4 AM |
1882 | Recd.

Camden, Aug: 6   Evening

Nothing specially new—I am well—pleasant weather—the 2d Phila ed'n was delay'd till Friday last—commenced coming in at noon—by noon next day (yesterday) 500 had been sold[28]—*Specimen Days* is jogging along —neither very fast, or slow—You will get a copy of the Phila. ed'n L of G to-morrow or next day, as I have requested one sent you—by what I can

26.   Grimm's article was included in *Essays on Literature*, translated by Sarah H. Adams (1886).

27.   The edition appeared on the following day (see the next letter).

28.   So far as I can discover, WW never stated the exact number of copies of the second Philadelphia impression. Since he referred to the "cautious 1000" copies of the first impression, presumably this printing was larger. On August 13 the second impression was "now nearly gone." On August 27 Rees Welsh & Co. was "now paying out their third edition." On September 17 "they are now on their *fourth* Phila: ed'n L of G." The fifth impression was run off in October (see 1163).

29.   See 1144.

30.   In his answer on August 19, O'Connor mentioned with resentment that J. B. Gilder, of *The Critic*, was supporting Chadwick and deplored the fact that *Leaves of Grass*, according to the New York *Tribune* on August 15, was now "proscribed by Trinity College, Dublin" (Feinberg; Traubel, II, 496).

31.   Burroughs had just returned from a two-month visit to England, as he informed WW in a post card on August 9 (Feinberg).

32.   Before Rees Welsh & Co. became his publisher, WW bound some of the

learn there is no *Florio Montaigne*²⁹ to be had for love or money—Have
been in all day finishing up copy of S. D. for the printers—Out now to p.o.³⁰

W W

1150. *To John Burroughs*   *8.13.* [*1882*]

Camden   Aug: 13—Evn'g
*Welcome home again*³¹—by no means forgetting 'Sula & the youngster—

I am well—have had a very fair summer, (though so much hot
weather) —

I commenced publishing L of G in June on my own hook, but found it
vexatious from the start,³² & having quite vehement proposals from Rees
Welsh, (2d hand book dealer & law book publisher) 23 South 9th St. Phila.
I pass'd the use of the plates into his hands—he printed it (the plates are
here in Phila) an exact copy of the Osgood edition—Welsh's first edition
(a cautious 1000) was ready ab't three weeks ago & was exhausted in a day
—the second came in ab't five days ago, & is now nearly gone—a third is
ordered—I am glad I let him have it—

I am throwing together a *prose* jumble, *Specimen Days*—(see slips
enclosed)—nearly 200 pages already cast—O'Connor sent me a copy of your
letter about visiting W M Rossetti³³—(O'C & I correspond now quite often,
& just on the same terms as of yore)³⁴—When you have a leisure hour reel
me off a letter—put in ab't Mrs Gilchrist and Herbert—Dr Bucke is keeping
back his book till *Specimen Days* comes out³⁵—will come out by winter
likely—

Walt Whitman

"sheets" which he had received from Osgood (see 1108). Goldsmith estimated that only
fifty copies of this "edition" were issued (Barrus, 210*n*.).

33. Late in June, apparently, Burroughs informed O'Connor that Rossetti now called
Leaves of Grass "nasty"; see O'Connor's letter to Burroughs on July 12 (Barrus, 220).
On the next day O'Connor wrote to WW of Rossetti's recantation: "It is sad and sicken-
ing" (Feinberg). On August 24 Burroughs explained the situation to WW: "Yes, I was
much put out with Wm Rossetti; it was not so much what he said about your poems, . . .
but his manner, his coldness, his indifference. He did not even ask about your health, or
any other human thing, & made me feel that my call upon him, miserable petrefied cock-
ney that he is, was an unwelcome interruption" (Feinberg). Apparently Rossetti and Burroughs, in WW's words, "did not seem altogether to hit it" (Traubel, I, 437). When
Rossetti wrote to WW on January 1, 1885, his praise of *Leaves of Grass* and *Specimen
Days* was unstinted (Feinberg; Traubel, I, 436–437).

34. This is WW's only reference to his estrangement from O'Connor.

35. According to Bucke's letter to O'Connor on October 14, he was withholding
his book at the suggestion of WW. In fact, although he carefully refrained from saying so,
Bucke was not happy about WW's vague plans for the publication of his study by Rees
Welsh & Co. (LC).

1151. *To Anne Gilchrist* [*8.13. 1882*][36]

ADDRESS: Mrs Gilchrist | Keats' Corner 12 Well
Road | Hampstead | London England. POSTMARK:
Camden | (?) | 14 | 7 AM | N.J.

I am well as usual—have had a good summer—John Burroughs has returned safely—rec'd your welcome letter[37]—

W W

1152. *To John Burroughs* 8.27. [*1882*]

ADDRESS: John Burroughs | Esopus-on-Hudson | New
York. POSTMARK: Camden | (?) | 27 | 5 PM | N.J.

Camden N J Aug 27

All going on well with me—Your good letter rec'd—The type-setting of "Specimen Days" will be all finished the coming week & the book out ten days afterward[38]—same sized vol: same sort of type, binding, general appearance &c. with L of G—same price—As I write (Sunday afternoon) up in my 3d story room, heavy clouds, the rain falling in torrents—

W W

Does not what you saw of English society explain a good deal of Carlyle's *cussedness?*

1153. *To Anne Gilchrist* 8.27. [*1882*]

ADDRESS: Mrs Anne Gilchrist | Keats Corner 12 Well
Road | Hampstead | London | England.
POSTMARKS: Camden | Aug | 27 | 6 PM | N.J.;
Philadelphia | Aug | 27 | 1882 | Pa.

Camden N J Aug: 27

All going on well with me—the type-setting of my new prose book "Specimen Days" will be all finished the coming week & the book out in

36. This note was written at the bottom of a post card announcement of the Philadelphia printings of *Leaves of Grass* and *Specimen Days*. Since Burroughs had just returned from England (see the preceding letter), and since the postmark is clearly "14 | 7 AM," the card was undoubtedly written on August 13.
37. Probably a reference to Mrs. Gilchrist's letter of June 18 (Pennsylvania).
38. *Specimen Days* was not ready until October 1 (*CB*).
39. O'Connor, on August 28, was pleased that the third printing was out: "I think by September we shall have a boom in full drive. I will do my best to keep up the controversy" (Feinberg).

ten days afterward—same size, price, type, binding & general appearance as last L. of G. The Phila: publishers (L of G) are now paying out their third edition. As I write, (Sunday afternoon) up in my 3d story room, heavy clouds & rain falling in torrents. My brother & sister well—I saw Mrs. Stafford yesterday—all well there—love to H[erbert] and G[race]—

W W

1154. *To William D. O'Connor*   *8.27. [1882]*

ENDORSED: "Answ'd Aug 28/82." ADDRESS:
Wm Douglas O'Connor | Life Saving Service Bureau |
Washington D C. POSTMARKS: Camden | Aug | 27 |
6 PM | N.J.; Washington, D.C. | Aug | 28 | 4 AM |
1882 | Recd.

Camden   N J   Aug: 27

All going on well with me—the type-setting of "Specimen Days" will be all done next week & the book out in ten days afterwards—A Volume ab't same size, same sort of type, binding &c as L of G—same price—as I write, (Sunday afternoon) up in my 3d story room, heavy clouds, the rain falling in torrents—R[ees] W[elsh] & Co: are paying out their 3d edition[39]—no signs of any trouble yet—

W W

1155. *To William D. O'Connor*   *9.3. [1882]*

ENDORSED: "Answ'd Sept 20." ADDRESS: Wm D.
O'Connor | Life Saving Service Bureau | Washington
D C. POSTMARKS: Camden | Sep | 3 | 6 PM | N.J.;
Washington, D.C. | Sep | 4 | 4 AM | 1882 | Recd.

Camden   Sept 3—Evn'g

The T[ribune] & your Monday's letter came[40]—wonder if A[nthony] C[omstock] don't feel the Knout & the blood trickling—the *reader* almost does—*Specimen Days* is all in type & receiving the finishing touches —is to be on the market the 15th[41]—will send you the earliest copy I can

    40. On August 28 O'Connor informed WW that his reply to Comstock, "Mr. Comstock as Cato the Censor," had appeared in the New York *Tribune* on the preceding day. Only his opening sentence had been deleted: "Mr. Anthony Comstock's hostility to the nude—of which an illustrious instance was his famous prosecution of three unfortunate women, whom he had hired to dance before him for over an hour, without clothing, in a New York brothel, appears to extend to even the naked truth" (Feinberg; Barrus, 225). See also *WWR*, v (1959), 54–56.
    41. On September 26 WW wrote in *CB*: " 'Specimen Days' done," but it was not distributed until October 1.

get—two moist, hot, close, unhealthy days here—but as I write the breeze is beginning to spirt up, lively & cool—

W W

1156. *To Brander Matthews*[42]　　　　　*9.6. [1882]*

Camden　N J　Sept: 6

I cheerfully give permission to print "O Captain My Captain" in your book—

Walt Whitman

1157. *To the Editors, Springfield* Republican　　[*9.8. 1882*][43]

ADDRESS: Editors | Republican daily newspaper | Springfield | Mass.

for your paper of Sunday 10th if wanted | book will be out 15th

"Specimen Days"

Walt Whitman's new volume of autobiography and collected prose writings, just being brought out by Rees Welsh & Co., of Philadelphia, the present publishers of "Leaves of Grass," contains the following:

1158. *To Helen Price*　　　　　*9.12. [1882]*

Camden　N J | Sept: 12

My dear friend

I just write to tell you that I have heard of your dear father's death,[44] & that you have my true sympathy—Love to Arthur and Emily & all—It is

42. Matthews (1852–1929), professor of English literature at Columbia University from 1892 to 1924, included the poem in *Poems of American Patriotism* (1882), 268–269.

43. On September 8 WW sent notices of the publication of *Specimen Days* to the Springfield *Republican* as well as to the New York *Times*, the New York *Tribune*, the New York *World*, and the Philadelphia *Press* (CB). The *Republican* printed two columns of excerpts on September 10 (SD, 133–136, 282–283); for this information I am indebted to Miss Margaret Rose, reference librarian of the City Library Association in Springfield, Mass. The *World* printed a brief announcement on the same date. Apparently the *Times* and the *Tribune* did not give WW's book publicity.

44. According to the Certificate of Death, Edmund Price (1809–1882) died on September 9 of a chronic cardiac disease.

no time now to write at length, but I will write soon, dear friends—or perhaps make you a call personally—

Walt Whitman

1159. *To William D. O'Connor*   *9.17.* [*1882*]

ENDORSED: "Answ'd Sept 20." ADDRESS: Wm Douglas O'Connor | Life Saving Service Bureau | Treasury Department | Washington D C. POSTMARKS: Camden | Sep | 17 | 6 PM | N.J.; Washington, D.C. | Se(?) | 18 | 5 AM | 1882 | Recd.

Camden   Sept 17—Evn'g

All salubrious—Sheets go to the binder Tuesday—I will try to send a book so you will get it Saturday[45]—After you read it, forward the "Modern Thought"[46] (I send by same mail with this) to Dr Bucke. They are now on *their fourth* Phila: ed'n L of G—a furious article in N. Y. "American Queen"[47] of yesterday—

W W

1160. *To William D. O'Connor*   *9.22.* [*1882*]

ENDORSED (by O'Connor): "Ruskin, &c." ADDRESS: Wm D O'Connor | Life Saving Service Bureau | Treasury Dept: | Washington D C. POSTMARKS: [Camd]en | (?) | N.J.; Washington, Recd. | Sep | 22 | 6 AM | 1882 | 13.

Camden   Friday Evn'g | Sept: 22

Dear William O'Connor

This is the best I can do about *the Ruskin*[48]—you will have to pick out from the letters (especially what I have lined with the red ink)—I get *lots of letters*—these are samples more or less[49]—I am well—(I can't send your book till Monday)—

W. W.

45. The book was delayed until October 1.
46. Fitzgerald Molloy, of London, was the "author of the friendly article" in *Modern Thought*, IV (Sept. 1, 1882), 319–326. WW sent *Leaves of Grass* to Molloy on September 15 (*CB*).
47. I have not been able to find a copy of the New York *American Queen*.
48. WW did more; see 1162.
49. On September 20, O'Connor wanted to know "just what Ruskin said about L. of G., for I discover that it was to you, or some near friend of yours, that he wrote" (Feinberg; Traubel, IV, 21). WW forwarded to O'Connor three letters from William Harrison Riley, dated March 5, April 2, and April 4, 1879, and one from Herbert J. Bathgate, written on January 31, 1880. Riley and Bathgate were friends of Ruskin (see 909 and 946). O'Connor returned these letters to WW on August 17, 1883 (Feinberg). O'Connor's copies are in the Berg Collection.

1161. *To Susan Stafford*

Camden   Sunday   Sept: 24 '82

Dear friend

Your letter of over a week ago rec'd—& I should have answer'd before, but I expected to come down myself, or send word—but one thing or another delays the publication of my new book, & I am waiting for that—it is all printed and ready, & will be out early this coming week—I will bring you one when I come down—there is lots in about the pond & the old lane &c. and my times there five or six years ago—(but there are ever so many subjects in it)—

I went round yesterday in the rain to make a short visit to Mrs Rogers[50]—She is pretty well, considering—complains of being weak in the limbs & flush'd with the heat, but sat in the parlor & talked very cheerful & friendly, some time—said she hoped you would come up very soon—I ask'd if she didnt intend going down to your house soon—She said no, she expected to go on east (Mass:) to see her daughter—she said Amos was to be home that Saturday evening, to stay over Sunday—ask'd me to come around & get acquainted with him—So I had a very pleasant little visit—Every thing there look'd about the same, nice & comfortable—Jane came to the door—

We have had nothing but rain, rain, here, the last three or four days—seems to pour down all day long—it is well I didn't come down early in the week as I had intended but now as I write (Sunday, late forenoon) it is very pleasant sunshiny again—as I sit here the bells are ringing for church, off aways—sounds very good—every thing quite delightful after the long dark equinoctial storm—but I just wish I was down *there* this minute—a day there in the woods—

Where my books are now publish'd is 23 South 9th Street, Philadelphia[51] (not far from Leary's book store)—and they have fixed me up a big table and arm chair, by a window upstairs, all to myself—& there I go for an hour or two or three, every day if I like—the whole building is stuff'd with books, some old, some very costly, some very rare—all the histories, dictionaries, &c. you can think of, & every thing else—

50. See 1114.
51. On September 24 the Springfield *Republican* said: "It is to be regretted that Whitman had not the patience to wait for some firm of consequence to take up the task Osgood so feebly laid down," and then cited an objectionable adversitement of *Leaves of Grass*, undoubtedly the one referred to in *The Critic* of October 7: "We learn from Messrs. Rees Welsh & Co., of Philadelphia, that 'the party who inserted the advertisement' in which Mr. W's 'Leaves of Grass' was characterized as 'a daisy' 'has no longer charge of that department.' "
52. Mrs. Stafford's son-in-law, Joseph L. Browning.
53. WW went to Glendale on September 30, Saturday, and remained there until

Nothing very new with me—I still keep well—eat my rations every time—I havn't seen or heard any thing of Harry or any of you for a long time—except I saw Joe[52] at the ferry over a week ago—I want to come down Friday next, to Kirkwood, in the usual 4 o'clock train—shall be down Friday[53]—Love to you and George, Ruthy & all—

Walt Whitman

1162. *To William D. O'Connor*   [*10.7. 1882*][54]

ENDORSED: "WW | Answd | Aug 17/83." ADDRESS: Wm D O'Connor | Life Saving Service Bureau | Treasury | Washington | D C. POSTMARKS: Philadelphia | Oct | 7 | 1 PM | Pa.; Washington, Rec'd | Oct | 8 | 5 30 AM | 1882 | 2.

The *worry* of Ruskin—he has at various times sent to me for six sets of my ($10, two Vol.) centennial Edition[55]—& sent the money for them—with *Leaves of Grass* is that they are *too personal*, too emotional, launched from the fires of *myself*, my spinal passions, joys, yearnings, doubts, appetites &c &c.—which is really what the book is mainly for, (as a type however for those passions, joys, workings &c *in all the race*, at least as shown under modern & especially American auspices)—Then I think he winces at what seems to him the *Democratic* brag of L. of G.—I have heard from R several times through English visitor friends of his—It is quite certain that he has intended writing to me at length—& has doubtless made draughts of such writing—but defers & *fears*—& has not yet written—R like a true Englishman evidently believes in the high poetic art of (only) making abstract works, poems, of some fine plot or subject, stirring, beautiful, very noble, completed within their own centre & radius, & nothing to do with the poet's special personality, nor exhibiting the least trace of it—like Shakspere's great unsurpassable dramas. But I have dashed at *the greater drama going on within myself & every human being—that is what I have been after*[56]—

October 3 (*CB*). See the jottings in *NB*, 76–77.
   54. The date is confirmed not only by the postmark but also by O'Connor's letter on August 17, 1883 (Feinberg).
   55. See 909 and 946.
   56. O'Connor disagreed with WW's evaluation of Ruskin in a letter dated August 17, 1883: "I was very much touched with what Ruskin wrote, which seemed to me to be very strongly on your side. . . . It seems a great thing to say, as Ruskin does, that your book 'is deadly true—in the sense of rifles—against our deadliest social sins'—and also that its fruit is 'ungatherable save by loving and gleaning hands, *and by the blessed ones of the poor.*' I understand this as a high endorsement" (Feinberg).

P.S. William, (as you seem to be destin'd to defend the banner) I say here once for all you have my permission to make any extracts, at any time, should you so like from any of my letters—

W W

1163. *To Sylvester Baxter*

ADDRESS: Sylvester Baxter | Daily Herald | newspaper office | Boston Mass:. POSTMARK: Camden | (?) | 8 | 6 PM | N.J.

Camden   Oct: 8 '82

Dear Baxter—the book is out & 1st edition quite exhausted[57]—

I send you same mail with this a paper-bound copy of "Specimen Days" for your printing office use—will send you a regularly bound copy in a day or two—the volume is issued in precisely the same style as "Leaves of Grass"—same cloth binding, same butterfly on the back, same size, &c.— It is a great jumble (as a man himself is)—Is an autobiography after its sort—(sort o' synonyms & yet altogether different—"Montaigne," Rousseau's "Confessions" &c)—is the gathering up, & formulation, & putting in identity of the wayward itemizings, memoranda, and personal notes of fifty years, under modern & American conditions, a good deal helter-skelter but I am sure a certain sort of orbic compaction and oneness the final result— dwells long in its own peculiar way on the Secession War—gives glimpses of that event's strange interiors, especially the Army Hospitals—in fact makes the resuscitating and putting on record the *emotional aspect* of the war of 1861–'65 one of its principal features.

The years from 1876 to the present date Whitman has been a partial paralytic. Very much of his days—(and nights also as it appears)—he has spent in the open air down in the country in the woods and fields, and by a secluded little New Jersey river—His memoranda on the spot of these days and nights fill a goodly portion of the Volume—Then comes the "Collect," embodying "Democratic Vistas," the Preface to L of G. of 1855, and much other prose.

---

57. On November 12 WW informed O'Connor that of 1500 copies of *Specimen Days* 400 remained unsold (see 1173). Perhaps he referred to a second printing; more probably WW overstated the success of the volume so that Baxter would have good copy for his review in the Boston *Herald*.

58. This notation refers to the preceding paragraph, which Baxter included verbatim in the second last paragraph of his "review" of *Specimen Days* in the Boston *Herald* on October 15. Baxter quoted from the first paragraph of WW's letter but then incorpo-

It is understood that Whitman himself considers "Specimen Days" the exponent and finish of his poetic work "Leaves of Grass," that each of the two volumes is indispensable in his view to the other, and that both together finally begin and illustrate his literary schemes in the New World. Talking lately in a half jocular vein to a friend he termed them his Adam and Eve, sent out in "this garden the world."

(don't fail to copy this—can't it conclude your notice?)[58]

Four Phila: editions of "Leaves of Grass" have been issued & sold within the last three months—they are now on the fifth—The first edition of "Specimen Days" has been exhausted in less than a week. They are now on the *second*—

Dear B, if you notice—send me a paper—don't fail—Send also one each to

Wm D O'Connor, Life Saving Services Washington D C

Dr. R M Bucke, London, Ontario, Canada

Dear B[59] I have dash'd off all this to help you—to use (incorporate) or not as you think fit—you will understand—

Of course use whatever of this you want—incorporate it I mean in your article.[60]

1164. *To Anne Gilchrist*

ADDRESS: Mrs: Anne Gilchrist | Keats' Corner 12 Well Road | Hampstead | London England. POSTMARKS: Camden | Oct | 8 | 6 PM | N.J.; Philadelphia | Oct | 8 | 1882 | Pa.

Camden—Sunday afternoon | Oct: 8 '82

Never have we had a week of more perfect, sunny, fresh, yet mellow and rich, autumn weather—to-day is the eighth day of it—("In this resplendent summer" began Emerson 25 years ago in an autumn lecture, "it has been a luxury *merely to live*")[61]—I suppose you have rec'd the "Specimen Days" I sent a while since[62]—I am well as usual—reeling out my weeks

rated the rest of the poet's letter without indicating the source.

59. This note appears in the upper corner of the first page of the letter.
60. This direction is in the margin opposite the first paragraph.
61. See the first sentence of *The Divinity School Address* (1838): "In this refulgent summer, it has been a luxury to draw the breath of life."
62. WW sent two copies to Mrs. Gilchrist on October 5 (*CB*). Herbert referred to the book on October (?) 20 (Feinberg), and Mrs. Gilchrist described her reactions to the work on November 24 (LC; Harned, 209–210).

& months about the same as ever—often think of you all—the books are selling quite well[63]—

W. W.

1165. *To Rudolf Schmidt*

ADDRESS: Rudolf Schmidt | Baggesen's Gate 3 | Copenhagen | Denmark. POSTMARKS: Camden | Oct | 8 | 6 PM | N.J.; K | Omb 1 | 3 10 82.

Camden, New Jersey—U S America | Oct: 8 '82
Your handsome *"Buster og Masker"*[64] has safely reach'd me—best thanks—I will soon send you a copy of my prose *"Specimen Days"*[65]—Dr Bucke's book is not printed yet—My volumes are now published in Philadelphia & are selling fairly—I rec'd. & acknowledg'd g'd Thorsteinsson's poems[66]—I am well as usual—

Walt Whitman

1166. *To Rudolf Schmidt*

Camden   New Jersey   U S America |
Oct: 13 '82   Evn'g
I send you by same mail with this my new prose vol: *"Specimen Days"*[67]—I wrote you some days since that I had rec'd your elegant little volume—Dr Bucke has also rec'd his[68]—I am well as usual—

Walt Whitman

63. Because the records of David McKay, successor to Rees Welsh & Co. as WW's publisher, are now in the University of Pennsylvania Library, exact figures on sales are available until the poet's death. As of December 1, 1882, 4,900 copies of *Leaves of Grass* had been printed, of which 3,118 were sold. WW's royalty was $1,091.30. Only 1,000 copies of *Specimen Days* were printed and 925 copies sold; the return to WW was $203.50—a total of $1,294.80. Because WW owed McKay money, the actual return was $1,230.78 (*CB*).
64. *Buster og Masker* contains a revised version of Schmidt's essay on WW originally published in 1872. Schmidt's book, inscribed, is now in the Feinberg Collection.
65. See the next post card.
66. See 1082.
67. Schmidt noted receipt of the book on November 3 and his desire to translate "The Death of Abraham Lincoln" (Feinberg).
68. Bucke mentioned receiving Schmidt's book in a letter to WW on October 11. In this letter he summed up his reactions to *Specimen Days* in a passage which WW marked with red ink: "As to S. D. it is a suitable finish up to your work, it is what we

Do I address my letters right?

1167. *To William D. O'Connor* 10.25. *[1882]*

ENDORSED: "Answd Oct | 26 & 27." ADDRESS:
Wm D O'Connor | Life Saving Service Bureau |
Treasury | Washington D C. POSTMARKS: Camden |
Oct | 25 | 5 PM | N.J.; Washington, Recd | Oct |
26 | 5 AM | 1882 | 2.

Camden   Oct: 25 Evn'g:
Quite sick the last ten or twelve days[69]—havn't been out of the house
—great bodily weakness & "misery" in head & stomach—the doctor says
from almost entire stoppage of the action of the liver, other causes—
malarial &c—I dont hear any thing particular. Do you? Did they send you
the Boston *Herald's* two criticisms on S. D.—very warm, eulogistic
(largely extracts)—I shall be all right in a week or less—
W W

1168. *To John H. Johnston* 10.26. *[1882]*

ADDRESS: J H Johnston | Jeweler | 150 Bowery |
New York City. POSTMARKS: Camden | Oct | 26 | 8
PM | N.J.; P Ö | 10–2(?)–82 | 6 I A | N.Y.

Camden   Oct: 26.   Evn'g
I have been quite sick for ten days—& am yet—but nothing serious
—Shall be about as usual in a week at farthest[70]—
Walt Whitman

(those who know something of you) have been wanting for a long time and what the future will want still more and will prize far more even than we can prize it now—it is all on
a low key (as it ought to be) no fine writing but plain prose giving just the insight that we
wanted into your common every day life, and your ordinary every day manner of looking
at things—I think you may now say that your work is done, I do not see any more for you
to do at all events though perhaps you will see something, when you have had time to
look about again abit" (Feinberg).
    69. WW suffered from a liver disorder from October 17 to 28 (*CB*). Dr. Dowling
Benjamin, his physician, began to practice medicine in Camden in 1877; see George R.
Prowell, *The History of Camden County, New Jersey* (1886). A newspaper report
alarmed the poet's friends: "Walt Whitman is so seriously ill of Bright's disease that few
if any hopes for his recovery are entertained." See Traubel, IV, 322–323, and Jeff's letter
to his brother on October 29 (Feinberg).
    70. Johnston called on WW in Camden on October 10 accompanied by an Aus-
tralian friend, John W. Tilton. On the following day the poet sent to Johnston a copy of
Leaves of Grass for Tilton and a copy of *Specimen Days* for Mrs. Johnston (*CB*).

1169. *To William D. O'Connor*

ADDRESS: Wm D O'Connor | Life Saving Service
Bureau | Treasury | Washington | D C. POSTMARKS:
Camden | Oct | 29 | 6 PM | N.J.; Washington,
Recd. | Oct | 30 | 4 30 AM | 1882 | 2.

Camden | Sunday Evn'g—Oct: 29 '82

Thanks for kind letter & the bit poem—like a real star-twinkle.[71] I continue sick but move slowly toward recuperation. The liver begins to act. It has not been an *engorgement* or any thing like it. The basic situation I take to be this—that just now the liver is the seat of, & concentrates, that *markedly defective enervation* which my paralysis of '73 to '7 &c. has left me for life. The doctor comes every day—(old school, but receptive & progressive—believes more in drugs & medicines than I do, but so far his diagnosis seems thorough, & his doses are justified by results)—About that Heywood, Boston, arrest, mustn't there be some mistake?[72] The Chainey affair certainly settled the U. S. mail part—but the Mass: statutes on printed "indecency" are sweepingly stringent I believe. Do you know that Rand & Avery refused to *print* an edition of L of G. for me, after the Osgood row?—afraid of indictment—Where is Charley Eldridge's address?

Walt Whitman

1170. *To Anne Gilchrist*   *10.30. [1882]*

ADDRESS: Mrs Ann Gilchrist | Keats' Corner 12 Well
Road | Hampstead | London England. POSTMARKS:
Camden | Oct | 30 | 5 PM | N.J.; Phila. Paid All |
Oct | 30 | 1882 | Pa.

Camden   Oct: 30   Evn'g

Have been quite ill the last two weeks[73]—jaundice & mark'd bodily prostration & lassitude—But I am better, & have just been out a few steps —the doctor comes every day, (old school) & has certainly done me good. I suppose you rec'd "Specimen Days" I sent (two copies)—

W W

71. O'Connor included in his letter of October 27 an extract from a newspaper entitled "L'Estranger," a poem not too unlike WW's own statements about adhesiveness (Yale; Traubel, IV, 323).
72. Ezra H. Heywood (1829–1893), a radical reformer and an advocate of free love, was arrested on October 26, because he printed "To a Common Prostitute" and "A Woman Waits for Me" in *The Word* and attempted to mail the journals. On October 27 O'Connor noted a newspaper report of Heywood's arrest: "I don't like Heywood's ways, and I don't like the Free-Love theories at all, but he has his rights, which these devils trample on" (Yale; Traubel, IV, 323). See 1173.

1171. *To William D. O'Connor*   *10.31.* [*1882*]

ADDRESS: Wm D O'Connor | Life Saving Service
Bureau | Treasury | Washington D C. POSTMARKS:
Philadelphia | Nov | 1 | 1 AM | Pa.; Washington,
Recd. | Nov | 1 | 9 AM | 1882 | 1.

Camden   Tuesday Evn'g | Oct: 31
I am decidedly better—feel well as I write this—was out three hours
to-day, crossing the river, for the first time in over two weeks—& taking a
ride.

W W

1172. *To Edward Dowden*

TRANSCRIPT.

431 Stevens Street | Camden | Nov 10 '82
Your valued letter rec'd, it *is* like a kindly living talk and hand
clasp[74]—I shall forward it to Burroughs—So good to hear you & yours
active, full of receptivity and well—I have lately had a bad spell, prostration &c again, but am now well as usual. Dont forget the *Academy*[75] if it
appears—

Walt Whitman.

1173. *To William D. O'Connor*

ADDRESS: Wm D O'Connor | Life Saving Service
Bureau | Treasury | Washington | D C. POSTMARKS:
Camden | (?) | 12 | 6 PM | N.J.; Washington,
Recd. | Nov | 13 | 4 30 AM | 1882 | 2.

431 Stevens Street Camden New Jersey |
Nov: 12 '82—Sunday a. m.
It is the *same publishing*, only under a different name. The man
who runs Rees Welsh's business, (the chief mate of the ship) and who first
proposed & put through the bargain last June with me—*David McKay*—has

73. WW wrote on the same day in *CB:* "Am slowly getting better." On November 6 he observed: "to-day, well as usual, before sickness." The Camden *Daily Post* on
November 1 noted the poet's "reappearance on the street"; and "Walt Whitman's Illness"
appeared in the *Progress* on November 9 (*CB*).
74. Dowden's letter was sent to O'Connor and others and is apparently lost. On
November 21 Dowden acknowledged WW's card and urged the poet to "try a voyage
across the Atlantic" (Feinberg; Traubel, II, 363).
75. Dowden's review of *Specimen Days* appeared in *The Academy* on November 18.
See also Barrus, 233.

formally bo't out & assumed R W's miscellaneous & publishing & second-hand books business—& is now & henceforth the publisher of L of G and S D—drops into Rees Welsh's shoes—It is just as well—& is indeed to me *no* change—for really my doings have been with McK all along from the beginning[76]—S. D. sales *rather* sluggish—(1500 were printed, towards 400 remain on the shelves in 23 Ninth St.)[77]—

I have rec'd a long letter from Ezra H Heywood—dated Princeton, Mass:[78]—Heywood has been arrested by Comstock—part at least of the *cause* appears to be sending printed slips by mail with "to a common prostitute" and "a woman waits for me"—supplements to Heywood's paper "the Word"—(I believe I will just enclose H's letter—slips & all)—My impression is that *Comstock's chief object is to get, (by snap judgment probably) a judicial decision on which he can base a show to go before the P. M. General,* (as per the late decision of P.M.G. in such questions)—the hearing is to come off before U.S. Commissioner Hallett in Boston, Nov 16 —(As to the vehement action of the Free religious & lover folk, in their conventions, papers &c in my favor—and even proceedings like these of Heywood—I see nothing better for myself or friends to do than quietly stand aside & let it go on)—what do you think?

As I write, it is a cloudy moist warmish Sunday, 10¼ a. m. pleasant—quiet here—I am up in my 3d story, south-front room, writing this—

There is a long & supercilious notice of S. D. in N. Y. World, Oct 30, I wonder if written by Hurlbert[79] himself?—an emanation of that New York nest of little malignants, (Stoddard, little Winter, and half a dozen

76. See 1164.

77. WW constantly gave out erroneous figures. Only 1,000 copies of *Specimen Days* were printed in 1882 (see 1164). On December 1, 925 copies had been sold. Yet *The Critic* reported on October 21 that the book had been sold out before publication.

78. Heywood's letter was published as "An Open Letter to Walt Whitman" in a broadside distributed by *The Word* (copy in Feinberg). Heywood informed WW that Benjamin R. Tucker, editor of the Boston *Globe*, was openly advertising *Leaves of Grass* in defiance of the post office. On the last page of Heywood's letter, which was sent to O'Connor, WW wrote: "I don't want this back again—Have you any thing to Suggest?—the more I think of it, the more I am convinced that is Comstock's game, (*see my letter*)" (Berg).

With this letter WW enclosed *The Truth Seeker* of November 4, "Whispers of Heavenly Death," and "Talks with Trelawney," dated August 4, who was quoted as finding in *Leaves of Grass* "the material of poetry, but not poetry itself" (Berg). Mounted in the lower corner of WW's letter is a newspaper advertisement of Miss Leslie Hinton's appearance in *Little Sunshine*.

79. William Henry Hurlbert (1827–1895) was editor of the New York *World* from 1876 to 1883. The review of *Specimen Days* in the newspaper began: "So painfully impressed is Mr. Whitman with the idea that every deed and experience of a man's life, nay, every sight and sound and touch and taste and smell, should be recorded that it is strange he has not sooner written his autobiography." Yet the *World* had printed on June 4, during the Boston fracas, some highly sympathetic reminiscences of WW by Thomas A. Gere, reprinted in Bucke, 32–34.

80. For WW's contributions to Baxter's review, see 1163.

81. O'Connor also planned to include *The Good Gray Poet;* see Bucke's letter to

more)—The Boston Herald some weeks since (Oct: 15) had a lengthy and very warm notice, very judicious extracts (Sylvanus Baxter, author)[80]—the best I have seen from the book's own standpoint (which of course is every thing)—Are you then going to make a brochure of the Tribune letters?[81] *Good*, if so—Shall I furnish you with more detailed and verbatim data of the Osgood transaction & correspondence—or have you them sufficiently?

Where is Ashton?[82] Is he there in W. & do you see him? If so tell him I have not forgotten him—& that I send him & Mrs. A. my love—In a late note I ask'd you, if eligible, to send me Charley Eldridge's address[83]—☞ Do you know what *ducks & drakes* are? Well, S. D. is a rapid skimming over the pond-surface of my life, thoughts, experiences, that way—the real area altogether untouch'd, but the flat pebble making a few dips as it flies & flits along—enough at least to give some living touches and contact-points—I was quite willing to make an immensely *negative* book.

I am holding my own in the recovery of my *half state* of health—am contemplating some change of base, (residence, domicile—sometimes I have thought of coming to Washington, settling there, getting a lot & small house in fee simple)[84]—Have you sent Dowden's letter to Dr Bucke? I got a letter from Dr Channing[85] asking me to lecture in the Tilton sisters'[86] course this winter in Boston—but I cannot lecture at present—besides I shall certainly not do any thing to identify myself specially with free love[87]—

W W

O'Connor, dated August 4 (LC). According to Bucke's letter to O'Connor on October 14, the latter decided not to reprint his pamphlet (LC). On March 21, 1883, O'Connor explained to Burroughs that the project had been delayed because of "my cares and griefs" (Doheny).

O'Connor's third letter to the New York *Tribune* on the Boston censorhip was refused by Reid; if possible, it was more choleric and longwinded than his published communications (see Barrus, 226–231). Apparently O'Connor forgave the editor of the *Tribune*, for, in replying to O'Connor on October 14, Bucke wrote: "I think as you do that Reid did well by you and that we should be satisfied" (LC).

82. J. Hubley Ashton was Assistant Attorney General when WW was employed in that office.

83. On December 18 O'Connor gave Eldridge's address as the Internal Revenue Service Office in Boston (Feinberg).

84. On November 9 WW sold his lot at 460 Royden Street for $525 (CB).

85. O'Connor's brother-in-law, Dr. William F. Channing (see 143). According to O'Connor's letter to WW on June 3, Channing had offered to reprint at his own expense *The Good Gray Poet* (Feinberg; Traubel, I, 54).

86. According to Heywood's letter to WW on November 5, Josephine S. Tilton, "the persistent Socialist, once imprisoned for her Faith," was selling copies of *Leaves of Grass* on the streets of Boston (Berg).

87. On May 28 and 29, the Free Love League adopted the following resolution: "That effort to suppress Walt Whitman's poems for their alleged obscenity, because officious exponents of 'law and order' lack wit to understand them, shows the continued lascivious stupidity voiced by pulpits and courts, the religio-political lewdness still mistaken for culture and purity . . ." (Boston Public Library; Asselineau, 252*n*.).

Write often as you can—the days are quite stagnant with me—(a spell at any rate)—

1174. *To Karl Knortz*   *11.14.1882*

ADDRESS: Karl Knortz | cor: Morris Av. & 155th
Street | New York City. POSTMARKS: Camden | Nov |
14 | 2 PM | N.J.; P. O. | 11–14–82 | 7–1P | N.Y.

Dear Sir

The return'd papers, slips, &c rec'd—I didn't want them again, as I have duplicates—☞ I only want R. Schmidt's book, Burroughs's *Notes*, *Scribner's Magazine*,[88] the *Good Grey Poet*, Leaves *Imprints*,[89] and the Scandinavian and Hungarian papers returned—(but am in no hurry about it.) John Burroughs lives about 50 miles up the Hudson, his address is Esopus-on-Hudson.

Walt Whitman

Noon   Nov 14 '82—
Did you get "Specimen Days"? If not yet, please write me, & I will gladly send you a copy—at once—

1175. *To Franklin B. Sanborn*

ADDRESS: F B Sanborn | Concord | Mass:. POSTMARK:
Camden | Nov | 14 | 5 PM | N.J.

431 Stevens Street | Camden New Jersey |
Nov: 14 '82

Dear friend S—
I have rec'd from Boston the *"Life of Thoreau"*[90]—(& suppose I am indebted to you for it—real thanks)—The telling of Life after all refuses to be put in a polish'd, formal, consecutive statement—better, living glints, samples, autographic letters above all, memoranda of friends &c—You have pursued this plan & the result justifies—Froude's late *"Carlyle"*, a precious book, pursues it too—& succeeds—

Walt Whitman

88. Undoubtedly Stedman's article on WW in November, 1880.
89. *Leaves of Grass Imprints* (1860).
90. Sanborn's *Henry D. Thoreau* appeared in the "American Men of Letters" series in 1882.
91. WW's letter to Lee (see 1084).

1176. *To Karl Knortz*

ADDRESS: Karl Knortz | cor: Morris Av: & 155th St: | New York City. POSTMARKS: Camden | Nov | 15 | 12 M | N.J.; P.O. | 11–15–82 | 5 P | N.Y.

431 Stevens Street | Camden New Jersey
Nov: 15 '82

The return'd Scribner, R Schmidt's book, the Danish papers &c. received. I think neither John Burroughs's *Notes* or O'Connor's pamphlet is now for sale. I send you (same mail with this) *Specimen Days* which please *keep* as a little present from me. (See pp. 316, '17 *Specimen Days*.)[91] Dr R M Bucke, of London, Ontario, Canada, is preparing a book about me, in which he is going to reprint O'Connor's pamphlet[92]—

Walt Whitman

1177. *To William Sloane Kennedy*

431 Stevens Street | Camden New Jersey
Nov: 28 '82

I have just returned from a two week's visit down in the Jersey woods where I go occasionally[93]—& find your most interesting "Whittier"[94] —Thank you heartily—I am again about as usual in health—

Walt Whitman

1178. *To an Unidentified Correspondent*[95]

431 Stevens Street | Camden New Jersey |
Nov: 28 '82

Dear Sir

I have just come up from a three weeks' visit[96] down in the Jersey woods, & find your card of 26th—The only copies of my complete poems "Leaves of Grass," in my control, are of a special autograph & portrait edition, 1882, including everything to date—384 pages, 12 mo—price $3 —I can furnish you with this. If you wish it, send p. o. order, & I will forward by mail immediately.

Walt Whitman

92. *The Good Gray Poet* was reprinted in Bucke's *Walt Whitman,* 99–132.
93. WW was with the Staffords at Glendale from November 18 to 27 (*CB*).
94. Kennedy's *John Greenleaf Whittier* (1882).
95. Perhaps this letter was sent to L. O. Bliss of Iowa Falls, Iowa, to whom WW sent a "gilt-top L of G" on December 18 (*CB*).
96. WW was inaccurate, perhaps deliberately (see note 93 above).

I also supply, when desired, my *prose* volume "Specimen Days & Collect"—price $2.—374 pages 12 mo—

1179. *To Jeannette L. Gilder*   *12.7.* [*1882*]

Camden   Dec 7⁹⁷

Dear Miss Gilder
      Yours rec'd—and I send you some thoughts of mine on Burns—(a much belabored subject—but I wanted to have my say)—Will make two & a half pages—I sh'd like $20 for it⁹⁸—
      If you take it to print in next send me proof by Monday or Tuesday of next week & I will return same evening—

Walt Whitman

1180. *To T. W. H. Rolleston*   [*12.10*(?).*1882*(?)]⁹⁹

ADDRESS: T W H Rolleston | Lange Strasse 29 | Dresden | Saxony. POSTMARK: Camden, N.J. | Dec | 1(?) | (?).

—There are no later or fuller prints of my books than those you have—I contemplate a final compacted handy-sized Vol: comprehending all & in an order of progression that will suit me better—but it may be some time yet . . .¹

1181. *To William D. O'Connor*   *12.14.* [*1882*]

ENDORSED: "Answ'd Dec. 15/82." ADDRESS: Wm D O'Connor | Life Saving Service Bureau | Treasury | Washington D C. POSTMARKS: Philadelphia | Dec | 14 | 2 PM | (?); Washington, Recd. | (?) | 5 AM | 1882 | 2.

Camden   Dec 14
      I fear you have been derelict in forwarding Dowden's *letter* I sent you two or three weeks since, as I requested—If so, *please send it now, to*

---

      97. Possibly an envelope in the Berg Collection belongs with this letter: ADDRESS: J L & J B Gilder | Critic | office | 30 Lafayette Place | New York City. POSTMARKS: Camden | Dec(?) | 7 | 5 PM | (?); P. O. | (?) 8(?)–82 | (?) | (?).
      98. "Robert Burns" appeared in *The Critic* on December 16. WW received $15 for the article (CB). With additions he republished it as "Robert Burns as Poet and Person" in *The North American Review*, CXLIII (1886), 427–435, and in NB (1888), 57–64.
      99. According to CB, on December 10, 1882, WW sent Rolleston "full set loose leaves L of G. with postal card." Rolleston noted receipt of the card and "printed sheets" on December 26 (LC; Frenz, 77). Rolleston lived at this address in 1882, but resided at

John Burroughs—(Send the printed *Academy* criticism to Dr Bucke.)²
I am well as usual—Just starting for Phila—fine, sunny, crispy forenoon—

W W

1182. *To Josiah Child*

ADDRESS: Josiah Child | at Trübner & Co's: | 57 & 59
Ludgate Hill | London England. POSTMARKS:
Camden | (?) | 17 | 8 PM | N.J.; E 7 | London (?) |
Ja (?) | 83.

                        Camden New Jersey   U S America   Dec: 17 '82
Real thanks for your thought & deed in sending me "Nineteenth
Century" criticism—you have probably seen my new prose jumble, "Specimen Days" but I forward you, (same mail with this) a special *family copy*
different from the general edition—The other copy accompanying it, would
you do me the favor to see if you can find G C Macaulay, the writer of
criticism in the N C—& send to him?³ I am now well again as usual—

Walt Whitman

1183. *To William D. O'Connor*

ADDRESS: Wm D O'Connor | Life Saving Service— |
Treasury | Washington | D C. POSTMARKS: Camden |
(?) | 17 | 8 PM | N.J.; Washington, Recd. | Dec |
18 | 4 30 AM | 1882 | 2.

Camden   Dec: 17 '82

Dear friend
    Yours of 15th rec'd⁴—J[ohn] B[urroughs] had written to me for
the letter—he heard of it from Dowden himself)—Yes I too think D's
words "sweet and beautiful"—I read yesterday the Dec. "Nineteenth Century" article (Josiah Child, of Trübner's, mailed me in sheets)—& like it

28 Terrassen Ufer in 1883 (Frenz, 71–72*n*.). For Rolleston's letters in 1882 to WW,
see Frenz, 56–70.
    1. The signature was apparently cut off and pasted on page 29 of Rolleston's
copy of *Leaves of Grass* (see Frenz, 72*n*.).
    2. Dowden's review of *Specimen Days* (see 1172).
    3. Macaulay's review of *Leaves of Grass* appeared in *The Nineteenth Century*,
XII (December, 1882), 903–918. Despite some reservations, Macaulay's was a fair and
judicious essay; he particularly admired "Out of the Cradle Endlessly Rocking" and
"When Lilacs Last in the Dooryard Bloom'd."
    4. I have not found O'Connor's letter. There is a letter from O'Connor to Dr.
Bucke on December 15 in the Feinberg Collection.

much—*You* may not, on acct of the author's *John Bull reservations*, but I think it decidedly the best English (or any foreign) criticism yet printed. I will send you a copy (of the cheap N Y reprint) in two or three days—it was not ready last night—

William, as you are going to collect the "Tribune" letters, &c.⁵ I suggest that *you ask Dr Bucke to give up the* "Good Gray," & you *include it*—make a cluster of *all* you have written (Have you the "Times" article you furnish'd Raymond Dec: 1866?⁶ I have a copy, & can send you)—I think it would be just as well for you to so include, as Dr B has enough otherways—I hope you will like the idea—shall I ask Dr. B to give it up? there is something to me quite preferable in these *collectanea* at first hand for a life, affair, even history, out of which the modern intelligent reader, (a new race unknown before our time) can take and adapt & shape for him or herself—I send you the "Critic" with my piece on Burns⁷—

Cold, cold—but very bright & sunny here to-day—I am well as usual—Wonder how the Heywood trial will eventuate—Somehow I feel clear that *however* it goes, we will "pluck the flower" &c &c from that *however*—So you must not feel anxious a bit—T W H Rolleston at Dresden, Saxony (with one or two German scholars) is translating L of G. into *full German version*⁸—expecting it to be ready next spring—He is an Irish gentleman, a college man, about 30 I think, married, & I suppose of some fortune—What I know of him (by quite considerable correspondence) I like much.

Merry Christmas—

W W

1184. *To Jeannette L. and Joseph B. Gilder*

Camden   Dec: 21 '82

My dear friends

Yes I will give you the autograph name & perhaps a sentiment⁹—but would like first to see the picture they would go under—Most of the

---

5. See 1173.
6. See 205 and Addenda in final volume of *Correspondence*.
7. See 1179. O'Connor acknowledged receipt of *The Critic* on December 19 (Feinberg).
8. See Frenz, 56–60, 69–70.
9. On January 13, 1883, *The Critic* printed WW's picture with four lines from *Leaves of Grass* in WW's hand. The issue also contained a review of *Specimen Days* (2–3).
10. A three-volume edition of Molière, translated by Henri Van Laun, is now in the Feinberg Collection. Interestingly, it was published in 1880 by Worthington.
11. From December 23 to 25 WW spent a "pleasant time at R. Pearsall Smith's

pictures that have been put out of me, quite warrant the alarming estimation so many folks entertain—(If it is the drawing F Fowler took two years
ago in Huntington L[ong] I[sland], *I dont like it at all.*) I send you some
samples—& should be entirely satisfied with a good bold simple rendering
of either of the three—If you do it at all why not try to do it *well.*

Walt Whitman

1185. *To William D. O'Connor*

ADDRESS: Wm D O'Connor | Life Saving Service—
Treasury | Washington | D C. POSTMARK:
Philadelphia | Dec | 27 | 7 PM | Pa.

Camden New Jersey | Dec: 27 '82

Thanks for the *Molière*—the Vols:—(vivacious & jaunty—& entirely new to me & not too deep)—will surely lighten many hours in a way
most opportune & desirable[10]—

I am well as usual—have been out in Germantown on a few days' visit
—have taken long rides & explorations along the Wissahickon, Indian
Rock, & all about that region[11]—*Happy New Year*—

Walt Whitman

and his wife Mrs Hannah W Smith (& dear daughter Mary) at 4653 Germantown avenue . . . . the fine, long, spirited drives along the Wissahickon, the rocks and banks, the
hemlocks, Indian Rock—Miss Willard, Miss Kate Sanborn, Lloyd Smith (R P's brother)
the librarian" (CB). WW was again with the Smiths from December 30 to January 2
(CB).

Mary Smith, a student at Smith College, forced her somewhat reluctant family to
visit the poet. Her father became very fond of WW, who, however, never "hitched" with
his wife, a famous Quaker leader (1832–1911). Mrs. Smith was not impressed with the
poet's Hicksite leanings or his verse. WW was very fond of the other two Smith children,
Alys and Logan Pearsall (1865–1946). Lloyd Smith (1822–1886) was a publisher
and a librarian. See Logan Pearsall Smith, *Unforgotten Years* (1939), 92–108, and
A Religious Rebel: The Letters of "H. W. S." (*Mrs. Pearsall Smith*) (1949), xvii–xviii.

1883

1186. *To Edward Sprague Marsh*[1]

431 Stevens Street | Camden   New Jersey |
Jan 11 '83

Dear Sir

Yours of 2d just rec'd. The Centennial or 1876 edition of "Leaves of Grass" and "Two Rivulets" (the ed'n preceding the last) is in two vols, price $6 the two—I have some copies & can furnish you with a set—Should you wish them send me p o order & I will forward them by mail—

Walt Whitman

1187. *To Jeannette L. and Joseph B. Gilder*

431 Stevens street | Camden | N J | Jan: 25 '83

My dear friends

Would "the Bible as Poetry" suit you for paper of Feb: 3d or 10th?[2] The price is $15—I would like 50 copies of the W W head with motto &c about same size as your issue, printed on heavier paper, with the "Critic" imprint left off—will pay (for paper & print) 4 cents a copy—$2.00—If put in type send proof of "Bible" here early in week—

Walt Whitman

1188. *To Harry Stafford*

Camden   Jan: 30 | '83

Dear Harry

Your letter came all right, & glad to hear from you, as always. There is nothing very new with me—I keep on about the same in most every

1883

1. Marsh (1857– ?) was a lawyer in Brandon, Vermont, the editor in 1894 of the Brandon *Chronicle*, and a book collector. See *The Encyclopedia of Vermont Biography* (c. 1912). For this information I am indebted to Mrs. William F. Schneider, librarian of the Brandon Free Public Library.

2. "The Bible as Poetry" appeared in *The Critic* on February 3. On February 8 WW sent copies to Mrs. Gilchrist, Dowden, Rolleston, Schmidt, and G. C. Macau-

respect—To-day, (Tuesday) as I write it is warm & bright, & I am going out to enjoy it—pretty much the same old round—over the ferry & up Market street, Phila, & stop occasionally at 23 south 9th st. where my books are pub'd. Now that my two books, prose and the poems, are out, I hardly know what to strike for—what to look forward to, as I used to—The Vols. are selling middling well—"Specimen Days" has been republished in Scotland[3] & L. of G. is being translated in Germany[4]—

Tuesday night 10½—I am finishing my letter, as I have been out & only got back late—This will be a dry letter—but you must take the will for the deed—I send you a package of papers &c. once in a while, which I suppose you get—I came over to-night through the thick ice, filling the river—one big cake, half an acre, or more, hard & thick, I thought would conquer us, but it didnt, we *crunch'd* our way thro'—but it was a high old *crunch* & fight for ten minutes—& I enjoy'd it I tell you—

I have just been looking for your last letter to see if there is any special thing I ought to answer—but I cant find the letter—Never mind, Harry, dear—we'll make it all right when we meet—I have just written to your mother—Well my space is out, & there goes the clock striking 11—Good night, dear son—& here's a buss for you—

W W

1189. *To Susan Stafford*

Camden   Jan: 30 '83 | Evening—

Dear friend

Your letter came & I ought to have written to you before, but one thing & another prevented. I was up to Germantown, to a friend's, where I have been a good deal lately—Spent the Christmas & New Year holidays there[5]—they came for me, so I went & was glad—a big house full of people, old & young folks, & plenty of fun & every thing good—lots of oysters—& cook'd so nice—I never knew how much there is in the cooking—Otherways I have been here in C. all the time, have done a little work writing, but nothing much—My brother from St Louis has been on here with us for a while—& I have callers & visitors quite often—

How are you all? I hope this will find you all well—little George[6] is all

lay (*CB*).

3. Wilson & McCormick, of Glasgow, Scotland, published *Specimen Days* (see 1198).
4. Rolleston's projected German translation.
5. WW was with the Smiths from December 30 to January 2 (*CB*). See also 1185.
6. Mrs. Stafford's son.

right again I trust by this time—I met two jolly & good-looking Jersey boys this afternoon over in Market Street, Phila.—it was Elmer and Ed Stafford⁷—we had a little talk—did me good to meet them—I dont think Jersey has two nicer looking boys—I was on my way to West Philadelphia to see about a Mr Anders, an elderly man sick with consumption. *Young* Mr Anders and I had got acquainted in Canada two years ago, & quite attached to each other—he was a soldier there—I got a letter from him from Montreal day before yesterday, asking me to go to a certain number in West Phila: & see his father, who had come on here some time ago quite sick—Young A. wanted me to see & write to him how the father was particular—So I went up to-day—when I got there I found the elder A was *dead & buried*—so I have just had to write the sad intelligence to my Canada friend⁸—love to you & all—I have written a few lines to Harry—

W W

Ruth, I got your letter—it was very acceptable—I will answer it before long—I want to come down soon—Is the coast clear?

1190. *To Jeannette L. and Joseph B. Gilder* (*?*)

Camden   Feb 6 '83

Yours with the $15 (13) just rec'd⁹—thanks—yes, I want some copies of last *Critic*—if convenient send me six copies—

Walt Whitman

1191. *To John Burroughs*   2.9. [1883]

ADDRESS: John Burroughs | Esopus-on-Hudson | New York. POSTMARK: Camden | Feb | 9 | 4 PM | N.J.

Camden   Feb: 9 p m

Too bad—too vexatious—Wednesday forenoon was so dismal & slippery—& I not at all well—(am having some bad spells lately)—thought you would on not finding me at McKay's come right over here, as it is only 20 minutes to get here, & the cars pass my door—look'd for you all the afternoon—the sorest pinch is I feel *now* it is all *my* bungling fault¹⁰—

7. Elmer (1861–1957) was Mrs. Stafford's newphew; Edwin was her son.
8. This letter is not known.
9. Payment for "The Bible as Poetry" (see 1187). The editors deducted $2 for the offprints which WW requested.

Nothing very new to write about—McKay and Dr Bucke are in treaty about the Dr's book, with the probability of Mc publishing it[11]—

To-day, afternoon, feels like a precursor of spring so fresh & sunny— I am not busy at any thing particular—(Seem to be like a skipper who has come into port at last & discharged cargo—& don't know what next.) Who did you see in New York? And exactly how are you? Write soon —& freely—

Yours as always

Walt Whitman

1192. *To William D. O'Connor*   *2.17.* [*1883*]

ENDORSED: "Answ'd Feb 19/83." ADDRESS: Wm D O'Connor | Life Saving Service Bureau | Treasury | Washington | D C. POSTMARK: Washington, Recd. | Feb | (?) 8 | (?) AM | 1883 | 2.

Camden—Saturday night Feb. 17th

The publisher of Dr Bucke's book wants your letter or preface to the *Good G[ray] P[oet]*[12]—If he had it, would put the copy in hand on the 20th—wants to put the copy in the printers' hands in a lump—Can't you send it immediately? Send to *me* here—

W W

1193. *To William D. O'Connor*

ENDORSED: "Answ'd Feb 20/83." ADDRESS: Wm D O'Connor | Life Saving Service Bureau | Treasury | Washington D C. POSTMARKS: Philadelphia | Pa. | Feb 19 83 | (?); Washington, Recd. | Feb | 20 | 4 30 AM | 1883 | 2.

Camden   noon   Feb. 19 | '83.

Dear friend

You will get a copious shower (Dr B[ucke] and me together) of these pestering messages. I have been looking through the G[ood] G[ray] P[oet] as Dr B sent it in his copy, & it comes to my soul over the dozen years more eloquent & beautiful than ever—seems to me, (as a passionate shooting shaft launched into those times, & indeed fitting to the whole situation then & since)—*it deserves to stand just as it is*—two

10. Burroughs was in Philadelphia on Wednesday, February 7 (*CB*).
11. WW noted on January 31 that McKay sent over Bucke's manuscript of his biography. On February 8 the poet returned to Bucke "$200 borrowed last fall" (*CB*).
12. Bucke's biography included a letter from O'Connor dated February 22, 1883, which served as a preface to his reprint of *The Good Gray Poet*.

passages in the last page only might be left out, & I should so suggest.[13] Seems to me all that is wanted is a brief preparatory ¶ dated present time, *distinctly confirming your faith &c.* that it is without diminution (it couldn't have "increase")[14]—*Tomorrow & next day the printers will be waiting for the copy.* It is intended to put the copy, whole book, in hand in force, & have it out soon—Send to me here—

I am pretty well this ending winter. Yes I rec'd the big Powell *Ethnology*[15] & have made more than one *courageous* attack on it (thought I acknowledged it)—The air here (human & other) all nervous from the pouring crowds of big disasters, floods, mine cavings, deaths, wrecks, big casualties from every quarter—

W. W.

1194. *To William D. O'Connor*

ADDRESS: Wm D O'Connor | Life Saving Service | Treasury | Washington | D C. POSTMARKS: Camden | Feb | 21 | 5 PM | N.J.; Washington, Recd. | Feb | 22 | 4 30 AM | 1883 | 2.

Camden   N J | Feb: 21 '83—p. m.

Have just been looking over the "Transfer" pamphlet you sent—pages 46, '7, to which you call'd my attention are (I allow myself to think) a latent flattering unction to me & the ways I suggest of looking at questions in America.[16] Indeed such things do me more good than you think for—I am just going over to Germantown to spend to-night, to-morrow & till Thursday noon in the big family & big house, wife, son, two splendid daughters of a Quaker friend, whose carriage comes for me presently.[17] The eldest daughter, age 20, an admirer of L. of G. who comes up even to you.[18] Thanks for the MS.—(as I write, has not yet arrived but will be here soon no doubt)—You shall see the proof—all your wishes shall be followed.

I am curious to see the Carlyle-Emerson letters—(had not heard

13. In his reply on February 20 O'Connor stated that although he wanted to delete the passages mentioned, he was in a "dilemma," since they were singled out for censure by his critics when the pamphlet appeared in 1866. For this reason he thought no deletions should be made (Feinberg; Traubel, I, 351).

14. O'Connor, who had Olympian contempt for brevity, added more than a paragraph—a letter of twenty-five pages.

15. Perhaps an unidentified work by Frederick York Powell (1850–1904), Froude's successor at Oxford, who wrote an eulogistic letter to WW on November 1, 1884 (Feinberg; Traubel, I, 356–357).

16. On February 20 O'Connor wrote: "The paper on Life-Saving Transfer is mine—some touches in the others. I was thinking of you when I wrote the first and third of my three reasons against transfer" (Feinberg; Traubel, I, 351).

17. The family of Robert Pearsall Smith.

before about my being in them)[19]—You hit long ago on the reason–why of the Emerson (apparent) change, or defection or cloud—whatever it is to be call'd—it was the interference, doubtless *hard lying*, of others—there was & is a little knot of my most malignant enemies, *deadly haters*, in & around Boston—some in high quarters–& they plied the man incessantly—Then above all that appears or he *appears* to say—you may be sure that E loved me—I believe more than he did any one—he showed it at first, & stronger still at *last*—that Saturday evn'g & Sunday afternoon he & I were (mostly silently) together in September, 1881, at Concord, told it—told better than ever can be put in words[20]—

1195. *To William D. O'Connor*   2.23. [*1883*]

ENDORSED: "Answ'd Feb 24/83." ADDRESS: Wm D
O'Connor | Life Saving Service | Treasury |
Washington D C. POSTMARKS: Philadelphia | Pa. |
Feb 23 83 | 6 30 PM; Washington, Recd. | Feb |
24 | 4 30 AM | 1883 | 2.

                                Camden   Feb 23   p m
I have just come back from my delightful Quaker visit—& find your MS roll, all right—It is all in good time—& if otherwise 'twould have been worth waiting for—

                                W. W.

1196. *To William D. O'Connor*   [*2.23. 1883*][21]

ENDORSED: "Answ'd Feb 24/83." ADDRESS: Wm D
O'Connor | Life Saving Service | Treasury |
Washington | D C. POSTMARKS: Philadelphia | Pa. |
Feb 23 83 | 6 30 PM; Washington, Recd. | Feb |
24 | 4 30 AM | 1883 | 2.

You appear to have dropped (have not sent) the *last* page—or pages—of the Stoddard-Lanman-Round Table finale—I enclose you the

18. Mary Whitall Smith, who was at the time a student at Smith College and who married B. F. W. Costelloe and later Bernard Berenson.
19. According to his letter of February 20, O'Connor had read in the New York *Tribune* excerpts from *The Correspondence of Thomas Carlyle and Ralph Waldo Emerson, 1834–1872* (1883). He particularly objected to Emerson's reference to WW in one of the letters (II, 251): "The letter, as printed, is very characteristic of Emerson—his reserve, his shrinking, like a woman's, because of rebuff; his deceptive concessions to the enemy, in a vein of pleasantry, almost like irony, almost like a sneer, when he says the book 'wanted good morals so much' that he did not send it" (Feinberg; Traubel, I, 352). In 1888 WW agreed with O'Connor: "Emerson should have said yes or no—not yes-no" (Traubel, I, 353).
20. See 1058 and 1059.
21. The date of this post card, obviously sent later than the preceding one, is es-

last page of MS as you sent it. Supply the missing concluding lines please
& return immediately—

WW

1197. *To John Burroughs*

ADDRESS: John Burroughs | Esopus-on-Hudson | New
York. POSTMARK: Philadelphia | Pa. | Feb 26 83 |
10 30.

Camden | Monday Evng   Feb 26 '83
At the breakfast table this morning we all agreed—my sister most
markedly—that your piece in the March *Century* is the best you have
written[22]—I think so, after two readings. Don't you go back however on
any positions (naturalistic & critical) you have taken in former essays &
books—*they are all just right & needed*—
Dr Bucke's book is in the printer's hands—I am well as usual—Best
love & remembrances to you & all—

Walt W

1198. *To Anne Gilchrist*

ADDRESS: Mrs. Anne Gilchrist | Keats' Corner | 12
Well Road | Hampstead | London | England.
POSTMARKS: Philadelphia | Feb | 27 | 1883 | Pa.;
London, N.W. | M E | Mr 9 | 83.

Camden   Feb: 27 '83
Your good words (Jan 27–Feb 13) just rec'd. Of course does me
good to hear from you—(that anecdote of Lady Dilke too pleased me)[23]—
Every thing goes on pretty much the same with us here in Camden—
my sister quite up to her standard of health—not *plus*, but not *minus*
either—my brother a little on the plethoric, & a little more *minus* than is
desirable, but goes forth as usual every day—is building a house for
their own occupancy on the little farm at Burlington—

tablished by O'Connor's endorsement, the postmark, and the reference to O'Connor's
manuscript. In his reprint of *The Good Gray Poet* Bucke included a reference to Richard
Henry Stoddard's review of the pamphlet in *The Round Table* on January 20, 1866,
and printed a letter written to the magazine by Charles Lanman and O'Connor's reply
(130–132).
  22. "Signs and Seasons," *The Century Magazine*, xxv (March, 1883), 672–682.
  23. Mrs. Gilchrist related how Lady Dilke handled a betrayer of a maid (LC;
Harned, 211–212).
  24. Mary Whitall Smith.
  25. Fred W. Wilson of this firm wrote to WW on February 27, 1884: "You may
be pleased to know that your *Leaves of Grass* is going very well here. I have been a

I go out quite a good deal as guest to a charming Quaker family, R Pearsall Smith & Mrs Smith at Germantown—a son & two fine daughters—dear friends all—have fine drives—the elder daughter, 20, is a great reader of L of G.[24]

My books doing—L. of G. sales have been good—*Specimen Days* not so good yet, but I am satisfied. (Wilson[25] & McCormick, St. Vincent St. Glasgow, are publishing S D for the British market)—Dr Bucke's book is in the hands of the printers here (Phila) & is to be published by David McKay, 23 South 9th St. Phila. Will be out in three or four weeks. The Vols. of *Carlyle's and Emerson's Letters* are out here (Boston)—I have just glanced at them[26]—I suppose you recd "the Bible as Poetry" in the "Critic"—

I don't know where I shall flit to the coming summer—if I am well enough—Even as I write I receive a letter from John Burroughs, & will just enclose it—dont want it again—(not as promising as I could wish)— if you can lay hands on the last *Century* (March) read J. B's piece—I think very fine—best love to you—& to dear Herb, and dear Giddy—The Staffords are all well—I havn't been down there in some months, but am going.[27]

W W

1199. *To Joseph M. Stoddart*

ADDRESS: J M Stoddart | 1018 Chestnut Street | Philadelphia. POSTMARK: Camden | Mar | 6 | 5 PM | N.J.

431 Stevens Street | Camden   New Jersey |
March 6 '83

My dear Stoddart

I have rec'd your letter enclosing Mr Kelly's[28]—Why yes I can give Mr K the sitting or two he desires—If he could come on here any time within the next two weeks, I would sit either in the forenoon say

reader of your writings for the last ten years or so and have in my humble way done my best to spread a knowledge of your work. (Indeed I have evinced the sincerity of my belief in you by going farther in its expression than most people have thought *prudent* in me— viz: by becoming your publisher in this country. Not in the slightest degree do I regret taking this step for I look upon you as one of my teachers and as such owe you my debt of gratitude) (LC).

26. See 1194.

27. Apparently WW did not visit the Staffords from November 27, 1882, to April 14, 1883. Harry called on the poet on March 5 (*CB*).

28. James Edward Kelly (1855–1933) was known as "the sculptor of American history."

10 to 12—or afternoon say 2 to 4—wish him to send me word a day or two beforehand.

Walt Whitman

1200. *To William D. O'Connor*   *3.9.* [*1883*]

ENDORSED: "Walt Whitman | Answ'd March 10/83."
ADDRESS: Wm D O'Connor | Life Saving Service |
Treasury | Washington D C. POSTMARKS: (?) |
Mar | 9 | 5 PM | (?); Washington, Recd. | Mar |
10 | 4 30 AM | (?).

Camden   March 9   P M

The publisher says he will hand me the proofs of your Introductory Letter, in a day or two, to send you[29]—very likely Sunday nights mail from here—if not Monday night—I am well as usual—

W. W.

1201. *To William D. O'Connor*   *3.11.* [*1883*]

ADDRESS: Wm D O'Connor | Life Saving Service |
Treasury | Washington D C. POSTMARKS: Camden |
Mar | 11 | 6 PM | N.J.; Washington, Recd. | Mar |
12 | 7 AM | 188(?) | (?).

Sunday Evng   March 11

I send you the proofs of the Introductory Letter. If you return them (send to me) by Wednesday Evng's mail from Washington—(or even Thursday's)—it will be time enough.

Every thing seems moving on—not unfavorably at any rate—I am well as usual—

W W

I wish you would in your next tell me ab't my dear friends Nelly and Jeannie[30]—

29. On March 6 Bucke's manuscript was "in the hands of the printers—Sherman & Co: Phila." Three days later WW sent galleys to Bucke (CB), who, on March 12, acknowledged receipt of them (Feinberg).
30. On March 10 O'Connor informed WW that he was leaving Washington for Providence, R. I., because of the illness of his daughter (Feinberg). It is an interesting sidelight on the relations of O'Connor and WW that after the resumption of their correspondence in 1882 almost a year passed before O'Connor referred to his family or WW inquired about Mrs. O'Connor and Jeannie. Until the quarrel WW was on intimate terms with the family; in fact, Mrs. O'Connor continued to write to him for four years after the estrangement. Despite Jeannie's critical illness the poet referred to her only in this letter and in 1203. O'Connor mentioned her death on May 23 (Lion). In 1888 WW ob-

1202. *To John Burroughs*

TRANSCRIPT.

March 12, 1883

[WW promised to read the *Century* proof when it arrived and to return it with suggestions.]

Chew on what I said in my last[31]—the position you occupy in your printed books is just what it should be *to last*—the paragraph or two of let-up or disclaimer in "Signs and Seasons" is right, too, "for reasons"— let it stand—but *nothing further of apology*—not a word.

1203. *To William D. O'Connor*

ENDORSED: "Answ'd March 15/83." ADDRESS: Wm D O'Connor | Care of Dr W F Channing | 98 Congdon Street | Providence | Rhode Island | p o box 393. POSTMARKS: Philadelphia | Mar | 14 | 7 PM | Pa.; Providence | Mar | 15 | 1 PM | R.I.

431 Stevens Street | Camden   New Jersey | March 14 '83

Dear friend

Your telegram just rec'd—Your letter rec'd last Monday—I had however sent proofs of the entire Introductory Letter by Sunday night's mail hence in a parcel to Washington—& I have just sent a letter directed to (Acting) Chief Clerk L S S, asking him (if not already done) to forward the parcel to you at Providence—

I last night forwarded proofs of good part of the G[ood] G[ray] P[oet] to you at Providence direct—will forward the rest in a day or two—

I send best love to Nelly, I send best sympathy and love to the dear sufferer Jeannie[32]—Love too to Dr and Mrs Channing,[33] & their children—

Beautiful sunny day here—noon—the window open as I write—Dr

served: "Jeannie's death was the tragedy of their history—and a tragedy in my history, too. Too much must not be said of that or the like of that—it gets down in you where words do not go." Traubel reported that WW's "eyes were full of tears" (Traubel, II, 261). Yet WW apparently did not write to O'Connor about her death or record it in *CB*.

31. See 1197. Burroughs commented on this letter: "In the essay I had over-hauled the poets. When I came to put it in book form I modified and excised a little" (Barrus, 241).

32. On March 14 O'Connor reported that "Jeannie is very ill, confined to her bed, perhaps never to be well again" (Syracuse; Traubel, IV, 407).

33. Mrs. Channing and Mrs. O'Connor were sisters. WW visited the Channings in 1868 (see 317–322).

B[ucke]'s book is half in type—Send the proofs back soon as convenient—(no immanent hurry)—

Yes, I like the letter very much—

I am well as usual—

Walt Whitman

1204. *To William D. O'Connor*   *3.15. [1883]*

ENDORSED: "Answ'd March 19/83." ADDRESS: Wm D O'Connor | Care Dr W F Channing | 98 Congdon Street | Providence | Rhode Island | p o box | 393. POSTMARK: Philadelphia | Mar | 15 | 1883 | 5 PM | Pa.

Camden   March 15

If you have, or can think of, or select any thing—(it may be a line or two—or a quarter or half a page)—*for a motto like, to back the appendix title page that precedes your letter* & G[ood] G[ray] P[oet][34] —send it to me—will do, if sent within a week—

W. W.

1205. *To William D. O'Connor*

ENDORSED: "Answ'd March 17/83." ADDRESS: Wm D O'Connor | Care Dr W F Channing | 98 Congdon Street | Providence | Rhode Island | p o box | 393. POSTMARKS: Camden | Mar | 16 | 12 M | N.J.; Providence | Mar | 17 | 6 AM | R.I.

Camden   March 16 '83 | Noon

My dear friend

Yours of 14th & proofs of 1883 Letter rec'd—All y'r marks will be attended to—the Emerson passages put in as you desire[35]—the text minutely adhered to—every correction carried out—with the single exception (if you will allow it, as I personally request you will) of restoring the italic non-quoted names of books, &c. The typographical plan was laid out by the Superintendant in the printing office & agreed to by the publisher & myself—I stipulated that your text should be adhered to

34. On March 19 O'Connor offered two suggestions: the lines referring to Longinus in Pope's *Essay on Criticism* and three lines from *Hamlet* (Feinberg). Either Bucke or WW decided not to follow his proposals, and inserted a quotation from "a letter to R. M. B., by W. F., Mobile, Ala., March, 1883" (Bucke, 72). Bucke wrote to O'Connor about the motto on March 30 (LC).

35. On March 14 O'Connor requested that Emerson's letter be printed in entirety (Syracuse; Traubel, IV, 406–407).

without the slightest variation—but gave in to the type & technique business, so as to have a certain system & uniformity which those names as
printed come under—But it does not involve any material point & I know
you will be entirely satisfied when you come to see the Letter and the
G[ood] G[ray] P[oet] in the printed book—Also I request you will
allow a few certain ¶ breaks in the G G P—not at all affecting the text
—but helping the typography & reader—I think most decidedly helping[36]—

The foot note (early part of G G P) is printed I see exactly as in
copy—If not the true note, send it on as you wish, & it shall appear
verbatim—(we have no fear of scarifying Lowell)[37]—If the exigencies of
the printing office allow I will have a revise sent you—but it is not
certain—

Walt Whitman

1206. *To William D. O'Connor* 3.18. [*1883*]

ENDORSED: "Answ'd March 19/83." ADDRESS: Wm D
O'Connor | care Dr: W F Channing | 98 Congdon
Street | Providence | Rhode Island | P O Box | 393.
POSTMARKS: Camden | Mar | 18 | 6 PM | N.J.;
Providence | (?) | 18 | (?) PM | R.I.

Camden March 18

Returned proofs all arrived safe—You shall have a revise[38]—may
take five days—possibly more—all goes well—

W. W.

1207. *To William D. O'Connor* 3.25. [*1883*]

ENDORSED: "Answ'd March 27/83." ADDRESS: Wm D
O'Connor | Care Dr W F Channing | 98 Congdon
Street | Providence | Rhode Island | P O box 393.
POSTMARK: Camden | Mar | 25 | 6 PM | N.J.

Camden March 25 p m

Dont be impatient because the second proof dont come—One
little thing or another delays—but you shall see the revise & have your

---

36. On March 17 O'Connor vehemently opposed any alterations in his paragraphs
(Feinberg; Traubel, IV, 354–355).

37. O'Connor wanted printed exactly the footnote which alluded, without mentioning Lowell by name, to a Cambridge author who had termed WW "nothing but a low
New York rowdy," "a common street blackguard" (Bucke, 100n.).

38. With his usual insistence O'Connor wrote on March 17, "*Do* let me have a revise" (Feinberg; Traubel, IV, 355).

say, before the pages are cast—I hope to send it to-morrow evening—or next—

Every thing moves on, & I keep well—

You appear *middling* largely in letter, & *mighty* largely in spirit, in the book[39]—& I *know* you are going to like the typographical presentation too—

W. W.

1208. *To Kristofer N. Janson*[40]

ADDRESS: [K]ristofer Janson | [1306] Franklin Ave. | [Mi]nneap[olis] | Minn:. POSTMARK: Camden | Mar | (?).

431 Stevens Street | Camden   New Jersey
March 26 '83

Glad to hear from you again, & hope some day I shall meet you personally—Yes, I gladly consent to your putting "To Him that was Crucified" in your book.

Walt Whitman

1209. *To John Burroughs*   *3.29.* [1883][41]

Camden   March 29

I have run over the Carlyle proof & being in the mood have thought best to mark (of course for your consideration—you may have something behind which I do not see) *out* certain passages just as they summarily imprest me—clearly though rapidly feeling as I went along that the article would be bettered & more unitary without them. What you set out mainly to say & have to say, seems to me very well said indeed, & *I like the article* —What you have to offer as the Carlyle-foil, in defence of America, I dont

---

39. WW referred to the prefatory letter which preceded *The Good Gray Poet* in Bucke's study.

40. Janson, a Unitarian clergyman and author, was born in Bergen, Norway, and went to Minneapolis in 1882. For information about Janson, I am indebted to Martina A. Brown, of the Minneapolis Public Library.

41. The year is established by the following: on March 31, 1883, WW noted in *CB* that he had "read John Burroughs's 'Carlyle' proof"; on May 20 Burroughs referred to his article to which he was "adding a page about Mrs. C. as revealed by her letters" (Syracuse; Traubel, IV, 510); and the article, entitled "Carlyle," appeared in *The Century Magazine* in August, 1883. After writing "Carlyle and Emerson" for *The Critic*, II (May 20, 1882), 140–141, and an unsigned review of Froude's *Thomas Carlyle* in *The Century Magazine*, XXIV (June, 1882), 307–308, Burroughs began to gather material for a more extended article, as he informed WW from London on June 16,

like so well—(besides it is unnecessary any how—Unless one has got something outsmashing C himself—a battery-ram that batters *his* ram to the dust)—

Write when you can—Do you want me to send you papers or any thing?—always yours

W W

1210. *To William D. O'Connor*   3.29. [*1883*]

ENDORSED: "Answ'd April 1/83." ADDRESS: Wm D O'Connor | Care Dr W F Channing | 98 Congdon Street | Providence | Rhode Island. POSTMARKS: Philadelphia | Mar | 29 | 5(?) PM | Pa.; Providence | Mar | 30 | 6 AM | R.I.

Camden   March 29

Yours just rec'd—The printers are very slow—but will be coming along in a day [or] two—have a sudden rush—the American reprint "Encyclopædia Brittanica"—I send you by express a little package of books—the three Vols. of my own writing you keep—& give away, or do what you are a mind to with[42]—The Elze? book[43]—(have you run foul of it before? I guess not)—I send to while away unoccupied hours—keep it as long as you stay in Providence—then return it to me here.

W W

Your 27th M[arch] letter has pleased me well—as all your letters do —Wm, let me know how the Heywood affair gets on, or turns out, as you hear from it—We (I and McKay) have been somewhat at a loss what to do in it—whether to send on some money ($20 or so)—or whether to remain entirely aloof & silent (& send no money)—I finally concluded on the latter—& I am quite clear that is the right course for me—mainly because it *satisfies* me best, upon the whole[44]—What you say *about Mrs Spofford's say* lubricates my soul like precious ointment[45]—

1882 (Feinberg; Traubel, II, 171).

42. In his reply on April 1, O'Connor informed WW that he had given copies of *Leaves of Grass* and *Specimen Days* to the Channings (Feinberg; Traubel, II, 258).

43. O'Connor was thoroughly acquainted with the writings of Karl Elze (1821–1889), whom he termed "a perfect Bismarck philistine" (Feinberg; Traubel, II, 259). Probably WW sent Elze's *Essays on Shakespeare* (1874). The question mark after Elze in the text is WW's.

44. See 1169. Though O'Connor considered Heywood "a stupendous jackass," he was anxious to have him acquitted (Feinberg; Traubel, III, 566). On April 1 he approved of WW's course of inaction (Feinberg; Traubel, II, 260).

45. On March 27 O'Connor reported that Harriet Prescott Spofford (1835–1921), novelist and poet, considered WW "the only poet that ever lived who has done justice to women" (Feinberg; Traubel, III, 564).

1211. *To William D. O'Connor*

ENDORSED: "Answ'd April 1/83." ADDRESS: Wm D
O'Connor | Care Dr. W F Channing | 93 Congdon
Street | Providence | Rhode Island | p o box | 393.
POSTMARKS: Camden | Mar | 31 | 12 M | N.J.;
Providence | Apr | 1 | (?) AM | (?).

Camden   1883   March   31   noon

My dear friend

I send you the second proofs—look over carefully for technicals, misspelling of names, & in the Italian text on Page 109 &c[46]—but make no changes or alterations. If we were to begin the setting of the copy *de novo* you should certainly be obeyed in every detail & minutest particular—& I know I should like the result well enough. But I like wonderfully well the whole presentations just as they appear here—& I know you will too, either right off, or soon as you get accustomed to them. Besides *the matter itself*, after being faithfully given as to text & with typographic cleanliness & propriety, *makes remaining points not worth dwelling on*. Taken together the Introductory Letter and the G[ood] G[ray] P[oet] are so tremendous & vehement, so beautiful & orbic in themselves—so fitting for the body of the volume (almost its heart & lungs)—so honest & subtle, as well as stupendous, a eulogy and dissertation, on L of G, & on certain primary & spinal literary laws—so assuring a pedestal for my future fame—& as here printed so satisfactory in their type, style & paragraphing &c. *as they stand* that any change in those particulars would be worse than unnecessary—would be fatuous[47]—

I keep well—Write me often as you can—tell me all the news—your own movements as much as you can—

Did you get the parcel of books?[48]

Walt Whitman

Keep the proof *two days* after you get it if you wish[49]—

46. A series of quotations from Dante appear on this page of Bucke's book.
47. Despite WW's praise, O'Connor, on April 1, felt *"dreadfully* at the prospect your letter opens, of my paragraphing being changed" (Feinberg; Traubel, II, 260).
48. See the preceding letter.
49. The typesetting of Bucke's biography was completed on March 31 (*CB*). This was WW's book in every detail: he altered the proofs at will. On March 20, Bucke, whose role was simply to acquiesce in WW's changes, wrote: "I open and read these parcels of proof in fear and trembling (you must go as easy as you can, you are the terrible surgeon with the knife & saw and saw the patient). You left out my remarks on 'Children of Adam', I believe they were good but I acquiesce—your additions are excellent as they have been all through" (Feinberg). On May 28 Bucke was pleased with the book he and WW had produced: "I believe it will do, and if it will the Editor will deserve more credit than the Author—I am really surprised at the tact and judgement you have

1212. *To William D. O'Connor* *4.5.[1883]*

ADDRESS: Wm D O'Connor | Life Saving Service |
Treasury | Washington D C. POSTMARKS:
Philadelphia | Pa. | Apr 5 83 | 5 30 PM; Washington,
Recd. | Apr | 6 | 4 30 AM | 1883(?) | 2.

Camden   April 5   p m

Proof arrived promptly & safely. All shall be carefully attended to[50]—

W. W.

1213. *To Susan Stafford* *4.12. [1883]*

ADDRESS: Mrs Susan M Stafford | Kirkwood |
Glendale | New Jersey. POSTMARK: Camden | Apr |
13 | 7 AM | N.J.

Camden   April 12

I will come down Saturday afternoon in the 4 o'clock train to
Kirkwood—& stay over till Sunday afternoon[51]—

W W

1214. *To William Sloane Kennedy* *4.13. [1883]*

ENDORSED (by Kennedy?): "1883."

431 Stevens St   Camden   N J | April 13—Afternoon
Your "Holmes" rec'd[52]—thank you kindly—The brief glance over
& through it I have given impresses me what a *clean* piece of work it is—
what a presentable book—Dr R M Bucke of Canada has just finished the
printing (type-setting) of his book "Walt Whitman"—to be published here
ab't end of this month by David McKay, 23 South 9th Phila.[53]—(Pub'r of

displayed in putting my rough M. S. into shape and I am more than satisfied with all
you have done" (Feinberg). Bucke, however, was not quite so pleased with WW's high-
handed treatment of his book as his letters to the poet indicate. For in a letter on August 19 to O'Connor, who on August 16 objected to "several omissions and commissions,"
Bucke wrote: "I do not care to go into these matters by letter but when you come [to
Canada] I will make every thing clear to your comprehension" (LC).
 50. O'Connor sent a list of typographical errors on April 4 (Feinberg; Traubel, I,
67–68).
 51. WW went to Glendale on April 14, Saturday, and stayed until Monday (CB).
 52. *Oliver Wendell Holmes* (Boston, 1883) contains a brief reference to the Boston censorship (256).
 53. Bucke's biography was bound on June 1 and was formally released on
June 20 (CB).

my books) I will send you one soon as it is out—I am well, for me—have had a pretty good winter—

Walt Whitman

thanks for your brief, flashing, indirect glances on me—not so indirect either—

1215. *To William D. O'Connor*   *4.14. [1883]*

ENDORSED: "Answ'd April 17/83." ADDRESS: Wm D O'Connor | Life Saving Service | Treasury | Washington | D C. POSTMARKS: Philadelphia | Pa. | Apr 14 83 | 1 PM; Washington, Recd. | Apr | 15 | 4 30 AM | 1883 | 2.

Camden   April 14

My dear friend

I wish you would apply to the Librarian of Congress's office for the copyright at once—take it out of course in your own name—send the enclosed printed title page—& ask for a certificate—it is $1—(50¢ for entry & 50 for cert[ificate].)[54]

Every thing is going on well—but slowly with the book. It will be out last of the month. I shall send you an earliest copy or two. The publisher McKay told me to say to you that you can have at half price ($1) whatever number of copies you want "for personal or literary use"—Dr Bucke is absent from London on official business—(though I believe it is about time for him to return)—At last accounts John Burroughs was home in Delaware county, recuperating in the maple sugar woods—he was better—

Do you see in the Heywood trial, the Judge peremptorily ruled out the L of G slips part of the indictment—(which ruling out "was received with applause") & H was afterwards on the remaining part or parts acquitted. So A[nthony] C[omstock] retires with his tail intensely curved in-

---

54. On February 19 Bucke wrote to O'Connor: "If you do not object we are going to copyright the book in America in *your name* as we cannot in *mine*—Shall of course copyright in own name in England" (LC).

55. O'Connor was vehement in his denunciation of Comstock on April 17: "He ought to be crushed, signally, publicly, in the interest of free letters and the rights of thought; he ought to be nailed up, like a skunk to a barn-door, as an example to deter. . . . It is nothing less than a public—national—infamy, that an infamous dog like this, convicted of such practices—a decoy duck, a dirty stool pigeon—should be in the employ of the United States" (Syracuse; Traubel, IV, 91).

wards.[55] I am just starting for two or three days down in my Jersey woods retreat.

W W

The Doctor took a decided dislike to having the Latin motto on title page—so at his request I left it out—(I partly coincided with him)[56]—

1216. *To Herbert Gilchrist*

ADDRESS: Herbert H Gilchrist | Keats' Corner 12
Well Road | Hampstead | London England.
POSTMARKS: Gibbsborough, N.J. | Apr | 16 | 1883;
Philadelphia | A(?) | 1(?) | 1883 | Pa.

Kirkwood (Glendale) America   April 15 | '83
I am down here for a few days—Mrs. S[tafford] has had a severe fit of illness—three weeks—*one week quite alarming*—but is now better—to-day is up—& has been down stairs once or twice for a few minutes—with luck & good weather the doctor thinks she will get around again as usual before long—
Nothing specially new with me—I keep about as usual—have had a fair winter—Dr Bucke's book is being printed & is to have your intaglio for a frontispiece[57]—it arouses the strongest opinions pro and con—(Dr B. & several, including myself, decidedly like it)—
Love to you, to your dear M[other] & to G[race].

W W

1217. *To William Sloane Kennedy*   5.26. *[1883]*

Camden   May 26
I congratulate you on the live and telling piece in to-day's C[ritic]. It is the best paper that has appeared at any time in that Weekly[58]—I am well—

W W

56. The title page originally contained a quotation from Lucretius, the excision of which disappointed O'Connor (Syracuse; Traubel, IV, 90). WW, however, fibbed, for on May 28 Bucke wrote: "I see now that you were right about the Latin motto (as about everything else)" (Feinberg).
57. A saccharine, Millet-like portrait of WW. In his reply on April 29 Herbert noted that "John Burroughs was very violent against my intaglio" (LC; Harned, 213).
58. Kennedy's "The Obsolescence of Barrel-Organ Poetry," which appeared in *The Critic* on May 26, attacked conventional rhyme and meter in poetry, and praised the new freedom in the music and poetry of Wagner and WW. See also 1219.

1218. *To Anne Gilchrist*

ADDRESS: Mrs. Ann Gilchrist | 12 Well Road
Hampstead | London England. POSTMARKS: Camden |
May | 27 | 5 PM | N.J.; Philadelphia | May | 27 |
1883 | Pa.

Camden   May 27 '83

Your good letter came four days ago—Herb's has also reached me[59]—both warmly appreciated & thanked—I keep well—am still here in C. but shall go off somewhere soon—Dr Bucke's book will be first published in England[60]—Josiah Child, (at Trübner's) will have some copies in a very few days, (to enter one at Stationers' Hall, London, to secure the English copyright: & to make the first sales)—You will see your pen & thought are in it[61]—Herb's picture intaglio forms the frontispiece—Mrs Stafford is about as well as usual again.[62] It is a very warm Sunday afternoon—as I write up in my third story south room—

W W

1219. *To William Sloane Kennedy*

Camden   May 31 '83

The publisher having placed a few advance copies in paper of Dr Bucke's WW at my disposal I send you one[63]—The book will be pub: here & in London in ab't ten days—May-be you could find a market (in some remunerative quarter) for some early notices of same—yours of 27th rec'd—

I don't think you appreciate the importance of that article of yours, (statement, position, signal for advance, &c) in the *Critic*. It entails on

59. Mrs. Gilchrist wrote on May 6 (LC; Harned, 215–216), and Herbert on April 29 (LC; Harned, 213–214). When Mrs. Gilchrist replied to WW on July 30, she was unexpectedly (and sensibly) critical of Bucke's biography: she particularly objected to "carefully gathering together again all the rubbish stupid or malevolent that has been written of you" and to "all that unmeaning, irrelevant clatter about what Rabelais or Shakespeare or the ancients & their times tolerated in the way of coarseness or plainness of speech" (LC; Harned, 217). She also forwarded to WW her recent biography of Mary Lamb (1883). She wrote again on October 13–21 (LC; Harned, 220–222). Apparently WW did not reply to either letter.
60. The biography was published in London on June 15 (CB).
61. Bucke included extracts from Mrs. Gilchrist's article in *The Radical* in May, 1870 (204–206).
62. WW was with the Staffords from May 12 to 15 (CB).
63. Kennedy's review of Bucke's study appeared in the Boston *Globe* on June 10. WW sent "Press copies" to the Philadelphia *Press*, in which a review appeared on May 27; to *The Critic*, where it was reviewed on June 9; to the Boston *Herald* (to Sylvester Baxter), in which a review was printed on May 27; to the New York *Evening Post*; and to the New

you deep responsibilities, & great wariness & determination in keeping it up. I mean exactly what I said in my last.[64]

W W

1220. *To William D. O'Connor*

ENDORSED: "Answ'd June 15/83." ADDRESS: Wm D
O'Connor | Life Saving Service | Treasury |
Washington | D C. POSTMARKS: Philadelphia | Pa. |
Jun 13 83 | 6 30 PM; Washington, Recd. | Jun | 14 |
4 30 AM | 1883 | 2.

Camden   June 13 '83 | Evn'g

My dear friend

The corrections you specified have been or will be made, for future printing—(I wish you would notify me of any others you see also)[65]— The book is to be published simultaneously here and in London Eng. on the 15th June.[66] Typographically, & in get up, binding &c. the experts all pronounce it a success—it is generally taken for an *imported* book, (if that is any compliment)—the wonder is not that there are a few errors & plate-breakages—but that there are *so* few—your part looks & *is* even better than I anticipated from the proofs—more tremendous—the 1883 Letter is *vitalest* of all—it is like the Old French Revolution of '93[67]—long, long its provocation & reason-why—stands there, something, *the only*—an immense prologue before it & an immense epilogue after, & it but a speck in the middle between—an exception—but *enough*, the mark, the inerasable warning, for a thousand years—

The printed notice enclosed is from a scholar & staunch friend—a Yankee *litterateur*—W. S. K.—if you feel to do so, *I wish you would*

York *Tribune* (Notebook, Yale; and Bucke's Scrapbook, Feinberg). The Camden *County Courier* noticed the book on June 2, the New York *Times* on July 1 (see 1226), and *The Nation* on July 26 (see 1237). Dowden published a review in *The Academy* on September 8 (see 1243).

Of his book Bucke wrote to O'Connor on February 26: "I am glad to . . . go to battle in a good cause, but I am not exultant about it, I have made up my mind to be attacked in every conceivable way, to be called an idiot, a lunatic, and all the rest of it, and I am prepared to stand it all" (LC).

64. See 1217.

65. Apparently a reference to the errors cited in O'Connor's letter of May 23 (Lion). WW did not allude to Jeannie's death which O'Connor reported in the same letter (see 1201). However, O'Connor on May 14 informed Bucke of the details of his daughter's death and of "a bad attack of inflammatory rheumatism," which incapacitated him for the rest of the year (LC).

66. The book was published on June 15 in London and on June 20 in Philadelphia (CB, and see the following letter).

67. O'Connor considered WW's comparison "magnificent and happy" (Syracuse; Traubel, IV, 162).

write him a few words—he is worthy—Say that I sent you the criticism —his address is

Wm Sloane Kennedy
Cambridge Mass:[68]

I am well. Did you see the *Critic* June 9?[69] I saw the *Tribune* notice.

W. W.

1221. *To William D. O'Connor*   6.18. [*1883*]

ENDORSED: "Answ'd June 19/83." ADDRESS: Wm D O'Connor | Life Saving Service | Treasury | Washington | DC. POSTMARKS: Philadelphia | Pa. | Jun 18 | 1 PM; Washington, Recd. | Jun | 19 | 4 30 AM | 1883 | 2.

Camden   June 18

The date of publication here has been further postponed *to the 20th* (to give the London pub'n precedence)—All goes well—A week of splendid weather here—See the *Critic* of June 16—"Walt Whitman in Russia"[70]—Yours of 15th rec'd.—You have just rec'd—havnt you?—a copy of the regular bound ed'n—Don't you like the looks of it?

W W

1222. *To Joseph B. Gilder*

ADDRESS: J B Gilder | *Critic* office | 30 Lafayette Square | New York City. POSTMARK: Philadelphia | Pa. | Jun 18 83 | (?) PM.

Camden   June 18 '83

Please send copy of *Critic* of June 9 to *Dr R M Bucke, London, Ontario, Canada*—also (if not already sent) copy of *Critic* of June 16, *to same*. Dr B. is a subscriber to the C. but tells me in a note rec'd this morning, he has not rec'd the paper of June 9 (?[71] or has his subscription run out?)—I know he will be deeply gratified & grateful for your notice of his book in that paper—

Walt Whitman

68. On June 15 O'Connor promised to write to Kennedy as soon as his hand healed (Syracuse; Traubel, IV, 162).

69. The June 9 issue of *The Critic* contained a review of Bucke's book.

70. The article was allegedly written by Dr. P. Popoff. In the margin of a copy, however, WW wrote: "my guess (at random) is that John Swinton is the writer of this

1223. *To Karl Knortz*

ADDRESS: Dr Karl Knortz | Cor: Morris Avenue | &
155th Street | New York City. POSTMARKS:
Philadelphia | Pa. | Jun 19 83 | 2 30 PM; P.O. |
6–19–83 | 7–1 P | N.Y.

431 Stevens Street | Camden New Jersey   June 19 '83

Thanks for the copy German rendering *"Cradle Endlessly Rock-ing"* & for all the other German renderings of my pieces which you have sent me, & which I carefully keep, & prize—Dr R M Bucke has just published a book about me & my poems—& having two or three advance copies (in paper) at my disposal I should like to send you one. Shall I send it as before (by mail) to cor: Morris av: and 155th Street? (See the N. Y. *Critic* June 16)—

Walt Whitman

1224. *To Karl Knortz*

ADDRESS: Dr Karl Knortz | Cor: Morris Avenue | &
155th Street | New York City. POSTMARKS:
Camden | Jun | 21 | 12 M | N.J.; R | 6–22–83 |
6–1 A | N.Y.

431 Stevens Street | Camden New Jersey |
June 21 '83

Thanks for the portrait, engraving. It is welcome. A copy of Dr B[ucke]'s book, in paper, goes to you same mail with this.

Walt Whitman

1225. *To William D. O'Connor*

ENDORSED: "Answ'd June | 83." ADDRESS: Wm D
O'Connor | Life Saving Service | Treasury |
Washington | D C. POSTMARK: Camden | Jun | 27 |
6 PM | N.J.

Camden   June 27 '83   Evn'g

As I was about mailing these to Dr. B[ucke] I thought I would send first to you—(tho' I dont really know why—for there is nothing to dwell on in the cuttings)[72]—please forward them to Dr Bucke. I continue

article" (Feinberg). On August 12, 1882, Swinton informed the poet that his lecture on American literature had been translated and printed in *Zagranichnyi Viestnik* (Feinberg; Traubel, II, 393). See also Allen, *Walt Whitman Abroad*, 145.
71. WW's question mark.
72. Reviews of Dr. Bucke's study.

quite well for me. The British publisher of the "W W" is Wilson & McCormick, St Vincent Street, Glasgow—they also issue (under their own imprint) L of G and Specimen Days—the new book somewhat sluggish yet—it will take to fall & winter before the news gets well around—but it is *secured* & *effectual*—

W W

1226. *To William D. O'Connor*

ENDORSED: "Answ'd Aug 12/83." ADDRESS: Wm D
O'Connor | Life Saving Service | Treasury |
Washington | D. C. POSTMARKS: Philadelphia |
Jul | 20 | 7 PM | Pa.; Washington, Recd. | Jul | 21 |
4 30 AM | 1883 | 3.

Camden   July 20 '83

Dear friend

Yours of 19th recd.[73] Thanks for the corrections, & if you notice any more errors mention them to me, as I want to make out a full list preparatory to next printing—I will speak to McKay ab't the 25 copies & tell him I will go security—I dont know of any "office editor" to the *N. A. Review*—I think Allen Thorndike Rice the editor (& owner, 30 Lafayette Place New York) keeps every thing (in reading articles, judgment, &c.) in his own hands—seems to like controversial articles, attacks, &c.—any thing but dulness—yet I sh'd say is naturally conservative, respectable & English—he pays well, when suited—he always paid me well & gave me lots of taffy besides—but *balked* at my Carlyle article (pp. 170 to 178 *Specimen Days*) & sent back the MSS.[74]—A fuller acc't of that Russian matter[75] is in the enclosed, wh: after reading, please send back to me. The *American* (same mail with this,) after reading please forward to Dr Bucke. Thanks for the Boston *Transcript* (I have sent it to Dr. B.) If George Edgar M[ontgomery][76] keeps on this way he will soon be among the avowed & emphatic advocates of L. of G. The N. Y. *Times* article of some three weeks since I have not yet seen.

I am well—have been down all this month at a secluded place I go in the Jersey woods[77]—pleasant weather here now—The stress, &c. ab't Dr Bucke's book will *begin next winter* here & in England.

W W

73. WW referred to the letter of July 12, in which O'Connor mentioned corrections in Bucke's book and referred to the "office editor" of *The North American Review* (Feinberg; Traubel, III, 129).
74. See 1113.
75. See 1221.

1227. To Susan Stafford   *8.6.* [*1883*]

ADDRESS: Mrs Susan Stafford | Kirkwood | Glendale |
New Jersey. POSTMARK: Philadelphia | Aug | 6 |
8 PM | Pa.

Germantown | Afternoon   Aug: 6

Dear friend,

Sitting here in the library, alone in a great big house, I thought I
would write you a few lines to pass for a letter—though the Lord only
knows what I shall write about, for I have no news to tell, & nothing
special to say—

I came out here on a visit to an old friend[78] a few days ago, & shall
stay here perhaps the ensuing week—The family, (& a fine one they are)
are at Newport for the summer—my friend, the father, goes to his business in Philadelphia, absent all day, & I am left here master of a large
house, garden, library &c. with servants, horses—a good dinner at 1
o'clock every day—have to eat it all by myself, but I enjoy it—It is a
Quaker family I am very much attached to—(I believe I have mentioned
them to you before)—all kind & good—but the ones that seem most to
me are the eldest daughter Mary (ab't 21) the brightest happiest sunniest
cutest young woman you ever saw, & probably you would say upon knowing her, a new & different combination of character from any you ever saw
—& one I am sure you would like—And then the father himself, my friend
—he is in business in Phila:—he has been a great traveler in Europe, &
something of a preacher—he is a good talker—& very kind—we always
have a good long ride, from 5 to 7½ afternoons—which I enjoy very much
—& then return to supper—& a couple of hours talking, reading &c.

Then there is (all now at Newport as I said) another daughter & a
son,[79] a young man—all dear friends of mine—I have been here quite a
good deal the last year & a half, when they were all home—but now no
one but the father & myself here—I wish you could have two or three
good drives with me about here—we have a fast, strong, gentle young
sorrel mare—first rate—the roads & views are the finest you ever saw—&
now they show at their best—Yesterday (Sunday) afternoon & evening
seem'd to me one of the most perfect for weather &c I ever knew—we
drove out to a hill, about an hour from here, & had a view over twenty
miles towards Bethlehem—fields & farms & rolling country—some woods

76. George Edgar Montgomery reviewed Bucke's book on July 1 in the New York
Times and on July 7 in the Boston *Transcript*.
77. WW visited the Staffords from July 3 to 17 (CB).
78. WW stayed with Robert Pearsall Smith from August 4 to 28 (CB).
79. Alys and Logan.

—the richest tract in Pennsylvania. It was an hour before sundown. It was like Paradise. (It will have a good effect upon me the rest of the summer.)

Mont was in to see me ab't a week ago—By his acc't you must have a house full. I hope you keep up health & spirits—Love to Ruth—Ed also —(I havn't forgot those rides evenings off among the *pea-pickers*)—Respects to Messrs. Wyld and Edwards[80]—Nothing specially new with me— I am only middling well—seem to be getting clumsier than ever, more *loguey*—rheumatic & other ailments—My loss (money, dues, &c) I alluded to, from the letter rec'd when I was down there, is worse than I expected[81]—(I knew all the spring & early summer there would be *something*, for I was feeling too well & prosperous & *sassy*)—

If I could only feel well & sleep well, though (which I do not), I should not care a straw for pecuniary botherations & losses. What a beautiful ten days we have had past! I hope Ed's things are all turning out well. So good bye for this time, dear friend—

W W

Ruth, fatten up some o' them chickens & have 'em ready for early fall—

1228. *To William D. O'Connor*   *8.14.* [*1883*]

ENDORSED: "Answ'd Aug 17/83." ADDRESS: Wm D O'Connor | Life Saving Service | Treasury | Washington D C. POSTMARKS: Philadelphia | Aug | 14 | (?) PM; Washington, Recd. | Aug | 15 | 7 AM | 1883.

Germantown Aug: 14 Evn'g

Your good letter rec'd[82]—welcomed as always—I am out here this month with a valued Quaker friend, & enjoying the experience & visit much—Ample quiet country, house, large library, garden—the family (they too special friends of mine) all away at Newport—my friend down

80. WW noted during his stay at Glendale from July 3 to 17 "the rides over to 'Charlestown' with Ed. evenings to engage 'pea–pickers.' " Wyld and Edwards were Mrs. Stafford's boarders (CB).

81. What loss WW sustained at this time is not known, unless he referred to the 200 shares of stock he purchased on February 26 in the Sierra Grande mines at Lake Valley, New Mexico. According to a prospectus mounted in CB, shares in the company had a par value of $25. He received his first dividend ($50) on March 6, but he did not receive the second dividend, evidently payable on July 6, when he was with the Staffords, until October 3 (CB). Perhaps the delay in payment made him think that he had lost his money. He may have fabricated this story because Mrs. Stafford wanted to borrow money. He lent her $50 on October 24, 1882 (CB).

82. The letter O'Connor wrote on August 12 (see 1226) is apparently lost.

in Phila. at business bulk of the day—I alone here writing, reading, loafing—Then every afternoon a long drive about this beautiful, wonderful,
never-ending variety of country, the long Wissahickon, roads, Indian Rock,
Mt Airy, Chestnut Hill—I find I don't need to go to Rocky Mts. or
Saguenay for natural beauty or grandeur—I am well—nothing very new—

W W

Address me [at] Camden—I go in there every other day—

1229. To John Burroughs 8.21. [1883]

ADDRESS: John Burroughs | Esopus-on-Hudson | New
York. POSTMARK: Philadelphia | Aug | 21 | 6 PM |
Pa.

Germantown   Phila: Aug 21

Yours of 17th rec'd[83]—I am out here this month on a visit to an old
Quaker friend—very pleasant quarters & plenty of room (the family all
away at Newport)—A large garden, library, every afternoon a long
drive, &c. Nothing very new—I am middling well—hot weather here—no
special plans for the fall—it is 4½ P M & I am just going out for an
evening drive—

W W

1230. To Edward R. Pease [8.21. 1883][84]

ADDRESS: Edw: R Pease | 17 Osnaburgh Street |
Regents Park | London England. POSTMARK:
Camden | Aug | 21 | 4 PM | N.J.

431 Stevens Street | Camden   New Jersey
U S America

In response to yours of July 20. I have just mailed you my two

83. In his letter Burroughs commented on Bucke's book: "I cannot say that I care
much for what Dr. Bucke has to say; he gives me no new hint or idea" (Feinberg; Traubel,
I, 403). Evidently Burroughs did not recognize WW's hand in the book.

84. According to CB, WW sent the two books on August 2, but the postmark is
clearly August 21. Perhaps there was a delay in mailing because WW was staying with
Smith in Germantown.

In a letter to Professor Rollo G. Silver in 1934, Pease wrote: "I called on W. W.
in Camden in the winter (i.e. November or December) of 1888. He was ill in bed, & I
was only allowed to see him for 5 minutes. He was living in what my memory pictures as
almost a slum, & his bedroom was not exactly tidy. He spoke of the devotion of Americans
to the worship of the dollar, which surprised me, as his usual attitude in his writings is
patriotic, & laudatory of his compatriots." See also 1274.

Volumes, *Leaves of Grass* and *Specimen Days*—Won't you kindly send me a postal card, notifying me, soon as they reach you safely?

                                                          Walt Whitman

1231. *To John H. Johnston*

                                   Germantown   Phila: | Aug: 28 '83

Dear friend

    I have been out here 9 or 10 miles from Phil. City Hall all this month at a very secluded place—good quarters, very quiet—on a visit to an old Quaker friend—his large family are all away at Newport—he is absent all day down town at business—& I have the whole premises, house, horse & carriage when I want, large garden, library &c to myself—*good grub*—with every afternoon a long & delightful drive exploring this beautiful region for miles and miles, Chestnut Hill, Indian Rock, the whole Wissahickon area, &c &c.

    I have rec'd (June,[85] July, &c) your and Alma's hospitable & affectionate letters, invitations—& I ought to be kicked for not answering them before—but "you know what a wretch I am about such things"—never mind, *I appreciate them gratefully*—I am well as usual this summer—nothing very new ab't my books or literary fortunes—

    I shall make a permanent move from Camden before many months—as my brother's folks are ab't changing to new quarters at Burlington N J—& I shall not accompany them—I don't know where I shall go.

    What a glorious summer we have had!—Never one so fine, seems to me—Best love to you all—Specially Alma and Albert.

                                                          Walt Whitman

85. On June 13 Johnston invited WW to meet Grover Cleveland, then governor of New York and "a great admirer of Walt Whitman": "It will boom another edition for you sure, pop, and I hope you will come right over and smell the June roses with us" (Feinberg).

86. O'Connor's endorsement is incorrect. I have not found the letter he referred to.

87. See 916.

88. WW was not accurate. He sent Bucke's book to John H. Johnston and to John Swinton on July 19 (*CB*).

89. Benjamin R. Tucker was a translator and friend of Ruskin as well as an editor. On May 25, 1882, Tucker offered to act as WW's publisher in order to test the banning of *Leaves of Grass* (Feinberg; Traubel, II, 253-254). As editor of *Liberty*, he followed the Boston controversy closely in editorial comments on May 27, June 10, and July 22. In the July issue he printed an advertisement in which he offered to sell and mail *Leaves of Grass* to any purchaser, and informed Stevens, Marston, Tobey, and Comstock,

1232. To William D. O'Connor   8.29. [1883]

ENDORSED: "Answ'd Sept 4/82."[86] ADDRESS: Wm D
O'Connor | Life Saving Service | Treasury |
Washington D C. POSTMARKS: Philadelphia | Pa. |
Aug 29 83 | 6 30 PM; Washington, Recd. | Aug |
30 | 4 30 AM | 1883 | 2.

Camden Aug 29

Have finished my Germantown visit & am back here. I did not
send Dr B[ucke]'s book to Mrs. Ritter[87]—have indeed not sent copies to
any except my sisters and neices.[88] Mrs. Gilchrist, however, has a copy—
John Burroughs also has—Glad you sent one to Tucker[89]—he is a good
friend—I have not heard any thing more of Rolleston's German translation.[90] Dr Karl Knortz, cor: Morris av. & 155th st. New York City, has
translated many of my poems in German, & published them.[91] Do you
know the *Nation* is made up of *Evening Post* matter?

W W

1233. To Thomas Nicholson

Camden   New Jersey   U S A | Evn'g   Sept: 5 '83

Tommy,[92] your letter come to hand this evening, & I will just
scratch off a few lines to answer at once—for I am ever so glad to
know you have not forgot me, as I have not you, Tommy boy. I heard by
some London boy I met quite a while ago that you was married & I
supposed since you had your hands full of business, new associations &c.

Tom, I will just tell you about things—I still live in the same
quarters in Camden, but shall soon break up permanently from here. I
keep pretty well—feel as well as when I last saw you, & I suppose look ab't
the same—(perhaps grayer & redder)—though young enough *in spirit*

all of whom were mentioned by name, that he was willing to have his offer tested in the
courts. On August 19 he commented: "We have offered to meet the enemy, but the enemy declines to be met. . . . We still advertise the book for sale, and sell it openly and
rapidly." The advertisement appeared again on September 16.

90. On September 27 and again on November 22 Rolleston discussed problems
connected with his translation (Frenz, 77–78; Traubel, IV, 111–112). On October 14
WW sent Knortz's translations to Rolleston, and on December 10 noted receipt of his
friend's "lecture pamphlet, 'Wordsworth and WW' from Dresden [*Ueber Wordsworth
und Walt Whitman*]" (CB). A translation of Rolleston's lecture, prepared by Horace
Traubel's father and corrected by WW, appeared in the Camden *Daily Post* on February
13, 1884. WW's corrections in purple crayon appear in Traubel's manuscript in the
Feinberg Collection.

91. See 1223.

92. One of the young men whom WW met at Bucke's asylum (see 976).

& now in my 65th year, I could easily pass for 75 or so—Ups and downs of course, but I thank God I have had two pretty good years—& especially this past summer (which has been a remarkably fine one here.) My two books bring me in a moderate income[93]—I am satisfied with very plain living—& bless the Lord I am likely to have enough for that as long as I need—

Tom, give my best regards to your wife, for all I have no acquaintance with her yet—I wish to be remembered to any of the Asylum boys I knew there who yet remain—I remember well the kindness of them all, & the gay old rides around—Tom, do you recollect that Sunday evening you drove the women in town to church, & we had a sociable drive all around? —that was the time we first got acquainted—I have been thinking a good while of coming on to visit Dr Bucke again, & then I will come & see you[94]—God bless you, Tommy boy—Your old friend,

Walt Whitman

1234. To William D. O'Connor

ADDRESS: Wm D O'Connor | Life Saving Service | Treasury | Washington D C. POSTMARKS: Philadelphia | Pa. | Sep 6 (?) | 1 30 PM; Washington, Recd. | Sep | 7 | (?) | 1883 | 2.

Camden   Sept: 6 '83

Seems to me you couldn't do better—(let me suggest, if there is nothing in the way & you have no other imperative destination)—than to go on for a week or so & see Dr. B[ucke] at London—I know if you do go you will be glad you went.[95]

W W

93. On June 1 WW received from McKay $227.15 in royalties (Pennsylvania) and on December 5 $102.51 (CB). The sale of books was: 867 copies of *Leaves of Grass* and 558 copies of *Specimen Days* (Pennsylvania).

94. Though WW spoke frequently of visiting Bucke, he did not go to Canada after his journey in 1880.

95. WW's post card was written in answer to a letter from O'Connor on September 4 which is not extant (see 1232). Apparently O'Connor planned a vacation in order to recuperate after the death of his child. On August 19 Bucke urged O'Connor to visit Canada (LC).

96. WW's question mark. In his reply, dated September 14 by WW, Knortz wrote that Dr. Adolf Stodtmann (1829–1879) had translated eight of WW's "smaller

1235. *To Karl Knortz*

ADDRESS: Karl Knortz | Cor: Morris avenue | & 155th
Street | New York City. POSTMARKS: Philadelphia |
Pa. | Sep 11 83 | 3 PM; P. O. | 9–(?)–83 | (?)–1P |
N.Y.

431 Stevens Street   Camden   New Jersey |
Sept: 11 '83

In a note rec'd from you quite a while ago (from Johnstown, Pa:)
you mention some German translations of my poems by Dr ?[96] at Berlin
(since dead)—Would you please give me the *Dr's name exactly*—& some
particulars ab't the translations? Did you get Dr. Bucke's volume, which
was sent you June 21, last? I have received the translations into German, (slips, papers, &c) you have so kindly sent me from time to time[97]—
have not (otherwise) heard from you for some four months—I continue
(though a half paralytic) well as usual—

Walt Whitman

1236. *To William D. O'Connor*

ENDORSED: "Answ'd Sept. 22/83." ADDRESS: Wm D
O'Connor | Life Saving Service | Treasury |
Washington | D C. POSTMARKS: Philadelphia | Pa. |
Sep 13 83 | 8 30 PM; Washington, Recd. | Sep | 14 |
4 30 AM | 1883 | 2.

Camden, Sept 13   '83

Looking to-day over an old bundle, I find this curious letter which
I meant to have sent you at the time, but missed somehow—I am well as
usual—

W W

(Salt Lake City letter.)[98]

poems" in *Amerikanische Anthologie* (Leipzig, 1870), 149–154: "the late Doctor did
not, I am very sorry to say, give you a favorable introduction to the German public"
(Yale). Knortz also informed the poet that in his "critical history of American literature
. . . a whole chapter (about 20 printed pages) will be devoted to your poetry." This
book, *Geschichte der Nord Amerikanischen Literatur*, did not appear until 1891.
    97. See 1223.
    98. The letter referred to is not with the manuscript. WW wrote this note to
O'Connor on the envelope of the letter, which, according to the postmark, was received
in Camden on April 27. On September 22 O'Connor wrote: "I return your Salt Lake
City letter about Bacon and Shakespeare, having carefully read it twice. It seems quite
crazy—though maybe only crude—yet has some good points in it, which I took in" (LC;
Traubel, IV, 191).

1237. *To William D. O'Connor*   9.17. [1883]

ENDORSED: "Answ'd Sept. 18/83." ADDRESS: Wm D
O'Connor | Life Saving Service | Treasury |
Washington D C. POSTMARK: Philadelphia | Pa. |
Sep 17 83 | 2 30 PM.

Camden N J   Sept | 17

I wish you would send me (if you have it) the piece in the N Y
Evening Post of a while since—the subject of your letter—rejected by the
P. & by N Y *Times* also[99]—Which piece I will return you—Marvin[1] spent
Saturday afternoon last with me, & has posted me up about many
things. (*You* have an immense accepter & champion in M.)

W W

1238. *To William D. O'Connor*   [9.19. 1883]

ENDORSED: "Answ'd Sept 22/83." ADDRESS: Wm D
O'Connor | Life Saving Service | Treasury |
Washington | D C. POSTMARK: Philadelphia | Pa. |
Sep 19 83 | 1 30 PM.

offered for the Sunday Edition

about Walt Whitman
Dr Bucke's Book
To the Editor of the Sun

The following answer of mine to an article in the *Nation* of July 26
having been refused publication by that paper, it is sent to you, not in any
controversial spirit, but because the facts I give are of current interest, and
should be kept well before the American public, especially the New
York portion of it. Washington Sept: 1883

99. O'Connor wrote an answer to the review of Bucke's biography in *The Nation*
of July 26, the first sentence of which read: "This is an unadulterated eulogy by a man
of very little culture or critical ability." According to O'Connor's letter on September 18,
the New York *Times*, rejected it for " 'professional reasons' " (Syracuse; Traubel, IV,
394). Bucke, writing to O'Connor on December 16, said of the article in *The Nation*: "don't see anything in it to get mad about—do you get in a passion every time you
hear a hog grunt out of time? If so I fear, old man, you have a bad time" (LC).
1. Marvin's criticism of *Leaves of Grass* was reprinted in Bucke's book (163–
165).
2. Dana, the editor of the New York *Sun*, who was one of WW's early admirers
(see 10), rejected the article, according to O'Connor's post card of September 24 (Feinberg).
3. On September 18 O'Connor spoke of "a vague wandering notion of sending it
to *The Critic*," but "I felt rather deterred by the remembrance of [Joseph L.] Gilder's
unfriendly sport at me when I was fighting the contemptible clergyman, Chadwick, and

I suggest that you send it to the N. Y. *Sun* for their Sunday edition—with the preceding note—Dana I think is more or less friendly[2]—

1239. *To William D. O'Connor*   9.25. [*1883*]

ENDORSED: "Answ'd Dec 2/83." ADDRESS: Wm D
O'Connor | Life Saving Service | Washington D C.
POSTMARKS: Camden | Sep | 25 | 4 PM | N.J.;
Washington, Recd. | Sep | 26 | 5 AM | 1883 | 2.

Camden   Sept 25   (noon)

I *shouldn't* advise trying the C[ritic].[3] Let it go for the present. I have rec'd a cheery letter from C W E[ldridge]—says he has hung out his shingle as lawyer—but two or three lines in it squint at going into publishing yet[4]—John Burroughs is at Ocean Grove N.J. temporarily for sanitary purposes.[5] A bright, sunny glorious day here as I write—

W W

1240. *To William D. O'Connor*   9.30. [*1883*]

ENDORSED: "Answ'd Dec 2/83." ADDRESS: Wm D
O'Connor | Life Saving Service | Treasury |
Washington | D C. POSTMARKS: Philadelphia, Pa. |
Oct | 1 | 11 AM | Transit; Washington, Recd. | Oct |
2 | 4 30 AM | 1883 | 2.

Ocean Grove N J   Sept: 30.

I have been down here the past week right on the sea[6]—am on the beach quite all day & the surf sings me to sleep every night. John Burroughs is here—he leaves to-morrow morning for N Y, but I shall stay a

---

was so clearly in the right" (Syracuse; Traubel, IV, 395).

4. Eldridge, who had lost his governmental position because of "an uncircumcized dog," and was about to establish a law practice in Boston, wrote to WW on September 22: "I am still in the prime of life, have health, some means and many friends, and if under these circumstances I did not cheerfully accept the situation I should be unworthy ever to have read Leaves of Grass, with its philosophy of hope and the morning" (Yale). O'Connor, as indicated in his letter to WW of September 22, wanted Eldridge to re-enter the publishing business, "so that we might start a magazine, and make it pleasant for the bats and owls and literary carrion generally, but he appears to have abandoned the idea" (LC; Traubel, IV, 191–192).

5. On September 21 Burroughs invited WW to join him at the seashore (Feinberg).

6. WW stayed at the Sheldon House at Ocean Grove from September 26 to October 10 (CB, and see Allen, 512–514). Before leaving Camden, WW met Simon B. Conover (1840–1908), a former senator from Florida, at Scovel's on September 16, and on September 23 he had dinner at Conover's (CB).

few days longer. Am stopping at the Sheldon House & like it well—very quiet here—fine weather—

W W

1241. *To Truman Howe Bartlett*[7]   [*10.14. 1883*]

ADDRESS: T H Bartlett | sculptor | 394 Federal
Street | Boston Mass:. POSTMARKS: Camden | Oct |
(?) | 5 PM | N.J.; Philadelphia, Pa. | Oct | 14 |
7 PM | Transit.

Rec'd your letter—I send three photo's by same mail with this—is the profile one something like what you want? I don't know but I have already sent you the front face with hand up, as I designed one for you—but as I am not certain I send this—I have just returned from two weeks down along the Jersey sea beach, & am well as usual—always glad to hear from you—hope we shall be together again one of these days—give my best love to Mrs. F[airchild] and to B[oyle] O'R[eilly][8]—

W W

1242. *To Harry Stafford*   *10.22.* [*1883*]

Camden   Oct: 22   Evn'g

Dear Harry

The spirit moves me to scribble off a few lines to you—but I don't know why, for I have no news to tell & nothing particular to write about any how. I returned to-day from a three days visit to my Quaker friends at Germantown—they have tip top horses & carriage, & we had good long drives Saturday afternoon & Sunday towards evening after the rain—After supper, & the things are removed, we all sit around the table—we sometimes keep it up an hour & a half—& have a good talk & discussions, & accounts of any thing that has occurred during the day, & somebody has questions to put or information to glean—perhaps some little recitation or singing, a good lot of us—eight or nine altogether—there are two just

7. Bartlett (1835–1923), an instructor in modelling at the Massachusetts Institute of Technology, was characterized by William Vaughan Moody as "a magnificent old goat and man of God . . . passing hours with immortal phrases"; see Herman Hagedorn, *Edwin Arlington Robinson* (1938), 254. Bartlett evidently affected the Whitman pose with his open collar and flowing tie. On June 8, 1884(?), Bartlett informed WW that "the cast of your hand I shall soon send to Paris to be cast in bronze" (LC). The plaster cast is in the Feinberg Collection; a bronze cast is at Yale. Probably WW met him at Colonel Johnston's studio on September 1, 1878 (CB).
8. Mrs. Charles Fairchild, wife of Colonel Fairchild, the president of a paper company, to whom WW sent the Centennial Edition on March 2, 1876 (CB). He mailed

grown daughters, as nice and jolly and 'cute as young women can be—one son—& always three or four others—making a good time—Sunday morning, they have family prayers—I was requested to read a chapter from the testament—(the Sermon on the Mount)—*which I did*—(I wish you could have all seen & heard me)—I never beheld such a merry, affectionate, hearty healthy family—nobly, too—

With me, this fall, everything just floats idly along, as far as writing and work are concerned—Down there at Ocean Grove and along Barnegat &c. I was moved to write a poem *on the ocean*[9]—I have turned it & turned it & rewritten it over & over again—but cant get it to suit me yet—Harry, how is it with you? & why didnt you come & tell me—before you left the printing offices here? Write me a line soon as you get this[10]—Sometimes I think you must be sick—

I am about as usual—I am writing this after 9 at night up in my room, sitting in the big ratan chair.

God bless you, Harry dear—

W W

1243. *To John Burroughs*   [*10(?).(?). 1883*][11]

TRANSCRIPT.

[WW had enjoyed his stay at Ocean Grove. He referred to the "long & friendly notices" in the September issue of *The Scottish Review* and in *The Academy* of September 8, the latter written by Dowden.]

1244. *To Jeannette L. and Joseph B. Gilder*

431 Stevens Street | Camden, New Jersey | Nov. 23, '83

My friends

I am puzzled considerably—Nov 12 I sent you from here the proof of "Eminent Visitors"[12]—See by the paper of 17th the errors I marked

her husband a copy of *Progress* in April, 1881, shortly after his visit to Boston, where he probably met the Fairchilds for the first time (*CB*). For O'Reilly, see 1027.
    9. "With Husky-Haughty Lips, O Sea" (see 1247).
    10. Harry called on WW on October 30 (*CB*).
    11. This letter, or note, must have been written shortly after WW left Ocean Grove on October 10 (*CB*). The *Scottish Review* discussed both of WW's books, Rossetti's selection of 1868, Burroughs' study, and Bucke's work (II, 281–300). In "A Salt Breeze," in *Outing and the Wheelman*, III (January, 1884), 275–279, Burroughs referred to WW as a poet of the sea.
    12. "Our Eminent Visitors (Past, Present, and Future)," *The Critic*, III (November 17, 1883), 459–460.

were not corrected—Same note I requested some proof slips of the E. V. article—None have reached me. Nov: 19 I wrote you (reiterating the above &) saying as I could probably not now be furnished with proof slips I would like a dozen copies of the paper—No response to either of the letters—Didnt they reach you?[13]

Walt Whitman

1245. *To George and Susan Stafford*   *12.1.* [1883]

ADDRESS: [G]eorge and Susan M. Stafford |
Kirkwood | (Glendale) | New Jersey. POSTMARK:
Ca[md]en | Dec | 1 | 12 M | N.J.

Camden   Dec: 1st   noon

I suppose Harry has written to you[14]—Still I will send you this for good measure—What H speaks of the "unearthly noises" &c. he will get used to in two or three days—it is like living near a railroad—I am well as usual—

WW

1246. *To Thomas Donaldson*[15]

TRANSCRIPT.

Camden | December 2, 1883

["Acknowledging receipt of an invitation to the reception of Henry Irving, which he declines; and expressing a wish to call on Donaldson soon."]

---

13. These letters are not known. The envelope of the letter written on November 17 is in the Feinberg Collection.

14. Harry Stafford was in London, Ontario, with Dr. Bucke (see 1248).

15. Donaldson, a Philadelphia lawyer, was the author of *Walt Whitman, the Man* (1896). WW noted meeting Donaldson, then an agent for the Smithsonian Institute, on October 10, 1882, and characterized him as "my stout, gentlemanly friend, free talker" (*CB*). WW had supper with the Donaldsons on December 4—"a very enjoyable evening, warm hospitality—fine children" (*CB*). Irving described a visit to Camden in *The Theatre*, v (April, 1885), 178–179.

16. On December 16 Bucke informed O'Connor that the book had sold "250 or 300" copies (LC).

17. Bucke came to Camden on November 5 and again on November 27 and 28, when the poet and he visited Robert Pearsall Smith (*CB*).

18. WW was in error: "Our Eminent Visitors (Past, Present, and Future)" appeared in *The Critic* on November 17.

1247. *To William D. O'Connor*   *12.3.* [*1883*]

ENDORSED: "Answ'd January 13/84." ADDRESS:
Wm D O'Connor | Life Saving Service—Treasury |
Washington D C. POSTMARKS: Philadelphia | (?) |
Dec 3 83 | 10 30 PM; Washington, D.C. | Dec 4 |
7 AM | 1883 | Recd.

Camden   Dec. 3   Evn'g
Yours rec'd & welcomed—will write at length soon—(meantime this card)—Dr B[ucke]'s book has some sale all the time—nothing
vehement, but the orders drop in lingeringly[16]—yesterday ten copies from
Trübner London, &c. &c. My opinion that the book is *a success* (in the
most important requisites) is to-day more decided than ever—*largely
thanks to you.* Dr B has been in N. Y. for a month—has been twice here
to see me.[17] Did you see my article in *Critic* of Nov. 24?[18] I have lately sent
a little 20 line poem to *Harpers*—accepted immediately & paid for
($50!)[19]—I am well as usual—write often—

W W

I sent your letter to Dr. B—he always wants to hear from you—

1248. *To Harry Stafford*   *12.8.* [*1883?*]

TRANSCRIPT.

Camden. Saturday night, Dec. 8
. . . It is dark & foggy & miserable outside weather—but I have
had a good supper & am sitting up here feeling jolly & thankful enough
(yet a little lonesome) . . .[20]

19. "With Husky-Haughty Lips, O Sea" was published in *Harper's Monthly* in
March, 1884. Henry M. Alden, the editor, accepted the poem on November 30 (Feinberg; Traubel, II, 220). WW began to write the piece while he was at Ocean Grove
(Traubel, I, 406; Barrus, 245).
20. Since WW wrote several post cards to Harry after he went to Canada, probably the fragment reproduced here was sent at this time, since December 8 fell on Saturday in 1883. In a letter to WW from Canada on November 28, Harry complained of his
work as "turnkey" in Bucke's asylum, asked for letters of recommendation, and concluded: "Your boy is away among strangers and a good long letter from his dear friend
will do him good" (Feinberg). On December 17 Harry asserted: "I am *determined* to
make a hit somewhere and dont forget it. I havent had a blue spell yet and think I can
get along without any . . . With lots of love and a good old time kiss I am ever your
boy Harry" (Feinberg). According to his letter to his father on January 12, 1884, Harry
was reading Haeckel and Darwin, but was not satisfied with his position at the hospital:
"The rules of the Asylum are absurdly strict and of a military form" (letter in possession
of the Stafford family).

1249. *To William D. O'Connor*

ENDORSED: "Answ'd Jan 13/84." ADDRESS: Wm D.
O'Connor | Life Saving Service—Treasury |
Washington | D. C. POSTMARKS: Camden | Dec |
9 | 5 PM | (?); Washington, D.C. | Dec (?) | 4 AM |
1883 | Recd.

Camden N J   Dec 9 '83

A young workingman & engineer, Edward Doyle, (brother of my dear friend Peter D.)[21] may call on you, before long, to see what chance if any for employment. He is healthy, strong, intelligent for a laboring man—no bad habits—single—hails from Washington. I am well as usual—Nothing new—I send you a paper—

W W

1250. *To Mary Whitall Smith*   12.11. [1883]

ADDRESS: Miss Mary W Smith | 4653 Germantown
Avenue | Philadelphia. POSTMARK: Philadelphia |
Pa. | Dec 11 83 | 10 30 PM.

Camden   Dec 11

Dear friend

Your father's kind note & yours recd—Yes with pleasure—I'll be there by 6 Saturday Evn'g.[22]

Walt Whitman

1251. *To O. S. Baldwin*

431 Stevens Street | Camden   New Jersey |
Dec. 15 '83

Dear Sir

In compliance with your letter of 12th I send a piece herewith[23]— It *is indispensable that I shall see the proof*—if convenient set it up & send me proof any time during next week. I reserve the right of publishing (including) the piece in future book—I shall want 30 papers.

Very respectfully &c
Walt Whitman

21. Doyle spent the afternoon of December 7 with WW (CB). He visited the poet again on June 4, 1884. When Doyle's mother was dying, on May 23, 1885, WW sent $10, and he lent Doyle $15 when he came to Camden on June 4, 1885 (CB). In the 1870's Edward Doyle, like Peter, had been a streetcar conductor.
22. WW was with the Smiths from December 15, Saturday, to December 17 (CB).
23. WW sent "An Indian Bureau Reminiscence" to *Baldwin's Monthly*, published by "Baldwin, the Clothier"; it was printed in February, 1884, and was reprinted in *To-*

1252. *To O. S. Baldwin*

ADDRESS: O S Baldwin | N E cor: Broadway &
Canal | New York City. POSTMARKS: Philadelphia |
Pa. | Dec 18 83 | 2 30 PM; P. O. | 12–18–83 | 9 P |
N.Y.

Camden New Jersey | December 18 '83

Yours of 17th with the pay ($10) for my piece has come safely to hand & the money is hereby receipted—

Walt Whitman

1253. *To George and Susan Stafford*   *12.21.* [*1883*]²⁴

Camden   Dec 21

Dear friends

Although I suppose you hear from Harry I will send you this letter rec'd by me last evn'g as it may interest you—I am about as usual. Susan, I rec'd your letter & was glad to get it. I am writing a little. The wintry weather & bad traveling keep me in more than I like—

Merry Christmas to you & George & all—

W W

Susan, I enclose an envelope with the right direction so you can write to Harry—

1254. *To Mannahatta and Jessie Louisa Whitman*

ADDRESS: Mannahatta | and | Jessie L Whitman | 2511
Second Carondelet avenue | St Louis | Missouri.
POSTMARK: Philadelphia | Pa. | Dec 28 83 | 7 PM.

Camden N J   Dec. 28   Evn'g

Dear neices²⁵

I have received the beautiful book-knife—Just the thing, & will be in my hands every day—All well here—

Uncle Walt

Day in May, 1884.

24. Since Harry Stafford wrote to WW on December 17 from London, Ontario, and since he enclosed an addressed envelope, the year would appear to be 1883 (see 1248).

25. Mannahatta and Jessie, Jeff's daughters, had visited Camden in August of this year, had gone to see Hannah Heyde in Burlington, Vt., and had returned to St. Louis at the end of November (CB).

1255. *To John H. Johnston*

Camden   Dec 29 '83 | Noon

Dear friend

Yours rec'd—The little poem you speak of was sent to *Harpers*, accepted at once & paid for[26]—when it will appear I know not—

I am well as usual. Don't know why I have not come on to N Y to visit you—but I think of you all—you, Alma & Ally[27]—with the same old love, & shall be with you again before long. John, I am *not* favorable to the select extracts plan you mentioned four or five weeks ago—Get the next *Baldwin's Monthly*—it has a little reminiscence of mine in it[28]—

I go out to Germantown quite frequently—have some very good Quaker friends there—long rides every afternoon[29]—A spell of real winter here, cold, snow, fog, &c—but bright and sunny to-day as I write.

Happy New Years to all—

Walt Whitman

1256. *To Mary Whitall Smith*

ADDRESS: Miss Mary W Smith | 4653 Germantown Avenue | Germantown | Philadelphia. POSTMARK: Camden | Dec | 30 | 5(?) PM | N.J.

Camden   Dec. 30 '83

Dear friend

I send you the picture I spoke of—it is an artist's proof & I mounted it myself. Happy New Years to you, & Alice & all.

Walt Whitman

---

26. "With Husky-Haughty Lips, O Sea" (see 1247).
27. Johnston's son, Albert.
28. "An Indian Bureau Reminiscence" (see 1251). WW published "Some Diary Notes at Random" in *Baldwin's Monthly* in December, 1885, for which he received $10 (CB).
29. WW was with the Smiths from December 15 to 17. He stayed with Francis H. Williams (1844–1922), a poet and dramatist, from December 22 to 26 (CB and 1257). Note also Traubel, II, 341, and *Proceedings of the New Jersey Historical Society*, LXXIII (1955), 298–299.

1884

1257. *To Harry Stafford*

Camden   Wednesday Evn'g   Jan 2 '84

Dear Son & Comrade

I have got word from you once or twice[1]—& glad to hear that you keep well & in good spirits—that's more than half the battle—& I'm sure its the *best half* too—I got a letter from Dr B[ucke] to-day—he mentions you in it, & speaks very friendlily indeed of you—I also rec'd a letter from your mother to-day, which I will enclose, as every thing from home is welcome, (even if she has written already to you, as is very likely)—I have written to your mother this evening—

I jog along very much in the old way—am pretty well, so far this winter—(they say I am fatter & more red-faced than ever)—I spent my Christmas over in Germantown at Mr and Mrs Williams's,[2] new friends, very nice, & a big family of children—was there four days—had a jolly time—a sleigh ride, or two—fine traveling, but too cold to enjoy it—Ruth and Burt[3] were up here to see me last week—Ruth is going to make a fine looking woman, & good-sized, like her mother (*Shape first, face afterward*, was the saying of a old sport I used to know)—I met Ed Stafford (John's son)[4] yesterday at the ferry—he asked about you—the boys are all curious to know about you—all wish you luck, sincerely—Well good bye for the present, my darling boy—Keep a good heart—we will be together yet & have good times yet—(I shall break up from here in the Spring & leave Camden—I don't know where)[5]—

Walt Whitman

1884
    1.   Harry was with Dr. Bucke in London, Ontario (see 1248).
    2.   See 1255.
    3.   Ruth was Harry's sister. I have not identified "Burt."
    4.   John Stafford (1825–1900), a cousin of Mr. Stafford, had a son named Edmund (1860–1939).
    5.   Since George was shortly to move to Burlington, N.J., WW had to make new living arrangements. According to O'Connor's letter to WW on February 22, the poet evidently discussed with Burroughs the possibility of going to Esopus (Yale).

1258. *To Jeannette L. and Joseph B. Gilder*

ADDRESS: J L & J B Gilder | *Critic* office | 20 Lafayette
Place | New York City. POSTMARK: Philadelphia |
Pa. | Jan 11 84 | 5 30 PM; P.O. | 1–11–84 | 12
(?) | N.Y.

Camden   Jan: 10 '84

The slips rec'd, (thanks) of course making it unnecessary for you
to send the ten copies C[ritic]—But did you mail the five copies of paper
to the addresses?⁶ Send me a postal telling me.

Walt Whitman

If not already mailed, you need *not* do it—I will attend to it—

1259. *To Karl Knortz*

431 Stevens Street | Camden New Jersey | Jan: 10 '84

Dear Sir

Yes, I have rec'd the Dresden pamphlet⁷—I enclose you a late article of mine from the *Critic*⁸—I keep about as usual in health this winter—
How do you get on with your new book?

Walt Whitman

1260. *To William D. O'Connor*   [*1.11. 1884*]

ENDORSED: "Answ'd Jan 13/84." ADDRESS: Wm D
O'Connor | Life Saving Service Treasury |
Washington | D C. POSTMARKS: Philadelphia | Pa. |
Jan 11 84 | 5 30 PM; Washington, D.C. | Jan 12 |
4 AM | 1884 | Recd.

I am about as usual—Havn't heard from you in quite a while⁹—
How are you getting along? Terrible weather here—I still go out to Ger-

6. WW on December 21, 1883, sent, "A Backward Glance on My Own Road"
to *The North American Review* and asked $40; it was returned. He then sent the piece
to *The Critic* on December 27 and requested $12, and it was printed on January 5,
1884 (CB). When the magazine failed to send, as requested, copies of the article to
Dowden, Symonds, Schmidt, Rolleston, and O'Connor, WW sent them himself on January 9 or thereabouts (CB). The article was later incorporated into "A Backward Glance
o'er Travel'd Roads" (NB, 5–18).
    7. Rolleston's lecture (see 1232).
    8. "A Backward Glance on My Own Road."
    9. O'Connor's last letter was evidently written on September 24 (Feinberg). WW
wrote this note on an offprint of "A Backward Glance on My Own Road." O'Connor's

mantown frequently—Did you get any "Eminent Visitors" article in *Critic* of Nov. 17 last? If not I will send you one.

1261. *To T. W. H. Rolleston*

ADDRESS: T W Rolleston | 28 Terrassen Ufer | Dresden | Saxony. POSTMARKS: (?) Paid | (?); Dresden (?)ltst. | 62 | 94(?) | 12–P N.

Camden New Jersey U S America | Jan. 22 '84—
Yours of New Year's day rec'd, with K[nortz]'s translations[10]—
I send you a little paper—Yes, I know Edward Carpenter—I am well as usual—A severe winter here—have had fine sleigh-rides, & enjoyed them—or some days on the river, the Delaware, on our powerful steam ferry-boat, pressing & crashing through the heavy ice.

Walt Whitman

1262. *To Harry Stafford*   2.10. *[1884]*

Camden   Sunday P M   Feb 10[11]

Dear Harry
At the request of your mother & from what you wrote some time ago I bundled up all the old letters I could find, & Edward Stafford[12] stopt here & took them to her—this is over a week ago, (Ed still comes up here to school in Phila. to learn bookkeeping)—I believe your folks are all as usual—but I suppose you have heard from there, latest particulars. I am jogging along pretty much the same as ever—was to the theatre last week, & enjoyed it, "Francesca da Rimini"—lots of love-making & hugging in the play, done first rate—I quite fell in love with the lady actress (Mary Wainwright)[13]—the actors spied me in front, & sent around to ask me to come behind the scenes, which I did at the end of the play,

reply on January 13 is not known.
    10. WW sent Knortz's translations from *Leaves of Grass* to Rolleston on October 14 (*CB*). In his letter of January 1 Rolleston asked WW about Carpenter, whose *Towards Democracy* (1883) he was reading (LC; Frenz, 81–82).
    11. The year is confirmed by the notes below. February 10 fell on Sunday in 1884. Stafford was still in Canada with Bucke (see 1248). On February 10 he informed the poet that he was suffering from an "abcess in my neck," and asked for a letter of introduction to any one WW knew in Detroit: "Don't get the blues worth a dam and don't aspect to" (Feinberg). See 1267.
    12. Possibly Edward L. Stafford, son of Richard C. Stafford, or perhaps WW meant Edmund D. Stafford (see 1257).
    13. Marie (not Mary) Wainwright.

& was made much of, especially by Barrett the star—was invited to go with him to the Continental to supper—which I declined[14]—

I am doing a little in writing—have a little poem in Harpers for March, forthcoming, which I will send you[15]—(I sent you the Indian piece,[16] I believe)—When you get ready to go on further, or to any Western city, or anywhere, I will furnish you with a general letter of recommendation, if you wish it—may serve to break the ice, possibly, somewhere. I suppose you get the Camden & other papers I send—

For over a month now we have had rough winter weather here—lately rain & fog, most a week—but to-day is bright & fine—I am sitting up in the 3d story room, Stevens street, in the afternoon sun writing this—Glad you write to me in such good spirits, & are well—*they two are every thing*—Keep on—explore the big western cities, Chicago, Cincinnati, St Louis—Denver—even to California—it will do you good to see the actual world, & men & affairs—God bless you, dear boy—

W W

1263. *To Herbert Gilchrist*

431 Stevens St. | Camden N J, U S A | Feb 12 '84

Dear Herb

Thanks for your affectionate letter—(thank your dear mother also for hers—a most welcome one)[17]—Nothing special or new to write about —health & every thing go on with me ab't as usual—I enclose a *piece* of cloth[18]—cannot find a coat that I think would serve you, (which is the garment I suppose you most want)—Dr Bucke has told me of a picture he got from you, he prizes immensely—I havn't seen it—Write whenever you can, dear boy, & I will to you—

Walt Whitman

14. WW noted this performance in CB on January 30: "B[arrett] sent for me behind the stage & I went at the close of the play & had a short interview with him in his dressing room. Acting good, especially Francesca's and her lover's." Lawrence Barrett (1838–1891), an American actor, was noted for his Shakespearean roles.
15. "With Husky-Haughty Lips, O Sea."
16. "An Indian Bureau Reminiscence."
17. Herbert's letter is not known. Apparently WW referred to Mrs. Gilchrist's letter of October 13–21 (LC; Harned, 220–222).
18. On January 26 Mrs. Gilchrist asked Louisa Whitman for an old suit of WW's which would be of use to her son for a painting entitled "The Poet's Tea Party," in which

1264. *To George and Susan Stafford*   *2.14. [1884]*

Camden   Feb. 14   P M

Dear friends

I send the within letter just rec'd from Harry[19]—I am about as usual, & nothing new in my affairs. Susan, this will be a mean short letter this time—better luck next time—It is heavy and bad outside, the wind blowing a gale—(I should like to put on my overshoes & old overcoat & *go off in the woods* for an hour or two)—

I havn't heard from Deb[20]—I hope she is all right—Well, bad as the weather is, I must up & go out & across the river, or I shall have the horrors. The Lord A'mighty bress[21] you all—good bye.

W W

1265. *To Robert Pearsall Smith*   *3.4. [1884]*

ADDRESS: R Pearsall Smith | 410 Race Street | Philadelphia | Lock Box | P. POSTMARK: Camden | Mar(?) | (?) | (?)M | N.J.

Camden   March 4   P M[22]

Thanks for your dear kind note of last week—I have been quite ill —the doctor says mainly a lesion or trouble, (physical,) brain centre, other botherations too—but as I write this towards evening I have the very definite feeling of the worst having passed, & that I shall be better in a day or two—I feel so to-day already—& soon about as usual—

No, my friend, there is nothing you can specially do for me (I should frankly tell you, if there was.) Mary's and Logan's visit Sunday through the storm was a real comfort to me—(more a help than they knew.) I wish dear Alys would take the earliest convenient opportunity to give my excuses & love to Mr and Mrs: Williams, and Churchy[23]—I have had this trouble on me now for over three weeks—

It is very lonesome here—If I had not been born with a happy-tending

appeared WW, Mrs. Gilchrist, Grace, and Herbert; see Amy Haslam Dowe, "A Child's Memories of the Whitmans" (unpublished). See also Harned, 223.

19. Harry's letter of February 10 (see 1262).
20. Mrs. Stafford's daughter, Deborah Browning.
21. A Negro expression; compare Melville's *The Confidence-Man* (1955), 22: "God bress 'em."
22. WW noted this letter in *CB*. He became ill on February 17 and was not able to leave the house until March 4. See also 1266.
23. F. Churchill Williams is cited in *CB;* evidently he was a brother of Francis H. Williams (see 1255).

natural disposition (I inherit it from my mother) the last few weeks—yes the last ten years—would have been unmitigated darkness & heaviness to me—As it is, the ennuyeed hours have been the rare exceptions—

Then about the shows of life & my experience in them I am deeper & deeper impressed the older I grow that

the real something has yet to be known—

It is well I am physically ballasted so strong, with weightiest animality & appetites, or I should go off in a balloon—Well luckily for you, my friend, I have come to the end of the paper—

W W

1266. *To Robert Pearsall Smith*   *3.10. [1884]*

ADDRESS: R Pearsall Smith | 4653 Germantown
Avenue | Philadelphia. POSTMARKS: Camden | Mar |
11 | 7 AM | 1884 | N.J.; Philad[elphia,] Pa | Mar |
11 | 8 AM | Recd.

Camden   March 10   Evn'g
I am getting better—slowly but decidedly—my young friend died yesterday at noon[24]—

W W

1267. *To George and Susan Stafford*   [*3.13. 1884*][25]

Camden | Thursday   4 afternoon
Thank you for the nice chicken—had some for my dinner—was glad to see Van & to hear from you all—

I am getting over my bad spell of health—but very slowly—& have been depressed a great deal by the sudden taking down & death by hasty consumption of a dear friend, a young man in his 19th year—I was there all Saturday and Sunday—till he died ab't noon—I hadn't been out of

---

24. On March 8 WW spent "all the day & evening" with Tasker Lay, who, when the poet met him in 1881, was "15 or 16." The young man died on the following day and was buried on March 12 (CB). About this time WW gave the boy's grandfather, Alfred, a laborer, various sums of money, including $16 for the rent due on the house at 328 Mickle Street (see CB and 1268). The Lays rented the house at the time (Allen, 516). According to entries in CB, WW paid Mrs. Lay $2 weekly from April 5 to September 27.

Smith called on WW on March 8—"earnest & friendly, deeply so" (CB). In May Dr. Bucke stayed with Smith, and during his visit there was discussion of a "project for the special ed'n L of G. backed by Mr. S. and Dr.   Mr S's sudden & peremptory withdrawal from the project (Mrs. S 'wouldn't allow the book to be brought in the house')" (CB). Evidently Mrs. Smith's censure did not extend to the poet himself since she and

the house for three weeks, before—& was only able to get there with as-sistance—he sent for me to be with him—The funeral was yesterday afternoon—I did not intend to go to the cemetery & burial, but his father wished me to so earnestly, I went—So all these things hang like a cloud for a while—but I shall without doubt soon be nearly as usual—(though I think likely a little weaker & clumsier [consequently?]).[26]

I have got to get out of this house too, & very soon—for the new tenants take possession April 1. Don't know yet what move I shall make—but shall have to do something in a few days—If it hadn't been for my sick spell should have been out before this—I will let you know—(most likely shall come down & tell you myself)[27]—

I am sorry I missed Harry—I want to see him & have him with me—was in hopes he would come up in the Friday (or Saturday) morning train—& still have some hopes—but I have just rec'd his postal card from Haddonfield that he would try to come up early next week—I send him my best love, & always welcome[28]—

Susan, I rec'd your good letter—If we only lived near, so I could come in & spend a couple of hours every day or two I know it would do me good—Harry, come up soon—

W W

1268. *To John Burroughs*   *3.27.* [*1884*]

ADDRESS: John Burroughs | Esopus-on-Hudson | New York. POSTMARKS: Camden | Mar | 27 | 8 PM | 1884 | N.J.; P. O. | 3-28-84 | 4-1A | N.Y.

328 Mickle street | Camden New Jersey   March 27

I am getting well towards my usual (late year) state of health—have had a bad time ever since I saw you in Phila[29]—my own illness, con-finement to the house (a chilly, stagnant lonesome three weeks)—sudden sickness & death, (hasty consumption) of a young fellow I was much at-tached to, a near neighbor, & now the flitting—I moved yesterday (above

her daughters on his birthday sent sheets and a bolster (see 1275).
    25. Since Tasker Lay was buried on Wednesday, March 12, this letter can be positively dated.
    26. The ink is smeared and only "uently" is clear. Perhaps WW wrote "sub-sequently."
    27. See the following letter.
    28. According to Harry's letter on February 10 he expected to go to Detroit about March 1 (Feinberg). Apparently he changed his mind suddenly, for in *CB* on March 8 WW wrote, "Harry S. left London, Canada—now in Detroit," but later interpolated after "Canada"—"for home in N. J."
    29. Apparently WW saw Burroughs shortly before he became ill on February 17. Burroughs was in Washington when O'Connor wrote to WW on February 22 (Yale).

address) & shall remain here for the present[30]—it is half way nearer the ferry—write—

W W

1269. *To John H. Johnston*

Camden   March 27, 1884

[WW acknowledged receipt of a letter and some money from his friend.][31]

1270. *To Anne Gilchrist*

ADDRESS: Mrs: Anne Gilchrist | 12 Well Road— Hampstead | London England. POSTMARK: Camden | Apr | 21 | 7 AM | 1884 | N.J.

328 Mickle Street | Camden New Jersey—
U S America | April 20, '84—Evn'g

Yours of April 5th just recd, & *very much welcomed*[32]—Some how it is a special comfort—I have not been well as usual for two months but am now better & shall soon be ab't as of late years—I have moved into a little old shanty of my own—(See new address above)—am much more contented—am writing this impromptu at P. O. so you will get it at once. Will write more fully soon—best love—

W W

30. On March 27 WW wrote in *CB:* "Am writing this in my new premises in Mickle Street—slept here last night—the plumbers are here at work at gas & water fixings, & the carpenter—Mr and Mrs Lay." On April 3 he "paid $1750 cash for the premises 328 Mickle Street, Camden, to Rebecca Jane Hare, & took the deed, which I left at the Register's office to be recorded" (*CB*). WW had royalties from the Philadelphia editions amounting to $1250, and he borrowed $500 from George W. Childs (Traubel, I, 291).

The bill of sale, in WW's hand, is in the Walt Whitman House at Camden: "Camden, March 19, 1884, Received Sixteen dollars from Mrs: Lay, the rent in advance for house in Mickle St.—It is understood that if Mr Whitman before the end of April buys the house, this $16 is to be deducted from the price $1800. | R Jennie Hare" "I agree to sell Walt Whitman the premises 328 Mickle Street for Seventeen Hundred and Fifty Dollars cash instead of 1800 dollars. | R Jenne Hare"

Howe's Camden City Directory for 1883 listed as the occupant at 328 Mickle Street Mrs. Ellen Hare, a dressmaker and a widow. No mention of "R Jennie" or "Rebecca Jane" appears in the directories in the 1880's.

On March 23 WW handed his sister-in-law a "rough statement" of the sums paid to her for board from June, 1873, to March, 1884, a period of 560 weeks, during which time he was not in Camden for 143 weeks. The total paid was $1501—"ab't $3.60 a week for the time boarded" (*CB*).

31. Johnston visited WW shortly before he moved to Mickle Street and at that time arranged to purchase Hine's portrait of the poet for $200. On March 25 Johnston

1271. *To T. W. H. Rolleston* [*4.22(?). 1884*]

ENDORSED: "April 22 '84—Sent to Rolleston |
Dresden, to put in his | preface." DRAFT LETTER.

I thought I would write a brief endorsement of your friendly enterprise, translating and publishing in Germany, some of the poems of my
Leaves of Grass.[33] It has not been for my own country alone—ambitious
as the saying so may seem—that I have composed that work. It has been
to practically start an internationality of poems. The final aim of the
United States of America is[34] the solidarity of the world. What fails so
far, may yet be accomplished by song, radiating, clustering, concentrating
from all the lands of the earth, into a new chorus and diapason. One
purpose of my chants is to cordially salute all foreign lands in America's
name. And happy, most happy shall I be, to gain entrance and hearing
among the great Germanic peoples.

1272. *To Charles W. Eldridge*

328 Mickle Street | Camden New Jersey | May 7 '84
Charley, you would do me a special service if you could get &
send me a good photo (or other picture) of *Father Taylor, the old sailor
preacher.* I want it to be engraved for a magazine article[35]—Picture will be
returned—also find out for me when Father T died—No particular
hurry—but hope you will be able to help me soon as convenient—

sent $100 (Feinberg; Traubel, III, 331). On August 10 WW noted receipt of an addi-
tional $25 (*CB*). (There is a check from Johnston for this amount, dated July 2, 1884,
however, in the Feinberg Collection). For Johnston's other payments see also 1302 and
1305.

32. In her letter of April 5 Mrs. Gilchrist mentioned "wistful thoughts" that, "were
not I & mine bound here by unseverable ties, . . . could I make America my home for
the sake of being near you in body as I am in heart & soul—but Time has good things
in store for us sooner or later" (LC; Harned, 223). She also wrote on May 2, August 5,
October 26, and December 17 (LC; Harned, 225–232).

33. After receiving Rolleston's letter of April 5, in which he spoke of his plans to
publish excerpts from *Leaves of Grass* and in which he asked for WW's authorization
(LC; Frenz, 87–88), WW wrote two letters to Rolleston. In the first, apparently sent
on April 20, he suggested again "the printing of the English text with the German"
(*CB*). The second letter, evidently mailed on April 22, though the entry in *CB* appears
under April 20, included an "endorsement to go in R's preface—& recommending that
Salut au Monde be included." The text given here is the "endorsement" which Kennedy
translated from the German in *The Fight of a Book for the World*, 249–250 (reprinted
by Frenz, 89). Rolleston on May 18 agreed to the poet's suggestions (*CB*).

34. WW deleted at this point: "entire humanity's good will."

35. The article, "Father Taylor and Oratory," did not appear until 1887. WW
heard Edward Thompson Taylor (1793–1871) preach in the Seaman's Chapel in Boston
in 1860 (Allen, 239).

I have had a bad spell nearly all the year—till ab't a month ago—when things turn'd favorably, & I am now about as usual with me—

With good old remembrances—

Walt Whitman

1273. *To Jeannette L. Gilder*   5.27. *[1884]*

Private

328 Mickle st   Camden   May 27

My dear friend

If convenient & you can print the following, *just as it is,*[36] put in & oblige your friend

Walt Whitman

1274. *To Elizabeth and Isabella Ford and Edward R. Pease*[37]

Camden New Jersey   U S America | 328 Mickle
Street | May 28, 1884

Your kind message received. I am as usual & in good heart.

Walt Whitman

1275. *To Mary Whitall Smith*   5.28. *[1884]*[38]

328 Mickle St: Camden | noon   May 28

Dear friend

Thank you & dear Alys for the nice sheets & cases, which arrived yesterday, were immediately assigned to use, & will be of more direct & continued comfort to me than you think.

I am well as usual, & in good heart. Got through those three hot days quite well—Remembrances to all, especially dear boy Logan—

Walt Whitman

Dark & raining heavily here as I write, but opportune & welcome—

36. *The Critic* printed on May 31 "A Fabulous Episode," in which WW, writing in the third person, repudiated an anecdote related by James Berry Bensel in the Lynn *Saturday Union* of May 24: when WW allegedly asked Longfellow for permission to dedicate to him the first edition of *Leaves of Grass*, the latter was ready to consent if certain passages were excised. The notice in the Lynn newspaper was sent to WW by S. W. Foss on May 26 (Feinberg; Traubel, II, 227).

37. Elizabeth Ford wrote to WW on February 16, 1875: "Your words that you have written are such a strength, it is so wonderful to find said, things that hover in one. I mean, to read things that one's heart cries out in answer to. This is what makes me so that I cannot help writing to you" (Feinberg). Her picture, inscribed June 20, 1877, is in the Feinberg Collection. WW sent *Leaves of Grass* and *Specimen Days* to Isabella on October 11, 1882, and to Elizabeth on June 27, 1883 (CB). For Pease, see 1230.

1276. *To Harry Stafford*   5.28. *[1884]*

328 Mickle St   Camden | Wednesday night   May 28
Dear Harry
    I recd your letter over two weeks ago—Am glad you have a good place at Marlton—such a spot is so much pleasanter than Phila. or Camden or any close city—Hank, I am sorry you have that trouble with your throat, but I have no doubt it will go over in time—Your mother was up here yesterday—bro't me a nice chicken—said every thing was all right with your folks home—I am pretty much as usual again after quite a long siege—I am here in a little old house I have bought—my room is a big one in the 2d story—get along well enough (nothing to brag of)—there is a couple of elderly folks, acquaintances of mine, Mr and Mrs Lay, they live in the house, & I take my meals with them. Any how I like it all ever so much better than the Stevens Street business—
    Am not doing any thing lately, & the sale of my books has been very slim for some time[39]—Met a lady on the ferry last week, she came up to [me] very pleasant & said "Your friend Jo Allen is in Laredo, Texas, keeping store, doing well, & has a family"—
    So long, Harry dear boy—write soon, & I will the same—I send you some papers[40]—

                                                         W W

1277. *To Peter Bolger*   5.29. *[1884]*

TRANSCRIPT.

                                              Camden, May 29.
    [WW sent a publicity release entitled "Walt Whitman's Birthday," referring to his sixty-fifth anniversary, for insertion in the Philadelphia *Times* on Saturday, May 31.][41]

    38. This letter can be assigned to 1884 on the basis of the following undated entry in CB after June 2: "rec'd a most kind & serviceable present, from Mary & Alys Smith & Mrs S. nice new sheets & pillow and bolster cases for my bed."
    39. WW continued to sell books to people who wrote directly to him. According to entries in CB, he received about $30 from these sales since the first of the year. McKay paid him $91.41 in royalties in June and $71.63 in December (Pennsylvania).
    40. In his letter Harry evidently mentioned his impending marriage, since WW noted it in CB. Interestingly, the poet ignored it in his letter, as he had done in the past when his soldier friends reported their matrimonial plans (see 230 and 344). On June 25 Harry was married to Eva Wescott by Claudius W. Bradshaw, mayor of Camden. The young man was accompanied by WW, who noted the fact in his diary and referred to the bridegroom's "throat trouble."
    41. According to a notation in CB, WW met Bolger in December, 1878.

1278. *To Henry Tyrrell*

328 Mickle Street | Camden   New Jersey   June 2 '84

Thanks, dear friend, for your loving note & beautiful little enclosure—I am about as usual—receive the *Weekly* you send & am glad to get it.[42]

Walt Whitman

1279. *To Dr. J. W. Bartlett*

328 Mickle street | Camden New Jersey |
June 11 1884

Dear Sir[43]

In answer to yours of yesterday recd (with enclosed check, pay for the Vol.—thanks—) I send you a copy of the $3 edition of *Leaves of Grass* —Would you kindly send me a word notifying me of its receipt?

Walt Whitman

1280. *To Mary Whitall Smith*

TRANSCRIPT.

328 Mickle Street | Camden N J   July 27 '84

Dear friend

Your letters have been rec'd & Alys's also—& have given me comfort—So full of living buoyancy & youth—I see those qualities—or the tally of them—are the important matter, & then the circumstances & happenings may be whatever may chance—The son (a friend of mine) of the proprietor of the paper here asked me to "help him out" in yesterday's paper[44] —so I gave him the letter to print—I enclose you the slip—how well & off-hand it reads—I am living here in my den in Mickle Street the same as ever—A little episode—the 9-month-old baby grandson of Mrs. Lay (my housekeeper) was attacked with cholera infantum & brain trouble a

42. Apparently Tyrrell was associated with Frank Leslie's Publishing House in New York City.

43. Early in June, Bartlett wrote to WW for his autograph, and received in reply a printed card advertising an autographed edition of *Leaves of Grass* for $3; the card and envelope as well as Bartlett's notation are in the Barrett Collection. On June 10 Bartlett sent the money for the book (LC), which on the following day WW sent to Chicopee Falls, Mass. (CB).

44. Probably Harry Bonsall, the son of the owner of the Camden *Daily Post*. I

week ago—the doctor insisted on a change of locale—they lived in hot close rooms—so the babe & mother & two other children are here the past week—& the babe (an exceptionally fine one) is out of danger—but it has been a close shave—the doctor comes twice a day—says it has been this house & back yard (very nice & breezy—we have had a hammock swung there) that has done most of the curing—Are you interested in the episode? I have been much.[45]

Love to Alys, Logan & all—

W W

1281. *To the Librarian of Congress*

ENDORSED (by WW): "Copy of | letter sent Librarian of Congress | July 30 1884 | renewal granted & | rec'd by me." DRAFT LETTER.

328 Mickle street | Camden New Jersey   July 30 '84

Dear Sir

Please give me, (as under Section 6 of your *Copyright Directions* of 1882), the 14 years renewal of my copyright to the edition of *Leaves of Grass* granted Sept 11, 1856—Printed title page herewith enclosed— Please send me a certificate of such renewal—One dollar herewith enclosed.

Respectfully &c
Walt Whitman

1282. *To Robert Underwood Johnson*

328 Mickle Street | Camden New Jersey |
August 4   1884

Dear Sir[46]

In answer to your letter & request a few days ago *Yes* I will gladly write for the *Century* an article on the Hospitals & Hospital Nursing of the

can find, however, no article by WW in the newspaper.

45. The baby, Harry Lay, died on August 7 and was buried three days later (CB). During June and July WW was having his new "shanty" repaired. Peter Doyle called on June 4, Edward Carpenter was in Camden from June 18 to 20, and his brother Jeff and his two daughters arrived on June 20 (CB).

46. Johnson (1853–1937) was on the staff of *The Century Magazine* from 1873 to 1913. On July 12 Johnson asked WW for an article on the Civil War (Feinberg; Traubel, II, 218). "Army Hospitals and Cases" was printed in the magazine in October, 1888. See also 1292.

Secession War, such as outlined by you—I will set about it immediately—

I enclose a short sketch & reminiscence of Father Taylor, with authentic portrait, (given me by his daughter). The price is $50—If you use it I would want to see proof, & would like to reserve the right of printing it in future book—Say after the lapse of a year—Respects to Watson Gilder[47]—

Walt Whitman

1283. *To Albert Johnston*   *8.10.* [*1884*]

ADDRESS: Al Joh (?) | J(?)er | (?)O Bowery, Cor: Broome | New York City. POSTMARK: (?)iladelphia | Pa. | (?)184 | (?) AM.

Camden   Sunday Evn'g Aug 10

Dear Boy Al

The 25 arrived safely[48]—thanks—I am about as usual, only extra lameness—I am coming soon—Love to father, mother, May and all—

W W

1284. *To William Sloane Kennedy*   *8.10.* [*1884*]

ENDORSED (by Kennedy?): " '84."

Camden   Sunday Evn'g | Aug 10

The *Wonders* &c has arrived safely[49]—& thank you for sending it —I am getting along pretty much in the old way—only an extra lameness —Love to you & Mrs: K—

W. W.

1285. *To Miss Elwell*

328 Mickle Street | Camden New Jersey Aug. 13 '84

Dear Miss Elwell

I thank Mrs. Taylor[50] heartily for her poem to me—not forgetting

47. Gilder, who was also associated with the magazine, thanked WW for "Father Taylor and Oratory" on August 9 (Feinberg; Traubel, II, 212). See also 1272.
48. Another payment for the purchase of WW's portrait (see 1269).
49. *Wonders and Curiosities of the Railway* was printed in Chicago in 1884.

you too for kindly sending it—I keep about as well as usual this summer.

Walt Whitman

1286. *To David McKay(?)*

328 Mickle street | Camden   Aug 18 '84

Dear Sir

Please send me over, by express package

25 Specimen Days
3 Leaves of G
2 Dr Bucke's WW

—Thirty copies altogether—which, as I make it, are yet coming to me—

1287. *To T. W. H. Rolleston*   [*8.20.1884*]

ENDORSED: "Aug 20 '84 Sent Rolleston | 28 Terrassen
Ufer Dresden Saxony." DRAFT LETTER.

Two or three little matters I will write to you about.[51] How is the publication of the German version getting on? My guess would be that when fairly afloat it might have quite as much sale here in the United States as in Germany—perhaps more. Would of course require a little while to get bruited about—but then I think quite probable a steady demand would set in. Two or three central book jobbing houses should be fixed upon, one in New York, one in Chicago, & one in San Francisco—

With an eye to this I would like early copies sent to

Wm Sloane Kennedy, Belmont, Mass:

J L & J B Gilder, Critic office, 18 Astor Place New York City

Prof. Edward Dowden, Temple Road Winstead Rathmine's, Dublin Ireland

Talcott Williams, Daily Press cor 7th & Chestnut Sts Phila

Editors, Daily Republican newspaper Springfield Mass

Dr Karl Knortz cor Morris av and 155th st New York

R W Gilder Century Magazine, Union Sq N Y

All the above would quite certainly announce and review the German trans.

50. Perhaps Mrs. Hannah L. Taylor, to whom WW wrote about December 10, 1880 (Feinberg).

51. On August 7 Rolleston informed WW of the progress of his translation (Syracuse; Traubel, IV, 113–114). Despite Rolleston's willingness to subsidize the German edition, he was not able to publish it (see 1291).

1288. *To Edwin Booth*

328 Mickle Street | Camden New Jersey | Aug: 21 '84

My dear Sir[52]

First begging your pardon & hoping "I dont intrude" (yet knowing I do)—I am writing for the magazine market—or rather have written—a reminiscence of the actors & plays & "the old Bowery" of my youthful days—the chief figure in it being your father—by far the greatest histrion I have ever seen in my life (& I have always been a theatre goer)—

What I write to you now for, I want a good characteristic portrait of your father either in citizen's costume, or, (if *very good*) in one of his dramatic characters, to wood-engrave an illustration from—say to make a picture to fill ab't the size of one of the Harper's Magazine pages. Can you help me to it?

I am disabled coop'd up here, & can't get about to get things for my-self—or I wouldn't trouble you—

Won't you allow me to send you an autograph copy of my "Leaves of Grass" as a nibble at recompense?

Walt Whitman

1289. *To Edwin Booth*

328 Mickle Street | Camden New Jersey |
September 3 1884

Dear Mr Booth

Thank you for sending me the volume *the Booths*—It does not furnish me the picture I wanted—(I am very particular & shall not be satisfied till I get one that fills the bill)—But the volume is more helpful to me (in touches, corrections, guidance &c to my piece) than I can de-scribe—& the reading of all about your father, of absorbing interest—He was a beautiful character.

Walt Whitman

52. Booth (1833–1893) wrote to WW on August 24 and 28 (Feinberg; *WWR*, vi [1960], 50), and sent a copy of Asia Booth Clarke's *The Elder and the Younger Booth* (1882), "containing," in Booth's words, "poor copies of the good portraits that are in some secure, forgotten place among my 'traps.'" The article, entitled "Booth and 'The Bowery,'" appeared in the New York *Tribune* on August 16, 1885 (see 1341).
53. "What Lurks Behind Shakspeare's Historical Plays?" appeared in *The Critic* on September 27. WW sent it to *The Nineteenth Century* on August 8 and to *The North American Review* on September 1, the asking price being $50 (CB). *The Critic* paid him $15 (see 1293).
54. When Rolleston wrote on September 9, he was in Ireland. Acknowledging his

1290. *To Jeannette L. and Joseph B. Gilder*

328 Mickle street | Camden New Jersey |
September 16 1884

My friends
Can you use this in the C[ritic]?[53]
The price would be $15—& 20 copies of the number—& of course
I should want to see proof—(reserving the right to include in my future
book)—

Walt Whitman

1291. *To T. W. H. Rolleston*   [*9.20. 1884*]

ENDORSED: "Sent to Rolleston, Ireland, | Sept. 20 '84."
DRAFT LETTER.

Write now to acknowledge yours from Ireland just rec'd.—to send
you congratulations on return home with wife and children—and prayers
for good future to you all—will write in time, what I have to say about the
new phase of the trans[lation] enterprise.[54] I am about as usual in health
—one point worse—thre[atened] with total and permanent loss of walking power—

1292. *To William D. O'Connor*

ENDORSED: "W. W. | Answ'd Oct 3/84."[55] ADDRESS:
Wm D O'Connor | Life Saving Service |
Washington | D C. POSTMARKS: Philad(?) | Pa. |
Sep 29 (?) | 7 PM; Washington, Rec'd. | Sep | 30 |
5 30 AM | 1884 | 1.

328 Mickle street | Camden New Jersey |
September 29 '84

Dear friend
Enclosed a little piece the whole idea of which I got from you—
as you see. It is in the *Critic* of Sept. 27[56]—Dry and warm and often

failure to persuade a German publisher to undertake the volume, he now wanted WW
to find "a willing publisher with some German connection" in America (Feinberg; Traubel, I, 18–21). The book was printed in 1889 in Switzerland. This draft letter was written on the verso of an envelope from John K. Randall, a Baltimore lawyer. According to
WW's reference to this letter in CB, he must have sent about this time a post card to
Rolleston in Switzerland.
    55. O'Connor's reply was dated October 2 (see the following note).
    56. "What Lurks Behind Shakspeare's Historical Plays?" (see 1290). O'Connor's
elation at the support he received from WW for his Baconian theories is evident in his
letter of October 2 (Feinberg; Traubel, I, 177–179).

oppressive weather here—a long spell—My lameness seems permanent like—I have promised to write a War Hospital Article for *Century* to supplement their forthcoming swell [of] war narratives by Grant & the rest.[57]

William, I wonder if you or Charles Eldridge couldn't help me to something there from the Medical Bureau—summaries, or statistics or any information—who do you know in the Surgeon Gen[eral]'s office?[58]

Walt Whitman

1293. *To Joseph B. Gilder*

ADDRESS: Joseph B Gilder | *Critic* office | 20 Astor Place | New York City. POSTMARK: Philadelphia | Pa. | Oct 1 84 | 5 PM.

Camden New Jersey | October 1 1884

Received from *Critic* Fifteen Dollars for my piece *"What Lurks"* &c—

Walt Whitman

The slips & papers came safely—thanks—

1294. *To Talcott Williams*

Thursday P M | Oct: 9 '84

My dear Williams

I leave you this in hopes you can use it in to-morrow's paper—(as the Red Jacket affair has come off to-day at Buffalo.) I should like $5 for it.

I am well as usual—only very lame—

Walt Whitman

Have the proof read carefully by copy[59]—

57. See 1282.
58. O'Connor informed WW on October 2 that he would have trouble in obtaining the material which was in the process of publication (Feinberg; Traubel, I, 178–179) *The Medical and Surgical History of the War of the Rebellion* appeared in instalments between 1870 and 1888.
59. "Red Jacket (from Aloft)," commemorating the reburial of the old Iroquois warrior on October 9 at Buffalo, appeared on the following day in the Philadelphia *Press*, of which Williams was the editor.
60. But see the following letter.

1295. To Talcott Williams

328 Mickle Street | Camden | Oct 11 '84

My dear friend

Thank you for your kind & warm invitation to write a Blaine poem—but I shall not be able to accept it[60]—

Thank you heartily too for the pay (more than I asked & more than it is worth) for the little *Red Jacket* bit[61]—but it has not yet come to hand—most likely will come soon—I am about as usual—only very lame.

Walt Whitman

I enclose my last screed in the *Critic*[62]—

1296. To Talcott Williams   10.12. [1884]

328 Mickle Street | Camden   Oct 12   P M

My dear Williams

After I sent your note in answer yesterday—& reading yours again—I have perpetrated this—do I understand you are to have a long varied Blaine melange like in sections—the Presidential canvas business, of course? If so you might find a spot in the course of it all, where this screed may come in[63]—

If that don't suit you, or is not practicable (though I hope it will be, as I should like it just as well) print it by itself, like the little piece of Friday last.[64]

I will call about 10. this evening to see proof.

Whitman

1297. To Talcott Williams   10.13. [1884]

328 Mickle Street | Camden Oct: 13

My dear Williams

I should like the little *Presidential canvass poem* to go in the paper

61. WW did not record the amount he received from Williams in CB. Since he was paid $10 for his next contribution to the Philadelphia *Press*, probably he received the same amount for "Red Jacket (from Aloft)."

62. "What Lurks Behind Shakspeare's Historical Plays?"

63. "If I Should Need to Name, O Western World" (later "Election Day, November, 1884") appeared in the Philadelphia *Press* on October 26. WW received $10 for the poem (CB). The manuscript, with instructions to the printer for putting it in type, is in the Feinberg Collection.

64. "Red Jacket (from Aloft)."

of Sunday Oct 26—I think that time would be opportune—Send me word (by note) if that suits you—& if so I will send it two or three days beforehand.

As I am writing to you I enclose the rec't for the Red Jacket bit—

Walt Whitman

1298. *To William C. Bryant*   *[10.18. 1884]*

DRAFT LETTER.

Thanks for your kind letter about the little *Red Jacket* bit &c.— Best wishes to you, wife, children & (unknown) friends there[65]—

1299. *To Robert Pearsall Smith*   *11.6. [1884]*

TRANSCRIPT.

Camden.   Thursday Evng., Nov. 6.[66]

My dear friend,

I should like to come over Saturday, be there about noon—will come up in the horse cars—will spend some hours with Mr. Clifford, and if you come home early enough and the weather good we may have a (longer or shorter) drive before supper—will leave the question of my stopping over Sunday, open.

Walt Whitman

1300. *To Susan Stafford*   *11.10. [1884]*

328 Mickle street | Camden   Monday 3 p m |
Nov 10[67]

Thanks, my dear friend, for the nice chicken—I have just had a part of it for my dinner—& the *honey in the comb* just like that is something I like—

65. Bryant (1830–1898), a lawyer and president of the Buffalo Historical Society, was responsible for placing the remains of Red Jacket and other Senecan chiefs in Forest Lawn Cemetery. For this information I am indebted to Ridgway McNallie, of the Buffalo and Erie County Public Library. WW's poem was printed in *Transactions of the Buffalo Historical Society*, III (1885), 105.
66. WW stayed at Robert Pearsall Smith's Germantown home from November 8 to 10 (*CB*). Edward Clifford made a drawing of WW on November 3 (*CB*). I am indebted to Professor Holloway for bringing this letter to my attention.

I had a very pleasant visit out in Germantown—I went partly at the request of a fine jolly young Englishman who is visiting there for a few days, & told me much about my friends in England (of whom I find I have far more than I knew of)—

I am about as usual—feel considerably better, more able to get around since the cool weather has set in—had rather a bad summer—my walking power gives out more this year, & I am afraid is destined to be worse, instead of better—otherwise I am about the same—appetite good—spirits ditto—

I am sorry I wasn't in when you stopped this forenoon—have been hoping you would stop this afternoon—Does George keep well this fall? Ruth, how do you like married life?[68] I rec'd *the cake*—very nice—Well, Ed, how are you about Cleveland?[69] I am just as well satisfied—

I have rec'd a long letter from Herbert[70]—nothing very new. The Lord bless you & be with you all—

Walt Whitman

1301. *To Harry and Eva Stafford*

ADDRESS: Harry L and Eva Stafford | RR Station | Marlton | New Jersey. POSTMARK: Camden | Nov | 19 | 1884 | N.J.

328 Mickle Street   Camden | Evn'g   Nov. 18 '84
My dear friends

Your kind letter (Eva's) came this afternoon & it gave me real comfort both to hear from you & have such loving remembrance & friendly invitation—Harry, dear boy, I hardly think I shall be able to come down & be with you this Thanksgiving[71]—but I will come one of these times—Since I have got into this shanty, although I go out every day, I don't go any distance—havn't been away this past summer, only one short trip to Cape May[72]—My lameness increases on me—it probably won't be long before I shall be unable to get around at all—General health otherwise about the same as usual—Eva, my dear friend, it would be a true comfort for me if it was so I could come in every few days, and

67. November 10 fell on Monday in 1884, and see the preceding letter.
68. Ruth Stafford married William Goldy on August 19.
69. A reference to the contested election between Blaine and Grover Cleveland.
70. Perhaps a reference to the letter Herbert Gilchrist wrote on September 30 (Feinberg).
71. WW was with the Smiths on Thanksgiving Day, November 27 (CB).
72. WW made a "jaunt" to Cape May on September 14 and had a "pleasant sail around the little inner bay" (CB).

you and Harry and I could be together—I am sure it would be good for me—

Nothing very new in my affairs—not much sale for my books at present, or for the last fifteen months—Harry, your Mother call'd here last Monday, but I was not in, was over to Germantown—I was sorry to be away—I am writing this up in my room—am alone most of the time—write a little most every day—sell a piece once in a while—maintain good spirits and a first-rate appetite—My dear friends, indeed I appreciate your loving wishes & feelings, & send you mine the same, for both of you—

Walt Whitman

Eva, would you like to have me send you some papers now & then? Write me whenever you can. Harry, I am sorry about the neck—I think it will get right & heal in time—

1302. *To John H. Johnston*

328 Mickle Street | Camden   Nov. 18 '84[73]

Dear friend
        Yours of yesterday just rec'd—with the $25—(making 150 in all)[74] —best thanks—So you like the Brignoli bit[75]—I was not sure it amounted to much, but it came from the heart—(it was first sent to the *Tribune* to be published the morning of B's funeral, but the T sent it back)—

How are you all? How is Al, under the new dispensation? I send my love specially to Alma and the girls & the new Mrs J—

Nothing very new with me—I am ab't as well as usual except an increasing lameness—Anticipate a time not remote when I shall be unable to walk at all—Have not forgotten the *Memorandum History of the Portrait* —have already outlined & partly prepared it—you shall have it soon[76]—

I am writing this up in my big den—the floor all around horribly *litter*-rary, but a cheery wood fire in the little stove—& I comfortable

---

73. This letter (or possibly draft) was offered in the C. W. Houghton sale at the Anderson Galleries on October 18, 1923, as a two-page manuscript. The first page is now in the Houghton Collection at the Library of Congress. The second page, which can be identified on the basis of the auction record, is now in the Feinberg Collection.
    74. Johnston's payments for the portrait (see 1269).
    75. Brignoli, the Italian tenor, was buried on November 3. "The Dead Tenor" appeared in *The Critic* on the following day. A newspaper clipping reporting the funeral and a proof of the poem are in the Feinberg Collection. WW heard Brignoli sing in 1867

in my great capacious rattan arm-chair—(which I may will to Al, if he cares for it)—

W W

1303. *To Talcott Williams*

328 Mickle Street | Camden   Dec. 14 '84

My dear friend

Upon the whole I shall have to beg off from Monday night. The doctor enjoins upon me that I am like an old wagon body—must keep rigidly to the smooth ordinarily traveled roads, & not cut across lots any how. Give my friendliest greetings & wishes to Miss Terry & Mr Irving —Should they, or either, feel any day—say from 2 to 3 in the afternoon— like calling upon me here, I should rate it a welcome honor.[77]

If you have not procured the tickets before receiving this let them go unprocured—Best remembrances to Mrs. Williams.

Walt Whitman

Show this note to Miss Terry and Mr Irving—& if Miss T has the least desire to keep it, please let her do so.

1304. *To Blaine and Mary Donaldson*[78]   *[12.25.] 1884*

ADDRESS: Blaine and Mary | Donaldson | 326 north 40th Street | Philadelphia. POSTMARK: Camden | Dec | 26 | 6 AM | 1884 | N.J.

Christmas—1884—'5 | 328 Mickle Street Camden | N J

Thanks, my loving young friends, for the magnificent chair—so opportune—will be so useful to me daily, hourly—Will soon come up & see you & your father & mother—

Walt Whitman

(see 231), in 1872 (see 435), and on September 16, 1876, at the Academy of Music in Philadelphia (CB).

76. Johnston had requested a history of the portrait by Hine on March 25 (Feinberg; Traubel, III, 331).

77. WW used his poor health as an excuse from all social occasions which he did not wish to attend. From December 2 to 4 he dined daily with Dr. Bucke in Philadelphia, and on December 4 and 5 Burroughs joined them for trips to Smith's home (CB).

78. The children of Thomas Donaldson.

1305. *To John H. Johnston*

December 28, 1884

[WW acknowledged receipt of money for his portrait.][79]

1306. *To Edmund Gosse*   *12.31. [1884]*

328 Mickle Street | Camden New Jersey | Dec: 31.

Dear Mr Gosse:

I shall be glad to see you—Call about 11 forenoon if convenient
—I live less than half a mile from the ferry landing here, crossing from
Philadelphia[80]—

Walt Whitman

79. In an undated entry but written about December 28, WW recorded the receipt of $50 from Johnston "for portrait—now paid in full, $200" (CB).

During the year Hannah Heyde had been seriously ill, emotionally more than physically. Heyde wrote on October 14, November 2 and 25, and December 20(?) to inform WW of his wife's breakdown, to complain of the additional burdens he had to assume, and to ask for money (Trent). WW sent $20 to Hannah on October 17, $20 to Heyde on November 13, and $10 to his sister on December 23 (CB). On December 19–20, he wrote in CB: "gloomy news from dear sister Hannah—letter worse than ever from the wretched cur, C L H[eyde]." On January 24, 1885, Heyde informed WW that Hannah's "disorder is mental, beyond medical aid" (Trent). Heyde continued to complain of medical bills and to pity himself; obviously he expected more financial aid than he received from WW or from George.

80. On December 29 Gosse asked permission to call on WW to deliver "to you in person the messages which I bring from Mr. Swinburne and other common friends in England" (Feinberg; Traubel, I, 40). Although WW vaguely recorded the visit as on January "7th or before" in CB, Gosse called on Saturday morning, January 3. The Philadelphia *Daily News* of January 6 reported the visit in detail, with additions supplied by WW. Gosse informed the poet that recently Tennyson had "delighted a considerable audience with recitations for half an hour from 'Whitman's Leaves of Grass.'" Gosse described the visit in *Critical Kit-Kats* (1896), 95–111.

1885

1307. *To Ellen M. Abdy-Williams*

ADDRESS: E M Abdy-Williams | Care of Messrs.
Sonnenchein | *Time* monthly office | White Hart
Street Paternoster Square | London EC England.
POSTMARK: Camden | Jan | 7 | 2 PM | 1885 | N.J.

> 328 Mickle Street | Camden New Jersey   U S
> America | Jan. 7 '85

Yours of Dec. 25 rec'd—with £1 for books—I forward them by this mail—*Leaves of Grass* and *Specimen Days*—two Vols—As soon as they reach you safely will you kindly send me a card notifying me?[1]

> Walt Whitman

1308. *To William Sloane Kennedy*

> 328 Mickle Street | Camden New Jersey—Jan 8 '85

Welcome letter—return'd books, &c. just rec'd (with slip—thanks)[2]—Am feeling well—Fine & sunny to-day—Have had a pleasant two-hours visit from Edmund Gosse[3]—

> Walt Whitman

1309. *To Charles M. Skinner*

ADDRESS: Charles M Skinner | Daily Times |
newspaper office | Brooklyn | New York. POSTMARK:
Camden | Jan | 19 | 8 PM | 1885(?) | N.J.

> 328 Mickle Street | Camden New Jersey | Jan: 19 '85

Dear Sir[4]

In hasty answer to your request asking me to specify over my own signature what years I worked as an editorial writer in the Brooklyn

1885

1. "The two volumes miscarried," as Miss Abdy-Williams informed WW on March 18 (Feinberg); he sent other copies on March 31 (CB).

2. On January 7 Kennedy returned a copy of Burroughs' book which he had read on the trip from Camden to Belmont, Mass.: "I shall cherish the memory of that blessed January 2nd '85 to the end of my days. My dear Whitman—I want you to regard me as a sort of son; tell me whenever I can do anything for you; let me loan you 5.00 if you get in a pinch, (& I have it) . . . & behave handsomely & intimately & affectionately to-ward me" (Feinberg). See also Kennedy, 4.

3. See 1306.

4. Skinner was editor of the Brooklyn *Daily Times*. The letter is in the Barrett Collection; the envelope and the note marked "Private" are in the Feinberg Collection.

Times office I would say that if I remember right it was along in 1856, or just before.[5] I recollect (doubtless I am now going to be egotistical about it,) the question of the new Water Works (magnificently outlined by Mc-Alpine,[6] and duly carried out and improved by Kirkwood,[7] first-class engineers both,) was still pending, and the works, though well under way, continued to be strongly opposed by many. With the consent of the proprietor, I bent the whole weight of the paper steadily in favor of the McAlpine plan, as against a flimsy, cheap and temporary series of works that would have long since broken down, and disgraced the city.

This, with my course on another matter, the securing to public use of Washington Park (Old Fort Greene,) stoutly championed by me some thirty-five years ago, against heavy odds, during an editorship of the Brooklyn *Eagle*, are "feathers in my wings" that I would wish to preserve.

I heard lately with genuine sorrow of the death of George C Bennett.[8] I remember him well as a good, generous, honorable man.

I send best greetings to your staff, and indeed to all the Brooklyn journalists.

Walt Whitman

Private
C M S—Dear Sir
You are at liberty to print letter, if you desire—If so *read proof very carefully & copy*—& don't forget to send me here a couple of papers—
W W

5. WW was the editor of the *Daily Times* from 1856 to 1859; see Allen, 208–216.
6. William Jarvis McAlpine (1812–1890), a civil engineer, planned the Riverside Drive in New York City.
7. James P. Kirkwood was a friend of Jeff and aided WW's hospital work during the Civil War (see 51).
8. Bennett was the proprietor of the *Daily Times*. Apparently he dismissed WW from the editorship in 1859 (Allen, 215).
9. O'Connor dated this post card correctly.
10. The Springfield *Republican* reprinted on January 24, from the New York *Mail and Express*, a jocular account by Henry Peterson in which he took exception to WW's descriptions of animals. Peterson was a friend of O'Connor (see Traubel, I, 29, and IV, 162).
11. Bucke visited WW from December 2 to 5, and Burroughs joined them on December 4 (*CB*).
12. "Of That Blithe Throat of Thine" appeared in the January issue of *Harper's Monthly*. WW sent the poem to the magazine on October 17, 1884, and asked $30 (*CB*).

1310. *To William D. O'Connor*   [*1.26. 1885*]⁹

ENDORSED: "Answ'd Feb 1, 1885" | "Jan. 26 1885."
ADDRESS: Wm D O'Connor | Life Saving Service |
Washington | D C. POSTMARKS: Camden | Jan |
(?) | 6 PM | 1885(?) | N.J.; Washington, Rec'd. |
Jan | 27 | 730 AM | 1885 | (?).

328 Mickle st.   Camden | Monday Evn'g
I am ab't as usual—All right, heart & spirits—I send *Springfield
Republican* with piece, more because I want to send *something* than because of any moment in it¹⁰—Send on to Dr B[ucke]¹¹ when you have
read. I write a little—sort o' sundown sonnets¹²—have some nice visitors—
Sometimes foreigners—two or three American girls now & then—great
comfort to me¹³—

W W

1311. *To Joseph B. Gilder*   *2.18.* [*1885*]

Camden   Feb. 18

My dear J B G
I have no feeling of objection to your substituting a *nom de
plume* in place of Mr Scovel's name¹⁴—

Walt Whitman

Henry M. Alden, the editor, rejected "After the Supper and Talk" on January 13 (Fein-
berg; Traubel, II, 211). "Washington's Monument, February, 1885" appeared as "Ah,
Not This Granite, Dead and Cold" in the Philadelphia *Press* on February 22. "Death of
General Grant," with the title "As One by One Withdraw the Lofty Actors," was sent on
April 2 at the "request" of the editor of *Harper's Weekly* and was printed on May 16
(*CB*). It appeared as "Grant" in *The Critic* on August 15.
    13. WW did not inform O'Connor of domestic details. On January 20 the Lays
moved out of 328 Mickle Street, and on January 25 he began to have his breakfasts at the
home of Mrs. Mary Davis at 412 West Street. For almost five weeks WW lived alone
until Mrs. Davis became his housekeeper on February 24 (*CB*).
    14. A reference to "Walt Whitman in Camden" which appeared in *The Critic* on
February 28 under the signature of George Selwyn. It was reprinted in *Authors at Home*,
ed. J. L. and J. B. Gilder (1888), and in *Critic Pamphlet No. 2* (1898), in which WW
was cited as the author and a page of the manuscript was reproduced in facsimile. Apparently WW's original intention was to use the name of James Matlack Scovel as he had
done in the article published in the Springfield *Republican* in 1875 (see 683). "Selwyn's" account was filled with factual errors.

1312. *To Alma and John H. Johnston*

ADDRESS: Mrs: Alma Johnston | 305 East 17th Street |
New York City. POSTMARK: Camden, N.J. | (?).

328 Mickle Street | Camden New Jersey |
March 4 '85

Dear dear friends[15]

Your letter comforts & touches me deeply, & I am not sure but it
w'd be a good arrangement not only for me, but all 'round—But for the
present I shall keep on here—Since you was here, Alma, I have had a
friend move in, Mrs. Davis, strong & hearty & good natured, a widow,
young enough, furnishes me my meals, & takes good care[16]—I am feeling
quite well for me as I write this. Soon as you get this write me how
John is getting along—Last Saturday's *Critic* has a piece about my *home*
which may interest you[17]—I have been *under the weather* myself for nearly
a fortnight, but am now all right—I shall never forget your kindness &
generosity to me—I am in good spirits as I finish this, feeling better
to-day than for some time past—Love to Al[18] and to May & to all—
Walt Whitman

1313. *To Anne Gilchrist*

ADDRESS: Mrs: Gilchrist | 12 Well Road | Hampstead |
London | England. POSTMARKS: Camden | Mar |
15 | 5 PM | 1885 | N.J.; London, N.W. | M C | Mr
26 | 85.

March 15 '85—328 Mickle street | Camden   New
Jersey—U S America

Dear friend

In a letter from John Burroughs a while since he writes me that
your article is to appear in *To-Day*[19]—When printed I wish Herby w'd
get ten copies & send me by mail, (in two packages, five in each) —Nothing

15. Mrs. Johnston visited WW on February 9 (*CB*).   16. See 1310.
17. "Walt Whitman in Camden."   18. Mr. Johnston's son, Albert.
19. Mrs. Gilchrist's "A Confession of Faith" appeared in *To-Day* in June. WW's
"Resurgemus" ("Europe") had appeared in the same magazine the previous September.
WW did not refer to Mrs. Gilchrist's letter of February 27, in which she spoke of
"bronchial & asthmatic troubles" and of her lasting affection—"you are in my thoughts
as constantly as ever though I have been so silent" (LC; Harned, 233).
20. The Lays (see 1310).
21. Apparently this letter was written on Tuesday, April 7, 1885, since Scovel
on that date informed WW that his note had arrived too late in the evening for the
"promised sour mash" (Feinberg). At this time Scovel was preparing an article about

very different with me—I am full as well as common—a new & good care-taker for me here in the house (the old ones gone),[20] Mrs. Davis, a sailor's widow, young & strong & good-natured, & very kind & attentive—according to indications a blessed change—I am writing a little—Shall probably add to next edition of L of G. at end not more than 30 or 35 pages—

After-Songs and A Letter of Parting

the "letter" (prose) a sort of résumé & talk in general—The old bulk part of the book left all the same as now. I am writing this Sunday afternoon up in my room by wood fire. I suppose you rec'd the Camden *Post*.

Love to you, & Herb & Grace—

W W

1314. *To James Matlack Scovel*   [*4.7(?). 1885(?)*]

328 Mickle St.   Camden | 11 a m Tuesday[21]

My *friend* J. M. S. | (for so I would have it)

Yours just rec'd. Come around right away & let me mix you a good generous *sour mash* to remove such *baseless & unworthy* constructions from your thought—Affectionate respects to Mrs. S.

Walt Whitman

1315. *To Karl Knortz*

ADDRESS: Dr Karl Knortz | 540 East 155th Street | New York City. POSTMARK: Camden | Apr | 27(?) | 2(?) | 1885 | N.J.

328 Mickle Street | Camden New Jersey
April 27 '85

My dear Dr Knortz

What is now the status of the Rolleston translation, with reference to publication?[22] I have seen your letter of some weeks since to Dr Bucke

WW for the Springfield *Republican*, and the poet was insisting upon alterations. On April 7 Scovel suggested that "to start *right* again I think you had better send me my MSS—and let me do as I d—n please with it" (Feinberg). On May 7 and again on May 12 Scovel asked WW to return the manuscript (Feinberg). The article, simply called "Walt Whitman," was sent to the newspaper on May 22 (CB) and appeared on June 16; it detailed WW's financial returns from the sale of articles and books with information obviously supplied by the poet. According to a letter dated "Monday," written about June 16, the newspaper paid Scovel $8 for the piece—"does not seem to me capable of division but I am ready to do whatever you say" (Feinberg).

22. See 1291 and 1344. Rolleston wrote to WW about Knortz's revision of his manuscript on February 11 (Feinberg; Traubel, III, 85–86).

—tell me of any thing new—or probabilities. I particularly hope it is intended to give the English text of the pieces, either on the left-hand page or running in smaller type at the bottom of every page & forming one third—

If you have some loose sheets (last proofs, or what not) of your new "Representative German Poems,"[23] send me three or four pages. (I dont want the book, but just want to see how it is made up, paged & printed)— My health is about as usual, except a worse lameness—

Walt Whitman

1316. *To the Editor, the New York* Graphic[24]

328 Mickle street | Camden New Jersey | May 21 | '85

Dear Sir

As I have lost the address of the young man[25] who call'd upon me yesterday from your paper, & to whom I promised some pictures and memoranda, I send them directly to you—If I can furnish you with any thing else, or any information I shall be happy to do so—

Walt Whitman

the best likeness in my opinion is the big photo—

1317. *To John Burroughs*   *5.24. [1885]*[26]

ADDRESS: John Burroughs | West Park | Ulster Co: | New York. POSTMARKS: Camden | May | 2(?) | 188(?) | N.J.; Philadelphia, Pa. | May | 24 | 7 PM | Transit.

328 Mickle Street | Camden N J   May 24

Dear J B—

I am ab't in my usual general health, but *lameness bad*—had a fall a month ago, & turned my ankle in—don't think I will be able to come up to West Park—

W W

23. *Representative German Poems: Ballad and Lyrical* apparently was not published until 1889.

24. The following letter was written to the editor of the New York *Daily Graphic*, which in a birthday tribute on May 31 printed part of it in facsimile as well as two portraits of WW and sketches by T. A. Teraud of Mickle Street and the Huntington birthplace.

25. Perhaps Andrew E. Murphy, described in CB as "the attaché [of the *Daily Graphic*] who wrote to me May '85."

1318. *To Richard Watson Gilder*

> 328 Mickle street | Camden New Jersey |
> May 24 '85

My dear Watson Gilder

I am in about my usual general health (which is nothing to brag of) but my locomotion is worse—had a fall a month ago & turned my ankle in, & at my age one dont recover from such things—Have no thought of coming to New York—If I did so, I should willingly give your friend the sittings for portrait.

> Walt Whitman

Were the artist to visit Philadelphia I would sit to him here in my own room—good place north-light—as many times as he wishes.[27]

1319. *To William Sloane Kennedy*

> 328 Mickle St: | Camden N J   May 24 '85

Dear friend

The long MS you sent me some months since is all right & I will return it to you forthwith—The whole drift of it is lofty, subtle & true— I would not put it *out by itself*—Such things never strike in so well in the abstract as in illustration, of *some definite personal, critical concrete thing* —I suggest to you a criticism on *Tennyson and Walt Whitman* (or if you prefer on *Victor Hugo, T and WW*) where they should be work'd in— What think you?[28]

> W W

1320. *To Sylvester Baxter*

> 328 Mickle Street | Camden New Jersey
> June 9 '85

My dear Baxter

I wonder if you could use this in the *Outing?* The price would be

26. The year is established by the reference to the sprained left leg which WW complained of from April 28 to June 8 (*CB*); see also the following letter.

27. Since Gilder's letter to WW is not extant, it is not possible to determine who the artist was. Perhaps it was John White Alexander (see February 20, 1886).

28. On January 16 Kennedy sent the manuscript of "The New Ars Poetica," in which he attempted to defend WW's poetic style (Feinberg). On June 2 he accepted WW's suggestion of expanding his article (Feinberg). This essay became part of *The Poet as A Craftsman* (see 1354).

12^{29}—I am ab't as usual of late years—I rec'd your kind note some months since—

Walt Whitman

1321. *To Harry and Eva Stafford*

328 Mickle St   Camden | June 9 '85

Dear Harry | & Dear Eva

I am still badly lamed by my *turned ankle* of six or seven weeks ago—otherwise about as good health as usual—Am much pleased at the nice little home & interested in the printing office venture—all right—But think twice about the monthly periodical project—

Nothing specially new with me—I like my new house lady Mrs. Davis —Eva, dear girl, when you come up to Camden for a day, come *here* & make your headquarters—I am sure you will like it, & be contented, as we should gladly be—

Harry, dear son, how is that throat?

God bless both of you & a good kiss for each from

W W

1322. *To Anne Gilchrist*

ADDRESS: Mrs: Anne Gilchrist | 12 Well Road | Hampstead | London | England. POSTMARKS: Camden | (?) | 1885 | N.J.; Philadelphia | Jun | 10 | 1885(?) | Paid; London, N.W. | Z A | Ju 22 | 85.

328 Mickle Street | Camden New Jersey   U S A |
June 10 '85

Dear friend

I have seen the "Confession of Faith" & read it over more than once[30]—it bears my great test of going deeper & better the second reading than the first, & deeper still the third—To have my poetry received by the emotional & the scientific spirit, each emulating the other & warmly endorsing—need I say how it comes to me?

I am still here in my nook in Mickle Street—a little change in the

---

29. On June 7 WW sent to *Harper's Monthly* "The Voice of the Rain," which was returned to him by Alden, the editor, on the following day (Feinberg; Traubel, 1, 28). It appeared in *Outing*, "An Illustrated Monthly Magazine of Recreation," in August.

30. It appeared in the June issue of *To-Day*. Herbert included it in his biography of his mother (1887).

31. WW did not inform Mrs. Gilchrist of his sprained leg in his letter of March 15, since the accident occurred on April 28. Perhaps one of his letters to her is missing.

domestic overseeing arrangements—Mrs Davis has now been here four months, (instead of the former folk,) & *the change is immensely in my favor*—I doubt if I could be better provided—

Summer is upon us—I shall probably remain *here*—I am lamed (I fear permanently) by my fall & turned ankle of two months since, of which I told you in my last[31]—& it is best for me to not get too far off my own chair & bed—Otherwise I am about in usual health—full-bodied & red-faced—Love to you & Herb & Grace—tell Herb I rec'd the *Standard*—if not already sent, send me a few numbers of the June *To-Day*—I suppose you get a paper from me occasionally with piece—a fine bright summer forenoon as I write—

Walt Whitman

I should like Dr Bucke to get the "Confession"[32]

Also John Burroughs
      West Park
      Ulster County   New York

Also Wm D. O'Connor
      Life Saving Service
      Washington   D C

A young lady *special friend of mine* Mary Whitall Smith is coming to London, (with her parents) & I want her to come & see you—I think of her as *thoroughly American*—(of Quaker stock) with the best English qualities added[33]

(If you or Herb send to Dr B[ucke] and the others mention it in letter or card to me)

1323. *To William Sloane Kennedy*

ENDORSED: "on MS of my | 'Poet As A | Craftsman.' "

328 Mickle St   Camden N J | June 10 '85

Dear K

I return the MS—It has a magnificence of strength, *originality & suggestion*—& I adhere fully to what I advised in my former note[34]—I

32. Although this part (at Pennsylvania) has been separated from the main body of the letter, which is in the Morgan Library, I have placed the two together. On June 21–22, when Mrs. Gilchrist received WW's communication, she referred to his request for copies for his three friends (LC; Harned, 239–240).

33. See 1326. On July 20 Mrs. Gilchrist informed WW that she was "on the lookout for Miss Smith" (LC; Harned, 242).

34. See 1319.

think a synopsis of V[ictor] H[ugo] and T[ennyson] with the other parts—& then this MS. brought in as the reason for writing synopsis—just the same as Homer?[35] compiles the first 18 books of the Iliad, purely to bring in the remain[in]g 6—your main matter—

W W

1324. To Sylvester Baxter

ADDRESS: Sylvester Baxter | *Outing* Office | 175 Tremont St: | Boston Mass:. POSTMARK: Philadelphia | Pa | Jun 11 85 | 7 30 PM.

328 Mickle Street | Camden N J   June 11 '85

Received from Sylvester Baxter (*Outing* magazine Boston) Twelve Dollars for piece[36]—

Walt Whitman

1325. To William D. O'Connor

ENDORSED: "Answ'd July 27/85."[37] ADDRESS: Wm D O'Connor | Life Saving Service | Washington | D C. POSTMARKS: Philadelphia | Pa. | Jun 11 85 | 7 30 PM; Washington, Rec'd. | Jun | 12 | 7 AM 1885 | 2.

328 Mickle Street | Camden New Jersey |
June 11 '85—noon

The picture arrived this morning—it is a splendid piece of work & I feel sure a good likeness—At any rate it is that rare bird a perfect photo —& I am mighty glad to get it—it leans against the wall before me this moment with *the Bacon*—(I am ashamed to say never before acknowledged—but it is in my little sitting room & before my eyes every day— more than half the time is taken for Shakspere)[38]—

I am about as well as usual in general health—full as well—but laid by with lameness—added to by a fall two months ago & turning my ankle in. I hear from Dr Bucke and John Burroughs—both well—Doctor busy as a bee—both vehement in hospitable invitations to me which I

35. WW's question mark.
36. "The Voice of the Rain" (see 1320).
37. O'Connor replied on July 25 (Syracuse; Traubel, IV, 67–70).
38. O'Connor sent "the picture of Lord Bacon by Vandyke" on March 7 (Syracuse; Traubel, IV, 477–478).
39. On April 5 Bucke insisted that WW spend the summer in Canada (Feinberg).
40. WW slipped: Mrs. Gilchrist's "An Englishwoman's Estimate of Walt Whitman" appeared in 1870 in *The Radical* (see 364).

should be most glad to accept—but I find it best not to stray too far from my own chair & bed[39]—Mrs Gilchrist has a strong article abt L. of G. &c printed in the "To-day," cheap radical English magazine for June—I shall probably have some soon & will send you one—It is equal to the 1872 piece[40]—

How are you? Any prospect of decapitation?[41] How is Nelly? Give my best love & remembrances to her? I am comfortable here in my shanty. I suppose you get the papers & pieces I send—*So long*, dear friend—

W. W.

1326. *To Richard Monckton Milnes, Lord Houghton.*

ADDRESS: Lord Houghton.

328 Mickle street | Camden New Jersey   U S A |
June 20 1885

Dear old friend[42]

If convenience helps I want to present two American girls, sisters, Mary Whitall and Alys Smith, of Quaker stock, special personal friends of mine—to you—They are traveling in Europe with their parents —Mary can tell you all about my perplexing self to latest dates—

Walt Whitman

To | Lord Houghton

1327. *To John Burroughs*

ENDORSED: "Just recd this | Looks as if W. was | not going to move. I | shall try him again by & by, | J. B."

328 Mickle Street | Camden New Jersey |
June 23 '85

Dear John Burroughs

Yours just received (with the 10—many thanks—)—the kind invitation reiterated[43]—&c—I am in pretty fair condition generally, but unable to walk or get around, except very small stretches, & with effort—somehow feel averse to leaving this shanty of mine—where I am probably getting along better than you think—

---

41. O'Connor referred to the possibility of losing his governmental post in the Cleveland administration on February 1 (Feinberg; Traubel, I, 33) and on July 25 (Syracuse; Traubel, IV, 70).

42. Milnes met WW in 1875 (see 696). The Smiths sailed on June 24 and arrived in England on July 3. When Mary called on June 20 (CB), WW undoubtedly gave her this letter of introduction.

43. Burroughs invited WW to visit him at West Park, N. Y., on May 18 (Feinberg). The letter reiterating the invitation is seemingly lost.

Mrs Gilchrist's essay has appeared in the *To-Day*—probably she will send it to you—if not, I will send you mine—It is a noble paper—I have a little poem to appear in the *Outing*, perhaps in the forthcoming number[44]— Mary Smith & all the family (our Germantown friends) start for Europe to-morrow to be gone over a year.

As I write it is a delightful day—temperature perfect—I take the car to the ferry, & get out on the river every pleasant day.

Walt Whitman

1328. *To John H. Johnston*

ADDRESS: J H Johnston | Jeweler | 150 Bowery | New York City. POSTMARK: Philadelphia | Pa | Jun 23 85 | 2 30 PM.

328 Mickle Street | Camden New Jersey |
June 23 '85

Dear friend

I have no idea of going abroad—couldn't do it anyhow—as I am very lame & find it difficult to get about here, even small distances— Otherwise I should have been on to see Alma and you—for my wishes have been with you both—My general health however is very fair. I am getting along here better than you think for—for very little suffices me—

As I write it is beautiful weather—temperature perfect—Love to Alma & all—

Walt Whitman

1329. *To Mary Whitall Smith*

ADDRESS: Miss Mary Whitall Smith | by R Pearsall Smith | Care J S Morgan & Co: | Bankers | London | England. POSTMARKS: Philadelphia | Jul | 20 | 1885 | Paid (?); London (?) | H | Jy 31 85 | AE.

328 Mickle Street | Camden   New Jersey | July 20 '85
—noon—

Dear Mary Smith

Your second letter (dated July 9) came an hour ago—welcomed,

---

44. "The Voice of the Rain."

45. WW's question mark. On September 6 he sent "photos &c" to the Rev. S. A. Barnett, of London, "for Toynbee Hall" (CB). This settlement house was established by young Oxford fellows and named for Arnold Toynbee, a friend of Mary Smith's future husband. It was described in a letter from Eldridge to O'Connor on August 10: "It is a sort of priesthood, but of course the vows are self imposed—Walt is their great exemplar

& read twice already—the acc't of the Toynbee?[45] Hall doings & chat deeply interesting to me—I think much of all genuine efforts of the human emotions, the soul & bodily & intellectual powers, to exploit themselves for humanity's good—the *efforts in themselves*, I mean (sometimes I am not sure but *they* are the main matter)—without stopping to calculate whether the investment is tip-top in a business or statistical point of view. These libations, ecstatic life-pourings as it were of precious wine or *rose-water* on vast desert sands or great polluted river—taking chances for returns *or no returns*—what were they (or are they) but the theory & practice of the beautiful God Christ? or of all divine personality?

We have had a week of furious hot weather here—& are having it yet —(Seems to have concentrated in & around Philadelphia)—I keep pretty well, considering—dont go out at all till toward sundown, but get on the river two or three hours afterwards every even'g—I send in Phil. Press my last little piece[46]—you must chew upon it a little—my inward idea in it being the least literary or *poetical*, & most physiological & scientific—

My last letter from Dr. Bucke spoke of his going off with a sick friend & relative to the Canadian Rockies, a jaunt of six or seven weeks—I have heard lately from John Burroughs—he has been writing quite a piece ab't Matthew Arnold, which I tho't at first I w'd send you, but I believe I won't—as it is not very clear or encouraging—rather *dis*couraging[47]—

Ab't myself & my own affairs there is nothing new or special to write, Mary dear. My house-lady Mrs. Davis continues to be in every respect (handiwork & atmosphere) the very best and most acceptable that could have befallen me—Hot as it is, & with several kind invitations away, I remain for the summer at my shanty in Mickle Street—upon the whole it is best for me—

Mary, I hope your next letter will tell me of a visit to Mrs. Gilchrist— As I close it suggests itself to me that I prepare one of the big photos (the one with hand up to mouth) & send you to give to the Toynbee? Hall folk—Love to you & all—

Walt Whitman

and teacher and they speak of him reverently as *Master*" (Berg). See also R. A. Parker, *The Transatlantic Smiths* (1959), 59.

46. Perhaps "Continuities," although I have not been able to find the "piece" in the *Press*.

47. Burroughs wrote to WW about his first meeting with Arnold on November 18, 1883 (Syracuse; Traubel, IV, 36). He discussed "Matthew Arnold's Criticism" in *The Century Magazine*, XXXVI (June, 1888), 185–194.

1330. *To John H. Johnston*

Camden, July 21, 1885

The watch (a beauty), the knives & forks & the china ware all reach'd me safely this afternoon[48]—thanks, thanks, & best love. . . . Am just going out for my evening sail on the Delaware. God bless you & yours.

1331. *To John H. Johnston*   7.31. [1885]

ADDRESS: John H Johnston | Jeweler | 150 Bowery Cor: Broome | New York City. POSTMARKS: Camden | Jul | 31 | 5 PM | 1885 | N.J.; A | 8–(?)–85 | (?) IA | N.Y.

Camden New Jersey | July 31   P M

I was affected by the heat—had vertigo fits—unconscious temporarily—fell—but really nothing serious[49]—Shall be out as usual in a day or two—Love to A[lma]—I suppose the book came—

W W

1332. *To Herbert Gilchrist*

ADDRESS: Mrs: Gilchrist[50] | 12 Well Road | Hampstead | London | England. POSTMARKS: Camden | Aug 1 | 5 PM | 1885 | N.J.; London N (?) | 7 U | Au 14(?) | (?).

328 Mickle Street | Camden New Jersey   U S America | August 1 '85

Dear Herbert Gilchrist

Yours of July 21 just rec'd, soliciting some definite word from me ab't an English or transatlantic "free will offering"—a proposed affec-

48. WW noted receipt of these articles in *CB* on July 19.
49. In an entry dated July 20 to 23 WW cited "the bad vertigo fits—bad fall." In another notation he described himself as "unwell" from July 20 to September 3 (*CB*). *The Critic* noted his prostration from the heat as well as the English "offering" on August 1.
50. WW made a mistake in addressing the envelope.
51. Mrs. Gilchrist on July 20, in what was to be her last letter to the poet, spoke of the eagerness of many young men in England to show their affection for WW. For this reason they inserted a paragraph in *The Athenaeum* on July 11 soliciting funds, but were disturbed by a notice in the Camden *Daily Post* of July 3 "which seems decisively to bid us desist!" (LC; Harned, 241). The *Daily Post* reprinted W. H. Ballou's interview with the poet from the Cleveland *Leader and Herald* on June 28, in which WW was quoted: "My income is just sufficient to keep my head above water—and what more can a poet ask?" *The Athenaeum* said in part: "The poet is in his sixty-seventh year, and has . . . maintained himself precariously by the sale of his works in poetry and prose, and by

tionate and voluntary gift to me from my friends there.[51] I feel deeply, even for the prompting of it, and should decidedly and gratefully accept any thing it produces. (My publisher David McKay, of Philadelphia, has just been over to pay the last half-annual royalty on my two Volumes *Leaves of Grass* and *Specimen Days*, which amounted to twenty-two dollars and six cents—this being the income to me from the sale of my books for the last six months.)[52]

Fearfully hot weather here. I have had a sunstroke which has made me weak, and kept me indoors for the last twelve days; but I move around the house, eat my rations fairly, write a little, and shall quite certainly soon resume my usual state of health, late times—(doubtless lower'd a slight notch or two, as I find that is the way things go on year after year.) Fortunately I have a good faithful young Jersey woman and friend, Mary Davis, who cooks for me, and vigilantly sees to me.

Give my love to Wm M. Rossetti[53] and to all enquiring friends, known or unknown.

You are at liberty to make any use of this letter you see fit.[54]

Walt Whitman

1333. *To Edward Carpenter*

ADDRESS: Edward Carpenter | Millthorpe | near Chesterfield | England. POSTMARKS: Camden | Aug | (?) | 8 PM | 1885 | N.J.; Philadelphia | Aug | 3 | 1885 | (?).

328 Mickle Street | Camden New Jersey   U S
America | Aug: 3 '85

Dear Edward Carpenter

Yours of June 9th with the draft for £50 has reached me & I have the money.[55] Hearty & affectionate thanks to you, dear friend, and to Bessie and Isabella Ford—

occasional contributions to magazines."

52. WW did not include his much larger income from the sales of poems and prose to magazines and newspapers (see 1353). On December 1, 1885, he received $20.71 in payment of royalties from McKay for the preceding six months (Pennsylvania).

53. On August 28 Rossetti wrote to WW: "You will believe that I received with pride & warm feeling the love wh. you sent me in a letter to Gilchrist, . . . & that I reciprocate your love with reverential affection" (Hanley).

54. A facsimile of this letter was made by Gilchrist and, according to his letter of September 5, was printed in *The Athenaeum* on August 22 and in the London *Daily News* on August 24 (Feinberg). The New York *Times* copied the article in *The Athenaeum* on September 4.

55. In American currency the gift amounted to $239.83 (CB). Although Carpenter dated his letter "9 June," and WW cited the same date, it was actually written on July 9, as the postmark on the envelope indicates (Feinberg).

I have suffered from the great heat here—have had two or three bad fits of vertigo (thermal fever the doctor calls it)—but shall soon almost certainly be around as usual—

Walt Whitman

1334. *To Elizabeth and Isabella Ford*

328 Mickle Street | Camden New Jersey   U S
America | Aug: 3d '85

Dear Bessie and Isabella Ford

I will at least write a line to say I have safely received your and Edward Carpenter's affectionate generous gift of £50. It has come very opportunely & I thank you all[56]—

I have been prostrated lately by sun-stroke, but am well recovering from it—

God bless you, dear friends,

Walt Whitman

1335. *To Edward Carpenter*

Camden New Jersey   U S America | Aug 5 '85

I wrote to you a few days since acknowledging with deepest thanks yours of June 9, safely rec'd—& stating that I had been prostrated by the heat, somewhat badly, but was on the mend—I still hold my own & consider myself recuperating—I hope you will meet my young American lady friend Mary Whitall Smith at Mrs. Gilchrist's—

W W

1336. *To William Sloane Kennedy*   *8.5.* [1885]

328 Mickle Street | Camden New Jersey   Aug: 5

Your card rec'd some days since—I had a sun stroke two weeks

56. The Ford sisters and Carpenter, in addition to this gift, sent a second check for $216.75 in May, 1886, and another one for £20 in July, 1887 (*CB*).

57. This card flattered Kennedy, who observed fervidly on August 8(?): "Your confidential item ab't royalties also makes me glad & wrings my heart at the same time." He enclosed $5, which, he declared, "is a pure *business* debt. $5000. represents my soul indebtedness to Walt Whitman, who is the only *god* I at present worship apart from the Universe as a whole" (Feinberg).

58. An envelope in the Feinberg Collection may belong with this letter: ADDRESS:

ago—makes me weak since (legs and bones like gelatine)—but I guess I am recuperating—My Phila: publisher McKay was just over here to pay me the income on the last six months' sales of my two Vols. L of G. and S Days—the am't was $22: & six cts.[57]

W W

1337. *To Mary Whitall Smith*[58]

TRANSCRIPT.

328 Mickle Street | Camden New Jersey   U S
America | Aug: 8 '85

Dear friend

Your *third* letter ab't the Tennyson visit arrived today—& has already been re-read with eager interest[59]—as was the Toynbee Hall one also. I now anticipate the one ab't your meeting Mrs. Gilchrist.—Thanks, dear girl, for the past & thanks for those to come—Since you left we've had over three weeks of extremely hot weather—it affected me badly, caused some fits, unconsciousness, falling &c—I can't go out, which is quite a cross—but no doubt in due time things will return to their usual routine. I am sitting here down stairs by the window in the little front room, writing this—Mrs. Davis has just brought me a beautiful perfect middling sized sun flower—it looks like a curious golden face turning toward me from its jar on the window sill—Fine day this for the Grant funeral show in New York which is going on as I write[60]—O I nearly forgot to mention the cyclone & destruction, brief but terrible, of last Monday[61]—they did not touch these premises—but came very near. Well, Mary, dear girl, I am making out a stupid letter—but I was determined to write something—Affectionate remembrances to Alys, the Father and Mother, Logan, and to Mr C[ostelloe][62]—

Walt Whitman

Miss Mary Whitall Smith | by R Pearsall Smith | Care J S Morgan & Co: | Bankers | London | England. POSTMARKS: Philadelphia, Pa. | (?) | 1885 | (?); London | A | 7 Sp | 85.

59. The Smiths went to see Tennyson with a letter of introduction from WW; see Mary W. Smith's letter on July 25 (Rollo G. Silver; Donaldson, 234–236).

60. The General died on July 23.

61. WW cited the cyclone in *CB* on August 3.

62. Benjamin F. C. Costelloe, Mary's future husband, called on WW with her on September 11, 1884 (*CB*).

1338. *To William Sloane Kennedy*

328 Mickle Street | Camden New Jersey
Aug: 10 '85 | noon

Dear W S K—

Just rec'd your cheering letter—with contents—all safe. Thanks—
I am getting along, but lack any thing like strength or alertness—No
probability of my visiting Boston—pleasant weather as I write seated
here & my little canary bird singing away like mad.

Walt Whitman

1339. *To Elizabeth and Isabella Ford*   *8.11. [1885]*

328 Mickle Street | Camden New Jersey   U S
America | Aug: 11

The letter from E[dward] C[arpenter] arrived, with contents—
all safe. I return heartfelt thanks—am only middling well in health, but
get about the house, & write a little[63]—

Walt Whitman

1340. *To Percy Ives*

328 Mickle street | Camden New Jersey
Aug: 11 '85

Dear Percy[64]

You cannot understand how comforted I was & am to hear from
you once more. I have been prostrated by the heat into even more than my
usual disability, but trust I am getting around—Respects to your father
—God bless you, dear boy—

Walt Whitman

63. Perhaps WW had forgotten his acknowledgment of the gift in 1334.
64. See 1053.
65. "Fancies at Navesink" was rejected by *Harper's Monthly* when WW submitted it on May 11; see Henry M. Alden's letter on May 12 (Feinberg; Traubel, I, 61).
He sent it on May 23 to James Knowles, editor of *The Nineteenth Century*, where it appeared in August. WW was paid $145.20 (*CB*).
66. James Redpath, at this time editor of *The North American Review*, was an old
friend of the poet (see 61). On June 30 Redpath asked WW to send to Rice, the proprietor of the magazine, his reminiscences of Abraham Lincoln and also requested an
article on "hospital life" during the Civil War for Rice's newspaper syndicate, which
printed popular articles in the Sunday editions of such papers as the New York *Tribune*
and the Philadelphia *Press* (Feinberg; Traubel, II, 73–74). Rice wrote on July 14 to
WW soliciting contributions for the syndicate (Syracuse; Traubel, IV, 329–330). Apparently WW accepted both proposals in his (lost) letter which Redpath received before
he wrote on July 16 (Feinberg; Traubel, II, 74–75).

Write whenever convenient—above address—I have a new poem in London *Nineteenth Century* for August—just out.[65]

1341. *To James Redpath*   [*8.12. 1885*]

ENDORSED: "Sent James Redpath | Aug. 12, '1885."
DRAFT LETTER.

All right, my dear J R—$60 for the Booth article will do, in full—(I reserve the right of printing it in future collections of my writings—this is indispensable.) I have been & am lingering under the miserable inertia following my sunstroke—otherwise should have sent you one or two articles—have them on the stocks—

Am very slowly gaining the tally of my previous strength—had none to spare before—

Thank you, dear friend, for your services & affectionate good will.[66]

1342. *To Charles Allen Thorndike Rice*   [*8.12. 1885*][67]

ENDORSED: "Aug: '85." DRAFT LETTER.

Received from Allen Thorndike Rice—by Mr. Ferris attorney and through James Redpath—Sixty Dollars for article *Booth and the Old Bowery*—which article I reserve the right to include & print in future collections of my writings.

1343. *To Charles W. Eldridge*[68]

TRANSCRIPT.

328 Mickle Street, Camden, | New Jersey,
Aug. 19, 1885

Glad to hear your mother is getting along, & better—give my respects and best wishes to her. . . .[69] Fine weather here—I got out

---

On August 11 Redpath informed WW that he was enclosing "a check for sixty dollars, which is payment for the article according to your own estimate of three thousand words, at the rate of twenty dollars a thousand, which is the very highest rate they [the syndicate] pay" (Feinberg; Traubel, II, 75). "Booth and 'The Bowery' " appeared in the New York *Tribune* on August 16. Redpath paid $50 for "Slang in America" on October 20 (Feinberg; Traubel, II, 232), which appeared in *The North American Review* in November, 1885.

67. It can be assumed that WW sent the receipt to Rice at the same time he wrote to Redpath. The transaction was recorded in *CB* on August 15.

68. Since Eldridge wrote to WW on August 17 (Feinberg) a letter which, according to his own notation, was "answ'd Aug 19," and since Eldridge was in Camden on August 5 (*CB*), he is the logical recipient of this letter. I have combined transcriptions from two auction records.

69. In the fragment of Eldridge's letter mounted in *CB*, there is no reference to his mother.

a little yesterday for the first time, but find myself weaker and lamer than ever—Your letter rec'd. If you see the Academy,[70] send it to me. I wrote yesterday (after receiving your letter) to Dr. Bucke, & for Wm. O'C[onnor][71]—have heard nothing at all from either since I saw you.

Walt Whitman

1344. *To Karl Knortz*   *9.10.* [*1885*]

Camden (328 Mickle st) Sept 10.

Dear Sir:

I send Rolleston's last letter to me—please look at the parts marked in blue—Did you get a note from me ab't two months ago?[72]

Walt Whitman

1345. *To Herbert Gilchrist*

ADDRESS: Herbert H Gilchrist | 12 Well Road | Hampstead | London | England. POSTMARKS: Philad(?) | S(?) | 18(?) | Pa(?); London N.W. | Z 7 | Sp 25 | 85.

Sept. 15 '85 | 328 Mickle Street | Camden
New Jersey | U S America

My dear friend

Yours of Sept: 5 just rec'd. Rossetti's remittance by P. O. drafts &c. duly reached me, & I have the money—(& very opportune it is.)[73] Edward Carpenter sent me £50 lately—the affectionate noble-hearted young man[74]—

As far as I can perceive & understand your scheme is managed admirably & to my entire satisfaction & deepest gratitude.

70. Buchanan's satirical poem "Socrates in Camden, with a Look Around" appeared in *The Academy* on August 15. The poem was an offshoot of his visit with WW on April 8 (*CB*), which he recorded in *A Look Round Literature* (1887). See also Blodgett, 84–85.
71. O'Connor was at Bucke's home in Canada in August (*CB*). When Bucke wrote to WW on September 15, O'Connor was about to leave Canada (Feinberg). He was with WW on September 24 and 25 (*CB*).
72. WW wrote this note on the last page of Rolleston's letter of August 4, and marked with a blue crayon those passages referring to Knortz's failure to revise Rolleston's translations (Feinberg; Traubel, III, 487–488). WW's last known communication in 1885 with Knortz was written on April 27 (see 1315).
73. On August 28 Rossetti sent the first instalment of £22.2.6, or $107.54 (Hanley).
74. See 1333.
75. Ruth Stafford married William C. Goldy (not Gouldy) on August 19, 1884, and left for Topeka, Kansas, on January 20, 1885 (*CB*). Her first child, born on June 27, 1885, was named Amy Whitman Goldy. See the following letter.

With me personally here every thing moves in pretty much the old current—not quite so well for bodily health of late & at present—yet not much different. The Staffords are well—Harry has a very fair situation (address RR Station, Marlton, New Jersey) & has a little printing office, besides his RR agency—Ruth is in Kansas, married to Wm Gouldy[75]— Ed called here a few days ago[76]—reported every one well[77]—

W W

Herbert, here are some names of friends (or used to be friends) of L of G. and W. W. for *your private information:*

Cyril Flower, Surrey House, Hyde Park Place—(used to read L of G, call'd upon me at Washington 14 years ago)[78]

John Addington Symonds, Davos, Platz—Switzerland

C Oscar Gridley, 9 Duke street, London Bridge—call'd on me here[79]

H Buxton Forman, 46 Marlborough Street, St John's Wood

G C Macaulay, Rugby

H J Bathgate, Oakenhold Hall, near Flint

1346. *To Herbert Gilchrist*   9.22. [1885]

ADDRESS: Herbert H Gilchrist | 12 Well Road | Hampstead | London | England. POSTMARKS: Camden | Sep | 22 | 12M | 1885 | N.J.; London. N.W. | 7 U | Oc 2 | 85.

Dear H—

This comes here, by absurd fault of address[80]—So I forward it to you—all goes on about the same with me[81]—I have rec'd a handsome present of horse & light wagon[82]—was down to Glendale all day last

76. Probably Harry's brother, Edwin.
77. WW did not inform Herbert that Deborah (Stafford) Browning gave birth to a daughter on February 2, 1885 (CB). The child, Ruth, died on July 26.
78. Flower, an English barrister, met WW in Washington in December, 1870 (see 427).
79. Gridley, who was the secretary of the Carlyle Society, called on WW in April, 1884 (CB). He contributed to the offering in 1885 (Traubel, IV, 210).
80. WW wrote this note on the verso of an envelope addressed to Gilchrist at Mickle Street.
81. On September 23 and 24 WW noted a "bad spell—lost eyesight—lost equilibrium." The attack must have been severe since Louisa and George visited him on September 24. O'Connor was in Camden for two days toward the end of September, and Burroughs came on October 1 (Barrus, 256) and Eldridge on the following day (CB). See also 1349.
82. On September 15 WW received a horse and wagon from Donaldson and twenty-eight friends, including Whittier, Mark Twain, Oliver Wendell Holmes, and Edwin Booth (Feinberg). Donaldson printed the letters from the donors (173–182). See also 1349.

406 THE COLLECTED WRITINGS OF WALT WHITMAN

Sunday—all well—Ruth home, with *her baby*, Harry home—trouble with throat—Mr and Mrs Stafford well—

Love to you and your dear mother—

W W

Sept 22

1347. *To Thomas Donaldson*

328 Mickle Street, | Camden, N.J., October 13, 1885.

Thank the Columbus Buggy Co., and their workmen, for the beautiful looking and practically perfect buggy furnished me. I get out in it every day—my only exercise—and I find it the easiest riding vehicle I ever sat in. Thank them for a most opportune kindness and generosity to me.

Walt Whitman.

1348. *To an Unidentified Correspondent*

328 Mickle Street, Camden, New Jersey,
October 30 | 85

[WW acknowledged with thanks receipt of a copy of "Bryant and his Friends" and wondered whether he should not have thanked General Wilson.][83]

83. General James Grant Wilson (see 920) was the author of *Bryant and His Friends* (1886).

84. Barrett, the actor (see 1262), sent $10 (*CB*). On November 9 WW received through Donaldson "Ferry pass for horse & buggy" (*CB*).

85. On October 19, accompanied by Dr. William Osler, WW went to see Professor Norris "ab't my eyes . . . satisfactory visit & examination—I had feared I was becoming blind. Dr N. decidedly discountenanced the idea" (*CB*).

86. William Duckett was the driver. After he received the carriage WW visited his friends more frequently. On November 1 he noted his "5th visit" to the Staffords. He went to see Harry Stafford and his wife later in the month, and had Thanksgiving Day dinner with Debbie Browning on November 26 (*CB*).

On either November 5 or 6 Sir Graham Balfour (1858–1929), the cousin and biographer of Robert Louis Stevenson, and Earl Russell, John Francis Stanley (1865–

1349. *To Thomas Donaldson*

ADDRESS: Thos: Donaldson | 326 North 40th Street |
Philadelphia. POSTMARKS: Camden | Nov | 9 |
1885 | N.J.; Received | Nov 9 | 3 PM | Phila.

328 Mickle St: Camden | Nov: 9 '85

Dear T D

Yours rec'd with L[awrence] B[arrett]'s check & the ferry
pass[84]—Many & best thanks—I will come over & see you all soon.

I am in good spirits, & somewhat better, but fearfully lame & disabled
yet[85]—go out with the horse & buggy every afternoon[86]—

W W

1350. *To Ernest Rhys*

328 Mickle Street | Camden New Jersey
U S America | Nov. 9 1885

My dear Sir[87]

Excuse the delay—I have rec'd the draft for 10 pounds, 10 shillings, & have drawn the money. As I understand it, the plan is to make a
selection from my Poems & put them in a Volume of your "Canterbury"
series, to be called *Walt Whitman's Poems*—you to select—& perhaps to
write Preface or Biographical notice, or what not—I am willing—on the
sole & specific condition that it is not to come for sale to this country,
without further & written permission from me.

Walt Whitman

1931), a barrister and brother of Bertrand Russell (who was later to marry Alys Smith),
called on WW. Russell contributed to the English offering; see Rossetti's letter on October 4 (Syracuse; Traubel, IV, 209).

87. Ernest Rhys (1859–1946), the English writer, wrote on May 31: "Let me
say simply in a young man's way to you who are an old man now, how dearly and
earnestly I think of you across the sea to-night, remembering the Past, looking on to the
great to-morrow, for perhaps of all young men you have helped me most powerfully &
perfectly" (Feinberg). On July 7 Rhys proposed a one-shilling edition of WW's poetry
in *The Canterbury Poets* series (Feinberg; Traubel, I, 451–453). On September 25–29
Rhys wrote for the third time after waiting "for a reply so far in vain," and included the
payment from Walter Scott, the English publisher of *The Canterbury Poets* (Feinberg;
Traubel, III, 162–164). On Rhys's letter WW wrote: "the little English selection from
L. of G. is out since, & the whole edition (10,000) sold."

1351. *To William Roscoe Thayer*

ADDRESS: Wm R Thayer | 68 Mt Auburn Street |
Cambridge | Mass:. POSTMARK: Philadelphia, (?) |
Nov 25 | (?) | 85.

> 328 Mickle Street | Camden New Jersey |
> Nov: 25 '85

My dear W R T[88]

Thanks for the $5. "remembrance." Nothing very new with me.
My sight is better—walking power slim, almost not at all—spirits buoy-
ant. Glad to get your letters. As I write, we here are just through a dark
November storm of three days, & the sun is coming out.

> Walt Whitman

1352. *To Herbert Gilchrist*

ADDRESS: Herbert H Gilchrist | 12 Well Road |
Hampstead | London | England. POSTMARKS:
Camden | Nov 30 | 4 PM | 1885 | N.J.; London,
N.W. | M Z | De 11 | 85.

> 328 Mickle street | Camden New Jersey |
> Nov: 30 '85   p m

Dear Herbert Gilchrist

What on earth can I say to you in response to the news about
your dearest mother in my[89] letter rec'd this morning?—words are such
weak things any how in so deep & solemn a case—makes me heavy
hearted indeed, & have been so, all the day. As it is I can only send best
best love & thoughts dwelling with her all the time[90]—

---

88. Thayer (1859–1923), the editor of John Hay's letters and the biographer of
Theodore Roosevelt, called on the poet on September 4 (*CB*). According to his "Personal Recollections of Walt Whitman" in *Scribner's Monthly*, LXV (1919), 674–687,
he visited WW with decided reluctance at the urging of Furness when he was on the
staff of the Philadelphia *Evening Telegraph*.

89. WW's error.

90. On September 29 Herbert reported to WW that "Mother is very sickly"
(Feinberg). On November 19 he said: "Her condition is critical. Four years ago our
dear mother was attacked by cancer with left breast. . . . Her strength seems daily
ebbing and her heart is very weak" (Feinberg). Mrs. Gilchrist died the day before WW
sent this letter. The son wrote with deep emotion on December 2: "The lovely spirit
fled on Sunday afternoon at five o'clock. . . . Ten days ago mother asked me if I had
written to you. . . . on her tomb I shall find a line from Leaves of Grass. In a little
memoranda addressed to us she noted your name down as the one friend in America
to whom we were to write to, in announcing darling mother's death. She died in my

I have seriously considered coming to London—but it seems impossible—I am still here—my eyesight is less disturbed, is nearly ab't as formerly—but my walking power worse than ever—they have to half carry me out to the wagon to take the only little exercise I get every day—but my spirits remain cheery & buoyant as ever—I eat and sleep fairly—am so far without any pain of violence—& still have my good & kind housekeeper Mrs. Davis—

Have just rec'd the third instalment (31 pounds 19 shillings) of the good English "offering" from Wm Rossetti—(some 49 pounds previously—making 81 pounds or thereabout altogether so far rec'd)[91]—and I can assure you it has been all most acceptable to me—& heart's thanks to you all—I was down yesterday to the Staffords' at Glendale.[92]

O how I wish I could see your dearest mother—again my best, dearest love to her.

                                                        Walt Whitman

1353. *To William Michael Rossetti*

                                        328 Mickle Street | Camden New Jersey |
                                                                Nov: 30 '85

My dear Wm Rossetti

        Yours of Nov: 13 with 31 pounds 19 shillings has been received—the third instalment of the "offering"[93]—my thanks are indeed deeper than words.

        I have just been writing to Herbert Gilchrist ab't his mother, & am filled with sadness—nothing new with me, only my eyesight is better—
                                                        Walt Whitman

arms" (Feinberg).
        91. See the following letter.
        92. WW was in Atlantic City on November 28 and at Glendale on the following day (CB).
        93. Up to this time WW had received three payments from Rossetti amounting to $446.18 (see 1355). Including the gift from Carpenter and the Ford sisters (see 1333) WW received in 1885 from his English admirers a total of $686.01. In contrast, his royalties from McKay for the year totalled $42.77 (Pennsylvania); he also received $24 from Worthington and about $47.50 from Scott (CB).
        In 1885 WW received at least $350.20 from sales of poems and articles: "Washington's Monument, February, 1885" ($10), "As One by One Withdraw the Lofty Actors" ($30), "Fancies at Navesink" ($145.20), "Booth and 'The Bowery'" ($60), "Slang in America" ($50), "Some Diary Notes at Random" ($10), "Abraham Lincoln" ($33), and "The Voice of the Rain" ($12). I have not ascertained how much he received from *The Critic* for the right to reprint the poem on Grant or from the New York *Star* for "How Leaves of Grass Was Made" (CHAL, II, 561).

1354. *To William Sloane Kennedy*

ENDORSED: "This letter relates to what now forms a
portion of Chap. III, of my 'Walt Whitman,'
W.S.K."

328 Mickle Street | Camden New Jersey |
Dec. 2 '85   noon

Dear W S K

Your "the Poet as a Craftsman" seems the best statement possible
of the modern scientific American point of view—as it certainly is the
highest & deepest (complimentary) statement of my theory & practise in
L of G—I only rec'd it an hour or so ago—so reserve most of what I have
to say for another letter[94]—

If you have them to spare, can you send copies by mail to following?
Wm M Rossetti, 5 Endsleigh Gardens, London n w Eng.
Prof. Edward Dowden, Temple Road, Winstead, Rathmines, Dublin,
  Ireland.
T W Rolleston, Dalgany, County Wicklow, Ireland
Lord Alfred Tennyson, Freshwater, Isle of Wight, Eng.
J. Addington Symonds, Davos, Platz, Switzerland
Edward Carpenter, Millthorpe near Chesterfield, Eng.
Ernest Rhys, 59 Cheyne Walk, Chelsea, London, Eng.
Dr Karl Knortz, 540 East 155th st., New York City
G. C. Macaulay, Rugby, England.
Richard Watson Gilder, Century office, Union Square, New York City
Wm D O'Connor, Life Saving Service, Washington D C
John Burroughs, West Park, Ulster Co. New York
Edmund C Stedman, author, New York City
Dr. R M Bucke, Asylum, London, Ontario, Canada
James Knowles, 1 Paternoster Square, London E C Eng:
—if you can send them, do it at your leisure—only let me know if you
cannot send—

I am getting along middling well. Eyesight improved again ab't as
well as of late years—Walking power quite gone—Spirits buoyant &
hearty—

The December sun is shining out wistfully as I finish, & I am going
out in my wagon, for a two or three hours drive—

Walt Whitman

94. *The Poet as A Craftsman* was printed as a twenty-page pamphlet by David
McKay in 1886.

1355. *To Herbert Gilchrist*

> 328 Mickle Street—Dec 4 '85 | Camden New Jersey
> U S America

Dear Herbert Gilchrist

As I doubt I made some small misfiguring in my last I send you an exact list of what I have rec'd of your good British "offering:"[95]

abt Sept. 8	£22.2.6—$107.54
Oct. 20th	37.12.—	183.11
Nov. 28	31 19—	155.53

—from which I am living—fuel, clothing, food, &c—personally living, this winter—

> Walt Whitman

You may as well hand this card to Mr Rossetti—

1356. *To Anne Gilchrist*

ENDORSED: "Received Dec: 18th/H H G." ADDRESS: Mrs: Anne Gilchrist | 12 Well Road | Hampstead | London | England. POSTMARKS: Camden | Dec | 8 | 2 PM | 1885 | N.J.; London N.W. | Z 7 | De 18 | 8(?).

> Camden   Tuesday noon | Dec: 8 '85

Dear friend[96]

I think of you very often, & cannot but trust your illness is less gloomy than Herbert states it—I know I have myself felt convinced several times during the last twelve or thirteen years of serious conditions & finálés that endurance has tided over—& O I so hope that you will surmount all—& that we may yet meet each other face to face.

I am middling well—the trouble in my eyesight (& very annoying it was to my *anchor'd* condition) seems to have pass'd over—We are having extremely cold weather here, & I do not get out of the house—but it is bright & sunny as I look out—I wrote a card to Herbert three days ago which I suppose he has rec'd—God's peace & blessing to you, beloved friend—

> Walt Whitman
> with best love

95. See 1352.
96. WW did not know that Mrs. Gilchrist had died on November 29.

1357. *To James Redpath*

ENDORSED: "Answered | ALLEN THORNDIKE RICE."

328 Mickle Street | Camden   New Jersey |
Dec: 10 1885

Thank you, my dear J R—& thank Mr Rice most heartily—for the copious & opportune supply of stationery sent me—It is just what I wanted—

Walt Whitman

Send proof of "Lincoln" article[97]—

1358. *To James Redpath*

328 Mickle Street | Camden New Jersey |
Dec: 15 '85—noon

My dear J R

I have rec'd the pay ($33) for the "Lincoln" article from Mr Rice, & sent a receipt for it[98]—

Your letter (12th) says you have sent the proof of "Lincoln" article same mail—*I have rec'd no proof.* It has evidently miscarried, or something. So please send me another—None was enclosed in the letter—I am ab't as usual—Come & see me whenever you can.

Walt Whitman

1359. *To Herbert Gilchrist*

ADDRESS: Herbert H Gilchrist | 12 Well Road | Hampstead | London | England. POSTMARKS: Camden | Dec | 15 | 4 PM | 1885 | N.J.; New York | Dec 16 | 1 30 AM | 85.

328 Mickle street | Camden New Jersey |
Dec. 15 1885

Dear Herbert

I have rec'd your letter. Nothing now remains but a sweet & rich memory—none more beautiful, all time, all life, all the earth—

97. See the following letter.
98. Probably the receipt was sent on the day WW received the money, December 4 (*CB*). This article, written at Rice's request (see 1341), was sent to Redpath on November 15 (*CB*), and was included in Rice's *Reminiscences of Abraham Lincoln* (1886), 469–475. WW was not proud of his "screed"; see his letter of March 18, 1886.
99. On January 25, 1886, Herbert wrote to WW: "You will be glad to hear that

I cannot write any thing of a letter to-day. I must sit alone & think.[99]

Walt Whitman

1360. *To Susan Stafford*   *12.15.* [1885]

ADDRESS: Mrs: Susan Stafford | Glendale | Ashland |
New Jersey. POSTMARK: Camden | Dec | 15 | 5
(?)M | 1885 | N.J.

328 Mickle Street   Camden | Dec: 15—Noon—
I got a letter from Herbert, this morning—death & burial of Mrs.
G[ilchrist]—gloomy, gloomy news. No doubt you will receive, or have
rec'd, a letter from H. but I tho't I w'd write. I am ab't as usual—the
rainy ride Sunday, has not done me any harm. Harry was here with me
yesterday. Looks & feels & is quite well—came up on a little business &
went back to Marlton on the 5 o'clock train—Bright & sunny here after a
long dark spell—hope George is better—

W W

1361. *To John Burroughs*

ADDRESS: John Burroughs | West Park | Ulster
county | New York. POSTMARK: Camden | Dec | 21 |
2 PM | 1885 | N.J.; New York | Dec 21(?) | 7 30
(?) | (?) | (?).

328 Mickle Street   Camden | Dec: 21 '85
My dear friend
Real glad to hear from you once more, as by yours of 18th—The
death of Mrs: Gilchrist is indeed a gloomy fact—she had cancer, &
suffered much the last three months of her life with asthma—for a long
time "every breath was a struggle," Herbert expresses it—the actual
cause of death was dilatation of the heart. Seems to me mortality never
enclosed a more beautiful spirit—
The trouble ab't my eyesight passed over, & I use both eyes now
same as before—I am living here, rather monotonously, but get along—

I am going to republish some of mother's essays; giving some account of her beautiful
life. May I quote from some of your letters to mother? and will you help me to the extent of lending me, mother's letters to you? those that you have kept? I should be glad
of them quite soon, as I have got to work already; at present thinking over her life is the
only thing that I take pleasure in: indeed I am unable to get my thoughts away, and I
don't want to. . . . never did son have such a sweet companionable dear mother as
mine" (Feinberg).

as I write, feel ab't the same as of late years—only the walking power seems quite gone from me, I can hardly get from one room to another—sometimes quite force myself to get out a few yards, but difficult & risky—

O'Connor seems to be holding on at Washington—I think he is middling well, except the leg power—his "gelatine legs" he calls them—will pass over I rather think—

I drove down yesterday (Sunday) to my friends the Staffords, 10 miles from here, & staid three hours, had dinner &c—I go *there* every Sunday—So I get stirr'd up some, but not half enough—three reasons, my natural sluggishness & the paralysis of late years, the weather, & my old, stiff, slow horse, with a lurking propensity to stumble down—

The "free will offering" of the English, through Rossetti, has amounted in the past year to over $400—I am living on it—I get a miserable return of royalties from McKay, my Philad. publisher—*not $50 for both books L of G. and S D for the past year*[1]—

John, I like *both the names* in your note—I cannot choose—if I lean at all it is in favor of "Spring Relish"[2]—either would be first rate—Did you get W S Kennedy's pamphlet "the Poet as a Craftsman"[3]—I hear from Dr Bucke quite often—he was the past season somewhat broken in physical stamina & health—but is better—he gives up for the present his European tour, but is coming here soon for a week—As I close, my bird is singing like a house afire, & the sun is shining out—I wish you were here to spend the day with me—

W W

Merry Christmas to you and 'Sula and the boy—

1. Actually $42.77 (see 1353).
2. "A Spring Relish" became the title of a chapter in *Signs and Seasons* (1886).
3. Burroughs liked what Kennedy had to say about WW in his pamphlet, but thought that the statements about style were unsound (Feinberg; Traubel, II, 86).

Undated Post Cards and Letters

1362. *To Peter Doyle*[1]

ADDRESS: Pete Doyle | M st South—bet 4½ & 6th |
Washington D C

431 Stevens   Camden | N. Jersey | March 17
All going on about as usual—

W. W.

1363. *To Peter Doyle*

ADDRESS: Pete Doyle | M street South bet 4½ & 6th |
Washington D C. POSTMARKS: Camden | Jun | 16 |
N.J.; Carrier | Jun | 8 AM | 17.

Camden   N J

Every thing still going on much the same—

WW

1364. *To Peter Doyle*

ADDRESS: Pete Doyle | M Street South—bet 4½ & 6th |
Washington | D C. POSTMARK: Camden | Oct | 6 |
N.J.; Carrier | 7 | Oct | 8 AM.

Camden   Oct 6

All goes about as usual—Was real glad to see Mrs & Mr N[ash][2]
and Mrs C—love to them—

W W

Undated Letters
   1. The following three post cards were probably written in the late 1870's. The
last known letter to Doyle was sent in 1880.
   2. The Nashes were old Washington friends (see 370).

1365. *To John Swinton*[3]

Editorial Office of the Galaxy, 40 Park Row,
New York. | Wednesday noon | 12th

John Swinton

Will call at 12, noon, to-morrow, 13th, to see you—
Will also call at 5 this afternoon—
At Galaxy office—

Walt Whitman

1366. *To John Swinton*[4]

ADDRESS: John Swinton | 134 East 34th Street | New
York City. POSTMARKS: Camden | Jun | (?); F |
6–11 | 7 P.

Camden New Jersey | June 11

Printed slips rec'd—much obliged—Am pretty well for me this
summer & having fair times as can be expected—

W W

1367. *To an Unidentified Correspondent*[5]

431 Stevens Street | Camden N J Oct 20

Hearty thanks for your beautiful little book which has just
reach'd me—

Walt Whitman

1368. *To Theodore Patterson*[6]

ADDRESS: Theodore Patterson | Courier Office | Federal
& Second | Camden. POSTMARK: Camden | Jul |
24(?) | 7 AM.

[J]uly

Upon seco[nd] thoughts you needn't make up my letter into two
pages. Leave it *in one long slip*, broadside, just as I saw it in first proof—
Send me up the revised by 9½ if convenient—

Whitman

3. This note was sent during one of WW's visits to New York, probably in the
years 1877 to 1879. The poet was in New York from March 2 to 27, 1877, from
June 13 to July 10, 1878, and from April 9 to June 14, 1879.
4. Probably this note was sent to Swinton before 1880, but it could have been
written later. Someone has dated the card "1878."
5. All that can be said of this note is that it was sent before April, 1884, when
WW moved to Mickle Street.
6. Since the Camden *County Courier* was established on June 2, 1882, the fol-

1369. *To Theodore Patterson*

ADDRESS: Theodore Patterson | *Courier* Office |
Federal near 2d | Camden. POSTMARK: C(?) | (?) |
7 AM | N.J.

If you have them, I should like about 20 of yesterday's *Couriers*—
Please roll them up & let Benner bring them up to me here—
                                    Walt Whitman
                                    431 Stevens St. cor West

1370. *To Theodore Patterson*

ADDRESS: Theodore Patterson | Daily *Courier*.

The: have you sent the 50 papers up to me at 431 Stevens? If not
please send right away—
                                                Whitman

1371. *To Theodore Patterson*

ADDRESS: Theodore Patterson.

Send up the printed slips to my house as soon as done—
                                    W Whitman
Tuesday afternoon

1372. *To Alma Johnston*[7]

TRANSCRIPT.

                431 Stevens St. | Thursday afternoon   half-past 2.
    This is the queer little book, perhaps you may remember I spoke
about, some weeks since. It is odd in form & may be without attractive-
ness at first—but somehow I think it real good & deep—(after you break
the crust & get a little used to it).
                                    Walt Whitman

lowing four notes were written after that date and probably not later than the end of
March, 1884. The note requesting "fifty papers" may have been sent after the appearance of the review of Bucke's book in the newspaper on June 2, 1883. Patterson was the
son of the editor and business manager of the newspaper. See George R. Prowell, *The
History of Camden County, New Jersey* (1886).
    7.   WW may have written to Mrs. Johnston after one of his visits to her home
in New York between 1878 and 1882, or he may have sent it after one of her trips to
Camden between 1878 and April, 1884.

Appendix A

A LIST OF MANUSCRIPT SOURCES AND PRINTED APPEARANCES

The locations of the manuscripts transcribed in this volume appear in the following list, through an abbreviation explained in the list of abbreviations in the Introduction. If the version in this edition is based upon a printed source, or is derived from an auction record, the fact is indicated by the word TEXT. Unless otherwise indicated, the manuscripts have not previously appeared in print. I record all earlier printed appearances through the abbreviations CT (Complete Text) and PT (Partial Text). The locations and printed appearances, if any, of draft letters are also noted. Occasionally the location of a letter is followed by a reference in parentheses to an envelope in another collection. In this way I have, artificially, restored the manuscript to its original state.

This list is followed by a list of the institutions and individuals whose manuscripts are represented in this volume, in order that scholars may readily tell which letters are to be found in a given collection.

708. Berg.
709. Berg.
710. Berg.
711. Robert H. Taylor.
712. Royal Library of Copenhagen. CT: *Orbis Litterarum*, VII (1949), 57.
713. TEXT: Transcription by Edward Dowden in Berg.
714. University of Texas.
715. Library of Congress. CT: *SB*, VIII (1956), 243.
716. Robert H. Taylor. DRAFT LETTER (in Feinberg).
717. Barrett. CT: *SB*, V, (1952), 206.
718. Berg.
719. Berg.
720. Trent. CT: Gohdes and Silver, 85–86. PT: Perry, 218.
721. Barrett. FACSIMILE: Bram Stoker, *Personal Reminiscences of Henry Irving* (1906), II, 96. DRAFT LETTER (in Lion): Traubel, IV, 185–186.
722. Robert H. Taylor. DRAFT LETTER (in Feinberg): *CW*, II, 257–259; Donaldson, 29–31; Holloway, 289–290; Nonesuch, 1024–1025.
723. Pennsylvania. CT: Nonesuch, 1023–1024. DRAFT LETTER (in Library of Congress): Harned, 145–146.
724. Columbia University.
725. Berg.
726. Hanley. DRAFT LETTER (in Feinberg).
727. Robert H. Taylor. DRAFT LETTER (in Feinberg).
728. Robert H. Taylor. DRAFT LETTER (in Feinberg).
729. Draft letter (?) in Feinberg.
730. Draft letter in Feinberg. CT: Traubel, II, 327; Nonesuch, 1025.
731. Feinberg.
732. Robert H. Taylor. DRAFT LETTER (in Feinberg).
733. Draft letter in Feinberg.
734. TEXT: Swann Auction Galleries, May 19, 1949.

735. TEXT: Barrus, 128.
736. Feinberg.
737. Draft letter in Feinberg.
738. Hanley.
739. Feinberg. CT: *The Emerson Society Quarterly*, I (IV Quarter), 8.
740. Draft letter in Feinberg.
741. TEXT: Typescript prepared by Will Monroe, Stanford University.
742. Draft letter in Feinberg.
743. Robert H. Taylor. DRAFT LETTER (in Feinberg).
744. FACSIMILE: G. M. Williamson, *Catalogue of A Collection of Books, Letters and Manuscripts written by Walt Whitman* (1903), 28.
745. Feinberg.
746. Draft letter in Barrett.
747. Draft letter in Feinberg. CT: Traubel, I, 369–371; Nonesuch, 1026–1027.
748. Barrett.
749. Feinberg.
750. Gregg M. Sinclair.
751. Lion.
752. Barrett. CT: Nonesuch, 1027–1028. PT: Barrus, 134–135.
753. Robert H. Taylor. PT: Gilchrist, 225.
754. Draft letter in Feinberg.
755. TEXT: Royal Cortissoz, *The Life of Whitelaw Reid* (1921), I, 312.
756. Smith College.
757. G. Ross Roy. PT: Perry, 244.
758. Library of Congress. CT: *SB*, VIII (1956), 244.
759. Royal Library of Copenhagen. CT: *Orbis Litterarum*, VII (1949), 56–57.
760. Hanley.
761. Feinberg. DRAFT LETTER (in Feinberg).
762. Draft letter in Feinberg. CT: Traubel, II, 326–327; Nonesuch, 1028.
763. A. J. Marino, who supplied a typescript.
763.1 Feinberg.
764. Feinberg.
765. Library of Congress.
766. TEXT: Typescript in Stanford University.
767. TEXT: American Art Association, November 5–6, 1923, and Edward Dowden's transcription in Berg.
768. Hanley. DRAFT LETTER (in Feinberg).
769. Feinberg. CT: Furness, 249–250.
770. Florence A. Hoadley.
771. Morgan.
772. Pennsylvania.
773. Feinberg.
774. Stillman Letters, Union College.
774.1 TEXT: Camden *Daily Post*, November 18, 1876.
775. Draft letter in Feinberg.
776. Pennsylvania.
777. Berg.
778. Library of Congress.
779. Pennsylvania.
780. NYPL.
781. Feinberg: CT: *Calamus*, 165–166; *CW*, VIII, 158–159.
782. Feinberg.
783. Feinberg.
784. Missouri Historical Society. CT: *Missouri Historical Society Bulletin*, XVI (1960), 104.
785. Trent. CT: *Calamus*, 170; *CW*, VIII, 163 (dated 1878).
786. Feinberg.
786.1 Feinberg.
787. Feinberg. CT: *Calamus*, 166–167; *CW*, VIII, 159–160.
788. Yale.
789. Draft letter owned by Louis H. Silver.
790. TEXT: Photostat in possession of Professor Emory Holloway.
791. Feinberg.
792. TEXT: Barrus, 139.
793. Pennsylvania.
794. Florence A. Hoadley.
795. Florence A. Hoadley.
796. Berg. PT: Barrus, 159.
797. Draft letter in Feinberg.
798. Feinberg.
799. Barrett. PT: Barrus, 159.
800. Pennsylvania.
801. Barrett. PT: Barrus, 110, 160.
802. Pennsylvania.
803. NYPL. PT: Barrus, 164.
804. Barrett.
805. Morgan.
806. Pennsylvania.
807. Barrett.
808. Pennsylvania.
809. Pennsylvania (Envelope in Feinberg).
810. Pennsylvania.
811. Barrett. PT: Barrus, 163–164; Nonesuch, 1029.
812. Feinberg.
813. Pennsylvania.

814. Pennsylvania.
815. Ben Bloomfield, who supplied a typescript.
816. Berg.
817. Feinberg. CT: *Calamus*, 167–168; *CW*, VIII, 160–161.
818. Feinberg. CT: Nonesuch, 1029–1030.
819. Professor Thomas Ollive Mabbott, who supplied a typescript. CT: Barrus, 144 (dated June 28).
820. TEXT: *The Modern School*, VI (April–May, 1919), 126. PT: Barrus, 166.
821. Trent. CT: *Calamus*, 168; *CW*, VIII, 161–162.
822. Morgan.
823. TEXT: Amy Haslam Dowe, "A Child's Memories of the Whitmans" (unpublished).
824. Feinberg. CT: *Eclectic*, LXVII (1898), 458.
825. Barrett.
825.1 Feinberg. CT: *Eclectic*, LXVII (1898), 458–459; *Bookman* (London), LXXII (1927), 204.
826. Berg.
827. Morgan.
828. Pennsylvania.
829. Feinberg. CT: *Calamus*, 168–169; *CW*, VIII, 162–163.
830. Morgan.
831. Pennsylvania (Envelope in Feinberg).
832. Pennsylvania.
832.1 Feinberg.
833. Missouri Historical Society. CT: *Missouri Historical Society Bulletin*, XVI (1960), 105–106.
834. TEXT: Typescript in Stanford University.
835. Trent. CT: Gohdes and Silver, 87.
836. Feinberg.
837. TEXT: Typescript in Stanford University.
838. Pennsylvania.
839. Pennsylvania.
839.1 TEXT: Anderson Galleries, October 18, 1923.
840. Yale.
841. Trent. CT: Gohdes and Silver, 87.
842. Trent. CT: Gohdes and Silver, 88.
843. Pennsylvania.
844. Pennsylvania.
844.1 Feinberg.
845. Pennsylvania (Envelope in Feinberg).

846. Berg.
847. Pennsylvania.
848. Doheny. CT: Barrus, 172. PT: *Memoranda During the War*, ed. Basler (1962), 27.
849. Feinberg. FACSIMILE: Charles N. Elliot, *Walt Whitman as Man, Poet and Friend* (1915), 82–83.
850. Hanley. CT: Barrus, 172.
851. Pennsylvania.
852. TEXT: Barrus, 172–173.
853. Pennsylvania (Envelope in Feinberg).
854. TEXT: Barrus, 173–174.
855. Pennsylvania (Envelope in Feinberg).
856. Barrett. PT: Barrus, 174.
857. Barrett.
858. Feinberg.
859. Feinberg.
860. Feinberg.
861. Yale.
862. Pennsylvania (Envelope in Feinberg).
863. Pennsylvania (Envelope in Feinberg).
864. Morgan (Envelope in Feinberg).
865. Feinberg.
866. Rosamond Gilder.
867. Whitman House, Camden. CT: *AL*, VIII (1937), 424–425; Nonesuch, 1030–1031.
868. Whitman House, Camden. CT: *AL*, VIII (1937), 425–427.
869. Pennsylvania.
870. Trent. CT: Gohdes and Silver, 88.
871. Berg.
872. Hanley. CT: Barrus, 176.
873. Pennsylvania.
874. Hanley.
875. Library of Congress. CT: *SB*, VIII (1956), 246.
876. Hanley.
877. Trent. CT: Gohdes and Silver, 142 (undated).
878. Feinberg.
879. Pennsylvania.
880. Berg. FACSIMILE (partial): *Bookman* (London), LXXII (1927), 204.
881. Feinberg.
882. Draft letter in Hanley. CT: Donaldson, 230–231; Nonesuch, 1031–1032.
883. Berg (Envelope in Feinberg).
884. University of Texas. FACSIMILE:

Donaldson, 194. CT: *Donaldson*, 232–233 (dated August 29).

885. Pennsylvania (Envelope in Feinberg).

886. TEXT: Typescript in Stanford University.

887. Berg.

888. Dr. R. J. H. DeLoach.

889. Library of Congress. CT: *SB*, VIII (1956), 247.

890. Library of Congress. CT: *SB*, VIII (1956), 247.

891. Trent. CT: Gohdes and Silver, 89.

892. Yale.

893. Pennsylvania.

894. Trent. CT: Gohdes and Silver, 89.

895. Library of Congress. CT: *SB*, VIII (1956), 247.

896. Pennsylvania.

897. Feinberg.

898. Doheny. PT (summary): Barrus, 180.

899. Pennsylvania.

900. Draft letter in Barrett.

901. Feinberg.

902. Barrett. CT: Nonesuch, 1035–1036 (dated [1879]). PT: Barrus, 180–181.

903. Pennsylvania.

904. TEXT: American Art Association, March 10–11, 1924.

904.1 Draft letter in Library of Congress.

905. Barrett. FACSIMILE: *Nocturne* (Spring, 1955), 11.

906. Historical Society of Pennsylvania. CT: *AL*, VIII (1937), 427; Nonesuch, 1032.

907. Pennsylvania (Envelope in Feinberg).

908. Pennsylvania (Envelope in Feinberg).

909. Feinberg.

910. Yale. CT: Barrus, 182.

911. Yale.

912. Pennsylvania.

913. Feinberg.

914. Yale.

915. TEXT: Typescript prepared by the secretary of Ogden Reid. CT: *SB*, VIII (1956), 247.

916. Pennsylvania.

917. Library of Congress. CT: *SB*, VIII (1956), 248.

918. Library of Congress. CT: *SB*, VIII (1956), 248.

919. Berg.

920. TEXT: Anderson Galleries, December 8, 1927.

921. TEXT: Catalog of Thomas Madigan (1930).

922. Berg. PT: Asselineau, 407*n*.

923. Pennsylvania.

924. Trent. CT: Gohdes and Silver, 90.

925. TEXT: Anderson Galleries, October 19–20, 1926.

926. Barrett. PT: Barrus, 146, 179, 186.

927. Feinberg.

928. Feinberg.

929. Barrett.

930. Feinberg.

931. Pennsylvania (Envelope in Feinberg). CT: Nonesuch, 1032–1033. PT: Gilchrist, 252; Harned, 186.

932. Doheny.

933. Doheny. PT: Barrus, 187; Nonesuch, 1033–1034.

934. Missouri Historical Society. CT: *Missouri Historical Society Bulletin*, XVI (1960), 106–107.

935. Missouri Historical Society. CT: *Missouri Historical Society Bulletin*, XVI (1960), 107–108.

936. Missouri Historical Society. CT: *Missouri Historical Society Bulletin*, XVI (1960), 108–109.

937. Berg.

938. Barrett. CT: R. U. Johnson, *Remembered Yesterdays* (1923), 335. DRAFT LETTER (in Feinberg).

939. Feinberg. CT: *Calamus*, 170–171; *CW*, VIII, 163–166; Nonesuch, 1034–1035.

940. Feinberg. PT: Gilchrist, 253.

941. Barrett. PT: Barrus, 188.

942. Feinberg.

943. Doheny. CT: Barrus, 189–190.

944. Pennsylvania.

945. TEXT: *AL*, IX (1937–1938), 243.

946. Feinberg. PT: Barrus, 190.

947. Harvard.

948. Library of Congress.

949. Furness Collection, Pennsylvania.

949.1 Furness Collection, Pennsylvania.

950. Feinberg.

951. Feinberg.

951.1 Library of Congress. FACSIMILE: *Memoranda During the War*, ed., Basler (1962), 31.

952. Feinberg.

953. Pennsylvania.

954. TEXT: Barrus, 191. (Envelope in Feinberg).

955. Berg. CT: Augustine Birrell, *Frederick Locker-Lampson—A Character Sketch* (1920), 135–136.
956. Pennsylvania.
957. NYPL.
957.1 John Mayfield.
958. Library of Congress. CT: *SB*, VIII (1956), 248–249.
959. Doheny.
960. TEXT: Chicago Book and Art Auction, April 29, 1931.
961. Camden County Historical Society.
962. Feinberg.
963. Feinberg.
964. Trent. CT: *Calamus*, 172; *CW*, VIII, 166.
965. TEXT: American Art Association, November 4–5, 1923.
966. Camden County Historical Society.
967. Walt Whitman House, Camden. CT: *AL*, VIII (1937), 428.
968. Feinberg.
969. Walt Whitman Birthplace, gift of Oscar Lion.
970. Hanley.
971. Pennsylvania.
972. Williams College.
973. Feinberg.
974. Royal Library of Copenhagen. CT: *Orbis Litterarum*, VII (1949), 57–58.
975. Pennsylvania.
976. Yale (Envelope in Feinberg). PT: William Lyon Phelps, *Howells, James, Bryant and Other Essays* (1924), 31–32.
977. Hanley.
978. University of Buffalo.
979. Berg.
980. Barrett.
981. Morgan (Envelope in Feinberg).
982. Berg.
983. Rosamond Gilder.
984. University of Texas.
985. Rosamond Gilder; Trent and Doheny. DRAFT LETTER (in Yale). PT: Barrus, 196–197.
986. Doheny. CT: A. E. Newton, *A Magnificent Farce* (1921), 152. PT: Barrus, 196.
987. Feinberg.
988. Barrett. CT: Barrus, 197.
989. Rosamond Gilder.
990. Trent. CT: Gohdes and Silver, 91–92.
991. Draft letter in Barrett.

992. TEXT: Swann Auction Galleries, April 4–5, 1951.
993. Morgan.
994. Berg.
995. Trent.
996. Feinberg.
997. Feinberg.
998. Feinberg.
999. Feinberg.
1000. Berg (Envelope in Feinberg). PT: Asselineau, 407n.
1001. Feinberg.
1002. TEXT: Barrus, 198–199.
1003. Library of Congress. CT: *AL*, VIII (1937), 428.
1004. Lion. CT: A. H. Joline, *Meditations of An Autograph Collector* (1902), 163.
1005. Feinberg.
1006. Berg (Envelope in the collection of the late Dr. Max Thorek).
1007. Lincoln Memorial Library.
1008. Berg.
1009. Harvard.
1010. Feinberg.
1011. Feinberg.
1012. Berg.
1013. Trent. CT: Gohdes and Silver, 92.
1014. Feinberg.
1015. Feinberg.
1016. Feinberg.
1017. Feinberg.
1018. Doheny. CT: Barrus, 200; Nonesuch, 1036–1037 (dated [March 29]).
1019. Trent. CT: Gohdes and Silver, 92–94.
1020. Pennsylvania. PT: Gilchrist, 263.
1021. Feinberg.
1022. TEXT: *Alpress Broadsides*, ed. Frank Ankenbrand, Jr. (1935).
1023. William E. Barton Estate. CT: *Putnam's Monthly*, V (1908), 168–169; Nonesuch, 1037.
1024. Feinberg.
1025. Feinberg.
1026. Professor Rollo G. Silver.
1027. Huntington. DRAFT LETTER (in Library of Congress): *CW*, VIII, 276–277.
1028. Feinberg.
1029. Yale.
1030. Hanley. DRAFT LETTER (in Library of Congress): *CW*, VIII, 277–278.
1031. Maine Historical Society.

1032. Hanley. DRAFT LETTER (in Library of Congress): *CW*, VIII, 278.
1033. Hanley.
1034. Hanley. DRAFT LETTER (in Library of Congress): *CW*, VIII, 279.
1035. Yale. DRAFT LETTER (in Library of Congress): *CW*, VIII, 280–281.
1036. Yale. DRAFT LETTER (in Library of Congress): *CW*, VIII, 281.
1037. Feinberg. DRAFT LETTER (in Library of Congress): *CW*, VIII, 281.
1038. TEXT: Barrus, 205–206.
1039. Berg.
1040. Draft letter in Library of Congress. CT: *CW*, VIII, 282.
1041. Barrett.
1042. Berg.
1043. State Historical Society of Wisconsin. DRAFT LETTER (in Library of Congress): *CW*, VIII, 282.
1044. Dr. R. J. H. DeLoach.
1045. NYPL. CT: *AL*, VII (1935), 80–81.
1046. TEXT: Sotheby & Company, May 13, 1935.
1047. Barrett.
1048. University of California (Berkeley).
1049. Feinberg.
1050. Feinberg.
1051. Missouri Historical Society. CT: *Missouri Historical Society Bulletin*, XVI (1960), 109–110.
1052. Feinberg.
1053. TEXT: *Detroit Historical Society Bulletin*, XVI (February, 1960), 6.
1054. Berg.
1055. Yale. DRAFT LETTER (in Library of Congress): *CW*, VIII, 283–284.
1056. Feinberg.
1057. Yale. DRAFT LETTER (in Library of Congress): *CW*, VIII, 284–285.
1058. Northwestern University. FACSIMILE: G. W. Allen, *Walt Whitman* (1961), 120.
1059. Barrett. CT: Barrus, 206; Nonesuch, 1038.
1060. Feinberg.
1061. Mr. and Mrs. Stephen Greene. FACSIMILE: Burroughs, *Whitman: A Study* (1896), 76. CT:

The Modern School, VI (April–May, 1919), 126–127. PT: Barrus, 206–207; Nonesuch, 1038–1039.
1062. Barrett (Envelope in Ohio Wesleyan).
1063. Draft letter in Library of Congress.
1064. Draft letter in Library of Congress. CT: *CW*, VIII, 286.
1065. Feinberg. CT: Nonesuch, 1039.
1066. Yale.
1067. Missouri Historical Society. CT: *Missouri Historical Society Bulletin*, XVI (1960), 110–111.
1068. Feinberg.
1069. Berg. FACSIMILE: *Walt Whitman's Correspondence: A Checklist* (1957), viii.
1070. Feinberg.
1071. TEXT: *The Autograph*, I (December, 1911), 33.
1072. Wesleyan University.
1073. Syracuse University.
1074. Morgan (Envelope in Feinberg).
1075. Trent. CT: Gohdes and Silver, 90 (dated 1880); Frenz, 51.
1076. Feinberg.
1077. TEXT: Anderson Galleries, April 19–20, 1933.
1078. Yale.
1079. Yale. DRAFT LETTER (in Library of Congress): *CW*, VIII, 288.
1080. Feinberg.
1081. Hanley.
1082. Royal Library of Copenhagen. CT: *Orbis Litterarum*, VII (1948), 58–59.
1083. Library of Congress.
1084. Yale. PT: *Specimen Days* (1882), 316–317; *CW*, V, 259–261; Boston *Herald*, October 15, 1882; Furness, 251–252; Nonesuch, 1039–1040.
1085. Trent. CT: Gohdes and Silver, 94.
1086. Draft letter in Library of Congress. CT: Furness, 252; Frenz, 52–53.
1087. Pennsylvania (Envelope in Feinberg).
1088. TEXT: American Art Association, January 31, 1939.
1089. TEXT: *The Collector*, LVII (1943), 38.
1090. Feinberg.
1091. Yale.
1092. Feinberg. CT: Allen, 503.

1093. Feinberg.

1094. Berg.

1095. Photostat at Pennsylvania. PT: Holloway, *Free and Lonesome Heart* (1960), 208–209.

1096. Hanley. DRAFT LETTER (in Library of Congress): *CW*, VIII, 290–291.

1097. Hanley. DRAFT LETTER (in Library of Congress): *CW*, VIII, 291.

1098. Barrett (Envelope in Feinberg). CT: *SB*, V (1952), 206.

1099. Hanley. DRAFT LETTER (in Library of Congress): *CW*, VIII, 292–293.

1100. Feinberg.

1101. Hanley. DRAFT LETTER (in Library of Congress): *CW*, VIII, 294. COPY (in Library of Congress): *CW*, VIII, 295.

1102. Feinberg.

1103. Pennsylvania.

1104. Professor Rollo G. Silver.

1105. Telegram in Hanley. DRAFT COPY (in Library of Congress): *CW*, VIII, 296.

1106. TEXT: Anderson Galleries, October 19–20, 1926.

1107. Hanley. DRAFT LETTER (in Library of Congress): *CW*, VIII, 296–297. ANOTHER DRAFT (in Library of Congress). COPY OF DRAFT (in Feinberg).

1108. Huntington. PT: Barrus, 209–210; Nonesuch, 1040–1041.

1109. TEXT: Dodd, Mead & Company, Catalog 59 (March, 1901).

1110. Berg.

1111. Berg.

1112. Berg.

1113. Dr. Cornelius Greenway, who supplied a typescript.

1114. Feinberg.

1115. Berg. PT: Perry, 233.

1116. Washington University, St. Louis.

1117. Draft letter in Library of Congress.

1118. Draft receipt in Library of Congress. CT: Philadelphia *Press*, June 16, 1882.

1119. Library of Congress. CT: *SB*, VIII (1956), 249.

1120. Trent. CT: Gohdes and Silver, 94.

1121. Feinberg.

1122. Berg.

1123. Feinberg.

1124. Berg. PT: Perry, 230–231; Barrus, 216*n*.

1125. Berg. PT: Barrus, 216*n*.

1126. Feinberg.

1127. TEXT: *SD*, 291. CT: the Boston *Herald*, October 15, 1882; *CW*, V, 38–39.

1128. Barrett.

1129. Lion.

1130. Feinberg.

1131. Historical Society of Pennsylvania.

1132. Berg.

1133. Draft letter in Pennsylvania.

1134. Berg.

1135. Feinberg.

1136. Berg.

1137. Barrett. CT: *This World*, July 1, 1882; Asselineau, 250*n*.

1138. Berg.

1139. Library of Congress.

1140. Berg.

1141. Berg.

1142. Berg.

1143. Berg.

1144. Berg.

1145. Pennsylvania.

1146. TEXT: Typescript in Stanford University.

1147. Draft letter in Library of Congress.

1148. Berg.

1149. Berg.

1150. Doheny. PT: Barrus, 99, 222; Nonesuch, 1042.

1151. Morgan.

1152. Doheny.

1153. Morgan.

1154. Berg.

1155. Berg.

1156. Columbia University. CT: *AL*, VIII (1937), 429.

1157. Abernethy Library of American Literature, Middlebury College.

1158. Feinberg.

1159. Berg.

1160. Berg.

1161. Feinberg.

1162. Berg. PT: Perry, 238–239 (dated 1883).

1163. Berg.

1164. Morgan.

1165. Royal Library of Copenhagen. CT: *Orbis Litterarum*, VII (1949), 59.

1166. Royal Library of Copenhagen. CT: *Orbis Litterarum*, VII (1949), 60.
1167. Berg.
1168. Feinberg.
1169. Berg.
1170. Morgan.
1171. Berg.
1172. TEXT: Dowden's transcription in Berg.
1173. Berg. PT: Nonesuch, 1042–1044.
1174. Barrett. CT: Knortz, 90; *AL*, XX (1948), 157.
1175. Massachusetts Historical Society. CT: *The Emerson Society Quarterly*, I (IV Quarter), 9.
1176. Barrett. CT: Knortz, 90; *AL*, XX (1948), 157–158.
1177. Trent. CT: Gohdes and Silver, 95.
1178. William Andrews Clark Memorial Library of the University of California, Los Angeles.
1179. Abernethy Library of American Literature, Middlebury College.
1180. Dr. Alma Howard (photostat in possession of Horst Frenz). CT: Frenz, 71–72.
1181. Berg.
1182. Feinberg.
1183. Berg.
1184. Berg.
1185. Berg.
1186. Yale.
1187. University of Chicago.
1188. Berg.
1189. Feinberg.
1190. Ohio Wesleyan.
1191. Feinberg. PT: Barrus, 240.
1192. Berg.
1193. Berg.
1194. Berg. PT: Perry, 237.
1195. Berg.
1196. Berg.
1197. Yale.
1198. Morgan (Envelope in Feinberg).
1199. Feinberg.
1200. Berg.
1201. Berg.
1202. TEXT: Barrus, 240–241.
1203. Berg. PT: *Harvard Studies and Notes in Philology and Literature*, XIV (1932), 32n.; Esther Shephard, *Walt Whitman's Pose* (1938), 352.
1204. Berg.
1205. Berg. PT: *Harvard Studies and Notes in Philology and Literature*, XIV (1932), 32n.; Shephard, 352.
1206. Berg.
1207. Berg. PT: *Harvard Studies and Notes in Philology and Literature*, XIV (1932), 32n.
1208. Barrett.
1209. Doheny. PT: Barrus, 111–112; Nonesuch, 1041 (dated 1882).
1210. Berg. PT: Holloway, *Free and Lonesome Heart* (1960), 200.
1211. Berg. PT: *Harvard Studies and Notes in Philology and Literature*, XIV (1932), 32n.; Shephard, 352–353.
1212. Berg.
1213. Feinberg.
1214. Trent. CT: Gohdes and Silver, 95. PT: Kennedy, 50.
1215. Berg. PT: Barrus, 225; Asselineau, 251.
1216. Pennsylvania.
1217. Trent. CT: Gohdes and Silver, 95.
1218. Morgan.
1219. Trent. CT: Gohdes and Silver, 96. PT: Kennedy, 50.
1220. Berg. PT: *Harvard Studies and Notes in Philology and Literature*, XIV (1932), 32n.
1221. Berg.
1222. Barrett.
1223. Barrett. CT: Knortz, 91; *AL*, XX (1948), 158.
1224. Feinberg.
1225. Berg.
1226. Berg. DRAFT LETTER (in Feinberg).
1227. Feinberg.
1228. Berg.
1229. Professor G. Ross Roy.
1230. Barrett.
1231. Barrett.
1232. Berg.
1233. Trent. CT: Gohdes and Silver, 96–97.
1234. Berg.
1235. Barrett. CT: *SB*, V (1952), 206–207.
1236. Berg.
1237. Berg.
1238. Berg.
1239. Berg.
1240. Berg.
1241. Amy Lowell Collection, Harvard.
1242. Feinberg.
1243. SOURCE: Barrus, 246.

1244. Slack Collection, Marietta College.
1245. Feinberg.
1246. SOURCE: Catalog of George J. C. Grasberger, Inc., 1924(?).
1247. Berg.
1248. TEXT: Sotheby & Company, May 13, 1935.
1249. Berg.
1250. Feinberg. CT: *WWN*, IV (June, 1958), 88.
1251. Barrett.
1252. Feinberg.
1253. Feinberg.
1254. Missouri Historical Society. CT: *Missouri Historical Society Bulletin*, XVI (1960), 111.
1255. Feinberg.
1256. Feinberg. CT: *WWN*, IV (June, 1958), 88.
1257. Berg.
1258. Wellesley College.
1259. Barrett. CT: Knortz, 91; *AL*, XX (1948), 159.
1260. Berg.
1261. Photostat in possession of Percy Muir.
1262. Berg.
1263. Pennsylvania.
1264. Feinberg.
1265. Feinberg. CT: *Colophon*, n.s., II (1937), 198. PT: Binns, 315.
1266. Feinberg. CT: *WWN*, IV (June, 1958), 88.
1267. Feinberg.
1268. Feinberg. PT: Barrus, 247–248.
1269. SOURCE: American Art Association, November 5–6, 1923.
1270. Morgan.
1271. Draft letter in Feinberg.
1272. Trent. CT: Gohdes and Silver, 97.
1273. Hanley.
1274. FACSIMILE: *Collection of Whitmaniana in the Reference Library Bolton* (1931), 15.
1275. Feinberg. CT: *Colophon*, n.s., II (1937), 199 (dated 1885).
1276. Feinberg.
1277. SOURCE: Stan V. Henkel's Catalog, February 26, 1912.
1278. Feinberg.
1279. Feinberg.
1280. Mrs. Barbara Halpern. TEXT: *Colophon*, n.s., II (1937), 199.
1281. Draft letter in Pennsylvania.
1282. Trent. CT: Gohdes and Silver, 98.

DRAFT LETTER (in Library of Congress).
1283. Feinberg.
1284. Trent. CT: Gohdes and Silver, 98.
1285. Whitman House, Camden.
1286. Pennsylvania.
1287. Draft letter in Library of Congress. CT: *AL*, VIII (1937), 429; Frenz, 92–93.
1288. The Walter Hampden Memorial Library, The Players, New York. CT: *WWR*, VI (1960), 49.
1289. The Walter Hampden Memorial Library, The Players, New York. CT: *WWR*, VI (1960), 50.
1290. Berg.
1291. Draft letter in Library of Congress. CT: Frenz, 98.
1292. Berg.
1293. Berg.
1294. Columbia University. CT: Elizabeth Dunbar, *Talcott Williams* (1936), 191; *AL*, VIII (1937), 430.
1295. Doheny.
1296. Columbia University. CT: *AL*, VIII (1937), 430.
1297. Doheny.
1298. Draft letter in Library of Congress.
1299. TEXT: Catalog of Edward C. Lowe, June, 1935.
1300. Feinberg.
1301. Feinberg.
1302. Library of Congress and Feinberg.
1303. Doheny.
1304. Whitman House, Camden.
1305. SOURCE: American Art Association, April 19–21, 1932.
1306. Feinberg. CT: *Victorian Studies*, I (1957), 182.
1307. Yale.
1308. Trent. CT: Gohdes and Silver, 98–99.
1309. Barrett and Feinberg. FACSIMILE: Brooklyn *Times*, April 2, 1892; S. M. Ostrander, *A History of the City of Brooklyn* (1894), II, 90. PT: Kennedy, *Walt Whitman's Diary in Canada*, 64–65; *I Sit and Look Out* (1932), 15.
1310. Berg.
1311. Ohio Wesleyan.
1312. Ohio Wesleyan. PT: Alma Calder Johnston, "Personal Memories of

Walt Whitman," *The Bookman*, XLVI (1917), 412.

1313. Pennsylvania (Envelope in Feinberg).

1314. Feinberg.

1315. Barrett. CT: Knortz, 91; *AL*, XX (1948), 159.

1316. Feinberg. FACSIMILE (in part): New York *Daily Graphic*, May 31, 1885.

1317. NYPL. CT: *AL*, VII (1935), 81 (dated 1888).

1318. Barrett.

1319. Rutgers University. CT: *Journal of the Rutgers University Library*, VIII (1944), 18.

1320. Berg.

1321. Feinberg.

1322. Morgan and Pennsylvania (Envelope in Feinberg).

1323. Trent. CT: Gohdes and Silver, 99.

1324. Barrett. CT: *SB*, V (1952), 207.

1325. Berg. PT: *Harvard Studies and Notes in Philology and Literature*, XIV (1932), 10.

1326. Feinberg. CT: *Colophon*, n.s., II (1937), 200.

1327. Trent. CT: Barrus, 252.

1328. Feinberg.

1329. Feinberg. CT: *Colophon*, n.s., II (1937), 200–201. PT: R. A. Parker, *The Transatlantic Smiths* (1959), 59–60.

1330. TEXT: Anderson Galleries, October 18, 1923.

1331. Feinberg.

1332. Pennsylvania. CT: *London Athenaeum*, August 22, 1885; *Letters of William Michael Rossetti*, ed. Gohdes and Baum (1934), 157–158.

1333. Hanley.

1334. FACSIMILE: *Collection of Whitmaniana in the Reference Library* Bolton (1931), 14.

1335. Trent. CT: Gohdes and Silver, 99.

1336. Trent. CT: Gohdes and Silver, 100. PT: Kennedy, 50.

1337. Mrs. Barbara Halpern. TEXT: *Colophon*, n.s., II (1937), 201–202.

1338. Trent. CT: Gohdes and Silver, 100. PT: Kennedy, 50.

1339. FACSIMILE: *Collection of Whitmaniana in the Reference Library* Bolton (1931), 15.

1340. FACSIMILE: Detroit *Sunday News-Tribune*, April 5, 1896.

1341. Draft Letter in Feinberg. CT: Traubel, II, 76; Nonesuch, 1044.

1342. Draft letter in Feinberg.

1343. TEXT: Anderson Galleries, October 18, 1923, and May 1, 1916.

1344. Feinberg. CT: Traubel, III, 488.

1345. Pennsylvania (Envelope in Feinberg).

1346. Hanley (Envelope in Feinberg).

1347. TEXT: Donaldson, 184.

1348. SOURCE: American Art Association, January 8–9, 1925.

1349. Hanley. CT: Donaldson, 190 (dated October 9).

1350. Robert H. Taylor.

1351. Barrett.

1352. Pennsylvania (Envelope in Feinberg).

1353. Hanley.

1354. Rutgers University. CT: *Journal of the Rutgers University Library*, VIII (1944), 19–20.

1355. Barrett. CT: *SB*, V (1952), 207–208.

1356. Pennsylvania (Envelope in Feinberg).

1357. John Carter Brown Library, Brown University.

1358. Feinberg.

1359. Pennsylvania (Envelope in Feinberg). CT: Gilchrist, 284; Harned, xxxvi; Holloway, 309; Nonesuch, 1045; Allen, 524.

1360. Feinberg.

1361. Berg. PT: Barrus, 152, 257–258; Nonesuch, 1050–1051 (dated 1888).

1362. William E. Barton Estate.

1363. British Museum.

1364. Feinberg.

1365. William E. Barton Estate.

1366. Yale.

1367. Morgan.

1368. Feinberg.

1369. Feinberg.

1370. Feinberg.

1371. Feinberg.

1372. TEXT: Catalog of George J. C. Grasberger, 1924(?).

Collections

904.1 (*draft*), 917, 918, 948, 951.1, 958, 997, 1003, 1027 (*draft*), 1030 (*draft*), 1032 (*draft*), 1034–1037 (*drafts*), 1040 (*draft*), 1043 (*draft*), 1055 (*draft*), 1057 (*draft*), 1063 (*draft*), 1064 (*draft*), 1079 (*draft*), 1083, 1086 (*draft*), 1096 (*draft*), 1097 (*draft*), 1099 (*draft*), 1101 (*draft and copy*), 1105 (*draft*), 1107 (*two drafts*), 1117 (*draft*), 1118 (*draft receipt*), 1139, 1147 (*draft*), 1182 (*draft*), 1287 (*draft*), 1291 (*draft*), 1298 (*draft*), 1302.
Lincoln Memorial University, 1007.
Oscar Lion Collection, New York Public Library, 751, 1004, 1129.
Amy Lowell Collection, Harvard University, 1241.
Professor Thomas Ollive Mabbott, 819.
Maine Historical Society, 1031.
A. J. Marino, 763 (*typescript*).
Massachusetts Historical Society, 1175.
John S. Mayfield, 957.1.
Missouri Historical Society, 784, 833, 934–936, 1051, 1067, 1254.
Pierpont Morgan Library, 771, 805, 822, 827, 830, 864, 981, 993, 1074, 1151, 1153, 1164, 1170, 1198, 1218, 1270, 1322, 1367.
Percy Muir, 1261 (*photostat*).
New York Public Library, 780, 803, 957, 1045, 1317.
Northwestern University, 1058.
Ohio Wesleyan, env. 1062, 1190, 1311, 1312.
University of Pennsylvania, 723, 772, 776, 779, 793, 800, 802, 806, 808–810, 813, 814, 828, 831, 832, 838, 839, 843–845, 847, 851, 853, 855, 862, 863, 869, 873, 879, 885, 893, 896, 899, 903, 907, 908, 912, 916, 923, 931, 944, 953, 956, 971, 1020,

1087, 1095 (*photostat*), 1103, 1133 (*draft*), 1145, 1216, 1263, 1281 (*draft*), 1286, 1313, 1322, 1332, 1345, 1352, 1356, 1359.
Historical Society of Pennsylvania, 906, 1131.
Professor G. Ross Roy, 757, 1229.
Rutgers University, 1319, 1354.
Louis H. Silver, 789.
Professor Rollo G. Silver, 1026, 1104.
Gregg M. Sinclair, 750.
Slack Collection, Marietta College, 1244.
Smith College, 756.
Stillman Letters, Union College, 774.
Syracuse University, 1073.
Robert H. Taylor, 711, 716, 722, 727, 728, 732, 743, 753, 835, 841, 842, 1350.
University of Texas, 714, 884, 984.
Dr. Max Thorek, env. 1006.
Trent Collection, Duke University, 720, 785, 821, 870, 877, 891, 894, 924, 964, 985, 990, 995, 1013, 1019, 1075, 1085, 1120, 1177, 1214, 1217, 1219, 1233, 1272, 1282, 1284, 1308, 1323, 1327, 1335, 1336, 1338.
Washington University, St. Louis, 1116.
Wellesley College, 1258.
Wesleyan University, 1072.
Walt Whitman Birthplace, Huntington, N.Y., 969.
Whitman House, Camden, 867, 868, 967, 1285, 1304.
Williams College, 972.
State Historical Society of Wisconsin, 1043.
Yale University, 788, 840, 861, 892, 910, 911, 914, 976, 985 (*draft*), 1029, 1035, 1036, 1055, 1057, 1066, 1078, 1079, 1084, 1091, 1186, 1197, 1307, 1366.

Appendix B

A CHECK LIST OF WHITMAN'S LOST LETTERS

It is sometimes of importance to biographers and critics to know about letters WW wrote, even though the letters themselves are not extant. The entries in this check list include (1) the date, (2) the name of the recipient of WW's letter, and (3) the source of information which makes possible the reconstruction, unless the source is the *Commonplace-Book* (Feinberg). Many of the dates are approximate because the information is based upon a letter addressed to WW, which simply informs us that the poet had written before the correspondent had replied. I have indicated the date and present location of correspondence addressed to WW. Allusions to lost letters in WW's own correspondence are designated WW and followed by the appropriate letter number. Auction records which contained no text are incorporated into this list, since the letters as of the moment are "lost." The abbreviations are explained in the table of abbreviations in the Introduction.

1876

About January 1. To Jeannette L. Gilder. Letter from Miss Gilder, January 2 (LC).

February 2. To Thomas Dixon. Letter from Dixon, February 16 (Feinberg).

About February 15. To Edward Dowden. Letter from Dowden, February 16 (Feinberg).

March 2. To Edward Dowden. WW 720.

March 5. to Thomas Dixon. WW's notation on letter from Dixon, February 16 (Feinberg).

April 5. to Thomas Dixon. WW's notation on envelope of letter from Dixon, February 16 (Feinberg).

About April 19. To the Postmaster, New York City. WW 736.

April 22(?). To the Editor, London *Times*.

About April 25. To D. Jardine. Letter from Jardine, April 26 (Feinberg).

April. To the Editor, London *Times*.

About May 1. To the Editor, New York *Herald*. WW 746.

May 5. To Richard Maurice Bucke.

May 5. To Laura Curtis Bullard.

May 5. To the Editor, Chicago *Tribune*.

Early June. To William Michael Rossetti. WW 753.

Early June(?). To Rudolf Schmidt. WW 759.

June 30. To John M. Rogers. WW's notation on envelope of letter from Rogers, March 28 (Feinberg).

July 13. To John Newton Johnson. Letter from Johnson, July 17 (Feinberg).

July 14. To John M. Rogers. LC #108.

September 6. To C. W. Sheppard.

September 14. To Jeannette L. Gilder.

September 14. To Alfred, Lord Tennyson. WW 882.

September 24. To Whitney & Adams, booksellers.

September 25. To Asa K. Butts.

November 1(?). To Robert Buchanan.
November 1(?). To C. W. Sheppard.
November 3. To William Michael Rossetti.
November. To Edmund Clarence Stedman. Catalog of Walter T. Spencer, 1934.
December 13 or 14. To Joe Allen.
December 13 or 14. To George W. Childs.
December 13 or 14. To Miss Nicholson.
December 14. To Philip Ripley.

1877

About January 30. To George and Susan Stafford. Letter from Mrs. Stafford, January 31 (Feinberg).
March 12(?). To John Burroughs. WW 803.
About March 26. To John Newton Johnson. Letter from Johnson, March 27 (Feinberg).
May 2. To John Trivett Nettleship.
May 3. To William Michael Rossetti. Letter from Rossetti, June 15–22 (Feinberg).
May 4. To Joseph C. Baldwin.
May 4. To Thomas B. Freeman.
May 4. To the Editor, London *Examiner*.
May 4. To the Editor, *Secularist* (London), care of George William Foote.
May 7. To Walt Whitman Storms. Letter from Storms, September 1 (Feinberg).
June (?). To Trübner & Company. WW's notation on letter from Trübner, May 31 (LC).
About July 8. To Susan Stafford. Letter from Harry Stafford, July 9 (Feinberg).
About July 21. To Thomas Jefferson Whitman. Letter from Jeff, July 22 (Feinberg).
July 21(?). To Susan Stafford. WW 824.
July 29. To Susan Stafford.
August 15. To Harry Stafford.
September 10. To Harry and Susan Stafford.
About September 20. To Joseph C. Baldwin. Letter from Baldwin, September 21 (Feinberg).
September 23. To John Newton Johnson.

September 24. To Thomas Jefferson Whitman.
September 24. To Mary Van Nostrand.
October 2. To Edward Cattell.
October 11. To William Michael Rossetti.
October 11. To the Editor, *Secularist* (London), care of George William Foote.
October 17. To Harry Stafford.
October 25. To Edward Cattell.
October 28. To Harry Stafford.
About October 30. To Harry Stafford. Letter from Stafford, November 2 (Feinberg).
November 4. To Harry Stafford.
November 10. To George Stafford.
November 19. To George Stafford.
November 29. To Elmer E. Stafford.
December 4. To Deborah Stafford.
December 5. To W. B. Clarke, bookseller.
December 6. To Joseph B. Marvin.
December 23. To Susan Stafford.

1878

About January 17. To Elmer E. Stafford. Letter from Stafford, January 18 (Feinberg).
January 20 To Harry Stafford.
January 31. To Reuben Farwell.
February 1. To John M. Rogers.
February 6. To George and Susan Stafford.
February 10. To Edward Cattell.
February 24. To Mannahatta Whitman.
February 24. To Fanny Raymond Ritter.
February 24. To General William J. Sewell.
February 24. To D. M. Zimmerman.
February 25. To Priscilla Townsend(?).
February 26. To George and Susan Stafford.
February 27. To John Burroughs.
March 5. To John Burroughs.
March 5. To W. H. Stennett.
March 14. To Richard Maurice Bucke.
March 14. To John M. Rogers. WW's notation on envelope of letter from Rogers, February 21 (Feinberg).
March 19. To Anne Gilchrist.
March 19. To John Newton Johnson.
March 19. To George and Susan Stafford.

March 20.   To Alma(?) Johnston.
March 20.   To Ben Pease.
April 3.   To Thomas Dixon.
April 8.   To John Burroughs.
April 8.   To Peter Doyle.
April 8.   To Katharine Hillard.
April 8.   To George and Susan Stafford.
April 11.   To Louisa Orr Whitman.
April 13.   To Hannah Heyde.
April 13.   To John Burroughs.
April 13.   To John Newton Johnson.
April 15.   To George and Susan Stafford.
April 22.   To Hannah Heyde.
April 22.   To Thomas Jefferson Whitman.
April 22.   To George and Susan Stafford.
April 29.   To George and Susan Stafford.
April 30.   To Priscilla Townsend.
May 3.   To Thomas Jefferson Whitman.
May 3.   To Beatrice Gilchrist.
May 3.   To Susan Stafford.
May 8.   To Thomas Dixon.
May 8.   To Beatrice Gilchrist.
May 10.   To John Newton Johnson.
May 13.   To Broadbent & Taylor.
May 15.   To Hannah Heyde.
May 19.   To George and Susan Stafford.
June 5.   To Deborah Stafford.
June 5.   To George and Susan Stafford.
About June 15.   To Anne Gilchrist. WW 869.
July 11.   To Peter Doyle.
July 12.   To Richard Maurice Bucke.
August 14.   To Bartram Bonsall.
September 1.   To Hannah Heyde.
September 1.   To Mary Van Nostrand.
September 1.   To Thomas Jefferson Whitman.
September 1.   To Smith Caswell.
September 1.   To George and Susan Stafford.
September 9.   To B. Westermann & Company.
September 20.   To Hannah Heyde.
September 20.   To Sarony, the photographer.
September 20.   To Edwin Stafford.
September 23.   To Joseph C. Baldwin.
October 2.   To George and Susan Stafford.

October 3.   To Peter Doyle.
October 8.   To William Taylor.
October 13.   To Anne Gilchrist.
October 30.   To Thomas Jefferson Whitman.
November 3.   To Hannah Heyde.
November 3.   To Mary Van Nostrand.
November 3.   To Peter Doyle.
November 3.   To Beatrice Gilchrist.
November 3.   To Harry Stafford.
November 24.   To Joseph B. Marvin.
November 24.   To Susan Stafford.
November 24.   To William H. Taylor.
November 26.   To John Newton Johnson.
November 27.   To Josiah Child.
November 27.   To John Fraser, *Cope's Tobacco Plant*.
November.   To John Burroughs. Barrus, 180.
December 8.   To John H. Johnston.
December 9.   To Richard Maurice Bucke.
December 15.   To George Coffman.
December 20.   To Mary Van Nostrand.
December 20.   To Jeannette L. Gilder.
December 22.   To Jeannette L. Gilder.
December 23.   To Hannah Heyde.
December 27.   To Mrs. Charles Stuart Pratt, *Wide Awake Pleasure Book*.
December 30.   To Herbert Gilchrist.
December 30.   To Jeannette L. Gilder.

1879

January 4.   To Mrs. James Matlack Scovel.
January 13.   To Anne Gilchrist.
January 22.   To Nancy Whitman(?).
February 10.   To Henry M. Alden, *Harper's Magazine*.
February 16.   To S. H. Morse.
February 18.   To James Vick.
March 18.   To Hannah Heyde.
March 27.   To John H. Johnston.
March 27.   To Joseph B. Marvin.
March 27.   To Daniel L. Proudfit.
April 18(?).   To Hannah Heyde. MS Notes for *CB*.[1]
April 18(?).   To Mary Van Nostrand. MS Notes for *CB*.
April 18(?).   To John P. Miller. MS Notes for *CB*.

---

1. WW prepared these notes for inclusion in the *Commonplace-Book* upon his return to Camden. The manuscript is in the Feinberg Collection.

April 18(?). To Fred W. Rauch. MS Notes for *CB*.

April 29. To Mary Van Nostrand. MS Notes for *CB*.

April 29. To Alfred Janson Bloor. MS Notes for *CB*.

April 29. To William Cannon. MS Notes for *CB*.

April 29. To Eugene Conley. MS Notes for *CB*.

April 29. To Peter Doyle. MS Notes for *CB*.

April 29. To Colonel John W. Forney. MS Notes for *CB*.

April 29. To Tilghman Hiskey. MS Notes for *CB*.

April 29. To Albert Johnston. MS Notes for *CB*.

April 29. To John R. Johnston, Jr. MS Notes for *CB*.

May 28. To Whitelaw Reid. Letter from D. Nicholson (for Reid), May 29 (LC).

June 15. To John H. Johnston.

June 25. To Richard Maurice Bucke.

June 27. To Trübner & Company.

June 27. To Josiah Child.

About July 16. To G. P. Putnam's Sons. Letter from Putnam's, July 17 (LC).

July 20. To Hannah Heyde.

July 20. To Mary Van Nostrand.

August 5(?). To P. Armáchalain. Letter from Armáchalain, August 25 (Feinberg).

August 9. To T. W. H. Rolleston.

August 14. To T. W. H. Rolleston.

August 30. To Leavitt & Company.

October 11(?). To Hannah Heyde. WW 936.

October 11(?). To Mary Van Nostrand. WW 936.

October 11. To the Postmaster, Camden, N. J. WW 936.

October 24. To Hannah Heyde. *St. Louis Diary*.[2]

October 25. To Mr. and Mrs. James Matlack Scovel. *St. Louis Diary*.

October 30. To Fred W. Rauch. *St. Louis Diary*.

October 31. To W. R. Wood. *St. Louis Diary*.

October(?). To Richard Worthington. WW 969.

November 1. To Edward Cattell. *St. Louis Diary*.

November 1. To George Washington and Louisa Orr Whitman. *St. Louis Diary*.

November 1. To Hannah Heyde. *St. Louis Diary*.

November 1. To Mary Van Nostrand. *St. Louis Diary*.

November 1. To Clarence ("Clarry") Whittaker. *St. Louis Diary*.

November 3(?). To John Hardie. *St. Louis Diary*.

November 4. To Smith Caswell. *St. Louis Diary*.

November 5. To Nat Jones. *St. Louis Diary*.

November 5. To Captain Respegius Edward Lindell. *St. Louis Diary*.

November 5. To Charles Wood. *St. Louis Diary*.

November 12. To Richard Maurice Bucke. *St. Louis Diary*.

November 12. To Joseph B. Marvin. *St. Louis Diary*.

November 16. To George W. Childs. *St. Louis Diary*.

November 20. To Louisa Orr Whitman. *St. Louis Diary*.

November 20. To Henry ("Harry") L. Bonsall, Jr. *St. Louis Diary*.

November 21. To John Burroughs. *St. Louis Diary*.

November 24. To George W. Childs. *St. Louis Diary*.

November 24. To Thomas Nicholson(?). *St. Louis Diary*.

November 24. To George Washington and Louisa Orr Whitman. *St. Louis Diary*.

November 28. To Honora E. Thompson. *St. Louis Diary*.

November 28. To James W. Thompson. *St. Louis Diary*.

November 29. To Ida Johnston. *St. Louis Diary*.

November 29. To Fred W. Rauch. *St. Louis Diary*.

December 4. To Hannah Heyde. *St. Louis Diary*.

December 4. To Mary Van Nostrand. *St. Louis Diary*.

December 9. To Erastus Brainerd. *St. Louis Diary*.

2. These notes, now among the Livezey-Whitman Manuscripts at the University of California at Berkeley, were published in *WWR*, VII (1961), 3–14.

December 11. To Louisa Orr Whitman. *St. Louis Diary.*
December 11. To Hannah Heyde. *St. Louis Diary.*
December 17. To T. & J. Johnston & Company. *St. Louis Diary.*
December 17. To Hannah Heyde. *St. Louis Diary.*
December 17. To Mary Van Nostrand. *St. Louis Diary.*
December 18. To Louisa Orr Whitman. *St. Louis Diary.*
December 19. To Henry ("Harry") L. Bonsall, Jr. *St. Louis Diary.*
December 19. To Richard Maurice Bucke. *St. Louis Diary.*

1880

January 6. To Thomas Jefferson Whitman.
January 6. To Henry ("Harry") L. Bonsall, Jr.(?).
January 6. To Captain A. B. Frazee.
January 6. To the New York *Tribune*(?).
January 6. To the Philadelphia *Public Ledger*(?).
January 10. To T. & J. W. Johnson & Company.
January 13(?). To the Camden & Atlantic Railroad.
January 17. To Thomas J. Hall.
January 17. To Charles Pope.
January 22. To John H. Johnston.
January 22. To Trübner & Company.
January 26. To Richard Maurice Bucke.
January 26. To Albert Johnston.
January 30. To Richard Maurice Bucke.
January 30. To F. Gutekunst, photographer.
February 4. To James W. Thomson.
February 8. To Charles W. Post.
February 16. To Herbert J. Bathgate.
March 4(?). To Trübner & Company.
March 13. To Richard Maurice Bucke.
March 13. To Mrs. Ellen E. Dickinson.
March 14. To Herbert J. Bathgate.
March 16. To Thomas Jefferson Whitman.
March 16. To John Addington Symonds.
March 16. To Alfred, Lord Tennyson.
March 18. To Herbert J. Bathgate.
March 18. To John Gilmer Speed.

March 18. To James W. Thomson.
March 21. To William Michael Rossetti.
March 21. To A. C. Wheeler, *Sunnyside Press.*
April 13. To the Editor, Chicago *Tribune.*
April 13. To the Editor, Cincinnati *Commercial.*
May 6. To Hannah Heyde.
May 6. To General William J. Sewell.
May 24. To the Editor, *The Literary World.*
May 30. To Thomas Gibbons.
June 5. To Louisa Orr Whitman.
June 5. To Elmer E. Stafford.
June 5. To George and Susan Stafford.
June 8. To Mary E. Wager-Fisher.
June 8. To Mrs. Elisa S. Leggett.
June 9. To Henry ("Harry") L. Bonsall, Jr.
June 9. To Peter Doyle.
June 9. To John R. Johnston, Jr.
June 9. To Whitelaw Reid.
June 9. To C. H. Sholes.
June 10. To George Washington and Louisa Orr Whitman.
June 10. To Mary Van Nostrand.
June 10. To Colonel John W. Forney.
June 10. To George and Susan Stafford.
June 12. To Hannah Heyde.
June 12. To Mannahatta Whitman.
June 12. To Mrs. James Matlack Scovel.
June 14. To William Reidel (Reisdell?).
June 15. To William Hamilton.
June 15. To John L. Peck.
June 17 or 18. To the Editor, Boston *Herald.*
June 17 or 18. To the Editor, Camden *Daily Post.*
June 17 or 18. To the Editor, Chicago *Tribune.*
June 17 or 18. To the Editor, Cincinnati *Commercial.*
June 17 or 18. To the Editor, Detroit *Free Press.*
June 17 or 18. To the Editor, Halifax (Nova Scotia) *Chronicle.*
June 17 or 18. To the Editor, Louisville (Ky.) *Courier Journal.*
June 17 or 18. To the Editor, Montreal *Witness.*
June 17 or 18. To the Editor, Philadelphia *Press.*

June 17 or 18. To the Editor, St. Johns (New Brunswick) *Globe*.

June 17 or 18. To the Editor, Washington *Post*.

June 17 or 18. To the Editor, Woodstown (New Jersey) *Register*.

June 20. To George Washington and Louisa Orr Whitman.

June 20. To Thomas Jefferson Whitman.

June 20. To Hannah Heyde.

June 20. To Mary Van Nostrand.

June 20. To Joseph C. Baldwin (?).

June 20. To John Burroughs.

June 20. To Smith Caswell.

June 20. To Edward Cattell.

June 20. To William Clark.

June 20. To Peter Doyle.

June 20. To Harry Scovel.

June 20. To Elmer E. Stafford.

June 20. To George and Susan Stafford.

About June 23. To C. A. J. Hueckberny. Letter from Hueckberny, June 24 (Manchester).

June 24. To Harry Stafford.

June 26. To Katie Macdonald.

June 26. To Charles Warren Stoddard.

June 28. To William Erving.

June 29. To T. W. H. Rolleston.

July 4. To Norman McKenzie.

July 4. To George and Susan Stafford.

July 7. To Louisa Orr Whitman.

July 12. To Louisa Orr Whitman.

July 13. To James and Priscilla Townsend.

July 13. To Elmer E. Stafford.

July 16. To Charles Warren Stoddard.

About July 17. To Deborah V. Browning. Letter from Mrs. Browning, July 18 (Manchester).

July 24. To Hannah Heyde.

July 24. To Mary Van Nostrand.

July 24. To Harry Stafford.

July 25. To Louisa Orr Whitman.

July 25. To Charles S. Gleed.

July 25. To J. B. Lippincott.

August 15. To Louisa Orr Whitman.

August 15. To Thomas Jefferson Whitman.

August 15. To John Burroughs.

August 15. To Peter Doyle.

August 16. To W. Curtis Taylor, photographer.

August 23. To Hannah Heyde.

About September 7. To Jack Richardson. Letter from Richardson, September 8 (LC).

September 17. To Jack Richardson.

September 19. To John H. Ingram.

September 19. To Richard Worthington.

September 28. To Thomas Jefferson Whitman.

September 28. To Hannah Heyde.

September 28. To Mary Van Nostrand.

September 28. To Smith Caswell.

September 28. To Josiah Child.

September 28. To Edward Dowden.

September 28. To Charles S. Gleed.

September 28. To John Newton Johnson.

September 28. To John H. Johnston.

September 28. To T. W. H. Rolleston.

September 28. To Elmer E. Stafford.

September 28. To George and Susan Stafford.

September 28. To John Addington Symonds.

October 5. To Richard Maurice Bucke.

October 8. To W. R. Balch, Philadelphia *American*.

October 8. To Richard Maurice Bucke.

October 9. To the Editor, *Cope's Tobacco Plant*.

October 9. To the Editor, *Harper's New Monthly Magazine*.

Between October 10–13. To the Postmaster General, Ottawa, Canada.

October 15. To Richard Maurice Bucke.

October 23. To Richard Maurice Bucke.

October 27. To Hannah Heyde.

October 27. To Richard Maurice Bucke.

October 27. To George and Susan Stafford.

October 31. To James Arnold.

October 31. To Charlotte F. Bates.

October 31. To John Burroughs.

October 31. To George and Susan Stafford.

November 2. To the Editor, London (Ontario) *Advertiser*.

November 16. To Richard Maurice Bucke.

November 17. To Edward Dakin.

November 17. To Colin Mackenzie.

November 19. To Susan Stafford.

December 3. To the Editor, *The North American Review*.

December 6. To John Burroughs. WW 988.

December 9. To George and Susan Stafford.

About December 9. To Hannah L Taylor. Letter from Mrs. Taylor, December 10 (Feinberg).

December 11. To Joseph Baron.

December 19. To Jack Richardson.

December 19. To Harry Stafford.

December 19. To the Century Club, New York.

December 21. To Hannah Heyde.

December 21. To Mary Van Nostrand.

December 21. To Richard E. Labar.

December 27. To Mrs. Elisa S. Leggett.

December 31. To James Hearne of the Century Club.

December. To Leon Richeton. WW's notation on letter from Richeton, December 10 (Lion).

1881

January 2. To Susan Stafford.

January 6. To D. M. Zimmerman.

January 16. To E. H. Hames & Company, *The Literary World*.

January 23. To Richard Maurice Bucke.

January 25. To Richard Maurice Bucke.

January 26. To William A. Millis.

February 2. To Frank H. Ransom.

February 7. To the Editor, *The Literary World*.

February 13. To Richard Maurice Bucke.

February 16. To Anson Ryder, Jr.

About February 27. To John Alcott. Letter from Alcott, February 28 (LC).

March 6. To Trübner & Company.

About April 10. To George Parsons Lathrop. Letter from Lathrop, April 11 (LC).

April 20. To Richard Maurice Bucke.

April 20. To Charles T. Dillingham.

April 26. To T. W. H. Rolleston.

May 3. To W. R. Balch, of *The American*.

May 3. To the Editor, *Cope's Tobacco Plant*.

May 4. To Emil Scholl.

May 5. To Richard Maurice Bucke.

May 5. To the Editor, *The Critic*.

May 6 To W. R. Balch.

May 6. To Susan Stafford.

May 8. To John Boyle O'Reilly.

May 20. To Innes Randolph, of the Baltimore *American*.

May 20. To Charles Allen Thorndike Rice.

May 20. To Albert D. Shaw.

May 20. To the Editor, *Harper's New Monthly Magazine*.

May 27. To W. R. Balch.

May 28. To Jeannette L. Gilder.

June 2. To Susan Stafford.

June 5. To Richard Maurice Bucke.

June 5. To James R. Osgood. WW's notation on draft of 1035.

June 6. To George and Susan Stafford.

June 9. To Hannah Heyde.

June 9. To Mary Van Nostrand.

June 16. To W. R. Balch.

June 16. To John Fraser.

June 19. To Edward Cattell.

June 23. To Richard Maurice Bucke.

July 3(?). To Joseph B. Gilder. Envelope in Feinberg.

July 15. To Richard Maurice Bucke.

July 17. To Richard Maurice Bucke.

August 5. To Louisa Orr Whitman.

August 5. To Richard Maurice Bucke.

August 5. To Captain Respegius Edward Lindell.

August 7. To Louisa Orr Whitman.

August 7. To Richard Maurice Bucke.

August 7. To the Postmaster, Camden.

August 7. To the Postmaster, New York City.

August 17. To Sylvester Baxter.

August 17. To the Postmaster, Camden.

August 20. To Louisa Orr Whitman.

August 20. To Richard Maurice Bucke.

August 20. To the Postmaster, Camden.

August 21. To Henry ("Harry") L. Bonsall, Jr. (?).

August 21. To Charles Brown.

August 21. To Willard K. Clement.

August 21. To Richard E. Labar.

August 21. To Helen E. Price.

August 21. To the Editor, the Philadelphia *Press*.

September 1. To Richard Maurice Bucke.

September 9. To Louisa Orr Whitman.

September 9. To Franklin B. Sanborn.

September 11. To the Editor, the New York *Tribune*.

September 14. To the Secretary of War.

September 28. To Richard Maurice Bucke.

October 4(?). To Louisa Orr Whitman.

October 4. To Richard Maurice Bucke.

October 6. To Hannnah Heyde.

October 21. To Sylvester Baxter. Envelope in Feinberg.

October 23. To Harry Stafford. WW 1068.

October 29. To the Editor, *The North American Review*.

October 31. To James R. Osgood & Company.

October 31. To the Editor, the Boston *Post*.

November 1. To Hannah Heyde.

November 6. To Arthur E. Lebknecker.

November 6. To James R. Osgood & Company.

November 6. To Charles E. Shephard.

November 6. To Harry Stafford.

November 7. To Moncure D. Conway.

November 7. To William Michael Rosssetti.

November 7. To John Addington Symonds.

November 8. To the Editor, *The Critic*.

November 9. To T. W. H. Rolleston.

November 10. To Rudolf Schmidt.

November 14. To Howard M. Jenkins, of *The American*.

November 15. To John Burroughs.

November 16. To Ruth Stafford.

November 20. To the Editor, the Boston *Globe*.

November 20. To the Editor, the New York *Sun*.

November 21. To Richard Maurice Bucke.

November 23. To R. M. Ware.

December 14. To Mrs. D. C. Peck.

December 20. To Thomas Nicholson.

December 20. To Benjamin Ticknor.

December 22. To C. H. Farnam.

December 25. To Ruth Stafford.

December 28. To Richard Maurice Bucke.

1882

January 9. To Hannah Heyde.

January 9. To Richard Maurice Bucke.

January 10. To the Editor, Worthington (Minnesota) *Advance*.

January 21. To Daniel G. Brinton.

January 26. To John H. Johnston(?).

January 26. To William S. Walsh.

January 28. To Josiah Child.

February 2. To Richard Maurice Bucke.

February 3. To Edwin Stafford.

February 5. To the Postmaster, Boston.

February 9. To Mrs. V. O. Coburn.

March 8. To West Jersey and Seashore Railroad Company.

March 19. To Arthur E. Lebknecker.

April 8. To the Editor, *The North American Review*.

April 17. To the Editor, *The Critic*.

April 19. To Richard Maurice Bucke.

April 27. To Richard Maurice Bucke.

May 3. To John Burroughs.

May 4. To the Editor, *The North American Review*.

May 7. To Richard Maurice Bucke.

May 18. To the Editor, *The North American Review*.

May 19. To Franklin B. Sanborn.

May 23. To the Editor, the Boston *Globe*.

May 23. To the Editor, the Boston *Herald*.

May 23. To the Editor, the Boston *Post*.

May 23. To Crosby Stuart Noyes.

May 25. To Sylvester Baxter. Catalog of John Heise (1935).

June 10. To Richard Maurice Bucke.

Before August 15. To Herbert Gilchrist. Letter from Gilchrist, August 16 (Feinberg; Traubel, I, 227).

September 8. To the Editor, the New York *Times*.

September 8. To the Editor, the New York *Tribune*.

September 8. To the Editor, the New York *World*.

September 8. To the Editor, the Philadelphia *Press*.

September 10. To Harry Stafford. Formerly in the possession of Alfred F. Goldsmith.

Before September 23. To T. W. H. Rolleston. Letter from Rolleston, September 24 (LC; Frenz, 67).

Before September 23. To T. W. H. Rolleston. Letter from Rolleston, September 24 (LC; Frenz, 67).

October 9. To Richard Maurice Bucke. Letter from Bucke, October 11 (Feinberg).

October 9. To Richard Maurice Bucke. Letter from Bucke, October 11 (Feinberg).

October 13. To T. W. H. Rolleston.

October 26. To Charles S. King & Company.

Before October 28. To John Burroughs. Letter from Burroughs, October 29 (Feinberg; Traubel, I, 333).

November 3. To Mrs. Charles Hine.

November 6. To Richard Maurice Bucke. Letter from Bucke, November 9 (Feinberg).

December 20. To Hannah Heyde.

December 20. To Mary Van Nostrand.

1883

January 27. To John Burroughs.

January 30. To Mr. Anders.

February 6. To Hannah Heyde.

February 8. To Richard Maurice Bucke.

March 9. To Richard Maurice Bucke.

March 14. To Richard Maurice Bucke. Letter from Bucke, March 20 (Feinberg).

March 14. To L. S. S.

March 27. To John Burroughs. American Art Association, March 17, 1931.

May 31. To Richard Maurice Bucke. Letter from Bucke, June 2 (Feinberg).

June 3. To Charles H. Farnam.

June 24(?). To Hannah Heyde.

July 19. To Hannah Heyde.

July 20. To Wilson & McCormick, publishers.

August 30. To Richard Maurice Bucke. Letter from Bucke, September 9 (Feinberg).

September 4. To Harry Stafford. Formerly in the possession of Alfred F. Goldsmith.

September 13. To Richard Maurice Bucke. Letter from Bucke, September 23 (Feinberg).

September 17. To Harry Wroth.

Before September 25. To T. W. H. Rolleston. Letter from Rolleston, September 27 (LC; Frenz, 77).

October 14. To T. W. H. Rolleston.

November 12. To Jeannette L. and Joseph B. Gilder.

November 15. To H. N. Whitman. Letter from Whitman, November 20 (Feinberg).

November 17. To Jeannette L. and Joseph B. Gilder.

November 27. To H. N. Whitman. WW's notation on letter from Whitman, November 20 (Feinberg).

November 28(?). To the Editor, Harper's New Monthly Magazine.

December 9. To John Newton Johnson.

December 21. To Hannah Heyde.

December 21. To Mary Van Nostrand.

December 21. To the Editor, The North American Review.

December 27. To Jeannette L. and Joseph B. Gilder. Envelope: Berg.

1884

January 2. To Susan Stafford. WW 1257.

January 9. To the Editor, The Critic.

January 11. To Richard Maurice Bucke. Envelope: Professor Harold Blodgett.

January 13. To Harry Stafford. Formerly in the possession of Alfred F. Goldsmith.

January 14. To an unidentified correspondent. Catalog of John Heise, 1935.

April 20. To T. W. H. Rolleston.

After June 3. To Mrs. Mattie Maxim. Letter from Mrs. Maxim, June 3 (LC).

About July 19. To Parker Pillsbury. Letter from Pillsbury, July 30 (LC).

August 8. To the Editor, The Nineteenth Century (London).

September 1. To the Editor, The North American Review.

October 17. To Hannah Heyde.

October 17. To the Editor, Harper's New Monthly Magazine.

November 13. To Charles L. Heyde.

December 23. To Hannah Heyde.

December 23. To Mary Van Nostrand.

1885

January 5(?). To A. B. Drake. Letter from Drake, January 9 (Feinberg).

January 12. To the Editor, Harper's New Monthly Magazine.

February 20. To the Editor, the Philadelphia Press.

March 4(?). To John Boyle O'Reilly. Letter from O'Reilly, March 5 (Feinberg; Traubel, II, 38).

April 2. To the Editor, *Harper's New Monthly Magazine.*

May 11. To the Editor, *Harper's New Monthly Magazine.* Letter from Henry M. Alden, May 12 (Feinberg; Traubel, I, 61).

May 23. To James Knowles, *The Nineteenth Century.*

May 28. To William C. Bryant.

May 29. To Hannah Heyde.

May 29. To Mary Van Nostrand.

June 7. To the Editor, *Harper's New Monthly Magazine.*

June 9. To William C. Bryant.

About July 15. To James Redpath. Letter from Redpath, July 16 (Feinberg; Traubel, II, 74).

About July 29. To Hannah Heyde. Letter from Charles L. Heyde, July 30 (Trent).

About July 30. To Thomas Jefferson Whitman. Letter from Jeff, July 31 (Feinberg).

August 7. To Leon & Brothers, New York.

August 18. To Richard Maurice Bucke. WW 1343.

September 8. To William Michael Rossetti. Letter from Rossetti, October 4 (Syracuse; Traubel, IV, 209).

September 13. To Richard Maurice Bucke. Letter from Bucke, September 15 (Feinberg).

September 22. To James Redpath.

September 30. To Richard Maurice Bucke. Letter from Bucke, October 2 (Feinberg).

October 20. To William Michael Rossetti. Letter from Rossetti, November 13 (Feinberg; Traubel, II, 330).

November 11. To O. S. Baldwin, of *Baldwin's Monthly.*

November 15. To James Redpath.

After November 17. To Lorenz Reich. WW's notation on Reich's letter, November 17 (Feinberg).

December 22. To Hannah Heyde.

December 22. To Mary Van Nostrand.

Appendix C

A CALENDAR OF LETTERS WRITTEN TO WHITMAN

This Calendar includes extant letters written to WW. The following information appears in the entries: (1) the date; (2) the name of the correspondent, sometimes with a brief identification in order to indicate the nature of the correspondence; (3) the location of the letter, if known; and (4) appearance in print, if applicable. The letters to WW which are reproduced in this volumes are marked WW with the appropriate letter number. Excerpts from many of these letters appear in the notes. Abbreviations are explained in the table of abbreviations in the Introduction.

1876

January 2. From Jeannette L. Gilder. LC.

January 3. From Edward Carpenter. Feinberg. PT: Traubel, III, 414–418.

January 18. From Anne Gilchrist. LC. CT: Harned, 139–140.

January 26. From H. Buxton Forman. Feinberg. CT: Traubel, II, 266–267.

February 6. From Edward Dowden. Feinberg. CT: Traubel, I, 299–301.

[February 7]. From John Newton Johnson. Feinberg.

February 14. From Abraham Stoker. Feinberg. CT: Traubel, IV, 180–181.

February 16. From Thomas Dixon. Feinberg.

February 16. From Edward Dowden. Feinberg. CT: Traubel, I, 301–303.

February 18. From Alfred Webb (ordering books). Feinberg.

February 25. From Anne Gilchrist. LC. CT: Harned, 141–142.

February 28. From William Michael Rossetti. Feinberg.

February 29. From Kenningale Cook (ordering books). Feinberg.

March 11. From Anne Gilchrist. LC. CT: Harned, 143–144.

March 15. From Nancy M. Johnson (ordering a book). Feinberg.

March 16. From Edward Dowden. Feinberg. CT: Traubel, I, 122–123.

March 17. From E. Mell Boyle(?) (willing to advertise *Leaves of Grass*). Feinberg.

March 20. From Henry Abbey(?). Feinberg.

March 28. From John M. Rogers. Feinberg.

March 30. From Anne Gilchrist. LC. CT: Harned, 147–148.

March 30. From William Michael Rossetti. Feinberg.

March 30. From Therese C. Simpson and Elizabeth J. Scott-Moncrieff, admirers. Feinberg.

April 2. From Albert G. Knapp, an ex-soldier. Berg.

April 4. From William Michael Rossetti. Feinberg.

April 7. From E. F. Strickland, Jr. (requesting an autograph). Feinberg.

April 8. From Edward Carpenter. Feinberg.

April 9. From C. W. Hine (ordering a book). Feinberg.

April 14. From B. G. Morrison (ordering books). Feinberg.

April 15. From Dr. Ferdinand Seeger (payment for a book). Feinberg.

April 16. From Joaquin Miller. Feinberg. CT: Traubel, II, 139–140.

April 18. From Robert Buchanan. Feinberg.

April 18. From Rudolf Schmidt. Feinberg.

April 18. From Dr. Ferdinand Seeger (ordering a book). Feinberg.

April 19. From Charles P. Somerby, a bookseller. Feinberg.

April 21. From Anne Gilchrist. LC. CT: Harned, 149–151.

April 22. From J. M. Green (requesting WW act as poet at Dickinson College). Feinberg.

April 23. From John Quincy Adams Ward. Feinberg. CT: Traubel, II, 278.

April 24. From Moncure D. Conway. Feinberg. CT: Traubel, I, 346–347.

April 24. From John Swinton (ordering books). Feinberg.

April 25. From the Rev. A. P. Putnam (ordering books). Feinberg.

April 26. From D. Jardine (ordering a book). Feinberg.

April 26. From John T. Trowbridge (payment for a book). Feinberg.

April 27. From A. J. Davis (ordering books). Feinberg.

April 28. From Robert Buchanan. Feinberg.

May 1. From Susan Stafford. Feinberg.

May 2. From Charles W. Eldridge. Feinberg. CT: Traubel, III, 483.

May 3. From Laura Curtis Bullard. Feinberg. CT: Traubel, III, 555–556.

May 3. From S. W. Green, a New York printer. Feinberg.

May 7. From John Newton Johnson. Feinberg.

May 10. From S. F. Michel(?), for the Chicago *Tribune* (returning a manuscript). Feinberg.

May 12. From Charles P. Somerby. Feinberg.

May 18. From Anne Gilchrist. LC. CT: Harned, 152–153.

May 24. From Miss R. M. Cox (ordering a book). Feinberg.

June 1. From John Quincy Adams Ward (payment for books). Feinberg.

June 3. From Edward Carpenter. Feinberg.

June 17. From Thomas Dixon. Feinberg.

July 5. From John Newton Johnson. Feinberg.

July 10. From Whitelaw Reid. Feinberg. CT: Traubel, II, 212.

July 17. From John Newton Johnson. Feinberg.

July 24. From Rudolf Schmidt. Feinberg.

July 25. From John Hay. Feinberg. CT: Traubel, I, 60 (dated July 22).

[August 5]. From John Newton Johnson. Feinberg.

August 21. From James Arnold (acknowledging receipt of books). Feinberg.

September 23. From Justin H. McCarthy, Jr. (acknowledging receipt of a book). Feinberg.

September 28. From Charles P. Somerby. Feinberg.

October 4. From Edward Dowden. Feinberg. CT: Traubel, II, 90–91.

[October 6]. From John Newton Johnson. Feinberg.

November 12. From William Gardner Barton (requesting an autograph). Feinberg.

November 17. From W. A. Stagg (requesting an autograph). Feinberg.

About December 20. From John Newton Johnson. Feinberg.

December (?). From William Michael Rossetti. Feinberg.

1876(?). From George Fraser. LC.

1877

January 1. From Eugene Benson, a painter. LC.

January 8. From Robert Buchanan. Feinberg. CT: Traubel, I, 2–3.

January 23. From John Addington Symonds. Feinberg. CT: Traubel, I, 458–459.

January 25. From D. M. Zimmerman (requesting an article). LC.

January 31. From Susan Stafford. Feinberg.

February 1(?). From Thomas B. Freeman (acknowledging receipt of a book). Feinberg.

February 20. From John Newton Johnson. Feinberg.

March 1. From Edward Carpenter. Syracuse.

March 27. From John Newton Johnson. Feinberg.

March 27. From W. A. B. Jones (requesting an autograph). Feinberg.

March 29(?). From Scribners, Armstrong Company. LC.

April 1(?). From Harry Stafford. Feinberg.

April 6. From Sarah E. Bowen (or Brown), a friend of Amelia Johnston. LC.

April 23. From Kenningale Cook. Feinberg. CT: Traubel, II, 219.

May 13. From Joseph C. Baldwin. Feinberg.

May 13. From Thomas B. and P. J. Freeman. Feinberg.

May 20. From John Newton Johnson. Feinberg.

May 21. From Harry Stafford. Feinberg.

May 31. From Trübner & Company. LC.

June 15–22. From William Michael Rossetti. Feinberg. CT: Traubel, III, 170–172.

July 9. From Harry Stafford. Feinberg.

[July 12]. From St. Loe Strachey (sending verses). Feinberg.

July 12. From John Addington Symonds. Feinberg. CT: Traubel, III, 197.

July 21. From Harry Stafford. Feinberg.

July 22. From Thomas Jefferson Whitman. Feinberg.

August 2. From Kate A. Evans, a "rather gushing" admirer. Feinberg.

August 6. From Harry Stafford. Feinberg.

August 10. From John Burroughs. Feinberg. CT: Traubel, II, 318–319. PT: Barrus, 168–169.

August 11. From Joseph C. Baldwin. Feinberg.

August 14. From Harry Stafford. Feinberg.

August 17. From William Michael Rossetti. Feinberg.

September 1. From Walt Whitman Storms. Feinberg.

September 11. From Joseph C. Baldwin (requesting a loan). Feinberg.

September 16. From John Newton Johnson. Feinberg.

September 17. From Professor R. B. Anderson (asking for an appointment). Feinberg.

September 17. From Edward Carpenter. Syracuse. CT: Traubel, IV, 204–205.

September 20. From Edward Carpenter. Location unknown. CT: Traubel, IV, 205.

September 21. From Joseph C. Baldwin (acknowledging receipt of money). Feinberg.

September 24. From Annie Talman Smith, an admirer. Feinberg.

[September 24]. From John Swinton (introducing Annie Talman Smith). Feinberg.

September 25. From Harry Stafford. Feinberg.

September 29. From John Burroughs. Location unknown. PT: *Cope's Tobacco Plant*, II (1879), 319; *CW*, IV, 192–193.

October 3. From Claxton, Remsen, & Haffelfinger, booksellers. LC.

October 4. From Harry Stafford. Feinberg.

October 10. From Charles L. Heyde. Trent.

October 17. From Harry Stafford. Feinberg.

October 24. From Harry Stafford. Feinberg.

October 29. From Harry Stafford. Feinberg.

November 2. From Harry Stafford. Feinberg.

November 4. From Richard Maurice Bucke. Feinberg.

November 7. From Harry Stafford. Feinberg.

November 9. From Elmer E. Stafford. Feinberg.

November 13. From Harry Stafford. Feinberg.

[November 15]. From Edward D. Bellows (ordering books). LC.

November 17. From Harry Stafford. Feinberg.

November 21. From Harry Stafford. Feinberg.

November [26]. From Edward Cattell. Feinberg.

November 27. From Harry Stafford. Feinberg.

December 2. From John T. Trowbridge. Feinberg. CT: Traubel, II, 224–225.

December 17. From William Michael Rossetti. Feinberg.

December 18. From William H. Taylor (inviting WW for a visit). LC.

December 19. From Edward Carpenter. Feinberg. CT: Traubel, I, 189–190.

December 23. From Susan Stafford. Feinberg.

[December]. From Joaquin Miller. Feinberg. CT: Traubel, III, 225.

1877(?). 21 Sunday. From Edward Cattell. Feinberg.

1878

January 5. From Claxton, Remsen, & Haffelfinger, booksellers. LC.

January 11. From Elmer E. Stafford. Feinberg.

January 18. From Elmer E. Stafford. Feinberg.

January 18. From Harry Stafford. Feinberg.

January 20. From Peter Doyle(?). LC #195.

January 24. From Harry Stafford. Feinberg.

January 26. From Susan Stafford. Feinberg.

January 29. From Harry Stafford. Feinberg.

January 29. From W. L. Tiffany. Feinberg.

January 31. From C. B. Whitman (asking for genealogical data). Feinberg.

[January]. From George William Foote. Feinberg.

February 3. From John Burroughs. Lion. CT: Barrus, 171; William E. Barton, Abraham Lincoln and Walt Whitman (1928), 192–193; Traubel, IV, 463–464.

[February 8]. From John Newton Johnson. Feinberg.

February 21. From John M. Rogers. Feinberg.

February 23. From James Matlack Scovel. LC.

February 25. From John Burroughs. Feinberg. PT: Memoranda During the War, ed. Basler (1962), 27–28.

February 28. From John Burroughs. Feinberg.

March [14]. From John Newton Johnson. Feinberg.

March 16. From Mary Van Nostrand. Trent. CT: Gohdes and Silver, 207–208.

March 26. From Harry Stafford. Feinberg.

March 27. From Charles A. Raymond(?). Barrett.

April 4. From Susan Stafford. Feinberg.

April 11. From members of Sarah Mead's family (announcing Mrs. Mead's death). Feinberg.

April 20. From George Parsons Lathrop. Feinberg. CT: Traubel, II, 315–316.

May 5. From John Newton Johnson. Feinberg.

May 5. From Sidney Lanier. Feinberg. CT: Traubel, I, 208. PT: Kennedy, The Fight of a Book for the World (1926), 59–60.

May 13. From Edward Carpenter. Barrett. CT: Traubel, IV, 391–392.

June 5. From Harry Stafford. Feinberg.

June 7. From Mrs. Walter Bownes, a relative. LC.

July 11. From John Burroughs. Feinberg.

July 17. From Whitelaw Reid. Mrs. Doris Neale.

July 27. From Harry Stafford. Feinberg.

August 3. From Benjamin Gurney(?) (acknowledging receipt of books for Mr. Sarony). Hanley.

August 11. From Oscar Tottie (acknowledging receipt of books). LC.

[August 12]. From Beatrice Gilchrist. LC. CT: Harned, 156–158.

August 24. From Alfred, Lord Tennyson. Hanley. WW 884.

August 26. From Harry Stafford. Feinberg.

September 3. From Anne Gilchrist. LC. CT: Harned, 159–160.

September. From Anne Gilchrist. LC. CT: Harned, 154–155 (dated 1877).

October 7. From George W. Bull (requesting an autograph). LC. CT: Furness, 200.

October 25. From Anne Gilchrist. LC. CT: Harned, 161–162.

October 27. From Thomas Jefferson Whitman. Feinberg.

November 13. From Anne Gilchrist. LC. CT: Harned, 163–165.

[December 14]. From John Newton Johnson. Feinberg.

1879

January 2. From Hannah Heyde. LC.
January 5. From Anne Gilchrist. LC.
CT: Harned, 166–168.
January 13. From John Burroughs.
Feinberg.
January 13. From Harry Stafford.
Feinberg.
January 14. From Anne Gilchrist. LC.
CT: Harned, 169–170.
January 23. From Nancy Whitman(?).
Feinberg.
January 27. From Anne Gilchrist. LC.
CT: Harned, 171–172.
February 2. From Herbert Gilchrist.
LC. CT: Harned, 173–174.
February 7. From James Matlack
Scovel. California. CT: WWR, VII
(1961), 7.
February 16. From Beatrice Gilchrist.
LC. CT: Harned, 175–176.
March 5. From William Harrison
Riley, a friend of John Ruskin. Fein-
berg.
March 18. From Anne Gilchrist. LC.
CT: Harned, 177–178.
March 26. From Anne Gilchrist. LC.
CT: Harned, 179–180.
April 2. From William Harrison Riley.
Feinberg.
April 4. From William Harrison Riley.
Feinberg.
May 29. From D. Nicholson (for the
New York Tribune). LC.
June 9. From Alfred Janson Bloor. LC.
June 20. From Anne Gilchrist. LC. CT:
Harned, 181–182.
July. From T. W. H. Rolleston. Man-
chester.
July 17. From G. P. Putnam's Sons.
LC.
August 2. From Anne Gilchrist. LC.
CT: Harned, 183–185.
[August 9(?)]. From S. H. Morse.
Feinberg.
August 13. From H. B. Wilson, the
Camden Postmaster. LC.
August 24. From John Burroughs.
Feinberg. CT: Traubel, III, 260–261.
PT: Barrus, 186–187.
August 25. From P. Armáchalain,
"the Hindoo." Feinberg.
August 27. From William H. Kelly
(ordering a book). LC.
September 3. From Charles T. Dilling-
ham (probably ordering books).
Fragment in CB.
September 29. From Richard Worth-
ington. Yale.
October 1. From Richard Watson
Gilder. Historical Society of Pennsyl-
vania. CT: Donaldson, 215–216.
October 6–12. From Anne Gilchrist.
Barrett. CT: Barrus, 147–148.
October. From Anne Gilchrist. Cali-
fornia. CT: WWR, VII (1961), 12.
November 9. From Richard Maurice
Bucke. Feinberg.
November 25. From E. Steiger (prob-
ably ordering books). Fragment in
CB.
December 5. From Anne Gilchrist. LC.
CT: Harned, 187–189.
December 29. From John Burroughs.
Manchester.

1880

January 19. From Richard Maurice
Bucke. Manchester.
January 20. From James W. Thom-
son (ordering books). Feinberg.
January 25. From Anne Gilchrist. LC.
CT: Harned, 190–192.
January 31. From Herbert J. Bath-
gate. Copy: Berg.
February 3. From Richard Maurice
Bucke. Manchester.
February 6. From Richard Maurice
Bucke. Manchester.
February 15. From William Mills
(acknowledging receipt of a book
and photograph). Feinberg.
March 9. From Herbert Gilchrist. Lo-
cation unknown. PT: Barrus, 148–
149.
March 18. From Richard Maurice
Bucke. Manchester.
March 23. From Richard Maurice
Bucke. Manchester.
March 25. From Robert G. Ingersoll.
Manchester.
[March 28]. From Edward Carpenter.
Manchester.
March 28. From Anne Gilchrist. Man-
chester.
April 3. From James Berry Bensel, a
young admirer. Feinberg.
April 7. From Frederick Locker-
Lampson. Location unknown. CT:
Donaldson, 236–237.

April or May(?). From T. W. H. Rolleston. Manchester.

June 5. From Katie Macdonald (ordering a book). Manchester.

June 9. From Katie Macdonald (sending payment for a book). Manchester.

June(?) 9. From William Taylor (requesting an article). Manchester.

June 10. From A. H. Whitaker, an admirer. Feinberg.

June 14. From Charles Warren Stoddard. Manchester.

June 15. From Anne Gilchrist. Whitman House, Camden.

June 15. From Frederick Locker-Lampson. Manchester.

June 18. From Mrs. Elisa S. Leggett. Manchester.

June 21. From James Matlack Scovel. Manchester.

June 22. From Harry Scovel. Manchester.

June 24. From C. A. J. Hueckberny(?) (effusively acknowledging receipt of WW's note). Manchester.

June 24. From Fred W. Rauch (concerning his travels in Germany). Manchester.

June 26. From John H. Johnston. Manchester.

June 27. From Norman McKenzie, a Canadian schoolboy. Manchester.

July 1. From Edward Carpenter. Manchester.

July 2. From Herbert J. Bathgate. Manchester.

July 3. From Frederick Locker-Lampson. Manchester.

July 4. From Respegius Edward Lindell. Manchester.

July 4. From Louisa Orr Whitman. Manchester.

July 7. From Charles Warren Stoddard. Manchester.

July 9. From Robert Elliott, a young Canadian admirer. Manchester.

July 10. From Josiah Child (sending a draft from Trübner & Co.). Manchester.

July 10(?). From Harry Stafford. Manchester.

July 16. From Susan(?) Stafford. Manchester.

July 17. From Elmer E. Stafford. Manchester.

July 18. From Deborah V. Browning. Manchester.

July 19. From Mrs. Elisa S. Leggett. Manchester.

July 21. From Franklin B. Sanborn. Manchester.

July 22. From Louisa Orr Whitman. Manchester.

August 1. From John H. Ingram. Feinberg.

August 4. From Vivas(?) Tully (furnishing data about the Great Lakes). Manchester.

August 22. From Anne Gilchrist. LC. CT: Harned, 193–194.

September 8. From Jack Richardson. LC. CT: *L'Ane d'Or*, V (1926), 44–45.

October 9. From Mrs. Elisa S. Leggett. LC. CT: Donaldson, 239–242.

October 13. From Frederick Locker-Lampson. Location unknown. CT: Donaldson, 237.

October 14. From William Davidge(?) (requesting an autograph). Feinberg.

October 16. From T. W. H. Rolleston. Feinberg. CT: Traubel, II, 67–69; Frenz, 15–18.

October 20. From E. C. Cheever (ordering books). Feinberg.

October 25. From C. L. Ehrenfeld (ordering books). Feinberg.

October 25. From George Heard (ordering books). Feinberg.

October 27. From Frederic Almy (enclosing payment for books). Feinberg.

November 2. From John Burroughs. Hanley.

November 10. From Jno. S. Stott. Feinberg.

November 11. From W. Colin Mackenzie. Feinberg.

November 11. From T. W. H. Rolleston. LC. CT: Frenz, 19–20.

November 20. From Helena de Kay Gilder. Feinberg. CT: Traubel, II, 118–119.

November 20. From David Hutcheson (ordering books). Feinberg.

November 22. From Titus M. Coan, The Century Club (ordering books). LC.

November 28. From Lizzie Westgate, a fervid young admirer. Feinberg.

November 30. From Herbert Gilchrist. LC. CT: Harned, 195–196.

December 2. From A. Williams (ordering books). Feinberg.

December 6. From James Matlack Scovel. Feinberg.

December 10. From Leon Richeton (requesting a photograph for an etching). Lion.

December 10. From Hannah L. Taylor (thanking the poet). Feinberg.

December 13. From Herbert Gilchrist. Feinberg.

December 29. From James Hearne, The Century Club (requesting a receipt). LC.

1881

January 20. From William Sloane Kennedy. Feinberg. CT: Traubel, I, 377–378.

January 21. From Charles Allen Thorndike Rice. Yale.

January 25. From the Camden & Atlantic Railroad Company. LC.

January 29. From T. W. H. Rolleston. LC. CT: Frenz, 21–24.

January 31. From Frederick Locker-Lampson. Historical Society of Pennsylvania.

February 10. From T. W. H. Rolleston. LC. CT: Frenz, 25–27.

February 16. From Anne Gilchrist. Pennsylvania.

February 21. From Mrs. Mollie W. Carpenter, an admiring young poet. LC.

February 22. From Henry Wadsworth Longfellow. Berg.

February 25. From Elihu Vedder (ordering books). Feinberg.

February 28. From John Alcott (acknowledging receipt of books). LC.

March 14. From John Burroughs. Feinberg. CT: Traubel, I, 43–44; Barrus, 199–200.

March(?). From T. W. H. Rolleston. LC. CT: Frenz, 28–29 (dated February–May, 1881).

April 4. From Harry Stafford. Feinberg.

April 15. From J. T. Cobb, a troubled admirer. Feinberg.

April 18. From Anne Gilchrist. LC. CT: Harned, 197–199.

April 26. From John Boyle O'Reilly. Huntington.

May 12. From James R. Osgood. LC. PT: *CW*, VIII, 277.

May 16. From Henry A. Beers. LC.

May 19. From Emma M. String, of the Pennington Seminary (inviting WW to a dedication). Feinberg.

May 22. From Richard Maurice Bucke. Feinberg.

May 23. From John Burroughs. Hanley.

May 23. From James R. Osgood. LC. PT: *CW*, VIII, 278 (dated May 28).

[May(?)] 24. From Henry M. Alden (returning a poem). LC.

May 31. From James R. Osgood. LC. PT: *CW*, VIII, 278–279.

June 3. From James R. Osgood. LC. PT: *CW*, VIII, 279–280.

June 4. From T. W. H. Rolleston. LC. CT: Frenz, 30–34.

June 5. From Herbert Gilchrist. LC. CT: Harned, 200–202.

June 8. From Benjamin Ticknor. LC.

June 10. From James R. Osgood & Company. LC.

June 17. From Anne Gilchrist. Pennsylvania.

June 21. From James R. Osgood & Company. LC.

June 22. From Mrs. Elisa S. Leggett. New-York Historical Society. CT: Donaldson, 242–246.

June 25. From James R. Osgood & Company. LC. PT: *CW*, VIII, 282.

July 1. From Edward Carpenter. Feinberg.

July 11. From T. W. H. Rolleston. LC. CT: Frenz, 35–37.

July 18. From James R. Osgood & Company. LC. PT: *CW*, VIII, 283.

August 30. From John Boyle O'Reilly (enclosing WW's article in the Boston *Pilot*). LC.

September 13. From James R. Osgood & Company. LC. PT: *CW*, VIII, 284.

September 17. From T. W. H. Rolleston. LC. CT: Frenz, 38–42.

September 21. From John Boyle O'Reilly. Location unknown. CT: Traubel, II, 136.

September 28. From John Ward Dean. Fragment in *CB*.

October 5. From Standish James O'Grady. Feinberg. CT: Traubel, I, 399–400.

November 4. From Louis Karpstyin(?) (requesting an autograph). LC.

November 14. From Benjamin Ticknor. LC. PT: *CW*, VIII, 287.

November 27. From Rudolf Schmidt. Feinberg.

November 28. From John Fitzgerald Lee. LC. CT: Frenz, 48–50. PT: Furness, 251.

November 28. From T. W. H. Rolleston. LC. CT: Frenz, 43–47. PT: Furness, 251.

November. From Hannah Heyde. LC. CT: *Life in Letters: American Autograph Journal*, II (1939), 104–106.

December 6. From Thomas Nicholson. Feinberg.

December 10. From Benjamin Ticknor. LC. PT: *CW*, VIII, 286–287.

December 13. From James R. Osgood & Company. LC.

December 14. From Anne Gilchrist. LC. CT: Harned, 203–204.

December 31. From Richard Maurice Bucke. Feinberg.

1882

January 7. From T. W. H. Rolleston. LC. CT: Frenz, 54–55. PT: Furness, 252.

January 11. From Joseph M. Stoddart. LC. CT: Barrus, 235n.

January 15. From Herbert Gilchrist. Feinberg.

January 25. From John H. Johnston. LC. PT: *CW*, VIII, 288.

January 29–February 6. From Anne Gilchrist. LC. CT: Harned, 205–206.

February 14. From T. W. H. Rolleston. LC. CT: Frenz, 56–60.

March 1. From Oscar Wilde. Feinberg. CT: Traubel, II, 288; *The Letters of Oscar Wilde*, ed. Hart-Davis (1962), 99–100.

March 4. From James R. Osgood & Company. LC. CT: *CW*, VIII, 289; Allen, 498.

March 16. From Edward Carpenter. Feinberg. CT: Traubel, I, 252.

March 20. From James R. Osgood & Company. LC. CT: *CW*, VIII, 292.

March 21. From James R. Osgood & Company. LC. PT: *CW*, VIII, 293–294.

March 29. From James R. Osgood & Company. LC. PT: *CW*, VIII, 295.

April 10. From James R. Osgood & Company. LC. CT: *CW*, VIII, 296.

April 13. From James R. Osgood & Company. LC. CT: *CW*, VIII, 297.

April 23. From H. S. Kneedler, an admirer. LC.

May 1. From John Burroughs. Feinberg. CT: Traubel, III, 350–351; Barrus, 211–212.

May 4. From James R. Osgood & Company. LC. CT: *CW*, VIII, 298.

May 8. From Anne Gilchrist. LC. CT: Harned, 207–208.

May 9. From Richard Maurice Bucke. LC (Bucke's transcription).

May 9. From William D. O'Connor. Syracuse. CT: Traubel, IV, 433–434.

May 9. From Joseph M. Stoddart. LC.

May 11. From Jacob Moller (requesting an autograph). LC.

May 20. From William D. O'Connor. Feinberg. CT: Traubel, II, 12–15.

May 20. From Benjamin Ticknor, for Osgood and Company. LC.

May 21. From Mrs. Jenny C. Croly (requesting a poem for *Demorest's Illustrated*). LC.

May 21. From Helen Wilmans. Feinberg. CT: Traubel, I, 49–50.

May 22–25. From Alfred Janson Bloor. Feinberg.

May 23. From John C. Everrett, a student. Feinberg.

May 25. From Benjamin Ticknor, for Osgood and Company. LC. PT: *CW*, VIII, 299.

May 25. From Benjamin R. Tucker. Feinberg. CT: Traubel, II, 253–254.

May 26. From Fred R. Guernsey, of the Boston *Herald*. Feinberg.

May 28. From Van Doran Stafford. Feinberg.

May 29. From William D. O'Connor. Feinberg. CT: Traubel, III, 282–284.

May 29. From John G. Willson (requesting WW's presence at the "Melancholy Club"). Feinberg.

June(?). From William Sloane Kennedy. Feinberg.

June 3. From George W. Christy, an offended reader. LC.

June 3. From William D. O'Connor. Feinberg. CT: Traubel, I, 52–54.

June 4. From Edwin H. Woodruff (enclosing a poem). Feinberg.

June 5. From Rees Welsh & Company. Pennsylvania.

June 10. From T. W. H. Rolleston. LC. CT: Frenz, 61–63.

June 15. From William D. O'Connor. Feinberg.

June 16. From John Burroughs. Feinberg. CT: Traubel, II, 171–172; Barrus, 217.

June 16. From Rees Welsh & Company. Pennsylvania.

June 18. From Anne Gilchrist. Pennsylvania.

June 19. From William D. O'Connor. Feinberg. CT: Traubel, I, 312–314.

June 21. From Rees Welsh & Company. Pennsylvania.

June 24. From William D. O'Connor. Feinberg. CT: Traubel, III, 349.

June 26. From Rees Welsh & Company. Pennsylvania.

June 29. From William D. O'Connor. Feinberg. CT: Traubel, III, 48–50.

July 5. From Rees Welsh & Company. Pennsylvania.

July 7. From William D. O'Connor. Feinberg.

July 10. From William D. O'Connor. Feinberg.

July 13. From William D. O'Connor. Feinberg.

July 20. From William D. O'Connor. Feinberg. CT: Traubel, II, 60–61.

July 25. From Richard Worthington. Yale.

July 27. From George Chainey. Feinberg.

August 2. From Ainsworth R. Spofford. LC.

August 9. From John Burroughs. Feinberg.

August 12. From John Swinton. Feinberg. CT: Traubel, II, 393.

August 14. From T. W. H. Rolleston. LC. CT: Frenz, 64–66.

August 16. From Herbert Gilchrist. Feinberg. CT: Traubel, I, 227–229.

August 19. From William D. O'Connor. Feinberg. CT: Traubel, II, 495–497.

August 24. From John Burroughs. Feinberg.

August 28. From William D. O'Connor. Feinberg.

September 20. From William D. O'Connor. Feinberg. CT: Traubel, IV, 20–21.

September 24. From T. W. H. Rolleston. LC. CT: Frenz, 67–68.

October 11. From Richard Maurice Bucke. Feinberg.

October 18. From James Arnold (ordering a book). Feinberg.

October(?) 20. From Herbert Gilchrist. Feinberg.

October 23. From W. Hale White (ordering a book). Feinberg.

October 26. From William D. O'Connor. Feinberg.

October 27. From William D. O'Connor. Yale. CT: Traubel, IV, 322–323.

October 29. From John Burroughs. Feinberg. CT: Traubel, I, 333–334; Barrus, 232–233.

October 29. From Thomas Jefferson Whitman. Feinberg.

October 29. From T. W. H. Rolleston. LC. CT: Frenz, 69–70.

November 3. From Rudolf Schmidt. Feinberg.

November 5. From Ezra H. Heywood. Berg.

November 9. From Richard Maurice Bucke. Feinberg.

November 21. From Edward Dowden. Feinberg. CT: Traubel, II, 363.

November 24. From Anne Gilchrist. LC. CT: Harned, 209–210.

December 10. From Richard Maurice Bucke. Feinberg.

December 16. From Charles de Kay (requesting that WW join a literary society). Feinberg.

December 18. From William D. O'Connor. Feinberg.

December 19. From Mrs. Elisa S. Leggett. Location unknown. CT: Donaldson, 246–248.

December 19. From William D. O'Connor. Feinberg.

December 26. From T. W. H. Rolleston. LC. CT: Frenz, 73–76.

1882(?). From Ingersoll Lockwood, for *The American Bookmaker* (proposing to print a sketch of WW's life). Feinberg.

1883

January 9. From G. C. Macaulay. Feinberg. CT: Traubel, II, 62.

January 27–February 13. From Anne Gilchrist. LC. CT: Harned, 211–212.

February 3. From John Russell Young. Feinberg. CT: Traubel, III, 311.

February 20. From William D. O'Connor. Feinberg. CT: Traubel, I, 350–353.

February 25. From John Burroughs. Location unknown. Cited in *A List of Manuscripts, Books, . . . from the Whitman Collection of Mrs. Frank Julian Sprague* (1939), 40.

March 10. From William D. O'Connor. Feinberg.

March 12. From Richard Maurice Bucke. Feinberg.

March 14. From William D. O'Connor. Syracuse. CT: Traubel, IV, 406–407.

March 14. From D. L. Proudfit (ordering books). Feinberg.

March 15. From William D. O'Connor. Syracuse. CT: Traubel, IV, 459–460.

March 17. From William D. O'Connor. Feinberg. CT: Traubel, IV, 354–356.

March 18. From Richard Maurice Bucke. Feinberg.

March 19. From William D. O'Connor. Feinberg.

March 20. From Richard Maurice Bucke (a letter). Feinberg.

March 20. From Richard Maurice Bucke (a post card). Feinberg.

March 25. From Albert G. Knapp, an ex-soldier (ordering a book). Feinberg.

March 27. From Richard Maurice Bucke. Feinberg.

March 27. From William D. O'Connor. Feinberg. CT: Traubel, III, 563–566.

April 1. From William D. O'Connor. Feinberg. CT: Traubel, II, 258–261.

April 4. From William D. O'Connor. Feinberg. CT: Traubel, I, 67–68.

April 8. From William D. O'Connor. Feinberg.

April 9. From William D. O'Connor. Feinberg. CT: Traubel, IV, 138–139.

April 17. From William D. O'Connor. Syracuse. CT: Traubel, IV, 90–92.

April 23. From V. D. Davis, a youthful admirer. Feinberg.

April 29. From Herbert Gilchrist. LC. CT: Harned, 213–214.

April 30. From Craig Maginnis, an admirer. Feinberg.

May 6. From Anne Gilchrist. LC. CT: Harned, 215–216.

May 9. From Richard Maurice Bucke. Feinberg.

May 20. From John Burroughs. Syracuse. CT: Traubel, IV, 509–510.

May 23. From William D. O'Connor. Lion.

May 28. From Richard Maurice Bucke. Feinberg.

June 2. From Richard Maurice Bucke. Feinberg.

June 7. From Richard Watson Gilder. Feinberg. CT: Traubel, II, 165–166.

June 13. From Elizabeth Ford (ordering books). Feinberg.

June 13. From John H. Johnston. Feinberg.

June 15. From William D. O'Connor. Syracuse. CT: Traubel, IV, 162 (dated June 13).

June 16. From Hannah Heyde. LC.

June 20. From Arthur Boyle, for the Santa Fé Tertio Millennial Celebration (requesting a poem). Feinberg.

June 26. From William Roscoe Thayer (asking about a letter written by Sidney Lanier). Feinberg.

July 12. From William D. O'Connor. Feinberg. CT: Traubel, III, 128–130.

July 14. From Hannah Heyde. LC.

July 20. From William D. O'Connor. Feinberg. CT: Traubel, III, 130–131.

July 20. From John Swinton (acknowledging "a beautiful book"). Feinberg.

July 30. From Anne Gilchrist. LC. CT: Harned, 217–219.

August 17. From John Burroughs. Feinberg. CT: Traubel, I, 403. PT: Barrus, 244.

August 17. From William D. O'Connor. Feinberg.

August 27–October 22. From Herbert Gilchrist. Feinberg.

September 9. From Richard Maurice Bucke. Feinberg.

September 14. From Karl Knortz. Yale.

September 18. From William D. O'Connor. Syracuse. CT: Traubel, IV, 394–395.

September 21. From John Burroughs. Feinberg.

September 22. From Charles W. Eldridge. Yale.

September 22. From William D. O'Connor. LC. CT: Traubel, IV, 191–192.

September 23. From Richard Maurice Bucke. Feinberg.

September 24. From William D. O'Connor. Feinberg.

September 27. From T. W. H. Rolleston. LC. CT: Frenz, 77–79.

September 30. From T. W. H. Rolleston. Feinberg.

October 13. From T. W. H. Rolleston. Feinberg.

October 13–21. From Anne Gilchrist. LC. CT: Harned, 220–222.

October 18. From Charles L. Heyde. Trent.

November 17. From T. F. Macdonald. Syracuse. CT: Traubel, IV, 197–198.

November 18. From John Burroughs. Syracuse. CT: Traubel, IV, 35–37.

November 20. From H. N. Whitman (acknowledging receipt of a book and requesting genealogical information). Feinberg.

November 22. From T. W. H. Rolleston. Syracuse. CT: Traubel, IV, 111–112.

November 23. From Emma Riley (requesting *Specimen Days*). Feinberg.

November 28. From Harry Stafford. Feinberg.

November 30. From Henry M. Alden, for *Harper's New Monthly Magazine*. Feinberg. CT: Traubel, II, 220.

December 17. From Harry Stafford. Feinberg.

December 23. From Mary Van Nostrand. Yale.

1884

January 1. From T. W. H. Rolleston. LC. CT: Frenz, 80–82.

January 4. From Alice G. Brown (requesting an autograph). LC.

January 8. From John Burroughs. Feinberg. CT: Traubel, I, 395; Barrus, 247.

January 8. From General William J. Sewell. Mrs. Doris Neale.

February 6. From Josephine Barkeloo (thanking WW for an article). LC.

February 10. From Harry Stafford. Feinberg.

February 16. From William Sloane Kennedy. Yale.

February 18. From William Sloane Kennedy. LC.

February 22. From William D. O'Connor. Yale.

February 27. From Fred W. Wilson, a publisher. LC.

March 2. From Edward Carpenter. Lion. CT: Traubel, IV, 76–77.

March 4. From T. W. H. Rolleston. LC. CT: Frenz, 83–86.

March 25. From John H. Johnston. Feinberg. CT: Traubel, III, 331.

April 5. From Anne Gilchrist. LC. CT: Harned, 223–224.

April 5. From T. W. H. Rolleston. LC. CT: Frenz, 87–88.

May 2. From Anne Gilchrist. LC. CT: Harned, 225–226.

May 5. From T. W. H. Rolleston. LC. CT: Frenz, 90–91.

May 11. From Eleanor M. Lawney, an admirer. Feinberg.

May 26. From S. W. Foss, of the Lynn (Mass.) *Saturday Union*. Feinberg. CT: Traubel, II, 227.

May 31. From Henry Tyrrell. Feinberg.

June 3. From Mrs. Mattie Maxim (ordering a book). LC.

June 8. From Truman Howe Bartlett. LC.

June 10. From Dr. J. W. Bartlett (payment for a book). LC.

June 10. From Folger McKinsey (requesting an autograph). Feinberg.

June 23. From George W. Ludwig (inquiring about the price of WW's books). LC.

June 25–26. From Mrs. M. B. Minchen, a mystical admirer. Feinberg.

June 27. From L. Birge Harrison (praising *Specimen Days*). LC.

June 30(?). From L. Birge Harrison. Feinberg.

July 12. From Robert Underwood Johnson. Feinberg. CT: Traubel, II, 218.

July 16. From Harry W. Gustafson, a youthful admirer. Feinberg.

July 21. From Anna M. Wilkinson (acknowledging receipt of books). Feinberg.

July 30. From Parker Pillsbury (acknowledging receipt of book). LC.

August 5. From Anne Gilchrist. LC. CT: Harned, 227.

August 7. From T. W. H. Rolleston. Syracuse. CT: Traubel, IV, 113–114.

August 9. From Richard Watson Gilder. Feinberg. CT: Traubel, II, 212.

August 11. From E. V. Garrison (inviting WW to spend the evening). LC.

August 16. From Pliny B. Smith (ordering books). LC.

August 20. From James Knowles, editor of *The Nineteenth Century* (returning a manuscript). Feinberg.

August 24. From Edwin Booth. Feinberg. CT: Traubel, I, 355; *WWR*, VI (1960), 50.

August 28. From Edwin Booth. Feinberg. CT: Traubel, I, 46; *WWR*, VI (1960), 50.

September 5. From Robert Pearsall Smith. LC.

September 9. From T. W. H. Rolleston. Feinberg. CT: Traubel, I, 18–21; Frenz, 94–97.

September 17. From Cupples, Upham & Company (ordering a book). Feinberg.

September 29. From R. Watson (requesting an inscribed book). LC.

September 30. From Herbert Gilchrist. Feinberg.

October 2. From William D. O'Connor. Feinberg. CT: Traubel, I, 177–179.

October 14. From Charles L. Heyde. Trent.

October 16(?). From William C. Bryant. LC.

October 20(?). From Hannah Heyde. LC.

October 22. From Henry M. Alden. Feinberg. CT: Traubel, II, 218–219.

October 26. From Anne Gilchrist. LC. CT: Harned, 228–229.

November 1. From Frederick York Powell. Feinberg. CT: Traubel, I, 356–357.

November 2. From Charles L. Heyde. Trent.

November 12. From Mary W. Smith. Feinberg. PT: *Smith Alumnae Quarterly* (February, 1958), 86–87.

November 14. From James Matlack Scovel. LC.

November 25. From Charles L. Heyde. Trent.

November 28. From John Addington Symonds. Feinberg.

December 17. From Anne Gilchrist. LC. CT: Harned, 230–232.

December 20. From Charles L. Heyde. Trent.

December 21. From Mary B. N. Williams (inviting WW to dinner). Feinberg.

December 29. From Edmund Gosse. Feinberg. CT: Traubel, I, 40 (dated 1887); *Victorian Studies*, I (1957), 181.

December 29. From John (?) B. Robinson, for the Delaware County Institute of Science (requesting a lecture). Feinberg.

[1884(?)]. From Charles W. Dailey (requesting an autograph). Feinberg.

1885

January 1. From William Michael Rossetti. Feinberg. CT: Traubel, I, 436–437.

January 7. From William Sloane Kennedy. Feinberg.

January 9. From A. B. Drake (acknowledging receipt of books). Feinberg.

January 13. From Henry M. Alden. Feinberg. CT: Traubel, II, 211 (dated January 3).

January 16. From William Sloane Kennedy. Feinberg.

January 17. From Charles L. Heyde. Trent.

January 24. From Charles L. Heyde. Trent.

February 1. From William D. O'Connor. Feinberg. CT: Traubel, I, 29–33.

February 5(?). From William C. Skinner (payment for a book). LC.

February 11. From John Boyle O'Reilly. Feinberg. CT: Traubel, I, 8–9.

February 11. From T. W. H. Rolleston. Feinberg. CT: Traubel, III, 85–86; Frenz, 99–100.

February 13. From John Swinton. Feinberg. CT: Traubel, III, 271.

February 19. From Charles L. Heyde. Trent.

February 20. From Professor G. H. Palmer. Feinberg. CT: Traubel, I, 112.

February 23. From Thomas Jefferson Whitman. Feinberg.

February 27. From Anne Gilchrist. LC. CT: Harned, 233–235.

February 27. From Charles L. Heyde. Trent. CT: Gohdes and Silver, 228–229.

March 5. From John Boyle O'Reilly. Feinberg. CT: Traubel, II, 38.

March 7. From William D. O'Connor. Syracuse. CT: Traubel, IV, 477–478.

March 10. From Gabriel Harrison (acknowledging receipt of a book). Feinberg.

[March 11]. From William Sloane Kennedy. Feinberg.

March 16.   From Charles L. Heyde. Trent.

March 17.   From Palin H. Sims, an ex-soldier (recalling Civil War experiences). Feinberg.

March 18.   From Ellen M. Abdy-Williams (concerning receipt of books). Feinberg.

March 31.   From George Parsons Lathrop (inviting WW to give readings to raise funds in aid of international copyright). Feinberg.

April 5.   From Richard Maurice Bucke. Feinberg.

April 7.   From James Matlack Scovel. Feinberg.

May 4.   From Anne Gilchrist. LC. CT: Harned, 236–238.

May 7.   From James Matlack Scovel. Feinberg.

May 11.   From M. Schuyler(?), of *Harper's Weekly*. Feinberg.

May 12.   From Henry M. Alden. Feinberg. CT: Traubel, I, 61.

May 12.   From James Matlack Scovel. Feinberg.

May 18.   From John Burroughs. Feinberg.

May 21.   From Samuel B. Wright (inquiring about WW's books). Feinberg.

May 31.   From Ernest Rhys. Feinberg.

[June 2].   From William Sloane Kennedy. Feinberg.

June 8.   From Henry M. Alden. Feinberg. CT: Traubel, I, 28.

June 9.   From Robt. Lutz (inquiring about a German translation of *Leaves of Grass*). Feinberg.

June 10.   From Carolan O'Brien Bryant (ordering books). Feinberg.

June 13.   From George Weaver (requesting an autograph). Feinberg.

About June 16 (Monday).   From James Matlack Scovel. Feinberg.

About June 16 (Thursday).   From James Matlack Scovel. Feinberg.

June 21–22.   From Anne Gilchrist. LC. CT: Harned, 239–240 (dated January 21).

June 23.   From Charles L. Heyde. Trent.

June 30.   From James Redpath. Feinberg. CT: Traubel, II, 73–74.

July 1.   From William J. Linton. Feinberg. CT: Traubel, II, 442–443.

July 7.   From Ernest Rhys. Feinberg. CT: Traubel, I, 451–453.

July 8.   From Charles Aldrich (requesting an autograph). LC.

[July] 9.   From Edward Carpenter (misdated June 9). Feinberg.

July 14.   From Charles Allen Thorndike Rice. Syracuse. CT: Traubel, IV, 329–330.

July 16.   From James Redpath. Feinberg. CT: Traubel, II, 74–75. PT: *Memoranda During the War*, ed. Basler (1962), 46.

July 20.   From Anne Gilchrist. LC. CT: Harned, 241–242.

July 21.   From Herbert Gilchrist. Feinberg.

July 25.   From William D. O'Connor. Syracuse. CT: Traubel, IV, 67–70.

July 25.   From Charles Parsons, of *Harper's Weekly* (requesting permission to publish WW's portrait). Feinberg.

July 25.   From Mary Whitall Smith. Rollo G. Silver. CT: Donaldson, 234–236.

July 30.   From Charles L. Heyde. Trent.

July 31.   From Alexander K. Reamer, a rhapsodic admirer. Feinberg.

July 31.   From Thomas Jefferson Whitman. Feinberg.

August 4.   From T. W. H. Rolleston. Feinberg. CT: Traubel, III, 487–488; Frenz, 101–103.

August 8(?).   From William Sloane Kennedy. Feinberg.

August 11.   From James Redpath. Feinberg. CT: Traubel, II, 75–76.

August 15.   From James Matlack Scovel. Feinberg.

August 17.   From Charles W. Eldridge. Feinberg.

August 17.   From Edw. Mawson (relating theatrical reminiscences). Feinberg.

[August 28].   From William Sloane Kennedy. Feinberg.

August 28.   From William Michael Rossetti. Hanley.

August [30].   From John Newton Johnson. Feinberg.

September 5.   From Herbert Gilchrist. Feinberg.

September 5.   From an unidentified correspondent (asking for a synopsis of a forthcoming book). Feinberg.

September 9. From John H. Johnston. Feinberg.

September 11. From Thomas Jefferson Whitman. Yale.

September 15. From Richard Maurice Bucke. Feinberg.

September 16. From A. B. Nourse (asking the price of a book). Feinberg.

September 19. From Houghton, Mifflin & Company (inquiring about the original edition of *Leaves of Grass*). Feinberg.

September 25–29. From Ernest Rhys. Feinberg. PT: Traubel, III, 162–164.

September 29. From Herbert Gilchrist. Feinberg.

October 2. From Richard Maurice Bucke. Feinberg.

October 4. From William Michael Rossetti. Syracuse. CT: Traubel, IV, 209.

October 6. From William Michael Rossetti. Feinberg. CT: Traubel, III, 65–66.

October 7. From John Burroughs. Feinberg. CT: Traubel, I, 404; Barrus, 257.

October 12. From William Roscoe Thayer. Feinberg.

October 15. From Richard A. Stuart (inquiring whether WW was willing to read his poetry at a meeting). Feinberg.

October 20. From Lionel Johnson. Feinberg. CT: Traubel, II, 180–181.

October 20. From James Redpath. Feinberg. CT: Traubel, II, 232.

October 23. From Edward Carpenter. Feinberg. CT: Traubel, III, 192–193.

October 23. From James Redpath. Feinberg.

November 13. From William Michael Rossetti. Feinberg. CT: Traubel, II, 330–331.

November 17. From Lorenz Reich, an admirer. Feinberg.

November 18. From Herbert Gilchrist. Feinberg.

December 2. From Herbert Gilchrist. Feinberg.

December 2. From William Sloane Kennedy. Feinberg. CT: Traubel, IV, 479–480.

December 6. From Marion Thrasher (requesting that WW tour the Midwest giving readings at $50 a night). Feinberg.

December 31. From John Burroughs. Feinberg. CT: Traubel, II, 86–87; Barrus, 258–259.

December. From B. P. Stewart, a young admirer. Feinberg.

Appendix D

CHRONOLOGY
OF WALT WHITMAN'S LIFE AND WORK

1819	Born May 31 at West Hills, near Huntington, Long Island.
1823	May 27, Whitman family moves to Brooklyn.
1825–30	Attends public school in Brooklyn.
1830	Office boy for doctor, lawyer.
1830–34	Learns printing trade.
1835	Printer in New York City until great fire August 12.
1836–38	Summer of 1836, begins teaching at East Norwich, Long Island; by winter 1837 - 38 has taught at Hempstead, Babylon, Long Swamp, and Smithtown.
1838–39	Edits weekly newspaper, the *Long Islander*, at Huntington.
1840–41	Autumn, 1840, campaigns for Van Buren; then teaches school at Trimming Square, Woodbury, Dix Hills, and Whitestone.
1841	May, goes to New York City to work as printer in *New World* office; begins writing for the *Democratic Review*.
1842	Spring, edits a daily newspaper in New York City, the *Aurora;* edits *Evening Tattler* for short time.
1845–46	August, returns to Brooklyn, writes for *Long Island Star* from September until March.
1846–48	From March, 1846, until January, 1848, edits Brooklyn *Daily Eagle;* February, 1848, goes to New Orleans to work on the *Crescent;* leaves May 27 and returns *via* Mississippi and Great Lakes.
1848–49	September 9, 1848, to September 11, 1849, edits a "free soil" newspaper, the Brooklyn *Freeman*.
1850–54	Operates printing office and stationery store; does free-lance journalism; builds and speculates in houses.
1855	Early July, *Leaves of Grass* is printed by Rome Brothers in Brooklyn; father dies July 11; Emerson writes to poet on July 21.
1856	Writes for *Life Illustrated;* publishes second edition of *Leaves of Grass* in summer and writes "The Eighteenth Presidency!"
1857–59	From spring of 1857 until about summer of 1859 edits the Brooklyn *Times;* unemployed winter of 1859 - 60; frequents Pfaff's bohemian restaurant.
1860	March, goes to Boston to see third edition of *Leaves of Grass* through the press.
1861	April 12, Civil War begins; George Whitman enlists.

1862	December, goes to Fredericksburg, Virginia, scene of recent battle in which George was wounded, stays in camp two weeks.
1863	Remains in Washington, D. C., working part-time in Army Paymaster's office; visits soldiers in hospitals.
1864	June 22, returns to Brooklyn because of illness.
1865	January 24, appointed clerk in Department of Interior, returns to Washington; meets Peter Doyle; witnesses Lincoln's second inauguration; Lincoln assassinated, April 14; May, *Drum-Taps* is printed; June 30, is discharged from position by Secretary James Harlan but re-employed next day in Attorney General's office; autumn, prints *Drum-Taps and Sequel*, containing "When Lilacs Last in the Dooryard Bloom'd."
1866	William D. O'Connor publishes *The Good Gray Poet*.
1867	John Burroughs publishes *Notes on Walt Whitman as Poet and Person;* July 6, William Michael Rossetti publishes article on Whitman's poetry in London *Chronicle;* "Democracy" (part of *Democratic Vistas*) published in December *Galaxy*.
1868	Rossetti's *Poems of Walt Whitman* (selected and expurgated) published in England; "Personalism" (second part of *Democratic Vistas*) in May *Galaxy;* second issue of fourth edition of *Leaves of Grass*, with *Drum-Taps and Sequel* added.
1869	Mrs. Anne Gilchrist reads Rossetti edition and falls in love with the poet.
1870	July, is very depressed for unknown reasons; prints fifth edition of *Leaves of Grass*, and *Democratic Vistas* and *Passage to India*, all dated 1871.
1871	September 3, Mrs. Gilchrist's first love letter; September 7, reads "After All Not to Create Only" at opening of American Institute Exhibition in New York.
1872	June 26, reads "As a Strong Bird on Pinions Free" at Dartmouth College commencement.
1873	January 23, suffers paralytic stroke; mother dies May 23; unable to work, stays with brother George in Camden, New Jersey.
1874	"Song of the Redwood-Tree" and "Prayer of Columbus."
1875	Prepares Centennial Edition of *Leaves of Grass* and *Two Rivulets* (dated 1876).
1876	Controversy in British and American press over America's neglect of Whitman; spring, meets Harry Stafford, and begins recuperation at Stafford farm, at Timber Creek; September, Mrs. Gilchrist arrives and rents house in Philadelphia.
1877	January 28, gives lecture on Tom Paine in Philadelphia; goes to New York in March and is painted by George W. Waters; during summer gains strength by sun-bathing at Timber Creek.
1878	Spring, too weak to give projected Lincoln lecture, but in June visits J. H. Johnston and John Burroughs in New York.
1879	April to June, in New York, where he gives first Lincoln lecture, and says farewell to Mrs. Gilchrist, who returns to England; September, goes to the West for the first time and visits Colorado; be-

cause of illness remains in St. Louis with his brother Jeff from October to January.

1880   Gives Lincoln lecture in Philadelphia; summer, visits Dr. R. M. Bucke in London, Ontario.

1881   April 15, gives Lincoln lecture in Boston; returns to Boston in August to read proof of *Leaves of Grass*, being published by James R. Osgood; poems receive final arrangement in this edition.

1882   Meets Oscar Wilde; Osgood ceases to distribute *Leaves of Grass* because District Attorney threatens prosecution unless the book is expurgated; publication is resumed in June by Rees Welsh in Philadelphia, who also publishes *Specimen Days and Collect;* both books transferred to David McKay, Philadelphia.

1883   Dr. Bucke publishes *Walt Whitman,* a critical study closely "edited" by the poet.

1884   Buys house on Mickle Street, Camden, New Jersey.

1885   In poor health; friends buy a horse and phaeton so that the poet will not be "house-tied"; November 29, Mrs. Gilchrist dies.

1886   Gives Lincoln lecture four times in Elkton, Maryland, Camden, Philadelphia, and Haddonfield, New Jersey; is painted by John White Alexander.

1887   Gives Lincoln lecture in New York; is painted by Thomas Eakins.

1888   Horace Traubel raises funds for doctors and nurses; *November Boughs* printed; money sent from England.

1889   Last birthday dinner, proceedings published in *Camden's Compliments.*

1890   Writes angry letter to J. A. Symonds, dated August 19, denouncing Symonds's interpretation of "Calamus" poems, claims six illegitimate children.

1891   *Good-Bye My Fancy* is printed, and the "death-bed edition" of *Leaves of Grass* (dated 1891 - 2).

1892   Dies March 26, buried in Harleigh Cemetery, Camden, New Jersey.

Index

Index

THIS BOOK is set in Monticello, a Linotype face designed after what was perhaps the first native American type face of real quality, cut by Archibald Binney probably in 1797. Printed on S. D. Warren Paper Company's University Text, the book was manufactured in its entirety by Kingsport Press, Inc.

The design and typography are by Andor Braun.

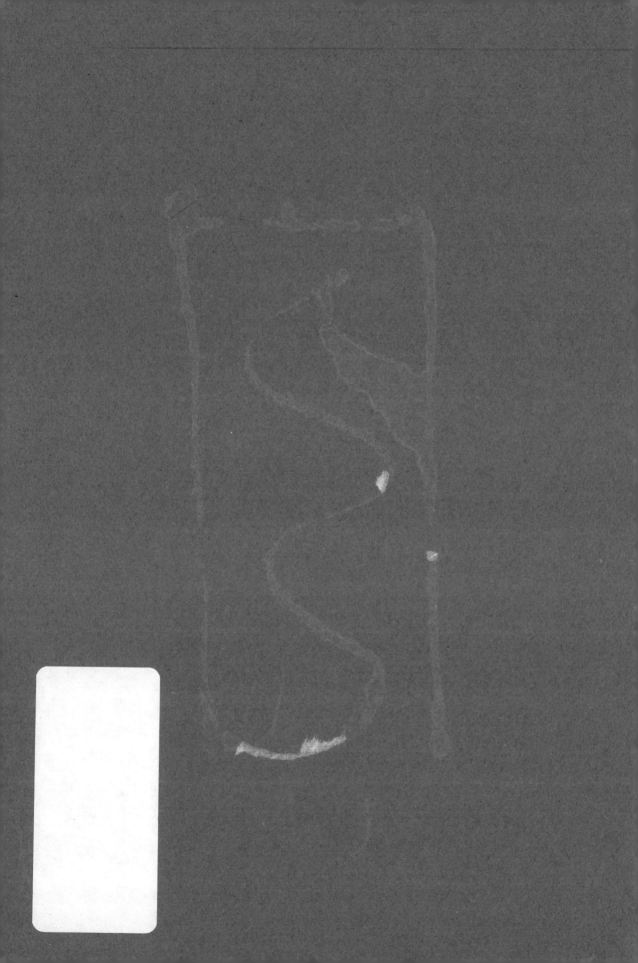